HANDBOOK OF MARKETING STRATEGY

T0329830

To Samita, Sara, Sujay, Shreya and Kamli . . . for all the inspiration and sacrifice.

To Lori, Ashley, Lacey and Dylan . . . for everything.

Handbook of Marketing Strategy

Edited by

Venkatesh Shankar

Texas A&M University, USA

and

Gregory S. Carpenter

Northwestern University, USA

Edward Elgar

Cheltenham, UK • Northampton, MA, USA

Published by
Edward Elgar Publishing Limited
The Lypiatts
15 Lansdown Road
Cheltenham
Glos GL50 2JA
UK

Edward Elgar Publishing, Inc.
William Pratt House
9 Dewey Court
Northampton
Massachusetts 01060
USA

A catalogue record for this book
is available from the British Library

Library of Congress Control Number: 2011942542

ISBN 978 1 84980 098 3 (cased)

Typeset by Servis Filmsetting Ltd, Stockport, Cheshire
Printed and bound by MPG Books Group, UK

Contents

Contributors

Todd J. Arnold is an associate professor of marketing and PhD Program Coordinator at Oklahoma State University. Dr Arnold's research focuses upon retailing and personal selling, as well as sales management. His work has appeared in top publications, including the *Journal of Consumer Research, Journal of Applied Psychology, Journal of the Academy of Marketing Science, Journal of Retailing, Journal of Service Research, Journal of Personal Selling and Sales Management, Journal of Management, Journal of Marketing Theory and Practice, Journal of Retailing and Consumer Services* and *Journal of Business Psychology*. He has been awarded the Richard W. Poole Research Excellence Award at Oklahoma State in 2007, 2008, 2009 and 2010. In addition, Dr Arnold is a member of the editorial review board for both the *Journal of Retailing* and the *Journal of Marketing Theory and Practice*. He also serves as an *ad hoc* reviewer for the *Journal of Marketing* and several other international publications. He received his PhD in marketing from the University of Missouri, Columbia.

Gregory S. Carpenter is the James Farley/Booz Allen Hamilton Professor of Marketing Strategy at the Kellogg School of Management at Northwestern University. Dr Carpenter's research on competitive marketing strategy has appeared in leading academic journals in addition to being featured by *Harvard Business Review, Financial Times* (London) and National Public Radio. The American Marketing Association has recognized his contributions to marketing with the William F. O'Dell Award, the Paul E. Green Award, the Donald R. Lehmann Award and the Marketing Science Institute/H. Paul Root Award, and his research has been cited in cases before the US Supreme Court. He received Kellogg's Sidney J. Levy Teaching Award and the Kellogg Managers' Program voted him Outstanding Professor of the Year. He is one of a handful of Kellogg faculty to be recognized by *Businessweek* as an outstanding faculty in its *Guide to the Best Business School*. He has advised many organizations on marketing strategy, including Advanced Micro Devices, Bacardi, Cadbury–Schweppes, Carnival Corporation, Coca-Cola, Cunard Lines, Diageo, Dow Chemical, Federal Reserve Bank, General Electric, Harley-Davidson, International Paper, Microsoft, Motorola, Procter & Gamble, Sara Lee, Unilever and Visa. He received his PhD degree from Columbia University.

Deepa Chandrasekaran is an assistant professor of marketing at Lehigh University. Her primary research expertise lies in the areas of new product growth, innovation management and global marketing strategies. Her research articles have been published in journals such as *Marketing Science* and *Review of Marketing Research*. She has also published book chapters in the *Wiley International Encyclopedia of Marketing* and the Marketing Science Institute's Relevant Knowledge Series. Dr Chandrasekaran has won several research awards, including the competitive Christian and Mary Lindback Foundation's Minority Junior Faculty award, and the Best Paper award at the Product Development and Management Association (PDMA) Research Forum. She has presented her work at major international conferences, including the Marketing Science conference, Winter

Marketing Educators' Conference, Summer Marketing Educators' Conference, PDMA research forum and the Marketing Dynamics conference. Her teaching interests include principles of marketing, global marketing, marketing strategy and product management. She received her PhD from the University of Southern California.

John A. Czepiel is a professor of marketing and Stern Teaching Excellence Fellow at the Leonard N. Stern School of Business at New York University. He has been named the Best Professor in Stern's top-ranked Executive MBA Program in 1992, 1996, 2000 and 2001. His prowess at teaching strategy led to his being cited in *Businessweek*'s *Guide to the Best Business Schools* as one of Stern's Outstanding Faculty. He received his MS and PhD degrees from Northwestern University's Kellogg School in 1972. His research has been published in such journals as the *Journal of Marketing, Journal of Marketing Research, Journal of Retailing, Journal of the Academy of Management, California Management Review, Journal of Business Research*, and in books and monographs. Dr Czepiel has extensive experience as a consultant and educator in industry.

Marnik G. Dekimpe is a research professor of marketing at Tilburg University, The Netherlands and Professor of Marketing at the Catholic University Leuven, Belgium. His work has been published in *Marketing Science, Management Science, Journal of Marketing Research, Journal of Marketing, International Journal of Research in Marketing* and *Journal of Econometrics*, among others. He has won best-paper awards from *Marketing Science* (1995, 2001), *Journal of Marketing Research* (1999), *International Journal of Research in Marketing* (1997, 2001, 2002) and *Technological Forecasting and Social Change* (2000). As of October 2009, he is the new editor of the *International Journal of Research in Marketing*, the leading European marketing journal. He also serves on the editorial boards of the *Journal of Marketing Research, Marketing Science, Journal of Marketing, Journal of the Academy of Marketing Science, Review of Marketing Science, Journal of Interactive Marketing* and *Marketing Letters*. His current research interests deal with the drivers of private label success, the internationalization of retail firms, the impact of product crises and the measurement of long-run marketing effects. He received his PhD in marketing from the University of California, Los Angeles.

Carly Frennea is a doctoral student in marketing at the Jones Graduate School of Business at Rice University. She received her MBA with a concentration in marketing from the Jones School in 2009 and holds a BS in public relations with a minor in business from the University of Texas at Austin. Her current research interest is in consumer behavior.

Gary F. Gebhardt is visiting Professor of Marketing at HEC, Montreal. Dr Gebhardt's research interests include marketing strategy and implementation, managerial decision making, organizational change, marketing processes within organizations, and research methods. His research has appeared in the *Journal of Marketing* and *Psychology & Marketing*. For his research, he has won the 2006 MSI/H. Paul Root Award from the *Journal of Marketing* Editorial Review Board based on his significant contribution to the advancement of marketing practice and the 2008 Robert D. Buzzell Marketing Science Institute Best Paper Award. He received his PhD from the Kellogg School of Management, Northwestern University.

Katrijn Gielens is an internationally recognized expert in the areas of international retailing and product innovation. The *International Journal of Research in Marketing (IJRM)*, *Journal of Marketing* and *Journal of Consumer Research* have published her research. She has twice won the prestigious *IJRM* Best Article Award. Dr Gielens teaches courses in international retail management and econometric and market response models. Before she joined UNC Kenan-Flagler, she served on the faculty of the RSM Erasmus University, one of UNC Kenan-Flagler's OneMBA partners, and Tilburg University. She serves on the strategy team of AiMark, a global center studying key marketing strategy issues, which brings together academics around the world, two of the top four market research agencies and brand manufacturers. She received her PhD in marketing from Catholic University Leuven.

Rajdeep Grewal is the Irving & Irene Bard Professor of Marketing at the Smeal College of Business at the Pennsylvania State University. He is also the Associate Research Director of the Institute for the Study of Business Markets. His research focuses on empirically modeling strategic marketing issues and has appeared in prestigious journals such as the *Journal of Marketing*, *Journal of Marketing Research*, *Marketing Science, Management Science*, *Journal of Consumer Psychology*, *MIS Quarterly* and *Strategic Management Journal*, among others. Currently he serves or has served on the editorial boards for the *Journal of Marketing*, *Marketing Science*, *International Journal of Research in Marketing*, *Journal of the Academy of Marketing Science* and *Decision Sciences*. He has received several awards for his research, including a doctoral dissertation award from the Procter & Gamble Market Innovation Research Fund. For his research, he has received the Honorable Mention Award at the prestigious MSI/JM competition, the year 2003 Young Contributor Award from the Society of Consumer Psychology, and the 2006 Paul E. Green Award and 2010 O'Dell Award for best article published in the *Journal of Marketing Research* in 2005. He received his PhD from the University of Cincinnati.

Dominique M. Hanssens is the Bud Knapp Professor of Marketing at the UCLA Anderson Graduate School of Management, where he has been on the faculty since 1977. He has served as the school's faculty chair, associate dean and marketing area chair. From 2005 to 2007 he served as executive director of the *Marketing Science Institute* in Cambridge, Massachusetts. His research focuses on strategic marketing problems. Dr Hanssens serves or has served as an area editor for *Marketing Science* and an associate editor for *Management Science* and the *Journal of Marketing Research*. His papers have appeared in the leading academic and professional journals in marketing, economics and statistics. Five of these articles have won best-paper awards. Dr Hanssens won distinguished teaching awards in the UCLA MBA and Executive MBA programs. In 2003 he was awarded the UCLA Anderson School's Neidorf "decade" teaching award, in 2007 he was the recipient of the Churchill Lifetime Achievement Award of the American Marketing Association, and in 2010 he was elected a Fellow of the INFORMS Society for *Marketing Science*. He received his PhD in marketing from Purdue University.

Kristiaan Helsen is an associate professor at the Hong Kong University of Science & Technology. His research interests include competitive marketing, hazard rate modeling, international marketing, new products modeling, product harm crises and empirical modeling. He serves on the editorial board for the *International Journal of Research in*

Marketing. Some of his research has appeared in the *Journal of Marketing, International Journal of Research in Marketing, Marketing Science, Journal of Retailing, Journal of Marketing Research* and *Marketing Letters.* Dr Helsen received his PhD in Marketing from the University of Pennsylvania.

Donna L. Hoffman is the Chancellor's Chair and Professor of Marketing at the A. Gary Anderson Graduate School of Management at UC Riverside. She has published widely in the top academic journals and has been awarded the Sheth Foundation/*Journal of Marketing* Award for long-term contributions to the discipline of marketing, the Stellner Distinguished Scholar Award from the University of Illinois, and the William O'Dell/ *Journal of Marketing Research* Award for long-term research impact. She also co-directs the UCR Sloan Center for Internet Retailing. She is also the co-founder of eLab, an internationally recognized, award-winning research lab for fielding online experiments and surveys regarding the Internet. *The New York Times* calls this pioneering effort "one of the premiere research centers in the world for the study of electronic commerce," and *The Wall Street Journal* recognizes the effort as the "electronic commerce pioneer among business schools." She was named a Distinguished Graduate Alumnus of UNC in 2002. Dr Hoffman has a PhD from the University of North Carolina at Chapel Hill.

Douglas B. Holt is President of the Cultural Strategy Group, a brand and innovation consultancy. He formerly held the chair in marketing at Oxford and also taught at Harvard Business School. In his academic research Holt works from a consumer culture theory perspective to examine sociological questions concerning social class, gender and brands. He has published widely on these issues in the *Journal of Consumer Research* and the *Journal of Consumer Culture.* He is former editor of the *Journal of Consumer Culture* and co-edited *The Consumer Society Reader* (with Juliet Schor). In his management research, Holt pioneered a cultural approach to branding and innovation in his books *How Brands Become Icons: The Principles of Cultural Branding* (Harvard Business School Press, 2004) and *Cultural Strategy: Using Innovative Ideologies to Build Breakthrough Brands* (Oxford University Press, 2010). Holt is now a Fellow at Colorado State University's Center for Fair and Alternative Trade, where he works on branding environmental issues including climate change. He earned a PhD from Northwestern's Kellogg School.

Katherine E. Jocz is a research associate at Harvard Business School. Previously, she was senior director of networks and relationships and thought leader at Marketspace, a Monitor Group company. Formerly, she was vice president of research operations at the Marketing Science Institute. She has served on the editorial review board of the *Journal of Marketing*, the board of directors of the Association for Consumer Research, committees for the annual Marketing and Public Policy conference, and the US Census Bureau Advisory Committee. Her publications include articles and books on marketing management and the discipline of marketing; the most recent is *Greater Good: How Good Marketing Makes for Better Democracy* (with John Quelch).

Kevin Lane Keller is the E.B. Osborn Professor of Marketing at the Tuck School of Business at Dartmouth College. Professor Keller has degrees from Cornell, Carnegie-Mellon and Duke universities. At Dartmouth, he teaches MBA courses on marketing management and strategic brand management, and lectures in executive programs on that topic. Professor Keller's general area of expertise lies in marketing strategy and planning. His specific research interest is in how understanding theories and concepts related to consumer behavior can improve marketing strategies. His research has been published in three of the major marketing journals: *Journal of Marketing*, *Journal of Marketing Research* and *Journal of Consumer Research*. He also has served on the editorial review boards of those journals. With over 60 published papers, his research has been widely cited and has received numerous awards. He has served as a consultant and advisor to marketers for some of the world's most successful brands. He has also served as an academic trustee for the Marketing Science Institute. His textbook, *Strategic Brand Management*, has been adopted at top business schools and leading firms around the world and has been heralded as the "bible of branding."

Roger A. Kerin is the Harold C. Simmons Distinguished Professor of Marketing at the Cox Business School at Southern Methodist University. Dr Kerin currently serves on the editorial boards of the *Journal of Retailing* and the *Journal of Business & Industrial Marketing*, and has served on the *Journal of Marketing*, *Journal of Marketing Research*, *Journal of the Academy of Marketing Science*, *Journal of Strategic Marketing* and *Marketing Letters* boards. During 1988–90, he served as the editor for the *Journal of Marketing*. He has consulted for numerous companies, such as Alcon Laboratories, Wal-Mart, Frito-Lay, Honeywell, Marion Laboratories and Club Corporation of America in the areas of brand management, market strategy, product management and strategic marketing. He received his PhD from the University of Minnesota, Minneapolis.

V. Kumar, or VK as he is more popularly known in academic and professional circles, is the Richard and Susan Lenny Distinguished Chair Professor in Marketing, the Executive Director of the Center for Excellence in Brand and Customer Management, and the Director of the PhD Program in Marketing at the J. Mack Robinson School of Business, Georgia State University. Dr V. Kumar's pioneering research on customer loyalty and customer lifetime value has received attention worldwide. His research has been widely published in premier journals such as the *Journal of Marketing*, *Harvard Business Review*, *Sloan Management Review*, *Journal of Marketing Research*, *Marketing Science* and *Operations Research*, to name a few. He was recently ranked as one of the top five scholars in marketing worldwide. VK also serves as a consultant for leading Fortune 500 corporations. Dr V. Kumar's latest book is titled *Managing Customers For Profit* (January 2008). Dr Kumar recently received two lifetime achievement awards. He was a finalist for 2006 & 2007 ISMS Practice Prize Competition and has been awarded twice the H. Paul Root Award by AMA and MSI.

Marvin B. Lieberman is a professor in the policy area at UCLA Anderson School of Management. From 1982 to 1989, he was Assistant Professor of Business Policy in the Graduate School of Business at Stanford University. Professor Lieberman's current research focuses on issues relating to market entry, and productivity and performance comparisons of US and foreign manufacturing firms. His broader teaching and research interests are in the areas of competitive strategy, industrial economics and operations management. He is the author of numerous articles in professional journals, on topics such as cost reduction and productivity improvement, market entry and exit, and strategic investment. His paper on "First-mover advantages" (co-authored with David

Montgomery) was awarded the 1996 Best Paper Prize by the Strategic Management Society. He received his PhD degree in Business Economics from Harvard University.

Vikas Mittal is the J. Hugh Liedtke Professor of Marketing at the Jones Graduate School of Business at Rice University. Before joining Katz, he was on the faculty at Kellogg Graduate School at Northwestern University. Dr Mittal's publications appear in leading marketing journals such as the *Journal of Consumer Research, Journal of Marketing, Journal of Marketing Research* and *Marketing Science*. He currently serves on the editorial boards of the *Journal of Consumer Research, Journal of Marketing, Journal of Marketing Research, Journal of Service Research, Journal of the Academy of Marketing Science, Journal of Interactive Marketing* and *Journal of Retailing*. In 2006 Professor Mittal was awarded the William F. O'Dell Award for making the most significant long-term contribution to the theory, methodology and practice of marketing. In 2001 his research was recognized with the FedEx Excellence in Service Research award at the *Journal of Service Research*. At Katz, he won the excellence in teaching award at the Katz Graduate School three years running, and was voted the best professor by executives in the 2003 IEMBA program in Brazil. Dr Mittal holds a PhD in Management from Temple University.

David B. Montgomery is the Kresge Professor of Marketing – Emeritus, Graduate School of Business, Stanford University and Dean – Emeritus at Singapore Management University. He has published over 100 articles and ten books and special journal issues relating to marketing science, marketing strategy, and global marketing and management. He is an INFORMS Fellow (2009) and is an Inaugural Fellow of the INFORMS Society for Marketing Science (2008) and was awarded the 2002 AMA Career Contributions to Marketing Strategy award. He has served on the editorial boards of seven leading marketing/strategy/management science journals. His interests include the analysis of competitor response and decision making, global strategic alliances, globalization of marketing, global account management, modeling business-to-business buyer behavior, empirical analysis of the manufacturing/marketing interface, methods and applications of meta-analysis.

Thomas P. Novak is the Albert O. Steffey Professor of Marketing and Co-Director of the Sloan Center for Internet Retailing at the University of California, Riverside. Novak's research has focused exclusively on Internet and Web-based commerce. His current research areas include measuring the online consumer experience, Internet marketing, societal impact of the Internet and social cognition. An internationally recognized academic researcher in Web-based commerce, Novak has published extensively on the topic in academic journals in a range of scholarly disciplines, including *SCIENCE, Marketing Science, Journal of Marketing, Communications of the ACM*, the *Information Society* and *Harvard Business Review*. He has also been a contributing writer to both *Wired* and *HotWired*. Novak received his PhD in quantitative psychology with a formal minor in Biostatistics from the University of North Carolina, Chapel Hill.

Robert W. Palmatier is an associate professor of marketing, John C. Narver Endowed Professor at the Foster School of Business at the University of Washington. His research interests include relationship marketing theory and strategy, customers' relationships in the business-to-business and retail markets and the role of customer relationships in services and innovation. His research has been published in the *Journal of Marketing*,

Journal of Marketing Research, Journal of Consumer Psychology and *Marketing Science*. He has won research awards including the American Marketing Association award for the Best Services Article for "Effect of service transition strategies on firm value," and the Harold H. Maynard Award for a significant contribution to marketing theory and thought in the *Journal of Marketing* (2008). Dr Palmatier has consulted for Microsoft, Telstra, Emerson, Littelfuse, Fifth Third Bank and Cincom. He received his PhD from the University of Missouri, Columbia.

John A. Quelch is a Distinguished Professor of International Management, Vice President and Dean at CEIBS. He was appointed as La Caixa Visiting Professor of International Management at CEIBS in 2009 and joined CEIBS officially in February 2011. Previously, he was Senior Associate Dean and Lincoln Filene Professor of Business Administration at Harvard Business School. Professor Quelch's research focus is on global marketing and branding in emerging as well as developed markets. Professor Quelch is the author, co-author or editor of 25 books, including *Greater Good: How Good Marketing Makes for Better Democracy* (2008), *Business Solutions for the Global Poor: Creating Social and Economic Value* (2007), *The New Global Brands* (2006), *Global Marketing Management* (5th edition, 2006), *The Global Market* (2005), *Cases in Advertising and Promotion Management* (4th edition, 1996) and *The Marketing Challenge of Europe 1992* (2nd edition, 1991). He has published 17 articles on marketing strategy issues in *Harvard Business Review*, and many more in leading practitioner and academic journals. Professor Quelch has served as an independent director of 12 publicly listed companies in the USA and UK. He received his DBA from Harvard University.

Bharath Rajan is research manager for the Center for Excellence in Brand and Customer Management at the J. Mack Robinson College of Business. He holds undergraduate and graduate degrees in Business and Economics. Bharath has published in business and marketing journals such as *Management Accounting Quarterly*, *Strategic Finance* and *Marketing Intelligence Review*. His current research interests include customer relationship management, group-buying behavior, international marketing research and international trade.

Jagmohan S. Raju is the Joseph J. Aresty Professor and Director of the Wharton–Indian School of Business Program. Professor Raju is internationally known for his research on pricing strategies, coupon programs, managing private labels and sales force compensation. He consults extensively with companies around the world, including Wyeth Pharmaceuticals, Medtronic, Warner Home Video, and Johnson & Johnson on designing pricing strategies and developing launch plans for new products. A prolific scholar, Professor Raju's research has been published in top-tier academic journals including *Management Science, Journal of Retailing* and *Marketing Science*. He also serves as the marketing editor of *Management Science* and is the President of the INFORMS Society for Marketing Science, a professional organization whose members include marketing academics and business executives who apply quantitative methods to solve marketing problems. He has received numerous teaching and research awards. He received his PhD from Stanford University.

Ram C. Rao is the Founders' Professor and Professor of Marketing at the University of Texas at Dallas. Dr Rao's research investigates how firms compete and how they should formulate competitive marketing strategies with emphasis on pricing. He has published numerous papers in leading marketing journals, and his research has received support from the National Science Foundation as well as Nortel Networks. He serves on the editorial boards of the *Journal of Marketing Research* and *Marketing Science*, and is past area editor of *Marketing Science* and associate editor for the *Journal of Business Economics and Statistics*. He is currently the co-editor of the Web-based marketing journal *Review of Marketing Science* (*ROMS*) and serves on the advisory boards of *Quantitative Marketing and Economics* and *Marketing Research Network*. Dr Rao received his PhD from Carnegie-Mellon University.

Brian T. Ratchford is the Charles and Nancy Davidson Professor of Marketing, University of Texas at Dallas. From 1999 to 2006 he was Pepsico Chair in Consumer Research, University of Maryland. From 1971 to 1999 he held various academic positions at State University of New York at Buffalo. His research interests are in economics applied to the study of consumer behavior, information economics, marketing productivity, marketing research and electronic commerce. He has published over 70 articles in marketing and related fields, including articles in the *Marketing Science, Management Science, Journal of Consumer Research* and *Journal of Marketing Research*. He was editor of *Marketing Science* from 1998 to 2002, is currently an associate editor of the *Journal of Consumer Research*, and is currently on the editorial review boards of the *Journal of Marketing Research, Journal of Marketing, Journal of Retailing, Journal of Interactive Marketing* and *Journal of Service Research*. He received his PhD degree from the University of Rochester.

John H. Roberts is a professor of marketing at the London Business School with a joint appointment with the School of Management, Marketing and International Business at the Australian National University. His research expertise is in marketing strategy, marketing models and their adoption in industry, new product marketing and brand equity, high-technology marketing and methods to measure its effect in the marketplace. He has published on this area in the *Harvard Business Review, Marketing Science* and *Journal of Marketing Research*. He also has extensive consulting and senior management experience in calibrating marketing strategies. Dr Roberts has served on the editorial board for *Marketing Science, Journal of Marketing Research, International Journal of Research in Marketing, Journal of Forecasting, Academic Trustee* and *Marketing Sciences Institute*. He received his PhD from the Massachusetts Institute of Technology.

Derek D. Rucker holds the Richard M. Clewett Professorship in Marketing at Kellogg School of Management at Northwestern University. His primary research focuses on study attitudes, persuasion and consumer behavior. His work has appeared in numerous leading journals in psychology and marketing, such as the *Journal of Personality and Social Psychology, Journal of Consumer Research, Journal of Marketing Research* and *Journal of Consumer Psychology*. In addition, his research has been covered in major media outlets such as *The New York Times, Time Magazine* and *ABC News*. In recognition of his passion for teaching, Dr Rucker was nominated as a finalist for the L.G. Lavengood Outstanding Professor of the Year Award. In addition to his work in the classroom, Dr Rucker is a co-instructor of the annual Kellogg Advertising Superbowl Review. The review is in the spirit of Kellogg's focus on experiential learning and is designed to cultivate basic principles learned in the classroom to critically evaluate advertising in a real-world and high stakes environment.

Gaurav Sabnis is Visiting Associate Professor of Marketing at the Fordham School of Business, Fordham University. His PhD is from Penn State University. His research focuses empirical modeling of marketing strategy issues related to competition, user-generated content and sales management. Before entering academia, he worked as a sales manager for IBM, India.

Raj Sethuraman is an associate professor of marketing and Department Chair at the Cox Business School at Southern Methodist University. Dr Sethuraman's research interests include the tradeoff between price promotion and advertising, competition between national brands and stores brands, and measuring brand equity. His research has appeared in *Marketing Science, Journal of Retailing, Journal of Business Research* and *Journal of Marketing Research*. He has served on the editorial boards of the *Journal of Retailing, Marketing Science, Review of Marketing Science* and *Journal of Modeling in Management*. He has consulted on the following topics: strategic marketing, price and advertising strategies, national brand versus store brand competition, marketing generalization and statistical analysis, and some of his consulting engagements include Samsung, KPMG, QUEST and the Center for Non-Profit Management. He received his PhD from Northwestern University.

Venkatesh (Venky) Shankar is Professor and Coleman Chair in Marketing and Marketing PhD Program Director, Mays Business School, Texas A&M University. He has a PhD from Kellogg Graduate School of Management, Northwestern University. His expertise areas include marketing strategy, innovation, e-business, international marketing, and retailing. His research has been published in *Journal of Marketing Research, Marketing Science, Management Science, Strategic Management Journal, Journal of Marketing, Harvard Business Review* and *Sloan Management Review.* Dr Shankar is the author of *Shopper Marketing* and co-editor of the *Handbook of Marketing Strategy.* He is an Academic Trustee of the Marketing Science Institute and winner of the Clarke Award for the Outstanding Direct Marketing Educator, the Green Award for the Best Article in *Journal of Marketing Research*, the Lehmann Award for the Best Dissertation-based Article in an AMA journal, and the Sheth Award for the Best Paper in *Journal of Academy of Marketing Science.* He is Editor Emeritus of the *Journal of Interactive Marketing*, ex-associate editor of *Management Science* and is on the editorial boards of *Journal of Marketing, Journal of Marketing Research, Marketing Science, International Journal of Research in Marketing, Journal of Academy of Marketing Science*, and *Journal of Retailing.* The Shankar-Spiegel Award from the Direct Marketing Educational Foundation is named in his honor. He is ex-President of the Marketing Strategy SIG, AMA and serves on the Chief Marketing Officers (CMO) council and Business-to-Business (B2B) Leadership Board. He is three-time winner of the Krowe Award for Outstanding Teaching and has been a visiting faculty member at MIT, INSEAD, Singapore Management University, SDA Bocconi, Nanyang Technology University, Indian School of Business, and Chinese European International Business School. He has been a keynote speaker in several conferences and has delivered over 150 presentations in different countries, including Australia, Belgium, China, Finland, France, Germany,

Hong Kong, India, Italy, Mexico, Netherlands, Singapore, the UK, and the USA. His work has generated about 4 000 citations and 10 of his articles have won best paper/ honorable mention/finalist awards. He has appeared as an international business expert on CNN and C-SPAN and has served as an expert witness in business cases. He has had working/consulting/executive education experience with companies such as ARINC, Allstate Insurance, Cap Gemini Ernst & Young, Colgate-Palmolive, Frito-Lay, Giant Food, Glaxo SmithKline, Halliburton, Hewlett Packard, Honeywell, HSBC, IBM, Intel, International Paper, Lockheed Martin, Lucent Technologies, Marriott International, Medtronic, Northrop Grumman, PepsiCo, Philips, Sirius, United Nations Foundation, Vodafone, Volvo Group, and Wegmans.

Gerard Tellis is a professor of marketing, Neely Chair of American Enterprise and Director of the Center for Global Innovation at the USC Marshall School of Business. He has been Visiting Chair of Marketing, Strategy and Innovation at the Judge Business School, Cambridge University, UK, and Distinguished Visitor, Erasmus University, Rotterdam. Dr Tellis specializes in the areas of innovation, global strategy, market entry, new product growth, advertising, promotion and pricing. He has published over 100 articles and four books, which have won 15 awards, including five of the most prestigious awards in the field of marketing: the Frank M. Bass, William F. Odell, Harold D. Maynard (twice), AMA–Berry and AMA Mahajan award for lifetime contributions to marketing strategy. He is an associate editor for the *Journal of Marketing Research* and has been on the editorial review boards of the *Journal of Marketing Research*, *Journal of Marketing* and *Marketing Science* for several years. He received his PhD from the University of Michigan.

Rajan Varadarajan is a Distinguished Professor of Marketing and holder of the Ford Chair in Marketing and E-Commerce in the Mays Business School at Texas A&M University. His primary teaching and research interests are in the area of marketing strategy. He is author of over 60 refereed journal articles on such topics as market strategy, marketing strategy, competitive advantage, corporate diversification and divestitures, e-commerce, global competitive strategy, innovation, market pioneering advantage, multi-market competition, strategic alliances, strategy typologies and taxonomies, and interdependencies between corporate, business and marketing strategy. His research has been published in such journals as the *Journal of Marketing*, *Journal of the Academy of Marketing Science*, *Academy of Management Journal*, *Strategic Management Journal* and *Management Science.* He currently serves on the editorial review boards of a number of journals, including the *Journal of Marketing*, *Journal of Marketing Research*, *Journal of the Academy of Marketing Science*, *Journal of Interactive Marketing*, *Journal of Strategic Marketing* and *Journal of Marketing Management*. Dr Varadarajan is a recipient of a number of honors and awards including the American Marketing Association Paul D. Converse Award for contributions to the field of marketing (2008) and the *Journal of Marketing* Harold H. Maynard Best Paper Award (2001). He received his PhD from the University of Massachusetts.

Peter C. Verhoef is a professor of marketing at the University of Groningen, The Netherlands. His research interests concern customer management, customer loyalty, multi-channel issues, category management and consumer well-being. He has extensively published on these topics and worked with multiple co-authors across the globe. His publications have appeared in several journals, including the *Journal of Marketing*, *Journal of Marketing Research*, *Marketing Science*, *Marketing Letters*, *Journal of Consumer Psychology*, *Journal of the Academy of Marketing Science* and *Journal of Retailing*. His work has been awarded with the Donald R. Lehmann Award for the best dissertation-based article in the *Journal of Marketing* and *Journal of Marketing Research* in 2003 and the Harold M. Maynard Award for the best article published in the *Journal of Marketing* in 2009. He is currently an editorial board member of the *Journal of Marketing*, *Marketing Science*, *Journal of Retailing*, *Journal of Service Research* and *Journal of Interactive Marketing*. He functions as area editor for the *International Journal of Research in Marketing*. Dr Verhoef is the founder and director of the Customer Insights Center University of Groningen, which now has more than 20 member companies. He obtained his PhD from Erasmus University Rotterdam, The Netherlands.

Russell S. Winer is the William H. Joyce Professor of Marketing and Chair at New York University, Stern. His research interests include customer relationship management, consumer choice models, information technology in marketing and the psychological aspects of price. Dr Winer has written three books, *Marketing Management*, *Analysis for Marketing Planning and Product Management*, and a research monograph, *Pricing*, and has authored over 60 papers in marketing on a variety of topics including consumer choice, marketing research methodology, marketing planning, advertising and pricing. He has served two terms as the editor of the *Journal of Marketing Research*, he is the past co-editor of the *Journal of Interactive Marketing* and is currently an associate editor of the *International Journal of Research in Marketing*. Dr Winer is the co-editor of the *Review of Marketing Science*, and he is on the editorial boards of the *Journal of Marketing*, *Journal of Marketing Research* and *Marketing Science*. He received his PhD from Carnegie-Mellon University.

Foreword

Philip Kotler

This book focuses on an important part of marketing, namely marketing strategy. It does not discuss marketing tactics, macro marketing, or other branches of marketing. I like to think of "strategy" as "a thoughtful plan by a company to produce desired outcomes in the marketplace vis-a-vis customers, channel members, and competitors." We can even think of certain companies that have developed an exemplary marketing strategy on which their business rests: Amazon, Apple, Facebook, Google, Harley Davidson, Southwest Airlines, and Starbucks, to name a few. Whether these companies developed their strategy by accident or by design doesn't matter. The incontestable fact is that each of these companies has a strategy, not just a set of tactics.

I don't want to diminish the role of marketing tactics. Without proper tactics, a strategy would fail. Starbucks knows this and its tactics include serving good coffee in many varieties; its baristas must be knowledgeable, quick, and motivated; its decor and furnishings must be earthy. Otherwise, poor tactics and poor implementation can destroy a good strategy. Herb Kelleher, founder of the successful Southwest Airlines, said, "We have a strategic plan. It is called doing things."

For a strategy to succeed, it should be unique. Unfortunately, strategies are converging and losing their uniqueness. If all competitors have the same strategy, then it isn't a strategy. You may be able to implement the same strategy better than your competitors, but it would be even more sustainable and profitable if it was different and unique. Bruce Henderson, a famous consultant, said, "Unless a business has a unique advantage over its rivals, it has no reason to exist."

A company must keep its strategy current. There is the danger of markets changing faster than the company's marketing. Sears, K-Mart, and GM were admirably responsive to the marketplace of yesterday, as they found out. To stay relevant, companies really need two marketing departments: one keeps furiously selling to the market of today; the other tries to figure out what the market of tomorrow will look like. Over time, the company carefully shifts its strategy toward what the market of tomorrow requires.

My observation is that companies are tactics-rich and strategy-poor. The reason for this book is to bring a greater consciousness into marketers' thinking about whether they are just dishing out tactics or have a firm strategy foundation on which to hang their tactics. Venky Shankar and Greg Carpenter, the editors of the *Handbook of Marketing Strategy*, have divided the chapters into seven major strategic topics in marketing strategy. For each topic, they searched for the most stimulating authors and articles. The result is 27 rich chapters on different facets of marketing strategy by 36 scholars in marketing strategy. My guess is that if each marketing department would assign a topic reading each week over a seven-week period, and discuss the articles, then the members of that marketing department would gain new insights and end up with a new and refined sense of marketing strategy.

Philip Kotler
S. C. Johnson and Son, Distinguished Professor of International Marketing
Kellogg School of Management, Northwestern University

Acknowledgments

A *Handbook* of this nature is not possible without the assistance of several people. We will be remiss if we do not acknowledge their assistance. First, a big "thank you" to all the authors of the chapters for their thoughtful contributions and patience during the publication process. Second, our sincere thanks to Faye Palmer of Kellogg Graduate School of Management, Northwestern University for her unwavering commitment to corresponding and following up with the authors. Finally, our heartfelt appreciation to Nicole Hanson, marketing doctoral student, Mays Business School, Texas A&M University for her diligent proofreading of a few chapters.

Venkatesh Shankar
College Station

Gregory S. Carpenter
Evanston

1 Introduction
Venkatesh Shankar and Gregory S. Carpenter

Since Peter Drucker first articulated it, the marketing concept has become central to marketing, it has been embraced by other fields such as strategic management, and it has become central to the practice of management. Drucker, of course, argued that products, brands or technologies do not produce profits. Customers do, and the purpose of business – not *a business* but *business* – is to create customers. From that process, profits flow. As the marketing concept has become more mainstream, it has become recognized as the engine driving the growth and success of many firms. As the global economic downturn continues, and firms seek growth, even more have embraced the marketing concept, seeking to enjoy the fruits of a sound marketing strategy.

Marketing remains a broad and dynamic field. Developments in the social sciences influence how we think about customers, markets and competition; technological innovations change how organizations reach customers, and organizational changes influence how marketing is practiced within firms. Our goal in this handbook is to provide an authoritative, comprehensive and accessible resource on the current state of marketing strategy. We intend the handbook to be an important resource guide for researchers, doctoral students, practitioners and consultants in the field of marketing strategy. Toward that end, the handbook provides a broad overview of marketing strategy with contributions from leading experts on the different facets of marketing strategy, including its evolution, competitor analysis, customer management, resource allocation, dynamics, branding, advertising, multichannel management, digital marketing and financial aspects.

We have selected seven broad topics for this handbook. Part I focuses on the conceptual and organizational aspects of marketing strategy and contains two chapters. Part II deals with understanding competition and comprises three chapters. Part III focuses on customers and customer-based strategy and includes two chapters. The eight chapters of Part IV deal with different marketing strategy decisions, ranging from the allocation of marketing resources to the management of customer satisfaction. Three chapters constitute Part V, which focuses on branding and brand strategies. Part VI deals with marketing strategy dynamics and consists of four chapters. The final section (Part VII) contains four chapters that discuss the impact of marketing strategy on performance variables such as sales, market share, shareholder value and stakeholder value.

In each part, each chapter is authored by expert(s) on the relevant topic. The authors focus on a number of managerially relevant concerns. These concerns include, What are some marketing strategy issues that keep strategy professionals awake? What decisions related to the focal topic are critical? How do managers currently make these decisions? What insights/tools on this topic will be most helpful to managers? The chapters in the handbook offer an in-depth analysis of research developments, provide frameworks for analyzing key issues, and highlight important unresolved problems in marketing strategy.

CONCEPTS OF MARKETING STRATEGY

What is marketing strategy? Although definitions abound, we view marketing strategy as a broad plan of managerial initiatives and actions relating an organization to its customers and markets. Three key aspects distinguish marketing strategy from marketing tactics. (1) Marketing strategy focuses on the strategic decisions necessary to allocate resources. (2) It concerns managerial actions that have long-term effects. (3) Decisions relating to marketing strategy are made by marketing executives in an organization and implemented by many others through the organization and beyond.

Part I begins with a discussion of the concepts of marketing strategy. Varadarajan (Chapter 2) first differentiates marketing strategy from strategic marketing. He views strategic marketing as a field of study and marketing strategy as an organizational construct. He further opines that the characterization of marketing decisions pertaining to segmentation, target market selection and positioning as "strategic marketing decisions" and decisions that pertain to product, promotion, price and distribution as "tactical marketing decisions" is arbitrary and conceptually flawed. He prefers that we simply refer to issues concerning all these decisions as more strategic or less strategic. He describes marketing strategy as "an organization's integrated pattern of decisions that specify its crucial choices concerning products, markets, marketing actions and marketing resources in the creation, communication and/or delivery of products that offer value to customers in exchanges with the organization and thereby enable the organization to achieve specific objectives."

One of the fundamental concepts of marketing is the concept of market orientation. In Chapter 3, Gebhardt discusses what market orientation means and how firms can be market-oriented toward better performance. He focuses on the characteristics of market-oriented firms, explains how and why such firms are able to achieve superior market performance, and outlines what managers can do to create greater levels of market orientation in their organizations.

UNDERSTANDING COMPETITION

An important component of market orientation is understanding competitors and competition. Part II covers competitor analysis. In Chapter 4, Czepiel and Kerin discuss the objectives of competitor analysis and lay out the processes involved in identifying important competitors and information needs, gathering necessary information and interpreting this information for gaining competitive advantage.

To attain competitive advantage, firms also need to understand the structure of the market. In Chapter 5, Sabnis and Grewal address this topic by reviewing the main themes of competition research in marketing and related fields such as economics, industrial organization, management and sociology. They elaborate on competitive market structure and on behavioral and structural approaches to understanding firms' responsiveness to competition, including the structure–conduct–performance and the new empirical industrial organization (NEIO) approaches. They also propose an agenda for further research, highlighting how Internet and user-generated content are changing the nature of competition among firms.

Much of the competition discussed in Chapters 4 and 5 relates to competition among manufacturers or service providers. What about retail competition and its implications for marketing strategy? In Chapter 6, Rao provides an overview of the models of retail competition, beginning with models between two or more retailers who compete on the price dimension and one or more of convenience, products, service and format dimensions. He discusses such retail competition topics as retail format, promotions, assortment, trade support, loyalty programs, e-tailing and new retailer entry.

CUSTOMER-BASED MARKETING STRATEGY

From understanding competition, we turn to understanding customers in Part III. Customers can be viewed as strategic assets. Each customer of an organization has a lifetime value for that organization. In Chapter 7, Kumar and Rajan discuss the concept of customer lifetime value (CLV) and its implications for marketing strategy. They highlight the need for measuring and managing CLV by contrasting the accuracy of CLV with the other traditional metrics used in managing customer value. They provide an integrated approach to manage CLV that accounts for the nature (B2B versus B2C) and the type (contractual versus non-contractual) of relationships between customers and firms.

Customer management takes place through multiple channels. In Chapter 8, Verhoef reviews the most recent developments in multichannel customer management (MCM), building on Neslin and Shankar (2009). He discusses a strategic framework for MCM, including its strategic foundations and formulation, implementation and evaluation of MCM strategy.

MARKETING STRATEGY DECISIONS

Armed with a good analysis of company, competition and customers, a firm needs a deep understanding of the different decisions underlying marketing strategy. Part IV focuses on these decisions. First, firms need to effectively allocate their marketing resources. In Chapter 9, Shankar reviews the issues, methods and models for allocating resources among marketing and non-marketing variables, products, markets, channels, customers and stages in the product life cycle.

With organizational resources effectively allocated, firms need to develop a successful strategy for launching and managing new products. In Chapter 10, Roberts reviews and discusses how to develop new products and services in the context of the overall strategic environment of the organization. He reviews the commonly used methods for developing new products, including the stage-gate system.

To be successful, products need to be supported by a strong advertising and communication strategy. In Chapter 11, Rucker reviews advertising strategies, discussing research findings that share the idea that persuasion can be enhanced by aligning consumer mindsets with the advertising message.

As communication efforts are increasingly reallocated to the new media (e.g. social media, mobile media), organizations can benefit from a thorough understanding of strategies related to such media. In Chapter 12, Hoffman and Novak discuss social media and their impact on marketing strategy and practice. They define social media as media that enable and facilitate conversations among consumers primarily through Web-based tools, including mobile applications that people use to create and share content. They point out that, in an effective social media strategy, marketers should not control these conversations, but must listen to, participate in, and influence the conversations.

In Chapter 13, Shankar introduces mobile marketing and proposes a framework for understanding mobile marketing strategy. He identifies the key features of mobile devices, outlines how mobile marketing strategy differs from traditional marketing strategy, and discusses its drivers, decision components and consequences.

In addition to developing appropriate strategies for social and mobile media, marketers require a good understanding of managing channel relationships. In Chapter 14, Arnold and Palmatier discuss the important issues relating to channel management strategy. They outline relationship theory, discuss the antecedents to a relational channel exchange, and describe the key drivers and consequences of channel relationships.

Together with channel relationship strategy, marketers need to develop sound pricing strategy. In Chapter 15, Winer lays out the behavioral issues in developing such a strategy. These issues include: price knowledge, digit pricing, price fairness, reference prices, price–quality relationship and context effect on price judgment.

Finally, managing customer satisfaction is a critical decision element of marketing strategy. Chapter 16 by Mittal and Frennea provides an overview of this topic. The authors view customer satisfaction (CS) as customers' post-consumption/purchase evaluation of a good or service based on a single experience (i.e. transactional) or a series of experiences (i.e. cumulative). They examine from three perspectives, each with its own insights: comparing a firm to other firms longitudinally and cross-sectionally (macro); understanding how CS affects the firm's entire customer base (meso) and examining the antecedents of overall CS (micro).

BRANDING AND BRAND STRATEGIES

From marketing strategy decisions, we proceed to strategies relating to brands. As intangible assets, brands have become recognized as increasingly important and valuable. Part V focuses on brands and branding strategies. In Chapter 17, Keller provides an overview of brand architecture strategies. He discusses three key issues underlying brand architecture strategy: (1) the potential of a brand viewed along the breadth of its "market footprint," (2) the types of product and service extensions that allow a brand to achieve that potential, and (3) the brand elements and positioning that are associated with the offerings of a brand as part of that extension strategy.

While Keller's chapter covers brand architecture and extension, Holt (Chapter 18) focuses on the cultural perspective of branding strategy. Holt views cultural brand strategy as a distinctive approach to strategy that is guided by theories of culture, society and politics. According to him, such a strategy helps develop new businesses and revive defunct enterprises. He illustrates cultural brand strategy through a case study involving the Jack Daniel's brand.

Finally, in the retail environment, private label brands have been growing substantially. In Chapter 19, Sethuraman and Raju offer an in-depth view of private label strategy. Starting with the view that store brand management is part of category management for retailers, they discuss five components of private label strategy, including decisions relating to the introduction, targeting, positioning, pricing and promotion of private label brands.

MARKETING STRATEGY DYNAMICS

From brand strategies we move to the dynamics of marketing strategy in Part VI. In Chapter 20, Lieberman and Montgomery discuss the ambiguities, misperceptions and myths concerning the advantages of being a first mover or pioneer. They present the fundamental mechanisms that may create or inhibit first-mover advantage and provide an overview of the empirical evidence relating to such an advantage.

There are some advantages of being a late mover as well. In Chapter 21, Shankar and Carpenter present these advantages, their sources and associated late-mover strategies. The authors show that although there are several arguments in favor of pioneering advantage, by adopting the right strategies later entrants can successfully overtake the pioneer and turn the conventional wisdom of pioneering advantage on its head.

As brands diffuse in the market over time, marketers need to develop appropriate marketing strategies during different periods in the life cycle. In Chapter 22, Tellis and Chandrasekaran discuss the diffusion of innovations and its implications for marketing strategy. They summarize the key research and findings relating to the diffusion of innovations, including the Bass model, its estimations and extensions, turning points in the product life cycle and diffusion patterns across countries.

Finally, researchers and managers need a good understanding of the dynamics of entering overseas markets. In Chapter 23, Gielens, Helsen and Dekimpe provide a detailed review of international market entry strategies. They review the antecedents and consequences of international entry decision components, including country selection, entry timing, entry mode and entry scale, and product adaptation. They also discuss the interrelationships among these components and their dynamics.

IMPACT OF MARKETING STRATEGY

From the dynamics of marketing strategy, we move in Part VII to focus on the impact of marketing strategy. We begin this section with Shankar's chapter (Chapter 24) on the relationship between marketing strategy and firm or shareholder value. It reviews what is known about the effects of marketing strategy components such as business-model changes, new product introductions, and communication strategy changes on firm value. It proposes a framework of how marketing strategy affects firm value, documents empirical evidence and highlights unexplored issues.

In assessing the effect of marketing strategy on the organization, a common concern for many marketers is the financial return on marketing strategy. In Chapter 25, Ratchford examines the productivity of marketing investments and returns to marketing efforts. He views productivity as a ratio of inputs to outputs and, in this context, as the ability of resources expended on implementing marketing strategies to affect some measure of output, such as sales, market share and profit. He reviews conceptual approaches to productivity measurement, discusses measurement techniques and reviews applications of the conceptual approaches to productivity and the resulting findings.

Marketing expenditures also need to be managed for long-term and profitable growth. In Chapter 26, Hanssens and Dekimpe discuss the long-term effects of marketing strategy on sales and market share. They define short- and long-term horizons and summarize the learning on marketing's impact on both short-term and long-term business performance, including on brand equity and customer equity. They conclude with some empirical generalizations on the long-term effects of the major elements of marketing strategy.

We close with Chapter 27, in which Quelch and Jocz discuss marketing, its relationship with and role in democracy. They propose a conceptual framework in which good marketing strategies create social capital, which, in turn, leads to a vibrant democracy. According to them, marketing is also connected to democracy through economic development and growth of social institutions. By highlighting six core benefits – exchange, consumption, choice, information, engagement and inclusion – that marketing and democracy share, they examine the effects of marketing strategy on consumer empowerment and corporate social responsibility.

Collectively, these chapters provide a deep understanding and a number of key insights into the foundations, antecedents and consequences of marketing strategy. As the domain of marketing strategy evolves, we anticipate that more research on this domain will continue to produce new insights and identify new challenges. We hope this handbook will serve as a catalyst in that process.

REFERENCE

Neslin, Scott and Venkatesh Shankar (2009), "Key issues in multichannel management: current knowledge and future directions," Tenth Anniversary Special Issue, *Journal of Interactive Marketing*, **23** (1), 70–81.

PART I

CONCEPTS AND ORGANIZATIONAL ASPECTS OF MARKETING STRATEGY

2 Strategic marketing and marketing strategy
Rajan Varadarajan

INTRODUCTION

Strategic marketing as a field of study has evolved over almost half a century and continues to evolve. The current body of knowledge is the result of the confluence of paradigms, theories, principles, constructs, relationships, models, methods, measures and findings, principally from the disciplines of marketing, management and industrial organization economics. Within the field of marketing, the evolution of strategic marketing thought precedes the addition of the term strategic marketing to the marketing lexicon, and can be traced to literature dating back to the 1950s, 1960s and 1970s focusing on strategic issues in the realms of differentiation, positioning, segmentation, branding, innovation and product life cycle, to list a few. Exemplars of more recent streams of inquiry in marketing contributing to the body of literature on strategic marketing include branding and managing and leveraging brand equity (see Keller, Chapter 17 in this volume), customer relationship management (see Kumar and Rajan, Chapter 7 in this volume), customer satisfaction (see Mittal and Frennea, Chapter 16 in this volume), e-commerce (see Hoffman and Novak, Chapter 12 in this volume; Shankar, Chapter 13 in this volume), global competitive strategy (see Gielens, Helsen and Dekimpe, Chapter 23 in this volume), inter-firm cooperative strategies such as strategic alliances, market orientation (see Gebhardt, Chapter 3 in this volume), market pioneering/first-mover advantage (see Lieberman and Montgomery, Chapter 20 in this volume), late-mover strategies (see Shankar and Carpenter, Chapter 21 in this volume), preemption and entry deterrence, product quality and signaling (Heil and Robertson 1991).

The evolution of the field during the 1970s and 1980s was also influenced by calls (e.g. Day 1984; Wind 1982; Wind and Robertson 1983) for marketing scholars to focus on issues relating to the role of marketing in charting the strategic direction of the firm (e.g. analysis, planning and strategy formulation at the corporate and business unit levels), and implicitly a broader construal of the field. Given the boundary-spanning nature of the marketing function, it was argued that marketing personnel in organizations are likely to be the most knowledgeable about the external environment, and, therefore, equipped to play an important role in charting the strategic direction of the firm. It is conceivable that at least some of the new research streams that emerged in the field of strategic marketing during the past three decades are a consequence of such calls for a broader construal of the domain of the field. An examination of extant marketing literature is indicative of a number of broad research streams with a strategic focus, including, but not limited to, the following:

1. Research focusing on marketing strategy related issues in the realms of product, price, promotion and place (4Ps), and segmentation, target market selection and positioning (STP).

2. Research focusing on organizational-level phenomena that influence marketing strategy in important ways (e.g. corporate culture, organizational learning and knowledge management).
3. Research focusing on issues at the interface of corporate and marketing strategy (e.g. synergy and horizontal acquisitions), business and marketing strategy (e.g. order of entry strategy and strategic alliances), and corporate, business and marketing strategy (e.g. multimarket competition; and financial valuation of brands in the context of mergers and acquisitions).
4. Research focusing on strategy at the corporate level (e.g. diversification and divestitures) from the perspective of how corporate strategy has an impact on and is impacted by marketing strategy, and the strategic role of the marketing function in organizations at the corporate level.
5. Research focusing on strategy at the business unit level (e.g. generic competitive strategies) from the perspective of how strategy at the business unit level influences and is influenced by marketing strategy, and the strategic role of the marketing function in organizations at the business unit level (see Varadarajan and Jayachandran 1999).

While literature provides evidence of the field having made impressive strides in a number of substantive areas as well as empirical issues, the literature is also indicative of certain shortcomings. For instance, there is considerable divergence in the context in which the terms "strategic marketing" and "marketing strategy" are used. For instance, these terms are widely used interchangeably to refer to a field of study in marketing. The term "marketing strategy" is also used to refer to an organizational strategy construct. Against this backdrop, this chapter provides a perspective on the domain of strategic marketing as a field of study, the scope of marketing strategy and definition of marketing strategy as an organizational strategy construct. The points of view advanced in this chapter on the above issues are intended to facilitate and promote debate and discussion and, thereby, the emergence of a shared understanding and consensus on the above issues among the community of marketing educators and practitioners.

The chapter is organized as follows. First, in an attempt to provide a context and perspective, an overview of the diverse contexts in which the terms marketing strategy, marketing tactics and marketing management are used in marketing literature is offered, followed by a discussion on marketing decisions and strategic marketing decisions. Third, a discussion on the domain of strategic marketing as a field of study is presented. Fourth, alternative definitions of marketing strategy are proposed. In the management discipline, the term "strategic management" refers to the field of study, and "corporate strategy" (strategy at the firm level in a multi-business firm) and "business strategy" (strategy at the business unit level in a multi-business firm) refer to two key organizational strategy constructs that are the focus of the field. Along similar lines, in this chapter, the term "strategic marketing" is used to refer to a field of study in marketing, and the term "marketing strategy" to refer to an organizational strategy construct that is germane to the field of strategic marketing.

MARKETING STRATEGY, MARKETING TACTICS AND MARKETING MANAGEMENT

A review of marketing literature is indicative of diverse points of view concerning the meaning and the conceptual distinction between marketing strategy, marketing tactics and marketing management. Consider, for instance, the distinction between marketing strategy and marketing tactics. An examination of journal articles and marketing textbooks (textbooks on principles of marketing, marketing management and marketing strategy) reveals diverse points of view including the following: (1) the marketing behaviors of firms in the realm of the 4Ps (product, promotion, price and place/distribution) are characterized as marketing strategy in some sources and as marketing tactics in other sources; in sources in the latter category, marketing behaviors pertaining to segmentation, target market selection and positioning are considered as the domain of marketing strategy and behaviors pertaining to the 4Ps as the domain of marketing tactics; (2) in yet other sources, some elements of the 4Ps are characterized as pertaining to marketing strategy (product and place/distribution) and others as pertaining to marketing tactics (price and promotion); and (3) in still other sources, certain marketing behaviors in the realm of each of the 4Ps are characterized as marketing strategy (e.g. promotion – push versus pull strategy; price – market-skimming price strategy versus market penetration price strategy) and others as marketing tactics (e.g. promotion tactics and pricing tactics). Three representative quotes (one each from the 1980s, 1990s and 2000s) are presented next to highlight this point.

In regard to the distinction between marketing management and marketing strategy, in an editorial essay, Cunningham and Robertson (1983, p. 5), stated:

> As presented in marketing literature today, marketing management is concerned with target market selection and the design of the marketing program. The marketing management literature addresses issues at the level of the individual product or brand . . . Marketing strategy, on the other hand, addresses issues of gaining long run advantage at the level of the firm or strategic business unit.

A potential problem with distinguishing between "marketing strategy" and "marketing management" along the above lines is that at the most fundamental level, while the former pertains to marketing behavior of organizations, the latter pertains to managing the marketing behavior of organizations. However, both an organization's decisions concerning target market selection (choice of where to compete) and design of the marketing program (choice of how to compete) are primarily concerned with its present and/or planned marketing behavior and not with managing marketing behavior.

In regard to the distinction between marketing strategy and marketing tactics, Webster (1992, p. 10) states:

> To consider the new role of marketing within the evolving corporation, we must recognize that marketing really operates at three distinct levels, reflecting three levels of strategy. These can be defined as the corporate, business or SBU and functional or operating levels . . . In addition to the three levels of strategy, we can identify three distinct dimensions of marketing – marketing as *culture*, marketing as *strategy* and marketing as *tactics* . . . Marketing as strategy is the emphasis at the SBU level, where the focus is on market segmentation, targeting, and positioning in defining how to compete in its chosen businesses. At the operating level, marketing

managers must focus on marketing tactics, the "4Ps" of product, price, promotion, and place/ distribution, the elements of the marketing mix.

In a more focused context (new product launch), Crawford and Di Benedetto (2008, p. 372) state:

> No matter how new-to-the-world the product is, the firm should think of product commer-cialization in two sets of decisions. **Strategic launch decisions** include both *strategic platform decisions* that set overall tones and directions, and *strategic action decisions* that define to whom we are going to sell and how. **Tactical launch decisions** are marketing mix decisions such as communication and promotion, distribution, and pricing that are typically made after strategic launch decisions and define how the strategic decisions will be implemented." (Italics and bold in original source)

The characterization of marketing decisions pertaining to segmentation, target market selection and positioning as "strategic marketing decisions" and decisions that pertain to product, promotion, price and distribution as "tactical marketing decisions" is arbitrary and conceptually flawed. Some marketing decisions made by organizations in every one of the above realms are bound to be strategic and others non-strategic. Also, given the dynamic and evolving nature of the field, circumscribing the scope of strategic marketing decisions as pertaining to specific issues, whether it's three (segmentation, target market selection and positioning) or seven (segmentation, target market selection, positioning, product, promotion, price and distribution) is inherently problematic. Drawing atten-tion to the problem with the strategy versus tactics dichotomy, Mintzberg (1987b, p. 14) notes:

> The point is that these sorts of distinctions can be arbitrary and misleading, that labels should not be used to imply that some issues are inevitably more important than others . . . Thus there is good reason to drop the word "tactics" altogether and simply refer to issues as more or less "strategic," in other words, more or less "important" in some context, whether as intended before acting or as realized after it.

STRATEGIC MARKETING DECISIONS

This section focuses on the nature and scope of strategic marketing decisions. Following a brief overview of the link between marketing decisions and actions, activities and behaviors, the defining characteristics of strategic marketing decisions are discussed; and the distinction between two broad types of strategic marketing decisions is highlighted.

Marketing Decisions, Actions, Activities and Behaviors

A cursory review of strategy literature is indicative of extensive reference to an organiza-tion's decisions, actions, activities and behaviors. For instance, Mintzberg (1987a) points out that while a statement of strategy that is future focused is an explicit guide for con-sistent future behavior of the firm, one that is past focused describes consistency in past behavior. Porter (1996) views the essence of strategy as activities – a business's decision to perform different activities (choice of activities to perform) and/or perform specific activities differently (the manner in which specific activities are performed) relative to its competitors. He points out that competitive cost advantage is the result of a business's performing specific activities more efficiently than competitors, and competitive differentiation advantage is a consequence of a business's choice of activities to perform and the manner in which they are performed. Day et al. (1990) note that marketing strategy focuses on marketing activities and decisions that are related to building and maintaining a sustainable competitive advantage.

Within reason, the terms actions, activities and behaviors can be used interchangeably. An organization's marketing decisions specify the marketing actions or activities or behaviors to engage in. While a number of marketing related activities may occur within the boundaries of an organization (e.g. new product development related activities), customers respond to and competitors react to an organization's marketing actions, activities or behaviors in the marketplace (e.g. actions such as the distinctive features of an organization's product offering, the channels through which the product is made available, and the price of the product offering).

Strategic Marketing Decisions

Amit and Schoemaker (1993, p. 36) define strategic assets as "a set of difficult to trade and imitate, scarce, appropriable and specialized resources and capabilities that bestow a firm with a competitive advantage." In reference to strategic capability, Teece et al. (1997, pp. 517–18) note: "To be strategic, a capability must be honed to a user need (so there is a source of revenues), unique (so that products/services produced can be priced without too much regard to competition) and difficult to replicate (so profits will not be competed away)." The reference to competitive advantage in Amit and Schoemaker's definition of strategic assets, and to profits not being competed away in Teece et al.'s conceptualization of strategic capabilities suggest that regardless of whether the focal construct is strategic assets or strategic capabilities or strategic marketing decisions, they are potentially of major consequence from the standpoint of an organization's long-term performance. These considerations suggest the following as a defensible definition of strategic marketing decisions:

> Strategic marketing decisions refer to an organization's marketing decisions that are potentially of major consequence from the standpoint of its long-term performance.

In the context of for-profit firms, decisions they are potentially of major consequence are those that are likely to have a major impact in respect of performance metrics such as long-term survival, growth and profitability. Chief among the distinguishing characteristics of strategic marketing decisions that stem by virtue of their implications for the long-term performance of an organization are the following. Strategic marketing decisions

- entail resource commitments that are either irreversible or relatively difficult to reverse (see Ghemawat 1991);
- entail resource commitments that are relatively larger in magnitude;
- entail resource commitments that are made with a relatively longer-term outlook;
- entail resource commitments that are spread over a relatively longer time period;

- entail resource commitments that are made with a relatively greater emphasis on the achievement of a competitive cost and/or differentiation advantage;
- entail tradeoffs (i.e. pursuing course of action "A" implying that courses of action "B", "C" and "D" must be foregone, in light of the relatively large resource outlays that pursuing any of these courses of action would entail);
- are made in the context of other strategic decisions, in light of interdependencies between them; and
- are made at higher levels in an organization (e.g. the top management level – the CEO and executives directly reporting to the CEO), and/or at higher levels within the marketing function (e.g. the CMO and executives directly reporting to the CMO).

Strategic Marketing Decisions and Associated Actions: Customer Interfacing Actions versus Precursors to Customer Interfacing Actions

A cursory examination of marketing literature suggests that the term "marketing strategy" is used in a wide variety of contexts. As evidenced by some of the other chapters in this handbook, marketing strategy has been explored in literature from a number of vantage points, including, but not limited to, the following:

- *the product dimension of the marketing mix* – brand strategy (Keller, Chapter 17), private label strategies (Sethuraman and Raju, Chapter 19), and new product development (Roberts, Chapter 10);
- *other dimensions and sub-dimensions of the marketing mix* – advertising (Rucker, Chapter 11), channels (Arnold and Palmatier, Chapter 14), and pricing (Winer, Chapter 15);
- *pattern of allocation of resources across marketing mix variables* – marketing resource allocation strategy (Shankar, Chapter 9);
- *market entry mode* – international market entry strategies (Gielens, Helsen and Dekimpe, Chapter 23);
- *market entry timing/order* – first-mover/pioneer strategies (Lieberman and Montgomery, Chapter 20) and late-mover strategies (Shankar and Carpenter, Chapter 21);
- *evolving market environment and enabling technologies* – social media strategy (Hoffman and Novak, Chapter 12) and mobile marketing strategy (Shankar, Chapter 24); and
- *customers* – cultural brand strategy (Holt, Chapter 18), multichannel customer management strategy (Verhoef, Chapter 8), customer lifetime value management (Kumar and Rajan, Chapter 7), and managing customer satisfaction (Mittal and Frennea, Chapter 16).

As summarized below, at one extreme, marketing strategy is broadly conceptualized as a multidimensional construct encompassing a broad array of integrated and internally consistent sets of coordinated behaviors by an organization in the marketplace – that is, behaviors directed at consumers, customers, competitors and/or other key constituencies in the marketplace. At the other extreme, narrow conceptualizations of marketing strategy essentially focus on specific aspects or subsets of the broad array of behaviors that in the upper limit may be envisioned as an organization's marketing strategy.

- A vector of marketing decisions (or marketing actions, activities or behaviors) encompassing multiple aspects of where to compete (e.g. markets to serve and market segments to target) and how to compete (e.g. differentiation by product features, positioning, channels etc.).
- A vector of marketing decisions encompassing numerous aspects of how to compete.
- A vector of marketing decisions concerning certain aspects of how to compete (e.g. push strategy versus pull strategy – pattern of allocation of resources among the advertising, personal selling, consumer sales promotion and trade sales promotion elements of the promotion mix).
- A marketing decision concerning a specific aspect of how to compete (e.g. market skimming price strategy versus market penetration price strategy, positioning strategy and branding strategy).

On the one hand, the use of the term marketing strategy in such myriad contexts is a reflection of the broad scope of marketing strategy. However, as proposed in Table 2.1, there may be merits in distinguishing between strategic marketing decisions and associated actions that are the basis for a business's actions or behaviors constituting the customer interfacing layer of marketing strategy from strategic marketing decisions and associated actions that are precursors to the customer interfacing layer of marketing strategy. As detailed in Table 2.1, elements of the customer interfacing layer of marketing strategy include actions such as brand name, product attributes, price, distribution intensity, advertising and sales promotion that have the potential to engender affective, cognitive and/or behavioral responses from customers.

In contrast to customer interfacing strategic marketing decisions listed in Table 2.1 and associated actions, consider the question of "how to enter a market," listed in Table 2.1 under precursors to the customer interfacing layer. Of the alternative entry strategies that may be available to a business (internal development, acquisition and strategic alliance), under certain environmental and organizational conditions, entering into a strategic alliance with another firm that possesses complementary skills and resources might be the preferred alternative, in light of its greater potential to enable a firm to offer to its customers a superior product offering relative to its competitors' product offerings. However, the response of the customers is to the attributes of the superior product offering and not to the strategic alliance. Therefore such strategic marketing decisions and associated actions are shown in Table 2.1 as precursors to an organization's customer interfacing actions.

It should be noted that the illustrative strategic marketing decisions enumerated in Table 2.1 represent only decisions that undergird an organization's actions or behaviors. The scope of an organization's strategic marketing decisions also encompasses decisions underlying cessation of a current course of action (e.g. brand deletion decisions and market exit decisions) as well as decisions *not* to make changes in the current course of action. For example, following careful analysis, an Internet-based retailer might decide to continue to remain an Internet-only retailer and not to become a multichannel retailer.

Table 2.1   Strategic marketing decisions and actions: customer interfacing actions versus precursors to customer interfacing actions[1]

A. Customer interfacing actions: strategic marketing decisions that are the basis for a business's customer interfacing actions or behaviors in the marketplace[2]

How to compete?	*Brand strategy*
	Single brand strategy versus multi-brand strategy
	Branding strategy
	Introduction of a new product (entry into a new product category) with an existing brand name in the firm's brand portfolio versus with a new brand name
	Channel strategy
	Single versus multichannel strategy
	Online versus online and offline
	Distribution (intensity) strategy
	Intensive versus selective versus exclusive distribution
	Positioning strategy
	Positioning of a firm's product offering relative to the positioning of its competitors' product offerings
	Positioning of a firm's offerings in individual market segments relative to the positioning of its offerings in the other market segments
	Pricing strategy
	Market penetration price strategy versus market skimming price strategy
	Product line strategy
	Broad versus narrow product line
	Promotion strategy
	Predominantly *push strategy* versus predominantly *pull strategy* [Pattern of allocation of promotion effort toward advertising and consumer sales promotion (pull elements of the promotion mix) versus trade sales promotion and personal selling (push elements of the promotion mix)]
How to compete in individual country markets?	*Multinational marketing strategy / global competitive marketing strategy*
	Standardization of specific competitive marketing variables (e.g. positioning, branding) across country markets versus partial standardization / partial adaptation across country markets versus adaptation to individual country markets

B. Precursors to customer interfacing actions: strategic marketing decisions and related actions that are precursors to a business' customer interfacing actions in the marketplace

Where to compete?[2]	*Target market strategy* Market(s) to serve and market segment(s) to serve
Where to compete and how to compete?[3]	*Business scope strategy* Customer groups to serve (markets and market segments to serve) Customer functions to serve (customer needs to satisfy) Technologies to utilize (Abell 1980) Stages of the value added system to participate in (Day et al. 1990, p. 27) *Product-market coverage strategy* Single product-market concentration versus market specialization versus product specialization versus selective product-market specialization versus full product-market coverage (Abell 1980)
What is the overarching strategy?	*Market driving strategy* (shaping / influencing / modifying the market environment) versus *market driven strategy* (adaptively responding to the market environment) *Primary demand stimulation strategy* (increasing the size of the market for a product) versus *selective demand stimulation strategy* (increasing the firm's share of the market)
When to enter a market?	*Order of market entry / market entry timing strategy* First-mover versus early follower versus late entry
When to enter a cluster of markets?	*Product launch (rollout) strategy across country markets* Simultaneous entry into major country markets (sprinkler model) Sequential entry into major country markets (waterfall / cascade model)
How to enter a product market?	*Market entry strategy* Internal development versus acquisition versus joint venture / strategic alliance

Table 2.1 (continued)

What should be the relative emphasis on alternative growth opportunities?	*Relative emphasis on product-market growth alternatives*
	Relative emphasis on market penetration strategy (promoting present products in present markets), *market development strategy* (promoting present products in new markets), and *product development strategy* (developing new products for present markets)
	Relative emphasis on innovation alternatives
	Relative emphasis on radical innovations versus incremental innovations
	Relative emphasis on new product development alternatives
	Relative emphasis on development of variety extension new products, replacement new products, competitive substitute new products, new to the firm new products, and new to the world new products
	Relative emphasis on present customers versus new customers
	Greater emphasis on retaining present customers (defensive strategy) versus greater emphasis on acquiring new customers (offensive strategy)
	Relative emphasis on customer relationship management (CRM) programs portfolio
	CRM programs for acquiring new customers, retaining present customers, recapturing lost customers, reactivating dormant customers, enhancing the profitability and/or revenue streams of relationships with present customers, etc.

Notes:
1. The marketing strategy and marketing strategy decisions delineated in the table are only representative and do not constitute a comprehensive list. For instance, strategic marketing decisions that pertain to whether to engage in a particular course of action (e.g. whether to enter into a particular product market) or disengage from a current course of action (e.g. whether to exit from a particular product market and how to exit a product market such as spin-off versus sell-off versus phase-out) are not shown in the table.
2. Customer interfacing behaviors of an organization refer to behaviors of the organization directed at customers to effect specific affective, cognitive and behavioral responses in them to facilitate their engaging in revenue generating transactional and relational exchanges with the organization.
3. The nature of issues pertaining to "how to compete" listed here (customer functions to serve, technologies to utilize and stages of value added to compete in) are at a higher level of aggregation compared those listed under "how to compete" in section "A" (i.e. customer interfacing layer of marketing actions).

Furthermore, while every marketing strategy decision is also a strategic marketing decision, not every strategic marketing decision is a marketing strategy decision. In other words, marketing strategy decisions constitute only one subgroup of strategic marketing decisions. Building on the foregoing sections, the next two sections focus on the domain of strategic marketing as a field of study and the definition of marketing strategy as an organizational strategy construct.

DOMAIN OF STRATEGIC MARKETING

On the one hand, how the content and direction the field of strategic marketing might be impacted as a consequence of (1) developments in the realm of marketing practice and (2) the directions in which researchers, individually and collectively, might take the field are unknowns. On the other hand, the boundaries of any proposed domain statement must be sufficiently broad to encompass the current body of literature, as well as accommodate at least some of the future directions in which the field might evolve. The proposed domain statement presented in this section constitutes a concerted effort to be responsive to the above issues. The conceptual domain of strategic marketing proposed here represents the perspective of a marketing strategy researcher, albeit based on insights gleaned from a review of relevant literature. Extant literature provides insights into other approaches that can be employed to gain insights into the conceptual domain of strategic marketing as a field of study. For instance, Nag et al. (2007) inductively derive a consensus definition for the field of strategic management. Building on extant literature that provides insights into the evolution of the field of strategic marketing and definitions of marketing, the following domain statement for the field of strategic marketing is proposed:

> The domain of strategic marketing is the study of organizational, inter-organizational and environmental issues that are potentially of major consequence from the standpoint of the long-term performance of organizations, and primarily concerned with the behaviors of organizations in the marketplace in the context of the creation, communication and delivery of products that offer value to customers in exchanges with organizations, and the general management responsibilities of the marketing function in organizations that align with its boundary spanning role.

A brief elaboration of some of the considerations underlying the proposed domain statement follows.

Understanding, explaining and predicting the behavior of firms, broadly construed, is of enduring interest to researchers in the fields of strategic marketing, strategic management and industrial organizational economics. Of particular interest to strategic marketing as a field of study is the behavior of organizations in the marketplace in their interactions with consumers, customers (both end-use customers and intermediate customers), competitors and other key external constituencies in the context of the creation, communication and delivery of products that offer value to customers engaging in exchanges (transactional and relational exchanges) with organizations. The creation, communication and delivery of products that offer value to customers in an exchange setting is a key element of AMA's 2007 definition of marketing (*Marketing News* 2008), as well as a number of other definitions. At an earlier point in time (e.g. 1960s, 1970s and 1980s), the scope of behaviors of organizations in the marketplace would generally have been construed as meaning behaviors that are directed or targeted at consumers, customers, competitors and other external constituencies.

In an Internet-enabled market environment, the scope of behaviors of organizations in the marketplace also encompasses interactive behaviors between the organization and specific external constituencies. The general management responsibilities of the marketing function that align with its boundary spanning role encompass activities such as monitoring and analysis of the environment and strategy formulation at the corporate and business unit levels. For instance, Day (1984, p. 3) notes: "As a general management responsibility, marketing embraces the interpretations of the environment and the crucial choices of customers to serve, competitors to challenge, and the product characteristics with which the business will compete." A conceptual framework that provides additional insights into the domain of strategic marketing as well as preliminary validation for the proposed domain statement is presented in the next section.

Domain of Strategic Marketing: Representative Organizational, Inter-organizational and Environmental Issues

Complementing the descriptive domain statement presented in the previous section, Figure 2.1 presents a figurative representation of the domain of strategic marketing. Here, the bidirectional links from Box A to Boxes 1 through 10 serve to denote that issues pertaining to the behavior of organizations in the marketplace and the general management responsibilities of the marketing function in organizations that align with its boundary spanning role are the principal concerns of the field of strategic marketing. In an attempt to highlight the role of theories, principles, concepts, methods, models, metrics and so on in the study of strategic marketing (describing, understanding, explaining and predicting phenomena of interest to the field), these are also listed in Box A. In Boxes 1 to 10, a number of representative organizational, inter-organizational and environmental issues are delineated. The bidirectional arrows shown in the figure denote conceptual links and not directional relationships. For example, the bidirectional arrow linking Box A and Box 4 denotes that issues pertaining to the marketing strategy formulation process, marketing strategy content and marketing strategy implementation are among the phenomena that are the focus of strategic marketing as a field of study. For purposes of simplicity of exposition, the conceptual links are shown only in reference to Box A in the figure. For example, while the issues enumerated in Box 3 are pertinent in the context of practically every one of the issues delineated in the other boxes (Boxes 1 and 2 and Boxes 4 to 10), they are not shown in the figure. A brief elaboration of two of the phenomena delineated in the boxes (Box 2 and Box 9) follows.

Marketing strategy behaviors

While certain aspects of firm behavior can be construed as specific to the domains of corporate, business and marketing strategy, certain other aspects of firm behavior span multiple levels. Varadarajan and Clark (1994) provide an overview of the distinctive and overlapping domains of corporate, business and marketing strategy. Although the term "firm behavior" is commonly used, it is decision makers in the firm who orchestrate its

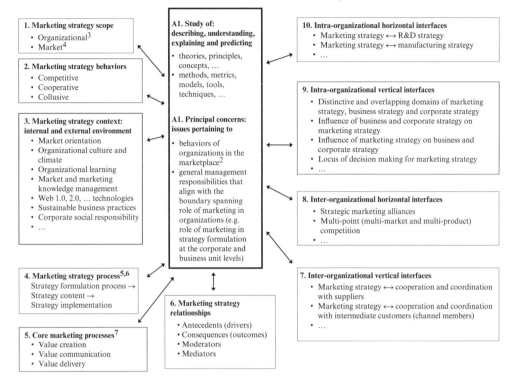

Notes:
1. The issues delineated in the figure are only representative of the domain of strategic marketing as a field of study, and do not constitute either an extensive or comprehensive mapping of the domain of the field.
2. At an earlier point in time (e.g. 1960s, 1970s and 1980s), the scope of behaviors of organizations in the marketplace would generally have been construed to mean behaviors targeted at consumers, customers, competitors and other external constituencies. In an Internet-enabled market environment, the scope of behaviors of organizations in the marketplace also encompasses interactive behaviors between the organization and specific external constituencies.
3. *Organizational scope of marketing strategy*: firm, business unit, product class, product category, brand etc.
4. *Market scope of marketing strategy*: geographic market scope, market types scope and market segments scope.
   Geographic market scope: global, multi-country, country, region of a country etc.
   Market types scope: business-to-business market, business-to-consumer market, business-to-business and business-to consumer markets, etc.
   Market segments scope: all market segments, subset of market segments, specific market segment etc.
5. Although, for ease of exposition, the marketing strategy process is shown as a linear sequence, in reality, it is an iterative process. For example, firms routinely make changes in strategy content in the aftermath of the outcomes of implementation.
6. Strategy content in Box 4 is the same as "Behaviors in the marketplace" in Box A and "Marketing strategy behaviors" in Box 2.
7. Also see Srivastava et al. (1999) for a discussion on core business processes that create value for customers: product development management process, supply chain management process and customer relationship management process.

Figure 2.1 Domain of the field of strategic marketing: representative organizational, inter-organizational and environmental issues[1]

behavior in the marketplace. That is, decisions made by managers and their subsequent execution manifest as a firm's marketing strategy behavior in the marketplace. For instance, in reference to innovation strategy, Ahuja and Lampert (2001) draw attention to organizational pathologies (managerial biases and inertia) that could inhibit breakthrough inventions. They include the familiarity trap (favoring the familiar), the maturity trap (favoring the mature) and the propinquity trap (favoring the search for solutions near to existing solutions). The role of factors such as managerial cognitions and biases on the behavior of firms in the marketplace is subsumed under "process" in the proposed framework. As noted earlier, bidirectional links such as between Box 2 and Box 3 implied by the above are not shown in the figure.

In Figure 2.1, cooperative and collusive marketing strategy behaviors refer to marketing strategy behaviors that are in accord with the prevailing legal and regulatory environment. While in certain instances, competitive, cooperative and collusive behaviors can persist as distinct behaviors, in other instances, cooperative and collusive behaviors are precursors to competitive marketing strategy behavior (e.g. alliances between subgroups of competitors manifesting as competition between alliances; signaling by competitors resulting in diminished intensity of competition). In addition to competitive, cooperative and collusive behaviors, Heil and Robertson (1991) list conciliatory and confirmative behaviors under the rubric of behavior of firms. However, these are not shown explicitly in Figure 2.1 in light of their conceptual overlap with cooperative and collusive behaviors, respectively.

Intra-organizational vertical interfaces
Diversified firms (multi-business firms) do not compete against each other; rather, individual businesses in the portfolios of multi-business firms compete in the marketplace (Porter 1987). However, the behaviors of multi-business firms at the corporate level (e.g. their diversification and divestitures related behaviors) are often precursors to the behaviors of individual businesses in their portfolios in the marketplace. Cases in point include the effects on the behavior of specific businesses in a firm's portfolio of (1) economies of scope (cost and demand interdependencies between various businesses in a firm's portfolio) that arise as a consequence of a firm's diversification into related businesses, and (2) economies of scale that arise as a consequence of a firm's horizontal acquisitions and/or geographic market extension acquisitions of its competitors in specific business domains.

A potential concern with the proposed domain statement is that it is linked to the definition of marketing as an organizational activity rather than to domain statement of marketing as a discipline. Hunt (1983) describes marketing science as the behavioral science that seeks to explain exchange relationships and focuses on four interrelated sets of fundamental explananda: (1) the behaviors of buyers directed at consummating exchanges; (2) the behaviors of sellers directed at consummating exchanges; (3) the institutional framework directed at consummating and/or facilitating exchanges; and (4) the consequences on society of the behaviors of buyers, the behaviors of sellers, and the institutional framework directed at consummating and/or facilitating exchanges. Day and Montgomery (1999) delineate the following as issues fundamental to the field of marketing: (1) How do customers and consumers really behave? (2) How do markets function and evolve? (3) How do firms relate to their markets? (4) What are the contributions of marketing to organizational performance and societal welfare?

In the context of the above perspectives on the domain of marketing as an academic discipline, the following alternative domain statement is proposed.

> The domain of strategic marketing is the study of organizational, inter-organizational and environmental issues concerned with an organization's present and potential product offerings, target markets, consumers, customers, competitors, collaborators and other stakeholders that are potentially of major consequence from the standpoint of the organization's long-term performance.

The above domain statement is framed in the context of constructs such as products, markets, customers and competitors that are central to the field of marketing. Illustrative of organizational, inter-organizational and environmental issues that are captured in the above domain statement are an organization's development of products that offer value to customers, interactions with customers, competitors and collaborators, leveraging of asset stocks that reside in the marketing function, and deployment of firm resources entrusted to the marketing function in order to achieve specific organizational objectives.

MARKETING STRATEGY: DEFINITIONS

At the broadest level, marketing strategy can be defined as

> an organization's integrated pattern of decisions that specify its crucial choices concerning products, markets, marketing actions and marketing resources in the creation, communication and/or delivery of products that offer value to customers in exchanges with the organization and thereby enable the organization to achieve specific objectives.

The proposed definition constitutes a broad definition in that it encompasses all of the strategic marketing decisions delineated in Table 2.1. For example, the term "crucial choices concerning markets" in the proposed definition encompasses an organization's strategic marketing decisions pertaining to questions such as where to compete (markets to serve and market segments to serve; see, in this volume, Czepiel and Kerin, Chapter 4; Gebhardt, Chapter 3; Sabnis and Grewal, Chapter 5), when to enter a market (see, in this volume, Lieberman and Montgomery, Chapter 20; Shankar and Carpenter, Chapter 21), and how to enter a market (see Gielens, Helsen and Dekimpe, Chapter 23).

In reference to a specific planned product offering of an organization, the above definition can be stated more succinctly as follows:

> Marketing strategy refers to an organization's integrated pattern of decisions that specify its crucial choices concerning markets to serve and market segments to target, marketing actions, and the allocation of marketing resources among markets, market segments and marketing actions toward the creation, communication and/or delivery of a product that offers value to customers in exchanges with the organization and thereby enable the organization to achieve specific objectives.

While organizations are faced with the need to address issues relating to "how to compete" on an ongoing basis and make mid-course changes as appropriate, the question of "where to compete" (choice of markets to serve and market segments to target) is an issue that is addressed relatively infrequently. Hence, in specific reference to a current product offering of an organization that is targeted at specific markets and market segments, the proposed definition can be stated even more succinctly as follows:

> Marketing strategy refers to an organization's integrated pattern of decisions that specify its crucial choices concerning marketing actions and the allocation of marketing resources among markets, market segments and marketing actions toward the creation, communication and/or delivery of a product that offers value to customers in exchanges with the organization and thereby enable the organization to achieve specific objectives.

The above definitions build on the proposed definition of strategic marketing decisions presented in the previous section and the following definition of marketing that was adopted by the American Marketing Association (AMA) in 2007 (*Marketing News* 2008, p. 28): "Marketing is the activity, set of institutions, and processes for creating, communicating, delivering, and exchanging offerings that have value for customers, clients, partners, and society at large." Building on the centrality of the creation, communication and delivery of products that offer value to customers in an exchange to the definition of marketing, marketing strategy is conceptualized as an organization's crucial choices concerning products, markets, marketing activities and marketing resources in the creation, communication and/or delivery of products that offer value to customers in exchanges with the organization.

The following alternative definition of marketing strategy builds on its role in engendering specific affective, cognitive and behavioral predispositions in target customers towards its product offering and thereby facilitating their engaging in revenue-generating transactional and relational exchanges with the organization:

> Marketing strategy is defined as an organization's integrated pattern of decisions that specify its crucial choices concerning marketing behaviors or actions directed at customers to effect specific affective, cognitive and behavioral predispositions in them towards its product offering in order to facilitate their engaging in revenue-generating transactional and relational exchanges with the organization and thereby enable the organization to achieve specific objectives.

The proposed definition can be adapted to various levels of market aggregation as illustrated here in reference to global marketing strategy:

> Global marketing strategy is defined as an organization's integrated pattern of decisions that specify its crucial choices concerning marketing behaviors directed at customers in multiple country markets to effect specific affective, cognitive and behavioral predispositions in them towards its product offering in order to facilitate their engaging in revenue-generating transactional and relational exchanges with the organization and thereby enable the organization to achieve specific objectives.

A brief discussion of the rationale underlying the proposed definitions and elaboration of the key elements of the definitions (the context in which specific key words and phrases are used in the proposed definition) follows.

Mintzberg (1987a) points out that a realized strategy can emerge in response to an evolving situation, or it can be brought about deliberately, through a process of formulation followed by implementation. The proposed definitions are stated in the latter context (i.e. intended strategy). The definitions of marketing strategy proposed here refer only to the behaviors of organizations directed at customers. This raises the question of the behaviors of organizations directed at competitors. Indeed, it is commonplace for firms to direct some of their behaviors such as new product preannouncements and signaling at competitors in order to either deter them from engaging in certain kinds of behaviors or encourage them to engage in certain kinds of behaviors. However, the behaviors of firms directed at competitors are not an end in themselves, but a means to an end, namely engendering specific affective, cognitive and behavioral predispositions in customers towards its product offering in order to facilitate their engaging in revenue-generating transactional and relational exchanges with the organization. What ultimately matters from the standpoint of the long-term performance of organizations is the behavior of the organizations in the marketplace directed at customers in a competitive environment and how customers respond to these behaviors.

In the proposed definitions, "organization" refers to both "for-profit" and "not-for-profit" organizations. However, some of the alternative definitions that refer to revenue-generating transactional and relational exchanges are pertinent only in the context of for-profit firms. From a unit of analysis perspective, the frame of reference for marketing strategy can either be the firm at large as in a single business firm, an organizational sub-unit such as a strategic business unit in a multi-business firm, a product category within a strategic business unit, a product within a product category, or a specific brand of a product. "Integrated pattern of decisions" denotes that at the broadest level, marketing strategy entails making a multiplicity of decisions that are interrelated and interdependent and must therefore be internally consistent. "Crucial choices" refers to choices that are potentially of major consequence from the standpoint of the long-term performance of the organization. An integrated pattern of actions, activities or behaviors in the marketplace logically follows from the integrated pattern of decisions that undergird them.

"Marketing resources" refers to all types of resources expended by an organization toward the creation, communication and/or delivery of products that offer value to customers in transactional and relational exchanges with the organization. They include financial resources expended toward specific marketing activities (e.g. advertising, personal selling, consumer sales promotion, trade sales promotion), the accumulated stock of marketing infrastructure assets (e.g. logistics and physical distribution infrastructure, sales force) and the stock of market-based relational assets (e.g. brand equity and channel equity). Although certain marketing strategy decisions per se and in isolation (e.g. markets to serve and market segments to target, pricing and positioning) may not entail expending marketing resources, acting on these decisions will necessarily entail expending marketing resources on an array of marketing activities.

Organizational objectives is broadly construed to encompass (1) the facilitation of the achievement of competitive positional advantage (cost and/or differentiation advantage), (2) the achievement of specific market responses from customers (e.g. affect and behavior) and competitors (including inaction or non-response), and (3) the achievement of specific marketplace performance objectives (e.g. market share, revenue, sales, sales growth, customer satisfaction, customer loyalty, and creation of market-based relational assets and intellectual assets), and financial performance objectives (e.g. profit, return on investment, market value creation). While an organization's stock of market-based relational assets constitutes marketing resources that are available for deployment in the marketplace, their creation falls within the realm of marketing strategy objectives. While an organization's marketplace related intellectual assets (i.e. market knowledge and marketing knowledge) play an important role in making effective marketing resource deployment decisions, per se they do not constitute marketing resources that can be deployed in the marketplace. The term and/or is used in the proposed definitions to signify that the scope of a specific marketing strategy can either be broad, encompassing creation, communication and delivery, or somewhat focused and limited. Of course, even in the latter context, the implication is commensurate behaviors with respect to other elements of marketing strategy, given the integrated, interdependent and multifaceted scope of the marketing strategy of an organization directed at entities in the marketplace such as customers and competitors.

CONCLUSION

In the broader context of this vast and expansive literature, this chapter presents a perspective on the domain of strategic marketing as a field of study and the scope of marketing strategy as an organizational strategy construct. Alternative statements of the domain of strategic marketing as well as definitions for marketing strategy are proposed. As noted in the introductory section, the perspectives advanced in this chapter in regard to the above are intended to facilitate and promote debate and discussion and, thereby, the emergence of a shared understanding and consensus on the above issues among the community of marketing educators and practitioners.

The proposed domain statements for strategic marketing as a field of study serve to highlight the importance of delineating the domain of any field of study. However, the attendant challenges and limitations of any such endeavor, and the need for periodically revisiting the issue given the evolving nature of any field of study, must be borne in mind. The following quote from Inkeles (1964, p. 1) is instructive in this regard:

> Any attempt to set limits to a field of intellectual endeavor is inherently futile. Whatever boundaries we set will inevitably omit men whose work should be included. Yet when we stretch the boundaries to bring these men and these works within the field, we inevitably incorporate some we otherwise would have excluded. And what seems to us today firmly entrenched as part of our little community, may yesterday have been an alien enclave and tomorrow may have set itself outside our walls as an independent discipline trying to define its own boundaries.
>
> To define the limits of a field of inquiry may prove, in the long run, to be only a gesture, but for a start, delimitation, however tentative, is indispensable. The danger is not too great if we keep in mind that any boundaries we establish are an aid to understanding.

Marketing strategy is a construct that is germane to the field of strategic marketing specifically, and to the discipline of marketing more broadly. Rather than providing *a* definition of marketing strategy and *a* statement of the domain of strategic marketing, this chapter provides multiple definitions of marketing strategy and alternative statements of the domain of strategic marketing. Given the centrality of marketing strategy to strategic marketing as a field of study, multiple definitions from different orientations can be valuable to practitioners and researchers from the standpoint of gaining better insights into a complex and dynamic field. As Mintzberg (1987b, p. 11) notes:

Human nature insists on a definition for every concept. The field of strategic management cannot afford to rely on a single definition of strategy, indeed the word has long been used implicitly in different ways even if it has been traditionally defined formally in only one. Explicit recognition of multiple definitions can help practitioners and researchers alike to maneuver through this difficult field.

REFERENCES

Abell, Derek (1980), *Defining the Business: The Starting Point of Strategic Planning*, Englewood Cliffs, NJ: Prentice-Hall.

Ahuja, G. and Lampert, C.M. (2001), "Entrepreneurship in the large corporation: a longitudinal study of how established firms create breakthrough inventions," *Strategic Management Journal*, **22** (June–July), 521–43.

Amit, R. and Shoemaker, P. (1993), "Strategic assets and organizational rent," *Strategic Management Journal*, **14** (1), 33–46.

Crawford, M. and Di Benedetto, A. (2008), *New Products Management*, 9th edn, New York: McGraw-Hill/Irwin.

Cunningham, William H. and Robertson, Thomas S. (1983), "From the editor," *Journal of Marketing*, **47** (Spring), 5–6.

Day, George S. (1984), *Strategic Market Planning: The Pursuit of Competitive Advantage*, St Paul, MN: West Publishing Co.

Day, George S., Weitz, Bart and Wensley, Robin (eds) (1990), *The Interface of Marketing and Strategy*, Greenwich, CT: JAI Press.

Day, George S. and Montgomery, David B. (1999), "Charting new directions for marketing," *Journal of Marketing*, **63** (Special Issue), 3–13.

Ghemawat, Pankaj (1991), *Commitment: The Dynamic of Strategy*, New York: Free Press.

Heil, Oliver and Robertson, Thomas S. (1991), "Toward a theory of competitive market signaling," *Strategic Management Journal*, **12** (6), 403–18.

Hunt, Shelby D. (1983), "General theories and the fundamental explananda of marketing," *Journal of Marketing*, **47** (Fall), 9–17.

Inkeles, A. (1964), *What is Sociology? An Introduction to the Discipline and Profession*, Englewood Cliffs, NJ: Prentice-Hall.

Marketing News (2008), "Marketing defined," *Marketing News*, **42** (January 15), 28–9.

Mintzberg, H. (1987a), "Crafting strategy," *Harvard Business Review*, **65** (July–August), 66–75.

Mintzberg, H. (1987b), "The strategy concept I: five Ps for strategy," *California Management Review*, **30** (Fall), 11–24.

Nag, R., Hambrick, D.C. and Chen, M.J. (2007), "What is strategic management, really? Inductive derivation of a consensus definition of the field," *Strategic Management Journal*, **28** (September), 935–55.

Porter, Michael E. (1987), "From competitive advantage to competitive strategy," *Harvard Business Review*, **65** (May–June), 43–59.

Porter, Michael E. (1996), "What is strategy?" *Harvard Business Review*, **74** (November–December), 61–78.

Srivastava, Rajendra K., Shervani, Tasadduq, A. and Fahey, Liam (1999), "Marketing, business processes, and shareholder value: an organizationally embedded view of marketing activities and the discipline of marketing," *Journal of Marketing*, **63**, 168–79.

Teece, D.J., Pisano, G. and Shuen, A. (1997), "Dynamic capabilities and strategic management," *Strategic Management Journal*, **18** (August), 509–33.

Varadarajan, Rajan and Clark, Terry (1994), "Delineating the scope of corporate, business and marketing strategy," *Journal of Business Research*, **31** (October–November), 93–105.

Varadarajan, Rajan and Jayachandran, Satish (1999), "Marketing strategy: an assessment of the state of the field and outlook," *Journal of the Academy of Marketing Science*, **27** (Spring), 120–43.

Webster, F.E., Jr (1992), "The changing role of marketing in the corporation," *Journal of Marketing*, **56** (October), 1–17.

Wind, Y. (1982), "Marketing and corporate strategy," *The Wharton Magazine*, **6** (Summer), 38–45.

Wind, Y. and Robertson, T.S. (1983), "Marketing strategy: new direction for theory and research," *Journal of Marketing*, **47** (Spring), 12–25.

3 Market orientation
Gary F. Gebhardt

The *Handbook of Marketing Strategy* explains and provides examples of a number of important marketing strategy topics, including competitive advantage (Czepiel and Kerin, Chapter 4; Sabnis and Grewal, Chapter 5), new product development (Roberts, Chapter 10), first-mover advantage (Lieberman and Montgomery, Chapter 20), positioning and branding (Keller, Chapter 17), brand communities (Holt, Chapter 18), and customer satisfaction (Mittal and Frennea, Chapter 16). Reading through these topics, some readers – particularly experienced managers – may wonder, "Why do some companies seem to be so much better at creating and implementing their marketing strategies than others?" More to the point, are there things that managers can do to help their organizations be better than their competition at: understanding their markets; identifying underserved segments or new competitive advantages; developing solutions that satisfy their target segments; and realizing the financial rewards of those activities? The answer is "yes". Studies of thousands of companies around the world have found that certain of them are consistently more successful at discovering and exploiting market opportunities than others. The primary characteristic that more successful companies have is that they are more market-oriented.

The idea that firms should be market-oriented, primarily focusing on understanding and meeting the needs of customers, has been around since at least Adam Smith's (1776) *Wealth of Nations*: "Consumption is the sole end and purpose of all production; and the interest of the producer ought to be attended to, only so far as it may be necessary for promoting that of the consumer" (p. 501). In other words, firms work best within the capitalist system when their primary focus is on meeting the needs of the market. Two centuries later, Peter Drucker (1954) moved the notion further along, observing that "Marketing is not only much broader than selling, it is not a specialized activity at all. It encompasses the entire business. It is the whole business seen from the point of view of its final result, that is, from the customer's point of view. Concern and responsibility for marketing must therefore permeate all areas of the enterprise" (pp. 38–9). In 1988, after more than two centuries of agreement that firms should be market-focused, a Harvard marketing professor published an article entitled "What the hell is 'market oriented'?" (Shapiro 1988). His point was that managers and academics kept using the term "market-oriented" or "customer-oriented," but no one seemed to agree on what, exactly, a market-oriented firm looked like or how managers could make their firms market-oriented. Around the same time as Professor Shapiro's article, several teams of researchers, funded by the Marketing Science Institute, began addressing just those questions (Deshpandé 1999; Deshpandé et al. 1993; Kohli and Jaworski 1990; Narver and Slater 1990).

In the 20 years since, an extensive amount of research by hundreds of academic researchers has investigated market orientation. "Market orientation" now means something fairly specific. Market orientation is defined as the seamless ability of all members of an organization to act in unison to (1) constantly collect information on the current and future needs of current and potential customers, (2) disseminate that information throughout the organization to create a shared understanding of the market, (3) develop strategies and tactics to meet the needs of a target population better than current market offerings, and (4) successfully implement those strategies and tactics to exceed the expectations of customers and create strategic competitive advantages. Since 1990, researchers have also found extensive empirical support regarding the advantages of a market orientation across a wide variety of organizations, markets and countries. The advantages that more market-oriented firms have over less market-oriented firms include: (1) more satisfied and loyal customers; (2) more innovative and successful new products and services; (3) more satisfied and intrinsically motivated employees, and (4) higher levels of profitability and stock market returns (Cano et al. 2004; Deshpandé and Farley 1998; Kirca et al. 2005; Kumar et al. 2011).

This chapter is composed of three major sections: (1) the characteristics of market-oriented firms; (2) an explanation of how and why market-oriented firms are able to achieve superior market performance, and (3) what managers can do to create higher levels of market orientation in their own organizations.

CHARACTERISTICS OF MARKET-ORIENTED ORGANIZATIONS

The first formal definition of market orientation focused on the behaviors of market-oriented organizations (Kohli and Jaworski 1990). Specifically, all of the members of market-oriented organizations act in a coordinated fashion to collect, disseminate and act on market intelligence. Over time, that definition continues to be a robust metric to identify market-oriented firms. That said, market-oriented firms are characterized and explained by much more than their behaviors. The behaviors are merely the visible consequences of a market-oriented organization.

Market orientation is an organizational culture that includes specific shared values and norms amongst all organization members, along with shared schemas (mental pictures or roadmaps) of the organization's markets and the processes used to understand and serve those markets (Gebhardt et al. 2006; Homburg and Pflesser 2000). Figure 3.1 illustrates the notion that organizational cultures are defined by a set of shared assumptions about the organization, which are codified in shared values, behavioral norms and, finally, the behaviors and artifacts that are visible (Schein 1985). Table 3.1 details the corresponding assumptions, values and behavioral norms that define market-oriented firms. The preeminent assumption shared amongst members of market-oriented firms is that everyone in the organization is there to make a living by serving the needs of the market. Anybody who doesn't share that assumption will have a difficult time getting along with others within a market-oriented culture. The codified value of this assumption is the "Market as the *raison d'être* (reason for being)," with the associated behavioral norm that "every decision and action must consider how it affects the market."

The five additional values of market-oriented firms include: (1) collaboration, (2) respect/empathy/perspective taking; (3) keep promises; (4) openness; and (5) trust. These values may strike readers as surprising – since they appear to have little to do with marketing. However, combined with the "Market as the *raison d'être*," they are

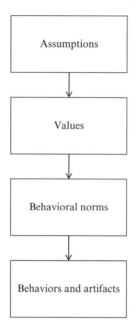

Figure 3.1   Hierarchy of attributes defining an organizational culture

Table 3.1   Values, assumptions and norms of market-oriented firms

Value	Assumption	Behavioral norm
Market as the *raison d'être*	We come together as an organization to serve the market and make a living	Every decision and action must consider how it affects the market
Collaboration	Working together, we can achieve more and do so faster and better than we could apart	Work is done collaboratively by teams. Teams are jointly responsible for outcomes
Respect/ empathy/ perspective taking	People are basically good and have reasons for their actions	Consider the perspectives, needs, training, expertise and experience of others when reacting to or interpreting their actions
Honoring promises	To succeed, everyone must do his or her part	Each employee is responsible for following through on commitments to others
Openness	Honestly sharing information, assumptions and motives allows others to understand and effectively collaborate with us	Proactively and honestly share information, assumptions and motives with others
Trust	Everyone is committed to the same goal. Therefore we can have positive expectations about their intentions and behaviors	Trust that your fellow colleagues are telling the truth and will follow through on commitments

essential for realizing the behaviors that define a market orientation: having everyone in the organization collect, disseminate and react to market information. The six market-oriented values provide the cultural rules and expectations for everyone in the organization. The more market-oriented a firm is, the more these values are universally shared within the organization and the more severe the consequences for members who do not act accordingly.

Members of market-oriented organizations also have shared schemas about markets and the processes for understanding and serving those markets. (Schemas are also known as "mental maps.") If everyone in the organization has the same market schema – including types of customers, competitors, channels, and so on – then it is much easier for people to collect, disseminate, discuss and act on information. For example, if someone at Harley-Davidson Motor Company talks about a "Harley Rider," everyone else in the organization understands what that means and doesn't mean. The importance of shared schemas for a market orientation is more evident when looking at organizations that do not have organizationally shared schemas. For example, imagine a technology company in which market researchers are the only people who interact with potential customers. When market researchers share their new insights with the engineers responsible for developing new solutions, the researchers will communicate the information based on their own market researcher schemas – but the engineers will comprehend the information based on their engineering-centric schemas. What often happens is that even though the same steps of collecting data and sharing information occur in more and less market-oriented firms, the shared schemas of market-oriented firms make the data more meaningful and useful.

Market-oriented firms also possess shared process schemas that define how an organization adapts to the market by updating its shared market schemas. In other words, shared process schemas provide the roadmap for how the organization collects market information and disseminates it, so that the new information updates everyone's shared market schemas. Hence, as markets change – including changes in customer needs, competitive offerings and channel structures – market-oriented firms adapt to those changes by relying on their shared process schemas to update their shared market schemas. Meanwhile, the core market-oriented cultural values remain unchanged.

WHY MARKET-ORIENTED FIRMS OUTPERFORM THEIR COMPETITORS

As mentioned earlier, more market-oriented firms are more successful than less market-oriented firms across a number of dimensions, including having: (1) more satisfied and loyal customers; (2) more innovative and successful new products and services; (3) more satisfied and intrinsically motivated employees, and (4) higher levels of profitability and stock market returns (Cano et al. 2004; Deshpandé and Farley 1998; Kirca et al. 2005; Kumar et al. 2011). A strong culture based on the six core market-oriented values, combined with organizationally shared market and process schemas, forms the basis for why more market-oriented firms are able to outperform their less market-oriented competitors. The overarching explanation for the superior performance of more market-oriented firms is that their cultures enable them to more effectively and efficiently coordinate the collection, dissemination and reaction to market information than firms that are less market-oriented. A market orientation ensures everyone in the firm focuses on the core reason why the firm exists – its customers – and provides communication and coordination mechanisms via cultural values and shared schemas.

The relationship between higher levels of market orientation and higher levels of performance becomes evident when considering specific activities that are affected by a market orientation. First, when collecting market information, the cultural value of "the market as the *raison d'être*" provides incentive and focus for all organization members to collect market data and share them in the course of their day-to-day activities. The fact that everyone shares the same understanding of the market makes exceptions easier to identify and new market information easier to convey across the organization.

Similarly, everyone in the firm is able to contribute to strategy development. Again, this is possible because (1) a market-oriented culture expects people to collaborate, openly and honestly, to figure out how to best serve the organization's customers, and (2) shared market schemas allow people from a variety of disciplines – and possibly working in different geographic locations – to effectively and efficiently communicate and collaborate in assessing strategic options. Compare this to the more typical approach of strategic planning, where a select few people are charged with developing a strategy, but often have little or no visibility of the challenges of implementing various options. This highlights another strength of market-oriented firms: because market strategies are developed collaboratively with firm-wide participation, market-oriented firms are able to implement those strategies much more quickly and effectively. This compares with one of the most frustrating aspects of more traditional top-down strategy development processes, in which a strategy cannot be implemented effectively – or at all – because strategy developers didn't consider (or understand) a number of implementation requirements and dependencies.

A market-oriented culture and shared market and process schemas also explain why more market-oriented firms are able to develop and launch more successful new products than their less market-oriented peers. The generally accepted best practices for developing new products include cross-functional teams that collaboratively collect and analyze market data, and then collectively develop and launch those new products or services (Hauser et al. 2006; Kelley and Littman 2001; Kelley and Littman 2005; Kuczmarski 1992; Roberts, Chapter 10 in this volume). Hence market-oriented firms clearly have an advantage in developing new products, since the culture of the firm and its everyday functioning already require people to work collaboratively.

It also follows that if market-oriented firms have a better understanding of the market, are better able to leverage that knowledge across the firm, and are better at developing and implementing solutions to meet the needs of their customers and partners, then they also have more satisfied customers than their competitors. Regarding quality, the first and most important step in quality assurance programs is understanding customer needs in order to design appropriate quality metrics (Griffin and Hauser 1993). If more market-oriented firms better understand their customers and are able to more effectively communicate customer needs throughout the organization, it makes sense that more market-oriented firms have higher-quality levels – as judged by their customers – than less market-oriented firms (Kirca et al. 2005). Likewise, the more satisfied customers are, the more likely they are to remain customers (Fornell et al. 1996). Hence customers of more market-oriented firms are more loyal than the customers of less market-oriented firms (Kirca et al. 2005; Kumar et al. 2011).

In addition to market performance advantages, more market-oriented firms are also more pleasant and fulfilling places to work. When everyone is working toward the same goal – meeting the needs of the market – it creates a much more positive environment than when trying to work across functional boundaries tied to competing objectives. Moreover, the cultural expectations of being open and honest, respecting differences, collaborating, keeping promises and trusting the people you work with make for a more pleasant and productive work environment. And the intrinsic motivation of accomplishing a common goal of making customers better off creates a workforce that is just better at meeting market needs than a workforce motivated solely by individual monetary payoffs. Hence employees at more market-oriented firms exhibit higher job satisfaction, higher levels of organizational commitment, higher levels of cooperation, lower levels of conflict, and lower turnover than employees at less market-oriented firms (Kirca et al. 2005).

Combining the market and organizational advantages of a market orientation, it becomes clear how more market-oriented firms are able to outperform their less market-oriented competitors across an array of metrics. They are better at collecting market information, disseminating it, analyzing it, using it to develop strategies, and implementing those strategies. As a result they are able to recognize untapped opportunities better than their competitors and leverage those opportunities into more successful new products and services. As a result of being more attuned to the needs of their customers – and by responding to those needs better than competitors – more market-oriented firms are better able to satisfy their customers and, thus, keep their customers for longer. Finally, working for market-oriented firms is preferable for most people and, thus, market-oriented firms enjoy higher employee satisfaction, organizational commitment and lower turnover among their workforces.

CREATING A MARKET ORIENTATION

Since a market orientation is an organizational culture coupled with shared market and process schemas, it follows that creating a market-oriented organization involves (1) changing the organization's culture; (2) instantiating the organization with an initial shared market schema; and (3) creating a shared process schema for updating the market schema in the future. Our understanding of how to create a market-oriented organization is based on the in-depth analysis of a number of firms that successfully changed to be more market-oriented (Gebhardt et al. 2006). Figure 3.2 illustrates the four-stage process for creating a market orientation, along with the individual steps comprising each stage.

Initiation

In the first stage, Initiation, top managers commit to the change process, create a coalition of committed managers to lead the cultural change process, and then plan for the cultural change process. Because cultural change is difficult, the executives/managers instigating the change must have the power to begin – and the wherewithal to follow

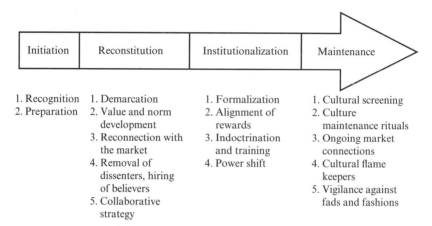

Initiation	Reconstitution	Institutionalization	Maintenance
1. Recognition 2. Preparation	1. Demarcation 2. Value and norm development 3. Reconnection with the market 4. Removal of dissenters, hiring of believers 5. Collaborative strategy	1. Formalization 2. Alignment of rewards 3. Indoctrination and training 4. Power shift	1. Cultural screening 2. Culture maintenance rituals 3. Ongoing market connections 4. Cultural flame keepers 5. Vigilance against fads and fashions

Figure 3.2   Process of creating a market orientation

through – the change process. In every case of a successful transformation, the instigator of the change was the most powerful person in the organization – whether the CEO, the heir apparent to the CEO, the executive in charge of the business unit who chose the next CEO and COO, or the lead investor and CEO in a leveraged buy-out.

Next, the change instigators create a coalition responsible for managing the organization's cultural transformation. (Oftentimes, one or more of the individuals instigating the change process will also be part of this team.) Since the purpose of this coalition is to guide the cultural change process, it is referred to as "the guiding coalition." Members of the guiding coalition include members from all the broad functions and geographies of the organization, but they are all similar in two respects: (1) they deeply believe in the notion that all of the organization's activities should be driven by the organization's current and future markets, and (2) they have a genuine respect for the ability of every organization member to contribute to the organization's future. Once the guiding coalition is formed, they plan and guide the cultural change process. Planning the change process involves tailoring the cultural transformation steps to the specific organization while ensuring the spirit and purpose of the steps are maintained. For example, while one firm may be able to send out a multitude of cross-functional teams with four of five members on each team to visit customers, some firms can only send out a few two-person teams to visit, observe and interview customers (particularly consumers) in the field.

Reconstitution

The Reconstitution stage represents the organization-wide implementation of the change process and comprises five steps: (1) demarcation, (2) value and norm development, (3) reconnection with the market, (4) removal of dissenters and hiring of believers, and (5) collaborative strategy. The demarcation step informs everyone in the organization about the cultural change process, why it's necessary, the benefits of creating a market-oriented organization, the market-oriented values and norms the organization will be adopting, the process for creating a market orientation, and the guiding coalition's expectations for participation in the process and, eventually, the strategic planning process. Although the demarcation event takes place at a certain time and is limited in its duration by an hour or two, its importance cannot be overstated. The very public, open and forthright nature of the event allows everyone to be involved, showcases the very values the coalition is trying to embed in the organization, and is the first step in creating shared market and process schemas. In addition to the demarcation event, the guiding coalition develops their organization's market-oriented values and norms using three mechanisms: (1) modeling the values and norms through the coalition's actions, (2) publicly encouraging and rewarding members' behaviors consistent with the values and norms, and (3) engaging all organization members to some extent in subsequent cultural transformation activities.

The step of reconnecting with the market differentiates the creation of a market-oriented organization from other types of cultural transformations. It entails sending a series of cross-functional teams into the market to visit and interview customers, channel members, influencers and partners. As cross-functional teams complete their visits, they document their findings and debrief other teams on what they found. Having multiple teams visit different sites and compare their findings highlights common themes across sites and also creates an initial organizationally shared market schema. Using cross-functional teams ensures that information that could be relevant to the organization is recognized. For example, a comment about an unmet need might trigger a thought or a solution in the mind of an engineer, whereas it might be unnoticed by a purchasing agent. The cross-functional team composition also encourages a unified understanding of the market in common terms, rather than the view of the market from one functional perspective (e.g. the sales team's view of the market). Finally, these cross-functional and collaborative customer visits encourage the market-oriented values of the market as the *raison d'être*, collaboration, respect/empathy/perspective taking, openness and trust. There is no better way to ensure mutual respect and understanding than having people with different perspectives interact on a shared task that is important to everyone.

In practice, it is not feasible for everyone within large organizations to visit with customers, channel members and so on in cross-functional teams. Therefore, once the teams have returned and compared their observations, they create some type of shared metaphor or mental map of the market to share with everyone else in the organization. Much like the demarcation event, it is essential that everyone in the organization be provided feedback on the teams' findings. This includes both an outline of the developed market schema and as many stories and artifacts as are practical to support the shared market schema. For example, team members can publicly share their experiences visiting customers and some of the requirements, needs and stories they heard from customers that support important aspects of the shared market schema. Additionally, having members representing a broad cross-section of functions/areas within the organization who share their insights reinforces that the developed schema is shared and not one person's or one function's perspective on the market.

Consistent with market-oriented values, everyone is given a chance to participate in the cultural transformation. However, during the Reconstitution stage, the organization begins to address the reality that some people are not interested or able to productively be a part of a market-oriented organization. After people have been notified of the cultural change process and given a chance to participate, those who cannot or will not participate are removed from the organization. Their departure is necessary to ensure they do not impede or sabotage the change process, either through explicit activities or by showing other organization members that there are no consequences for not acting consistent with cultural norms. Likewise, the selection of new organization members now includes an assessment as to whether the new members can thrive in a market-oriented organizational culture. Removing people who don't fit the culture and hiring people who do fit the culture strengthens a market-oriented culture.

As the market-oriented values and norms become stronger within the organization and the organization develops a shared understanding of the market, the organization is able to effectively develop a marketing strategy that leverages insights and strengths from across the organization. As mentioned earlier, everyone involved in developing a marketing strategy is now using the same shared market schema when considering strategic options, what is required to implement them, and the likelihood of market success. Also, by developing the strategy with broad participation from every group/area within the organization, the ability to successfully implement – and/or adapt – the strategy going forward is far superior to that of organizations without a market orientation. Finally, the collaborative nature of developing marketing strategies continues to reinforce market-oriented values and norms.

In summary, the steps within the Reconstitution stage create a firm that is much more market-oriented than it was before beginning the change process. At the end of the stage, members of the organization behave in a manner more consistent with market-oriented values, they have developed a market schema that is shared throughout the organization, they understand how they developed that market schema and how to adjust it in the future, and they have jointly developed a marketing strategy that leverages shared market data and is more likely to be implemented successfully, due to participation from across the organization. In essence, the organization is now market-oriented: it is collecting, disseminating and acting on market intelligence in a unified manner.

Institutionalization

Once the organization has made its initial change to become market-oriented, the guiding coalition takes steps to ensure the organization institutionalizes its market orientation. These include: (1) formalizing structures, (2) aligning rewards, (3) developing indoctrination and training processes, and (4) shifting power from the guiding coalition to the organization.

The formalization of structures includes ensuring the processes for annual planning, personnel evaluations, hiring of new employees and so on are all modified to be consistent with a market-oriented culture. For example, personnel evaluations are based on organizationally shared market goals to ensure employees are collaborating toward a common purpose. Similarly, the process for allocating rewards is revised to encourage a market-oriented culture. This entails having rewards – such as bonuses, salary increases and promotions – determined by how well individuals contributed to the shared goals of the organization. This also means that the majority of everyone's variable compensation is based on meeting group, team or organization objectives, rather than individual objectives. In other words, compensation is altered to be consistent with the shared values of a market-oriented culture.

The Reconstitution stage effectively changes the organization to be market-oriented through shared experiences of market understanding and collaborating on strategy development and implementation. However, as new members join the organization and the memory of the transformation fades for existing members, there is a need to formalize that organizational learning to ensure that people continue to work in a market-oriented manner. This is done through (formal or informal) indoctrination programs that share those collective experiences and market understandings with new members. This allows newer members to clearly understand how a market-oriented organization works and how they fit into a strong market-oriented culture.

In the final step of Institutionalization, the guiding coalition transfers its decision-making and cultural power to the organization at large. In effect, the major work of transforming the organizational culture has been completed and effectively maintaining the culture is the joint responsibility of everyone in the organization. This does not eliminate the need for formal leadership, but strong market-oriented cultures are much more clannish and organic, which allows them to adapt to market changes more quickly than their competitors. Once everyone in the organization shares the same cultural values and norms, and has a shared understanding of the market and how the organization is going to serve the market, individual organization members are trusted to make decisions without having to engage the formal hierarchy.

Maintenance

Once the organization has transformed itself to be market-oriented and the formal organizational structures have been changed to encourage market-oriented behaviors going forward, the organization is likely to become even more market-oriented with more experience. However, there are a number of actions that can cause a market-oriented culture to become less market-oriented. These threats include (1) hiring new members who do not fit the culture; (2) losing the organizational understanding of the importance and role of culture and shared schemas; (3) not updating market schemas to reflect market changes, (4) organizational changes that conflict with a market-oriented culture, and (5) adopting new management fads or fashions without considering their impact on the organization's culture. These threats need to be consciously kept in check through: (1) continued cultural screening of new members; (2) ongoing training and rituals to remind members of the importance of a market orientation; (3) ongoing market visits by cross-functional teams who share their findings across the organization; (4) charging a few powerful organization members with the role of ensuring new policies and processes are appropriate for a market-oriented organization; and (5) explicit consideration of whether policies or systems adopted by other organizations would positively or negatively impact the market-oriented culture.

SUMMARY

Market orientation is an organizational culture that encourages the organization-wide collection, dissemination and response to market information. In addition to shared cultural values, market-oriented firms have shared market schemas that facilitate market-based behaviors, as well as shared process schemas that permit the organization to adapt to market changes over time. Market-oriented firms enjoy a number of market and organizational advantages relative to their less market-oriented competitors. These advantages translate into superior financial performance. Given that market orientation is an organizational culture, it is possible for managers to make their firms more market-oriented through a process of cultural change.

REFERENCES

Cano, Cynthia Rodriguez, Francois A. Carrillat and Fernando Jaramillo (2004), "A meta-analysis of the relationship between market orientation and business performance: evidence from five continents," *International Journal of Research in Marketing*, **21** (2), 179–200.

Deshpandé, Rohit (ed.) (1999), *Developing a Market Orientation*, Thousand Oaks, CA: Sage Publications.

Deshpandé, Rohit and John U. Farley (1998), "Measuring market orientation: generalization and synthesis," *Journal of Market-Focused Management*, **2** (3), 213–32.

Deshpandé, Rohit, John U. Farley and Frederick E. Webster, Jr (1993), "Corporate culture, customer orientation, and innovativeness in Japanese firms: a quadrad analysis," *Journal of Marketing*, **57** (1), 23–37.

Drucker, Peter Ferdinand (1954), *The Practice of Management*, New York: Harper & Row.

Fornell, Claes, Michael D. Johnson, Eugene W. Anderson, Jaesung Cha and Barbara Everitt Bryant (1996), "The American customer satisfaction index: nature, purpose, and findings," *Journal of Marketing*, **60** (4), 7–18.

Gebhardt, Gary F., Gregory S. Carpenter and John F. Sherry, Jr (2006), "Creating a market orientation: a longitudinal, multifirm, grounded analysis of cultural transformation," *Journal of Marketing*, **70** (4), 37–54.

Griffin, Abbie and John R. Hauser (1993), "The voice of the customer," *Marketing Science*, **12** (1), 1–27.

Hauser, John, Gerard J. Tellis and Abbie Griffin (2006), "Research on innovation: a review and agenda for marketing science," *Marketing Science*, **25** (6), 687–717.

Homburg, Christian and Christian Pflesser (2000), "A multiple-layer model of market-oriented organizational culture: measurement issues and performance outcomes," *Journal of Marketing Research*, **37** (4), 449–62.

Kelley, Tom and Jonathan Littman (2001), *The Art of Innovation: Lessons in Creativity from IDEO, America's Leading Design Firm*, New York: Currency/Doubleday.

Kelley, Tom and Jonathan Littman (2005), *The Ten Faces of Innovation: IDEO's Strategies for Beating the Devil's Advocate & Driving Creativity Throughout your Organization*, New York: Currency/Doubleday.

Kirca, Ahmet H., Satish Jayachandran and William O. Bearden (2005), "Market orientation: a meta-analytic review and assessment of its antecedents and impact on performance," *Journal of Marketing*, **69** (2), 24–41.

Kohli, Ajay K. and Bernard J. Jaworski (1990), "Market orientation: the construct, research propositions, and managerial implications," *Journal of Marketing*, **54** (2), 1–18.

Kuczmarski, Thomas D. (1992), *Managing New Products: The Power of Innovation*, 2nd edn, Englewood Cliffs, NJ: Prentice Hall.

Kumar, V., Eli Jones, Rajkumar Venkatesan and Robert P. Leone (2011), "Is market orientation a source of sustainable competitive advantage or simply the cost of competing?," *Journal of Marketing*, **75** (1), 16–30.

Narver, John C. and Stanley F. Slater (1990), "The effect of a market orientation on business profitability," *Journal of Marketing*, **54** (4), 20–35.

Schein, Edgar H. (1985), *Organizational Culture and Leadership*, San Francisco, CA: Jossey-Bass Publishers.

Shapiro, Benson P. (1988), "What the hell is 'market oriented'?," *Harvard Business Review*, **66** (6), 119–25.

Smith, Adam (1776), *An Inquiry into the Nature and Causes of the Wealth of Nations*, 5th edn; 1930 edn, London: Methuen & Co., Ltd.

PART II

UNDERSTANDING COMPETITION

4 Competitor analysis
John A. Czepiel and Roger A. Kerin

Competitive marketing strategies are strongest either when they position a firm's strengths against competitors' weaknesses or choose positions that pose no threat to competitors. As such, they require that the strategist be as knowledgeable about competitors' strengths and weaknesses as about customers' needs or the firm's own capabilities.

This chapter is designed to assist the strategist understand how to gather and analyze information about competitors that is useful in the strategy development process. It discusses the objectives of competitor analysis and proceeds through the processes involved in identifying important competitors and information needs, gathering necessary information, and interpreting this information.

THE OBJECTIVES OF COMPETITOR ANALYSIS

The ultimate objective of competitor analysis is to know enough about a competitor to be able to think like that competitor so the firm's competitive strategy can be formulated to take into account the competitor's likely actions and responses. From a practical viewpoint, a strategist needs to be able to live in the competitor's strategic shoes. The strategist needs to be able to understand the situation as the competitor sees it and to analyze it so as to know what actions competitors would take to maximize their outcomes to be able to calculate the actual financial and personal outcomes of the competitor's strategic choices. They must be able to:

1. estimate the nature and likely success of the potential strategy changes available to a competitor;
2. predict each competitor's probable responses to important strategic moves on the part of the other competitors; and
3. understand competitors' potential reactions to changes in key industry and environmental parameters.[1]

What then should one expect from competitor analysis? Underneath all of the complexities and depth of competitor analysis are some basic practical questions, of which the following are typical:

- Which competitors does our strategy pit us against?
- Which competitor is most vulnerable and how should we move on its customers?
- Is the competitor's announced move just a bluff? What does it gain if we accept it at face value?
- What kind of aggressive moves will the competitor accept? Which moves has it always countered?

IDENTIFYING COMPETITORS

Identifying competitors for analysis is not quite as obvious as it might seem. Two complementary approaches are possible. The first is demand-side based, involving firms satisfying the same set of customer needs. The second approach is supply-side based, identifying firms whose resource base, technology, operations and the like are similar to those of the focal firm. However, the firm must pay attention not only to today's immediate competitors but also to those that are just over the horizon (such as cellphones once were to cameras, social networking sites once were to web portals, or the Internet once was to video rental stores). There are three domains for recognizing the sources and types of direct and less direct competitors to which the firm must also attend. These domains represent (1) the areas of influence, (2) the contiguous area and (3) the areas of interest.[2]

- The area of influence is the territory, market, business or industry in which the firm is directly competing with other firms to serve the same customer needs using the same resources. It is the arena in which Ford, Honda, Toyota, Kia and General Motors compete with each other; where Nokia competes with Samsung and Motorola in cellphones. These are a firm's direct competitors.
- Immediately contiguous areas are those in which competition is close but indirect; they comprise those firms that serve the same customer need but with different resources. Many food products fit into this category, such as snack foods (potato chips versus pretzels versus peanuts), or packaging (glass versus plastic versus aluminum). They may serve the same need but through differing distribution channels (direct such as Avon versus retail such as Revlon). These are a firm's indirect competitors.
- Areas of interest are composed of firms that do not currently serve the same customer base but have the same resource base or, in broader terms, have capability equivalence – the ability to satisfy similar customer needs.[3] For example, many firms possess the necessary capabilities to produce a wide range of digital electronic devices whether cellphones, PDAs, cameras or "pad" computers. These comprise a firm's potential competitors.

We will first examine product/market level competition – serving the same needs to the same customer group. Next we will examine firm-level competition.

Identifying Competitors at the Product-Market Level

The most direct competitor competes for the exact same customers in exactly the same way as the subject firm. It sells the same product made by the same technology to the same customers via the same marketing channels. If the firm cannot win customer patronage versus such an identical competitor, then it is unlikely that it can do any better competing against its indirect or potential competitors. Why? If the firm's exact counterpart can win in direct competition, then that same competitor should also win more against the less direct competitors.

Companies per se do not compete with each other in the marketplace. Rather, their individual businesses compete with each other. The strategic marketing literature denotes a business as a division, product line or other profit center with a company that produces and markets a well-defined set of related products and/or services, serves a clearly defined set of customers, and competes with a distinct set of competitors.[4]

A business is further defined in terms of a number of key dimensions, which reflect the ways and places in which it has chosen to compete. Primary among these are the products it offers and the types of customers to whom it chooses to sell.

The products a firm offers can be defined along three dimensions: functions, technology and materials:

- Customer function is concerned with what need is being satisfied. This is the most natural way to think about a product. Electromechanical devices, for example, can frequently be designed to satisfy any size set of functions from very narrow to very wide. For example, some cooking appliances are single function (microwave ovens), others are dual function (combination convection–microwave ovens), while others are multifunction (combination convection–microwave–conventional ovens). Another example concerns over-the-counter medications, which, although identical in ingredients, may be positioned or sold for the relief of colds or allergies or sinus symptoms. Others, such as Nyquil, are sold for even more specific usage applications (night-time cold relief).
- Technology tells us how the customer function(s) are being satisfied. For example, kitchen ranges may use two sources of thermal energy (gas or electric) or, alternatively, microwave energy to cook. X-rays, computerized axial tomography (CAT scan machines) and NMR (nuclear magnetic resonance) are three different technologies used in medical diagnostic imaging.
- The materials used in the manufacture of the product may also differ, producing slight differences in products that are otherwise identical. Cabinets may be made of chipboard versus plywood; bottles of glass or of such plastics as PET, polypropylene or polyethylene; and beverage cans of aluminum or steel.

The customer group being served is a key dimension. Automobile parts manufacturers, for example, may choose to serve either the original equipment manufacture (OEM) market or the automotive aftermarket, or both. One competitor may focus on serving urban markets while another serves rural markets. Wal-Mart's initial success came from its focus on serving small, rural markets that traditional discounters had thought too small and too poor to serve. In contrast, J.C. Penney has defined its customers as those households in the middle 80 percent of the US income distribution. Lane Bryant stores cater to women in need of larger sizes. There are obviously many ways of defining a firm's targeted customer groups.

A marketing strategist needs to understand the exact extent of competition among the products available on the market. At this level, competitors are best identified by customers – the demand side – rather than by supply characteristics.

Substitution-in-use

Current thinking about identifying the competitive structure for any given product is based on the idea of substitution-in-use. Three premises underlie the idea:

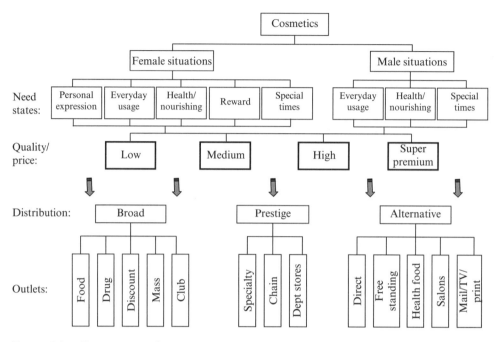

Figure 4.1   Cosmetics market structure

1. People seek the benefits that products provide rather than the products per se.
2. The needs to be satisfied and the benefits that are being sought are dictated by the usage situations or applications being contemplated.
3. Products and technologies are considered part of the set of substitutes if they are perceived to provide functions that satisfy the needs determined by intended usage.[5]

Determining a product's direct competition, then, may provide an answer that says, "It depends." It depends on (1) the number of separate and different uses or applications for the products in the market; (2) the number of different usage situations that customers encounter; and (3) user characteristics, including the number of product types or brands that a customer would evoke and choose among.[6] Some markets are relatively simple because the offerings within them provide only a single function for one or a few uses. Travelers' checks or bathroom tissue are two such products. Other examples include home pasta makers and irons, both of which perform a specific function across a small number of different usage situations. At the other extreme are complex markets in which each customer has many uses for the product and many alternatives to consider. Snack foods or dessert foods are examples. Depending on the intended usage occasion or situation, each of those product categories has many different kinds of products in competition. In the snack category, potato chips, pretzels, and various kinds of nuts, among others, compete. In the dessert realm, cakes, pies, ice cream, cookies and brownies, among others, compete.

Consider the cosmetics market structure shown in Figure 4.1. Consumers have a number of different need states ranging from personal expression, everyday usage, health or nourishing, reward, or special times. Depending on both their own economics

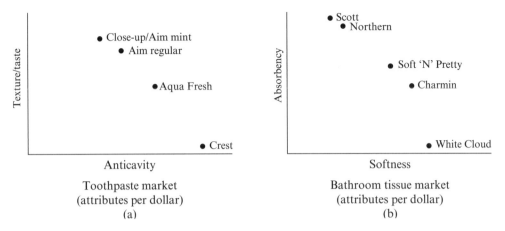

Source: Adapted from Steven M. Shugan, "Estimating brand positioning maps using supermarket scanning data," *Journal of Marketing Research*, **24** (1).

Figure 4.2 Brand positioning maps

and the need state, they may seek different price points and distribution outlets for their purchase. For any given need state, then, the competitive set will vary depending on price points, distribution and exact type of outlet chosen or encountered. Consider the cosmetics brand Aveda. Aveda distributes its cosmetics and personal care products through its own stores. While its products compete at a high level with those offered by such firms as Revlon or L'Oréal, the competition is not as direct as it is between brands whose products are next to each other on the drugstore shelf.

Financial services offer a similar example. One study, for example, defined a product market as "the set of products judged to be substitutes within those usage situations in which similar patterns of benefits are sought by groups of customers."[7] In the study, upscale customers were asked to judge the appropriateness of 24 different financial services across each of 12 different usage situations. One such usage situation was described thus: While you are out of town on a trip you have some unexpected problems with your car. The repair bill, at a small independent garage, is about $100 and must be paid immediately.

Using purchase behavior to identify competitors
No matter how much logical sense an analysis such as the foregoing makes, it is based on what customers say, not on what they do. Several researchers have developed techniques which are based on actual purchase data. Figure 4.2, for example, depicts the competitive structure of the toothpaste and bathroom tissue markets estimated on the basis of supermarket scanning data.[8] In this instance, the map positions products on the basis of their attributes on a per-dollar basis. As the map shows clearly, all toothpastes are not alike. Customers preferring taste over anti-cavity qualities are more likely to buy Close-Up or Aim than Crest. Furthermore, Close-Up and Aim are closer competitors than either is with Crest. The bathroom tissue market shows a similar positioning along its two primary dimensions: absorbency and softness. To say that Scott and White Cloud compete is true and not true at the same time. One might better say that Scott and Northern are in closer competition than either is with White Cloud or Charmin.

Identifying Potential Competitors

Depending on the purposes of the competitive analysis, it may also be important to identify potential competitors. The process starts by identifying firms for whom the various barriers to entry to the industry are low or easily surmountable. These may include the following:

- Technology: Firms which possess the technologies necessary to operate in an industry represent one source of potential competitors. Analysis of patent activity frequently signals intentions well prior to actual entrance.
- Market access: In businesses where market access is a key factor for success, firms with that access frequently attempt to leverage it by acquiring additional product lines to be sold in that channel or to those customers.
- Reputation and image: Brand extension strategies are based on the use of a firm's reputation in one product area to leverage its entry into another. Clairol used its reputation in hair coloring to enter into the hairdryer business.
- Operating knowledge and skills: Regional competitors in a business often expand geographically. Entenmann's Bakeries moved into Florida and Midwestern markets from their original Northeastern base, similar to the path taken by Thomas's English Muffins. Folger's Coffee was originally a regional brand on the West Coast until purchased by Procter & Gamble, which expanded its distribution nationwide.

Identifying Competitors at the Firm Level

The concept of interfirm rivalry extends beyond the product/market level. Competition can also occur as firms use related resources to bear on individual product/market level rivalry. The theory of multimarket competition describes those situations in which firms compete against each other in multiple markets.[9] For example, in 1989, America West entered the Houston, Texas market – Continental Airline's home base – with low introductory fares.[10] Continental retaliated, not by lowering prices in Houston but by lowering prices in Phoenix, Arizona, America West's home base and then communicated its displeasure with America West's actions in Houston. As a result, America West rescinded its low prices in the Houston market and, subsequently, Continental ceased its low-price counter-attack in Phoenix. Such behavior requires that the strategist understand the broader firm-level competitive set capable of such competitive behavior. One approach is to identify the different strategic groups in an industry.

The strategic group approach to identifying competitors is based on the differences in firms' strategies for competing in an industry. As such, it is a more general concept than the business definition approach. Like the business definition approach, the concept is intuitively appealing and understandable. For example, a hypothetical industry may be composed of three strategic groups:

1. A set of large firms pursuing a strategy of low-cost production of a full line of standardized products through mass-market outlets;

2. Another set of firms whose strategy emphasizes high-quality, differentiated and branded products sold through specialty shops; and
3. A group of smaller firms that have gained strategic advantage by specializing in serving either specific customer groups or producing a very narrow range of products.[11]

The strategic group concept is useful in identifying and analyzing firm-level competitors because members of a strategic group not only resemble each other but are also affected similarly by any given event or change in the environment. Given that they are playing the same game in the same way, their economics can be seen as similar. The commonality in their strategies means that they will likely respond in a similar manner to competitive threats or moves.

A further point should be noted about strategic groups. While all of the firms in an industry are in competition at a broad level, those in the same strategic group compete more closely among themselves than with those in other groups.[12] For example, Procter & Gamble, Unilever and Colgate-Palmolive in the household and personal care products markets are in closer competition with each other than they are with direct sellers of household and personal care products such as Amway or Avon. Further, the competition between and among groups is not equal – the various pairs of groups may compete more or less intensely. By observing the successes of the different strategic groups, one can better understand the potential for multimarket competition.

Competitive Blind Spots

Much competitor information is bounded by the assumptions that managers have with respect to their industry and these assumptions may lead to blind spots. The effect of these blind spots may cause the strategist to not recognize the significance of events, interpret them inappropriately, or see them only slowly.[13] There are six serious blind spots in competitor analysis:[14]

1. *Misjudging industry boundaries*   Too often firms define their industry around their current products, customer groups and geographies, blinding themselves to adjacent competitors that subsequently enter their current space.
2. *Poor identification of competitors*   Strategists frequently focus on only the largest and best-known companies to the exclusion of other viable competitors – those potential competitors noted earlier in this chapter.
3. *Overemphasis on competitors' visible competence*   Competitor analysis often focuses on competitors' hard assets and technology skills and ignores equally potent capabilities such as logistics, product design or human resources.
4. *Emphasis on where, not how, to compete*   Strategists too often assume that competitors' strategies will shift only incrementally to the exclusion of radical repositioning in how they could compete.
5. *Faulty assumptions about competitors*   Assumptions about competitors – the overuse of stereotypes – cause strategists to misjudge competitors' competences and competitive advantages.

6. *Paralysis by analysis*   Obsession with the task of data collection results in informa-
    tion overload, to the detriment of analysis and insight.

IDENTIFYING COMPETITOR INFORMATION NEEDS

The goal of competitor analysis is to be able to predict a competitor's probable future
actions, especially those made in response to the actions of the focal business. This
requires information that is both quantitative and factual (what the competitor is doing
and can do) as well as that which is qualitative and intentional (what the competitor is
likely to do). There are four key knowledge areas:

1. The competitor's marketplace strategy in terms of scope, posture and goals;[15]
2. The sources of competitive advantage that give its marketplace strategy potency,
    including resources and capabilities, organization, mindset and its place in the indus-
    try ecosystem;
3. The interpretation of the signals being sent by the competitor both by its actions and
    communications; and
4. A competitive response profile that analyzes the competitor's possible future moves.

The Competitor's Marketplace Strategy

The competitor's marketplace strategy defines the way the competitor is currently competing in the marketplace.[16] It defines the strategic choices the competitor has made
about where, how and why it seeks to attract, win and retain customers. A competitor's
marketplace strategy has three elements:

1. *Scope* – the product–customer segments the organization is in or wants to be in;
2. *Posture* – how it competes or wants to compete in those marketplace segments;
3. *Goals* – its purpose in being in those segments.

"Scope" defines the products offered to the market and the customers that purchase
them. It needs to incorporate both "static" and "dynamic" analyses. A static analysis
defines where the competitor is and what it is doing at the present time; dynamic analysis
refers to the moves the competitor has or is making over time in its choice of products or
customers or both. Customer segments may be identified by needs or the demographics
tied to those need states.

"Posture" defines how a competitor plays in the marketplace to win customers; most
importantly it is about how it differentiates itself from competitors in the eyes of customers. As with scope, it needs to be both static and dynamic. There are eight common
means of defining how the competitor competes.

1. Product line width – the number of types and items
2. Product features – the sizes and shapes available
3. Functionality – performance levels, reliability, durability
4. Service – technical assistance, installation, training

5. Availability – delivery speed, channels
6. Image and reputation – company reputation, brand image
7. Selling and relationships – customer coverage, relationships with distributors or customers
8. Price – list and street prices, price–performance relationship.

Successful competitors generally employ a number of interrelated modes to compete. Seldom is the reliance on one dominant mode (e.g. low price) a successful strategy.

"Goals" address the "why" of the scope and posture strategies that a competitor uses. Goals are the end whereas scope and posture are the means to that end. While it is easy to say that the goal is to generate profit, that is an end result several steps beyond the scope and posture actions being taken. Goals may be at the highest level of the business's intent and vision, such as Apple's intention to integrate voice, data and video. It may be at a lower level, focusing on the short to medium term such as penetrating each major channel of distribution or the attainment of a specific gross margin objective. Or it may be even more short term as achieving market share goals, cost efficiencies, or cash flow targets. Unless the goals have been publicly announced as a signal to the marketplace or to competitors, the analysis often must infer the competitor's goals from the flow of observable actions it has taken. At the heart of such an analysis is the question: "Why is the competitor taking the observed action?"

The Competitor's Source(s) of Competitive Advantage

Beneath a competitor's marketplace strategy lie the organization and the functional operations and processes that make the strategy possible. If the competitor is rational, then its marketplace strategy will have been built around those functions and activities where it is competitively advantaged versus competitors.[17] The ability to assess the economics of a competitor is key to competitive analysis. Incorporating knowledge about the competitor's advantages is key to understanding its strengths and weaknesses and its likely moves in the marketplace.

"Inputs" are a key source of advantage in many industries. Since very few businesses are completely vertically integrated, but simply add value to purchased inputs through their operations, assessing a competitor's source and costs of its raw materials is an important analysis. Identifying a competitor's suppliers and estimating such items as transportation costs is the first step. In businesses for which labor is a large part of the cost structure, that is the second step. Labor contracts are one source of such information, as are the various wage surveys available. The third element of inputs is the firm's weighted average cost of capital (WACC). A firm with a lower WACC can invest at a lower hurdle rate – the rate of return an investment must earn to gain corporate approval – and expand faster than one with a higher WACC. Equity analysts and many financial data services calculate the WACCs of firms.

"Technology" is the second focus, especially in industries that are still evolving. Assessing competitors' current operations and product technology is one step. Assessing the direction of their technology investments is the second. Many firms announce the present and future state of their technology to signal to competitors their competitive advantages. In other instances, following a competitor's published patents and scientific publications can give the analyst good indications of its direction. Estimating the number of R&D personnel is another common technique. As a generalization, a competitor that puts more resources against a given technology will create better technology faster than competitors giving it better products and operations.

"Operations" is the third focus. Many aspects of a competitor's operations can be accessed simply by buying its products and examining or reverse-engineering them. Quality, fit and finish, durability and the like can give the analyst insight into aspects of its operations. In service businesses, it is not difficult to benchmark one's own operations versus competitors' to understand how customers experience those operations. Comparing the cost of goods sold line of competitors' operating statements is another route.

"Products" are the primary locus of marketplace strategy. There are many ways to assess the advantage of competitors' products. The important task is to assess the products as customers see them. Customer surveys are a key and frequently used tool in this analysis. While many of the technical performance features are easy to measure, understanding the sources of customer value indicate what aspects of the products to analyze.

"Access, segments and customers" are the final considerations in understanding a competitor's sources of competitive advantage. Analyzing the type, number and quality of channel members serving a competitor, and its coverage in different channels of distribution, are key to assessing a competitor's advantage. For example, Anheuser-Busch, which sells almost 50 percent of the beer in the USA, has been able to attract the highest-quality distributors. In fact, some 60 to 70 percent of those distributors carry only Anheuser-Busch products. Other brewers, therefore, are not able to attract the same quality or must settle for distributors that also sell competing beers. Knowledge of competitors' penetration of the various segments is also important. Competitors who have a large share of growing customer segments are advantaged. Similarly, the customers a firm chooses to sell to can be a source of competitive advantage or disadvantage. One supplier to the slow-growing personal care market, for example, chose to target as its customers the small number of firms that were growing in the otherwise stagnant market, thereby growing while its competitors lost volume. In the early 2000s, Mitsubishi targeted the youth market in the USA with fast, small and sporty cars. Unfortunately, their customers' credit was poor and too many defaulted on the car loans.

Assessing and Interpreting Competitive Signals and Actions

Competitor analysis is not merely a static activity.[18] It requires more than the creation of a comprehensive report detailing the apparent strategies of the key industry competitors. It often means having only an hour or two to interpret the meaning of a competitor's 10 percent across-the-board price cut and to formulate a response. It often means being able to predict the reaction of competitors to your announcement of a major joint venture with the technology leader from an adjacent industry, or to your preannouncement of a major new product.[19] It means being able to understand what the leading competitor's chief executive means when quoted as saying of his company, "We must absolutely be as competitive as we possibly can." Is the message intended to rally the troops or to warn competitors?

Table 4.1   The domain of competitive signaling

FORM	PURPOSE (UNDERLYING OSTENSIBLE	VERACITY	FORUM OR MEDIUM	MESSAGE CONTENT
• Prior announcement • Announcement after the fact • Public discussion of industry • Discussion of own moves	• Preemption • Communicate strategic advantages • Threat of contingent action • Express pleasure or displeasure • Test of competitor's sentiments • Minimize provocative potential of own action • Avoid simultaneous actions • Inform financial community • Gain internal support	• True/untrue • Bluff • Misleading • Over/ understand	• Broad, prestigious industry audience • Financial analysts meeting • Interview in major industry/ business publication • Press release • Letter to customers or suppliers • Private communication with competitor	• Firm's goals • Internal situation of firm • Firm's intention • Expectations of competitor behavior • Rules of game/nature of dilemma

Source: John A. Czepiel, *Competitive Marketing Strategy*, Englewood Cliffs, NJ: Prentice-Hall, 1992, p. 361.

Interpreting competitor signals

Table 4.1 represents the domain of competitive signaling. Interpreting a competitor's message requires that one simultaneously consider the form of the message, its probable function, the forum or medium in which it is communicated, and the probable veracity of the message.

Message form   Prior announcements are perhaps the most often used form of competitive signaling because of their absolute versatility and ambiguity. One can announce with complete truthfulness the intention to expand capacity at some future point in time and change one's mind at some point thereafter. Prior announcements admit to the largest range of purposes and forums.

   Announcements of accomplished facts or results, on the other hand, admit to a smaller range of application, perhaps, but gain in the willingness of the receiver to believe that what has been announced has actually happened. Of course, this belief does not necessarily extend to swallowing whole the exact numbers, market shares and so forth that are offered in the announcement.

Public discussions of the state of the industry or competition within it rival prior announcements in their frequency and breadth of purpose. Speeches made at industry conferences, especially those attended exclusively by top-level executives, are carefully crafted to convey messages to participants and just as carefully dissected by rivals. Some, of course, need little interpretation. In an article in the *Wall Street Journal*, a portfolio manager with large holdings of Alcatel-Lucent stock was quoted as saying:

> the debilitating price wars between Alcatel-Lucent and its rivals could be "stabilizing," citing statements by Ericsson's (an Alcatel-Lucent competitor) management that the firm wouldn't push to gain market share in wireless equipment by cutting prices as it had early last year.[20]

Discussing one's own move in terms of its intent or rationale happens with less frequency than prior announcements, but possibly with greater impact. The apparent openness with which a competitor discusses the rationale underlying a given strategic move adds a luster of truth to the message, especially if it is shared in whispered tones with key customers or suppliers. Few public relations campaigns can spread news through an industry faster than sharing a strategy "in confidence, of course," with a customer whose greatest benefit is served by keeping competition for his or her business at a high pitch.

Message function The range of functions served by signaling is wide, and any given message may fulfill several simultaneously. Attempts to preempt competitors are certainly a leading function. During periods of shortages, industry publications are replete with competitors trying to prevent others from adding capacity by announcing their own capacity additions first. Announcing the future availability of major product developments to postpone customer purchase of competitors' products is another form of preemption. To the extent that they can be achieved, preemptive announcements are also used as the occasion to communicate strategic advantage to discourage less advantaged competitors from cluttering up the playing field.

Some messages are intended to minimize competitive provocation by explaining the rationale behind projected actions that could otherwise be interpreted as aggressively competitive. Consider, as an example, the announcement for lowering CD prices by the Universal Music Group in 2003:

> We're going to reinvigorate the record business in North America. Our new pricing policy will allow us to take the initiative in making music the best entertainment value and most compelling option for consumers. UMG is responsible for almost 30 percent of album sales in the U.S. so we are uniquely positioned to try this new strategy . . . We strongly believe that when prices are dramatically reduced on so many titles, we will drive consumers back to stores and significantly bolster music sales.[21]

Some external signals are given to gain internal support. Announcements in the public press by a company's president or chairman of its new drive to provide the highest level of quality are frequently more credible to employees than many internal communications programs. A variation is the external announcement that is made to cut off further internal discussion of a given strategy or specific action. Along the same lines, some announcements are made primarily to communicate indirectly with the financial community. Signals such as these may indeed carry little of import for competitors.

Message content   The actual content type of the message is important. One researcher has studied the various messages allowed in experimental studies of negotiation, cooperation and competition built around the various forms of the prisoner's dilemma and was able to discern different types of content.[22] Communication about the firm's goals has the potential to remove the dilemma in a situation in which the motivations are not clear. For example, if both are cooperatively disposed and both are aware of that, the obvious choice is to cooperate. Signals that communicate information about the internal situation of the firm, its health, success, and feelings about its outcomes and situation give others that knowledge necessary to infer its payoff matrix.

Signals about a firm's intentions give competitors information about how best to plan their own actions; this is especially so if the statement reveals commitment as well. Such knowledge is clearly important if the goal is to chart nonintersecting strategies. Communications or signals that state expectations of the competitor's behavior may be helpful in situations in which competition or cooperation are the choices and it is not clear to others how they should act.

It has been said that discussing the rules of the game and nature of the dilemma is particularly relevant in competitive interfirm situations because this message content contains more information than any of the others. Not only are statements about the nature of the game the most innocuous, but a cooperative equilibrium typically requires that competitors have a common view of how the game is played. Ultimately, of course, all competitors must limit their competitive behavior, and public discussions about how the buyer is the only winner in price wars are one way of signaling the need to cool the competitive state. David Steiner, the then CEO of industry-leading Waste Management, made the following statements during a conference call with investors:

> If you are going to continue to raise prices as an industry you've got to have all the industry players acting consistently. We're going to continue to raise price. We would certainly hope that the industry follows along with us.[23]

Forum or medium   Where and how a message is delivered is of key importance to its interpretation. Messages delivered before prestigious industry audiences or to a formal meeting with financial analysts are taken to contain higher truth content than those delivered in other forums. This is simply because both groups have good memories and require relationships based on personal trust.

Interviews in industry and business publications, on the other hand, are taken for what they are – the attempt by the competitor to deliver a carefully crafted message to a specific audience. The reality of the situation is that no executive has to consent to be interviewed and that consent is only given when there is some purpose to be served. Press releases are in a similar category. Letters to customers, on the other hand, carry a great deal of weight.

Veracity   Truth in strategic communication is a relative concept. While a communication may indeed be just what it is and says, the strategist is better off asking how it would benefit the sender if it were to be accepted by the receiver as true. Some signals are bluffs that will not be implemented if the bluff is successful in deterring competitive action but probably would not have been implemented anyway. Too many bluffs, however, and all parties suspend belief: the firm has lost a valuable tool through overuse. More often, the content of communications contains some aspects that are misleading or simply over- or understated. These aspects require the analyst to cross-check all numbers and to analyze every statement for possible alternative interpreta-tions. Sometimes ambiguity is intentional to allow one to read a possible worst-case scenario into an otherwise innocuous message. Some signals carry as much contradic-tory and hidden meaning as the gambits and contrivances one finds in the best of the Cold War spy novels.

Interpreting competitor actions

Interpreting a competitor's actions follows a similar analysis, beginning with the over-riding question: "Why is the action being taken?" In seeking to answer that question, the first step is to characterize the type of action. A frontal attack is one in which the competitor directly attacks with an identical or similar product. In the 1990s, Unilever directly attacked P&G's Joy brand dishwashing liquid with an identical product under the brand name Sunlight. Both were yellow, lemon scented products in iden-tical bottles promising shiny dishes. A flanking attack, on the other hand, is one in which the competitor enters an adjacent product–customer segment rather than going head-to-head. In the 1980s, for example, Bic entered the men's shaving business with a disposable razor rather than the traditional razors offered by Gillette. Pricing actions are of a number of types. They may simply be meeting the competition, undercutting the competition, a cross-parry in order to retaliate, or a widely announced increase. Alternatively, a pricing action may be a "non-action" – that is not following a price leader's announced price increases. Northwest Airlines (now Delta) frequently acted as a spoiler by not following competitors' price increases in the early 2000s, causing them to be rescinded.

The nature of the action is the next step. The analyst needs to ask the following questions:

- What was the action relative to the potential actions that could have been taken? Was it more or less severe?
- How was the action taken? Was it announced? Quietly implemented?
- How did it match or differ from the competitor's past actions and strategies? Does it suggest a continuation of past policies or does it mark a change in its strategy or mode of action?
- Does the action follow accepted industry practice? Is the competitor seeking to lead the industry into a new competitive territory?
- Does the competitor expect other firms to follow it?
- Is the move aggressive or does it suggest a more "cooperative" way of compet-ing?

It should be noted that competitive actions can be outside of the marketplace. Legal actions are a case in point. Lawsuits over trademarks and brands are frequent and can tie up a firm's executive and managers for long periods of time. Private antitrust suits are another form of competitive action. In both instances, a deep-pocketed competitor can cause great harm to smaller, less wealthy firms.

The Competitor's Response Profile

The likelihood of competitor reactions depends on:

1. the characteristics of the firm taking the action, for example its size and reputation for competitiveness;
2. the characteristics of the action. It could be a new market entry or price change;
3. the characteristics of the rival – its size, performance or desired reputation;
4. environmental characteristics such as market turbulence or growth.[24]

Given some insight into these four factors, the firm or analyst needs to ask the following questions about competitors.

1. What drives the competitor? What are their objectives?
2. What is their current strategy? How do they compete?
3. What assumptions and capabilities drive their actions?
4. What would provoke the greatest and most effective retaliation from them?

The combination of this analysis of competitors' goals and assumptions together with competitors' current strategies and capabilities allows one to estimate their response profiles.[25] A response profile tells one what kinds of actions a competitor is likely to take, if any, in response to the firm's own actions. Again, what this means is that a strategist has to be able to think like the competitor.

It may sound simplistic, but one of the most powerful determinants of a competitor's future actions is the set of economic outcomes that would result from each different competitive response. To the extent, then, that one can calculate the financial results that would flow from different actions, one should be able to predict competitors' actions.

One approach is to estimate the competitor's reactiveness to a competitive move on a particular product in a given geographical (or other defined market) market and the relative *clout* it has with which to respond to a competitive move.[26] Reactiveness is simply the competitor's incentive to counter competitive moves. It can be measured by estimating the contribution (revenues, profits etc.) that the product delivers in that market and that it delivers to the business unit of which it is a part adjusted for the strategic importance of the product and market to the competitor. Take, for example, a move against P&G's Tide laundry detergent product in the USA. With its leading market share it contributes both book profits and strong cash flow to the division of which it is a part and to the corporation as a whole. As the anchor product of the detergent aisle in supermarkets it is of strategic importance in maintaining the support of the channel. One can say with reasonable certainty that P&G would exhibit high reactiveness to any competitive move against Tide. Relative clout asks which of the competitors is in a better position to make a strategic move in that specific product/market arena. It is the ability to fight or to fight back. As with reactiveness, relative clout can be estimated from the competitors' relative sizes, cash positions, distribution coverage, and the relative number of salespeople.

Theoretically, the issue goes beyond reactiveness and clout. It is more complex. Economists use the term "conjectural variation" to refer to what is known about the likelihood and the intensity of competitors' responses. Specifically, a conjectural variation is what is believed about the relationship between a firm's own behavior and the corresponding return-maximizing action that will be taken by the competitor.[27] The interesting aspect is that estimating a competitor's actions requires the recognition that the competitor's decision involves more than simply choosing the action that yields it the highest relative financial result from among the set of actions available to it. This is because those financial results themselves are simultaneously affected by the competitor's own conjectures concerning the acting firm's reaction to its response.

In more practical terms for the strategist, this means working two moves ahead – estimating whether the competitor would see its action choices as leading to more or less effective countermoves. Game theory provides one framework for analyzing the situation. The main point, however, is to attempt to calculate the relative financial implications of the competitor's possible responses. A second approach suggests that one analyze the past effectiveness of the competitor's marketing mix elements. As theory would suggest, a competitor's response to, say, the market entry of a new product will be to adopt the approach that has shown the greatest response elasticity in the past.[28]

SUMMARY

Competitive marketing strategy requires that the strategist position the firm's offerings such that they minimize direct competition either by choosing vulnerable competitors or by pitting strength against weakness. The goal of competitor analysis is to provide the strategist with the means to achieve that result. As such, competitor analysis is critical for understanding competition and its implications for marketing strategy as detailed by Sabnis and Grewal, Chapter 5 in this volume.

This chapter portrays competitor analysis as a dynamic, not a static, process. The identification of competitors and gathering information pertaining to each competitor is viewed as an ongoing effort. It reflects not only competitor behavior, but the focal company behavior as well. This chapter also highlights the importance of competitor analysis as a critical component of strategic thinking and decision making in shaping a competitive marketing strategy. In particular, the role of competitor analysis in informing the focal company of both proactive and reactive moves of competitors is emphasized. Finally, this chapter repeatedly avers that a strategist must think like a competitor and avoid competitive blind spots.

NOTES

1.   John A. Czepiel, *Competitive Marketing Strategy*, Englewood Cliffs, NJ: Prentice Hall, 1992, p. 10.
2.   William L. Sammon, Mark A. Kurland and Robert Spitalnic, *Business Competitor Intelligence: Methods for Collecting, Organizing, and Using Information*, New York: John Wiley and Sons, 1984; Mark Bergen and Margaret A. Peteraf, "Competitor identification and competitor analysis: a broad-based managerial approach," *Managerial and Decision Economics* (June–August 2002), 157–69; Bruce H. Clark and David B. Montgomery, "Managerial identification of competitors," *Journal of Marketing* (July 1999), 67–83.
3.   Margaret A. Peteraf and Mark E. Bergen, "Scanning dynamic competitive landscapes: a market-based and resource-based framework," *Strategic Management Journal*, **24**, 2003, 1027–41.
4.   Roger A. Kerin, Vijay Mahajan and P. Rajan Varadarajan, *Contemporary Perspectives on Strategic Market Planning*, Boston, MA: Allyn & Bacon, 1990.

5. George S. Day, "Strategic market analysis: top-down and bottom-up approaches," Cambridge, MA: Marketing Science Institute, Report No. 80–105, August 1980, p. 14.
6. Day, "Strategic Market Analysis," p. 20; see also Glen L. Urban, Philip L. Johnson and John R. Hauser, "Testing competitive market structures," *Marketing Science*, **3** (2) (Spring 1984), 83–112.
7. Rajendra K. Srivastava, Mark I. Alpert and Allan D. Shocker, "A customer-oriented approach for determining market structures," *Journal of Marketing* (Spring 1984), p. 32.
8. Steven M. Shugan, "Estimating brand positioning maps using supermarket scanning data," *Journal of Marketing Research* (February 1987), 1–18; see also Steven M. Shugan, "Brand positioning maps from price/share data: the case of bathroom tissue," unpublished working paper, University of Chicago Graduate School of Business, July 1986, revised, and Terry Elrod, "Choice map: inferring a product-market map from panel data," *Marketing Science*, **7** (1) (Winter 1988), 21–39.
9. Aneel Karni and Birger Wernerfelt, "Multiple point competition," *Strategic Management Journal*, **6** (1985), 87–96 and Satish Jayachandran, Javier Gimeno and P. Rajan Varadarajan, "The theory of multi-market competition: a synthesis and implications for marketing strategy," *Journal of Marketing* (July 1999), 49–66.
10. Asra Nomani, "Airlines may be using a price-data network to lessen competition," *The Wall Street Journal*, June 28, 1994, A1.
11. This hypothetical industry in fact resembles the home appliance industry in the 1960s as described by Michael S. Hunt in his dissertation. Hunt coined the phrase "strategic groups" to explain the differences in profitability he observed within the industry. Michael S. Hunt, "Competition in the major home appliance industry, 1960–1970," unpublished doctoral dissertation, Harvard University, 1972.
12. The biological analogy predicts this. As Bruce Henderson (the founder of the Boston Consulting Group) noted, "The more similar competitors are to each other, the more severe their competition. This observation was made by Darwin in *The Origin of Species*." Bruce Henderson, "The anatomy of competition," *Journal of Marketing*, (Spring 1983), p. 8.
13. Michael E. Porter, *Competitive Strategy*, New York: The Free Press, 1980, p. 59.
14. Shaker A. Zahra and Sherry S. Chaples, "Blind spots in competitive analysis," *Academy of Management Executive*, **7** (2) (1993), 7–28; E.J. Zajac and M.H. Bazerman, "Blind spots in industry and competitor analysis: implications of interfirm (mis) perception for strategic decisions," *Academy of Management Review*, **16** (1) (1991), 37–56.
15. Liam Fahey, *Competitors: Outwitting, Outmaneuvering, and Outperforming*, New York: John Wiley & Sons, 1999.
16. This section is based on Liam Fahey, *Competitors*, pp. 108–18.
17. George S. Day and Prakash Nedungadi, "Managerial representations of competitive advantage," *Journal of Marketing* (April 1994), 31–44.
18. This section is based on Czepiel, *Competitive Marketing Strategy*, p. 360.
19. Jehoshua Eliashberg and Thomas S. Robertson, "New product preannouncing behavior," *Journal of Marketing Research* (August 1988), 282–92.
20. *The Wall Street Journal*, "Alcatel-Lucent deal, revisited," February 7, 2007, p. C2.
21. Ethan Smith, "Universal slashes CD prices to revive music industry," *The Wall Street Journal*, September 4, 2003, pp. B1, B8.
22. Marian Chapman Bourke, "Signalling and screening: tactics in negotiations across organizations," in Blair Sheppard, Max Bazerman and Roy Lewicki (eds), *Research on Negotiations in Organizations* (Greenwich, CT: JAI Press, 1988).
23. Lan Brat, "Garbage haulers raise prices: truce allows Waste Management, Allied, and Republic to push higher," *The Wall Street Journal*, September 18, 2008, p. B1.
24. David B. Montgomery, Marian Chapman Moore and Joel E. Urbany, "Reasoning about competitive reactions: evidence from executives," *Marketing Science* (Winter 2005), 138–49.
25. Michael Porter, *Competitive Advantage*, New York: The Free Press, 1980, p. 49.
26. Ian C. MacMillan, Alexander B. van Putten and Rita Gunther McGrath, "Global gamesmanship," *Harvard Business Review*, **81** (May 2003), pp. 62–71.
27. Raphael Amit, Ian Domowitz and Chaim Fershtman, "Thinking one step ahead: the use of conjectures in competitor analysis," *Strategic Management Journal*, **9** (1988), 431–42.
28. Kevin P. Coyne and John Horn, "Predicting your competitor's reaction," *Harvard Business Review* (April 2009), pp. 90–97.

5 Competition and its implications for marketing strategy
Gaurav Sabnis and Rajdeep Grewal

1. INTRODUCTION

In August 2009, at the World Athletics Championships in Germany, Tyson Gay clocked 9.71 seconds, his personal best, running the 100 meters faster than any man in previous rounds of the tournament. However, it was not enough to make him the tournament record holder, nor did it win him the gold medal. Running in the same race, Usain Bolt, with a time of 9.58 seconds, captured the gold medal, the tournament record, the world record and the news headlines. This example of a phenomenal athletic performance by Gay, overshadowed by Bolt's, underlines a truism that is as applicable to business as it is to sports: Performance is always evaluated relative to competitors'.

Market share, a key performance metric of a firm's marketing activities, measures the firm's sales relative to those of its competitors. Reibstein and Wittink (2005) stress the importance of measuring firm performance in relative terms. That is, competition plays a role not only in measuring but also in determining performance. As Day and Reibstein (1997) recognize, the success of marketing activities depends on how a firm's activities compare with those of its competitors. For example, whether customers respond to a firm's sales promotions and buy the firm's product often depends on the sales promotions offered by the firm's competitors. Managers thus are mindful of competitors' present and possible future actions when they devise and execute their marketing strategies (Leeflang and Wittink 1996). In this sense, competition affects almost every aspect of firm strategy – from devising and executing strategies, to the success of those strategies, to the evaluation of firm performance, and also critically influences a firm's allocation of resources (Shankar, Chapter 9 in this volume).

Competition has received ample attention from academics, in both business research and allied social sciences. Competitor analysis and competitive analysis have been extensively examined by marketing scholars (e.g. Czepiel and Kerin, Chapter 4 in this volume; Shankar 2010a, b). In this chapter, we take a detailed look at extant literature on competition in marketing and in related disciplines, such as strategic management, industrial organization (IO), economics and sociology. Researchers in these disciplines have studied in depth various questions related to competition, which we broadly classify into two categories: competitive market structures and competitive interactions. Market structure reflects the configuration of competing firms in an industry with respect to some key dimensions. Diverse perspectives serve to investigate market structures, including a demand-based perspective (in marketing), supply-based perspective (IO and strategic management) and environment-based perspective (IO and sociology). In section 2, we discuss these three perspectives to offer an integrated perspective and lay out an agenda for further research. Competitive interactions, which we outline in section

3, entail dynamic managerial strategic decision making that accounts for competitors' actions. We end in section 4 by elaborating on the emerging topics that researchers should consider to understand competition.

2.   MARKET STRUCTURE AND COMPETITION

Market structure refers to the configuration of competing firms in an industry, generally with regard to who competes with whom at a given level of the value chain. The study of competitive market structures started with a regulatory policy perspective (Demsetz 1973), according to which governments use market structure information to formulate public policy to protect the interests of stakeholders, including customers. One of the basic tenets of capitalist societies is that competition benefits the customer by spurring firms to improve quality and keep prices low. Governments, keen to protect this tenet, consider the market structure to ensure that competition is not stifled by the unfair practices of a few dominant players. Such research provides details about different types of market structures (e.g. monopoly, duopoly, oligopoly, monopsony) and their relative advantages and disadvantages (e.g. Perry 1984; Posner 1975).

From a managerial perspective, market structures influence important decisions related to advertising, branding, promotions, innovation and R&D. These market structures are asymmetric (e.g. Amit and Schoemaker 1993; Carpenter et al. 1988; DeSarbo et al. 2006; Shankar et al. 1998, 1999), such that the degree to which one firm competes with another is not the same as the degree to which the second firm competes with the first. Such asymmetries may arise from supply-based factors, such as differences in firm resource endowments or geographic scope of operations, as well as demand-based perspectives, such as differences in customer loyalty. Managers clearly must take such asymmetries into consideration when devising and executing marketing strategies.

2.1   Demand-based Perspective of Competition

The demand-based perspective on market structure assumes that competitive market structures rest in the minds and hearts of customers, and customers end up deciding which firms compete with one another. Not surprisingly, with its focus on customers, the demand-based perspective has received significant attention from marketing researchers (e.g. Blattberg and Wisniewski 1989; Cooper and Inoue 1996; DeSarbo et al. 2006).

From a demand-based perspective, market structures are "a *set of products* judged to be substitutes within those usage situations in which similar patterns of benefit are sought, and the *customers* for whom such usages are relevant" (Day et al. 1979, p. 10, emphasis in original). The complexity of the process by which consumers decide which products or brands to purchase provides myriad customer data that can uncover market structures, including but not limited to perceived brand similarities (e.g. DeSarbo and Manrai 1992), brand-switching probabilities (e.g. Carpenter and Lehmann 1985), panel data on purchase choices (e.g. Hansen and Singh 2009), customer knowledge structures (e.g. Alba and Chattopadhyay 1985) and price elasticity (e.g. Blattberg and Wisniewski 1989). Depending on the nature of the data, their granularity and the stage of the customers' decision-making process, assessments of market structure can and often do vary.

Through a review of literature that contains a demand-based perspective on competition, we have identified three broad research approaches that identify market structure according to customers' attitudes and behaviors: (1) knowledge structure approach, (2) consideration set approach, and (3) purchase decision approach. These approaches differ in terms of the stage of the purchase process the respondents are at when the data are collected: (1) no immediate purchase intended, (2) purchase intended in the near future, and (3) purchase concluded, respectively.

2.1.1　Knowledge structure approach

Consider consumers who own a laptop or have used one in the past. Their knowledge about laptop brands likely is an outcome of their past purchase and usage, the opinions and experiences of their friends and family, their exposure to laptop advertising, and what they have read or heard about laptops in the media, such as reviews and descriptions. However, these customers do not have an immediate need for a laptop. Data collected from them – by asking them to imagine a hypothetical purchase scenario and respond with their perceptions of brand similarities, brand preferences, price sensitivity and so on – will give researchers a picture of the market structure according to the knowledge structure of customers (e.g. Sinha and DeSarbo 1998). Therefore, in this knowledge structure approach, market structure represents the composition of a set of products, according to customers' perceptions of the competing players in the market (e.g. Alba and Chattopadhyay 1985).

2.1.2　Consideration set approach

When customers have an active need for a laptop, the set of products in their consideration set likely differs from those they perceive in the absence of an active need. For example, customers who otherwise would consider Windows-based, Mac-based and Linux-based laptops as substitutes may limit their consideration set when faced with an actual decision to, say, just Windows-based laptops. This alteration in the consideration set could have manifold reasons, such as switching costs, recent advertising or budget constraints. The resulting market structure provides information about competition based on the consideration sets of potential customers (e.g. Urban et al. 1984). The consideration set approach thus is based on data collected from customers who have an expressed intention to purchase in the near future. DeSarbo and Jedidi (1995), for example, use personal interviews with customers who intend to purchase an automobile within six months to measure consideration sets.

2.1.3　Purchase decision approach

Consumers think differently in the initial stage of their decision-making process versus the final stage when they make the purchase (e.g. Grewal et al. 2003). Thus, if customers have eliminated Apple from their consideration set, they may consider Lenovo, HP, Toshiba and Acer laptops, but their final choice may focus on HP versus Acer. Their final purchase features only one brand, of course. Thus customers' perceptions about the set of products in the initial stage of the purchasing process differ from those in the final stage (Shocker et al. 1991). Research on customer structure from a demand perspective based on data about final purchases, such as panel data, brand switching in repeat purchase setting and so on, therefore indicates a competitive market structure based on the purchase decision, which we call the "purchase decision approach" (e.g. Hansen and Singh 2009).

Each of these three approaches can offer useful insights for researchers, managers and policy makers, depending on the stage of the customer purchase cycle. The demand-based perspective is particularly useful for high-velocity industries, whose market composition and patterns change rapidly. Assessing the nature of competition, including the make-up of asymmetry, on the basis of what customers think can lead to insights that otherwise might not be salient. We therefore encourage researchers who examine competition from a demand-based perspective to consider the pros and cons of these three approaches to data collection carefully and study their interdependencies from a market structure perspective. Perhaps triangulating across these methodologies would also be useful.

2.2 Supply-based Perspective of Competition

The supply-based perspective assumes that competitive market structures reflect the minds of managers, who run the firms, and the collective structure results from how firms view one another as competitors, which determines the final competitive market structure in an industry (DeSarbo et al. 2006). Scholars from the domains of industrial organization (IO) and strategic management primarily view the competitive market structure of an industry through the lens of firms' and managers' perceptions of whom they compete with, and who competes with them.

This supply-based perspective has its roots in the IO school of economics (Mason 1939), which stresses the importance of industry structure and observes that firm profitability depends directly on competitive market structure factors, such as industry concentration (e.g. Scherer and Ross 1990) and the oligopolistic/monopolistic nature of competition (e.g. Stigler 1964). However, IO scholars view the composition of the market as purely structural, in that just by existing in the same industry, all firms compete. Strategic management scholars (e.g. Barney 1986) have drawn heavily on the IO view but also questioned the assumption that all firms in an industry are *de facto* competitors. Instead, competitive market structures may arise from managerial perceptions, which requires the incorporation of managers' demographic and psychological factors into any competitor identification or analysis (e.g. Porac and Thomas 1990; Zajac and Bazerman 1991). Thus the supply-based perspective identifies and analyzes competitive market structures on the basis of the perceptions of managers pertaining to which firms are their competitors and which are not. Scholars identify competitive market structures primarily through perceptual cognitive data obtained from managers and textual analyses of company reports and shareholder letters, as well as strategic firm variables (e.g. available from financial databases), with the assumption that these variables reflect managerial cognitions.

Industrial competition is dyadic (i.e. the struggle between two firms for customers and resources), but because the supply-based perspective charts market structure according to the firm-level perceptions of managers, there could be a mismatch in how two firms view each other. Managers from Firm A might view Firm B as a competitor, whereas managers from Firm B do not consider Firm A competition, which leads to asymmetric competition (e.g. DeSarbo et al. 2006). In the 1960s and 1970s, US automobile and electronics firms did not view Japanese firms as competitive threats, but Japanese firms considered US firms as their primary competitors. Thus competitive market structures derived from managerial perceptions can provide insights into the asymmetric nature of competition in the market.

Asymmetry in managers' views of competition suggests that not all firms in an industry compete equally; rather, there are subsets of firms that compete more intensely with each other than firms in other subsets. These subsets within an industry are called "strategic groups", a term first used by Hunt (1972) and adopted by many others (e.g. Ketchen et al. 1997; McGee and Thomas 1986). Strategic groups consist of firms in an industry that are similar in factors such as their product portfolio or cost structure, so they adopt similar strategies. Firms in a strategic group compete more intensely than firms across strategic groups, and strategic groups help explain performance differences across firms (e.g. Cool and Schendel 1987; Dranove et al. 1998).

Although strategic groups help analyze market structure, growing recognition notes heterogeneity in the degree to which firms comply with the strategic recipes of their groups (e.g. Ketchen et al. 1993). Scholars studying market structures from a supply-based perspective recently have sought to understand the complexities of strategic group compositions, as well as within-group differences in strategies and performance outcomes. For example, McNamara et al. (2003) study differences within strategic groups and find variations in the way core and secondary members perform. DeSarbo and Grewal (2008) propose the notion of "hybrid strategic groups" that consist of firms that blend strategies from two or more groups. Similarly, a recent focus has been to study the dynamics of strategic groups (e.g. Fiegenbaum et al. 2001; Mascarenhas 1989), using models for evolutionary paths of strategic groups (DeSarbo et al. 2009) and hidden Markov models to reflect firm switching across strategic groups (Ebbes et al. 2010).

2.3   Environment-based Perspective of Competition

The competitive market structure may evolve as a result of environmental factors, such as government regulations, legal environment, infrastructure, institutions and technological advancements. Apart from strategic management, two disciplines have also examined the role of the environment: the political economy (PE) school of economics (e.g. Bresnahan and Reiss 1991) and organizational sociology (e.g. White 1981).

The PE school draws on theories in economics, law and political science to explain how political institutions in an environment influence economic activity (e.g. Gaynor and Vogt 2000; Neven and Röller 2005). With regard to competition, PE scholars examine how aspects of the environment, shaped by political institutions such as public policy, regulations and the legal system, affect the competitive market structure of an industry. The best-known and conspicuous element of the environment (as related to political institutions) that influences competitive market structure is antitrust legislation. Antitrust legislations (such as the US antitrust law and the European Union (EU) competition law) are enacted by governments to protect their citizens' interest by maintaining market competition and regulating or curbing what governments view as "anticompetitive conduct." The rationale behind such legislation is that if a certain firm grows in size and uses its relative size advantage to undermine its competitors, the overall level of competition in the market declines, leaving consumers vulnerable to undesirable outcomes such as price gouging and poorer quality of products or services. Antitrust legislation is the tool governmental regulatory bodies use to stop companies from engaging in, or penalize them for conduct that could suppress, robust competition.

Antitrust legislation can play several influential roles in shaping market structure. As a direct influence, the government might step in and force a firm it deems too big and powerful to break up into smaller firms, which changes the market structure radically. Perhaps the most famous example of this exertion of government force was the breakup of "Ma Bell" (AT&T) in the 1980s, which by US government mandate became several smaller firms popularly referred to as "Baby Bells," transforming the market structure of the telephone industry from a monopoly to an oligopoly. Regulatory bodies also can use antitrust laws to prevent a change to the existing market structure by stopping mergers if regulators believe the resulting market concentration will harm competition and thus consumers.

The legal environment influences market structure beyond just antitrust legislation, though. In economies in which the legal environment provides relatively easy recourse for firms that are victims of unethical or illegal practices (e.g. patent violations, intellectual property disputes, misleading advertising), it is difficult for dominant firms to engage in predatory practices or increase their power. A well-functioning legal system can stop the market structure from being held hostage by dominant firms. However, in economies whose legal system is not as robust, dominant firms often shape the market structure to their benefit by engaging in rent-seeking behaviors and moral hazard (e.g. Hainz 2003).

Other aspects of the external environment that can influence market structure include the infrastructure and technological advancements. Technological advancements and the related intellectual property can shape the market structure, depending on, for example, whether the advances are driven by dominant big players or newcomers. The cellular phone industry's competing technological standards – GSM (developed by existing dominant players) versus CDMA (developed by newer firms) – have prompted several studies on the resulting market structure evolution (e.g. Bekkers et al. 2002).

Infrastructure, such as roads, freight, airports, electricity, telecommunications and financial systems, also influences competitive market structures. In economies with a well-developed infrastructure, companies of varying sizes can compete, leading to a market structure that is amenable to greater competition. However, in economies with poor infrastructure, big companies with access to capital have an advantage. For example, in India, the power infrastructure falls short of meeting demand, so firms often build power plants within their manufacturing units to ensure reliable power supplies, which requires significant access to capital and thus erects barriers to entry.

Organizational sociologists argue that market structure results from as well as reflects the position of the relevant industrial actors (firms, suppliers, regulators etc.) in the social structure that connects these industrial actors. Sociologists view economic activity and the resultant market structure as determined primarily by socially defined positions in the market context (e.g. Granovetter 1985; White 1981). Thus market structure is socially constructed, as perceived by all market participants and influenced by factors related to the participants' position in the social structure, their roles and their status (e.g. Podolny 1993). Sociologists regard competition among firms as relationships, the resulting competitive market structure as a network of relationships, and the market structure as an evolving entity that reflects levels of embeddedness in the network (e.g. Uzzi 1996), including structural holes (e.g. Burt 1995) or cliques (e.g. White 1981). A full understanding of the structural aspects of the network of relationships among market participants can reveal the nature of the market structure, its antecedents, and its consequences for all the participants.

2.4   Integrating the Three Perspectives

Thus far, we have discussed three broad perspectives on competitive market structure: consumers', managers' and the environmental perspective. Although market structure has been studied in detail by scholars in several fields, each producing its own perspective, we believe that the way forward is to integrate these three perspectives.

As DeSarbo et al. (2006) argue, there are shortfalls in the demand- and supply-based perspectives, and it would be beneficial to view them as complements. The supply-based perspective, which relies only on managerial perceptions, likely reflects asymmetry in competition and ignores some firms that consumers might view as competitors; thus its picture of the precise nature of the market structure is incomplete. The demand-based perspective relies only on consumer perceptions and thus likely excludes newcomers that eventually will become potent forces in the competitive market structure but are not yet on equal footing with other firms. DeSarbo et al. (2006) integrate these two approaches to conceptualize asymmetric market structures.

We stress the need for more integrative work that combines not only the supply- and demand-based perspectives but also the environment-based approach. The study of competitive market structures should not be a choice among the influences of managers, consumers or the environment; rather, it should treat all these perspectives as complementary and draw from phenomena suggested by all of them to develop a complete picture of the market structure.

The market structure in a given industry can and should be regarded as the interplay of the actions of managers, consumers and the environment. For example, in the cellular phone industry, the market structure clearly has been shaped by managers, consumers and the environment. From a supply-based perspective, the exclusive agreements between phone manufacturers and service providers (e.g. Apple and AT&T for the iPhone) determine who competes with whom. From a demand-based perspective, consumers appear to perceive the Blackberry as a functional phone primarily used by professionals, whereas the iPhone and Android phones are "cool toys" used by non-professionals, such that the latter two phones appear closer to in the perceptual space than does the Blackberry. Finally, from an environment-based perspective, technological advances such as 3G and 4G services have drastically changed the landscape, allowing a new entrant such as Apple to achieve a strong position quickly.

Any approach that studies an industry from only one of the three perspectives will fail to recognize the impact of the other two perspectives. However, the observations from these three perspectives clearly are related. For example, the technological advancements allowed Apple to enter the cellular phone industry with the iPhone, and consumers who previously used other Apple products such as iPods and Macs viewed it as a desirable product, unlike existing Blackberry phones, which enabled AT&T to attract this significant chunk of Apple fans by entering into an exclusive agreement with it. Integrating the three perspectives should provide a richer understanding of competitive market structures than does focusing on just one of them.

2.5   Agenda for Further Research on Competitive Market Structures

Research on competitive market structures, in both marketing and related fields, has been plentiful and insightful, but several areas show promise for ongoing research. Although every aspect of market structure can benefit from further research, we focus on a few areas we consider most important for marketing scholars and practitioners, given the state of extant literature.

As we noted previously, integrating the three perspectives of market structure can lead to new insights. However, the integration of all three perspectives poses several challenges, conceptually (e.g. integrating the differing theories on which the three perspectives rely), methodologically (e.g. developing models that can capture phenomena from all three perspectives and their interactions) and in terms of the data (e.g. gathering data on managerial perceptions, consumer perceptions and environmental constructs). Tackling these challenges will be difficult but also will lead to insights regarding the identification, antecedents and consequences of market structure that hitherto have been unknowable.

In our review of market structure literature across various fields, we have noticed that empirical studies overwhelmingly are cross-sectional (although notable exceptions exist, e.g. Ebbes et al. 2010). Although cross-sectional studies can identify the market structure and related phenomena in the short run, they cannot capture the evolution of the market structure over time. We call for studies that investigate the temporal aspects of market structure, using longitudinal data and appropriate time-dynamic models. Most industries undergo structural breaks or shocks (e.g. radical innovation, regulatory changes, recession) that shake up the market structure; we argue for the need to incorporate these structural breaks into longitudinal studies of market structure. Such longitudinal studies can provide insights into how market structures evolve over time and why. For example, a longitudinal study of changes in the airline industry's market structure over the past three decades, driven by antecedents such as oil price fluctuations, Internet booking, the entry of budget airlines, regulatory changes, the 9/11 attacks, mergers and so on, could clarify how that market structure evolved and reveal the relative impact of the various antecedents.

3.   COMPETITIVE INTERACTIONS

Research on competitive interactions addresses questions that fit under the broad question that Weitz (1985) articulates as follows: "How do competitive actions affect market decisions?" This stream of research considers how firms react to the actions of their competitors, the extent of their responsiveness to competitors, and the efficacy of these competitive reactions. We classify research on competitive reactions into three broad categories, based on their conceptual and methodological approaches: behavioral, structural, and game-theoretic approaches. The behavioral approach, as used primarily in strategic management literature (e.g. Chen 1996) and frequently in marketing literature (e.g. Bowman and Gatignon 1995), attempts to predict the competitive reactions of firms on the basis of their characteristics and those of their competitors. The structural approach, from IO but also gaining ground in marketing, uses economic models of the competitive strategy choices of firms, according to profit maximization goals. Finally, the game-theoretic approach models the optimum competitive reactions of firms with an equilibrium analysis (as explained in greater detail in Moorthy 1985; Rao, Chapter 6, this volume). In the following sections, we focus on the behavioral and structural approaches to competition and their main themes, using research from marketing, IO and strategic management.

3.1   Behavioral Approach to Competitive Reactions (Interfirm Rivalry)

The dominant approach in strategic management literature (e.g. Chen 1996), which also appears frequently in marketing literature (e.g. Gatignon et al. 1989), draws from organizational theory to predict the strategic behavior of firms that react to competitive actions, as well as the results of their interfirm rivalry. The underlying principle is the structure–conduct–performance (SCP) paradigm (Bain 1951), which holds that a firm, in the interest of sustaining its performance, reacts to its competitors' actions in the form of an action–response dyad (Chen et al. 1992) or a series of moves and countermoves (e.g. Porter 1980). Strategic reactions to competitive actions depend on antecedents specific to the competitor who employed the competitive attack, the firm that reacts, and the market conditions. Management scholars typically analyze competitive reactions using firm- or industry-level antecedents; marketing scholars typically study brand-level antecedents (Chen 1996).

A firm's competitive behavior is motivated by its goal of capturing market share from competitors (in the case of a firm undertaking a competitive attack) or defending or improving existing market share (in the case of a firm responding to a competitor's action). The perceived utility of strategically attacking competitors to capture market share has been demonstrated through strategies such as garnering the first-mover advantage by introducing a new product first, price cuts and discounts, aggressive promotions, increased advertising budgets and so on. Although such competitive attacks seem to work in the short run, evidence for their long-term utility is mixed. For example, Young et al. (1996) find that firm performance increases with more competitive attacks, but Pauwels et al. (2002) uncover virtually no long-term effects of aggressive price promotions introduced to capture market share. Evidence is similarly mixed about the efficacy of a swift competitive response, such that some studies show that early and aggressive responses to competitive attacks benefit the reacting firms (e.g. Chen and MacMillan 1992), whereas others indicate that competitive responses harm retaliating firms (e.g. Steenkamp et al. 2005). Yet competitive attacks and responses seem permanent phenomena that show no signs of declining.

In marketing literature, a behavioral approach to competitive reactions typically uses market share as the dependent variable, with marketing mix variables such as price, advertising and innovation as explanatory variables (e.g. Blattberg and Wisniewski 1989; Eckard Jr 1987; Lynch Jr and Ariely 2000). Descriptive studies attempt to determine the nature of competitive reactions and their antecedents (e.g. Gatignon et al. 1989), and normative studies use tactics such as decision calculus models to suggest the best course of action for firms in a given situation (e.g. Hauser and Shugan 1983). Most such studies use firm-level factors and model reactions in terms of those factors. Some marketing scholars also attempt to identify and demonstrate behavioral underpinnings for why firms (i.e. managers) react as they do to competitive actions or what the strategic competitive reasoning might be (e.g. Montgomery et al. 2005). Marketing managers' behavioral responses do not appear to include the heterogeneity of the situation, often because of the difficulty of obtaining necessary information and the uncertainty of predicting competitor outcomes.

Strategic management literature examines the antecedents of competitive reactions and their effectiveness at a higher level of abstraction than in marketing. The primary theoretical basis has been the resource-based view (Barney 1991), which scholars have used to derive constructs related to firms' resources as antecedents of competitive reactions. Other theoretical bases include firms' conceptualization of competitors (e.g. Porac and Thomas 1990), awareness of the interdependence among competitors (e.g. Amit et al. 1988), the relational nature of their competition (e.g. Barnett 1993), and recently the dynamic capabilities perspective (e.g. Teece et al. 1997).

Strategic management scholars also conceptualize constructs that help them predict competitive reactions. For example, Chen (1996, p. 107) defines resource similarity as "the extent to which a given competitor possesses strategic endowments comparable, in terms of both type and amount, to those of the focal firm." Typically, competitive actions and responses by firms with high levels of resource similarity will be similar and constrained, such that the firms have similar competitive vulnerabilities. In contrast, firms with low resource similarity should exhibit greater variety in the competitive strategies they use, because of their unique strategic resources. Resource similarity is a construct useful for predicting competitive reactions.

A construct used to predict patterns of competitive interaction that has gained popularity in recent years with management and marketing scholars is multimarket or multipoint competition. Karnani and Wernerfelt (1985) describe multimarket or multipoint competition as a situation in which firms compete simultaneously in several markets. The airline industry is the most common example: all airlines do not compete on all routes, and there is a difference in the degree to which they have markets in common. The degree of multimarket competition, also termed market commonality (e.g. Chen 1996), reveals competitive reactions in strategic management literature (e.g. Anand et al. 2009) and marketing literature (e.g. Kang et al. 2010). Studies across industries show that greater multimarket competition actually deters aggressive competitive actions, a phenomenon referred to as "mutual forbearance". Such forbearance is driven by the awareness that greater multimarket competition leaves the attacker open to counterattacks in multiple markets. Firms that compete in a majority of their markets tend not to attack each other but instead pursue competitors with whom they have a moderate degree of multimarket contact.

The dominant view of the behavioral approach to competitive reactions relies on the school from IO known as SCP. This SCP-based view assumes that engaging in aggressive competitive behavior or rivalry is counterproductive, and over the long term, firms engaged in multimarket competition should eschew aggressive competitive behavior. However, most industries also are becoming dynamic, seeing shorter business cycles, and confronting a new kind of competition known as "hypercompetition" (D'Aveni

1995). This concept of hypercompetition extends the idea of Schumpeterian competition, which is characterized by "creative destruction" (Schumpeter 1934). That is, businesses are in a state of flux, and the only way for firms to grow and keep growing is to destroy old technologies and products and develop new ones. A sustainable competitive advantage that might have been enough to help firms stave off competitive attacks in the past cannot really be sustained. Thus an aggressive competitive action does not necessarily suppress performance, as suggested by the SCP model, but rather spurs growth, and continuous aggressive hypercompetition helps firms. The hypercompetition view also implies that competition is not varying but rather something that firms should accept as a given, and then act accordingly. Demonstrations of hypercompetition mainly appear in "high-velocity" (Eisenhardt 1989) environments such as software and computer technology, among others. Scholars such as Ilinitch et al. (1996) and Wiggins and Ruefli (2005) demonstrate, though, that an increasing number of industries display high-velocity and dynamic characteristics, such that hypercompetition extends beyond high-tech industries.

Finally, the behavioral approach focuses mainly on a firm's behavior, treating the firm or a specific industry as the unit of analysis. However, the decisions a firm makes essentially are decisions by its managers, so some scholars have tried to study competitive reactions using managers as the unit of analysis (e.g. Montgomery et al. 2005). These studies investigate how competitive reactions might be determined by characteristics specific to individual managers. Competitive actions and responses undertaken by firms thus result from the way managers perceive the competition and what they believe is the best course of action. Theories to predict managerial behavior in competitive scenarios include regulatory focus theory (e.g. McMullen et al. 2009), competitive reasoning (e.g. Montgomery et al. 2005), the awareness–motivation–capability perspective (e.g. Chen et al. 2007), and the upper echelons perspective (e.g. Hambrick et al. 1996), among others. These studies indicate that heterogeneity among managers influences the kind of competitive moves firms make. For example, Hambrick et al. (1996) find that managerial teams that are diverse in terms of education, background and experience are more prone to make competitive attacks but slower to react to them than are homogeneous teams. Similar studies that link competitive reactions to managerial heterogeneity could shed further light on the nature of the process that drives competition.

3.2   Structural Approach to Competitive Reactions (NEIO Model)

The structural approach from IO has gained considerable ground in marketing as a means for studying competitive reactions. This approach relies on the new empirical industrial organization (NEIO) framework and uses structural economic models to consider the competitive strategy choices of firms, according to some kind of optimizing behavior, typically profit maximization (e.g. Chintagunta et al. 2006; Kadiyali et al. 2001).

In particular, NEIO scholars (for reviews see Ackerberg et al. 2007; Bresnahan 1989; Reiss and Wolak 2007) address several limitations of the SCP paradigm, such as its inability to capture heterogeneity in the structural characteristics across firms and industries, and thus marketing strategies, fully. Studies using the SCP paradigm also tend to pool data across industries and, even if the analysis is limited to one industry, fail to account for heterogeneity across firms. Some studies run separate regressions (e.g. Prescott et al. 1986) or allow for fixed effects in panel data (e.g. Boulding and Staelin 1993), but, as Kadiyali et al. (2001) point out, differences across and within industries, and their impact on performance, run deeper than the SCP variables. The SCP paradigm also suffers from the issue of endogeneity arising from simultaneity (Wind and Lilien 1993); although conduct influences performance, there also is ample evidence of performance influencing conduct too (e.g. sales affecting advertising). Thus the endogeneity inherent to the SCP paradigm creates a problem with regard to studying competitive reactions. Furthermore, the SCP paradigm considers cost data only in terms of accounting costs and resulting profits, which do not give a complete picture of costs compared with economic profits.

The structural approach, that is, the NEIO model, seeks to overcome these limitations of the SCP paradigm by estimating effects at the industry level and then, within industries, at the firm level. The NEIO model consists of three main specifications: (1) a demand specification that expresses the relationship of demand with strategic variables; (2) a cost specification that expresses economic costs (not just accounting costs) that the firm incurs by undertaking the available strategies; and (3) a specification for competitive reactions, which shows how competing firms react to one another. Using these three specifications, the model derives first-order conditions from different equilibria, according to the context. To estimate the model, researchers can use approaches that allow for simultaneous equation estimation to account for endogeneity, such as 3SLS, GMM (generalized method of moments), or the instrumental variable approach (e.g. Kadiyali et al. 2001; Shankar 1997). With such rich, robust and flexible models to specify the demand, cost and competitive interaction functions, as well as appropriate models to account for endogeneity, the NEIO approach provides relatively unbiased, more complete findings about competitive reactions than does the SCP paradigm.

Moreover, NEIO models provide other benefits compared with the SCP paradigm (see Chintagunta et al. 2006; Kadiyali et al. 2001). Researchers using NEIO models compare empirically alternative theoretical frameworks and select the most appropriate framework according to model fit (e.g. Knittel and Stango 2003; Porter 1983). The variables in NEIO models, such as demand, cost and strategy variables, link to existing theories on firm behavior and lend themselves to simple interpretation. Because the NEIO models account for industry and firm effects, the estimated parameters are independent of the changes in the levels of strategic variables and can be used for managers' "what-if" analyses (e.g. Dunne et al. 2009; Goolsbee and Petrin 2004). Finally, NEIO models allow for a fine-grained analysis of the antecedents of firm profitability, which makes it possible to determine the proportion of profit that came from each strategic action.

In recent years, NEIO models have appeared in marketing literature as a means to study competitive reactions and optimum competitive strategies in diverse contexts, focusing not only on marketing mix variables such as price, advertising and promotions (e.g. Shankar 1997; Sun 2005; Vilcassim et al. 1999) but other strategic variables as well. For example, Shankar and Bayus (2003) apply the NEIO framework to the video game industry and find that consumer network strength effects decrease with greater consumer network size, such that firms in small networks can overtake the sales of firms in large networks.

3.3   Agenda for Further Research on Competitive Interactions

Through this summary of the extensive work done on competitive reactions in marketing and allied fields such as strategic management and industrial organization (see Table 5.1), we identify promising avenues for further research that can contribute significantly to the field. We arrange these suggestions into two categories, conceptual and methodological.

Conceptually, as Chen (1996) has noted, the greatest promise for research likely involves building a solid theoretical basis for understanding what drives competitive actions and reactions, as well as why some competitive strategies work better than others. Although well-regarded theoretical frameworks such as the SCP paradigm and the resource-based view provide insights into the processes that drive competitive behavior, we argue that a complete, if not comprehensive, theory of competitive behavior has not yet been formulated. The need for a comprehensive theory can be gauged from the diversity of empirical findings related to the desirability and efficacy of competitive strategies across contexts and industries. The path to stronger theoretical frameworks should be paved by incremental contributions that describe phenomena related to competitive behaviors at increasing levels of abstraction compared with empirical findings. For example, multimarket competition research has helped explain competitive phenomena in terms of market commonality. Such theoretical contributions will add to our understanding of competitive behavior and competition in general.

Methodologically, the advances in the structural approach using NEIO models have been promising and should be extended by incorporating newer variables and interaction effects. Specifically, robust functional forms for the cost and competitive interaction specifications in NEIO models might increase insights into how competitors react and interact. The importance of better functional forms for the specifications involved extends beyond NEIO modeling and into game-theoretic and empirical modeling as well (for a review and assessment, see Leeflang 2008). Our understanding of competitive reactions and behavior also might benefit from the use of longitudinal data with dynamic models, which allow for convincing analyses of causality and can address the issue of endogeneity.

The ubiquity of the Internet has fundamentally changed the way business is done. Not surprisingly, the Internet has changed the nature of competition, in terms of both market structure and competitive reactions (Varadarajan et al. 2008). In particular, the phenomenon of asymmetric competition, as we described in Section 2, denotes a difference in the degree to which two firms view each other as competitors, arising from factors such as firm size and market reach. However, the Internet, by fundamentally changing market reach, has reduced asymmetric competition in several industries. Barnes & Noble, a firm more than a century old and still the largest book retailer in the USA, would not have considered smaller players as direct competitors prior to the 1990s, and certainly did not worry about Amazon.com, an online company that started in 1994 out of a tiny office with minimal funding. Yet the expansion of the Internet reduced market reach and access barriers, such that consumers could buy books from Amazon.com more easily than by driving over to a Barnes & Noble store. Asymmetry declined because of the Internet, and Amazon.com is now Barnes & Noble's biggest competitor. The market structure of the book industry changed fundamentally and in

Table 5.1 A summary of research on competition and key insights

Core concepts in competition research	Perspectives on competition concepts	Discipline	Research examples	Key insights
Market structure and competition	1. Demand-based perspective of competition	Marketing	Day et al. (1979)	Market structure resides in the minds of consumers
	• Knowledge structure approach		Sinha and DeSarbo (1998)	Consumers' knowledge about competing brand yields market structure
	• Consideration set approach		Urban at al. (1984)	Information on brands considered by consumers during initial stages of purchasing process yields market structure
	• Purchase decision approach		Hansen and Singh (2009)	Consumers' final decisions on which brands to buy yield market structure
	2. Supply-based perspective of competition	IO economics, strategic management	Mason (1939) Barney (1986)	Market structure resides in the minds of firms' managers
	• Asymmetric competition		DeSarbo et al. (2006)	Market structure should reflect asymmetry in the way firms view each other as competitors
	• Strategic groups		Ketchen at al. (1997)	Firms with similarities in product portfolio or cost structure compete more intensely than firms with dissimilarities
	3. Environment-based perspective of competition	Political economy, organizational sociology	Bresnahan and Reiss (1991) White (1981)	Competitive structure reflects environmental factors Competitive structure reflects social structure

Table 5.1 (continued)

Core concepts in competition research	Perspectives on competition concepts	Discipline	Research examples	Key insights
	• Government regulations		Gaynor and Vogt (2000)	Competitive structure is shaped by antitrust legislation and policies
	• Legal and technological environment		Hainz (2003) Bekkers et al. (2002)	Competitive structure reflects the impact of legal and technological environment on firms
Competitive interactions	1. Behavioral approach (interfirm rivalry)	Strategic management, marketing	Chen (1996) Gatignon et al. (1989)	Firms react to competition in an action–response manner to sustain their performance
	• Market share battle		Chen and MacMillan (1992) Steenkamp et al. (2005)	Firms react to competitive attacks to defend their market shares. Evidence on efficacy of retaliation is mixed.
	• Multimarket competition		Karnani and Wernerfelt (1985)	Competitive reactions and their efficacy depend on how many markets firms compete in. High market commonality results in mutual forbearance.
	• Hyper competition		D'Aveni (1995)	In rapidly evolving industries, reacting to competitive attacks and initiating attacks on competitors is necessary
	2. Structural approach (NEIO model)	Microeconomics, marketing	Ackerberg et al. (2007) Chintagunta et al. (2006)	Competitive interaction decisions are driven by optimizing behavior of firms, and can be modeled analytically using structural economic factors

72

a relatively short period of time. This market structure in an Internet-enabled environment deserves further research.

Although market reach is the strongest driver of changing market structures, it is by no means the only one resulting from the Internet. The explosion of user-generated content (e.g. blogs, YouTube, twitter) has created a new arena for firm competition, in which user involvement reaches unprecedented levels. Reviews of products and services in blogs or consumer forums hold nearly as much weight as, if not more than, reviews posted in newspapers and magazines. These reviews force firms that never competed with others to do so, undermining the market leader and first-mover advantages. For example, Microsoft's and Yahoo's search engines existed well before Google's, but Google, mainly through word of mouth on online forums, quickly became the market leader. Greater research on late-mover and first-mover advantages in the Internet-enabled environment is desired (e.g. Lieberman and Montgomery, Chapter 20 in this volume; Shankar and Carpenter, Chapter 21 in this volume; Varadarajan et al. 2008).

The Internet also has introduced new challenges and avenues for competitive actions and reactions. The reduced costs for distribution and marketing communication give firms new ways to attack their competitors, and competitors have newer ways to respond. For example, firms recognize the importance of appearing on the first page of relevant results on search engines, which has led to the burgeoning field of search engine optimization (in 2008, worth US$15 billion) for firms that must improve their search engine visibility relative to their competitors. Firms also encourage user-generated content to involve loyal consumers in attacks on the competition, as evidenced by the pitched battles in the blogosphere between users of Apple's Macintosh computers and PCs running Microsoft's Windows. Such phenomena are clearly worthy of greater and ongoing scrutiny.

REFERENCES

Ackerberg, D., C. Lanier Benkard, S. Berry and A. Pakes (2007), "Econometric tools for analyzing market outcomes," *Handbook of Econometrics*, **6**, 4171–276.

Alba, J.W. and A. Chattopadhyay (1985), "Effects of context and part-category cues on recall of competing brands," *Journal of Marketing Research*, **22** (3), 340–49.

Amit, Raphael and Paul J. Schoemaker (1993), "Strategic assets and organizational rents," *Strategic Management Journal*, **14** (January), 33–46.

Amit, R., I. Domowitz and C. Fershtman (1988), "Thinking one step ahead: the use of conjectures in competitor analysis," *Strategic Management Journal*, **9** (5), 431–42.

Anand, J., L.F. Mesquita and R.S. Vassolo (2009), "The dynamics of multimarket competition in exploration and exploitation activities," *Academy of Management Journal*, **52** (4), 802–21.

Bain, J.S. (1951), "Relation of profit rate to industry concentration: American manufacturing, 1936–1940," *Quarterly Journal of Economics*, **65** (3), 293–324.

Barnett, W.P. (1993), "Strategic deterrence among multipoint competitors," *Industrial and Corporate Change*, **2** (1), 249–78.

Barney, Jay B. (1986), "Types of competition and the theory of strategy: towards an integrative framework," *Academy of Management Review*, **11** (4), 791–800.

Barney, Jay B. (1991), "Firm resources and sustained competitive advantage," *Journal of Management*, **17** (1), 99–120.

Bekkers, R., G. Duysters and B. Verspagen (2002), "Intellectual property rights, strategic technology agreements and market structure: the case of GSM," *Research Policy*, **31** (7), 1141–61.

Blattberg, Robert C. and Kenneth J. Wisniewski (1989), "Price-induced patterns of competition," *Marketing Science*, **8** (Fall), 291–309.

Boulding, William and Richard Staelin (1993), "A look on the cost side: market share and the competitive environment," *Marketing Science*, **12** (2), 144–66.

Bowman, Douglas and Hubert Gatignon (1995), "Determinants of competitor response time to a new product introduction," *Journal of Marketing Research*, **32** (February), 42–53.

Bresnahan, T.F. (1989), "Empirical studies of industries with market power," in Richard Schmalensee and Robert Willing (eds), *Handbook of Industrial Organization*, Amsterdam: North-Holland, vol. 2, pp. 1011–57.

Bresnahan, T.F. and P.C. Reiss (1991), "Entry and competition in concentrated markets," *Journal of Political Economy*, **99** (5), 977–1009.

Burt, Ronald S. (1995), *Structural Holes: The Social Structure of Competition*, Cambridge, MA: Harvard University Press.

Carpenter, Gregory S. and Donald R. Lehmann (1985), "A model of marketing mix, brand switching, and competition," *Journal of Marketing Research*, **22** (August), 318–29.

Carpenter, Gregory S., Lee G. Cooper, Dominique M. Hanssens and David F. Midgley (1988), "Modeling asymmetric competition," *Marketing Science*, **7** (Fall), 393–412.

Chen, Ming-Jer (1996), "Competitor analysis and interfirm rivalry: towards a theoretical integration," *Academy of Management Review*, **21** (1), 100–34.

Chen, M.J. and I.C. MacMillan (1992), "Nonresponse and delayed response to competitive moves: the roles of competitor dependence and action irreversibility," *Academy of Management Journal*, **35** (3), 539–70.

Chen, M.J., K.G. Smith and C.M. Grimm (1992), "Action characteristics as predictors of competitive responses," *Management Science*, **38**, 439–55.

Chen, M., K. Su and W. Tsai (2007), "Competitive tension: the awareness–motivation–capability perspective," *Academy of Management Journal*, **50** (1), 101–18.

Chintagunta, Pradeep, Tülin Erdem, Peter E. Rossi and Michel Wedel (2006), "Structural modeling in marketing: review and assessment," *Marketing Science*, **25** (6), 604–16.

Cool, Karel O. and Dan Schendel (1987), "Strategic group formation and performance: the case of the U.S. pharmaceutical industry, 1963–1982," *Management Science*, **33** (9), 1102–24.

Cooper, Lee G. and Akihiro Inoue (1996), "Building market structures from consumer preferences," *Journal of Marketing Research*, **33** (3), 293–306.

D'Aveni, Richard A. (1995), *Hypercompetitive Rivalries*, New York: Free Press.

Day, G.S. and D.J. Reibstein (1997), *Dynamic Competitive Strategy*, New York: John Wiley & Sons.

Day, George S., Allan D. Shocker and Rajendra K. Srivastava (1979), "Customer-oriented approaches to identifying product markets," *Journal of Marketing*, **43** (4), 8–19.

Demsetz, H. (1973), "Industry structure, market rivalry, and public policy," *Journal of Law and Economics*, **16** (April), 1–9.

DeSarbo, Wayne S. and Rajdeep Grewal (2008), "Hybrid strategic groups," *Strategic Management Journal*, **29** (3), 293–317.

DeSarbo, Wayne S. and Kamel Jedidi (1995), "The spatial representation of heterogeneous consideration sets," *Marketing Science*, **14**, 326–42.

DeSarbo, Wayne S. and Ajay K. Manrai (1992), "A multidimensional scaling methodology for the analysis of asymmetric proximity data in marketing research," *Marketing Science*, **11** (1), 1–20.

DeSarbo, Wayne S., Rajdeep Grewal and Rui Wang (2009), "Dynamic strategic groups: spatial evolutionary paths," *Strategic Management Journal*, **30**, 1420–39.

DeSarbo, Wayne S., Rajdeep Grewal and Jerry Wind (2006), "Who competes with whom? A demand-based perspective for identifying and representing asymmetric competition," *Strategic Management Journal*, **27** (2), 101–29.

Dranove, David, Margaret A. Peteraf and Mark Shanley (1998), "Do strategic groups exist? An economic framework for analysis," *Strategic Management Journal*, **19** (11), 1029–44.

Dunne, T., S.D. Klimek, M.J. Roberts and D. Xu (2009), "Entry, exit, and the determinants of market structure," NBER Working Paper.

Ebbes, Peter, Rajdeep Grewal and Wayne S. DeSarbo (2010), "Modeling strategic group dynamics: a hidden Markov approach," *Quantitative Marketing and Economics*, **8** (2), 241–74.

Eckard Jr, E.W. (1987), "Advertising, competition, and market share instability," *Journal of Business*, **60** (4), 539–52.

Eisenhardt, K.M. (1989), "Making fast strategic decisions in high-velocity environments," *Academy of Management Journal*, **32** (3), 543–76.

Fiegenbaum, Avi, Howard Thomas and Ming-Je Tang (2001), "Linking hypercompetition and strategic group theories: strategic maneuvering in the US insurance industry," *Managerial and Decision Economics*, **22** (4, 5), 265–79.

Gatignon, Hubert, Erin Anderson and Kristiaan Helsen (1989), "Competitive reactions to market entry: explaining interfirm differences," *Journal of Marketing Research*, **26** (February), 44–55.

Gaynor, M. and W.B. Vogt (2000), "Antitrust and competition in health care markets," *Handbook of Health Economics*, **1**, 1405–87.

Goolsbee, A. and A. Petrin (2004), "The consumer gains from direct broadcast satellites and the competition with cable TV," *Econometrica*, **72** (2), 351–81.

Granovetter, Mark (1985), "Economic action and social structure: the problem of embeddedness," *American Sociological Review*, **15** (3), 478–99.

Grewal, Rajdeep, Thomas W. Cline and Anthony Davies (2003), "Early entrant advantage, word-of-mouth communication, brand similarity, and the consumer decision-making process," *Journal of Consumer Psychology*, **13** (3), 187–97.

Hainz, C. (2003), "Bank competition and credit markets in transition economies," *Journal of Comparative Economics*, **31** (2), 223–45.

Hambrick, D.C., T.S. Cho and M.J. Chen (1996), "The influence of top management team heterogeneity on firms' competitive moves," *Administrative Science Quarterly*, **41** (4), 659–84.

Hansen, K. and V. Singh (2009), "Market structure across retail formats," *Marketing Science*, **28** (4), 656–73.

Hauser, John R. and Steven M. Shugan (1983), "Defensive marketing strategies," *Marketing Science*, **3**, 327–51.

Hunt, M.S. (1972), "Competition in the major home appliances industry, 1960–70," Doctoral Dissertation, Harvard University.

Ilinitch, A.Y., R.A. D'Aveni and A.Y. Lewin (1996), "New organizaational forms and strategies for managing in hypercompetitive environments," *Organization Science*, **7** (3), 211–20.

Kadiyali, Vrinda, K. Sudhir and Vithala R. Rao (2001), "Structural analysis of competitive behavior: new empirical industrial organization methods in marketing," *International Journal of Research in Marketing*, **18** (1–2), 161–86.

Kang, W., B.L. Bayus and S. Balasubramanian (2010), "The strategic effects of multimarket contact: mutual forbearance and competitive response in the personal computer industry," *Journal of Marketing Research*, **47** (3), 415–27.

Karnani, A. and B. Wernerfelt (1985), "Multiple point competition," *Strategic Management Journal*, **6** (1), 87–96.

Ketchen, David J., James B. Thomas and Charles C. Snow (1993), "Organizational configurations and performance: a comparison," *Academy of Management Journal*, **36** (6), 1278–313.

Ketchen, David J., James G. Combs, Craig J. Russell, Chris Shook, Michelle A. Dean, Janet Runge, Franz T. Lohrke, Stefanie E. Naumann, Dawn Ebe Haptonsthal, Robert Baker, Brenden A. Berkstein, Charles Handler, Heather Honig and Stephen Lamoureux (1997), "Organizational configurations and performance: a meta-analysis," *Academy of Management Journal*, **40** (1), 223–40.

Knittel, C.R. and V. Stango (2003), "Price ceilings as focal points for tacit collusion: evidence from credit cards," *American Economic Review*, **93** (5), 1703–29.

Leeflang, P.S.H. (2008), "Modeling competitive responsiveness," in Berend Wierenga (ed.), *Handbook of Marketing Decision Models*, New York: Springer, pp. 211–51.

Leeflang, P.S.H. and D.R. Wittink (1996), "Competitive reaction versus consumer response: do managers overreact?," *International Journal of Research in Marketing*, **13** (2), 103–19.

Lynch Jr, J.G. and D. Ariely (2000), "Wine online: search costs affect competition on price, quality, and distribution," *Marketing Science*, **19**, 83–103.

Mascarenhas, Briance (1989), "Strategic group dynamics," *Academy of Management Journal*, **32** (2), 333–52.

Mason, E.S. (1939), "Price and production policies of large-scale enterprise," *American Economic Review*, **29** (1), 61–74.

McGee, John and Howard Thomas (1986), "Strategic groups: theory, research and taxonomy," *Strategic Management Journal*, **7** (2), 141–60.

McMullen, J.S., D.A. Shepherd and H. Patzelt (2009), "Managerial (in)attention to competitive threats," *Journal of Management Studies*, **46** (2), 157–81.

McNamara, Gerry, David L. Deephouse and Rebecca A. Luce (2003), "Competitive positioning within and across a strategic group structure: the performance of core, secondary, and solitary firms," *Strategic Management Journal*, **24** (2), 161–81.

Montgomery, David B., Marian Chapman Moore and Joel E. Urbany (2005), "Reasoning about competitive reactions: evidence from executives," *Marketing Science*, **24** (1), 138–49.

Moorthy, Sridhar (1985), "Using game theory to model competition," *Journal of Marketing Research*, **22** (3), 262–82.

Neven, D.J. and L.H. Röller (2005), "Consumer surplus vs. welfare standard in a political economy model of merger control," *International Journal of Industrial Organization*, **23** (9–10), 829–48.

Pauwels, K., D.M. Hanssens and S. Siddarth (2002), "The long-term effects of price promotions on category incidence, brand choice, and purchase quantity," *Journal of Marketing Research*, **39** (4), 421–39.

Perry, M. K. (1984), "Scale economies, imperfect competition, and public policy," *Journal of Industrial Economics*, **32** (3), 313–33.

Podolny, Joel M. (1993), "A status-based model of market competition," *American Journal of Sociology*, **98**, 829–72.

Porac, Joseph F. and Howard Thomas (1990), "Taxonomic mental models of competitor definition," *Academy of Management Review*, **15** (2), 224–40.

Porter, Michael E. (1980), *Competitive Strategy: Techniques for Analyzing Industries and Competitors*, New York: Harper & Row.

Porter, R.H. (1983), "A study of cartel stability: the joint executive committee, 1880–1886," *Bell Journal of Economics*, **14** (2), 301–14.

Posner, R.A. (1975), "The social costs of monopoly and regulation," *Journal of Political Economy*, **83** (4), 807–27.

Prescott, J.E., A.K. Kohli and N. Venkatraman (1986), "The market share–profitability relationship: an empirical assessment of major assertions and contradictions," *Strategic Management Journal*, **7** (4), 377–94.

Reibstein, David J. and Dick R. Wittink (2005), "Competitive responsiveness," *Marketing Science*, **24** (1), 8–11.

Reiss, P.C. and F.A. Wolak (2007), "Structural econometric modeling: rationales and examples from industrial organization," in James Heckman and Edward Leaner (eds), *Handbook of Econometrics*, Amsterdam: North-Holland, pp. 4277–415.

Scherer, Frederic M. and David R. Ross (1990), *Industrial Market Structure and Market Performance*, Boston, MA: Houghton-Mifflin.

Schumpeter, Joseph A. (1934), *The Theory of Economic Development*, Cambridge, MA: Harvard University Press.

Shankar, V. (1997), "Pioneers' marketing mix reactions to entry in different competitive game structures: theoretical analysis and empirical illustration," *Marketing Science*, **16** (3), 271–93.

Shankar, V. (2010a), "Competitive analysis," *Wiley's Encyclopedia in Marketing*, Hoboken, NJ: John Wiley & Sons, pp. 24–31.

Shankar, V. (2010b), "Competitor analysis," *Wiley's Encyclopedia in Marketing*, Hoboken, NJ: John Wiley & Sons, pp. 31–2.

Shankar, V. and B.L. Bayus (2003), "Network effects and competition: an empirical analysis of the home video game industry," *Strategic Management Journal*, **24** (4), 375–84.

Shankar, Venkatesh, Gregory Carpenter and Lakshman Krishnamurthi (1998), "Late mover advantage: how innovative late entrants outsell pioneers," *Journal of Marketing Research*, **35** (1), 54–70.

Shankar, Venkatesh, Gregory Carpenter and Lakshman Krishnamurthi (1999), "The advantages of entering in the growth stage of the product life cycle: an empirical analysis," *Journal of Marketing Research*, **36** (2), 269–76.

Shocker, Allan D., Moshe Ben-Akiva, Bruno Boccara and Prakash Nedungadi (1991), "Consideration set influences on consumer decision making and choice: issues, models, and suggestions," *Marketing Letters*, **2** (August), 181–98.

Sinha, Indrajit and Wayne DeSarbo (1998), "An integrated approach toward the spatial modeling of perceived customer value", *Journal of Marketing Research*, **35** (2), 236–49.

Steenkamp, J.-B., V.R. Nijs, D.M. Hanssens and M.G. Dekimpe (2005), "Competitive reactions to advertising and promotion attacks," *Marketing Science*, **24** (1), 35–54.

Stigler, G.J. (1964), "A theory of oligopoly," *Journal of Political Economy*, **72** (1), 44–61.

Sun, B. (2005), "Promotion effect on endogenous consumption," *Marketing Science*, **24** (3), 430–43.

Teece, David, Gary Pisano and Amy Schuen (1997), "Dynamic capabilities and strategic management," *Strategic Management Journal*, **18** (7), 509–33.

Urban, Glen L., Philip L. Johnson and John R. Hauser (1984), "Testing competitive market structures", *Marketing Science*, **3** (2), 83–112.

Uzzi, Brian (1996), "The sources and consequences of embeddedness for the economic performance of organizations: the network effect," *American Sociological Review*, **61** (August), 674–98.

Varadarajan, Rajan, Manjit Yadav and Venkatesh Shankar (2008), "First-mover advantage in the Internet-enabled environment: a conceptual framework and propositions," *Journal of Academy of Marketing Science*, **36** (3), 293–308.

Vilcassim, N.J., V. Kadiyali and P.K. Chintagunta (1999), "Investigating dynamic multifirm market interactions in price and advertising," *Management Science*, **45** (4), 499–518.

Weitz, Barton A. (1985), "Introduction to special issue on competition in marketing," *Journal of Marketing Research*, **22** (August), 229–36.

White, Harrison C. (1981), "Where do markets come from?," *American Journal of Sociology*, **87**, 517–47.

Wiggins, R.R. and T.W. Ruefli (2005), "Schumpeter's ghost: is hypercompetition making the best of times shorter?," *Strategic Management Journal*, **26** (10), 887–911.

Wind, Y. and G.L. Lilien (1993), "Marketing strategy models," in Jehashua Eliashberg and Gary L. Lilien (eds), *Handbook in Operations Research and Management Science*, Amsterdam: North-Holland, pp. 773–826.

Young, G., K.G. Smith and C.M. Grimm (1996), "'Austrian' and industrial organization perspectives on firm-level competitive activity and performance," *Organization Science*, **7** (3), 243–54.

Zajac, Edward J. and Max H. Bazerman (1991), "Blind spots in industry and competitor analysis: implications for interfirm (mis)perception of strategic decisions," *Academy of Management Review*, **16** (1), 37–46.

6 Models of retail competition
Ram C. Rao

1. INTRODUCTION

Peterson and Balasubramanian (2002), in defining retailing, say that "the present [their] article will not propose a new definition of retailing . . ." So what is retailing? Retailing is an intermediating function that helps manufacturers deliver goods to end consumers. How do retailers deliver goods efficiently? Think of a consumer desiring a single product. The product manufacturer can make it convenient for consumers to shop at a close location. Lower cost of shopping can support a higher price and greater demand. So, in modeling retail competition, relative convenience of competing retailers is important. Convenience is commonly modeled by exogenously locating retailers at distinct points on a straight line of finite length, often at either end. Consumers located along the line incur a cost to visit either retailer, so a consumer may find one retailer more convenient. This model, labeled the Hotelling model, follows Hotelling (1929) and is used to model not only physical location but often also location of consumers and brands in the space of benefits.

Consumers buy many products, so shopping economies accrue at a one-stop retailer. Thus competitive strategies of retailers span multiple products that are not necessarily substitutes in consumption (competing brands of toothpaste) or complements in consumption (chip and dip, shirt and tie). Retailers carry products like detergent and bread or children's clothes and men's shirts that are complements in purchase (Betancourt and Gautschi 1990). The multi-product nature of retailing translates into two tasks for retail success: create traffic, using part of the assortment, and effect high level of sales to arriving consumers using another part of the assortment. Retail competition on multiple products can be modeled by incorporating two products, or baskets, that are complements in purchase.

Consumer choice usually needs information on competing products, information that a retailer often provides tailored to the consumer. The retailer may also "customize" the product, and so competition on providing service reflects an important aspect of retailing (Betancourt and Gautschi 1988). Modeling service is tricky: service incurs a variable cost, increasing with level of service and possibly also fixed costs. Consumers are assumed to derive positive utility from service, substituting it for costly consumer effort.

Finally, consumers are heterogeneous in what they buy, their shopping cost, size and composition of shopping basket, need for service and other dimensions. To meet their needs, retailers can differentiate on multiple dimensions: location, assortment, service, product delivery – all captured by the retail format, which becomes an important element of competition. The essential feature of a format such as its key positioning message or location, say on the Internet, can be exogenously specified to model format.

Price competition is central to retailing. Prices are modeled as being chosen conditioned on location, product assortment and service. Thus prices are chosen in the second (or last) stage of a multi-stage game with other strategic choices made earlier. Consumers can learn of prices by engaging in costly search or from retailers' advertisements that are assumed to be credible and contractual in nature. Retailer advertising may be limited to a subset of assortment, it being costly to advertise all of numerous products.[1]

This chapter elaborates on models of competition between two or more retailers who compete on price and one or more of convenience, multiple products, service and format.[2] I have set aside models that focus on retailer pricing strategies and study the strategic relationship retailers have with manufacturers, either of a single retailer or of competing retailers. These models study double marginalization and, more broadly, channel coordination. An early and important work in this area is McGuire and Staelin (1983), which has led to numerous investigations subsequently. See Moorthy (2005) for a comprehensive treatment of channel margins.

I have organized this chapter by the basis of competition: price, format, promotions, assortment, trade support, loyalty programs, Internet retailing and entry. There is a section on directions for future work followed by references.

2. PRICE COMPETITION

2.1 Store Traffic and Shopper Retention

The inconvenience of visiting a store can be modeled as a cost, variously termed transportation cost, shopping cost or search cost. If consumers incur a search cost to learn price at a store, a celebrated result known as the "Diamond paradox" (named after Diamond, 1971, who came up with it) arises. The idea behind this paradox has important practical implications for retail competition. Assume that two stores sell a homogeneous good to consumers, all of whom seek one unit of it. Let $s > 0$ denote the consumer's cost of going from one store to another (labeled search cost). Assume also that going to at least one store – the first store – is costless. Consumers don't know a store's price until they visit it. Imagine a shopper arriving randomly at one store. If p, the store's price, is higher than r, his willingness to pay, then he might go to the other store, or forgo buying the product. Suppose $p \leq r$ and he expects the other store's price to be $p_c \leq r$. Then he could buy the product or decide to visit the other store.[3] The first store can retain the shopper even if its price is higher than the competitors', up to $p_c + s$. Its optimal pricing rule, p^*, is therefore given by: the price should neither exceed the consumer's willingness to pay nor make it attractive for him to go to the competing store. Mathematically,[4]

$$p^* = \min\{r, p_c + s\}$$

Since half the customers would land up in it, the competing store's optimal pricing rule, p^*_c, is

$$p^*_c = \min\{r, p + s\}$$

The two pricing rules imply that each retailer would like to price higher than its competitor's price by search cost s, ensuring that it does not exceed r. Clearly, each retailer would end up charging r, exactly the price that a monopolist retailer would have charged. Even under competition, the mere existence of consumer search cost ratchets retail prices up to the monopolist price, a paradoxical result (the Diamond paradox).[5]

It is important to note that the Diamond paradox arises in the first place because retailers in the model are not allowed to advertise. What would advertising do in this model if it leads to transportation cost to go from one store to another replacing the search cost for price? Upon reflection, we obtain an important insight central to retailing. The transportation cost gives the Diamond paradox force *after* a shopper has arrived at a store. Thus advertising's critical role is to attract shoppers to the store. More generally, competition to generate store traffic is critical in retailing. Competition to retain shoppers is attenuated by transportation costs. The next model, a model of loss leaders, illustrates this dramatically.

2.2   Price Advertisements and Loss Leaders to Build Store Traffic

Can competition to generate store traffic lead to loss leaders, defined as products priced below cost resulting in negative retail margins? Lal and Matutes (1994) offer a model with two competing multi-product retailers, 1 and 2, each offering the same two products, A and B, that are complements in purchase. Stores are located at the ends of a Hotelling line with consumers uniformly distributed on it. Consumers are willing to pay R for each product, and incur transportation cost of c per unit distance.[6] Stores can advertise the price of one of the products. Consumers have rational expectations of unadvertised prices.

This model has two equilbiria in pure strategies. In one, both stores advertise the price of good A, and in the other of good B. Prices are set to be: unadvertised good is set at the maximum (monopoly) price of R, advertised at $c - R$ and so price of the basket of the two goods is c, yielding each store a profit of $0.5c$.[7] If $R > c$, the advertised good, designed to build store traffic, is a "loss leader." Essentially, competition for store traffic results in loss leaders. Think of the advertised good as the one on promotion at the store. The unadvertised good, on the other hand, exhibits the Diamond paradox since consumers incur a cost to visit an additional store. It is priced high, and following the assumption of rational expectations, consumers are aware of this. Note that it does not pay stores to advertise different products as that would result in some consumers, located in the middle of the line, buying the low-priced product at each store, transferring some surplus from the stores to consumers.

2.3   Unadvertised Specials and Competing Intelligently for Store Traffic

Unadvertised promotions can't affect store traffic, and yet supermarkets have them, as Rao and Syam (2001) note. Could they then help retain shoppers arriving at a store? Rao and Syam examine equilibrium in mixed strategies applied to the Lal–Matutes model, leading to two cases: first, stores advertise price of one good in stage 1, and choose price of other good in stage 2; second, stores choose both the good to be advertised and the price of the unadvertised good in a single stage.

Equilibrium in the two-stage case has both stores advertising each good with probability 0.5, setting price of the advertised good at $c - 0.5R > 0$. Think of this as stores mixing "promotions across products." When stores advertise the same good in stage 1, the price of unadvertised good is R, as in Lal–Matutes, a consequence of the Diamond paradox. If, on the other hand, stores advertise different goods in stage 1, each has a promotion in stage 2 on the unadvertised good priced at $1.5c - R$.[8] This unadvertised promotion on the good that is advertised by the competitor helps retain all shoppers visiting the store. The expected basket price is $0.25\,(7c - R)$, and each store's profit is $0.25\,(3.5c - 0.5R)$, which is greater than store profits under the pure strategy equilibrium in Lal–Matutes, $0.5c$. Why does this happen?

Randomizing promotions across products by a mixed strategy means stores don't know which good the competitor is advertising; so head-to-head competition for store traffic using the same good occurs only half the time. However, because half the time stores advertise different goods, they offer a promotion on unadvertised good to retain shoppers. Consumers end up buying both goods priced below R. Still, the reduced intensity of competition for store traffic leads to higher profits. The key insight of this is that to obtain higher profits stores must find ways to build traffic without engaging in head-to-head competition. Rao and Syam further show that if only one good is advertised, profits increase monotonically with number of goods stores carry because the probability of head-on competition for traffic declines.

In the one-stage equilibrium, for certain values of the parameters, profits remain higher with mixed strategy advertising combined with unadvertised promotions than in the pure strategy equilibrium. In equilibrium some consumers, in the middle of the Hotelling line, split their shopping basket by buying the lower-priced good at each store whenever stores advertise different goods.[9]

2.4   Price Matching to Attenuate Competition for Store Traffic

A promise by one store to match its competitors' prices may eliminate the incentive for competitors to cut price to attract traffic (Edlin 1997). So price matching could be a way for competitors to collude implicitly by making the reaction functions positive sloped. Hess and Gerstner (1991) find that supermarket prices indeed went up in one market after a store instituted price matching.

In practice, competitors have several ways of lowering aggressive price competition for store traffic. So, why price matching? Png and Hirshleifer (1987) model a market with two types, or segments, of customers. Type 1 has a very high search cost while type 2 has zero search cost. Consumers arrive at first store without incurring cost. Demand by type 1 consumer is assumed to be inelastic while by type 2 it is elastic.[10] Suppose there is just one store. Denote r to be price that maximizes store profits were it to serve only type 1 consumers. Serving both types of consumers with no way to discriminate on price requires optimal price to be $p_m < r$. Now, if a competitor enters the market, the first store can serve both types and discriminate on price by offering to match the competitor's price if it is lower. In equilibrium the first store chooses price r, the second store p_m and consumer behavior is as follows: half of type 1 arrive at each store and buy from that store; half of type 2 arrive at first store and decide (at zero cost) to check out the other store and end up buying there at price p_m; the other half arrive at the second store and decide to check out the other store and end up buying there at price p_m by invoking the price matching policy. In contrast to the monopoly case, now half of type 1 consumers end up paying *r* instead of the lower p_m because store 1 engages in price discrimination. In this model, price matching raises the price at one store, and combined profits of the stores also is higher.[11] The key point is that price matching helps to retain some price-sensitive customers visiting the high-priced store. It has no impact on traffic generation.

Png and Hirshleifer's model does not have consumers with a small non-zero search cost a realistic possibility. Price matching policies then may actually result in greater search than in their absence, thus increasing competition for store traffic. Chen et al. (2001) analyze a model of rich consumer heterogeneity and show that price matching policies can, indeed, lead to lower prices in their model. If price-sensitive consumers have positive search cost, a store could offer to match competitor with lowest price without consumers incurring search cost to attract traffic. This is the essential argument in the "Automatic Price Protection" policy pursued by the specialty electronics retailer Tweeter Inc. (Gourville and Wu 1996). Moorthy and Zhang (2006) offer another communication implication of price matching policies by considering stores offering different service levels. A high-service store needing to credibly communicate this differentiation could signal its service level by eschewing price matching while the low-service store benefits from the offer to match price. Thus price matching may help in gaining traffic from the right type of consumer.

3.   COMPETITION BETWEEN STORE/RETAIL FORMATS

3.1   EDLP and Store Positioning

Positioning allows firms to differentiate themselves and pursue segmentation. Retailers, particularly supermarkets, know that convenience determines store choice and so they prefer not to completely forgo traffic from any consumer segment. Store positioning then determines the product mix that each segment buys at the store, and the relative proportion of each segment served, which is the clientele mix. Lal and Rao (1997) show how the EDLP strategy accomplishes this for supermarkets.

The Lal–Rao model of supermarket competition assumes two stores located at either end of a Hotelling line serving two consumer segments. One segment, labeled time constrained, has consumers with high search costs and the other, labeled cherry pickers, with low search costs. Each store carries the same two goods that are complements in purchase. All consumers are willing to pay *R* for each good. Competition is modeled as a multi-stage game as shown in Figure 6.1. The stage 1 decision is whether each wants to be EDLP or PROMO store, which determines the message each can employ: EDLP can communicate value by offering a "savings" relative to PROMO store on the two-good basket; PROMO, on the other hand, can communicate the price of one of the two goods. Thus neither store can reveal prices of both goods to consumers. In stage 2, firms set prices and communicate them: EDLP communicates the basket savings δ and PROMO the price *p* of one good. In stage 3, consumers in both segments form rational expectations of prices at EDLP and price of the unadvertised good at PROMO, allowing them to make utility-maximizing shopping choices.

The sub-game-perfect Nash equilibrium to this game is as follows: one store chooses

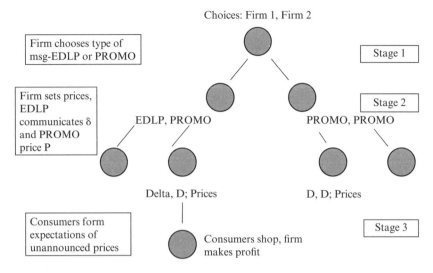

Figure 6.1   Lal–Rao model of retail competition

to be EDLP and the other PROMO; PROMO follows a mixed strategy of communicating with probability 0.5 price of each good set at $p < R = R - D$ with D interpreted as a discount, and sets the unadvertised good price at R; EDLP chooses δ, $0 < \delta < D$, and each good is priced equally at $R - 0.5(D + \delta) > R - D$. In equilibrium, time-constrained consumers shop in greater proportion at EDLP than PROMO, while cherry pickers split their basket, buying the "discounted" good at PROMO and the other good at EDLP.[12] The EDLP store has higher profits.

The key insight of Lal and Rao is that EDLP is not merely a pricing strategy but instead a positioning strategy encompassing pricing and communication. The *ED* implementation consists of a constant price, equal across products: neither product is "promoted" either randomly or always to build store traffic. This is a best response to PROMO's mixed strategy because it ensures that cherry pickers always visit EDLP.[13] The *LP* part is implemented by announcing savings on the basket that are attractive to time-constrained consumers.[14] Thus EDLP strategy addresses both consumer segments. The PROMO store, by randomizing discount across the two goods, ensures it has at least one good at a lower price, to attract cherry pickers. Time-constrained shoppers who only care about basket price prefer EDLP except for location. Extending this model with time-constrained consumers valuing time and therefore service, Lal and Rao show that, in equilibrium, PROMO provides higher-level service than EDLP, which in turn attracts time-constrained consumers to PROMO. In this way we can see that EDLP and PROMO are not merely pricing strategies. Hoch et al. (1994) reported a finding they deemed puzzling. Specifically, a test EDLP implementation at a Chicago supermarket chain yielded no noticeable change. But then the implementation consisted merely of following a pricing pattern. Lal–Rao analysis resolves the puzzle.

3.2   Outlet Malls and Segmentation

Manufacturers often sell through own (exclusive) retailers, independent retailers and outlet malls, inducing retail differentiation and competition.[15] Coughlan and Soberman (2005) model a market with two differentiated manufacturers or brands, indexed by i, located at the ends of a Hotelling line along which consumers live. Manufacturers sell through a single independent, exclusive retailer. Retailer i, corresponding to manufacturer i, sets retail price p_i and service level s_i to maximize its profits. The manufacturer may choose to also distribute its product through a store at an outlet mall, owned by it, setting price $p_{i, \text{OUTLET}}$. Service level at the outlet store is assumed to be zero. Consumers are of two types of, indexed by j. A consumer located at a distance x from brand 1 (and $1 - x$ from brand 2) values the product at v_j; service at $\theta_j s$ for service level s; and has a disutility of $x\, t_j$ for brand 1 and $(1 - x)\, t_j$ for brand 2. Type 1 consumer has a high cost of time and so values service more, so $\theta_1 > \theta_2$. Also it is assumed that $v_1 > v_2$ and $t_1 > t_2$. The consumer is assumed to incur a travel cost of TC_j, $TC_1 > TC_2$ to a store at the outlet mall of either manufacturer. Store prices and service levels are known to consumers. Consumer surplus CS to type j consumer from shopping at different places is then given by

$$\text{Retailer 1: } CS_{j1} = v_j + \theta_j s_1 - x\, t_j - p_1$$

$$\text{Retailer 2: } CS_{j2} = v_j + \theta_j s_2 - (1 - x)\, t_j - p_2$$

$$\text{Outlet store, manufacturer 1: } CS_{j1, \text{OUTLET}} = v_j - x\, t_j - p_{1,\text{OUTLET}} - TC_j$$

$$\text{Outlet store, manufacturer 2: } CS_{j2, \text{OUTLET}} = v_j - (1 - x)\, t_j - p_{2,\text{OUTLET}} - TC_j$$

Finally, it is assumed that there is a fraction λ of type 1 (and $1 - \lambda$ of type 2) consumers.

The key insight from Coughlan–Soberman relates to segmentation. By not offering service at outlet mall stores, can competing manufacturers gain by segmenting a market where the primary dimension of consumer heterogeneity is service sensitivity?[16] The answer is "not really". In these conditions, competing manufacturers do not benefit by diverting service-insensitive consumers to the outlet mall stores: the reason is that the level of competition in the primary market for service-sensitive consumers (who remain there) intensifies, dissipating potential gains. However, when the market is heterogeneous along two dimensions – service and price sensitivity – the answer is different. Here, diverting price-sensitive/service-insensitive consumers to the outlet mall can increase profit even in a competitive setting. In this situation, segmentation with outlet mall stores facilitates higher equilibrium prices, higher service levels and higher profitability in the primary market.

4.   PROMOTIONS COMPETITION

4.1   Using Promotions to Attract Consumers with Different Price Sensitivities

How should a retailer price to attract consumers differing in price sensitivity? Retailers that sell many products could use product assortment intelligently to attract different consumer segments. Increasingly, with the growth of the Internet, retailers often must compete on one product and face lower consumer search costs. A basic building block for modeling price competition in such cases is due to Varian (1980) and Narasimhan (1988).[17]

Varian considered competition among many retailers competing for two types of consumers: one type uninformed of prices, presumably because of high search costs and another perfectly informed, having zero search costs. All consumers are assumed to have a willingness to pay R. Uninformed consumers, U in number, buy with equal probability from any one of N stores. Informed consumers, I in number, buy at the store with the lowest price. So each store is assured of a profit of $R\,U/N$, assuming zero marginal costs. If all stores charge a price of R, one store can cut price by a small amount say to $R - \varepsilon$ and get all informed consumers to buy and obtain a profit of $(R - \varepsilon)(I + U/N)$. A small price cut by one store would invite a further price cut by another store, and so on. Define a price p_L that satisfies

$$p_L(I + U/N) = R\,U/N$$

No store would charge a price below p_L or above R. A symmetric Nash equilibrium to this pricing game then is in mixed strategies consisting of each store choosing a price drawn from a cumulative distribution function (cdf) $F(p)$ that leaves the store indifferent across all prices in the interval (p_L, R), and satisfies

$$p\,[\,(1 - F(p))^{N-1}\,I + U/N] = R\,U/N$$

The left-hand side of the foregoing equality is the expected profit from choosing a price p, taking into account the probability that the store has the lowest price. The right-hand side is the assured profit from choosing a price of R and selling only to its share of the uninformed consumers.

The probability density function (pdf) $f(p)$ associated with $F(p)$ turns out to be U-shaped.[18] This implies that a store chooses a low price close to p_L to attract the informed consumers, or a high price close to R and remain content to sell only to the uninformed consumers. The key insight from Varian's model is that randomized low prices are part of the equilibrium outcome. It is useful to think of prices below R as promotions that are necessarily random. Another insight is that the low prices are on average just as profitable as the maximum price R. In other words, all promotions on average yield the same profit as the maximum price, to be thought of as regular price. Contrast this with the mixing of reduced prices across products in the Rao–Syam model. There, promotions raise profits by more intelligently generating store traffic than using with certainty one product to generate traffic.

Narasimhan's model differs from Varian's by positing that each store (brand, in his model) has a loyal segment of consumers, and a pool of switching consumers who buy a lower-priced brand, as in Varian. He studied a duopoly with one brand having a larger loyal segment and characterized the equilibrium pricing consisting of mixed strategies. Once again promotions in his model are just as profitable on average as high prices.

4.2   Interpreting Mixed Strategies in Retailing

The mixed strategies of Section 4.1 imply that prices across retailers vary, independently of each other. Another interpretation is that store price varies, with no serial correlation, across time. What is random is the price or the depth of promotion if mixing is interpreted as promotions. How might this affect retailers? For example, if two manufacturers initiate promotions as in Narasimhan, then retailers cut price on the brand that yields them highest profits and they do not pass on the promotion on the other brand (Lal and Villas-Boas 1998). Turning to consumers, some of them may find it optimal to buy extra units of a product on promotion, especially of a large depth, anticipating higher future prices, affecting the mix of a store's clientele over time. Retailers must also understand that for promotions to increase store traffic they must be communicated. Advertising a low price can be costly, though frequently manufacturers may bear the cost. Finally, changing price incurs a cost, known as menu costs,[19] and so any interpretation of mixed strategies as drawing from a distribution of prices every time period is probably a simplification of the true pricing challenge facing a retailer.

A different interpretation of mixed strategies in retailing is that randomization is across products rather than the depth of promotion. In this case what differs is the product on promotion across stores or over time within a store, as we saw in Sections 2.3 and 3.1. This interpretation is consistent with the view of retailers as being concerned with store profits and so promotions are meant primarily to generate traffic to profit from sale of other products in the consumer's basket. Now it would be important to recognize differing incentives for manufacturers and retailers. The role of manufacturers, strategic consumers and menu costs would play a role even with this interpretation of mixed strategies.

Chen et al. (2010) show that randomized pricing with only a discrete number of prices, as opposed to a continuum of prices, can be part of competitive strategies if consumers have limited memory. In such a case lower prices, because those are what consumers choose to recall, have a higher probability of being charged. For empirical evidence of mixed strategy pricing see Rao et al. (1995) and Villas-Boas (1995).

4.3   Double Coupons, Store Traffic and Product Pricing

A retailer wants to attract consumers of different types – some that are very sensitive to price, and others less so; and he would like to charge a low price to the first type, and a high price to the second type through a good screening device. Coupons often are such a device for manufacturers (Narasimhan 1984). So a retailer could offer to cut price to users of manufacturer coupons. A common implementation is through double and triple couponing in which retailers pay consumers an additional (over the coupon value) amount equal to, or twice, the face value of a redeemed manufacturer coupon. Such a strategy eliminates the cost of distributing store coupons. However, products used to attract traffic now are those with manufacturer coupons. Manufacturers of products that are not traffic builders could then drop coupons to cut the price to consumer without lowering their margin. How can retailers then adapt their pricing strategy?

Krishnan and Rao (1995) found that the way retailers adapt differs depending on their format and whether or not they follow a double couponing policy. In the market they examined, the leading EDLP store did not double the face value of coupons, while the leading PROMO store did. Compare how the two stores react to manufacturer coupons. Suppose, for example, brand A toothpaste has a coupon for $0.30 in a week. This will draw many consumers, some of brand A and some of other brands willing to switch to brand A given the large price cut of $0.60, to the PROMO store, which incurs a cost of $0.30 for every coupon redeemed. Having generated the traffic, the store could consider a small price cut of, say, $0.05 on another brand B if that would prevent some consumers from switching brands and so save $0.30 on them while losing $0.05 on consumers of brand B. Now let us see what the EDLP store can do. It does not offer to double coupons so it offers $0.30 to users of the coupon. But it could prevent store switching by lowering the price on brand A. Based on data from a variety of product categories, Krishnan and Rao found exactly this kind of behavior: PROMO making a non-couponed brand attractive through a price cut, and EDLP making a couponed brand attractive. In evidence is the interplay of traffic generation strategies and individual product pricing of competing retailers of different formats.

5. PRIVATE LABELS AND PRODUCT ASSORTMENT COMPETITION

5.1 Private Labels, Store Loyalty and Store Traffic

National brands generate traffic because they have a large clientele base, offer the retailer incentives in return for favorable merchandising and promotions, and their quality is not controlled by the retailer so a low price at one retailer does not affect how consumers perceive its quality in choosing a store, something that may not be true of private labels. The main disadvantage of national brands to build traffic is also precisely the fact that consumers can begin to see store choice as merely an exercise in frugality, making it costly to generate traffic using national brands. And so, can private labels, or store brands, generate store traffic more profitably, at less expense, than national brands?[20]

Corstjens and Lal (2000) analyze a two-period model with consumers exhibiting brand choice inertia. A fraction γ of the population has low inertia, δ, and fraction $1 - \gamma$ has high inertia, Δ. Inertia affects consumers' relative willingness to pay for brands bought or not in the prior period. Low-inertia consumers are also assumed to have a low transportation cost of εc while high-inertia consumers' cost is c, $\varepsilon c < c$. Consumers are uniformly distributed on a Hotelling line at the ends of which is located a store. Stores carry a single product category that includes the same national brand and a unique private label of comparable quality across stores. Quality of all brands, q_m of national brand and q_s of private label, is common knowledge. However, consumers don't know in period 1 if the private label is to their liking, and so will buy it only if their inertia can be overcome. They can learn their liking by purchasing and using it. A fraction β of those that try is known to end up liking it. In each period, consumers choose the store offering them the greater surplus. They value a brand of quality q at $v(q)$. Retailers can advertise the price of one good, either the national brand or the store brand. Consumers learn advertised prices and form rational expectations of unadvertised prices. To retain focus on traffic

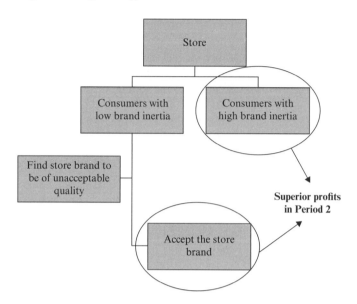

Figure 6.2   Equilibrium in Corstjens–Lal model

generation by private labels, national brands are assumed to have no cost advantage over private labels, meaning the marginal cost $mc(q)$ satisfies: $mc(q_m) - mc(q_s) = v(q_m) - v(q_s)$.[21] Let P denote price and subscripts refer to brand.

The interesting equilibrium to this model is the following: in period 1 both stores generate traffic by advertising national brand. Since all consumers have inertia to switch to the private label, some low and some high, each store prices the private label below the national brand such that low-inertia consumers buy the private label: $P_s = P_m + v(q_s) - v(q_m) - \delta$; some buyers will like it. All high-inertia consumers end up buying the national brand in period 1. In contrast to period 1, in period 2 there are three segments of consumers: high-inertia types liking the national brand, low-inertia consumers, some liking the private label, that have inertia to switch to national brand or the competitor's private label, and others liking the national brand with inertia to switch to either private label. In period 2 stores advertise private label prices: $P_s = mc(q_s) - \Delta + \gamma(1 - \beta) + (1 - \gamma)$ $\varepsilon c/c$. Consumers form expectations of national brand price: $v(q_m) - v(q_s) + P_s + \Delta$, these expectations being rational since prices are optimal given consumer expectations.

Private label helps raise store profits from two of the consumer segments in period 2 over period 1. Figure 6.2 depicts this. How does it happen? First turn to low-inertia consumers that like the store brand. For them stores are differentiated, helping to support higher store brand prices. Turing to high-inertia consumers, attracting them to the store is no longer by directly comparing national brand prices. Instead, the price of the private label, by bounding the national brand price from above, makes the value promise. High-inertia traffic is generated without head-on comparison of prices of identical products at the two stores. This is the key insight. A different version of this is given in Section 2.3: mix price announcements across products; in Section 3.1 EDLP and PROMO stores use different communication strategies; in all these cases strategies comprehend all consumer segments without head-on competition for traffic.

5.2 Assortment Reduction, Store Differentiation and Segmentation

Imagine that store assortments are different, making it hard for consumers to compare prices across stores. Electronic appliance retailers, for example, often carry different manufacturer lines, and even different models of the same manufacturer. Assortment differentiation helps minimize use of direct price comparison of traffic builders to generate traffic. However, a store carrying systematically higher-end (vertically differentiated) products at higher prices could be at a disadvantage in communicating value and building traffic. Possibly a good strategy for the high-end store is to carry some low-end items, creating competitive product overlap to facilitate value communication (Gourville and Moon 2004).

Reducing assortment could lower costs. Manufacturers certainly can trim manufacturing and supply chain costs by reducing the number of SKUs offered. Will this be profitable under retail competition? Dukes et al. (2009) assume that marginal cost of retailing increases with product varieties carried. A single manufacturer has two products for sale through independent retailers: one product is more popular than the other, modeled as realizing higher demand at the same price. Two competing retailers, facing a linear demand curve, choose quantities to sell while the manufacturer chooses wholesale price.[22] One retailer, termed dominant, decides in stage 1 of the game whether to carry one or both products. Of interest is the equilibrium outcome in which one retailer carries only the more popular product, and the other both products, incurring a higher cost. The insight here is that a dominant retailer can render the competitor's cost high, and thereby soften price competition for the popular product. There is also partial segmentation because for one of the products the retailer carrying both products is rendered a monopolist.[23]

5.3 Consistency in Assortment, Search, Segmentation and Store Differentiation

Consumers visiting a store, and not finding the item sought, must decide whether to search further. Heterogeneity in their search cost could serve as a basis for segmentation by offering different levels of certainty of assortment at the store: by positioning the store on commitment to being consistent in the expected assortment. This segmentation goes beyond just pricing strategy as illustrated by Krishnan et al. (2002). They posit that a store can adopt the strategy *C*, denoting consistent, offering a fixed and full assortment. Alternatively the store can adopt *NC*, not consistent, offering an assortment that entails a probability that the consumer must incur an additional travel cost to a second store following *C*. The store having *C* cannot take advantage of opportunistic buying and so has a higher marginal cost than the store having *NC*. For example, Ross Dress for Less in the USA carries name brands but not in all sizes or colors. A consumer takes a chance shopping there as opposed to a department store such as Macy's. However, the former stocks only what is inexpensive to source, and so has lower costs than the latter. Krishnan et al. use the Dutch flower market to find support for the findings of their analytical model. In the flower market some retailers stock whatever flowers they are able to acquire inexpensively at auctions. They are *NC* stores. Other retailers are *C* because they buy from a distributor who stocks all types of flowers, but this entails a higher cost of sourcing. There are two stores located at the ends of a Hotelling line along which consumers of every type are uniformly distributed.

Krishnan et al. assume two customer types: type 1 with high need for a particular variety of flowers (novices when it comes to flowers) and type 2 who, because of their expertise, do not depend on finding a specific flower. Type 2 can buy at the first store they visit, making their transportation cost certain, but type 1 may have to visit an additional store if they visit an *NC* store first. It is also assumed that within each type a fraction of the consumers has a need for service. A consumer who needs service and shops at a store that does not offer service is assumed to incur a cost (could be time or out-of-pocket). Retail competition is modeled as a multi-stage game. In stage 1, stores decide on *C* or *NC*; in stage 2 on whether or not to offer service that entails a fixed cost; in stage 3 prices; also in stage 3 consumers make shopping decisions. With this structure it is possible to ask what set of model parameters would support a sub-game-perfect Nash equilibrium in which: one store chooses to be *C* and chooses to offer service while the other chooses to be *NC* and does not offer service. Krishnan et al. inferred the Dutch market parameters and found them to be consistent with this equilibrium outcome. A little over half the florists sourced from auctions and their assortment exhibited significantly greater randomness in composition than stores that sourced from distributors. In other words, sourcing at auctions is an important feature of the *NC* florists. Additionally, while 75 percent of the *C* florists were rated highly for their service and special bouquets and so on, a little over 50 percent of the *NC* stores were rated highly for their service. Thus we see that segmentation as a part of retail competitive strategy involves dimensions beyond price and location: in this case sourcing, assortment and service provision all unified in a particular way.

6.   TRADE PROMOTIONS/SUPPORT COMPETITION

6.1   Cooperative Advertising Allowances

Competing retailers realize that any marketing that they undertake affects not only demand at their store but also at other stores. In particular, advertising of a product by one store might draw consumers' attention to the product that has the potential to increase demand for the product but at a competing retailer. The effect of spillover of advertising makes advertising less productive for the retailer, leading to a reduced level of advertising relative to the situation with no spillovers. Is there a way to overcome the negative effects of spillover? That is especially important to a manufacturer.

Bergen and John (1997) analyze a model of *n* retailers located equally spaced along a circle, a ring road. Consumers are uniformly distributed over the circle and incur a cost tz to shop at a store located at a distance z from the store. Prices at the stores are known to all. Given prices p_i at a store i and p_k at an adjacent store k, the fraction of consumers between the two stores that shops at store i is $0.5(1/n) + (p_k - p_i)/2t$. The number of such consumers who shop is assumed to depend on advertising, specifically the reach r_i of store i and the reach of all other stores. The cost of reach r denoted by $A(r)$ is assumed to be differentiable and convex. Higher reach leads to shopping by more consumers; and reach has a positive effect on all stores, implying positive advertising spillover. Demand at store i is then[24]

$$D_i = [(1 - \beta) r_i + (1/(n - 1)) \Sigma_{k \neq i} \beta r_k] 2 [0.5(1/n) + (p_k - p_i)/2t]$$

Each retailer incurs a fixed cost F_r of operation. A single manufacturer chooses the wholesale price w, a fixed fee F_f the retailer must pay and an advertising allowance α so that retailer's cost of advertising is $(1 - \alpha) A(r)$, the remaining cost being borne by the manufacturer. Retailers then choose retail prices and the reach to maximize their profits given by

$$(p_i - w) D_i - (1 - \alpha) A(r) - F_r - F_f$$

Bergen and John first ask how a vertically integrated manufacturer would choose n, p_i and r.[25] This corresponds to a fully coordinated channel. They then solve for the optimal triplet w, F_f and α so that the vertically integrated manufacturer's solution can be implemented. Such a triplet exists because w and F_f can be chosen to implement the coordinated price and α the coordinated level of advertising. The key insight is that cooperative advertising can coordinate actions of competing retailers. Exploring the model fully, they arrive at several insights into how a manufacturer can coordinate competing retailers.

6.2 Slotting Allowances and Retailer Costs

Slotting allowances can arise in the presence of information asymmetry as a way for a manufacturer to inform the retailer the true potential of a new product (Chu 1992; Lariviere and Padmanabhan 1997; Desai, 2000). Other arguments that favor slotting allowances include manufacturer competition (Shaffer 1991; Sullivan 1997) and retailer bargaining power (Chu 1992). But can slotting allowances also be seen as a way of sharing retailer costs? Can a manufacturer induce them to carry its product by providing slotting allowances so as to obtain the "optimal" level of distribution, in particular, under retail competition?

Kuksov and Pazgal (2007) consider a market with two retailers located at the ends of a Hotelling line along which consumers, totaling 1, are located such that the density of consumers is symmetric about the midpoint and concave in shape. The density of consumers at the midpoint is denoted by μ_0. If μ_0 is very large, most consumers are located at the midpoint and so retailers must compete heavily on price in that case. So μ_0 can be thought of as a measure of retail competition. A consumer has a travel cost of t per unit distance and so he would be willing to buy from a retailer if the price, p, and distance to the retailer, z, are such that the surplus he obtains, $V - p - tz \geq 0$. A single manufacturer contemplates distributing its product through one or both retailers, who are free to decide whether they wish to carry the product. Retailers incur a fixed cost C of distribution if they decide to carry the product, which must be offset by the gross profits. The manufacturer sets wholesale price w and a transfer from the retailer to the manufacturer of T that can be thought of as the fixed fee in a two-part tariff. If $T < 0$, we interpret it as a slotting allowance. The gross profits of retailer i are a share of the channel profits net of what the other retailer obtains. For example, retailer 1's profits, π_1, are $\lambda(\pi_{channel} - \pi_2)$, λ (0,1) being the retailer's bargaining power. The channel profits depend on how many retailers carry the products and the prices set, and the consumer demand given these prices, generated by consumers maximizing surplus and ensuring it is non-zero.

What might lead to slotting allowances in the Kuksov–Pazgal model? The mathematical condition is $C < t/2$ and $(1 - \lambda) C + \lambda t/2 > t/2 \mu_0$. These conditions have an intuitive meaning. The first condition says the fixed costs should not be too high to elicit retailer participation. The second condition says that, among other things, μ_0 should be sufficiently high. In other words, retail competition should lead to low margins to the retailers. If that were to occur, then slotting allowances could be used to raise retailers' net profits to zero, so as to elicit retailer participation. It is interesting to see that even if retailers have no bargaining power, $\lambda = 0$ in the model, slotting allowances may arise; higher retailer bargaining power along with high retail competition always results in slotting allowances. An extension of the model with competing manufacturers finds that if C is high enough, $C > t/\mu_0$, retailers prefer to carry a single product; otherwise, they carry multiple products.

7.   LOYALTY AND REWARD PROGRAMS COMPETITION

7.1   Frequency Rewards and Cherry Picking

To achieve their objectives, retailers use loyalty programs, for example by "rewarding" customers based on shopping frequency or purchase volume. Higher purchase volume may point to a loyal customer who shops at a single store for much if not all of the shopping basket. Is it then worthwhile to induce loyalty by encouraging shoppers to shop at a single store, taking into account retail competition and cost of implementing such a program?

Lal and Bell (2003) analyze Frequent Shopper Program's (FSP's) impact on store profitability and consumer behavior. They model two stores, A and B, located at the ends of a Hotelling line along which all consumers are uniformly distributed. Consumers desire an identical basket of goods, and incur a unit cost of c to travel to a store.[26] Shopping cost depends on consumer's location and c. The basket is conceptualized as consisting of two sub-baskets, or equivalently two goods, with each store offering one good cheaper. Denote price of more expensive good at store by P_A and less expensive by $P_A - d$. A similar situation applies to store B. It is assumed that d is determined exogenously and so acts as a parameter in the model.[27] Stores choose prices P_A and P_B and the Nash equilibrium outcome depends on size of d and c. Three cases arise: if $d < c$, all consumers buy the entire basket at a single store and each store makes profits of c, a result we have seen in Section 2.2 in the Lal–Matutes model; if $d > 2c$, all consumers split their basket buying the cheaper good at each store, and profits are less than or equal to zero;[28] the third case is the interesting one when $c < d < 2c$. In that case, consumers close to either end shop at a single store for their basket and consumers in the middle cherry pick. The equilibrium profits to each store, as a result of this are now less than c. What would happen if one store offered a loyalty reward? To analyze this, assume stores choose prices as before but one store, say store A, offers a reward of L to all consumers buying their entire basket in A. Store A now chooses both P_A and L, while store B chooses P_B. It turns out that as long as $d < 2c$, store A can choose L so as to prevent any cherry picking, thus making the situation identical to $d = 0 = L$.[29] Without cherry picking, store profits are restored to c. In other words, the loyalty reward program is profitable. Would the profits change if store B also had a reward program? No, that would still leave the profits at c.

A final question that Lal and Bell address is what happens if there are two types of consumers, some with transportation cost higher than others' transportation cost. Stores are now better off competing for only type 1 customers, as that would yield a profit of c_1 from that segment and possibly zero from the other. In effect the marginal customer that stores compete for is of type 1 with a higher transportation cost, raising profits. But with a loyalty program rewarding both types of customers, the marginal customer is of type 2, hurting profits. The key insight then is that it is important to reward some customers but not others. The next section examines a variation of this idea applied to pricing based on customers' differing basket size rather than transportation costs.

7.2 Basket Heterogeneity and Intelligent Pricing

One of the key dimensions of heterogeneity among consumers is the size and composition of the shopping basket. Humby and Hunt (2004) point out that the data gathered from reward programs can be used to design intelligent pricing strategies for different segments of the market. Exactly what might this mean?

Kumar and Rao (2006) model competing retailers located at ends of a Hotelling line along which consumers live. Some consumers are in the market for one of three goods (small basket) and others for two of three goods (large basket). Two possibilities arise: the large basket customer buys goods different from the one good bought by the small basket shopper, denoted DG for different goods. Alternatively there is a common good in both baskets, denoted CG. All consumers have unit transportation cost c to go to a store and return. We know that maximum store profits correspond to basket price of c for each type of customer. Therefore, for DG, goods in the small basket should be priced at c; and goods in the large basket priced so that basket price is c.[30] Retailers must know the composition of both baskets to implement the optimal pricing strategy.

What if retailers don't know basket composition? Then, all goods would be priced at a price P such that in equilibrium $P < c < 2P$. This means that the small basket shopper is paying less than c, the optimal basket price, while the large basket customer is paying more than c. Might this lead to higher profits than basket price of c for each type, especially if most of the customers are large basket customers? No, as Kumar and Rao (2006) show. Regardless of the proportion of small basket consumers in the population, profits are always lower than what the retailer would obtain were he endowed with basket composition knowledge. Would it help if both retailers were to collect information on shopping baskets? Unambiguously, yes. Profits with no basket information are lower than profits when basket information is with one store, in turn lower than when it is with both stores.

8.   E-TAIL COMPETITION

8.1   Non-digitized Attributes, Retail Support and Online Retailing

Should a manufacturer who sells through a traditional retailer decide to sell also through an own outlet on the Internet? What advantage would such a move have? And what would happen to equilibrium prices and profits under competition?

Lal and Sarvary (1999) model two manufacturers selling through their own retail store by competing on price. Consumers' willingness to pay for either offering is r. A consumer i is assumed to know that store i's offering is satisfactory. Consumers are assumed to know prices before shopping.[31] To buy either product, consumers must make a trip to the mall at a cost of k_1. At the mall, the consumer could visit store i first, and then pay price p_i to buy a known product. This is option 1. Instead of this the consumer can visit competitor j first and learn specifically about a non-digitized attribute of j, such as fit of clothing. The outcome of the store j visit is uncertain and could result in a good fit, yielding additional utility f with probability q; then the consumer could buy product j for p_j. This is option 2. Store j visit might result in a bad fit, yielding an additional utility $-f$. Again, the consumer could buy product j for p_j. This is option 3. Depending on the fit at j, the consumer may decide to go to i, incurring an additional travel cost of k_2, $k_2 < k_1$, if this yields a higher surplus, since at this point there is no uncertainty. This is option 4. Or the consumer may decide not to incur extra cost k_2 and decide not to buy any product. This is option 5. Finally, the consumer may decide not to go to either store. This is option 6. Figure 6.3 displays the options that the consumer has and utility U associated with each.

Now suppose that i decides to have a store on the Internet. The force of the Internet is twofold. First, to learn about j, the consumer i must visit j at a cost of k_1 since he cannot learn from the Internet because of the non-digitized nature of the attribute. Second, the consumer could save cost k_1 of visiting store i were he to forgo learning about j. This has

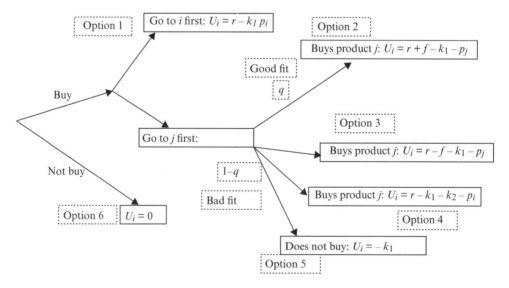

Figure 6.3   Consumer decisions in Lal–Sarvary model

the effect of raising the utility of option 1 by k_1 and option 4 by k_2. The Internet causes a wedge between utility that consumer i (and similarly consumer j) derives from the two products. Naturally, this will raise equilibrium prices. Thus we see an Internet retail presence causing prices to rise in situations in which consumers have experience with one product or brand, and must visit a store to learn about a competitive offering. Lal–Sarvary also demonstrate that under certain conditions, consumers that found it optimal to learn of a competitor product will choose not to do so when faced with the possibility of purchasing on the net.

8.2   Segmentation and Service Provision through Online Retailing

When would it profit a manufacturer to add their own Internet store to independent brick-and-mortar retailers carrying competitor products also? How would competition between the multi-brand retailer and their own Internet outlet affect equilibrium outcomes? Kumar and Ruan (2006) answer these questions by considering a manufacturer who distributes product through independent retailers. Retailers in this model have two important roles, in addition to setting price. First, by carrying competitor products, they offer consumers a choice, and enhance efficiency. Second, they provide a service to consumers, depending on the relative margin manufacturers offer. Competition in this model is between the independent retailer and the manufacturer-owned Internet retailer. Thus it resembles Coughlan and Soberman (2005), as we saw in Section 3.2. Also, in this model competing manufacturers' actions are exogenous.

The Kumar–Ruan model has two types of consumers: type 1, fraction α_r of the market, is loyal to the retailer and chooses between the two brands based on price and the service (think of it as recommendation) of the retailer to either. Type 2, a fraction α_m of the market, is loyal to the brand and buys either at the Internet store or at the retailer, depending on prices and their relative preference for the two outlets, captured by parameter δ, with δ uniformly distributed over interval $(-d, d)$. The manufacturer–retailer interaction is modeled as a three-stage game. In stage 1, the manufacturer decides on whether or not to have an Internet presence. In stage 2 the manufacturer chooses wholesale price to the independent retailer. In stage 3, the retailer chooses service level and retail price, and the manufacturer chooses price at the store on the Internet, if one exists.

Equilibrium outcomes in the model tell us what effect the online store has. Broadly two situations obtain. First, if margins on competitor products are low, the retailer provides a relatively high level of service to the manufacturer. An online store then allows the manufacturer to more effectively price discriminate by pricing higher to brand-loyal consumers. In the second scenario, if margins on competitive products are high, an online store, by catering to brand-loyal consumers, allows reduction in wholesale price, incentivizing the retailer to provide higher levels of service and capture sales from the store-loyal segment. In this way, we see that the profitability of the online store depends on the relative importance of price discrimination and service provision by the retailer.

8.3   Internet Shopping Agents and Online Retailing

The growth of the Internet has brought the ubiquitous Internet shopping agent (ISA), which enables quick price comparison of alternatives. How does ISA affect online

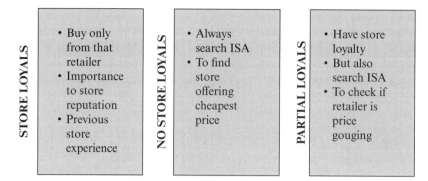

STORE LOYALS
- Buy only from that retailer
- Importance to store reputation
- Previous store experience

NO STORE LOYALS
- Always search ISA
- To find store offering cheapest price

PARTIAL LOYALS
- Have store loyalty
- But also search ISA
- To check if retailer is price gouging

Figure 6.4   Consumer types in Iyer–Pazgal model

retailers' pricing strategies? And, should a retailer have its prices displayed by ISA, or prefer to have consumers come to its site to learn of its price? A retailer joining ISA is called an inside retailer and one that does not an outside retailer. For a more general discussion of price dispersion on the Internet and across types of retailers see Pan et al. (2004) and Pan et al. (2002).

Iyer and Pazgal (2003) provide answers to the foregoing questions. They posit three kinds of consumers: type 1, a fraction α of the market, is loyal to some specific retailer, preferring to shop at retailer site; type 2, a fraction β, is not loyal to any store, is focused on price, and so likely to benefit from the information at the ISA. In Iyer–Pazgal an innovation is the existence of a third type, of size γ, assumed to be partially loyal to a store, meaning it prefers to buy at its favorite store as long as price at the store is no higher than the average price across all stores listed in the ISA. The consumer types are shown in Figure 6.4.

Retailers sell a homogeneous product to consumers all willing to pay R, normalized to 1. So competition is mainly on price. Each retailer is assured of selling to its loyal customers of size α/n, where n represents the number of firms, and so α/n is the security level of profits for each retailer both inside and outside the ISA. By joining an ISA, a retailer can hope to add to its loyal customers the type 2 consumers. But competition among the retailers in the ISA will make their profits equal to the security level. The partially loyal consumers are also equally distributed across the firms in the ISA if the average price charged by the ISA retailer is lower than that of any outside retailer.[32] Finally, the reach of the ISA r is defined as $\beta + \gamma$. It is possible that both r and α for the ISA stores are functions of the number of stores joining the ISA. This can be termed as the ISA's reach being endogenous. Alternatively, if the ISA's reach is fixed, its reach is exogenous. The authors examine both cases.

When reach is exogenous, retailers in the ISA mix their prices in equilibrium, as in Varian (1980) and Narasimhan (1988), and obtain expected profits of α/n. What is the equilibrium pricing strategy of outside retailers? The outside retailer charges a price of 1 and obtains its security level of profits. Or it could cut the price below the expected price of a retailer in the ISA, denoted by E_k, where subscript k refers to number of inside retailers. If $(\alpha + \gamma) E_k < \alpha$ the outside retailer's optimal strategy is to charge price of 1. How does E_k depend on k? Iyer and Pazgal show that it is monotonically increasing in k. So there exists a critical number k^* of inside retailers such that if $k < k^*$, outside retailers' optimal price is 1 and if $k > k^*$, it is

$E_k - \varepsilon$, where ε is positive, arbitrarily close to zero. So, the equilibrium outcome is: number of retailers joining ISA is $k < k^*$ and they follow mixed strategy pricing; the remaining $n - k$ retailers stay outside and follow a pure strategy of pricing at 1.[33] Essentially, the ISA can't be too large. Iyer and Pazgal go on to analyze several interesting extensions of this basic model, in particular treating reach as endogenous and allowing the ISA to share with inside retailers its advertising revenues, which increase as k increases.

9.   COMPETITION AND NEW RETAIL ENTRY

9.1   Rising Prices in Face of Entry

Entry of a competing retailer means that incumbent retailers lose market share, and prices and profits of incumbent firms are likely to fall. Are there situations in which prices may not fall, but rise instead? New entry may lead to a different segmentation of the market, or a different clientele mix of incumbent stores. This change in clientele mix can lead to higher prices.

Thomadsen (2010) considers the following situation. Suppose two retail chains, indexed by b, locate their stores on a Hotelling line, say McDonald's denoted by $b = M$ and Burger King, denoted by $b = B$. The price at a store is p. Consumers, indexed by i, located on the line at a distance d_{ij} from store j obtain utility U_{ij} from outlet j, $U_{ij} = \gamma_{b(j)} - \beta p_j - t d_{ij} + \varepsilon_{ij}$ where $\gamma_{b(j)}$ is the utility for band b, t is the unit cost of travel and ε_{ij} is a random error capturing consumer heterogeneity in utility conditioned on location. Now suppose another McDonald's outlet enters the market. If we had the estimates for the consumer utility model and marginal costs, we could calculate the effect of the entry on profits for various locations of outlets. This is what Thomadsen does, assuming that Burger King is located at the center of a 10-mile-long line and using estimates from Thomadsen (2005). He finds that profits can increase, especially in those cases in which the new entry is adjacent to an existing McDonald's, and neither too close to it nor too far away from it. Why might this occur?

The easiest way to conceptualize entry in this kind of model is to imagine B at the left end of a long line and M at some distance from it. The equilibrium price of B reflects the competition between B and M. The equilibrium price of M, on the other hand, must take into account not only competition with B but also the market to its right. Entry by an additional store from M can cause the price at the first M store to rise because it now does not serve the "far-away" customers on the right. Essentially, the mix of customers changes at the first M store with relatively fewer far-away customers and more nearby customers, resulting in price rise. In turn, this leads to higher sales at B and a higher equilibrium price. Thomadsen and Pazgal (2010) offer a more complete analysis of how entry can cause prices to rise.

9.2   What Happens after Wal-Mart Entry

Imagine a traditional supermarket that is facing inevitable entry by Wal-Mart. Would it be better if Wal-Mart located next to it, or further out but next to a competitor? Zhu et al. (2010) analyze this problem and provide interesting answers.

They consider a model with two traditional supermarkets *A* and *B* located at the ends of a Hotelling line, each of which carries two products: products 1 and 2, to be thought of as produce and dry groceries respectively. Both stores incur marginal cost of *K* for either product. They face entry by a discounter, like Wal-Mart, labeled *C* that might locate next to either *A* or *B*. Suppose it locates next to *A*. Store *C* is assumed to carry products 2 and 3; the latter might be appliances. So the assortment overlap is partial. Consumers are assumed to be heterogeneous in three ways: location relative to the stores; transportation and shopping costs; and basket size. Convenience (or basket) shoppers have a transportation cost *t* > 0 to visit a location, and a shopping cost *s* > 0 to actually shop at a store. In contrast, value shoppers (cherry pickers) have zero transportation and shopping costs. Convenience shoppers are willing to pay an amount greater than value shoppers, for either 1 or 2. While all are in the market for 1 and 2, a fraction β, labeled large basket shoppers, also buys product 3. A fraction α of the market is made up of convenience shoppers. All consumers are assumed to know prices at the stores.

The authors' analysis compares equilibrium profits of *A* and *B* before and after entry of *C*. Before entry, the situation is identical to Lal and Matutes (1989), with each retailer offering one good at a price lower than its competitor. Convenience shoppers split in equal proportion between the stores, and visit only the store nearest to them. Value shoppers split their basket and visit both stores. Profits to each retailer are $\pi = 0.5\,\alpha\,t + (1-\alpha)\,(L-K)$. What happens after entry? It is assumed that retailer *C* is non-strategic and chooses the price of product 2 to be less than or equal to *K*. Assuming that the fraction α of convenience shoppers is sufficiently large, and for the convenience shoppers *H* is sufficiently large so they all buy, *t* is sufficiently large so they don't cherry pick and *s* is sufficiently large so small basket shoppers don't visit *C*, the equilibrium outcome is as follows: large basket convenience shoppers visit *C* to buy 2 and 3, and then go to *A* to buy 1; small basket convenience shoppers split between *A* and *B*; and value shoppers buy 1 and 2 at *B* and *C* respectively. The first thing to note is the new segmentation of shoppers with *A* catering only to convenience shoppers while *B* caters to both convenience and value shoppers. Given this segmentation, the price of 1 is higher at *A* than at *B* because it ignores the value shoppers altogether. This is the "segmentation effect." Instead it benefits from the large basket convenience shoppers attracted to *C*. This is the "agglomeration effect," due to the one-stop consequence of *C* locating next to *A*.[34] Finally, the equilibrium profits are higher for *A* than for *B*. Thus we see that, faced with inevitable entry of *C*, a traditional retailer prefers to have it locate next to it, because of the advantage that gives it in competing for store traffic with another traditional retailer. Having obtained the traffic, there is also segmentation that leads to higher prices on product 1, which is not carried by *C*.

10.   FUTURE RESEARCH AND CONCLUDING COMMENTS

Studies of retail competition have produced several insights. A summary of insights from models of retail competition appears in Table 6.1. However, there is ample scope for future research on a number of important yet unexplored or unresolved issues.

In modeling retail competition it is necessary to consider multiple aspects of competition and go beyond just pricing. An urgent need is for future modeling efforts to develop

Table 6.1   Summary of key insights from models of retail competition

Topic	Key insights
Price competition	• Retail competition by advertising prices is all about generating traffic • Loss leaders are an extreme case of pricing to generate traffic • Randomizing advertised promotions across products to generate traffic accompanied by unadvertised specials can improve retail profits by reducing head-to-head competition by retailers • Price matching can help in price discrimination and customer retention if consumers differ in search costs
Competition between store formats	• Choice of format such as EDLP is a positioning strategy that demands consistency across advertising, pricing, assortment and service • Alternative formats can help segment consumers that differ not just in price sensitivity but an additional dimension such as need for service. Outlet stores are an example of this
Promotion competition	• Retail promotions that result from competing to attract price sensitive customers follow from stores employing mixed strategies or randomized pricing • The interplay of manufacturer promotions such as coupons and retailer strategies such as doubling coupon value to generate traffic requires retailers to focus on pricing all brands in the category
Private labels and assortment	• Using store brands rather than national brands to generate traffic can increase profits and raise national brand prices by reducing head-to-head competition by retailers • Limiting product assortment and reducing costs thereby or carrying full assortment to serve more customers but at higher costs are differentiation strategies that can lead to higher profits under competition • Competing retailers can differentiate by offering to guarantee product assortment or not, and choose the corresponding service strategy to effectively segment the market
Trade support	• By offering cooperative advertising allowances a manufacturer can help competing retailers to coordinate their strategies to mimic those of a vertically integrated manufacturer • When competition leads to low retail margins, manufacturers can use slotting allowances to elicit retail participation
Loyalty programs	• Frequent shopping program can improve profits by reducing cherry picking if only some stores implement it. However, all stores implementing the program is not profitable • When consumers use reward cards the information gathered that is most useful for pricing is the basket size and composition of consumers. Profits increase when all retailers have reward cards
E-tail competition	• Internet retail presence causes prices to rise in situations in which consumers have experience with one product or brand • For competing manufacturers, profitability of an online store depends on the relative importance of price discrimination and service provision by the retailer • In equilibrium, not all competing e-tailers would want to be part of an Internet Shopping Agent (ISA) and those that are part of ISA use mixed strategy pricing
Entry	• Entry by a competitor changes equilibrium clientele mix at an existing retailer that can cause prices to increase • If Wal-Mart or a similar store were sure to enter, an existing traditional retailer is better off if Wal-Mart located next to it because of the advantage in generating store traffic

various ways of accommodating more than one element in strategy. In addition, it is important to focus on retailers that carry more than one product so that traffic generation strategies play the important role that they do in practice. Game-theoretic models with multiple products and multiple strategy elements will pose many technical challenges.

The retail landscape is influenced by advances in technology such as the Internet that affect both the demand side through consumer shopping behavior and the cost side through supply chain and service provision innovations. In turn, this will affect both format and positioning of retailers. So an interesting direction for future research is exploring how technological advances lead to altered segmentation of the market, taking into account both demand cost side effects.

Finally, there are many retail innovations, so we shall have to develop models that reflect them. Exciting areas include the design of communication strategies such as mobile marketing, product customization at the retail store, and development of cross-selling opportunities.[35] I hope the extant models discussed in this chapter can provide a sound basis for analyzing competition in these situations.

ACKNOWLEDGMENTS

I thank Nanda Kumar, Ganesh Iyer, Dmitri Kuksov, Sridhar Moorthy, Paddy Padmanabhan, Anthony Dukes, Raphael Thomadsen, Chakravarti Narasimhan, Richard Staelin, Preyas Desai, Debu Purohit, Miguel Villas-Boas, David Soberman and Vishal Singh for their input in preparing this. All shortcomings are my responsibility.

NOTES

1. Some forms of communication such as sale signs can be modeled as signals (Anderson and Simester 1998).
2. See Chapter 5 in this volume.
3. The consumer would consider visiting the other store only if $p_c + s \leq r$.
4. Since shoppers arrive at the first store randomly, the role of price is only to retain shoppers and not to attract them to the store.
5. Kuksov (2006) shows that retailers' uncertainty of each other's knowledge about consumer valuations may lead to a more competitive price.
6. The cost is for a round trip, so that it costs $c\,x$ for a consumer to shop at a store located at a distance x from that consumer.
7. Marginal costs are set to zero.
8. Rao–Syam impose the assumption that $2c > R > c$.
9. See also Chapter 15 in this volume.
10. Png and Hirshleifer assume that type 1 will buy one unit at a price less than or equal to r and zero at higher prices.
11. In a symmetric equilibrium in which all stores offer to match competitor prices, all stores price according to a mixed, or randomized, strategy over the interval (p_m, r) and the expected price at each store is greater than p_m, in turn resulting in lower quantity sold, but the expected combined profits of the stores remain the same as that of a monopolist.
12. Note that since $R - 0.5(D + \delta) > R - D$, the "discounted" good at the PROMO store is priced lower than at the EDLP store, so it makes sense to split the basket.
13. If the PROMO store announced the price of one of the goods with probability 1, the EDLP store would want to lower the price of that good below the price at the PROMO store.

14. The EDLP strategy of announcing savings also has a price matching element to it.
15. For an analysis of competition between direct marketers and conventional retailers see Balasubramanian (1998).
16. Of course, a monopolist would greatly benefit by segmenting a market that is primarily differentiated on the basis of service sensitivity. The monopolist could offer higher levels of service at primary retailers and charge those customers who value the service a higher price.
17. Shilony (1977) and Raju et al. (1990) also model price competition in ways that are similar.
18. This is a consequence of modeling free entry, with a fixed cost K, and letting the number of stores be determined endogenously.
19. See Dutta et al. (1999).
20. See also Chapter 19 in this volume.
21. The authors note that their results would remain unaffected were the private label to have a cost disadvantage relative to the national brand.
22. Presumably the authors have in mind varieties of package sizes, or flavors, for example of consumer packaged goods. One flavor may be more popular than the other. They additionally assume that these are not substitutes.
23. See also Kuksov and Villas-Boas (2010) and Kuksov and Lin (2010) for issues considering the provision of product information to reduce consumer evaluation costs when a retailer carries a wide assortment.
24. The parameter β determines the weight of own versus competitor advertising, and demand is multiplied by 2 to account for two neighboring stores for each store.
25. Note that n affects convenience, and so willingness to pay and optimal prices.
26. Unlike in Section 2.2, here the cost is for a one-way trip and not for a round trip.
27. The set-up is similar to Rao and Syam in Section 2.3 except for the exogenously determined d.
28. At $d = 2c$, profits are zero.
29. Picking L to prevent cherry picking here is identical to the analysis in Rao and Syam (2001) when stores can commit to advertising opposite goods, and an unadvertised special is offered to prevent cherry picking. The reward L here plays the same part as the unadvertised special in Rao and Syam.
30. So the prices of the individual goods can be $k\,c$ and $(1-k)\,c$, $0 \leq k \leq 1$. For the CG situation, the common good has to be priced at c and the other two goods at 0.
31. Prices are assumed to be known to the consumer from advertisements before visiting stores.
32. All retailers in the ISA are assumed to follow a symmetric mixed strategy. If retailers are asymmetric in the size of loyal customers, then the price of the retailer with the smallest loyal segment has the lowest expected price, and this would be the basis for comparison for the partially loyal consumers.
33. There cannot be an equilibrium in which an outside retailer charges the price of $Ek - \varepsilon$, as that would lower profits and provide an incentive to some inside to leave the ISA.
34. See also Datta and Sudhir (2009). Consumers may also exhibit store loyalty for a subset of their shopping basket; see Zhang et al. (2010).
35. See also Chapter 13 in this volume.

REFERENCES

Anderson, E.T. and Simester, D.I. (1998), "The role of sale signs," *Marketing Science*, **17** (2), 139–55.
Balasubramanian, Sridhar (1998), "Mail versus mall: a strategic analysis of competition between direct marketers and conventional retailers," *Marketing Science*, **17** (3), 181–95.
Bergen, M. and John, G. (1997), "Understanding cooperative advertising participation rates in conventional channels," *Journal of Marketing Research*, **34** (3), 357–69.
Betancourt, R.R. and Gautschi, D. (1988), "The economics of retail firms," *Managerial and Decision Economics*, **9**, 133–44.
Betancourt, R. and Gautschi, D. (1990), "Demand complementarities, household production, and retail assortments," *Marketing Science*, **9** (2), 146–61.
Chen, Y., Iyer, G. and Pazgal, A. (2010), "Limited memory, categorization and competition," *Marketing Science*, **29** (4), 650–70.
Chen, Y., Narasimhan, C. and Zhang, J. (2001), "Consumer heterogeneity and competitive price matching guarantees," *Marketing Science*, **20** (3), 300–314.
Chu, W. (1992), "Demand signaling and screening in channels of distribution," *Marketing Science*, **11** (4), 324–47.
Corstjens, M. and Lal, R. (2000), "Building store loyalty through store brands," *Journal of Marketing Research*, **37** (3), 281–91.

Coughlan, A.T. and Soberman, D.A. (2005), "Strategic segmentation using outlet malls," *International Journal of Research in Marketing*, **22** (1), 61–86.

Datta, S. and Sudhir, K. (2009), "Sleeping with the frenemy: the agglomeration–differentiation tradeoff in spatial location choice," Working Paper, Yale School of Management.

Desai, P.S. (2000), "Multiple messages to retain retailers: signaling new product demand," *Marketing Science*, **19** (4), 381–9.

Diamond, P.A. (1971), "A model of price adjustment," *Journal of Economic Theory*, **3**, 156–68.

Dukes, A., Geylani, T. and Srinivasan, K. (2009), "Strategic assortment reduction by a dominant retailer," *Marketing Science*, **28** (2), 309–19.

Dutta, S., Bergen, M.E., Levy, D. and Venable, R. (1999), "Menu costs, posted prices, and multiproduct retailers," *Journal of Money, Credit, and Banking*, **31** (4), 683–703.

Edlin, A. (1997), "Do guaranteed-low price policies guarantee high prices, and can antitrust rise to the challenge?," *Harvard Law Review*, **111**, 528–75.

Gourville, J.T. and Moon, Y. (2004), "Managing price expectations through product overlap," *Journal of Retailing*, **80** (1), 23–34.

Gourville, J.T. and Wu, G. (1996), "Tweeter etc.," *Harvard Business School Premier Case Collection*, 597028.

Hess, J.D. and Gerstner, E. (1991), "Price-matching policies: an empirical case," *Managerial and Decision Economics*, **12**, 305–15.

Hoch, S.J., Dreze, X. and Purk, M.E. (1994), "EDLP, hi–lo and margin arithmetic," *Journal of Marketing*, **58**, 16–27.

Hotelling, H. (1929), "Stability in competition," *Economic Journal*, **39** (1929), 41–57.

Humby, C. and Hunt, T. (2004), *Scoring Points*, London: Kogan Page.

Iyer, G. and Pazgal, A. (2003), "Internet shopping agents: virtual co-location and competition," *Marketing Science*, **22** (1), 85–106.

Krishnan, T.V. and Rao, R.C. (1995), "Double couponing and retail pricing in a couponed category," *Journal of Marketing Research*, **32** (November), 419–32.

Krishnan, T.V., Koelemeijer, K. and Rao, R. (2002), "Consistent assortment provision and service provision in a retail environment," *Marketing Science*, **21** (1), 54–73.

Kuksov, D. (2006), "Search, common knowledge, and competition," *Journal of Economic Theory*, **130**, 95–108.

Kuksov, D. and Lin, Y. (2010), "Information provision in a vertically differentiated competitive marketplace," *Marketing Science*, **29** (1), 122–38.

Kuksov, D. and Pazgal, A. (2007), "The effects of costs and competition on slotting allowances," *Marketing Science*, **26** (2), 259–67.

Kuksov, D. and Villas-Boas, J.M. (2010), "When more alternatives lead to less choice," *Marketing Science*, **29** (3), 507–24.

Kumar, N. and Rao, R.C. (2006), "Using basket composition data for intelligent supermarket pricing," *Marketing Science*, **25** (2), 188–99.

Kumar, N. and Ruan, R. (2006), "On manufacturers complementing the traditional retail channel with a direct online channel," *Quantitative Marketing Economics*, **4**, 289–323.

Lal, R. and Bell, D. (2003), "The impact of frequent shopper programs in grocery retailing," *Quantitative Marketing Economics*, **1** (2), 179–202.

Lal, R. and Matutes, C. (1989), "Price competition in multi-market duopolies," *RAND Journal of Economics*, **20** (4), 516–37.

Lal, R. and Matutes, C. (1994), "Retail pricing and advertising strategies," *Journal of Business*, **67** (3), 345–70.

Lal, R. and Rao, R.C. (1997), "Supermarket competition: the case of everyday low pricing," *Marketing Science*, **16** (1), 60–80.

Lal, R. and Sarvary, M. (1999), "When and how is the internet likely to decrease price competition?," *Marketing Science*, **18** (4), 485–503.

Lal, R. and Villas-Boas, M. (1998), "Price promotions and trade deals with multi-product retailers," *Management Science*, **44**, 935–49.

Lariviere, M. and Padmanabhan, V. (1997), "Slotting allowances and new product introductions," *Marketing Science*, **16** (2), 112–28.

McGuire, T.W. and Staelin, R. (1983), "An industry equilibrium analysis of downstream vertical integration," *Marketing Science*, **2** (Spring), 161–92.

Moorthy, S. (2005), "A general theory of pass-through in channels with category management and retail competition," *Marketing Science*, **24** (1), 110–22.

Moorthy, S. and Zhang, X. (2006), "Price matching by vertically differentiated retailers: theory and evidence," *Journal of Marketing Research*, **43** (May), 156–67.

Narasimhan, C. (1984), "A price discrimination theory of coupons," *Marketing Science*, **3** (2), 128–47.

Narasimhan, C. (1988), "Competitive promotional strategies," *Journal of Business*, **61** (4), 427–49.

Pan, Xing, Brian Ratchford and Venkatesh Shankar (2004), "Price dispersion on the Internet: a review and directions for future research," *Journal of Interactive Marketing*, **18** (4), 116–35.

Pan, Xing, Venkatesh Shankar and Brian Ratchford (2002), "Equilibrium e-tailer prices: pure play vs. bricks-and-clicks e-tailers," *Advances in Applied Microeconomics*, Vol. 11, *Economics of Internet and E-Commerce*, pp. 29–61.

Peterson, R.A. and Balasubramanian, S. (2002), "Retailing in the 21st century: reflections and prologue to research," *Journal of Retailing*, **78** (1), 9–16.

Png, I.P. and Hirshleifer, D. (1987), "Price discrimination through offers to match price," *Journal of Business*, **60**, 365–83.

Raju, J.S., Srinivasan, V. and Lal, R. (1990), "Effectiveness of brand loyalty on competitive price promotional strategies," *Management Science*, **36** (30), 276–304.

Rao, R.C. and Syam, N. (2001), "Equilibrium price communication and unadvertised specials by competing supermarkets," *Marketing Science*, **20** (1), 61–81.

Rao, R.C., Arjunji, R.V. and Murthi, B.P.S. (1995), "Game theory and empirical generalizations concerning competitive promotions," *Marketing Science*, **14**, G89–G100.

Shaffer, G. (1991), "Slotting allowances and retail price maintenance: a comparison of facilitating practices," *RAND Journal of Economics*, **22** (1), 120–35.

Shilony, Y. (1977), "Mixed pricing in an oligopoly," *Journal of Economic Theory*, **14** (April), 373–88.

Sullivan, M.A. (1997), "Slotting allowances and the market for new products," *Journal of Law and Economics*, **40** (2), 461–93.

Thomadsen, R. (2005), "The effect of ownership structure on prices in geographically differentiated industries," *RAND Journal of Economics*, **36** (4), 908–29.

Thomadsen, R. (2010), "Seeking an aggressive competitor: how product line expansion can increase all firms' profits," Working Paper, University of California, Los Angeles.

Thomadsen, R. and Pazgal, A. (2010), "Profit-increasing entry," Working Paper, University of California, Los Angeles, Anderson Graduate School of Management.

Varian, H. (1980), "A model of sales," *American Economic Review*, **70** (4), 651–9.

Villas-Boas, J.M. (1995), "Models of competitive price promotions: some empirical evidence from the coffee and saltine crackers markets," *Journal of Economics and Management Strategy*, **4** (1), 85–107.

Zhang, Q., Gangwar, M. and Seetharaman, P.B. (2010), "Examining store loyalty as a category specific trait," Working Paper, The University of Iowa.

Zhu, T., Singh, V. and Dukes, A. (2010), "Local competition, entry and agglomeration," Working Paper, University of Southern California.

PART III

CUSTOMER-BASED MARKETING STRATEGY

7 Customer lifetime value management: strategies to measure and maximize customer profitability

V. Kumar and Bharath Rajan

> All customers are created equal, but some are more equal than others.
> (Inspired by George Orwell, *Animal Farm*, 1945)

1. INTRODUCTION

Customer lifetime value (CLV) is an indicator of the total financial contribution a customer is likely to give the company over his/her lifetime with the company. It can serve as the basis for formulating and implementing customer-specific strategies for maximizing customers' lifetime profits and increasing their lifetime duration. In other words, CLV helps firms treat each customer differently based on his/her contribution, instead of treating all the customers in a similar fashion. Implementing the CLV framework has tremendous implications for profitable customer management and firm profitability.

Increasingly, companies are focusing on building and maintaining profitable individual-level customer relationships in order to maximize firm profitability. This is not an easy task as managers have to keep up with the changing face of customers. This calls for keeping track of customers, maintaining consistency within the organization and satisfying customers' needs in order to enjoy continued patronage. This task becomes even more difficult in non-contractual settings where customers are not bound by contracts/agreements to stay with the firm (such as grocery store purchases). To address all of these challenges, companies have adopted innovative customer relationship management (CRM) strategies to effectively manage customers and ensure higher profitability.

We begin this chapter with a discussion on the concept and definition of CLV. The subsequent section explores the need for measuring and managing CLV by contrasting the accuracy of CLV with the other traditional metrics used in managing customers' value. We then discuss the drivers of CLV in a B2B and a B2C setting. In the subsequent section, we provide an integrated approach to managing CLV that accounts for the nature (B2B versus B2C) and the type (contractual versus non-contractual) of relationships between customers and firms. In this approach, we consider B2B and B2C companies that vary distinctly in the nature of relationships between the company and its customers. Within this distinction, we also recognize the type of relationships characterized as contractual or non-contractual. Integrating these distinctions, we provide an approach for companies to managing CLV that is applicable to both B2B and B2C companies. The strategies discussed here are tried and tested by companies across various sectors, and have helped the companies increase profitability significantly. We also offer managerial guidelines for the implementation of the CLV strategies in an organization. Finally, we outline areas and topics for future research opportunities.

2.   CUSTOMER LIFETIME VALUE – CONCEPT AND DEFINITION

We can define CLV as follows:

> The sum of cumulated future cash flows – discounted using the weighted average cost of capital (WACC) – of a customer over their entire lifetime with the company. (Kumar 2008b, p. 37)

As is evident from this definition, CLV measures the worth of a customer to the firm. Once companies calculate the CLV of their customers, they can rank-order them on the basis of their contribution to the firm's profits. Such an exercise will lay the foundation for the development and implementation of customer-specific strategies that can maximize each customer's lifetime profits and increase each customer's lifetime duration. In other words, a customer management approach based on CLV will help the firm treat each customer differently based on their profit contribution, rather than treating all customers the same.

Further, CLV provides an indication to the company on how much it can invest in retaining the customer in order to achieve a positive ROI (return on investment). Given that firms are always constrained by resources, their objective will therefore be to focus on investing in those customers who will bring maximum return to the firm. Achieving this objective is made possible by knowing the cumulated cash flow of a customer over his or her entire lifetime with the company, or the lifetime value of the customers.

While the definition of CLV involves calculating the lifetime value of a customer over his/her "lifetime", in reality we compute the CLV over a three-year time period for most applications. This "shortened lifetime" consideration is due to the following reasons:

1. In many instances, a customer's needs and preferences change after three years. In such situations, a full lifetime CLV computation may not yield valuable insights into customer profitability.
2. In many product categories, the product's place in the product life cycle changes. For instance, a product may have entered the "maturity" phase from a "growth" phase. In this case, considering a future revenue stream beyond three years from the product that has changed its stage in the life cycle may not yield relevant results.
3. Prior studies have estimated that nearly 80 percent of profit from customers comes in three years if the discount rate is in the range of 15 percent to 18 percent (Gupta and Lehmann 2005).
4. If longer time periods are considered for computing CLV, the models' predictive accuracy tends to decline.
5. Owing to the discount factor, contributions discounted beyond a three-year window will yield a smaller value and will therefore be of little use to decision making.

However, there are exceptions to this three-year measurement period. For instance, the auto industry has a different purchase pattern from the other industries. Here, for at least three purchases to occur, we suggest 20 years for the future time horizon. Therefore, the lifetime period for automobile customers would be 20 years. Similarly, the insurance industry takes up to seven years to recover its acquisition costs. Therefore we suggest the lifetime period for insurance customers to be between seven and ten years. So, why is it important to compute CLV?

3.   NEED FOR MEASURING AND MAXIMIZING CUSTOMER LIFETIME VALUE

To understand the need and importance of measuring CLV, we should consider how it performs with respect to the traditionally used metrics for measuring customer value. The traditionally used metrics are based on various concepts and procedures that are used to compute the value of a customer. Some are based on simple notions, whereas some require the application of mathematical techniques. While there are over 50 important metrics that every executive should know (Farris et al. 2006), in this section we review only a few that are popular. Table 7.1 provides a review of some of the popular marketing metrics used by practitioners.

Despite the area and scope covered by the metrics given in Table 7.1, they are not as comprehensive as the CLV metric. Let us now look into the shortcomings of each of the three classes of metrics.

The traditional marketing metrics have been adopted by marketing professionals for years and are used in measuring performance of brands, products and firms in a given geographical region. Even though these metrics (a) convey an important piece of information and can be readily computed, and (b) act as a flag for the management and serve as an indicator of the current health of the firm, they only give an aggregate view of performance and do not help companies in identifying which customers grew and which ones did not.

The primary customer-based metrics help managers determine the value each individual buyer brings to the customer base of the firm. These metrics were developed since managers were very sensitive toward balancing acquisition and customer retention activities. However, these metrics do not reveal the total value that a customer can provide to a firm.

The strategic customer-based value metrics are the popular metrics of customer value used in the industry. Despite providing a much improved way of estimating the value of a customer over the other two classes of metrics, this class of metrics still suffers from some drawbacks. Since share of wallet (SOW) is based on a set of responses from a representative sample of customers, it does not provide a way to clearly determine future revenues and profits from a customer. While recency, frequency and monetary value (RFM) accounts for the timing and value of purchases better than SOW, it fails to consider other factors that affect the future purchase behavior of the customer. The RFM, past customer value (PCV) and SOW metrics, apart from not accounting for future purchase behavior, also do not consider the costs in managing future customer relationships. In essence, these metrics are backward-looking, and lack the ability to look into the future and predict the value that a customer is likely to bring into the firm.

When we contrast these three classes of metrics with CLV, we can see that the last incorporates both the probability of a customer being active in the future and the marketing dollars to be spent to retain the customer. Further, CLV helps managers make

Table 7.1   Review of some popular marketing metrics

Class of metrics	Name of the metric	Description of the metric
Traditional marketing metrics	• Market share	Share of a firm's sales in relation to the sales of all firms in the industry – across all customers
	• Sales growth	Increase or decrease in sales volume or sales value in a given period to sales volume or value in the previous period
Primary customer-based metrics	• Customer acquisition	"Acquisition rate" is the proportion of prospects that is converted to customers "Acquisition cost" is the acquisition campaign spending divided by the number of acquired prospects
	• Customer activity	"Average inter-purchase time" is the average time between purchases, measured in terms of time periods (days, weeks, months etc.) "Retention rate" is the percentage of customers making a purchase in a given time period, given that they have purchased in the previous time period "Defection rate" is the percentage of customers actually defecting in a given time period, given that they have purchased in the previous time period. Also defined as $(1 - \text{Retention rate})$. "P(Alive)" is the probability of the customer being active at time t
	• Customer win-back	Proportion of acquired customers in a particular period that the company had lost in an earlier period
Strategic customer-based value metrics	• Share of wallet (SOW)	Degree to which a customer meets his/her needs in the category with a focal brand or firm
	• Recency, Frequency and Monetary value (RFM)	Recency is the time since a customer last placed an order with the firm. Frequency is how often a customer purchases from the firm in a particular time period. Monetary value is the value of purchases by a customer in an average transaction
	• Past customer value (PCV)	Present value of a customer as determined by his/her profit contribution in the past, after adjusting for the time value of money

Source: Adapted from Kumar and Reinartz (2006).

an informed decision as to when a customer buys, how much a customer buys and how much it costs to make the sale. Additionally, the purpose of calculating customer value is to design customer-level strategies so that firms can maximize ROI. After establishing that CLV is a conceptually better metric to manage customers, the following section discusses how CLV can be measured.

4. MEASURING CUSTOMER LIFETIME VALUE

Customer lifetime value looks at a customer's value to the organization, based on predicted future costs and transactions. So, managers would be interested to know how the value of a client has evolved over time. In other words, CLV is a multi-period evaluation of a customer's value to the firm, and it assists managers to allocate resources optimally and develop customer-level marketing strategies.

When computing CLV, managers have to consider the setting in which the customer purchases are being made, that is, contractual and non-contractual. A contractual setting is one where the customers are bound by a contract, such as a mobile phone subscription. On the contrary, in a non-contractual setting the customers are not bound by a contract, such as grocery store purchases. That is, in a contractual setting, the firm gets fixed monthly revenue through the subscription. But this would be missing in a non-contractual setting. Therefore, these differences will have to be included while computing CLV. To cover both the situations, CLV can be expressed in the following form:

$$CLV_i = \sum_{t=1}^{T} \frac{Base\ GC}{(1+r)^t} + \sum_{t=1}^{T} \frac{\hat{p}(Buy_{it} = 1)*\hat{GC}_{it}}{(1+r)^t} - \frac{\hat{MC}_{it}}{(1+r)^t} \tag{7.1}$$

Where:
CLV_i = lifetime value for customer i
$\hat{p}(Buy_{it})$ = predicted probability that customer i will purchase additional product(s)/service(s) in time period t
$\hat{GC}_{it}$ = predicted gross contribution margin provided by customer i in time period t
$\hat{MC}_{it}$ = predicted marketing costs directed toward customer i in time period t
t = index for time periods; such as months, quarters, years, etc.
T = the end of the calibration or observation timeframe
r = monthly discount factor
Base GC = predicted base monthly gross contribution margin
Equation (7.1) above can also be written as follows:

$$CLV_i = Baseline\ CLV + Augmented\ CLV$$

As is evident from Equation (7.1), this formula can be applied in both the contractual and non-contractual settings. Now, let us look how it works in each of the settings.

In a contractual setting, the first term ($\Sigma_{t=1}^{t} Base\ GC/(1+r)^t$) or the baseline CLV corresponds to the constant gross contribution that the customer is going to give to the firm. This could be either on a monthly, quarterly or annual basis. This term includes the marketing cost to retain the customer. The second term ($\Sigma_{t=1}^{T} \hat{p}(Buy_{it} = 1)*\hat{GC}_{it}/(1+r)^t$) corresponds to the predicted net present value of future purchases by the customer at a particular time period. The third term ($\hat{MC}_{it}/(1+r)^t$) corresponds to the additional marketing costs incurred to sell more product(s)/service(s) to the customer. The final value of these three components would yield the CLV in a contractual setting.

In a non-contractual setting, the first term ($\Sigma_{t=1}^{T} Base\ GC/(1+r)^t$) would not be valid as there is no constant flow of base income from a customer on a periodic basis. In short, there is no assured income due to subscriptions. Therefore there would be no baseline CLV for the firm. As with the previous case, the second term $(\Sigma_{t=1}^{T} \hat{p}(Buy_{it} = 1)*\hat{GC}_{it}/(1 + r)^t)$ corresponds to the predicted net present value of future purchases by the customer at a particular time period. The third term $(\hat{MC}_{it}/(1 + r)^t)$ corresponds to the additional marketing costs incurred to sell more product(s)/service(s) to the customer. The final value of these three components would yield the CLV in a non-contractual setting.

Once CLV has been computed, the summation of the lifetime values of all the customers results in the customer equity (CE) of the firm (Gupta et al. 2004). Given the changes and challenges in data availability and business needs, several other approaches to modeling and computing CLV have been developed. Kumar (2008a) provides a broad overview of alternative approaches to model CLV. With respect to customer equity, Villanueva and Hanssens (2007) provide an extensive and in-depth review of all the approaches to model CE, and provide a typology of the models. Table 7.2 provides a summary of the key insights from select CLV literature.

Now that we have learnt the concept of CLV and the various approaches to measure it, we need to clearly understand the factors that drive a profitable relationship with the customer and how they affect CLV. The identification of drivers benefit the firm in (a) providing a better understanding of a profitable customer relationship, and (b) helping managers take proactive measures to maximize a customer's lifetime value.

5.   DRIVERS OF CUSTOMER LIFETIME VALUE

The drivers of CLV are the main factors that affect the lifetime value of a customer. These drivers determine the nature of the relationship between the firm and the customer, and they help estimate the level of profitability and the CLV of each customer. The factors that drive profitable customer relationship are classified into exchange characteristics and customer heterogeneity. The profitable duration of customer–firm relationship depends, differentially, on the exchange characteristics at time t and on customer heterogeneity. The profitable lifetime duration can be expressed as (Reinartz and Kumar 2003):

   Profitable Lifetime Duration$_i$ = f (Exchange characteristics$_{it}$, Customer heterogeneity) (7.2)

   The exchange characteristics broadly include all the variables that affect and influence the customer–firm relationship, such as the customer spending level, cross-buying behavior, purchase frequency, product returns, marketing contacts made by the firm, and loyalty instruments. Customer heterogeneity refers to the demographic variables such as location of the customer, age, income levels, among others. As expected, the nature of business (whether B2B or B2C) determines the exchange characteristics and customer heterogeneity factors. Table 7.3 shows some of the typical CLV drivers in B2B and B2C settings. Other CLV drivers will have to be considered in other contexts. The following section provides a set of important CLV-based strategies that both B2B and B2C companies can adopt and implement.

Table 7.2 Summary of selected CLV literature

Name of the study	Study objective	Type of relationship	Nature of relationship	Type of drivers studied	CLV modeling approach	Type of model used	Focus on CLV maximization strategies (Yes / No)	Study outcome
Keane and Wang (1995)	Illustrate the application of the CLV concept to a newspaper	Contractual (stream revenue)	B2C	None	Aggregate	Deterministic	No	Computed the CLV of newspaper readers at the regional level that answered important questions related to regional sales performance, advertising spend, pricing strategy and spending on acquisition
Blattberg and Deighton (1996)	Propose a criterion to determine the optimal balance between acquisition and retention efforts	Contractual	B2B & B2C	Behavioral	Aggregate	Deterministic	Yes	Used a tool called "decision calculus" to build a model of relationship to identify a balance between acquisition and retention efforts
Berger and Nasr (1998)	Present a series of mathematical models for determination of CLV	Contractual	B2B & B2C	None	Aggregate & individual	Deterministic	No	Introduced five general classes of CLV models and used one of them to illustrate how to optimize the allocation of a promotional budget between acquisition and retention

Table 7.2 (continued)

Name of the study	Study objective	Type of relationship	Nature of relationship	Type of drivers studied	CLV modeling approach	Type of model used	Focus on CLV maximization strategies (Yes / No)	Study outcome
Pfeifer and Carraway (2000)	Introduce Markov chain models (MCM) for modeling customer relationships and calculating CLV	Non-contractual	B2C	None	Individual	Stochastic (Customer migration model, CMM)	No	Introduced and demonstrated that MCM could handle a wide variety of the customer relationship situations, including complicated situations for which algebraic solutions will not be possible
Reinartz and Kumar (2000)	Propose a method of computing CLV to test propositions about loyal customers that they: (a) are profitable customers; (b) contribute more profits over time; (c) cost less to serve; and (d) are willing to pay higher prices	Non-contractual	B2C	None	Individual	Deterministic	No	Demonstrated that loyal customers (a) are *not always* profitable, (b) do not contribute more profits over time, (c) demand premium service as they know their value to the company, and (d) believe they deserve lower prices

Libai et al. (2002)	Introduce a segment-based approach (as an alternative to an individual model) for customer profitability analysis	Non-contractual	B2C	Behavioral	Customer segment	Stochastic (CMM)	No	Demonstrated this segment-based approach in a retail environment to estimate long-run customer equity profitability using switching probabilities between segments with relative ease
Drèze and Bonfrer (2003)	Understand the impact of communication frequency on customer retention and ultimately on lifetime value	Non-contractual	B2C	Behavioral	Aggregate	Stochastic	Yes	Intercommunication time affects both attrition and consumer surplus and thus has a critical impact on the value of customers
Reinartz and Kumar (2003)	Develop a framework to compute CLV and identify factors that explain the variation in the profitable lifetime duration	Non-contractual	B2B & B2C	Behavioral	Individual	Deterministic	Yes	Illustrated the superiority of the proposed CLV framework by comparing other traditional frameworks used for evaluating customer value

Table 7.2 (continued)

Name of the study	Study objective	Type of relationship	Nature of relationship	Type of drivers studied	CLV modeling approach	Type of model used	Focus on CLV maximization strategies (Yes / No)	Study outcome
Venkatesan and Kumar (2004)	Develop a dynamic framework to maintain or improve customer relationships through optimal allocation of marketing resources and maximize CLV simultaneously	Non-contractual	B2B	Behavioral	Individual	Stochastic	Yes	Marketing contacts across various channels influence CLV nonlinearly. Customers who are selected on the basis of their lifetime value provide higher profits in future periods than do customers selected on the basis of several other customer-based metrics
Rust et al. (2004)	Present a unified strategic framework that enables competing marketing strategy options to be traded off on the basis of projected financial return	Non-contractual	B2C	Behavioral	Aggregate	Stochastic (Markov)	No	Demonstrated the validity of the framework by using data from the airline industry. The framework enables what-if evaluation of marketing return on investment, given a particular shift in customer perceptions

Thomas et al. (2004b)	Examine the optimal pricing strategy when the customer has decided to reinitiate the relationship	Contractual (stream revenue)	B2C	Behavioral	Individual	Stochastic	No	The optimal pricing strategy involves a low reacquisition price and higher prices when customers have been reacquired
Fader et al. (2005)	Propose a new model that links the RFM (recency, frequency, and monetary value) metric with CLV using "iso-value" curves	Non-contractual	B2C	Behavioral	Individual	Stochastic	No	Demonstrated that for low recency values, customers with high frequency present less CLV than other customers with lower frequency, suggesting that iso-value curves are highly nonlinear
Rust et al. (forthcoming)	Propose the adoption of Monte Carlo simulation algorithm that provides predictions on customer purchase propensity, customer profit (conditional on purchase), and firm marketing actions	Non-contractual	B2C	Behavioral	Individual	Stochastic	Yes	Demonstrated that the proposed model provides large improvements in prediction over the simpler models that previously have been shown to be best in the literature

Table 7.3   Drivers of CLV in B2B and B2C settings

	In a B2B firm (Kumar et al. 2008)	In a B2C firm (Reinartz and Kumar 2003)
Exchange characteristics	• Past customer spending level • Cross-buying behavior • Purchase frequency • Recency of purchase • Past purchase activity • Marketing contacts by the firm	• Past customer spending level • Cross-buying behavior • Focused buying behavior • Average inter-purchase time • Participation in loyalty programs • Customer returns • Frequency on marketing contacts • Customer initiated contacts
Customer heterogeneity	Includes variables such as industry, annual revenue and location of the business	Includes variables such as age, gender, spatial income and physical location of the customers

6.   DEVELOPING CUSTOMER-FOCUSED MARKETING STRATEGIES FOR B2B AND B2C FIRMS

When developing marketing strategies, companies have long since focused on products rather than customers (Kumar et al. 2009). That is, they have adopted a product-centric approach as opposed to a customer-centric approach. In a product-centric approach, the firm attempts to solve the needs and problems of their customers by developing appropriate product solutions. This involves building a portfolio of products and conducting the business on transactions. In this type of strategy, the manager most likely thinks and acts on the following lines: (a) How many customers can we sell this product to? (b) How can we develop the product(s) and increase market share? (c) What product features and advantages can we promote and highlight? (d) How can we identify and develop successful products and sales teams? In this approach, the performance is typically measured by the number of new products developed, profitability per product, and the market share at the product/brand level. The drawback of such a strategy is that companies tend to overlook the customer-specific needs that can often lead to dissatisfaction and defection to competition. Of course, it would not be wise or viable for companies to produce products that satisfy every single need of every customer. So what can they do?

The solution to this is a customer-centric approach to develop marketing strategies. In a customer-centric approach, the intention is to serve customers rather than sell products. This would involve serving a portfolio of customers and conducting the business on relationships. In such an approach, the managers' focus will be on: (a) How many products can we sell to *this* customer? (b) How can we develop profitable customer relationships? (c) How can we highlight those product benefits that satisfy customer needs? (d) How can we identify profitable customer segment(s) and develop CRM teams? The performance of a customer-centric approach is often evaluated by the SOW of customers, customer satisfaction, CLV and customer equity. The significance of the customer-centric approach can be seen in companies like Wells Fargo, IBM, Texas Instruments and Harrah's that have successfully migrated from a product-centric approach.

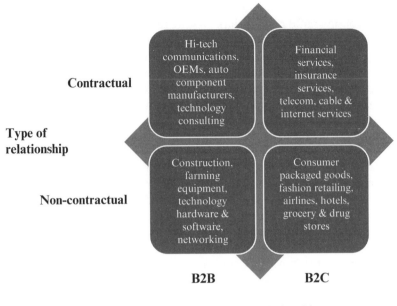

Construction, farming equipment, technology hardware & software, networking

Nature of relationship

Figure 7.1   Applications of CLV-based strategies

Given the scope and importance of a customer-centric approach, the need for a customer-focused metric becomes clear. Research has shown that CLV is the metric best suited to develop a customer-centric strategy owing to its ability to not only focus on the individual customer but also to look ahead and predict future customer profitability. If a company truly understood each customer's lifetime value, it could maximize its own value by increasing the number, scope and duration of value-creating relationships through customer-focused strategies.

So, what customer-focused strategies can firms develop in order to implement a truly customer-centric business relationship? Before we learn about the various customer-focused strategies, it is important to know where and how CLV is applicable. Figure 7.1 contains a 2 × 2 matrix that lists the several applications of the CLV metric along contractual, non-contractual, B2B and B2C business relationships.

As is evident from Figure 7.1, the matrix provides a flavor of those industries across B2B and B2C settings that can benefit by measuring and managing CLV. It is important to recognize the differences in the nature of relationships between B2B and B2C settings in order to develop appropriate CLV-based strategies.

While the basic tools and concepts of marketing may apply to both B2B and B2C companies, the considerable differences between the two settings have a significant impact on the design, evaluation and implementation of marketing strategies. For instance, a B2B firm may typically be characterized by the following: (a) fewer customers concentrated in specific geographic regions, (b) customized products/services that are highly technical, (c) shorter channels of distribution, (d) usage of rich communication modes (such as face-to-face, trade event meetings and telephone), and (e) availability of product/service upgrades to customers. Adopting rich modes of communication is a vital component in developing a profitable B2B relationship. Despite the high costs involved, the rich modes of communication offer a high level of personalization in retaining current customers and acquiring new ones. Rich modes are also preferred in situations when there is uncertainty in the relationship with the customers. Further, the rich modes are also helpful in converting transaction-based customers into relationship-based customers. Some of the classic examples in this setting are aircraft manufacturers, tractor manufacturers, brewers of hops and mining companies.

When contrasted with a B2C firm, the typical company may be characterized by: (a) large consumer segments spread over large regions; (b) largely standardized products, (c) larger distribution channels involving several channel partners; (d) usage of standardized communication modes (such as email, catalogs and direct mails); and (e) providing cross-buying opportunities to consumers. Here, standardized modes of communication are best suited owing to a widespread consumer market. They offer a cost-effective solution to communication with the individual customers. This mode can be used effectively to communicate the various cross-buying initiatives and current promotions offered by the company. Even for transaction-based customers, standardized modes can be used in conjunction with the rich modes to improve the effectiveness of the marketing initiatives. For example, direct mail (standardized) can be used along with telephone sales (rich mode) to improve the return on investment. Additionally, even trade shows and exhibitions may be useful. In the case of relationship-based customers, standardized modes can be used to maintain commitment and trust by regularly communicating the relationship benefits to these customers.

Similarly, the distinction between a contractual versus a non-contractual type of relationship has important implications for the calculation of CLV and the subsequent development of CLV-based strategies. For instance, a contractual relationship is characterized by: (a) the presence of a baseline CLV or a regular future stream of revenue contribution in addition to periodic revenue contribution from a consumer; and (b) the opportunity to model up-sell and cross-sell initiatives that can advise companies about the right time to pitch the right product(s) to the right customer(s). A classic example of this type of relationship is the mobile phone subscription. As noted earlier in the numerical example, a mobile phone subscriber provides a constant revenue stream every month until she remains a customer of that service provider. Even at the time of signing up for the subscription, the service provider will cross-sell phone accessories such as phone cases, screen protectors, hands-free and Bluetooth devices, and car charging kits among others. During the contract period of the customer with the service provider, cross-sell initiatives such as unlimited text messaging plans and mobile broadband plans and up-sell initiatives such as moving to a higher plan that offers more talk-time minutes and offers for better phones, are very common. Finally, as the subscriber approaches the end of her subscription period, the service provider sends up-sell offers such as an additional free phone(s) with renewal of the subscription or free additional lines/upgrades to a family plan with a subscription renewal, all in an effort to retain the customer.

A non-contractual relationship, on the other hand, is characterized by: (a) the presence of only the augmented CLV, as there is no regular flow of revenue contribution; and (b) the opportunity to model the inter-purchase time of products by the consumers.

This is perhaps the most common type of business relationship that exists between businesses and between businesses and consumers. Even if there is a contract between the firm and its customers, it is only for a specific order or for a specific time period. In the B2B setting, examples of this type of relationship could range from technology hardware and software purchases, office supplies, business and technology consulting, office maintenance services, equipment hiring and leasing services, advertising and PR services, staffing and recruitment services, financial and tax planning services, to travel desk services. In the case of B2C relationships, examples include grocery and drug purchases, clothing purchases, media and entertainment purchases, vacation and travel purchases, restaurant services, car rental services, among others. In both types of relationships, firms would be interested in modeling the average inter-purchase time (AIT) of their customers. AIT refers to the average time (in days, weeks, months etc.) between two purchases. Past research studies have shown that the CLV tends to be smaller when the AIT is either too short or too long. For instance, consider a customer of a catalog retailer. It is unlikely that the customer who makes several purchases within a very short period of time will continue to do so over extended periods. Such items are purchased in continuous, regularly spaced intervals. This customer might be stocking up on the merchandise that should last for a long time, and is unlikely to come back to the firm. There is a lower limit for the average purchase time as well. Customers who do not make a purchase over long periods of time are more likely to have switched to a competitor or stopped using the product altogether, and hence have a low CLV.

Therefore it is clear that the CLV metric is applicable to a wide variety of business relationships. When companies recognize these distinctions in business relationships, they will be in a better position to make informed decisions about profitable customer management. This also leads to the development of efficient and effective customer-focused marketing strategies. The following section provides some of the most popular and proven strategies developed based on the CLV metric.

7. CLV-BASED MARKETING STRATEGIES

Once the computation of CLV is completed, firms progress to maximizing it in order to reap the full benefits of the metric. It is important to note that the CLV metric is not just about the dollar value of future customer profitability. It extends beyond that and holds important implications for the marketing initiatives for a company and enables them to address marketing issues with greater confidence. Some of the strategic implications of adopting the CLV-based approach are spelt out below:

- How do firms decide which customers should be provided with preferential and sometimes personal treatment?
- How can firms ensure profitable customer loyalty among their customers?
- Which customers should the firms contact through inexpensive channels like the Internet or the touch-tone phone, and which let go?
- How do firms decide the timing of an offering to a customer?
- How do firms decide which prospect will make a better customer in the future, and is therefore worthwhile to acquire now?

- Having got the customer to transact with the firm, what kind of sales and service resources should the firm allocate to conduct future business with that customer?
- How should firms monitor customer activity in order to readjust the form and intensity of their marketing initiatives?
- How do firms leverage the CLV metric to drive their stock price and provide more value to their stakeholders?

Recent research studies in the area of CRM have provided answers to the above set of questions. The answers have been in the form of actionable marketing strategies. The starting point for all these strategies is selecting the right customers based on future profitability or CLV. Past research has shown that customers who are selected based on the CLV score generate about (a) 40 percent greater average revenue, (b) 42 percent more gross value, and (c) 45 percent more net value than customers selected through other traditional metrics like RFM, PCV and SOW (Kumar et al. 2008).

The next step is to manage loyalty and profitability of these customers simultaneously. Reinartz and Kumar (2002) show that loyal customers know their value to the company and demand premium service, believe they deserve lower prices, and spread positive word-of-mouth only if they feel *and* act loyal. All these would lead managers to identify those customers who provide the most value to the company and prioritize the marketing efforts accordingly. When resources are reallocated based on the optimal mix and frequency of communication channels, Venkatesan and Kumar (2004) show that in the case of a B2B company revenue realized increased by 100 percent and profits increased by 83 percent across selected customer segments. Further, it was identified that if the firm were to adopt similar resource allocation strategies for the entire customer base, the additional revenue generation would amount to $1 billion.[1] These insights can then be used as the basis for deciding which customers to pursue in the future. The remainder of this section describes select strategies that have enabled companies to manage their customers profitably.

7.1   What Products to Offer, to Which Customers, and at What Time?

The business problem
Managers are often confounded by the acceptance rate of the marketing offers they promote. That is, when promoting up-sell and cross-sell initiatives, managers would want all the customers to accept the offers provided to them. However, this seldom happens. So, what can managers do to predict what product a customer is going to buy and when, and approach her with a customized offer or promotion for all the product/services she is likely to buy?

The strategy
Estimate (a) the sequence in which a customer is likely to buy multiple products or across multiple product categories, (b) the time at which the customer expected to buy each product, and (c) the expected revenue from that customer.

How it works
Traditionally, a company estimates the purchase sequence by accounting for product choice (the probability that a customer will choose to purchase a particular product) and purchase timing (probability that a customer will make a purchase at a particular time) independently. By modeling these two simultaneously using Bayesian estimation, managers can estimate the purchase sequence more accurately.

How it measures up
This strategy was implemented in a high-tech B2B firm involving 20 000 customers. Results showed that the simultaneous modeling approach was able to improve profits by an average of $1600 per customer, representing an increase in ROI of 160 percent (Kumar et al. 2006). It was also found that while the traditional model can accurately predict which products customers will buy, it performs poorly in predicting the purchase timing.

What's in it for the managers
Predicting customer behavior is a crucial step in designing an effective marketing strategy. These predictions will enable managers to not only target the customers who are most likely to make a purchase, but also to pitch the right product. Additionally, this will avoid alienating customers by inundating them with promotions and offers. The benefits derived by reducing the mailing and other marketing costs more than compensate for the cost of customizing the promotions sent out, thus ensuring higher ROI on the marketing budget.

7.2   How Can Companies Retain Customers and Prevent Churn?

The business problem
When faced with customer attrition, managers face several important questions such as: (a) How do we identify the customers who are likely to defect? (b) When are they likely to defect? (c) Should we intervene and, if so, when? and (d) How much should we spend to avoid the attrition of a particular customer?

The strategy
The above-listed questions can be answered by building a "propensity to quit" model. These models give us the probability of a customer quitting at a particular point in time. Based on when the customer is likely to leave and his/her ability to contribute profits, firms can provide appropriate intervention strategies that will aid retention.

How it works
As mentioned earlier, the propensity to quit model provides firms with the likelihood that a customer will quit at a particular point in time. Standing in May, let us assume that the model indicates the likelihood of Customer A to quit in July is 0.4 and in August is 0.7. Then, managers would have to determine whether Customer A is worth retaining. This can be answered by applying the CLV metric. Business wisdom suggests that only profitable (positive CLV) customers should be intervened with offers. In this case,

if Customer A is profitable, then she has to be intervened with an offer at the beginning of August. Regarding the details of the intervention offer, managers can again use the CLV metric to guide them. If Customer A has a CLV of $100, it would not be appropriate to intervene with a $150 offer. Therefore the intervention offer will have to be less than $100.

How it measures up
This strategy was tested in a B2C telecommunications firm on test and control groups containing 2601 customers in each group having the same likelihood to quit (Kumar 2008b). While the control group did not receive any intervention offers, the test group received intervention offer(s). At the end of one year, the control group lost 833 customers. However, the test group lost only 190 customers. Controlling both groups of customers that were behaviorally the same, the test group saved 643 customers. At an average revenue contribution per customer of $600, these 643 saved customers translated into a revenue gain of $385 800 for the firm. When the cost of the intervention offer of $40 000 was deducted from this revenue gain, the firm gained an incremental profit of $345 800 with an ROI close to 860 percent.

What's in it for the managers
Identifying those customers likely to quit and reaching them with appropriate marketing messages holds the key to a favorable retention strategy. This strategy helps managers in more ways than one. First, managers can now prevent the loss of revenue by retaining the customers. Second, it gives them the extended duration in which initial customer acquisition costs can be recouped. Third, it provides them with important implications on the up-sell/cross-sell strategies and how they can be used as intervention offers. Finally, it helps them prevent the possible negative word-of-mouth instances from customers who quit.

7.3   Does Multichannel Shopping Lead to Revenue Growth?

The business problem
Having prevented customer attrition, managers need to know how to realize revenue growth from their customers. Given the overwhelming empirical evidence, a popular method of increasing revenue growth is adding more channels for customers to shop in. However, with the proliferation of channels for shopping, firms worry that it will lead to spreading the same revenue across multiple channels, that is, cannibalization of sales. Does this concern hold water? If not, can multiple shopping channels help firms to realize revenue growth?

The strategy
To effectively manage multiple channels, firms have to first identify who the multichannel shoppers are. This calls for identifying the drivers associated with purchase behavior across multiple channels. After identifying the drivers, firms have to determine whether multichannel shoppers: (a) are more likely to buy in the future; (b) spend more money; and (c) are more profitable than single-channel customers. The answers will help firms determine the profitability of the multichannel customers. Finally, managers also

need to ascertain which channel a customer is likely to adopt next and when this is likely to happen.

How it works

Identifying the drivers of multichannel shoppers holds the key to understanding the differences between multichannel and single-channel shoppers. The association of customer-specific characteristics (e.g. how many categories a customer purchases in), supplier-specific characteristics (e.g. how often a customer receives marketing communications) and demographic information (e.g. the income level of the customer) with multichannel shopping is empirically evaluated using an ordered logistic regression. This statistical model captures the differences in the effect of each of the preceding drivers on the probability of a customer buying from a single channel or multiple channels. After obtaining the weights for each of the drivers by estimating the model, we can see how each driver influences a customer's decision to shop in a single channel or multiple channels.

To determine whether multichannel shoppers are profitable or not, we have to compare the performance of single and multichannel customers along a set of customer-based metrics commonly used by firms. These metrics include how much a customer spends (revenue), the percentage of money a customer spends on that firm's products versus a competitor's products (SOW), the customer's past profitability (PCV), the likelihood that a customer will buy in the future (likelihood of staying active), and the customer lifetime value (CLV).

To determine which channel a customer is likely to adopt next and when this is likely to happen, the following behavioral and psychological factors regarding choice and timing of channel adoption have to be considered: (a) the travel cost involved in purchasing and immediate product availability; (b) the total quantity of items a customer purchases in a single shopping trip, in which product categories, the level of price discounts, and the amount of product returns; (c) the customer's purchase frequency and the frequency of marketing communications; and (d) customer demographics such as age, gender and income.

How it measures up

The strategy was tested with a large B2B computer hardware and software manufacturer to identify the drivers and customer-based metrics (Kumar and Venkatesan 2005). Results for the customer-specific drivers showed that: (a) customers who buy across multiple product categories are likely to purchase across multiple channels and are good prospects for adopting new channels; (b) up to a certain threshold product returns are positively related to multichannel shopping, beyond which they are negatively related with multichannel shopping; (c) customers who initiate contacts with the supplier are more inclined to shop across multiple channels; (d) customers who use the online medium are also inclined to shop across multiple channels; (e) customers who have been with the firm for a longer period of time are more likely to shop across multiple channels than new customers; and (f) customers who have a high purchase frequency are associated with multichannel shopping.

With respect to the supplier-specific drivers, the results showed that: (a) the number of different channels used to contact the customer, (b) the type of contact channel, and

(c) the channel mix are strongly associated with multichannel shopping. Regarding customer demographics, variables such as the number of customer-service employees, the annual sales of the company and the industry category it belongs to can be used to profile customers who are likely to shop across multiple channels. While the customer demographic variables may not be helpful in building theoretical models, they are useful for identifying customers to acquire.

When the study compared the value of single-channel and multichannel shoppers across various customer-based metrics, the results showed that as a customer shops across more channels (from one channel to four channels), she spends more revenue with your firm, spends a higher proportion with your firm (rather than with a competitor), has a higher past profitability (which is correlated with future profitability), and has a higher likelihood of buying in the future. This shows that multichannel shoppers are more profitable than single-channel shoppers.

To determine the choice and timing of channel adoption, a B2C firm that sells apparel in discount stores, full-price stores and through the Internet was studied (Venkatesan et al. 2007). The results indicated that the time taken to adopt another channel is shorter when: (a) the travel cost involved in the current channels is higher; (b) customers' basket sizes (purchase quantities in a single shopping trip) are either very small or very large; (c) the level of buying across product categories is higher; (d) the level of price discounts a customer obtains is higher; (e) single-channel customers make intermediate levels of returns compared with customers who make very few or too many returns; (f) the purchase frequency is higher; and (g) the frequency of marketing communications to the customers is at an intermediate level. However, the time taken to adopt another channel is longer when: (a) the proportion of products the customer is able to consume immediately after purchase in the customer's current channels is higher; and (b) the number of returns made by a customer shopping across two channels is higher. With respect to customer demographics, the study found that: (a) the male customers were found to have shorter channel adoption duration and the female customers took 17 percent longer than the time taken by male customers to adopt a new channel; and (b) income is not related to channel adoption behavior.

When the channel adoption model was tested in the B2C firm using test and control groups, the results showed that adding one more channel resulted in an average net gain of about 80 percent. After accounting for the marketing costs, the increase in revenue translated into a return on investment increase of about eight times, or 800 percent.

What's in it for the managers
The results from the two field studies discussed above clearly demonstrate that adding more channels and encouraging customers to shop across more channels does not cannibalize sales revenue. On the contrary, it leads to a gain in revenue.

Additionally, by providing customers with multiple channels to research and purchase, firms have the chance to create channel synergies. An excellent case in point is the online retailer, Zappos.com. They have a 24/7 customer service number displayed on every page of their website. While this was done primarily as a part of their superior customer service program, it also creates another channel in which customers can shop. For an online shopper at Zappos.com, providing another contact channel (such as telephone) is likely to encourage him/her to adopt the new channel for research and/or purchase. Verhoef et al. (2007) refer to this feature as cross-channel synergy in a research-shopper perspective. Cross-channel synergy refers to increased effectiveness of a channel for a customer because the customer has used another channel from the same firm. For example, a customer may use the online help desk to understand the features of a personal computer, so the customer knows how to compare products and interact with salespersons once he/she is in the store to make the final purchase.

Finally, customers who shop in multiple channels tend to have a deeper relationship with the firm and are more loyal to the firm, and get more utility out of doing business with the firm. This strengthens the relationship between the firm and the customers and thereby increases the customer's profitability with the firm. The marketing literature provides many empirical studies that have found that the average multichannel customer buys more and is more valuable than the single channel (Neslin et al. 2006; Kumar and Venkatesan 2005; Kushwaha and Shankar 2007; Thomas and Sullivan 2005). These studies have found that multichannel customers are much more valuable than single-channel customers. However, Thomas and Sullivan (2005) note that in the case of a major multichannel US retailer, not every two-channel combination is better than every single combination, but the addition of another channel to a given channel is associated with a more valuable customer. Further, Neslin and Shankar (2009) present a multichannel customer management decision (MCMD) framework that structures the process by which the firm can develop and implement a multichannel strategy, and to use the framework to identify key customer management issues. Similarly, Kumar (2010) proposes a CLV-based multichannel, multimedia communications framework that also accounts for the marginal effect of marketing communications on profitability for each customer. Since this approach considers the marginal effect of marketing communications, it provides a dynamic view of individual customer profitability. Additionally, by including customer information from the company's database and the value they provided by the customers to the company, this framework advocates sending targeted messages using differentiated modes of communication and also identifies the appropriate modes of inbound communication.[2]

Considering all these results, managers can explore the option of creating reward and incentive programs that encourage customers to purchase across more product categories and channels. Such an exercise is sure to increase the bottom line of the firm.

7.4   Path to Customer Profitability – Customer Acquisition or Customer Retention?

The business problem
Each year companies spend billions of dollars on advertising to try to acquire new customers. For instance, the Newspaper Association of America reports that the combined newspaper, print and online advertising expenditures in 2009 amounted to nearly $28 billion, with retail organizations spending as much as $15 billion.[3] Despite these high levels of spending, a recent study found that a 68 percent reduction in marketing investment per customer would increase average customer profitability by 42 percent for a B2B service provider! Findings from a pharmaceutical company and a catalog retailer also showed that the marketing spending was not at the optimal level that maximized profitability (Thomas et al. 2004a). So why do companies end up overspending or

underspending on their customers, and what can they do to prevent such undesirable results? Should managers focus on customer acquisition or customer retention to ensure profitability?

The strategy
This business problem can be avoided when managers realize that: (a) after a certain point, the cost of acquiring and/or retaining an additional customer outweighs the future stream of profit accrued from that customer; (b) focusing on customers who are easy to acquire and easy to retain may improve short-term profitability, but will not hold out in the long run; and (c) acquiring all possible customers and retaining all customers will lead to wastage of marketing resources on some customers who will never be profitable. Many firms still practice one or all of the above three as part of their customer management strategies. The right approach therefore lies in balancing resources between acquisition and retention that will lead to profit maximization.

How it works
The key to developing a profit-maximizing resource allocation strategy is in answering the following three questions:

- How do we allocate resources between the different contact modes for acquisition and retention, under a budget constraint?
- Between acquisition and retention expenditures, which is more critical to ensure profitability?
- What is the impact of choices in communication channels on investment effectiveness?

The answers to these three questions lie in adopting a framework that can reveal the true relationships between acquisition, retention and profitability. The true relationships are learned by analyzing how firm actions, customer actions competitor actions and customer characteristics play a role in enhancing customer profitability.

Firm actions refer to the various controls that a firm has when marketing to customers. These include acquisition expenses, retention expenses and the contact mix for each customer. Customer actions refer to any actions that a customer takes to begin or continue a relationship with the firm. These include any form of customer-initiated contacts, buying across product categories and frequency of purchases. Competitor actions refer to the amount of access competitors have to a given customer. In a B2B setting, this can be determined by calculating the customer's SOW. If the SOW for a customer is high, the customer purchases almost exclusively from a focal firm and likely has a low probability of switching to a competitor. However, customers with a low SOW are already purchasing from competitors and could potentially be swayed to purchase more (or exclusively) from a competitor. Finally, customer characteristics represent either the firmographics (for B2B companies) or the demographics (for B2C companies) of a customer. These characteristics help managers in profiling of prospects or current customers and thereby help in launching specific marketing campaigns. After identifying these actions and characteristics, managers can determine the relative impact on profitability by each driver by running these following models as a simultaneous regression model.

$$\text{Acquisition} = f(\text{FirmActions}_{\text{acquisition}}, \text{Customer Actions}_{\text{acquisition}}, \text{Demographics}_{\text{acquisition}})$$
$$(7.3)$$

$$\text{Retention} = f(\text{Firm Actions}_{\text{retention}}, \text{Customer Actions}_{\text{retention}}, \text{Competitor Actions}_{\text{retention}})$$
$$(7.4)$$

$$\text{Profitability} = f(\text{Firm Actions}_{\text{profit}}, \text{Customer Actions}_{\text{profit}}, \text{Competitor Actions}_{\text{profit}})$$
$$(7.5)$$

When the weights for each of the drivers are obtained for the above three models, they can be plugged into these models and solved simultaneously subject to the profit maximization condition. This will yield the optimal amount of spending for acquisition and retention activities that can maximize profitability.

How it measures up
This strategy was implemented across three firms (a B2B service provider, a pharmaceutical company and a catalog retailer) by a recent study (Reinartz et al. 2005). With respect to the question on allocating resources between acquisition and retention, the study found in the case of the pharmaceutical company that a maximum profitability of $1603 was realized when $10 was spent on acquisition and $60 on retention per customer. Even though spending $70 on retention was found to yield the highest retention rate, it did not provide the highest level of profitability. This finding proves that retention rates are not the most accurate predictors of profitability.

The question of focusing on acquisition versus retention often arises when managers are faced with budget cuts. When the pharmaceutical company is faced with a 5 percent total marketing budget cut, one way to tackle this is to cut 5 percent from the acquisition and retention budgets. When both budgets are reduced in such a fashion, the study found that for every $1 underinvested in the relationship, optimal long-term profitability was reduced by $1.25.[4] However, if the firm chose to cut only the acquisition budget (say, a 25 percent cut) and not touch the retention budget, the study found that every $1 underinvested in the relationship would reduce the customer's optimal long-term profitability by $3.03. Further, the study found that reducing the acquisition and retention budgets by 10 percent (a $2 profit loss for every $1 cost savings) is better than reducing the total budget by reducing acquisition budget only (a $3 profit loss for every $1 acquisition cost savings). While this study shows that the equal decrease in spending for acquisition and retention results in a higher long-term customer profit (than a budget cut in acquisition spending alone), it is important for companies to perform analysis internally of how deviations in spending affect overall profitability.

Regarding the impact of choices in communication channels on investment effectiveness, the study found that if the B2B service provider allocated 80 percent of the number of communication instances to e-mail, 11 percent to telephone contacts, 7 percent to Web-based contacts and 2 percent face-to-face contacts, it would maximize customer profitability. In the case of using multiple channels to communicate, the study also found that profits are maximized when telephone interactions and e-mail messages are used simultaneously in 37 percent of the time telephone contacts are used. Additionally, sending e-mail messages 67 percent of the time a face-to-face contact is employed would maximize profitability.

What's in it for the managers

This strategy advises managers that it is imperative to consider acquisition and retention spending at the same time, and not independently. Equally important is to understand that profitability is based on how acquisition and retention spending interact. This implies that considering how much to spend on acquisition and retention alone may not be sufficient. The more important decision is how to balance acquisition and retention spending together to maximize profitability. By determining the drivers described here, managers should be able to allocate the right resources to the right customers by correctly linking acquisition and retention spending to each customer.

Having incorporated the above strategies, CLV can then be used to link the outcome of marketing initiatives to the firm's market capitalization, as measured by the firm's stock price. Kumar and Shah (2009) demonstrate that after the implementation of CLV-based strategies, the percentage increases in stock price for a B2B firm and a B2C firm were approximately 32.8 percent and 57.6 percent, respectively. In sum, the performance of the above-mentioned strategies illustrates the power of CLV in strengthening the role of marketers and in aligning the CMO's objectives with the CFO's agenda.[5]

8.   FUTURE RESEARCH DIRECTIONS

Thus far, we have reviewed the concept of CLV, the relevant theories that lead to the concept of CLV, and the various ways to measure and manage CLV. While the strategies discussed here may have been tried and tested across a wide range of B2B and B2C industries having contractual and non-contractual types of relationships, there still are some areas that can serve as the basis of future research. These areas include (but are not limited to):

- Considering business settings that involve resellers or agents would lead to richer and deeper insights on the applicability of CLV. One such area of future research could focus on identifying the lifetime value of dealers (e.g. car dealerships). In the case of US car dealerships, auto manufacturers sell their cars either through exclusive dealerships and/or dealerships that carry multiple brands. While both types of dealerships have their own advantages and disadvantages, the auto manufacturers need to find a reliable method of (re)allocating scarce marketing resources to the "best" performing dealerships. In this regard, a dealer lifetime value (DLV) would help manufacturers solve the reallocation problem. Specifically, the DLV would help manufacturers identify the "high-value" and "low-value" dealers and place them in appropriate deciles. And based on these dealer deciles, manufacturers can make decisions on resource (re)allocation and dealer promotions.

  Another area of future research could be the determination of performance potential of a salesperson. Traditionally, salesperson performance has been measured using qualitative measures such as teamwork, ability, motivation and personal skills, among others. Quantitative measures to evaluate salesperson performance include number of sales conversions, sales volume and profit. While the above measures may provide an indicator of salesperson effectiveness, there is no "hard" metric that directly links salesperson performance and the bottom line of the company. This calls for the estimation of salesperson lifetime value (SLV). Stated simply, SLV refers to the net present value of future cash flows from his/her customers after accounting for training and incentive expenses incurred on the salesperson. The identification of SLV would help managers to uncover the true potential of each salesperson, aid in personnel selection and recruitment, design training programs and training needs, and design incentive structure for the sales force.

- Integrating consumers, opinions and attitudes into the behavioral database (Bolton 1998). When information such as customer satisfaction and customer attitudes is incorporated into the customer database, it is interesting to observe their roles in determining the lifetime duration of the customers. In other words, literature has shown that customer behavior influences CLV (Reinartz and Kumar 2003). It is also known that customer attitudes influence customer behavior (Anderson 1998, Verhoef et al. 2002, and Hogan et al. 2003, to name a few), which in turn influences CLV. But do customer attitudes directly influence CLV? Answering this question is bound to provide insights into the reasoning behind customer behavior and how it affects customer profitability.

- Considering the impact of competitor actions on the focal firm's customer behavior. While past research studies have considered the customer's SOW with the focal firm as an indicator of competitor action, more specific data on competitor actions can lead to more accurate results. That is, a firm's ability to track competitive actions and to react appropriately has been modeled in the past (Narver and Slater 1990, Kumar 1994). However, modeling the customer reactions as a result of competitor actions has not been done. This stream of research would shed more light on marketing strategy and profitable CRM.

- Accommodating the impact of macroeconomic trends and new product introductions by competitors is likely to have important implications on CLV implementation. For instance, most CLV implementation studies have accounted for marketing and financial variables, but have not factored in macroeconomic trends that are bound to affect the results. By accounting for macroeconomic factors such as GDP growth rate, rate of unemployment, consumption and investment spending, and the international trade balance, the CLV implementation is likely to be more accurate and reflect market realities.

- Determining the optimal balance of resource allocation between traditional and new media and how they can maximize ROI. With the introduction of new media, the choice of communication platforms for marketing managers has increased. This calls for revisiting the ways in which marketing resources have been allotted between the traditional and new media channels. For instance, many companies assign yearly budgets for each communication channel, and design communication plans within those budgets to target customers. This approach leads to a sub-optimal allocation of resources and companies end up communicating poorly with their target customers. Therefore it is important for firms to consider individual customers' responsiveness to each marketing communication channel as well as the costs involved across various channels of communication when making resource allocation decisions. The challenge here for researchers lies in deciding on the optimal mix of media options and how they should be prioritized among the customer deciles in order to maximize ROI.

Given these and many more potential research areas, we can expect the CLV framework discussed here to undergo further sophistication. Specific refinements and improvements are expected in (a) the approach to measure CLV, (b) better understanding of the drivers of CLV, and (c) more empirical evidence regarding the application of CLV for resource allocation, product promotions, preventing customer attrition and managing multichannel shopping. Finally, all these future trends can be expected to facilitate marketing's accountability to the corporate boardroom.

9.   CONCLUSION

It is no secret that firms have started to treat customers differentially. This chapter only accentuates this fact by providing proven research studies that combine the nature (B2B versus B2C) and the type (contractual versus non-contractual) of relationships between customers and firms. By adopting the concept of CLV as a basis of profitable customer management and initiating strategies to maximize CLV, firms will be able to increasingly customize their marketing messages based on the customer's expected response and value to the firm.

Looking into the future, firms will be challenged to obtain a 360-degree view of the customer the moment he/she walks into the firm. This is only possible when firms have the necessary data and controls to generate actionable marketing strategies. Given the advances in data storage and processing, firms are on the right track to achieve this. However, with more refinements to the type of information to be collected and a better understanding of CLV concepts and strategies listed here, firms will be in a position to generate a customized marketing plan for every customer as soon as the information is provided.

NOTES

1.   For general information on resource allocation, see Shankar, Chapter 9 in this volume.
2.   For general information on multichannel strategy, see Verhoef, Chapter 8 in this volume.
3.   Newspaper Association of America, http://www.naa.org/TrendsandNumbers/Advertising-Expenditures. aspx. Accessed on June 17, 2010.
4.   It is important to note that acquisition and retention expenditures represent different proportions of the total budget. For instance, a 10 percent deviation in the acquisition budget from the optimal level would represent only a 2.11 percent deviation from the optimal budget.
5.   For general information on this topic, see Shankar, Chapter 24 in this volume.

REFERENCES

Anderson, Eugene W. (1998), "Customer satisfaction and word of mouth," *Journal of Service Research*, **1** (1), 5–17.

Berger, Paul D. and Nada I. Nasr (1998), "Customer lifetime value: marketing models and applications," *Journal of Interactive Marketing*, **12** (1), 17–30.

Blattberg, Robert C. and John Deighton (1996), "Manage marketing by the customer equity test," *Harvard Business Review*, **74** (4), 136–44.

Bolton, Ruth N. (1998), "A dynamic model of the duration of the customer's relationship with a continuous service provider: the role of satisfaction," *Marketing Science*, **17** (1), 45–65.

Drèze, Xavier and André Bonfrer (2003), "To pester or leave alone: lifetime value maximization through optimal communication timing," in Lee Kong Chian School of Business, *Research Collection*, Paper 1915, Wharton–SMU Research Center, Singapore Management University.

Fader, Peter S., Bruce G.S. Hardie and Lee Ka Lok (2005), "RFM and CLV: using iso-value curves for customer base analysis," *Journal of Marketing Research*, **42** (4), 415–30.

Farris, P.W., Neil T. Bendle, Philip E. Pfeifer and David J. Reibstein (2006), *Marketing Metrics: 50+ Metrics Every Executive Should Master*, New Jersey, NJ: Wharton School Publishing.

Gupta, S. and Donald R. Lehmann (2005), *Managing Customers as Investments: The Strategic Value of Customers in the Long Run*, New Jersey, NJ: Wharton School Publishing.

Gupta, Sunil, Donald R. Lehmann and Jennifer Ames Stuart (2004), "Valuing customers," *Journal of Marketing Research*, **41** (1), 7–18.

Hogan, John E., Katherine N. Lemon and Barak Libai (2003), "What is the true value of a lost customer?," *Journal of Service Research*, **5** (3), 196–208.

Keane, Timothy J. and Paul Wang (1995), "Applications for the lifetime value model in modern newspaper publishing," *Journal of Direct Marketing*, **9** (2), 59–66.

Kumar, V. (1994), "Forecasting performance of market share models: an assessment, additional insights, and guidelines," *International Journal of Forecasting*, **10** (2), 295–312.

Kumar, V. (2008a), "Customer lifetime value–the path to profitability," *Foundations and Trends in Marketing*, **2** (1), 1–99.

Kumar, V. (2008b), *Managing Customers for Profit: Strategies to Increase Profits and Build Loyalty*, Upper Saddle River, NJ: Wharton School Publishing.

Kumar, V. (2010), "A customer lifetime value-based approach to marketing in the multichannel, multimedia retailing environment," *Journal of Interactive Marketing*, **24** (2), 71–85.

Kumar, V. and Werner J. Reinartz (2006), *Customer Relationship Management: A Databased Approach*, Hoboken, NJ: John Wiley & Sons.

Kumar, V. and Denish Shah (2009), "Expanding the role of marketing: from customer equity to market capitalization," *Journal of Marketing*, **73** (6), 119–36.

Kumar, V. and Rajkumar Venkatesan (2005), "Who are the multichannel shoppers and how do they perform? Correlates of multichannel shopping behavior," *Journal of Interactive Marketing*, **19** (2), 44–62.

Kumar, V., Rajkumar Venkatesan and Bharath Rajan (2009), "Implementing profitability through a customer lifetime value framework," *Marketing Intelligence Review*, **2** (October), 32–43.

Kumar, V., Rajkumar Venkatesan and Werner Reinartz (2006), "Knowing what to sell, when, and to whom," *Harvard Business Review*, **84** (3), 131–7, 50.

Kumar, V., Rajkumar Venkatesan, Tim Bohling and Denise Beckmann (2008), "The power of CLV: managing customer lifetime value at IBM," *Marketing Science*, **27** (4), 585–99.

Kushwaha, Tarun L. and Venkatesh Shankar (2007), "Single channel vs. multichannel customers: determinants and value to retailers," Working Paper, Texas A&M University.

Libai, Barak, Das Narayandas and Clive Humby (2002), "Toward an individual customer profitability model," *Journal of Service Research*, **5** (1), 69–76.

Narver, John C. and Stanley F. Slater (1990), "The effect of a market orientation on business profitability," *Journal of Marketing*, **54** (4), 20–35.

Neslin, Scott A. and Venkatesh Shankar (2009), "Key issues in multichannel customer management: current knowledge and future directions," *Journal of Interactive Marketing*, **23** (1), 70–81.

Neslin, Scott A., Dhruv Grewal, Robert Leghorn, Venkatesh Shankar, Marije L. Teerling, Jacquelyn S. Thomas and Peter C. Verhoef (2006), "Challenges and opportunities in multichannel customer management," *Journal of Service Research*, **9** (2), 95–112.

Pfeifer, Phillip E. and Robert L. Carraway (2000), "Modeling customer relationships as Markov chains," *Journal of Interactive Marketing*, **14** (2), 43–55.

Reinartz, Werner J. and V. Kumar (2000), "On the profitability of long-life customers in a non-contractual setting: an empirical investigation and implications for marketing," *The Journal of Marketing*, **64** (4), 17–35.

Reinartz, Werner J. and V. Kumar (2002), "The mismanagement of customer loyalty," *Harvard Business Review*, **80** (7), 86–94.

Reinartz, Werner J. and V. Kumar (2003), "The impact of customer relationship characteristics on profitable lifetime duration," *The Journal of Marketing*, **67** (1), 77–99.

Reinartz, Werner, Jacquelyn S. Thomas and V. Kumar (2005), "Balancing acquisition and retention resources to maximize customer profitability," *Journal of Marketing*, **69** (January), 63–79.

Rust, Roland T., Katherine N. Lemon and Valarie A. Zeithaml (2004), "Return on marketing: using customer equity to focus marketing strategy," *Journal of Marketing*, **68** (1), 109–27.

Rust, Roland T., Rajkumar Venkatesan and V. Kumar (forthcoming), "Will the frog change into a prince? Predicting future customer profitability," *International Journal of Research in Marketing*.

Thomas, Jacquelyn S. and Ursula Y. Sullivan (2005), "Managing marketing communications with multi-channel customers," *Journal of Marketing*, **69** (4), 239–51.

Thomas, Jacquelyn, Werner Reinartz and V. Kumar (2004a), "Getting the most out of all your customers," *Harvard Business Review*, **82** (7–8), 116–23, 88.

Thomas, Jacquelyn S., Robert C. Blattberg and Edward J. Fox (2004b), "Recapturing lost customers," *Journal of Marketing Research*, **41** (1), 31–45.

Venkatesan, R. and V. Kumar (2004), "A customer lifetime value framework for customer selection and resource allocation strategy," *Journal of Marketing*, **68** (4), 106–25.

Venkatesan, Rajkumar, V. Kumar and Nalini Ravishanker (2007), "Multichannel shopping: causes and consequences," *Journal of Marketing*, **71** (2), 114–32.

Verhoef, Peter C., Philip Hans Franses and Janny C. Hoekstra (2002), "The effect of relational constructs on customer referrals and number of services purchased from a multiservice provider: does age of relationship matter?," *Journal of the Academy of Marketing Science*, **30** (3), 202–16.

Verhoef, Peter C., Scott A. Neslin and Björn Vroomen (2007), "Multichannel customer management: understanding the research-shopper phenomenon," *International Journal of Research in Marketing*, **24** (2), 129–48.

Villanueva, J. and D.M. Hanssens (2007), "Customer equity: measurement, management and research opportunities," *Foundation and Trends in Marketing*, **1** (1), 1–95.

8 Multichannel customer management strategy
Peter C. Verhoef

INTRODUCTION

Modern firms confront the options of multiple channels they can use to get in touch with their customers. Customers in turn can utilize multiple channels to search, purchase and receive after-sales services for those offerings. Prior to the widespread emergence of the Internet in the 1990s, though, firms typically used only a limited number of channels, unlike today, when their sales channels include the store, the Web, catalogs, sales forces, third-party agencies, call centers and so on (Neslin and Shankar 2009). And the number of channels just keeps increasing. New channels, such as mobile or smart phones (e.g. Shankar and Balasubramanian 2009) and new social media, such as social networking sites (e.g. Facebook, LinkedIn), create new challenges and opportunities (Hennig-Thurau et al. 2010). By 2014, as much as 8 percent of retail sales likely will occur online and 53 percent will be enabled by a website (Techcrunch 2010).

The arrival and expansion of these channels have created various complexities for firms that need to address the concept of channel multiplicity (Van Bruggen et al. 2010). Imagine a mobile phone manufacturer, such as HTC for example, that wants to get in touch with its customers. Not only does it need to run advertising campaigns in multiple media, but it also has to maintain its own Internet sites, manage its presence in retail chains and stores (which demands careful account management) and review evaluations of its company and products on various of independent websites and blogs – and so on. If it hopes to maintain relationships with its customers, it also needs to gather customer data, run a call and service center, host an Internet service platform, communicate directly with customers through the mobile channel and so on again. As this partial listing of responsibilities clearly shows, firms face nearly innumerable complexities as they attempt to manage their customer relationships through multiple channels. As a consequence, multichannel customer management has become a hot topic for firms in industries spanning consumer goods, services and retailing (Neslin and Shankar 2009).

Therefore in this chapter I discuss key issues for multichannel management. To provide a framework for this discussion, I outline the conceptual foundations and important topics of the field. Then I detail, for each topic, the most recent insights, key research questions and primary managerial implications. I close the chapter with a summary and discussion.

CONCEPTUAL FOUNDATIONS AND STRATEGIC FRAMEWORK

Channels have prompted long-standing interest among marketers (e.g. Coughlan et al. 2001), though most attention in traditional sales channel research centers on how

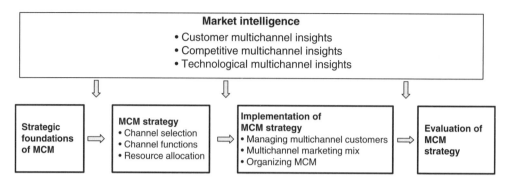

Figure 8.1   Strategic MCM framework

firms manage different distributor channels (Rangaswamy and van Bruggen 2005). Multichannel management demands a much broader range of activities and greater customer centricity. Neslin et al. (2006, p. 96) therefore introduce the concept of multi-channel customer management (MCM), which they define as "the design, deployment and evaluation of channels to enhance customer value through effective customer acquisi-tion, retention and development." In their conceptualization, channels represent customer contact points, that is, a medium through which the firm and the customer can interact.

Several proposed MCM frameworks (e.g. Neslin et al. 2006; Neslin and Shankar 2009; Wilson et al. 2008) in turn share certain common characteristics, as reflected in the summary framework I provide in Figure 8.1, consisting of four main components. Firms start by establishing a foundation for their MCM strategy and only then develop, imple-ment and evaluate their MCM strategy.

The entire process should be fueled by insights about customers, competitors and channel technologies. The use of customer insights to develop customer-centric MCM strategies should offer firms a competitive advantage (Hoekstra and Verhoef 2010; Jayachandran et al. 2005). One of the core issues for MCM customer insights involves data quality and data integration – extremely difficult goals for multichannel firms that collect their customer data across multiple channels. Ideally these data should be integrated across channels to provide a single view of customers (Zahay and Griffin 2002), although Neslin et al. (2006) argue that the marginal benefits of improved data quality decrease as costs increase, such that the profit-maximizing level of data quality features imperfect data. Competitor insights are required to observe which channels are deployed by competition. Firms might feel forced to adopt new channels because competitors adopt them (Neslin et al. 2006). However, they might also aim to create a first-mover advantage with early deployment of new channels. Finally, as multichannel operations are heavily influenced by technological innovations, firms need to constantly monitor new technological developments. Developments such as behavioral targeting may influence how firms operate their online operations, while also recent new develop-ments in mobile technology and social media strongly affect MCM strategies. [1]

In the following sections I shall focus on the four main blocks in the framework, on the basis of insights from marketing intelligence, as well as relevant issues with this approach.

STRATEGIC FOUNDATIONS OF MCM

Strategic Embedding of MCM

An MCM strategy should be based on the overall strategy of the firm. Firms that pursue a cost leadership strategy should have different MCM strategies than firms that pursue a differentiation strategy overall (Jindal et al. 2007). Among cost leaders, efficiency reasons are primary, but for differentiators, the creation of customer satisfaction is the most important goal. Similarly, firms that adopt customer relationship management (CRM) strategies with a focus on customer intimacy have different MCM strategies than firms that apply CRM to attain operational excellence (Langerak and Verhoef 2003).

Researchers offer several foundations or criteria for a MCM strategy. For example, Wilson et al. (2008) suggest the following strategic criteria: access (i.e. ability to reach sufficient number and range of potential customers), cost (to serve a customer through all steps of the life cycle) and experience (perceptions of the quality of the experience in the channel). Neslin and Shankar (2009) similarly discuss whether an MCM strategy pertains to efficiency, segmentation or customer satisfaction. From a managerial perspective, it is critical to establish the focus of the strategy, which guides its development. A strategy focused on lower costs to serve, for example, should attempt to move customers from costly (i.e. in-store) to low-cost (i.e. Internet) service channels.

Yet there is insufficient research into the foundations of MCM strategies. Jindal et al. (2007) consider the impact of business strategy on the number of channels that a firm uses. Their study shows that firms pursuing both a cost leadership strategy and a differentiation strategy tend to use more channels, whereas those firms that pursue a focused strategy or target a specific (niche) segment tend to use fewer channels. They also find that the customer orientation of a firm reduces the number of channels it uses. These findings at least provide evidence of a relationship between the pursued firm strategies and MCM strategies. Moreover, prior research offers some evidence that MCM strategies positively influence customer experiences, such that multichannel availability improves customer satisfaction (e.g. Danaher et al. 2003; Hitt and Frei 2002; Shankar et al. 2003). Improved customer satisfaction does not necessarily create greater loyalty though; rather, adding a channel potentially erodes customer loyalty (Ansari et al. 2008). Therefore firms that hope to improve customer satisfaction by adding channels to their multichannel strategy should take care to assess whether this improved customer satisfaction is also profitable.

Further Research

The preceding discussion demonstrates the need for additional research into the link between corporate strategies and MCM strategies. Researchers should investigate not only the number of channels used (e.g. Jindal et al. 2007) but also the effects of combining various channels across different phases. Other research could investigate the impact of a specific focus manifested in MCM strategies (i.e. cost versus experience focus) on customer responses and firm performance; research that investigates the contextual factors that may moderate these relationships seems particularly interesting. For example, what effects do market characteristics, such as the presence of alternatives, competitive intensity and customer involvement have on these relationships?

MCM STRATEGY

To develop their MCM strategy, firms need to select which channels to deploy, determine the functions of these deployed channels and allocate budgets and customers across the channels.

Channel Deployment

Which channels should a firm use? This question contains two sub-questions. First, should any channel new to that firm be added? Second, should any of the firm's existing channels be deleted? Thus far, research has mainly investigated the first sub-question.

Firms can take several theoretical factors into account in their channel addition decision: cross-channel synergy or cannibalization, competition, customer and market characteristics, potential channel conflicts, internal resources and strategy fit. For example, adding channels might cannibalize sales in other channels (cross-channel cannibalization) instead of creating synergies between them or growing the market by serving new market segments. Existing empirical evidence suggests minimal cross-channel cannibalization between online and offline channels in business-to-consumer (B2C) markets (Biyalogorsky and Naik 2003; Deleersnyder et al. 2002; Pauwels and Neslin 2008), but adding an online information channel may hurt retail sales in stores (van Nierop et al. 2011). Retail stores also cannibalize catalog sales (Pauwels and Neslin 2008); according to Shankar and Kushwaha (2008), some insurance industry channels can complement one another (Web, call center, exclusive agents), even as other channels offer substitutes (independent and exclusive agents). In addition, marketing efforts in one channel often enhance sales in another (Pauwels and Neslin 2008). Thus current research suggests that cannibalization (or negative cross-channel synergies) exist, but they depend on the channel combinations and the function of the channels.

Competition also may dictate the decision to add a new channel. Neslin et al. (2006) propose a potential prisoner's dilemma regarding the addition of new channels. Geyskens et al. (2002) notably suggest that in terms of order of entry, early followers gain a competitive advantage over both innovators and later followers in the addition of a new channel.[2] Their results suggest that firms should not be the first, but neither should they be the last, to add a new channel.

With regard to customer and market characteristics and their effects on new channel addition, Vinhas and Anderson (2005) show that firms are more likely to add a channel to their portfolio in response to greater customer heterogeneity, as well as when they operate in growing and larger markets. Their explanation indicates that greater market size and growth and more customer heterogeneity cause fewer problems with current channel partners. However, more customer heterogeneity in the market (i.e. heterogeneous channel preferences) also may offer more opportunities to create successful channel additions and larger and growing markets likely to provide more resources to firms to invest in a new channel. For example, Konus et al. (2008) show that channel preference segments differ across product categories, which can explain why in some markets, channel additions are more common than in others (i.e. banking versus supermarkets).

Potential channel conflict provides another important reason that firms might avoid adding a new channel, particularly in the context of transaction channels that could cannibalize the sales of existing channel partners.[3] Vinhas and Anderson (2005) specifically study the use of concurrent channels in a business-to-business (B2B) setting and find, in addition to the effects of market and customer factors, that firms that offer standardized products or brands are less likely to use concurrent channels. The channel literature also stresses the importance of supplier power (e.g. Gaski 1984), although Geyskens et al. (2002) show that powerful firms are more successful when they add an online channel. In this sense, channel conflict has received only limited attention, which constitutes an important gap in multichannel management literature. Van Bruggen et al. (2010) take a step toward filling that gap by noting how new multichannel environments may create different channel ownership structures, in which new players (e.g. Google) take ownership of customers.

Further issues relate to the presence of internal resources and fit with the chosen strategy (as discussed previously). Adding new channels requires huge investments, which means that firms must have sufficient (financial) resources. Geyskens et al. (2002) show that adding a well-supported Internet channel has greater performance potential. But firm experience with related channels (e.g. catalog and Web) may be just as important as financial support, although this relationship does not appear as straightforward. According to Geyskens et al. (2002), powerful firms with a few direct channels should achieve greater financial performance gains than less powerful firms with a single, broader direct channel when they add an online channel.

Beyond channel addition decisions, firms could face channel elimination decisions. For example, traditional catalog firms that have migrated to online business models may confront a decision about whether to continue their traditional catalog operations. Research on this topic is fairly limited. Konus et al. (2010) investigate the behavioral consequences of eliminating a catalog as an information channel; it has negative effects on purchase probabilities both off- and online, though these impacts vary across customers.

Channel Functions

The functions of a channel usually relate to the buying process. Yet firms need to decide exactly what use a channel serves: information search, transactions or after-sales services (Neslin et al. 2006). Most extant research focuses on transaction channels, especially how adding a transaction channel or migrating customers to a different transaction channel affects their behavior (e.g. Ansari et al. 2008; Gensler, Böhm and Verhoef 2010). As Van Nierop et al. (2011) show, customers' use of an information channel may negatively affect their shopping behavior in a department store. Pauwels et al. (2011) also find that the revenue impact of adding an information channel depends critically on the product category and customer segment. For example, an online information channel mainly benefits revenues in sensory product categories and customers who are distant from the store. The after-sales function of a channel unfortunately has received virtually no attention (cf. Frambach et al. 2007; Gensler, Böhm and Verhoef 2010).

From a customer management perspective, I might also distinguish among acquisition channels, and retention and development channels. Some research notes the impact of acquisition channels on customer lifetime value (e.g. Verhoef and Donkers 2005; Villanueva et al. 2008), but the use of multiple channels for retention and customer

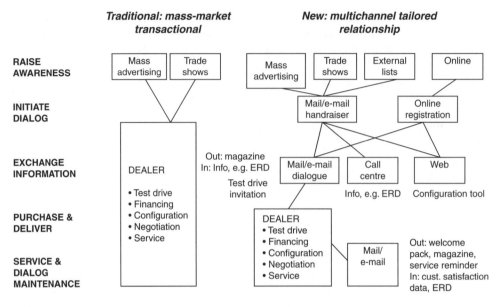

Source: Wilson et al. (2008).

Figure 8.2   The multichannel strategy of General Motors Europe

development has prompted far less attention. Rust and Verhoef (2005) provide some insights into the greater effectiveness of direct mailers for improving customer value compared with magazines. But a lack of knowledge persists about which channels are more suited for retention purposes.

Channel Allocation

One of the most important and perhaps most complex decisions related to a multi-channel strategy is how firms should allocate their resources and customers across channels. Wilson et al. (2008) attempt to define the appropriate channel combinations to offer; firms must determine the optimal channel mix per buying phase and per customer (segment). For this effort, it is crucial to understand customers' channel needs according to the segment to which they belong. These authors provide some interesting examples of how firms might define specific channel combinations, such as that for General Motors Europe (see Figure 8.2). This example suggests that firms take either a segmentation approach (for a specific segment, the firm chooses a specific channel) or a buying phase approach (a channel for each stage in the buying cycle). Most channel combinations arise from a careful examination of current channel usage patterns, which do not necessarily reflect the ultimate objective of optimizing customer lifetime value and/or the customer experience. Kushwaha et al. (2011) are unique in their efforts to optimize the allocation of marketing efforts across channel–customer segments. They develop response models for firm profit, purchase frequency, purchase quantity, product return propensity and contribution margin. Using a forward-looking optimization model, they also show that firms can improve their profits substantially if they optimally reallocate marketing efforts across the different customer–channel segments.[4]

Further Research

Thus far, research on channel additions mainly has addressed the addition of an online channel, but the arrival of even more recent channels (e.g. mobile smart phones) requires further studies. In particular, research attention should investigate the effects of channel conflict and channel additions, as well as channel eliminations. Along similar lines, companies need guidelines on how to channel their customers appropriately. Furthermore, a research gap persists regarding channels in specific phases of the customer life cycle. Attention should focus particularly on channel use in the retention and customer development phases. There is also still insufficient research into optimal channel combinations during the various purchase phases. New models should work to provide optimal multichannel solutions.

MCM IMPLEMENTATION

Managing Multichannel Customers

A crucial issue within MCM pertains to how firms might drive customers through channels during the customer purchase process. Managers thus face four important questions: (1) How can I attract customers to (new) channels? (2) Can I channel customers appropriately and should I proactively push customers to specific channels? (3) How do I keep customers within channels throughout the purchase process? and (4) Should I encourage customers to become multichannel customers?

Extensive research considers how specific channel attributes, such as risk, convenience and quality, might affect channel choice (Neslin et al. 2006; Verhoef et al. 2007). Researchers have shown that specific customers are more inclined to adopt a new channel faster (Venkatesan et al. 2007). Moreover, vast empirical evidence reveals that direct marketing communications (e.g. e-mail) drive channel choice (Ansari et al. 2008; Thomas and Sullivan 2005). These results in combination suggest that firms should create channels with good attributes, target specific customers to migrate and use communication to get customers into a channel.

If firms adopt a specific MCM strategy, with a strong focus on a specific channel, they likely want to send the appropriate customers into that channel. But Konus et al. (2009) warn that forcing customers into a specific channel (e.g. for cost reasons) creates customer reactance and dissatisfaction. Rewarding customers can help mitigate these negative effects. Overall, though, more research is required on channel elimination, especially as I expect that more firms will confront these decisions in coming years. Channel migration itself seems rewarding for firms, largely because customers usually move to less costly channels, though migrating customers to a certain channel also may inhibit their activity. For example, Gensler, Leeflang and Skierra (2010) show that bank customers who have been migrated to the online banking channel become more profitable, controlling for selection effects. However, Ansari et al. (2008) find that in a catalog context, customers migrated to online channels tend to become less loyal than those who continue to use the catalog channel. The nature of the services may explain these contrasting results; that is, whereas banking is a contractual service, catalog retailing involves no required contract.

An important problem that firms face is that customers often search in one channel and buy in another, in a process known as research shopping (Verhoef et al. 2007). Neslin and Shankar (2009) discuss three related shopper types: (1) competitive research, (2) loyal research and (3) one-stop shoppers. The first and second types are research shoppers and the competitive research shopper harms firms because he or she searches among and buys from different channels and different firms. To manage the research shopper phenomenon, firms need to understand how to design their channels to increase, or at least maintain, their loyal research shopper base while still ensuring they get a share of the competitive research shoppers (Neslin and Shankar 2009). Channel attribute differences, channel lock-in and cross-channel synergies all can drive research shopping (Verhoef et al. 2007). Specifically, channel attribute differences reflect the inherent differences between channels in different purchase phases. For example, the Web has excellent search attributes compared with the store channel, but the store offers stronger purchase attributes than the Web. Channel lock-in refers to the inherent capabilities of channels to retain customers in particular shopping phases (i.e. in a store, employees might convince customers to purchase). Finally, cross-channel synergies occur when it benefits the customer to search in one channel and buy in another. For example, searching the Web might provide customers with more information about prices, which better equips them to negotiate lower prices in the store. Notably, cross-channel synergies may reflect psychological processes, in that customers come to perceive themselves as smart shoppers when they engage in research shopping.

For firms, it is beneficial if the customers use multiple transaction channels, as long as all those channels are associated with a single firm. Empirical research consistently shows that such multichannel customers are more profitable (e.g. DoubleClick 2004; Kumar and Venkatesan 2005; Kushwaha and Shankar 2011; Thomas and Sullivan 2005). One important but still unresolved issue is whether this link is causal; that is, is it the case that heavy users and more brand loyal customers tend to use multiple channels, or does the use of multiple channels increase customer experiences and result in higher volume and profitability? Furthermore, multichannel research has been narrowly focused on transaction channels only. More research is required to determine if multichannel usage across different purchase phases benefits firms; the elucidation of research shopping already has pointed to some potential dark sides of multichannel customers. Moreover, Van Nierop et al. (2011) find that customers using a search channel tend to buy less frequently in the store.

Multichannel Marketing Mix

The marketing mix decision in a multichannel context mainly involves pricing and promotions, assortment, communication and service decisions across different channels in specific stages. The main issue is whether these mix strategies should be similar for all channels or could entail distinct strategies. Pricing decisions have attracted the most attention in prior academic research and extensive research considers price dispersion in online channels (for a review, see Pan et al. 2004). Zettelmeyer (2000) recommends that multichannel retailers should charge less in online outlets than in offline outlets, perhaps because multichannel customers tend to be more price sensitive than in-store customers

(Konus et al. 2008). Empirical evidence accordingly indicates that online prices tend to be lower than offline prices (for an extensive discussion, see Ratchford 2009) and analytical and empirical investigations (e.g. Ancarani and Shankar 2004; Pan et al. 2002; Xing et al. 2006) show that multichannel sellers can charge higher prices than pure online sellers.[5] The reasons for this finding might include the different customer segments the channels attract; multichannel retailers also provide additional attributes (i.e. customers can still visit the store if they want more service) and appear more trustworthy because of their presence in multiple channels.

Research on the assortments offered across different channels is almost nonexistent, though firms certainly can offer different products across different channels. However, such a strategy might be risky; if customers search for specific products online and do not find them, they naturally might conclude the store will not offer them either. In most cases, though, the Web grants opportunities for firms to offer more products because of its unlimited "shelf space." Firms might offer products for specific niches that could not affordably be offered in stores (i.e. the long tail; Anderson 2006).

The presence of different service levels across channels has also received insufficient attention. Customers clearly perceive service differences (Verhoef et al. 2007) and firms may purposefully maintain different service levels. For example, in the store, a customer can easily gain support from service employees, whereas the Web channel may offer only self-service and e-mail support. Such inconsistencies could have detrimental effects on the customer experience though (Verhoef et al. 2010), as discussions of integrated service quality across channels, a new dimension of service quality in a multichannel service context, propose (Sousa and Voss 2006). Moreover, van Birgelen et al. (2006) uncover interaction effects between satisfaction with traditional (bank office) and technology-mediated channels on loyalty intentions.

Organization of MCM

A final implementation issue regarding the MCM strategy pertains to its organization. How should multichannel operations be organized – as separate organizations or as one integrated activity? Who is responsible for the different channels across the organization?

The first question focuses on the external organization of multichannel operations. Firms might decide to maintain separate online operations that even operate under a different brand name. Research thus far has focused mainly on the coordination of marketing spending across channels and Berger et al. (2006) find that full integration in spending is more profitable than either partial integration or complete separation. Neslin and Shankar (2009) analytically show that coordinated marketing spending across different channels produces superior profits compared with independent marketing spending per channel.

The second organization issue clearly relates to the first. Academic findings suggest a coordinated approach, but in practice, channels are usually governed by different managers and/or departments, such as an e-commerce manager and store channel manager, for example. Each manager must optimize the profitability of the channel for which he or she is responsible, which likely induces only partial integration of channel policies, despite the greater profitability of full integration (Neslin and Shankar 2009). Moreover, marketing is usually responsible for customer relationships, but the sales department is frequently in charge of channel and distribution decisions (Verhoef and Leeflang 2009). To add even more complexity, customer data might not be well integrated across channels, as is necessary to create a single view of the customer (Neslin et al. 2006; Verhoef et al. 2010), especially if the IT department, instead of marketing, owns the customer data (Bijmolt et al. 2010). As a consequence, firms may be incapable of optimizing the value of their customers across channels.

Further Research

This discussion suggests ample opportunities for ongoing research. Most important, more research is required on the causal link between multichannel usage and profitability. Researchers should also consider the purchase and profit consequences of multichannel behavior in different buying phases. The existence of and processes that underlie research shopping are pretty clear; what remains uncertain are the specific forms of research shopping and which strategies are most effective in reducing detrimental research shopping. Further research on the persistence and developments in research shopping patterns would also be helpful. Will the Web-to-store route remain dominant among research shoppers? Will research shopping become even more fragmented and subtle as new media enter the mix? Imagine a customer in an electronics store who checks a smart phone to visit websites that offer alternative suppliers or price differences. Within the marketing mix domain, research specifically should address assortment decisions and service experiences across channels. Empirical research on multichannel organization could focus on the performance implications of nonintegrated or dispersed channel responsibilities across departments.

MCM EVALUATION

Finally, any MCM strategy must be evaluated. In this phase, firms must address two main issues: (1) Is our MCM strategy rewarding? and (2) What does each channel contribute to our performance?

Effectiveness of MCM Strategy

Prior research shows that on the individual customer level, MCM strategies seem rewarding for firms, in that multichannel customers tend to be more profitable (Kumar and Venkatesan 2005). Yet no strong evidence confirms whether such a strategy is rewarding. Neslin and Shankar (2009) discuss whether a MCM strategy provides a potential competitive advantage and suggest multiple ways to make it one (e.g. a customer satisfaction-based MCM strategy). Geyskens et al. (2002) further show that online channel additions tend to represent positive net present value investments, though the result depends of course on certain conditions (i.e. time of entry, power).

Channel Contribution

Another important assessment entails the contribution of each channel to the firm's performance, such as sales and profitability. Research on this topic is rather limited. Wiesel et al. (2011) use a variance autoregressive (VAR) model to measure the contribution of each applied sales channel in a B2B context. Their findings suggest that firms should reallocate their marketing resources from catalogs to search engines.

Further Research

It seems self-evident to call MCM evaluation an important domain for additional research, especially studies that determine whether companies with multichannel strategies enjoy better performance. It also would be relevant to understand which factors moderate performance consequences. Researchers could develop models to evaluate the contribution of each channel to performance, for which purpose a decomposition approach is probably necessary.

CONCLUSION

This chapter offers a strategic MCM framework that demonstrates how the development of an MCM strategy relates to the firm's overall pursued strategy. In their MCM strategy, firms should determine which channels to employ in which phases of the buying process and customer life cycle. In the implementation phase, customers should be managed across channels and firms should decide on their pricing, assortment and service levels. Beyond that point, they should determine an appropriate level of integration for their channel activities. Finally, firms need to evaluate their MCM strategy, in which context the contribution of each channel to performance is critical.

To discuss these varied management issues, I have incorporated insights from developing academic literature on MCM. In turn and on the basis of these discussions, I have provided some general directions for further research. In Table 8.1, I provide a summary of the main research questions per MCM strategy phase, the current findings per research question and important future research questions. This should stimulate further research in this interesting and relevant field.

Overall, the move to multiple channels has been one of the major developments regarding how firms can connect to their market and customers. It is very likely that this development will continue. The increasing number of channels that can be deployed provides huge opportunities and challenges for firms. Especially developments in the area of mobile channels and social channels will create opportunities (Hoffman and Novak, Chapter 12 in this volume; Shankar, Chapter 13 in this volume). Firms can use the existing insights on channel deployment to understand how they should create value with these new channels. Importantly, existing research suggest that firms should carefully evaluate whether the use of these channels can provide them with a competitive advantage. For example, being the first to deploy a mobile channel might not be the wisest strategy (e.g. Geyskens et al. 2002). One could also learn from existing research on how channels should be utilized in a coordinated manner in such a way that each channel has its function in the buying process and complements each other.

In sum, the provided framework and discussed findings in the literature may be very useful for firms in relation to how to develop their MCM strategy. Furthermore, they show academic researchers how they can position their research and which studies they

Table 8.1   Overview of key questions, extant findings and future research questions per MCM Topic

Topic	Key-Question(s)	Extant Findings	Future Research Questions
Strategic foundations of MCM	1. How are MCM strategies related to (generic) business strategies?	• Differentiators and cost leaders tend to use more channels • Firms can use different strategic criteria to develop their MCM strategy	• Do business strategies really drive MCM strategies, such as the deployment of specific channels? • How do strategic objectives (i.e. improve customer value) translate into MCM strategies?
MCM strategies	1. Which channels should a firm deploy? And how do channel additions affect performance?	• Channel additions do not cannibalize on sales; nor do they increase sales • Channel additions are positively valued by shareholders. Channel power, order of entry and investment moderate this effect • Channel conflict is an important determinant of channel additions	• What is the effect of channel eliminations on firm performance? • What is the effect of the addition of more specific channels, such as the mobile channel, on firm performance?
	2. Which functions should deployed channels have?	• Firms decide on which functions a channel should have (information search, transaction, after-sales) • Adding an information search channel may negatively affect purchase behavior • Acquisitions channels affect customer retention	• How can firms channel their customers appropriately in different phases of a customer life cycle? • How do channels affect customer retention and customer development?
	3. How can a firm allocate resources over channels?	• Firms can improve their profits if they optimally reallocate marketing resources over different customer-channel segments	• What are optimal channel combinations during the various purchase phases?
MCM implementation	1. How can multichannel customers be managed?	• Firms should create channels with good attributes, target specific customers to migrate and use communication to get customers into a channel	• What is the effect of multichannel usage in different buying phases on customer profitability?

	• Forcing customers into a channel may create negative customer attitudes, such as reactance • Migrating customers to another channel may impact customer profitability and loyalty in diverse ways • Customer research shop across channels and this can be explained by channel attribute differences, cross-channel synergies and lack of channel lock-in	• Which strategies could firms use to reduce potential detrimental effects of research shopping? And how can firms benefit from research shopping? • How persistent is research shopping and how will it develop in the future with even more deployed channels?
2. How should the MC marketing mix be managed?	• Multichannel retailers should charge less in online outlets than in offline outlets • Multichannel sellers ask higher prices than pure online sellers • Customers perceive service differences across channels	• How do differences in assortments and service levels across channels affect customer metrics?
3. How should MCM be organized?	• Coordinated marketing strategies across channels should provide superior profits	• What are the exact profit implications of nonintegrated or dispersed channel responsibilities across departments? • Do multichannel companies enjoy a stronger performance?
MCM evaluation 1. What is the effectiveness of an MCM strategy?	• Multichannel customers tend to be more profitable • MCM strategy can provide a potential competitive advantage through for example a customer-satisfaction-based strategy	
2. What does each channel contribute to firm performance?	• Contribution of each applied channel in the sales funnel can be measured using econometric models	• How can we measure the effects of each deployed channel in different phases of the buying process on performance metrics, such as sales and customer equity?

should execute in order to contribute to the existing MCM literature. However, I note explicitly that this chapter does not aim to provide a complete review of existing literature. I gladly refer readers to some extensive discussions and very specific directions for further research that have been published elsewhere (e.g. Dholakia et al. 2010; Neslin et al. 2006; Neslin and Shankar 2009; Verhoef et al. 2010).

ACKNOWLEDGMENT

The author acknowledges the two editors for their helpful comments.

NOTES

1. For more details on: (1) customer centric business, see Gebhardt, Chapter 3; (2) competitive analysis and the role of competition in creating marketing strategies, see Czepiel and Kerin, Chapter 4 and Sabnis and Grewal, Chapter 5; and (3) technological advances in MCM, see Chapters 12 and 13.
2. For a more extensive discussion on entry decisions, see Chapters 23, 20 and 21.
3. For more details on channel relationships, see Chapter 14.
4. For an extensive discussion on customer profitability, CLV models and marketing resource allocation models, see Chapters 7 and 9.
5. For more details on pricing issues, see Chapter 15.

REFERENCES

Ancarani, F. and V. Shankar (2004), "Price levels and price dispersion within and across multiple retailer types: further evidence and extension," *Journal of the Academy of Marketing Science*, **32** (2), 176–87.

Anderson, C. (2006), *The Long Tail: Why the Future of Business Is Selling Less of More*, New York: Hyperion.

Ansari, A., C. Mela and S. Neslin (2008), "Customer channel migration," *Journal of Marketing Research*, **45** (1), 60–76.

Berger, P.D., J. Lee and B.D. Weinberg (2006), "Optimal cooperative advertising integration strategy for organizations adding a direct online channel," *Journal of the Operational Research Society*, **57** (8), 920–27.

Bijmolt, T.H.A., P.S.H. Leeflang, F. Block, M. Eisenbeiss, B.G.S. Hardie, A. Lemmens and P. Staffert (2010), "Analytics for customer engagement," *Journal of Service Research*, **13** (3), 341–56.

Biyalogorsky, E. and P. Naik (2003), " The effect of on-line activities on off-line sales," *Marketing Letters*, **14** (1), 21–32.

Coughlan, A.T., E. Anderson, L.W. Stern and A.I. El-Ansary (2001), *Marketing Channels*, Upper Saddle River, NJ: Prentice-Hall.

Danaher, P., I. Wilson and R. David (2003), "A comparison of online and offline consumer brand loyalty," *Marketing Science*, **22** (4), 461–76.

Deleersnyder, B., I. Geyskens, K.J.P. Gielens and M.G. Dekimpe (2002), "How cannibalistic is the internet channel? A study of the newspaper industry in the United Kingdom and the Netherlands," *International Journal of Research in Marketing*, **19** (4), 337–48.

Dholakia, U.M., B.E. Kahn, R. Reeves, A. Rindfleisch, D. Stewart and E. Taylor (2010), "Consumer behavior in a multichannel, multimedia retailing environment," *Journal of Interactive Marketing*, **24** (1), 86–95.

DoubleClick (2004), *Retail Details: Best Practices in Multichannel Integration*, New York: DoubleClick Inc.

Frambach, R.T., H.C.A. Roest and T.V. Krishnan (2007), "The impact of consumer internet experience on channel preference and usage intentions across the different stages of the buying process," *Journal of Interactive Marketing*, **21** (2), 26–41.

Gaski, J.F. (1984), "The theory of power and conflict in channels of distribution," *Journal of Marketing*, **48** (3), 9–29.

Gensler, S., M. Böhm and P.C. Verhoef (2010), "Modeling customers' channel choice across different stages of the buying process," Working Paper, University of Groningen.

Gensler, S., P.S.H. Leeflang and B. Skierra (2010), "Effect of channel use on customer profitability," Working Paper, University of Groningen.

Geyskens, I., K.J.P. Gielens and M.G. Dekimpe (2002), "The market valuation of internet channel additions," *Journal of Marketing*, **66** (2), 102–19.

Hennig-Thurau, T., E. Malthouse, C. Friege, S. Gensler, L. Lobschat, A. Rangaswamy and B. Skiera (2010), "The impact of new media on customer relationships," *Journal of Service Research*, **13** (3), 311–30.

Hitt, L.M. and F.X. Frei (2002), "Do better customers utilize electronic distribution channels? The case of PC banking," *Management Science*, **48** (6), 732–48.

Hoekstra, J.C. and P.C. Verhoef (2010), "The customer intelligence–marketing interface: its effect on firm performance in services organizations," Working Paper, University of Groningen.

Jayachandran, S., S. Sharma, P. Kaufman and P. Raman (2005), "The role of relational information processes and technology use in customer relationship management," *Journal of Marketing*, **69** (4), 177−92.

Jindal, R., W. Reinartz, M. Krafft and W. Hoyer (2007), "Determinants of the variety of routes to market," *International Journal of Research in Marketing*, **24** (1), 17–29.

Konus, U., D. Trampe and P.C. Verhoef (2009), "Customer responses to forced channel migration," Working Paper, University of Groningen.

Konus, U., P.C. Verhoef and S.A. Neslin (2008), "Multi-channel customer segmentation," *Journal of Retailing*, **84** (4), 398–413.

Konus, U., P.C. Verhoef and S.A. Neslin (2010), "The effects of catalog elimination on customer purchase behavior," Working Paper, University of Groningen.

Kumar, V. and R. Venkatesan (2005), "Who are the multichannel shoppers and how do they perform?: Correlates of multichannel shopping behavior," *Journal of Interactive Marketing*, **19** (2), 44–62.

Kushwaha, T. and V. Shankar (2011), "Are multichannel customers always the most valuable customers? An empirically generalizable multicategory analysis," Working Paper, University of North Carolina.

Kushwaha, T., V. Shankar and J.Z. Huang (2011), "A customer-channel segment decomposition approach to optimal marketing effort allocation," Working Paper, University of North Carolina.

Langerak, F. and P.C. Verhoef (2003), "Strategically embedding CRM," *Business Strategy Review*, **14** (4), 73–80.

Neslin, S.A. and V. Shankar (2009), "Key issues in multichannel customer management: current knowledge and future directions," *Journal of Interactive Marketing*, **23** (1), 70–81.

Neslin, S.A., D. Grewal, R. Leghorn, V. Shankar, M.L. Teerling, J.S. Thomas and P.C. Verhoef (2006), "Challenges and opportunities in multichannel customer management," *Journal of Service Research*, **9** (2), 95–112.

Pan, X., B.T. Ratchford and V. Shankar (2002), "Can price dispersion in online markets be explained by differences in e-tailer service quality?," *Journal of the Academy of Marketing Science*, **30** (4), 433–45.

Pan, X., B.T. Ratchford and V. Shankar (2004), "Price dispersion on the internet: a review and directions for future research," *Journal of Interactive Marketing*, **18** (4), 116–35.

Pauwels, K. and S.A. Neslin (2008), "Building with bricks and mortar: the revenue impact of opening physical stores in a multichannel environment," MSI Working Paper.

Pauwels, K., P.S.H. Leeflang, M.L. Teerling and K.R.E. Huizingh (2011), "Does online information drive offline revenues? Only for specific products and consumer segments!," *Journal of Retailing*, **87** (1), 1–17.

Rangaswamy, A. and G.H. van Bruggen (2005), "Opportunities and challenges in multichannel marketing: an introduction to the special issue," *Journal of Interactive Marketing*, **19** (2), 5–11.

Ratchford, B.T. (2009), "Online pricing: review and research directions," *Journal of Interactive Marketing*, **23** (1), 82–90.

Rust, R.T. and P.C. Verhoef (2005), "Optimizing marketing interventions mix in intermediate CRM," *Marketing Science*, **24** (3), 477–89.

Shankar, V. and S. Balasubramanian (2009), "Mobile marketing: a synthesis and prognosis," *Journal of Interactive Marketing*, **23** (2), 118–29.

Shankar, V. and T. Kushwaha (2008), "An empirical analysis of cross-channel effects in a multichannel environment," Working Paper, Texas A&M University.

Shankar, V., A.K. Smith and A. Rangaswamy (2003), "The relationship between customer satisfaction and loyalty in online and offline environments," *International Journal of Research in Marketing*, **20** (2), 153–75.

Sousa, R. and C.A. Voss (2006), "Service quality in multichannel services employing virtual channels," *Journal of Service Research*, **8** (4), 356–71.

Techcrunch (2010), http://techcrunch.com/2010/03/08/forrester-forecast-online-retail-sales-will-grow-to-250-billion-by-2014/ (Forrester).

Thomas, J.S. and U.Y. Sullivan (2005), "Managing marketing communications with multichannel customers," *Journal of Marketing*, **69** (4), 239–51.

van Birgelen, M., A. de Jong and K. de Ruyter (2006), "Research note: multi-channel service retailing: the effects of channel performance satisfaction on behavioral intentions," *Journal of Retailing*, **82** (4), 367–77.

van Bruggen, G.H., K. Antia, S. Jap, F. Pallas and W. Reinartz (2010), "Managing marketing channel multiplicity," *Journal of Service Research*, **13** (3), 331–40.

van Nierop, J.E.M., P.S.H. Leeflang, M.L. Teerling and K.R.E. Huizingh (2011), "The impact of introducing and using an informational website on offline customer buying behavior," *International Journal of Research in Marketing*, **28** (2), 155–65.

Venkatesan, R., V. Kumar and N. Ravishankar (2007), "Multi-channel shopping: causes and consequences," *Journal of Marketing*, **71** (2), 114–32.

Verhoef, P.C. and B. Donkers (2005), "The effect of acquisition channels on customer retention and cross-buying," *Journal of Interactive Marketing*, **19** (2), 31–43.

Verhoef, P.C. and P.S.H. Leeflang (2009), "Understanding the marketing department's influence within the firm," *Journal of Marketing*, **73** (2), 14–37.

Verhoef, P.C., S.A. Neslin and B. Vroomen (2007), "Multichannel customer management: understanding the research shopper phenomenon," *International Journal of Research in Marketing*, **24** (2), 129–48.

Verhoef, P.C., R. Venkatesan, L. McAllister, E.C. Malthouse, M. Krafft and S. Ganesan (2010), "On CRM in data-rich multi-channel retailing environments," *Journal of Interactive Marketing*, **24** (2), 121–37.

Villanueva, J., S. Yoo and D.M. Hanssens (2008), "The impact of marketing-induced versus word-of-mouth customer acquisition on customer equity growth," *Journal of Marketing Research*, **45** (1), 48–59.

Vinhas, A.S. and E. Anderson (2005), "How potential conflict drives channel structure: concurrent (direct and indirect) channels," *Journal of Marketing Research*, **42** (4), 507–15.

Wiesel, T., K.H. Pauwels and J. Arts (2011), "Marketing's profit impact: quantifying online and offline funnel progression," *Marketing Science*, **30** (4), 604–11.

Wilson, H., R. Street and L. Bruce (2008), *The Multichannel Challenge: Integrating Customer Experiences for Profit*, Amsterdam: Butterworth Heinemann.

Xing, X., Z. Yang and F. Tang (2006), "A comparison of time-varying online price and price dispersion between multichannel and dotcom DVD retailers," *Journal of Interactive Marketing*, **20** (2), 3–20.

Zahay, D. and A. Griffin (2002), "Are customer information systems worth it?: results from B2B services," Marketing Science Institute Working Paper No. 02–113.

Zettelmeyer, F. (2000), "Expanding to the internet: pricing and communications strategies when firms compete on multiple channels," *Journal of Marketing Research*, **37** (3), 292–308.

PART IV

MARKETING STRATEGY DECISIONS

9   Marketing resource allocation strategy
Venkatesh Shankar

INTRODUCTION

Firms view allocating marketing resources as a strategic priority. According to a report by CMO Council, the primary task for most CMOs is to allocate marketing resources to improve the value of marketing investments (CMO Council 2007). Key marketing resource allocation decisions include those between marketing and product-related variables such as research and development (R&D); among products and brands, marketing mix elements, markets, countries, customers, channels, stages in the product life cycle. An overview of these types of decisions appears in Figure 9.1 (Shankar 2008). These decisions are critical to effective marketing strategy formulation (Shankar and Carpenter, Chapter 21 in this volume 2011; Varadarajan, Chapter 2 in this volume)

TYPES AND PRINCIPLES OF RESOURCE ALLOCATION MODELS

Regardless of the allocation context, firms can use one or more of four types of normative models of resource allocation: (1) a set of optimization rules applied to an econometrically estimated model; (2) empirical models that offer norms for strategic decision making; (3) analytical models with or without empirical estimation of market-specific parameters; and (4) decision calculus models with managerial judgment (Gatignon 1993). Although overall optimal budget determination and allocation may be related (Lodish et al. 1988; Mantrala et al. 1992), we address only the issue of marketing allocation in this chapter. Among the four types of models, we examine the first three types of models as they are most commonly used. For decision calculus models, see Little (1970).

Optimal resource allocation in all the models is based on the fundamental microeconomic principle that an optimal level of spending on an element of resource allocation is that at which the marginal return from an investment in that element equals the marginal costs of that investment. Many resource allocation decisions are based on elasticities

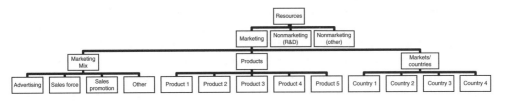

Source: Adapted from Shankar (2008).

Figure 9.1   An overview of the types of resource allocation decisions

or responsiveness and costs or margins associated with the variables involved in the allocation problem. The elasticity of a variable is the percentage change in the outcome variable (sales or profits) in response to a percentage change in that variable. A key decision rule is to allocate most resources to the variable with the highest elasticity.

ALLOCATION OF MARKETING RESOURCES

Managers make decisions on allocating resources to both marketing activities and non-marketing activities, such as R&D at different levels, corporate, business unit or product line. They base such decisions on factors such as past decisions, the type of industry, whether the product is new or existing, market responsiveness and the interrelation among the different variables.

Allocation between R&D and Marketing

Allocation between R&D and marketing is a strategic decision. Consider, for example, the pharmaceutical industry. In 2010, American pharmaceutical companies spent roughly $67.4 billion on R&D, or 17 percent of sales (PhRMA 2011), and $39.6 billion on marketing expenditures, or approximately 10 percent of sales, against industry sales of $396.5 billion. Because R&D and marketing spending are at high levels, allocating resources between them has critical implications for pharamaceutical firms' return on investment.

An effective model for allocation between these two (or more) strategic variables involves a deep understanding of the industry, the competitive context, the unique effects of each variable on firm profits and the effects of interactions among the variables. The formulation of an allocation model for R&D and marketing is challenging for two reasons. R&D investments typically have a long-term effect on firm profits (Erickson and Jacobson 1992), while marketing expenditures have both short-term and long-term effects on firm sales and profits (Dekimpe and Hanssens 1999). Furthermore, the interactions between R&D and marketing investments and their impact on firm profits are complex. On the one hand, higher marketing expenditures can enhance the effectiveness of R&D spending, leading to increased R&D spending. On the other hand, greater marketing spending can leave lower resources available for R&D when resources are fixed.

Most models do not deal directly with strategic allocation at the highest level of the organization. There are, however, descriptive models that study the effects of R&D and marketing variables on returns and profits (e.g. Bayus et al. 2003; Erickson and Jacobson 1992) and offer implications for resource allocation between these variables. Erickson and Jacobson (1992) estimate an econometric model of the effects of R&D and advertising expenditures on stock market returns and return on investment. They find that after controlling for unobservable firm-specific factors and the feedback between discretionary expenditures and profitability, the accounting and stock market returns to both R&D and advertising expenditures are substantially lower than previously believed. Their findings imply that companies tend to overallocate expenditures to either R&D or marketing. Bayus et al. (2003) analyze financial returns from new product introductions in the computer industry. They find that greater R&D spending and launch of new products coexist with lower marketing spending.

In practice, however, many firms set their R&D and marketing budgets according to one of the following methods: objectives and task; percentage of sales revenues; percentage change from the previous period; and competitive parity. These methods do not address the optimality of allocation between R&D and marketing, so there is a strong need for optimal models of and insights into resource allocation between R&D and marketing expenditures.

Allocation to R&D is higher for high-tech firms, while allocation to marketing is higher for consumer goods firms (Shankar 2008). During 2001–05, expenditures on R&D and marketing remained stable for most industries. However, for service firms, both R&D and marketing expenditures increased significantly over this period (Shankar 2008).

When firms decide their marketing budgets, they also decide how to spread those dollars across different marketing elements, such as advertising, sales force support and sales promotion. Marketing mix allocation is widely practiced by many firms, although the marketing mix variables vary considerably across industries.

In the pharmaceutical industry, for example, a majority of allocation is toward sales force efforts. In contrast, in the consumer packaged goods (CPG) industry, the bulk of the allocation is divided between advertising and sales promotion. For example, Procter & Gamble shifted approximately $400 million of its 2005 marketing budget of $4.3 billion to advertising in the new media, and Clorox moved its allocation from advertising to sales promotion (Neff 2004).

Allocation between Advertising and Sales Force

Advertising and sales force expenditures form a big part of firms' marketing spending in markets such as those for industrial, high-tech and pharmaceutical products. Lilien (1979) performed a descriptive analysis of marketing expenditure allocation data obtained during the 1970s on 131 diversified industrial products from 22 companies through the ADVISOR, a joint project of Massachusetts Institute of Technology and the Association of National Advertisers. The findings from Lilien's analysis show that firms' allocation toward the sales force relative to advertising depends on its size, the size of an average order, the stage in the product's life cycle, the complexity of the product, the fraction of the product's sales made-to-order, and the purchase frequency of the product.

Often, marketing mix variables, such as advertising and sales force, are correlated. Rangaswamy and Krishnamurthi (1991) propose an equity estimator for estimating regression models of sales response in which the marketing mix variables are typically multicollinear. Their application to pharmaceutical data shows that firms should spend more on the sales force than on advertising because sales force elasticities are much higher than those for advertising for ethical drugs.

Gatignon and Hanssens (1987) develop an econometric model of the effects of local advertising and sales force in the context of Navy recruitment. They show that sales force effectiveness in the hiring of Naval personnel increased with local advertising support, suggesting a synergy between advertising and personal selling efforts.

Gopalakrishna and Chatterjee (1992) develop and estimate a customer account level sales response model to capture the separate and joint effects of advertising and personal selling (sales force) on the sales of a mature industrial product in the presence of passive competitors. Although they do not directly address the allocation between advertising and personal selling, they suggest that if customer accounts are equally responsive to communication effort, then greater personal selling effort should be directed to the segment with the greater average business potential.

Shankar (1997) develops optimal allocation rules based on a decoupled multiplicative sales response model of allocation between advertising and the sales force. The model allows for the interaction of advertising and the sales force and the result extends the D–S (Dorfman and Steiner) (1954) theorem on price and advertising elasticities. The D–S theorem states that profit is maximized when the sum of price elasticity of demand and the marginal value product of advertising is zero. Shankar's (1997) result states that the ratio of optimal advertising and sales force expenditures is equal to the ratio of their effective elasticities. The effective elasticity of advertising or sales force is a function of the type of game between two competitors, market growth, margin and changes in these due to the entry of a new competitor. This result holds (1) if both the competitors play a Nash game or make their marketing mix decisions simultaneously or (2) if the competitor is a Stackelberg follower or makes the decision after the focal brand in one or all of the marketing instruments. His results show that, in general, a follower (leader) role in a marketing mix variable, a static (growing) market, a decrease (increase) in own elasticity, and margin all lead to a reduction of spending in that variable. Shankar's model and results offer insights into the allocation between advertising and the sales force. The allocation strategies proposed by his model are both theoretically and empirically driven, so they have important normative implications for managers.

Collectively, these models offer some generalizable insights into allocation between advertising and the sales force. The spending level on a marketing variable, such as advertising or sales force, is typically directly proportional to the elasticity of the variable and the contribution margin. Managers should allocate spending between advertising and the sales force according to their competitively relative elasticities. These elasticities may differ across industries, markets and firms.

Allocation between Advertising and Sales Promotion

In many markets, marketers need to decide the levels of expenditures for advertising and sales promotion. This decision is particularly important for consumer products and services. For CPGs, during the past two decades, the spending on advertising relative to sales promotion has steadily declined. For some CPGs, sales promotion constitutes two-thirds or more of marketing spending.

Many practitioners follow different rules of thumb in allocating marketing resources. For CPGs, they spend more on sales promotion over advertising for the following reasons. First, most consumers make purchase decisions at the point of purchase, leading marketers to spend more on in-store features, display and other merchandising activities. Second, retailers have become more powerful and demand strong trade promotions. Third, mass media advertising has become less effective with the advent and growth of the Internet, digital video recorders, and social and mobile media.

A few studies have examined the allocation between advertising and trade promotions. Sethuraman and Tellis (1991) incorporate two facets of trade promotions (price cuts) into the Dorfman and Steiner (1954) model of allocation: the opportunity loss from buyers who would have bought at the regular price and the loss from retailers' fractional pass-through of promotions to consumers. They find that when both promotion and advertising are profitable, the allocation between them is determined by their relative elasticities. Specifically, they find that for consumer nondurable goods, price cut elasticity is approximately 20 times that of advertising elasticity, while for durable goods, the corresponding ratio is only five. Their study did not examine differences in short- and long-run elasticities.

Neslin et al. (1995) analytically extend the substitutability of advertising and trade promotion in optimal allocation to a dynamic context that includes a retailer's forward-buying behavior and carryover effects of advertising. Such a lopsided ratio of promotion to advertising elasticities may explain the migration of marketing dollars toward sales promotion for CPGs during recent years. However, because advertising has long-term effects (Dekimpe and Hanssens 1999), companies may be myopic in overallocating to sales promotion on the basis of short-term effects.

Many of the rules of thumb and marketing mix models that guide the allocation of marketing spending between advertising and sales promotion, however, are not based on optimization principles. A major challenge in developing optimal allocation models between advertising and sales promotion is that often these two variables have synergistic effects on sales and profits, making it difficult to disentangle their unique effects.

Naik and Raman (2003) develop a dynamic advertising model (with advertising carryover effects) that captures synergy between communications in multiple media, using the Kalman filtering methodology. They estimate their model on data from Dockers brand and show a synergistic effect between television and print advertisements. They conclude that as the synergistic effect increases, a firm should raise its advertising budget and also increase its allocation to the less effective medium. They generalize the model to include differential advertising carryover and asymmetric synergy among media elements.

Naik et al. (2005) propose a model for allocation between advertising and sales promotion when the two have interaction effects and when managers can incorporate strategic foresight about competitor behavior. They use an extended Lancaster model and develop a continuous-discrete estimation method to calibrate dynamic models of oligopoly using market data.

Solving this dynamic optimization model using data on five detergent brands, Naik et al. (2005) find that large brands underadvertise and overpromote, while small brands underadvertise and underpromote, and that competitor responses to advertising and promotion are asymmetric.

In summary, consumer goods companies increasingly allocate more toward sales promotion and nontraditional media relative to advertising in the mass media, mainly because short-term mass media advertising elasticities are much smaller than elasticities of promotion or targeted media advertising. When interactions between advertising and sales promotions are included, large brands tend to underadvertise and overpromote, while small brands appear to advertise less and promote more.

Other Marketing Mix Allocations

A number of models of marketing mix allocation across other elements exist (Mantrala 2002). These elements include media and communications mix (Montgomery and

Silk 1972), sales territory allocation (Rangaswamy et al. 1990), direct mail campaigns (Elsner et al. 2004), and product and nonproduct marketing elements (Shankar 2006). In today's environment, the marketing mix involving nontraditional media is gaining ground. According to A.G. Lafley, former chief executive officer of Procter & Gamble, although the company still invests mostly in television, the media mix for major brands now includes a greater focus on in-store, Internet and nonmeasured media (Tode 2007).

Insights on media and communication mix allocation are somewhat limited. Using a distributed lag model of market share response on expenditures related to journal advertising, direct mail, samples and brochures for a company's ethical drug, Montgomery and Silk (1972) find that market share elasticities are highest for journal advertising and lowest for direct mail. They observe, however, that the company's actual allocation was inversely proportional to the suggested allocation mix. Strictly speaking, their model is based on market share response and would need to be extended to sales and profits to determine optimal allocation. Nevertheless, the findings suggest that many firms are still in search of an optimal communications mix. Given the expanded mix of communication vehicles available to marketers, optimal communication mix models are likely to be more complex than before.

Furthermore, managers need to make allocation decisions that are simultaneously related to product line length, channel coverage and pricing. Shankar (2006) develops a simultaneous model of demand and supply with product line and other marketing actions, which can be used to identify reaction and anticipation elasticities through the rational expectations approach. He estimates the model using data from the computer printer market, which comprises the market leader, Hewlett-Packard, and followers, Epson, Canon and Lexmark. The results show a firm is more likely to allocate more to expanding a product line when its competitors changed their product lines in the past, when the firm is large, and when its price is high.

ALLOCATION ACROSS PRODUCTS

Marketers make decisions on the allocation of funds toward different products and brands in their product portfolio. Models on allocation across products range from product portfolio models to models for a specific industry context (e.g. Mantrala et al. 1992). Among product portfolio models, the Boston Consulting Group (BCG) matrix (Henderson 1998) is the best-known tool. This matrix begins by identifying the positions of a firm's or a business unit's products along two dimensions: relative market share and market growth rate. Products can fall under four possible quadrants: (1) "cash cows" are products that are characterized by high relative market share but low market growth rate, (2) "stars" are those that have both high growth rate and relative market share, (3) "question marks" or "problem children" refer to products that have low relative market share in high-growth markets, and (4) "dogs" are products that have low relative market share in low-growth markets. The main resource allocation guidelines are to use the surplus cash from "cash cows" and "stars" (if any) to fund "question marks" so as to help them become "stars" for the future and to divest "dogs" unless they are strategic complements to other products or have substantial exit barriers.

Many firms employ variants of this tool. The enhancements to the BCG model go beyond relative market share as a proxy for competitive strength and market growth as a measure of market attractiveness. For example, General Electric uses a model that has broader dimensions based on multiple indicators that include relative market share and market growth.

Despite their widespread use, product portfolio models suffer from several limitations. First, they do not explicitly incorporate profits or margins as a major criterion. They implicitly assume that profits are correlated with relative market share. Second, the allocation rules from these models are based on a static view of the business universe. In reality, fast movement in markets and competitive dynamics may alter some product positions in the matrix, calling for changes in allocation rules that are difficult to make after investments are made on analysis of the original matrix. Third, the definitions of high- and low-growth rates or relative market shares are subjective, driving the categorization of products as "stars," "question marks," "cash cows" or "dogs" and the allocation rules. Therefore, although the portfolio models provide a useful high-level basis for resource allocation across products, they should be supplemented with more granular resource allocation models that are more detailed and specific to the industry and the firm.

Richardson (2004) develops and applies a linear programming model to allocate marketing funds for Reckitt and Coleman's (now Reckitt and Benckiser's) products, including Lysol. His approach involves weighing several company-specific criteria such as market growth, brand share, brand sales, contribution and market size against the budget constraints of the project, group, business unit and firm levels. He claims that the model led to improved profits, simultaneous examination of alternatives, fast response to unexpected situations and better utilization of the data at the firm.

Taken together, models and studies of allocation across products offer interesting insights. Firms should use the profits generated by "cash cows" to allocate more funds toward products with greater future potential. In deciding which products have greater future potential, firms should use multiple factors that reflect the attractiveness of the markets and the firm's competitive position.

ALLOCATION ACROSS CUSTOMERS AND CHANNELS

As firms become more customer-oriented, the allocation of resources by customers and customer segments is gaining greater importance than ever before. As companies increasingly offer their products through multiple channels, such as retail stores, the Web, and catalog or direct mail, and as more consumers buy them through different channels, the allocation of marketing efforts targeted at customers across channels is also becoming a critical issue for many marketers.

Models of marketing resource allocation across customers are primarily based on customer lifetime value (CLV). Venkatesan and Kumar (2004) identify low- and high-value customer segments on the basis of CLV and determine the optimal allocation of marketing resources to these segments. Applying a CLV model to data from a large multinational computer hardware and software company, Venkatesan and Kumar find that the effect of marketing communication on CLV is nonlinear across channels and that marketers can improve profits by maximizing CLV. Prior research using the CLV approach has also examined the allocation between customer acquisition and retention (Reinartz et al. 2005) and between retention and reacquisition of lost customers (Thomas et al. 2004).

As the practice of allocation by customer segment has evolved, allocation across customer-channel segments has become the next key development in resource allocation practice (Kushwaha and Shankar 2011a, 2011b). A study by McKinsey & Company calls for developing resource allocation metrics across channels (Myers et al. 2004). Neslin et al. (2006) and Neslin and Shankar (2009) emphasize the need to develop models for the allocation of marketing resources across channels.

Anderson et al. (1987) study the impact of variables associated with a financial portfolio model and the channel relationship on the selling time allocated by 71 independent sales agencies to the principals they represent. They find that the time (and resource) allocated to principals is consistent with an optimal microeconomic model, but channel relationship elements such as communication, participation and feedback also influence resource allocation.

Kushwaha and Shankar (2011b) propose an approach and model for optimal allocation of marketing efforts to each customer-channel segment. Their approach comprises marketing response models for each component of firm profit, purchase frequency, purchase quantity, product return propensity and contribution margin. Their purchase frequency model is an extended beta geometric/negative binomial distribution model, purchase quantity and product return propensity is a conditional negative binomial distribution model, and contribution margin is a gamma–gamma model. The optimal marketing effort allocation to each customer-channel segment is a function of the model parameters for that segment. They estimate the models using customer-level purchase, cost and promotional data from a large marketer of shoes and apparel accessories across the catalog, the store and the Web, and solve the optimization model in Excel using simulation. Their results show that consumer response to the company's marketing efforts varies significantly across the customer-channel segments for the different profit components, purchase frequency, purchase quantity and contribution margin. Using a holdout sample analysis, they show that firm profits can be substantially improved by optimally reallocating marketing efforts across the different customer-channel segments. In their revised allocation, the multichannel segment exhibits the highest percentage growth in budget and profit, highlighting the high profit potential of the multichannel segment.

Overall, there are some useful insights into allocation by customers and channels. Firms should allocate more to customers and customer segments that have higher CLVs than others. Multichannel customer segments are most profitable, so an optimal allocation model based on the responsiveness of customer-channel segment by profit components, such as purchase frequency, quantity, contribution and return propensity, can help marketers improve the returns to marketing efforts.

ALLOCATION ACROSS COUNTRIES

Allocation across different markets or countries is an important but challenging task. It requires a deep understanding of the response behavior of customers in different regions. Differences in responses across markets and countries increase the complexity of decision making. However, resource allocation based on a careful analysis of the factors that drive the differences across countries can result in substantial improvements in allocation decisions. These market- or country-specific factors include the population of target buyers, spending power per capita, per capita spending on product category, category penetration rate, category growth, category profitability, share of the company's brand, media costs, previous marketing expenditures and competitor actions.

Lilien and Rao (1976) propose a model for allocating retail outlet building resources across different markets for a consumer product. Lilien and Rao maximize the net present value of expected returns from a construction plan, comprising a different number of outlets in different markets subject to size constraints and determine the optimal plan. The model is based on an S-shaped relationship between outlet share and market share. Lilien and Rao implemented their model in a consumer goods firm in which it went on to become an integral part of the planning process.

In addition to market-specific factors, some cross-market factors such as diffusion, market learning and multimarket competition may drive allocation rules. Chintagunta and Desiraju (2005) develop a structural model that incorporates both cross-market contact effects, in addition to interaction effects, across marketing instruments and within-market competitive interaction effects, consistent with the theory of multimarket contact competition. They estimate their model using data from multiple European countries for a blockbuster category of ethical drugs. They find that detailing elasticities are comparable across the USA, Germany and Italy, but are higher in the UK and France, suggesting a greater allocation of the detailing budget to the latter regions.

Fischer et al. (2005) propose a market response model for entry timing across countries. Although they do not explicitly address allocation of marketing expenditures across countries, their results on marketing expenditures have implications for such allocation decisions. They find that a waterfall international entry strategy (entering markets sequentially) enhances marketing spending effectiveness. The normative implication for a brand that sequentially enters multiple markets or countries is that it should allocate greater spending to the later countries of entry than what would be appropriate based on market response in those countries if there were no prior entries in other countries.

Thus, although allocation across market or countries is a critical task, little practical guidance is available. The allocation criteria should go beyond country-specific factors, such as target market population, category growth and profitability to include cross-country effects that may be due to diffusion, market learning and multimarket competition.

ALLOCATION AMONG PRODUCT LIFE CYCLE STAGES

As a product goes through different stages in the product life cycle, marketers' strategic allocation decisions heavily influence its growth. Prior research offers insights on marketing spending by order of entry or by time horizon (see, in this volume, Hanssens and Dekimpe, Chapter 26; Lieberman and Montgomery, Chapter 20; Shankar and Carpenter, Chapter 21). Prior empirical analyses offer conflicting evidence or guidelines on changes in advertising spending over the product life cycle. Lilien and Weinstein (1984) and Parsons (1975) suggest that firms should reduce advertising expenditures over the life cycle, while Winer (1979) suggests that companies should increase advertising spending over the life cycle. However, Farris and Buzzell (1979) find no evidence for the main effect of the product life cycle on advertising expenditures. These studies do not consider any interaction or moderating effects of the product life cycle, nor do they study the allocation between advertising and other marketing mix variables, such as sales force.

Shankar (2011) develops a model to examine the effects of the product life cycle stages on a brand's strategic marketing allocation between advertising and the sales force. He allows the parameters to be moderated by the stage in the product life cycle. He estimates his model on data obtained from 29 brands in eight leading pharmaceutical categories over their life cycles. The results show that a brand's strategic marketing (pull versus push, or emphasis on advertising versus sales force expenditures) is moderated by its market position and the stage it is at in the product life cycle. The results also show that dominant brands significantly shift their resource allocation toward a push strategy or sales force while moving from the growth to the mature stages of the product life cycle; in contrast, weak brands shift their allocations toward a pull strategy or advertising from the growth to the mature stages. Shankar's (2011) data cover large therapeutic categories over long periods, making the analysis empirically generalizable to the pharmaceutical industry.

Taken together, the models offer some useful insights for effective resource allocation decisions over the product life cycle. A dominant (weak) brand shifts its strategic resource allocation toward a push (pull) strategy as it moves from the growth to the mature stages of the life cycle. Therefore allocation to advertising relative to the sales force may decrease (increase) for dominant (weak) brands over their life in markets that are more elastic to sales force than advertising.

A summary of selected resource allocation models, the associated data, key findings and limitations appears in Table 9.1 (Shankar 2008). The models range from econometric models to optimization models to game-theoretic or other analytic models. The data cover a broad spectrum of industries, including CPGs, durables, pharmaceutical drugs and industrial products. The key insights include optimal allocation based on competitively relative elasticities and several factors such as target population, category profitability and growth potential. A key limitation of most models is that competitor responses – particularly anticipated competitor actions – are not captured well. Furthermore, interaction effects among allocation variables are not often explicitly incorporated into the optimization approach.

ALLOCATION BETWEEN OLD AND NEW MEDIA

With the emergence and rapid growth of unmeasured and new media, the allocation of marketing resources to these avenues is becoming a challenging task for marketers of all products (Shankar and Hollinger 2007). Spending on unmeasured media includes expenditures on search engine marketing, Internet search ads, mobile media, social networking media, events, contests, in-store ads and product placement (Shankar, Chapter 13 in this volume). Although the proportion of the marketing budget allocated to such media is still low for many products, it is rising. While advertising spending on traditional media declined from $165.8 billion in 2007 to $127.2 billion in 2010,

Table 9.1 Summary of selected marketing resource allocation models

Paper / work	Model type	Data	Key findings / guidelines	Key limitations
Allocation across marketing and product-related resources				
Erickson and Jacobson (1992)	Econometric model	99 firms from S&P database during 1972–86	After controlling for firm-specific factors and the feedback between discretionary spending and profitability, stock marketing spending is significantly lower, so firms should not overspend on R&D or marketing	Residuals approximate unanticipated discretionary spending (R&D and marketing)
Bayus et al. (2003)	Econometric model	PCs	Higher new product introductions and R&D spending are associated with lower marketing and advertising support	Not generalizable to products in the mature and decline stages of the PLC. Results could be due to commoditization of product
Allocation across products and markets/countries				
Lilien and Rao (1976)	Optimization model	Consumer product	The optimal number of outlets across geographic markets can be determined based on an underlying S-shaped relationship between outlet share and market share	Simulation-based without a closed-form solution. Not validated on empirical data
Henderson (1998) (The BCG matrix)	Conceptual model	Not applicable	Milk the cash cows and feed question marks to upgrade them into stars and stars if needed. Stars self-finance themselves. Get rid of dogs unless they are strategic complements or have substantial exit barriers	Too simplistic dimensions. Assumes profits correlated with relative market shares. Assumes a static view of the business universe

Table 9.1 (continued)

Paper / work	Model type	Data	Key findings / guidelines	Key limitations
Allocation across products and markets/countries				
Chintagunta and Desiraju (2005)	Econometric (structural empirical industrial organization) model	Pharmaceuticals	Detailing elasticities are comparable across USA, Germany and Italy, but are higher in UK and France, suggesting greater allocation of detailing budget to UK and France	Not an explicitly normative model of resource allocation across countries
Fischer et al. (2005)	Econometric model	Pharmaceuticals	Marketing efficacy is higher in later countries of entry if firms follow a waterfall strategy, so firms should allocate more in later countries than that suggested by independent country response behavior	Not an explicitly normative model of resource allocation across countries
Marketing mix allocation and allocation over the PLC				
Lilien (1979)	Econometric (logit and linear regression) models	ADVISOR2 survey data from 22 companies for 131 products	Allocation to sales force determined by firm size, order size, stage in the product life cycle, product complexity and purchase frequency	Inappropriate for new products, narrow sample composition, US-centric data
Montgomery and Silk (1972)	Econometric (distributed lag) model	Time series data for an ethical product	Journal advertising has the highest and direct mail advertising has the lowest elasticity. The company's allocation is inversely related to these elasticities	Market share model. Needs to be extended to sales and profits to make conclusions on resource allocation

Study	Model type	Data/Context	Findings	Limitations
Gatignon and Hanssens (1987)	Econometric model	Time series data from US Navy	Sales force effectiveness in hiring of Naval personnel increased with local advertising support, suggesting a synergy between advertising and personal selling efforts	Specialized context (Navy hiring). Potential multicollinearity between advertising and sales force may hinder estimation of true synergy
Gopalakrishna and Chatterjee (1992)	Econometric model	Mature industrial product	Optimal marketing budget increases with number of accounts and the business potential of the accounts. Greater personal selling effort should be directed to the segment with the greater average potential	Competitors assumed to be passive. Do not directly address relative allocation between advertising and personal selling
Shankar (1997)	Analytical and econometric (game-theoretic and empirical industrial organization) model	A large drug product category	Brands should allocate resources between advertising and sales force in the ration of the competitive relative elasticities	Decoupled response function
Sethuraman and Tellis (1991)	Analytical and econometric model	Nondurable and durable goods	Promotions (price discounts) are more profitable than advertising for mature products, so allocate more to promotions	Other marketing variables not considered. Interaction effect ignored
Neslin et al. (1995)	Analytical model	Not applicable	Advertising and trade promotion expenditures are substitutes and balance each other	No empirical evidence

Table 9.1 (continued)

Paper / work	Model type	Data	Key findings / guidelines	Key limitations
Marketing mix allocation and allocation over the PLC				
Naik and Raman (2003)	Optimization model	Apparel	Synergy between media elements can be estimated using a dynamic advertising model. As synergy increases, a firm should raise its advertising budget and allocate more funds to the less effective media element	Results relevant for a monopoly; the role of temporal aggregation of data on optimal levels is unknown; potential multicollinearity between the media elements may hinder estimation of true synergy
Naik et al. (2005)	Optimization (differential game) model with continuous-discrete estimation method	Detergents	Advertising and promotion have significant interaction effects. Large brands underadvertise and overpromote. Small brands underadvertise and underpromote	Model ignores category sales changes; ignores carryover effects; other mix variables omitted; role of retailer absent
Shankar (2011)	Econometric (market response) model	Pharmaceuticals	Marketing expenditures and moderated by the stage in the PLC. Dominant brands shift allocation of sales force over the PLC	R&D decision not considered

Allocation across customers and channels

Venkatesan and Kumar (2004)	Optimization model at customer-cohort level	B2B customer data from a multinational computer hardware and software firm	Optimization based on CLV yields improved profits relative to other optimization approaches	Competitor responses not included in the model; indirectly relate costs and margins to CRM efforts
Anderson et al. (1987)	Econometric (S-shaped effort allocation) model, factor analysis of survey responses	Survey data from 95 firms belonging to Electronic Representatives Association (ERA)	Allocation of time by sales agencies to principal consistent with microeconomic model, but is also affected by communication, participation and feedback	Self-reporting bias; common method variance; key informant bias; one industry view
Kushwaha and Shankar (2011b)	Optimization model decomposed into purchases frequency, quantity and margin models	Shoes and accessories	The model produces a 32% increase in total profits in a holdout sample. Multichannel customers are most responsive to marketing mailers	Models applied in only one industry

Source: Adapted from Shankar (2008).

spending on online advertising increased to $25.8 billion (Perrin 2011). Furthermore, online advertising on social networking sites is likely to exceed $3 billion by 2011 (Perrin 2011).

Retailers are using different forms of the new media. Many retailers use e-mail to alert shoppers about new products, promotions and store openings. Some retailers like Kroger (http://shortcuts.com/?promo=kroger) even offer coupons on their websites for customers to download onto their loyalty card, saving the need to identify and clip coupons. Consumers can automatically redeem these coupons at the store checkout when they present their loyalty card. Retailers like American Eagle have Facebook applications, while retailers like Wal-Mart and Target have Facebook-sponsored groups, Urban Outfitters has MySpace pages, 1-800-Flowers has second-life e-stores, Buy.com, Radioshack and Overstock.com have YouTube/Video podcasts, and Officemax, Burger King and Taco Bell have viral micro sites (Bustos 2008). Social shopping services such as Groupon and Livingsocial offer special coupons that are based on the volume of customers buying on the deal.

There is, however, a dearth of formal models of allocation to new media. Effective allocation models in the context of the new media require a detailed understanding of the effectiveness of these media. Although improved data availability in the new media enables firms to measure their effectiveness more accurately than before, existing metrics are still in their infancy. For example, in the initial years of the Internet, marketing allocation to the Web was based primarily on eyeballs. With the advent and growth of targeted search advertising, click-through has become the key metric for allocating advertising dollars on the Web. Marketers, however, are still searching for a more appropriate measure because click-through still suffers from limitations, such as the inability to control for click-fraud.

The core principle of allocating resources in proportion to their competitively relative elasticities is the same for new media as it is for traditional media. However, the key metrics used for measuring customer responsiveness to marketing through new media are different from those through traditional media. As the metrics for new media evolve, the resource allocation models will become more specific to new media.

IMPLICATIONS FOR RESEARCHERS AND MANAGERS

Implications for Researchers

Marketing resource allocation models have a number of implications for researchers. First, resource allocation models that incorporate the relationship between marketing spending and shareholder value will be a useful addition to those based on the link between marketing expenditures and profits.

Second, additional research is needed on the linkages between different types and levels of allocation decisions. Existing research allocation models focus on a single allocation type or level or context (e.g. marketing versus sales force allocation, allocation across products) in isolation. Because many resource allocation decisions are interdependent, we need models that simultaneously optimize across different types of decisions. For example, a model that simultaneously optimizes allocation between R&D and marketing and within the marketing mix could offer more effective and precise allocation rules. Such models would likely be complex and simulation based.

Third, there should be greater research on allocation of resources to the new media. Models should incorporate interaction effects between the two types of media and the different media vehicles that make up these media.

Fourth, resource allocation models that incorporate different scenarios of anticipated competitor responses would be helpful. Such models require data from different contexts that involve different types of competitor responses.

Finally, research on the convergence of insights from the different types of allocation models is desirable. The allocation rules that result from a triangulation of insights from different models would offer greater confidence to the decision makers.

Implications for Managers

Resource allocation contexts and elements will likely become more complex. Although the basic principles of resource allocation and fundamental concepts will likely stay the same, the actual allocation rules will be based more on simulation than before. In many cases, closed-form analytical expressions for optimal resource allocation decisions may not be available, so managers will need to rely more on simulations for deriving the optimal decisions. Such simulations will not be as onerous a task as in the past, given the availability of richer data and greater computing power than before. In the future, managers will be more likely to use simulators and decision support systems for resource allocation than in the past.

CONCLUSION

The allocation of marketing resources continues to be a strategic priority for marketing executives. Allocation of marketing resources includes those between marketing and nonmarketing (e.g. R&D) variables; across marketing mix, products, markets, countries, customers and channels; and over the product life cycle. The core principle of allocation in different models is that the relative responsiveness or elasticity of the outcome variable (e.g. sales, profits) drives the changes in the allocation elements (e.g. marketing versus R&D, products and channels). The relative elasticity is driven by factors such as the industry, company size, strengths and weaknesses, and stage in the product life cycle.

Although marketing resource allocation models offer important guidance to managers, they can be improved to incorporate greater complexity, interactions among variables, anticipated competitor responses, relationship of spending with shareholder value, effects of new media and linkages between different types and levels of allocation.

REFERENCES

Advertising Age (2010), "100 Leading National Advertisers," June 20.
Anderson, Erin, Leonard M. Lodish and Barton A. Weitz (1987), "Resource allocation behavior in conventional channels," *Journal of Marketing Research*, **25** (February), 85–97.

Bayus, Barry L., Gary Erickson and Robert Jacobson (2003), "The financial rewards of new product introduction in the personal computers industry," *Management Science*, **49** (2), 197–211.

Bustos, Linda (2008), "110 ways retailers are using social media," http://www.getelastic.com/social-media-examples, last accessed July 20, 2008.

Chintagunta, Pradeep K. and Ramarao Desiraju (2005), "Strategic pricing and detailing behavior in international markets," *Marketing Science*, **24** (1), 67–80.

CMO Council (2007), *CMO Council 07 Outlook Report* (accessed December 10, 2007), available at http://www.cmocouncil.org.

Dekimpe, Marnik G. and Dominique M. Hanssens (1999), "Sustained spending and persistent response: a new look at long-term marketing profitability," *Journal of Marketing Research*, **36** (November), 397–412.

Dorfman, Robert and Peter O. Steiner (1954), "Optimal advertising and optimal quality," *American Economic Review*, **44** (5), 826–36.

Elsner, Ralf, Manfred Krafft and Arnd Huchzermeier (2004), "Optimizing Rhenania's direct marketing business through dynamic multilevel modeling (DMLM) in a multicatalog-brand environment," *Marketing Science*, **23** (2), 192–206.

Erickson, Gary and Robert Jacobson (1992), "Gaining comparative advantage through discretionary expenditures: returns to R&D and advertising," *Management Science*, **38** (9), 1264–79.

Farris, Paul and Robert Buzzell (1979), "Why advertising and promotional costs vary: some cross-sectional analyses," *Journal of Marketing*, **43** (Autumn), 112–22.

Fischer, Marc, Venkatesh Shankar and Michel Clement (2005), "Can a late mover use international market entry strategy to challenge the pioneer?", MSI Report No. 05-004, Marketing Science Institute.

Gatignon, Hubert (1993), "Marketing mix models," in J. Eliashberg and Gary L. Lilien (eds), *Handbook in Operations Research and Management Science: Marketing*, Amsterdam: Elsevier Science, pp. 697–728.

Gatignon, Hubert and Dominique M. Hanssens (1987), "Modeling marketing interactions with application to salesforce effectiveness," *Journal of Marketing Research*, **24** (August), 247–57.

Gopalakrishna, Srinath and Rabikar Chatterjee (1992), "A communications response model for a mature industrial product: application and implications," *Journal of Marketing Research*, **29** (May), 189–200.

Henderson, Bruce (1998), "The product portfolio," in Carl W. Stern and George Stalk Jr (eds), *Perspectives on Strategy from the Boston Consulting Group*, Boston, MA: BCG Publications, pp. 35–7.

Kushwaha, Tarun and Venkatesh Shankar (2011a), "Single channel vs. multichannel customers: determinants and value to retailers," Working Paper, Mays Business School, Texas A&M University.

Kushwaha, Tarun and Venkatesh Shankar (2011b), "Optimal allocation of marketing efforts by customer-channel segment," Working Paper, Mays Business School, Texas A&M University.

Lilien, Gary L. (1979), "Advisor 2: modeling the marketing mix decision for industrial products," *Management Science*, **25** (2), 191–204.

Lilien, Gary L. and Ambar G. Rao (1976), "A model for allocating retail outlet building resources across market areas," *Operations Research*, **24** (1), 1–14.

Lilien, Gary L. and David Weinstein (1984), "An international comparison of the determinants of industrial marketing expenditures," *Journal of Marketing*, **48** (Winter), 46–53.

Little, John D.C. (1970), "Models and managers: the concept of decision calculus," *Management Science*, **16** (8), B466–B484.

Lodish, Len, E. Curtis, M. Ness and M.K. Simpson (1988), "Sales force sizing and deployment using a decision calculus model at Syntex Laboratories," *Interfaces*, **18** (January–February), 5–20.

Mantrala, Murali K. (2002), "Allocating marketing resources," in Barton A. Weitz and Robin Wensely (eds), *Handbook of Marketing*, Thousand Oaks, CA: Sage Publications, pp. 409–35.

Mantrala, Murali K., Prabhakant Sinha and Andris A. Zoltners (1992), "Impact of resource allocation rules on marketing investment-level decisions and profitability," *Journal of Marketing Research*, **29** (May), 162–75.

Montgomery, David B. and Alvin J. Silk (1972), "Estimating dynamic effects of marketing communication expenditures," *Management Science*, **18** (June), B485–501.

Myers, Joseph B., Andrew D. Pickersgill and Evan S. Van Metre (2004), "Steering customers to the right channels," *McKinsey Quarterly*, **4** (December 7), 36–48.

Naik, Prasad A. and Kalyan Raman (2003), "Understanding the impact of synergy in multimedia communications," *Journal of Marketing Research*, **15** (November), 375–88.

Naik, Prasad A., Kalyan Raman and Russell S. Winer (2005), "Planning marketing-mix strategies in the presence of interaction effects," *Marketing Science*, **24** (1), 25–34.

Neff, Jack (2004), "P&G, Clorox discover modeling: marketing mix analytics gain new proponents," *Advertising Age* (March 29), 10.

Neslin, Scott and Venkatesh Shankar (2009), "Key issues in multichannel management: current knowledge and future directions," Tenth Anniversary Special Issue, *Journal of Interactive Marketing*, **23** (1), 70–81.

Neslin, Scott, Stephen G. Powell and Linda Schneider Stone (1995), "The effects of retailer and consumer response on optimal manufacturer and trade promotion strategies," *Management Science*, **41** (5), 749–66.

Neslin, Scott A., D. Grewal, R. Leghorn, V. Shankar, M.L. Teerling, J.S. Thomas and P.C. Verhoef (2006), "Challenges and opportunities in multichannel management," *Journal of Service Research*, **9** (2), 95–113.

Parsons, Leonard J. (1975), "The product life cycle and time varying advertising elasticities," *Journal of Marketing Research*, **12** (November), 476–80.

Perrin, Nicole (2011), *Traditional Media: Dollars and Attention Shift to Digital*, eMarketer Report, May.

PhRMA (2011), *Pharmaceutical Industry Profile 2011*, Washington, DC: PhRMA.

Rangaswamy, Arvind and Lakshman Krishnamurthi (1991), "Response function estimation using the equity estimator," *Journal of Marketing Research*, **28** (February), 72–83.

Rangaswamy, Arvind, Prabhakant Sinha and Andris Zoltners (1990), "An integrated model-based approach for sales force structuring," *Marketing Science*, **9** (4), 279–98.

Reinartz, Werner, Jacquelyn S. Thomas and V. Kumar (2005), "Balancing acquisition and retention resources to maximize customer profitability," *Journal of Marketing*, **69** (January), 63–79.

Richardson, Robert J. (2004), "A marketing resource allocation model," *Journal of Business & Economic Studies*, **10** (1), 43–53.

Sethuraman, Raj and Gerard J. Tellis (1991), "An analysis of the tradeoff between advertising and price discounting," *Journal of Marketing Research*, **27** (May), 160–74.

Shankar, Venkatesh (1997), "Pioneers' marketing mix reactions to entry in different competitive games structures: theoretical analysis and empirical illustration," *Marketing Science*, **16** (4), 271–93.

Shankar, Venkatesh (2006), "Proactive and reactive product line strategies: asymmetries between market leaders and followers," *Management Science*, **52** (2), 276–92.

Shankar, Venkatesh (2008), "Strategic allocation of marketing resources: methods and insights," in Roger Kerin and Rob O'Regan (eds), *Marketing Mix Resource Allocation and Planning: New Perspectives and Practices*, Chicago, IL: American Marketing Association Publication, pp. 154–83.

Shankar, Venkatesh (2011), "The role of the product life cycle and market dominance in marketing expenditures of products," Working Paper, Mays Business School, Texas A&M University.

Shankar, Venkatesh and Marie Hollinger (2007), "Online and mobile advertising: current scenario, emerging trends, and future directions," MSI Report No. 07-206, Marketing Science Institute.

Thomas, Jacquelyn, Robert C. Blattberg and Edward Fox (2004), "Recapturing lost customers," *Journal of Marketing Research*, **41** (February), 31–45.

Tode, Chantal (2007), "Procter & Gamble marketing looks to Internet," *DMNews* (May 3).

Venkatesan, Rajkumar and V. Kumar (2004), "A customer lifetime value framework for customer selection and resource allocation strategy," *Journal of Marketing*, **68** (October), 106–26.

Winer, Russell S. (1979), "An analysis of the time-varying effects of advertising: the case of Lydia Pynkam," *Journal of Business*, **52** (4), 563–76.

10 New product development in a strategic context
John H. Roberts

This chapter considers how to develop new products and services in the context of the overall strategic environment of the organization.[1] Strategy aims to take an overall and long-term view of the firm and so provides a useful framework within which to understand both the dynamic and cross-sectional aspects that must be considered when the development of a single new product is undertaken.

THE ELEMENTS OF STRATEGY

Marketing strategy sits beneath corporate strategy, coordinating the customer-facing aspects of the firm (e.g. Walker et al. 1999). Marketing strategy can be thought of in three separate, but interrelated stages: the marketing audit (addressing where the firm is), option generation (identifying where it might go), and option realization (determining how it could get there).

The Marketing Audit

Marketing is the management of exchange – from both the customer's and firm's perspectives. To meet the needs of the customer, the firm must first understand them and second have the capabilities to meet them. Day (1994) terms the first of these requirements "market sensing" abilities and the second as "market relating" capabilities. This linking requirement is illustrated by the arrow between the top two boxes in Figure 10.1 ("the customer matching process"). To realize the firm's objectives, it must participate in markets that enable it to achieve them ("the company matching process"), the bottom two boxes in Figure 10.1. Thus the marketing audit has four elements: company strengths (and weaknesses), target market needs, firm objectives, and market characteristics (including competition, channels of distribution and climate – technological, regulatory, infrastructure, economic etc.).

The audit performs two functions for the firm. First, it provides the information indicating where a firm can and cannot go. The eight italicized questions in Figure 10.1 enable any strategic initiative, including new product development, to be assessed for feasibility. Second, the framework provides the two criteria against which any potential strategic opportunity can be calibrated.

Strategic initiatives, including new products, will not succeed unless the firm can meet a need in the marketplace. Nor will they be successful if the firm is unable to meet at least some of its objectives by undertaking the activity. Note that the popular directional policy matrix (also known at the GE matrix and McKinsey 9 box matrix) presents a way of calibrating these two matching processes and plotting them in two dimensions (Coyne 2008). It plots the competitive capability against market attractiveness of the firm's different business units, products or other strategic groups. It is a simple and clear way of

Customer matching process

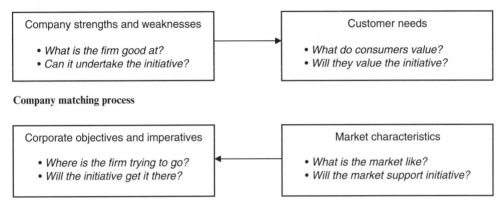

Company matching process

Figure 10.1   Elements of the marketing audit

representing the extent to which an initiative succeeds in achieving these dual impera-
tives. Thus the two matching processes in Figure 10.1 provide two rulers against which
we can calibrate any strategic opportunity: "Will the firm be good for customers in this
market?" and "Will the market assist the strategic mission of the firm?"

Option Generation

The audit provides a static view of the firm. Option generation is a way of introducing
dynamics to planning, addressing the question "Where can the firm go?" Option generation has two parts: defense (ensuring persistence of current incomes streams) and growth
(generating new ones). Defense largely addresses the question as to what the environment can do to the firm (forcing a consideration of the defensive strategies it can use
to insulate itself from such trends), while growth is about what the firm can do to the
environment (e.g. Roberts et al. 2005).

Option Realization

Having decided where the firm is and where it might go, the final stage of strategy, particularly new product strategy, is option realization – that is, how it might get there. This
aspect has attracted less attention than the previous two. Exceptions include Bonoma
(1985) and Walker and Ruekert (1987) on implementation. However, the importance of
execution has been recognized in both the academic and industry press. See Barwise and
Meehan (2004) for an academic call for excellence in execution.

NEW PRODUCT DEVELOPMENT STRATEGY

Having examined the broad components of marketing strategy (see Shankar and
Carpenter, Chapter 21 in this volume and Varadarajan, Chapter 2 in this volume for a

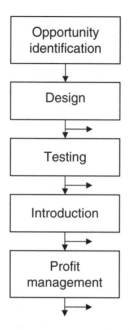

Figure 10.2   The new product development process (Urban and Hauser 1983)

detailed overview), the chapter now proceeds to examine their application to the new product development process in particular. There has been much work in this area in academic journals, texts and references, and industry guides. For example, the *Journal of Product Innovation Management* focuses entirely on new product and service development. There are many excellent texts that describe the new product development process, such as Urban and Hauser (1983). Finally, many industry guides to new product development explain in detail the steps required for success in this area (see, e.g. Caris-McManus 1991).

These books typically use a stage gate approach to new product development, describing the process as a series of sequential steps with feedback loops allowing return to previous processes. The stages that Urban and Hauser (1983) propose are illustrated in Figure 10.2.

Note that while such a framework guides the entire process, the strategic formulation part of the new product development process occurs primarily in the opportunity identification stage. The remainder of this chapter will focus on one particular part of the strategic nature of new product development: applying the two criteria for new product success. As such, this chapter does not cover new product introduction strategies (for further details on this topic, see Gatignon et al. 1990; Shankar 1999). Our two criteria were identified earlier, using Figure 10.1: the ability of any initiative to meet a need in the market; and its potential to realize one or more of the organization's objectives. In the specific case of new product development, the customer matching process (the ability of a new product to fill an unmet customer need) is captured by the value proposition, while I describe the company matching process (the new product's ability to achieve a set of objectives for the firm) as the product or brand role.

OPPORTUNITY IDENTIFICATION

In considering growth, Igor Ansoff (1965) suggested that a useful way to classify growth opportunities is whether they use new or existing products and whether they address new or existing markets. This idea of analyzing growth by looking at what the firm does (products) and to whom it does it (markets) has been supplemented by David Aaker (2005) to also include vertical integration (how much of the value chain the firm provides), illustrated in Figure 10.3. The strategy literature has considered growth options along similar strategic dimensions. For example, Strebel and Ohlsson (2006) classify growth options along the dimensions of innovation (value proposition maturity), intimacy (valuable customer diversity) and efficiency (value chain efficiency). These are close analogs to the three dimensions of Aaker's extension of the Ansoff matrix: products (what the firm does), markets (for whom it does it) and vertical integration (by what means) respectively.

New product opportunities for growth may arise from meeting the needs of either existing or new markets. In terms of existing markets (Box II in Figure 10.3), line extensions form one important source of growth. Existing products may be extended by adding features (e.g. a battery to Gillette's Mach range of shavers), new varieties (e.g. Dannon's "adult" flavored yoghurts), or new product forms (e.g. Saab's launching of a Cabriolet 9-3 auto). The benefit of line extensions is that they leverage off a strong market asset: the brand name. Potential disadvantages are that cannibalization may be maximized, and that there may be a risk to the parent brand. Changes in product

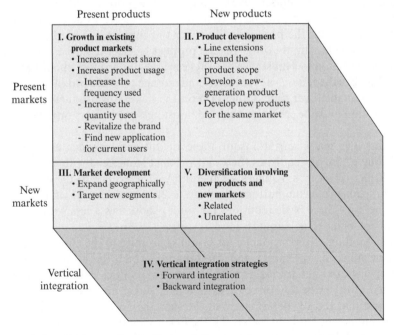

Source: From Aaker (2005), reproduced with permission.

Figure 10.3 Aaker's extension to the Ansoff matrix

scope may offer ways to increase both the unit sales and the margins that a product can command. For example, when Procter & Gamble launched Tide with Bleach, it captured a large part of the bleach market, as well as the consumer's heavy-duty detergent needs. Finally, other new products for the same markets may meet a set of unrelated needs that leverage off capabilities of the firm. For example, when American Hospital Supply (AHS) allowed its customers to order online it inserted a field where they could request products not in the firm's catalog. AHS used the information advantage from these data to determine new products for which the greatest pent-up demand existed among hospitals. Developing new products for new markets (diversification, Box V in Figure 10.3) is often described as high risk–high potential reward, and indeed it can be. Related diversification, by definition, does leverage off an existing strength of the firm (e.g. Philips used its light technology to enter the hair removal market). Unrelated diversification such as British American Tobacco entering the food and beverage market requires considerably more thought as to whether it makes sound strategic sense and, if so, how it can be undertaken successfully.

VALUE PROPOSITIONS

The concept of the value proposition of a product, service or brand is well established in the marketing literature (e.g. see Vargo and Lusch 2004). It goes by a large number of names, which include "customer promise" (Parasuraman et al. 1991), "core benefit proposition" (Urban and Hauser 1983), "unique selling proposition" (Laskey et al. 1989) and many others. However, the basic concept is similar: the value proposition tries to capture the benefit that the product will deliver the consumer. That benefit must have a number of characteristics in order for the product to meet the needs of the customer. For example, Urban and Hauser (1983) suggest that the product should provide (1) a benefit that is (2) salient at (3) a competitive advantage to other products in the market, that is (4) sustainable over time. Other criteria for successful products include that the value proposition must be credible, it should not suggest fatal flaws or major weaknesses and so on.

Combining the many variations of these definitions provides a highly nuanced understanding of the prerequisites for a new product to succeed with the customer. For example, Keller (2008, p.61) suggests a hierarchy of relevance to the customer from a basic level of salience at the bottom to a high level of attachment, which he calls resonance, at the top. These basic requirements for a product's success with consumers are useful, and are included as Table 10.1.

An understanding of the product's (or brand's) promise to the customer provides the basis to determine the categories and variants into which the product may be taken. The subject of brand extensions as a means of new product development and launch has attracted a very large amount of attention (e.g. Aaker and Keller 1990). Aaker and Keller suggest that the key determinant of the success of a brand extension (other than the criteria outlined in Table 10.1 above) is the fit between the associations held about the parent brand and desirable attributes in the area to which it is being extended.

While the general attributes required for a product to be successful (Table 10.1) provide useful guidance for new product strategy, their relative importance may vary

Table 10.1   Criteria to assess the value proposition of a brand

Criteria for successful value proposition	Explanation	Typical Reference
Benefit	The brand does make a promise	Urban and Hauser (1983)
Salient, resonant	The promise is valuable to customer	Keller (2008)
Competitive advantage	The promise offers some advantage	Urban and Hauser (1983)
Sustainability	The advantage can be maintained	Aaker (1991)
Points of parity	Weaknesses are mitigated	Keller (2008)
Credibility/believability	The promises must be believable	Aaker (1991)

considerably from application to application, and other attributes not included may be important in specific situations. Therefore it is useful to have a methodology with which to identify the customer needs criteria in a given situation, allowing the creation of a customized list. The directional portfolio matrix (DPM) provides us with exactly such a tool.

The way in which the competitive capability axis of the DPM is constructed is that the marketing analyst must first identify the dimensions of customers' needs. Those dimensions will then dictate the critical success factors that the firm must possess to succeed in the product category. If the firm has strengths in these critical success factors, then it will have a source of competitive advantage. (For a primer on the calculation of competitive capability, see Parmalee 1993.)

Marketing has considerable experience in calibrating the transformation between consumers' perceptions of a product and their preference and probability of choice of it in terms of choice-based conjoint analysis (see DeSarbo et al. 1995 for an overview). Thus this approach to determining the degree to which a firm's product has a compelling proposition is based on well-established tools in strategy and marketing analysis. Of course, the manager must distinguish between the design of a value proposition that is compelling to consumers and its delivery in practice. For example, in the branding literature (Aaker and Joachimsthaler 2000, p.40), a useful distinction is made between the value proposition that the firm aims to deliver (the brand identity) and the value proposition that the consumer perceives that she receives (the brand image).

BRAND ROLES

While the concept of the value proposition has received considerable attention, that of brand roles (the objectives of the firm that the product aims to assist) has received considerably less. The use of products to fulfill different roles has a long pedigree in the popular press, but its assessment in a systematic way is not well established in academia. In industry publications, we are used to reading about loss leaders (products whose job for the company is to generate cross-selling opportunities), flanker brands (products to protect market leaders) and cash cows (products without a long-term future that should be milked for the immediate cash flow that they can generate). Hess and Gerstner (1987) discuss loss leaders, Day (1977) describes cash cows, and Ritson

(2010) analyzes the role of flankers. However, there appears to be no work that synthesizes the different roles that products and brands can take on for the company in a comprehensive way.

One reason why brand roles have not attracted more attention in academia is that, for a value-maximizing firm, presumably all products should have the same aim: to maximize the total expected net present value of future income streams to the firm. However, there are two reasons to move beyond this somewhat narrow, finance-based view of individual products. The first is that many organizations do not have the single objective of value maximization. The concept of the triple bottom line (Elkington 1994) in which the three criteria of value to shareholders, responsibilities to employees, and obligations to the environment are balanced, suggests that we must move to multidimensional organizational objective functions (and thus towards a focus on having "horses for courses" for different products). With the rise of corporate social responsibility on firms' agendas (Carroll 1999), multidimensional performance has become considerably more important, as has its measurement (Raghubir et al. 2010).

Another reason to move beyond the idea that each product should be assessed on its incremental financial contribution to the value of the firm is that while it may make good sense in principle, in practice it can be extremely difficult to assess all of the cross-sectional and longitudinal externalities of a product. In their article "Beware the silver metric", Ambler and Roberts (2006) warn of the dangers of just examining single measures of success and note that such measures tend not to be very diagnostic in guiding the manager in achieving her long-term value maximization goal. That is, it may be much easier for a manager to understand that her primary goal is to maximize the cross-sell generated by a loss leader than to look at the marginal financial effect of her actions on the entire firm (data about which she almost certainly cannot access). It will be simpler for her to gauge her actions against intermediate criteria such as cross-sell generated, and also to reward her for performance against them.

Therefore it is useful to consider what different roles products can play in furthering the objectives of the organization. The literature, both academic and business, is ominously quiet on this subject.

To understand the different firm objectives that a product or brand can meet, it is useful to return to those objectives. The primary objective for most firms will be value (measured, e.g. by market capitalization), although obligations to employees and the community may also figure.

Expected value (measured in dollars) in time t (EV_t) can be measured by the expected net present value of future income streams. That is:

$$EV_t = \Sigma_j \, E_{t+j}/(1+d_{t+j})^j + PS_t - NS_t \tag{10.1}$$

where E_{t+j} = Expected earnings in dollars in time period $t + j$
d_{t+j} = Discount rate in time period $t + j$
PS_t = Positive synergies in dollars (externalities) with the rest of the portfolio
NS_t = Negative synergies in dollars (externalities) with the rest of the portfolio.

It is useful to further decompose the elements of future earnings, E_{t+j}, into their constituent elements:

Table 10.2   Product and brand roles: possible roles a product can undertake to meet the firm's objectives

Firm objective targeted	Product role	Example
Direct value creating products		
Time value		
Value created early	Cash cow	IBM pc
Value created later	Investment product	Nokia voice recognition
Value with less volatility	Counter cyclical product	College summer classes
Value through margin leverage		
Cost leverage	Capacity utilization product	Bark chips from lumber
Price leverage	Premium product	Buick Park Avenue
Value through volume leverage		
Category development	Innovation	Swatch watch
Share enhancement	Market coverage	Accor Base Hostels
Indirect value creating products (positive synergies with other products)		
Protect other products' earnings	Flanker product	Highland sticky notes
	Pre-emptive product	TAB Clear
Enhance other products' earnings	Value adding (synergistic)	iTunes and iPod
	Loss leaders (cross sell)	Microsoft Xbox
Address non-financial value objectives		
Products for community	CSR services	UK Transport Seniors card
Products for employees	Employee services	United Airlines staff tickets

$$E_{t+j} = I_{t+j} * S_{t+j} * (P_{t+j} - V_{t+j}) - F_{t+j} \qquad (10.2)$$

where I_{t+j} = Industry size in time period $t + j$ (in units)
S_{t+j} = Market share of the firm in time period $t + j$
P_{t+j} = Average price in time period $t + j$
V_{t+j} = Variable costs in time period $t + j$
F_{t+j} = Fixed costs in time period $t + j$

This formulation allows us to understand where different products will gain the ability to meet the firms' overall objective of value maximization. The classification of product roles that emerges from it is provided in Table 10.2. Equations (10.1) and (10.2) show that value may be created by changing the timing and volatility of new product earnings (the discount factor, $(1+d_{t+j})^j$), or it may come from commanding higher margins $(P_{t+j} - V_{t+j})$, generating higher volumes $(I_{t+j} * S_{t+j})$ or exploiting firm synergies $(PS_t - NS_t)$. The firm must be aware of what the role(s) of a product is in this framework.

One implication that follows from this analysis is that a product that makes sense to one firm might not make sense to another from the perspective of its objectives. (We know that the first matching process may provide a barrier to entry to a firm finding an opportunity attractive, despite its appeal to another firm with better matched resources.

We spend less time thinking about, given the different situation and objectives of different organizations, the same product equally well executed may be more appealing to one firm than another.) A good example of this is provided by Urban et al. (1984, p. 108). They showed how there was a highly profitable opportunity in the US caffeinated ground coffee market that was attractive to Nestlé (with a strong instant presence but no ground coffees), while it made little sense to General Foods, which would cannibalize its Maxwell House and Yuban brands. Indeed, Nestlé did subsequently launch a new caffeinated ground coffee, while General Foods did not.

Table 10.2 takes a series of different types of product in column 2 that will be familiar to most readers and attempts to classify them according to the firm objective that they address (in column 1). Examples of each are given in the third column. These examples are briefly elaborated on below.

Products may deliver value at different points in time. When IBM launched its PS2 range of computers in 1987, it maintained the IBM PC in its product line. It was highly cash flow positive and was not cannibalizing the PS2. It was a cash cow. Conversely, many firms have products that they know will not make money in the foreseeable future but are investment brands for the medium to long term. Nokia's efforts on voice recognition software fall into that category. With respect to timing, Unilever used to classify all of its products as "harvest" (cash cow), invest to maintain and invest to build (investment products). Products that reduce volatility of earnings will also increase value (Shankar, Chapter 24, this volume; Srivastava et al. 1997). Companies with highly seasonal sales, such as an educational college for example, will value the even cash flow of countercyclical products.

Products may meet the firm's objective of higher margins, either by reducing variable costs, or by commanding higher price levels. Capacity utilization products may use a by-product such as the bark chips generated in the process of milling lumber because of the low marginal cost incurred. Telecommunications networks that must dimension to peak load traffic will value any service that requires large amounts of bandwidth in off-peak hours. Products that use high fixed cost, low variable cost resources are becoming prevalent in perishable service industries such as hotels and transport. Products may alternatively attempt to extract higher prices from segments with lower price elasticities. For example, Buick used the Buick Park Avenue to create a higher priced version of the Buick Electra for many years.[2]

Increased contribution comes from either higher margins or higher volume. Higher volume may come from a product either expanding the category (generally through innovation) or by gaining a higher share of the category. In 1982, the Société Suisse pour l'Industrie Horlogère used the Swatch watch to greatly grow the size of the global watch market, encouraging consumers to buy multiple watches for different occasions. Accor, the French hotel group, has grown its share by using products to maximize market coverage including the Sofitel, Novotel, Mercure, Ibis, Motel Formula 1, and more recently Base Backpackers product ranges.

While the above examples relate to a product maximizing its own direct value, products can also be used to increase the value of other products. This can occur when they defend others' income streams or generate new ones for them. 3M Post IT Notes lead the sticky note category and are highly profitable. Highland Sticky Notes are also owned by 3M and are used as a flanker to send market signals that might prejudice the brand equity of Post IT Notes, if undertaken by that brand. One specific form of flanker product is the pre-emptive product. When Pepsi launched a clear cola, Pepsi Crystal, Coca-Cola was there with TAB Clear to cover the possibility that even such an unlikely move might prove successful. In terms of generating new earnings for other products, one product role can be that of value adding. The iTunes store added considerable value to Apple's iPod. Alternatively, the product can increase the user base of another product, and that is what loss leaders aim to do. Microsoft expected to lose money from every XBox 360 it sold (Hesseldahl 2005), but it hoped to make up that money on the sale of games.

Finally, a firm may have non-value-related objectives for its products. Discounts or special products for disadvantaged members of society fall into this category. Interestingly, we have seen very little activity in this area, despite the growing interest in corporate social responsibility.

A number of implications stem from considering the various roles that different products can address for the firm. The first is one of measurement. While the varying roles of different products is recognized in the management accounting literature, which endorses the idea that products can be loss making in their own right, there is little guidance to the chief financial officer or chief marketing officer as to how to determine the net effect of such products on the firm's overall value (e.g. Atkinson et al. 2007). Guilding and McManus (2002) propose that one way to account for cross-selling and product migration strategies is to move to regarding individual customers as the unit of analysis, allowing an assessment of the customer lifetime value, an approach now popular in marketing (e.g. Rust et al. 2001). Calibration of the externalities generated by individual products starts with the identification of those effects and then modeling and estimating their magnitude. A further advantage of understanding the magnitude of such positive and negative spillovers is that such information allows the manager and those above her to focus on the key objective. Rather than complaining about how much money a loss leader is costing (and trying to limit it), key performance metrics will look at the level of cross-selling attributable to the product and concentrate on how to increase it.

The second issue emerging from a consideration of product roles is the range of objectives addressed. It is possible for a product to undertake a number of different roles. For example, for many years, the Windows platform has played a defense role for Microsoft, minimizing competitive new service entry by using bundling as a barrier to entry. However, it has also acted as a major cash cow, generating large margins on very high sales volumes. It is necessary to balance the varying objectives that a product can address. Of course, a product may have positive effects on some aspects of its own earnings and those of other products, but a negative impact on other aspects (as illustrated in equation 10.1). For example, the IBM PCjr aimed to have the positive effects of generating volume at the low end of the desktop market, but it also had the negative effects of cannibalization and brand dilution on IBM's image.[3]

Another issue worthy of consideration is that of aggregation across products. The analysis proposed above is all at the individual product level, predicated on the relationship between the product and other products in the firm's portfolio. Clearly, some form of aggregation is required. A corporate view of the firm (by assessing all of its products) is necessary to consider the externalities between its different elements. At its simplest, this analysis will calibrate interactions to detect overlap (and thus the negative externalities that arise due to cannibalization), synergies (and thus positive interactions that arise due to issues such as economies of scale) and gaps (and thus areas in which further new product development is required). We know quite a lot about response functions and profit maximization for individual products (see, e.g, Hanssens et al. 2003). However, despite early attention from Day (1977), the literature on maximizing the value of portfolios of products is considerably less well developed. (For exceptions, see Bayus and Putsis 1999; Draganska and Jain 2005; Chen and Hausman 2000; and Shankar 2006.) This is an extremely difficult problem from an analytical perspective, but it is one that is very important to the manager. The CEO of Kellogg, for example, should be a lot less worried about how reducing non-consideration of a niche brand like Cocoa Krispies by broadening its appeal will increase its profits (a question that we are well equipped to answer) and much more about its net effect on Kellogg's total profit in the ready-to-eat breakfast cereal category, after considering all of the interactions with Kellogg's other products.

NEW PRODUCT METRICS, MONITORING AND TRACKING

New product development, like other areas in marketing, has come under increasing pressure to make investments in it accountable. Figure 10.1 provides a framework for us to consider the metrics we need to ensure the success of new products, both before and after launch. New products must meet the needs of the firm (objectives) and the requirements of the customer (needs). The market must support them (characteristics) and the firm must have the resources to allocate these resources and successfully execute them (strengths) (Shankar, Chapter 9 in this volume). The resultant measures are illustrated in Table 10.3.

These metrics, particularly those relating to market acceptance, will evolve during the launch process. Prior to launch, measures of attitudes (perceptions and associations) will provide an early indicator of likely market acceptance. As the product diffuses, behavioral measures such as level of trial and (still later) repeat will dictate the degree of market acceptance of the new product more accurately.

Table 10.3   Key new product development metrics (measurement analog to Figure 10.1)

	Internal performance measures	External performance measures
Customer value delivery performance measures	Production capacity and quality control Staffing levels: service support and sales force Adverting spend and communications budget	**Prelaunch metrics:** ● Perceptions ● Willingness to pay ● Purchase intentions **Additional post-launch metrics:** ● Awareness and consideration ● Trial, repeat, share of wallet ● Customer satisfaction/ recommend
Company objective performance measures	Profitability, margins and costs Cannibalization and category development	Distribution and availability Likely competitive response Regulatory barriers

FUTURE RESEARCH

The strategic roles of new products and brands in meeting the needs of a firm's target market and realizing a firm's objectives raise many interesting research questions. Perhaps the four most interesting ones are:

- *Product role calibration* How do we calibrate within the firm the degree to which a new product has the potential to fulfill different objectives of the firm?
- *Accounting for heterogeneity* When the firm plans and launches a new product, how should it determine the breadth of the target market to which it should appeal relative to the depth of appeal it seeks in that target?
- *Product portfolio maximization* How should a firm like Kellogg, the ready-to-eat breakfast cereal manufacturer, maximize profits across the whole category, as opposed to individually maximizing the value of Cornflakes, Rice Krispies, Special K and so on individually?
- *Customer value co-creation* As customers become more strongly networked, how can we harness their creative talents and word of mouth to ensure new products' success?

While there is a considerable amount of work on calibrating the appeal of new products to consumers prior to launch and over time (e.g. Roberts and Urban 1988), the same cannot be said of our ability to calibrate the different expected benefits of products in realizing different objectives of the firm. We do not adequately understand product externalities, which limits our ability to focus on product or brand roles.

This chapter has not focused on the marketplace phenomenon of customer heterogeneity. With the consideration of individual differences, the firm will be faced with a tradeoff between lower market share at a higher price, for example, and higher share at a lower price. Different distributions of heterogeneity will lead to different optimal product strategies. Ailawadi et al. (2003) talk in terms of a revenue premium for products, rather than a price premium, to allow for the fact that firms may capture the economic rents from strong products in terms of either higher prices or higher sales.

Next, product portfolio optimization presents a nettlesome problem. In marketing we are a long way from understanding how a firm should account for product interactions to maximize its within- and cross-category performance, as opposed to that of individual products. Why is it that Kellogg has a need for 25 sub-brands in its US ready-to-eat cereal portfolio (ignoring variants), whereas Anheuser Busch has only three major US beer brands? While factors such as the nature of consumer heterogeneity, competition, cost of product proliferation and the like are obviously important, how are they important?

Finally, many firms, both B2B and B2C are now trying to harness the ideas and resources of their customers in the new product development process (e.g. Morrison et al. 2000). We still do not understand the prerequisites for the successful harnessing of the firm's customer base in this area.

SUMMARY

This chapter has attempted to understand new product and service development from a strategic perspective. The foundation on which strategy is developed, the marketing audit, consists of two matching processes, in line with the idea of marketing being the study of exchange: what the firm can do to meet its customers' needs on the one hand, and the benefit that will accrue to it by doing so on the other. In the specific case of new product development, these two matching processes lead to a consideration of the value proposition of a product and the product or brand roles. Thus this chapter has stressed that different products should attempt to meet different needs of the customer on the one hand and address different objectives of the firm on the other. The resultant specialization leads us to then consider how to aggregate all of the firm's products to ensure consistency at the corporate level. That is, the firm ensures that the targeted needs of customers are cost-effectively addressed and all of the objectives of the company are covered by the entire portfolio of company products on the other.

NOTES

1. I shall use the term "product" to describe both products and services. While there are important differences between a consumer offering that consists totally of tangible features and one that is 100 percent service (and all combinations between), most of the concepts in this chapter may be applied to both. For a discussion of product–service differences see, for example, Lovelock (1983).
2. http://en.wikipedia.org/wiki/Buick_Park_Avenue.
3. http://en.wikipedia.org/wiki/IBM_PCjr.

REFERENCES

Aaker, D. (1991), *Managing Brand Equity*, New York: The Free Press.
Aaker, D. (2005), *Strategic Market Management*, 7th edn, Hoboken, NJ: John Wiley & Sons.
Aaker, D. and E. Joachimsthaler (2000), *Brand Leadership*, New York: The Free Press.
Aaker, D. and K. Keller (1990), "Consumer evaluations of brand extensions", *Journal of Marketing*, **54** (1), 27–41.
Ailawadi, K., D. Lehmann and S. Neslin (2003), "Revenue premium as an outcome measure of brand equity," *Journal of Marketing*, **67** (4), 1–17.
Ambler, T. and J. Roberts (2006), "Beware the silver metric: marketing performance measurement has to be multidimensional," Report 06–113, Cambridge, MA: Marketing Science Institute.
Ansoff, I. (1965), *Corporate Strategy*, New York: McGraw Hill.
Atkinson, A., R. Kaplan, E. Matsumura and S. Young (2007), *Management Accounting*, 5th edn, New York: Pearson.
Barwise, P. and S. Meehan (2004), *Simply Better: Winning and Keeping Customers by Delivering What Matters Most*, Boston, MA: Harvard Business School Press.
Bayus, Barry and William Putsis Jr (1999), "Product proliferation: an empirical analysis of product line determinants and market outcomes," *Marketing Science*, **18**, 137–53.
Bonoma, T. (1985), "Case research in marketing: opportunities, problems, and a process," *Journal of Marketing Research*, **22** (2), 199–208.
Caris-McManus, J. (1991), *The New Product Development Planner*, New York: AMACOM (American Management Association).
Carroll, A. (1999), "Corporate social responsibility: evolution of a definitional construct," *Business and Society*, **38** (3), 268–95.
Chen, K. and W. Hausman (2000), "Mathematical properties of the optimal product line selection problem using choice-based conjoint analysis," *Management Science*, **46** (2), 327–32.

Coyne, K. (2008), "Enduring ideas: the GE–McKinsey nine-box matrix," *McKinsey Quarterly*, **4**, 142.

Day, G. (1977), "Diagnosing the product portfolio," *Journal of Marketing*, **41** (2), 29–38.

Day, G. (1994), "The capabilities of market-driven organizations," *Journal of Marketing*, **58** (4), 37–52.

DeSarbo, W., V. Ramaswamy and S. Cohen (1995), "Market segmentation with choice-based conjoint analysis," *Marketing Letters*, **6** (2), 137–47.

Draganska, M. and D. Jain (2005), "Product-line length as a competitive tool," *Journal of Economics and Management Strategy*, **14** (1), 1–28.

Elkington, J. (1994), *Cannibals with Forks: The Triple Bottom Line of 21st Century Business*, Gabriola Island, BC: New Society Publishers.

Gatignon, H., B. Weitz and P. Bansal (1990), "Brand introduction strategies and competitive environment," *Journal of Marketing Research*, **27** (November), 390–401.

Guilding, C. and L. McManus (2002), "The incidence, perceived merit and antecedents of customer accounting: an exploratory note," *Accounting, Organizations and Society*, **27**, 45–59.

Hanssens, D., L. Parsons and R. Schultz (2003), *Market Response Models: Econometric and Time Series Analysis*, (International Series in Quantitative Marketing), Norwell MA: Kluwer Academic Publishers.

Hess, J. and E. Gerstner (1987), "Loss leader pricing and rain check policy," *Marketing Science*, **6** (4), 358–74.

Hesseldahl, A. (2005), "Microsoft's red-ink game," *Business Week* (November 22).

Keller, K. (2008), *Strategic Brand Management*, 3rd edn, Upper Saddle River, NJ: Pearson.

Laskey, H., E. Day and M. Crask (1989), "Typology of main message strategies for television commercials," *Journal of Advertising*, **18** (1), 36–41.

Lovelock, C. (1983), "Classifying services to gain strategic marketing insights," *Journal of Marketing*, **47** (3), 9–20.

Morrison, P.D., J.H. Roberts and E. von Hippel (2000), "Innovation by lead users in a second tier market: patterns in product modification and information sharing," *Management Science*, December, 1513–27.

Parasuraman, A., L. Berry and V. Zeithaml (1991), "Understanding customer expectations of service," *Sloan Management Review* (April), 39–48.

Parmalee, D. (1993), *Evaluating Marketing Strengths and Weaknesses*, American Marketing Association Marketing Toolbox Series, Chicago: NTC Books.

Ragubhir, P., J. Roberts, K. Lemon and R. Winer (2010), "Why, when and how should the effect of marketing be measured? A stakeholder perspective for corporate social responsibility metrics," *Journal of Public Policy & Marketing*, **20** (1), 66–77.

Ritson, M. (2010), "Should you launch a fighter brand?," *Harvard Business Review* (October), Reprint R0910K.

Roberts, J. and G. Urban (1988), "Modeling multiattribute utility, risk, and belief dynamics for new consumer durable brand choice," *Management Science* (February), 167–85.

Roberts, J., C. Nelson and P. Morrison (2005), "A prelaunch diffusion model for evaluating market defense strategies," *Marketing Science*, **24** (1), 150–64.

Rust, R., V. Zeithaml and K. Lemon (2001), *Driving Customer Equity: How Customer Lifetime Value is Reshaping Corporate Strategy*, New York: The Free Press.

Shankar, Venkatesh (1999), "New product introduction and incumbent response strategies: their interrelationship and the role of multimarket contact," *Journal of Marketing Research*, **36** (3), 327–44.

Shankar, Venkatesh (2006), "Proactive and reactive product line strategies: asymmetries between market leaders and followers," *Management Science*, **52** (2), 276–92.

Srivastava, R., T. Shervani and L. Fahey (1997), "Driving shareholder value: the role of marketing in reducing vulnerability and volatility of cash flows," *Journal of Market Focused Management*, **2** (1), 49–64.

Strebel, P. and A.V. Ohlsson (2006), "The art of making smart moves," *Sloan Management Review*, **47** (2), 79–83.

Urban, G. and J. Hauser (1983), *Design and Marketing of New Products*, 2nd edn, Englewood Cliffs, NJ: Prentice-Hall.

Urban, G., P. Johnson and J. Hauser (1984), "Testing competitive market structures," *Marketing Science*, **3** (2), 83–112.

Vargo, S. and R. Lusch (2004), "Evolving to a new dominant logic for marketing," *Journal of Marketing*, **68** (1), 1–17.

Walker, O. and R. Ruekert (1987), "Marketing's role in the implementation of business strategies: a critical review and conceptual framework," *Journal of Marketing*, **51** (3), 15–33.

Walker, O., H. Boyd and J Larreché (1999), *Marketing Strategy: Planning and Implementation*, 3rd edn, Boston, MA: Irwin McGraw-Hill.

11 Advertising strategy: consumer mindsets and message alignment
Derek D. Rucker

For many brands, producing a superior product is not enough to achieve success in the marketplace. Brands must motivate trial of their product and fend off the competition. Often such objectives require communicating and convincing consumers that a brand has a competitive or superior offering on some dimension of value to the consumer (see Czepiel and Kerin, Chapter 4 in this volume; Keller, Chapter 17 in this volume). As a consequence, at the crux of many thriving brands one should not be surprised to find a successful advertising campaign. However, this does not mean that advertising inevitably will benefit a brand. Indeed, Lodish and colleagues (1995) looked at 389 advertising experiments and found that in a number of cases advertising had no discernible impact on sales.

The findings of Lodish and colleagues do not mean that advertising has no effect. Rather, one interpretation of the data is that some messages are likely to be very successful, other messages to have little effect and other messages to have the potential to actually work against the brand. Put bluntly, there is much variance in the sea of advertising appeals when it comes to winning over the consumer. As a consequence, one of the greatest challenges faced by brand managers, advertisers and academics remains the issue of how to design communications that are persuasive. Although there is no simple answer to this problem or golden rule to follow, our understanding of the science of persuasion continues to advance with each generation and offers new insights to better design communications to consumers.

This chapter focuses on several recent research findings that have the common idea that persuasion can be enhanced by the creation of an alignment between consumers' mindsets and the copy or message of an advertisement. The chapter is organized as follows. To begin, the notion of consumer mindsets is introduced and discussed. Subsequently, the importance of aligning messages to consumers' mindsets is discussed with respect to effects of alignment on consumers' preferences, information processing and behavior. Different types of mindsets, as well as the information that resonates with that mindset, are revealed. Finally, future directions for research in this domain are discussed.

CONSUMER MINDSETS

The term 'mindset' in this chapter is used broadly to describe a psychological state of being. Examples of mindsets include emotional states that range from jubilation to depression (Labroo and Rucker 2010; Wegener et al. 1995), hierarchical considerations with respect to having or lacking power (Rucker and Galinsky 2008, 2009), a sense of confidence versus doubt (Gal and Rucker 2010; Tormala et al. 2008) and motivations associated with advancement versus security (Aaker and Lee 2001; Higgins 1997).

Mindsets can be both chronic (i.e. the natural state of an individual) and situational (i.e. brought about by one's immediate social environment). Consider the construct of psychological power – a state that arises from the asymmetrical control over other people or valued resources. The state of psychological power can be triggered by the actual hierarchical roles one possesses in a task; for example, whether an individual is assigned to be an employee (low power) or a boss (high power; Briñol et al. 2007; Galinsky et al. 2003; Rucker and Galinsky 2009, experiment 3). At the same time, there are chronic differences such that some individuals naturally feel more or less powerful (Anderson and Galinsky 2006; Rucker and Galinsky 2009, experiment 1).

The importance of mindsets for marketers and practitioners resides in the fact that mindsets affect how people interpret and respond to their world. Depending on consumers' mindset, certain types of information become more motivating, salient, focal or important than others. This has significant consequences, from affecting consumers' preferences to consumers' processing of information to consumers' actual behavior. As a result, marketers can design their advertisements to align with consumers' mindsets to increase efficacy. The term "message alignment" is hereafter used to refer to the fit or resonance between what is salient due to a consumer's mindset and what is presented in a message. For example, if a mindset orients a consumer to think more about status (versus quality), an advertisement that focuses on status will be more aligned with the mindset than an advertisement that focuses on quality. Indeed, consumers' responses to different types of advertising represent one means by which mindsets can be identified if unknown or not activated by the advertiser.

Of course, the type of information that aligns with a consumer's mindset is dependent upon the specific nature of the mindset. Given the sheer number of possible mindsets that can be present in consumers or activated by advertisers, the present chapter focuses on mindsets that have received recent empirical attention related to (a) different emotions, (b) promotion versus prevention, (c) power versus powerlessness, and (d) confidence versus doubt. Importantly the goal here is not to provide an exhaustive review of the literature in each of these areas, but to use these examples in an effort to familiarize the reader with the concept and importance of consumer mindsets and message alignment.

EMOTIONS

Emotions are often strong states accompanied by both physiological and psychological manifestations. Emotions can be categorized broadly by their valence (i.e. positive or negative) but also by the specific nature of the emotion. For example, sadness, anxiety, fear and embarrassment are all distinct negative emotions. Similarly, happiness, calmness, elation and pride are all distinct positive emotions. Both valence and the specific nature of the emotion have been shown to produce mindsets that predispose consumers towards processing or preferring certain types of information.

Happiness and Information Processing

Research on the valence of emotions has examined what types of information receive more or less scrutiny as a function of individuals' experiencing a positive or negative emotion. For example, work by Wegener and colleagues (1995) proposed that the experience of happiness on consumers' information processing of subsequent messages depends on how that message is framed or presented to the individual. The authors suggested that, as happiness is typically a desired state, individuals would be inclined to carefully attend to and process information that they perceived would maintain their happiness, but less inclined to attend to information that might undermine their happiness. This hypothesis suggests that, provided an individual has compelling arguments, positioning a message as reinforcing one's happiness, rather than as saddening, would be more effective in garnering attention and thus should enhance persuasion.

To test this idea, Wegener and colleagues first had individuals watch a ten-minute videotape designed to induce happiness or sadness. Subsequently, participants were presented with two articles. The first was designed to further reinforce participants' moods (i.e. a sad article in the sad condition or a happy article in the happy condition). The second article was presented as a tuition plan. However, at the outset of this second article participants were told the article was designed to either make them feel happy or sad. Importantly, this second article contained either strong and compelling reasons for the tuition plan or weak and specious reasons for the tuition plan. This latter manipulation is a standard for gauging information processing, as individuals should be more persuaded by strong relative to weak arguments as their attention to the message increases (for reviews see Petty and Wegener 1998; Rucker and Petty 2006).

Wegener and colleagues found evidence consistent with their proposed hypothesis: happy individuals showed a stronger differentiation between strong and weak arguments when they were informed that reading the message would make them happy, but showed little differentiation when informed that the article would make them sad. In contrast, individuals who were sad showed similar levels of differentiation. This finding suggests that, when people are happy, information that is presented as maintaining that happiness aligns better than information that is viewed as potentially undermining that happiness. This can be understood from the perspective of message alignment as a message focused on making people happy aligns with the goal produced by a pre-existing state of happiness.

Of course, the finding that sad participants processed information extensively regardless of how the message was framed does not mean that there is no information that aligns better with negative emotions. Rather, this outcome simply means that, when it comes to information processing, the hedonic value of the message is a source of alignment or misalignment for the mental mindset associated with happiness, but not for sadness. As detailed next, different negative emotions can also affect consumers' preference for different types of information.

Specific Negative Emotions and Preferred Positive Emotions

Recent work has tested how specific negative emotions can differentially affect consumers' preferences (Labroo and Rucker 2010; Rucker and Petty 2004). For example, Labroo and Rucker suggested that different negative emotions, such as anger and anxiety, are associated with either an approach or an avoidance orientation. For example, anxiety arises from failure to avoid an undesired outcome, whereas anger arises from failure to approach a desired outcome. They suggested these orientations would produce a preference among consumers such that individuals would tend to prefer positive outcomes that aligned with the nature of their negative emotions. If people were experiencing an approach-oriented negative emotion (e.g. sadness, anger), Labroo and Rucker predicted people would prefer a positive outcome that was approach oriented (e.g. happiness); conversely if experiencing an avoidance-oriented negative emotion (e.g. anxiety, embarrassment), they predicted people would prefer a positive outcome that was avoidance-oriented (e.g. calmness).

To test their hypothesis, Labroo and Rucker (2010) had participants first recall a past event in their lives where they felt sad, angry, anxious or embarrassed. Subsequently, as part of an ostensibly unrelated task, they exposed participants to an advertisement for a vacation destination. All participants were instructed to read the advertisement carefully and thus it was not expected that there would be an opportunity for differences in information processing. The copy for the execution was nearly identical, except that in one condition it stressed that the destination would offer consumers happiness and in the other it would offer consumers calmness. After reading the execution, participants were asked to indicate how much they liked the destination and their intention of visiting the destination.

Labroo and Rucker found that when participants had recalled a negative emotion associated with avoidance (i.e. anxiety, embarrassment), they reported liking the vacation destination associated with a positive avoidance emotion (i.e. calmness) more than the vacation destination associated with a positive approach emotion (i.e. happiness). In contrast, when participants had recalled a negative emotion associated with approach (i.e. sadness, anger), they reported liking the vacation destination associated with a positive approach emotion (i.e. happiness) more than the vacation destination associated with a positive avoidance emotion (i.e. calmness). Consistent with the notion of message alignment, these findings suggest that based on the orientation of consumers' negative emotion, different positive emotions better align with this preexisting state and are thus preferred.

PROMOTION AND PREVENTION

Regulatory focus theory (Higgins 1997) distinguishes between two major categories of desired goals: promotion and prevention. Promotion goals relate to attaining positive outcomes and are associated with concepts such as advancement, achievements and aspirations. Prevention goals relate to avoiding negative outcomes and are associated with concepts such as responsibilities, obligations and security. When there is a natural correspondence or alignment between regulatory focus and how information is presented, this produces "regulatory fit," which has implications for a wide variety of measures including information recall and brand evaluation.

Self-views and Recall of Promotion versus Prevention Information

Aaker and Lee (2001) put forth the proposition that matching the content of a message with the self-regulatory focus that is consistent with one's accessible view enhances attention to such information. Specifically, the authors suggested that activating an independent view of the self would be more consistent with a promotion-focused message (i.e. produce regulatory fit), whereas activating a view of the interdependent self would be more consistent with a prevention-focused message (see Lee et al. 2000). As such, Aaker and Lee predicted that when the independent self-view was activated, promotion-focused messages would be attended to more carefully compared to prevention-focused messages, but the reverse should be true when an interdependent self-view was activated. One consequence of greater attention should be a greater recall of information.

To test their hypotheses, Aaker and Lee (2001) asked participants to look at some ideas for an advertising campaign for a new tennis racket. Participants were given one of four different scenarios that described a tennis tournament and manipulated both self-views and promotion versus prevention. To manipulate self-views, the scenario used language describing the individual (e.g. "You are playing in a tennis tournament . . ." or describing the role of others (e.g. "Your team is playing in a tennis tournament"). To manipulate promotion versus prevention, the copy in the execution was varied to either emphasize prevention (e.g. "If you lose this last match, you will lose the championship title and not bring home the huge trophy") or promotion (e.g. "If you win this last match, you will win the championship title and bring home the huge trophy"). Subsequently, participants were asked to recall aspects of the scenario they read (e.g. the reward for winning the tennis match).

Consistent with the notion that regulatory fit can facilitate or direct one's attention, Aaker and Lee found that participants whose independent self-view was activated had better recall for the promotion-focused information than the prevention-focused information, whereas the reverse occurred among participants whose interdependent self-view was activated.

Regulatory Fit and Persuasion

Cesario et al. (2004) suggested that regulatory fit can also arise from a match between whether one is promotion or prevention focused and whether goals are pursued in an eager or vigilant manner. Furthermore, these authors suggest that regulatory fit can lead an individual to feel right about what they are doing and produce value. In the persuasion domain, Cesario and colleagues suggested that when the arguments in a message fit the regulatory focus of the message recipient, the recipient should experience regulatory fit and feel right. As a consequence, the individual should show more favorable attitudes with respect to the message advocacy.

As a test of their hypothesis, Cesario and colleagues (2004, experiment 2) first measured participants' chronic regulatory focus to identify participants as promotion or prevention oriented. Subsequently, all participants were exposed to a message about the benefits of a new after-school program. The arguments of the message were framed in terms of either an eager (e.g. "this program . . . will *advance* children's education and *support* more children to *succeed*") or vigilant means (e.g. "this program . . . will *secure* children's education and *prevent* more children from *failing*").

The authors found that those who were promotion focused were more persuaded by eager means than by vigilant means. In contrast, those who were prevention focused tended to be more persuaded by vigilant compared to eager means. In short, simply framing a message to align with individuals' chronic mindset had clear implications for persuasion.

POWER AND POWERLESSNESS

Power has been defined as asymmetrical control over others or resources (see Magee and Galinsky 2008; Rucker and Galinsky 2008). And, although there are chronic differences in power in society (e.g. bosses versus employees), power is also a psychological state or mindset that can be easily activated. For example, psychological states of power can be achieved merely by assigning individuals to the role of a boss or employee, asking them to recall a time they had or lacked power, or even through basic semantic priming procedures. Several recent experiments have suggested that the activation of a temporary state of power or powerlessness has important ramifications for the type of information that aligns with the mindset.

Power and Preference for Status versus Functionality

Rucker and Galinsky (2009) postulated that, because a state of low power is aversive, individuals placed into a temporary state of low power would seek to remedy that state. And, as status is a signal of one's place in the social hierarchy (Magee and Galinsky 2008), they further reasoned that individuals experiencing a state of powerlessness would have an increased preference for status-related objects. In contrast, a state of high power signals that one should follow his or her own beliefs and need not worry about the opinion of others (e.g. Briñol et al. 2007). Therefore individuals experiencing power should not be persuaded by high-status objects but instead should care about objects that offer the best experience for them personally (i.e. highly functional objects).

To test these hypotheses, Rucker and Galinsky first had participants recall a time they possessed power, lacked power or went to the grocery store (baseline). Then, as part of a supposedly unrelated task, participants received, and were asked to carefully evaluate, one of two advertisements for a pen. One advertisement described the pen in terms of the status it afforded (e.g. the copy stated the pen conveyed respect and esteem), whereas the other described the pen in terms of function and performance (e.g. the copy stated the pen was of fine craftsmanship and superior quality). Participants were asked to report how much they liked the pen.

Although all participants received an identical picture of the product, when the pen was framed in terms of status, Rucker and Galinsky (2009) found that low-power participants had significantly more favorable attitudes towards the pen that high-power and baseline participants, which did not differ from one another. In contrast, when the pen was framed in terms of performance, high-power participants had significantly more favorable attitudes towards the pen than low-power and baseline participants, which did not differ from each other. In short, the experience of a temporary state of power or powerlessness significantly affected participants' desirability for the product as a function of how the product was positioned in the marketing effort (i.e. advertisement). A status appeal aligned better with a low-power mindset, whereas a quality appeal aligned better with a high-power mindset.

Power and Spending on Oneself versus Others

One important point about mindsets is that they typically offer a series of associations. For example, an emotion, such as sadness, might have both an approach orientation but also have associations of certainty or uncertainty (Tiedens and Linton 2001). Consequently, it is not the case that there is only a singular dimension on which marketing efforts or advertisements can be matched. As an example of this, Rucker et al. (2011b) suggested that power might not only affect people's preferences for status or functionality (Rucker and Galinsky 2008, 2009), but might also affect people's preferences for how they spend on themselves versus others. Specifically, the authors argued that states of power tend to increase one's self-importance and, as a result, should foster a greater willingness to spend on gifts for oneself. In contrast, states of powerlessness tend to increase one's dependence on others, which should lead to greater spending on others. Thus they suggested that not only does power affect the type of product positioning consumers are sensitive to (i.e. status versus performance), but power might affect how consumers spend on gifts for themselves or others.

This is another hypothesis of alignment, as individuals should be most interested in a product for themselves when in a state of power, but more interested in a product for others when in a state of powerlessness. To test their hypothesis, Rucker and colleagues first assigned participants to a state of low or high power by informing them they would take on the role of a boss or employee in an upcoming task. Importantly, it was made clear to participants that in this task the boss would have authority and control of rewards and decisions, whereas the employee would have no control. Next, prior to engaging in the boss or employee task, participants were asked to bid on products, a mug and a t-shirt as a gift for either themselves or for another person. Specifically, when bidding for themselves participants wrote their own name down as the recipient, but when bidding for another person participants wrote that individual's name down.

Consistent with their hypothesis, Rucker and colleagues (2011b) found that low-power individuals, compared to high-power individuals, had a significantly higher bid price when the recipient of the products was another person. However, when the recipient of the products was the participant, high-power individuals had a significantly higher bid price than low-power individuals. Thus, for states of power, messages can be aligned both with respect to whether they focus on status versus functionality and whether they are focused on oneself or others.

PSYCHOLOGICAL CONFIDENCE AND DOUBT

Classic work on information processing suggests that people attend to information, in part, as a function of whether they feel confident or doubtful (e.g. Chaiken et al. 1989; Maheswaran and Chaiken 1991). People typically process information more carefully when in a state of doubt as opposed to confidence. The traditional explanation for this effect has been that when people feel confident, they attribute this to the fact they have sufficient knowledge, which renders further processing unnecessary. In contrast, when people feel doubt, they infer they lack sufficient knowledge and careful processing of information is one solution to this problem. However, researchers have begun to ask whether the information processing triggered by incidental states of confidence and doubt (i.e. states unrelated to the message topic) can be swayed by how a message is positioned. Rather than confidence or doubt inevitably reducing or increasing processing, recent findings suggest that how a message is framed can provide a signal of the relevance of the message due to one's state of certainty or doubt.

Confidence Framing

Tormala et al. (2008) suggested that when in a state of confidence, individuals actually attend to and process more carefully, information framed as conveying confidence because such information is viewed as more relevant since it aligns with individuals' current state. Furthermore, information framed as conveying confidence would mismatch the state of individuals experiencing doubt, which might ironically lead them to process the information less, despite their need for confidence.

To test their hypothesis, Tormala and colleagues (2008) first had participants list five experiences in which they felt either a great deal of confidence or a great deal of doubt. Subsequently, participants were told they would read a message for a new comprehensive exam policy supposedly being considered for implementation at their university. Before the message was delivered, approximately half the participants learned that the message was intended to build confidence, whereas the remaining participants received no such frame. Finally, all participants read a persuasive message in favor of the exam policy that contained either weak or strong arguments (see Petty and Cacioppo 1986). Tormala and colleagues found that, when there was no frame, a temporary state of confidence led to less differentiating among weak and strong arguments than a state of doubt, replicating the commonly observed effects of confidence and doubt on information processing. If the message was framed as offering confidence, however, the reverse occurred, a temporary state of confidence led to more differentiating among weak and strong arguments than a state of doubt.

These findings suggest that a confidence frame aligned with individuals who felt confident, which enhanced information processing, but misaligned with doubtful individuals, which actually decreased processing.

Confidence and Level of Construal

Recent work by Wan and Rucker (2011) suggests that confidence and doubt do not merely govern the depth of people's information processing, but affect how people think about information. Specifically, the authors suggested that doubt leads people to view objects at a low level of construal (i.e. emphasizing means-related, secondary and low-level representations), whereas confidence leads individuals to view objects at a high level of construal (i.e. emphasizing goal-relevant, schematic and high-level representations). Based on this observation, as well as a pre-test demonstrating such a relationship, the authors proposed that confidence might increase attention to a message that is framed at an abstract level of construal, whereas doubt would increase attention to a message framed at a concrete level of construal.

To test their hypothesis, participants were first asked to list experiences in which they experienced confidence or doubt (see Gal and Rucker 2010; Tormala et al. 2008).

Subsequently, participants were told they would read a message describing a hotel. In the high construal condition participants were told to think about booking this hotel for a trip that was six months away (i.e. distant future), whereas in the low construal condition they were told to think about booking the hotel trip next week (i.e. near future), a typical manipulation of construal (see Fujita et al. 2006). Participants then received a message that contained either weak or strong arguments. Consistent with expectations, Wan and Rucker found that participants' state of confidence interacted with level of construal. When the message was presented at a low level of construal (i.e. near future), a state of doubt led to a stronger differentiation between weak and strong arguments than confidence; when the message was framed at a high level of construal (i.e. six months), a state of confidence led to a stronger differentiation between weak and strong arguments than doubt. Thus incidental states of confidence and doubt do not always reduce and increase information processing respectively; rather, information processing is affected by whether the message aligns with their psychological state.

GENERAL DISCUSSION AND FUTURE DIRECTIONS

The present chapter has reviewed findings from four distinct areas to make a general point about the importance of aligning messages to consumers' mindsets. Although the evidence for message alignment seems clear, there remain a number of important issues and directions for future research. A selection of such possibilities is now discussed.

Traversing the World of Message Alignment: An Elaboration Perspective

Although the present research has summarized consistent evidence that suggests message alignment can affect consumers' behavior from information processing to recall and preferences, one might wonder when the various types of effects will be observed. For example, how can one predict, *a priori*, whether alignment will lead to greater processing of a message or simply predispose individuals to be more favorable towards the message?

There are likely many answers to this question worthy of exploration, but one potential answer lies in the elaboration likelihood model of persuasion (Petty and Cacioppo 1986). According to this model, the amount of thinking, or elaboration, done by an individual influences how a variable affects persuasion. For example, consider the credibility of the source. Sources that are credible (i.e. are trustworthy and possess expertise) can be used as a simple cue for persuasion when individuals are not thinking carefully and elaboration is low (e.g. if a credible source says it then it must be right!). However, when elaboration is moderate, the credibility of the source is more likely to affect whether people process information (e.g. individuals may feel a greater need to scrutinize the arguments of a less credible source). Finally, if elaboration is high, because people are already engaged in thoughtful scrutiny of a message, they will not use variables as heuristics nor do they need to decide whether to process the message. Rather, under high elaboration, variables, such as source credibility can bias processing, serve as arguments, affect thought confidence, or produce correction (see Rucker et al. 2011a). For example, the credibility of the source might lead individuals to feel more confident in their thoughts, which in turn would enhance persuasion to strong messages compared to weak messages (e.g. Tormala et al. 2007).[1]

Instances of message alignment or nonalignment could be examined through the lens of the elaboration likelihood model. When individuals are not paying careful attention, they might use message alignment as a simple cue, being more persuaded by a message that aligns with their mindset than a message that does not. When elaboration conditions are moderate, message alignment might be used as a signal to process the message more carefully. Finally, when elaboration is high, message alignment might serve to bias their thoughts, affect their confidence, produce correction processes, or serve as arguments. Indeed, a similar argument for multiple roles as a function of elaboration has been made for mood (e.g. Petty et al. 2001). Future research could aim to systematically test whether different types of message alignment affect persuasion through unique processes depending on level of elaboration as well as examine other possible moderators of the precise influence of message alignment or nonalignment.

Mapping Associations of Mindsets

As indicated in several of the examples used in this chapter, the same mindset can have multiple associations. For example, a state of power, compared to powerlessness, leads people to be more persuaded by a message advertising the functionality of the product compared to the status of a product (Rucker and Galinsky 2009). However, a state of power, compared to a state of powerlessness, also leads to an increased willingness to spend on oneself compared to others (Rucker et al. 2011b). Similarly, a state of certainty leads people to attend more to messages that are either framed in terms of building confidence (Tormala et al. 2008) or framed at a more abstract level (Wan and Rucker 2011).

The recognition of multiple associations to mindsets raises several interesting topics for further pursuit. For example, for any particular mindset, researchers are likely to benefit from pushing beyond an initial demonstration of an alignment effect and looking at the different types of alignment that can occur. The value in such an approach is not only does it hold potential practical applications, but by understanding what information aligns with various mindsets academics and practitioners also acquire a better understanding of the mindset itself. Another interesting issue is whether there are additive or interactive effects of alignment when more than one dimension is varied in a message. For instance, if a message talks about building confidence and is framed at an abstract level, would this produce even more processing by individuals experiencing confidence than either of these forms of alignment on their own? Such questions would help provide a richer understanding of both mindsets and message alignment.

Is Message Alignment Always Beneficial?

Many of the reported findings here suggest that aligning message content to consumers' mindsets is beneficial to the marketer in terms of enhancing persuasion or positively affecting behavior. From this perspective, the prescription is clear: measure or manipulate the consumers' mindset and provide information that aligns with it to enhance persuasion. However, the present discussion should not be taken as evidence that message alignment unilaterally increases persuasion. Most notably, in cases where individuals are deciding whether to process information, message alignment, which would increase information processing, could reduce persuasion if the ultimate arguments for buying the product are unconvincing (see Tormala et al. 2008). This observation underscores the importance of not simply understanding whether a message aligns with consumers' mindset, but *what process* is being affected by the alignment.

Similarly, message alignment might negatively affect persuasion if it leads people to be more likely to rely on their reactions to a message and those reactions happen to be negative. Indeed, in a subsequent experiment on regulatory fit, Cesario and colleagues (2004) found that if negative thoughts were elicited by a message, regulatory fit reduced persuasion. The authors suggested that the experience of fit led participants to not simply like the proposal more, but to be more likely to utilize their message-related thoughts, which led to more or less persuasion depending on whether participants' message-related thoughts were positive or negative. Future research should examine other boundary conditions to message alignment.

CONCLUSION

Persuasion is a powerful but complex tool in attempting to influence consumers' behavior. The present research demonstrates that the strategic alignment of one's message with consumers' mindsets is a powerful factor in the efficacy of one's persuasive attempts. Given how easily mindsets seemed to be activated (e.g. simple recall tasks, being assigned to a role), an exciting element from the perspective of practitioners should be that marketing communications and advertisements can be strategically designed with the goal of both activating the appropriate mindset and providing the response in the message that best aligns to that mindset (e.g. Aaker and Lee 2001). Message alignment is not only a powerful idea to leverage in one's communications, but message misalignment is often a pitfall that must be avoided. Indeed, the mixed results reported regarding advertising appeals (Lodish et al. 1995) might be partially remedied through greater attention to the alignment between consumers' mindsets and message content.

NOTE

1. A full discussion of the multiple roles for variables under different degrees of elaboration is beyond the scope of this chapter, but this topic is covered in depth elsewhere (see Petty and Wegener, 1998; Rucker and Petty 2006; Rucker et al. 2011a).

REFERENCES

Aaker, Jennifer L. and Angela Y. Lee (2001), "'I' seek pleasures and 'we' avoid pains: the role of self-regulatory goals in information processing and persuasion," *Journal of Consumer Research*, **28** (June), 33–49.
Anderson, Cameron and Adam D. Galinsky (2006), "Power, optimism and risk-taking," *European Journal of Social Psychology*, **36**, 511–36.
Briñol, Pablo, Richard E. Petty, Carmen Valle, Derek D. Rucker and Alberto Becerra (2007), "The effects of message recipients' power before and after persuasion: a self-validation analysis," *Journal of Personality and Social Psychology*, **93** (Dec.), 1040–53.

Cesario, Joseph, Heidi Grant and E. Tory Higgins (2004), "Regulatory fit and persuasion: transfer from 'feeling right'," *Journal of Personality and Social Psychology*, **86**, 388–404.

Chaiken, S., A. Liberman and A.H. Eagly (1989), "Heuristic and systematic information processing within and beyond the persuasion context," in J.S Uleman and J.A Bargh (eds), *Unintended Thought*, New York: Guilford Press, pp. 212–52.

Fujita, Kentaro, Yaacov Trope, Nira Liberman and Maya Levin-Sagi (2006), "Construal levels and self-control," *Journal of Personality and Social Psychology*, **90**, 351–67.

Gal, David and Derek D. Rucker (2010), "When in doubt, shout! Paradoxical influences of doubt on proselytizing," *Psychological Science*, **21** (October), 1701–7.

Galinsky, Adam D., Deborah H. Gruenfeld and Joe C. Magee (2003), "From Power to Action," *Journal of Personality and Social Psychology*, **85**, 453–66.

Higgins, E. Tory (1997), "Beyond Pleasure and Pain," *American Psychologist*, **52** (December), 1280–300.

Labroo, Aparna A. and Derek D. Rucker (2010), "The orientation-matching hypothesis: an emotion specificity approach to affect regulation," *Journal of Marketing Research*, **47** (5), 955–66.

Lee, Angela Y., Jennifer L. Aaker and Wendi L. Gardner (2000), "The pleasures and pains of distinct self-construals: the role of interdependence in regulatory focus," *Journal of Personality & Social Psychology*, **78**, 1122–34.

Lodish, Leonard M., Magid Abraham, Stuart Kalmenson, Jeanne Livelsberger, Beth Lubetkin, Bruce Richardson and Mary Ellen Stevens (1995), "How T.V. advertising works: a meta-analysis of 389 real world split cable T.V. advertising experiments," *Journal of Marketing Research*, **32**, 125–39.

Magee, Joe C. and Adam D. Galinsky (2008), "Social hierachy: the self-reinforcing nature of power and status," *Academy of Management Annals*, **2**, 351–98.

Maheswaran, D. and S. Chaiken (1991), "Promoting systematic processing in low-motivation settings – effect of incongruent information on processing and judgment," *Journal of Personality and Social Psychology*, **61** (Jul.), 13–25.

Petty, Richard E. and John T. Cacioppo (1986), *Communication and Persuasion: Central and Peripheral Routes to Attitude Change*, New York: Springer-Verlag.

Petty, Richard E. and Duane T. Wegener (1998), "Attitude change: multiple roles for persuasion variables," in Daniel T. Gilbert, Susan T. Fiske and Gardner Lindzey (eds), *The Handbook of Social Psychology*, 4th edn, vol. 1, New York: McGraw-Hill, pp. 323–90.

Petty, Richard E., David DeSteno and Derek D. Rucker (2001), "The role of affect in attitude change," in Joseph P. Forgas (ed.), *Handbook of Affect and Social Cognition*, Mahwah, NJ: Lawrence Erlbaum, pp. 212–33.

Rucker, Derek D. and Adam Galinsky (2008), "Desire to acquire: powerlessness and compensatory consumption," *Journal of Consumer Research*, **35**, 257–67.

Rucker, Derek D. and Adam Galinsky (2009), "Conspicuous consumption versus utilitarian ideals: how different levels of power shape consumer behavior," *Journal of Experimental Social Psychology*, **45**, 549–55.

Rucker, Derek D. and Richard E. Petty (2004), "An emotion specificity approach to consumer decision making," *Motivation and Emotion*, **28** (Mar.), 3–21.

Rucker, Derek D. and Richard E. Petty (2006), "Increasing the effectiveness of communications to consumers: recommendations based on the elaboration likelihood and attitude certainty perspectives," *Journal of Public Policy and Marketing*, **25** (Spr.), 39–52.

Rucker, Derek D., Pablo Briñol and Richard E. Petty (2011a), "Metacognition: methods to assess primary from secondary cognition," in Kanl C. Klauer, Andreas Voss and Christophe Stahl (eds), *Handbook of Cognitive Methods in Social Psychology*, New York: Guilford Press, pp. 236–64.

Rucker, Derek D., David Dubois and Adam D. Galinsky (2011b), "Generous paupers and stingy princes: power drives consumer spending on self and others," *Journal of Consumer Research*, **37**, 1015–29.

Tiedens, Larissa Z. and Susan Linton (2001), "Judgment under emotional certainty and uncertainty: the effects of specific emotions on information processing," *Journal of Personality and Social Psychology*, **81**, 973–88.

Tormala, Zakary L., Pablo Briñol and Richard E. Petty (2007), "Multiple roles for source credibility under high elaboration: it's all in the timing," *Social Cognition*, **25**, 536–52.

Tormala, Zakary L., Derek D. Rucker and Charles R. Seger (2008), "When increased confidence yields increased thought: a confidence-matching hypothesis," *Journal of Experimental Social Psychology*, **44**, 141–7.

Wan, Echo Wen and Derek D. Rucker (2011), "In confidence you see the forest, in doubt you see the tree," unpublished manuscript, Northwestern University.

Wegener, Duane T., Richard E. Petty and Stephen M. Smith (1995), "Positive mood can increase or decrease message scrutiny: the hedonic contingency view of mood and message processing," *Journal of Personality & Social Psychology*, **69**, 5–15.

12 Social media strategy
Donna L. Hoffman and Thomas P. Novak

As the Internet approaches nearly 20 years as a consumer medium, it is evolving into a distinctly social medium for communication, information and commerce. The Alexa rankings of the top 20 websites in the USA[1] as of August 2010 show that nine of the top sites (Facebook, YouTube, MySpace, Wikipedia, Blogger, Craigslist, Twitter, LinkedIn and WordPress) are pure social media sites driven by user-generated content. Only two sites in the Alexa top 20, Amazon and eBay, are retailing sites. This does not mean that online retailing is not successful; on the contrary, online retailers like Amazon and eBay are successful in large part because they incorporate strong social components such as user reviews and other user-generated content.

With the emergence of the Web as a social medium comes the concomitant rise of user control over this medium. In the early Web, we will call it "Web 1.0," consumers were required to navigate through relatively inflexible and often rigid online paths. In contrast, the key feature of the new Web, what we like to think of as "Web 2.0+," is that consumers can create and control their online navigational experiences and have much more freedom to engage in the behaviors that best suit their interests, which, it turns out, are not necessarily the behaviors marketers want them to have.

With consumers in control of their marketing experiences for the first time in modern history, managers are facing some distinct marketing challenges. To overcome these challenges, marketers need to focus on the fundamentals of *why* consumers use the Web. By focusing on the basic principles of how consumers behave online, not just current best practice, managers will be better prepared when Web 2.0 morphs into Web 3.0 and beyond.

In this chapter we discuss frameworks grounded in academic research that provide insight into online consumer behavior. These insights can be applied to develop and improve a company's social media strategy and help marketers prepare themselves for the next evolution in Web commerce.

THERE IS NO MARKETING WITHOUT INTERNET MARKETING

Most marketing strategy textbooks describe how marketing has moved through four stages – mass production, push selling, brand management and customer management – and note the basic trend that marketing is becoming increasingly consumer focused. With the advent of the commercial Internet in the mid-1990s, managers now have the capability to interact with, understand and build relationships with customers in ways never before possible. Internet marketing represents a fifth stage in the evolution of marketing, one in which the consumer is increasingly in control of much of the marketing process.

With each new stage of marketing, market segment sizes have become smaller and smaller. With Internet marketing, marketers increasingly attempt to target individual consumers, effectively reaching market segments of one. The ball would appear to be in the marketer's court, but there is a twist. At the same time, it is important to note that the consumption experience of the Internet is unique for each person, and as such it is impossible for marketers to control the way individual consumers actually experience the Internet. Consumers of 200+ cable or satellite TV systems have a much more uniform interface experience than individual consumers creating their own experiences online. Researchers and practitioners have to accept that on the Internet every consumer's experience is unique. This may not be true on a single website, but it is true of a consumer's overall use of the Internet and its role in her life.

The Roots of Internet Marketing are Instructive

It may be instructive to provide a brief pre-Internet view of Internet marketing by early proponents. Paul Baran, one of the "fathers of the Internet" due to his invention of "packet switching," gave a controversial talk to the American Marketing Association (AMA) in 1996:

> Around December '66, I presented a paper at the American Marketing Association called "Marketing in the Year 2000." I didn't talk about packet switching, but I described push-and-pull communications and how we're going to do our shopping via a television set and a virtual department store. If you want to buy a drill, you click on Hardware and that shows Tools and you click on that and go deeper. In the end, if you have two drills you're interested in, then you hit your Consumers Union button, and their evaluation goes up on the screen. Pretty much what WebTV is. Some in the audience were furious. They said, "People don't go shopping to buy things. They go there because of the enjoyment. You don't understand shoppers." I could see a few people going for it, but most of them were shaking their heads. (Brand 2001)

Traditional marketers were largely skeptical about claims regarding the capabilities and changes the Internet would herald. This skepticism persisted through the mid-1990s when online shopping started, and peaked around 2000 during the dot-com bust. However, a decade later Internet marketing has hit its stride. When one compares the AMA's current definition of marketing (see Box 12.1) with post-dot-com bust definitions of Internet marketing, they do not really look all that different. To us this says the field has for some time reached the point where there is no marketing without Internet marketing.

Despite these similarities, the recent incorporation of social media into the fabric of the Internet has introduced some important differences into the discussion of what is marketing. In a nutshell, online consumers can now create their own content and control their own online experiences. In a broad sense the purpose of this chapter is to explore what this means for (Internet) marketers.

Internet marketing has now been around for nearly two decades. It started in 1993 with the release of the Windows version of Mosaic and the National Science Foundation's decision to privatize its Internet backbone network NSFNET to allow commercial traffic. Yahoo, Amazon and eBay, launched in February 1994, July 1995 and September 1995 respectively, are now considered Internet old-timers, while YouTube, launched in February 2005, is considered a relative newcomer.

BOX 12.1   SOME DEFINITIONS

Definition of Marketing:
Marketing is the activity, set of institutions, and processes for creating, communicating, delivering, and exchanging offerings that have value for customers, clients, partners, and society at large.

Source: American Marketing Association (2007).

Definition of Internet Marketing:
Internet marketing is the process of building and maintaining customer relationships through online activities to facilitate the exchange of ideas, products, and services that satisfy the goals of both parties.

Source: Mohammed et al. (2002, p. 4).

The Internet is Increasingly about Social Media

What exactly is social media? Social media are interconnected media, and today have emerged as the dominant perspective to view the Web. Wikipedia defines social media as "media for social interaction, using highly accessible and scalable publishing techniques."[2] Most definitions integrate technology, communications and social interactions. Putting social media to work in search of a definition, Mashable recently posed the question, "What is social media?," requiring that all answers be submitted through Twitter in 140 characters or less (Lavrusik 2010). The hundreds of replies addressed the question from many perspectives, including collaboration, networking, conversations, sharing, relationships, information, community, personalization, content, discovery and, above all, people.

We define social media as media that enable and facilitate conversations among consumers. These social media conversations occur through Web-based tools, including mobile applications that people use to create and share content (see Shankar, Chapter 13 in this volume). We note that marketers cannot control these conversations. But they can listen to, participate in and influence the conversations. Social media are not so much about specific technologies, but rather what the technologies let people *do*. Thus marketers need to focus on the fundamental aspects of how consumers behave online, rather than the "buzz" surrounding any particular technology or application.

It is interesting to note that the Web was not originally designed to support social media. But human beings have a natural desire to communicate and share their experiences with each other, and the Web is not the first communication technology that was shaped by its users into a social media platform. Electronic "Bulletin Board Systems" or BBSes allowing people to dial in to a server via a telephone modem were developed and opened to the public in the late 1970s and offered opportunities for social discussions on message boards, community-contributed file downloads and online games. Online services like Prodigy and CompuServe were the first large-scale corporate attempts in the

1980s and early 1990s to bring a moderated interactive, "social" online experience to the mainstream public. Later, America Online (AOL) gained critical mass with aggressive direct marketing campaigns.

Even tweeting is not new. People have been broadcasting their real-time status updates (complete with hash tags (#) and at-signs (@)) since the late 1980s through Internet Relay Chat, many staying logged in continuously to keep in touch with friends in their network, just as Twitter is used today. By the mid-1990s ICQ, an instant messenger system for desktop computers, was invented and later purchased by AOL and offered to its broader market of Internet subscribers. Instant messaging is notable for the development of the emotional lexicon of social media, including avatars, abbreviations and emoticons as mechanisms to express attributes of one's self or feelings.

As the Internet Further Evolves, Marketers may Regain some Influence

Parallel to our brief history of the Internet, we can trace the history of the Web. This is a useful exercise because it gives insight into where the Web might be headed. We have noted that due to increased consumer control in social media, the balance of power has shifted to consumers. The early Web was largely static with fairly limited opportunities for interactivity, and consumers were required to follow set, relatively inflexible paths and existing, often rigid navigational structures. In this Web 1.0 environment the basic infrastructure of the Web was built and the environment was treated largely as a conduit for text and image-based data.

After nearly 20 years of commercial development we are in the middle of Web 2.0, the "next generation" of the Internet. In Web 2.0, consumers have much more control over their online navigational experiences and the Web is rapidly evolving into a platform or operating system in which applications and services are seamlessly connected or "mashed up" into a system that facilitates sharing and participation. This has been referred to as the "Lego phase" of the Internet with interactive parts that connect (Markoff 2006). The most basic implementation of "network as platform" has been to offer old applications via the network. For example, from one perspective Skype is simply telephone service served up on the Web.

But the social web is more than a new delivery system for old applications or services. One key feature of Web 2.0 applications is that they rely on network effects to acquire users, learn from them and build on their contributions; in the process, Web 2.0 applications get better the more people use them (O'Reilly and Battelle 2009). In this way Web 2.0, what we will call the social web, harnesses the collective intelligence of its users to co-create value in complex ways as witnessed with Wikipedia, eBay, YouTube, Facebook and Twitter.

Although we emphasize the strategic implications of the social web in its current incarnations, it is important to recognize that the Web continues to evolve rapidly. And while marketers are largely focused on how to implement, say, a "Facebook strategy," the social networking technologies pioneered in Web 2.0 are beginning to evolve into Web 2.0+ and Web 3.0 applications. These applications represent an extension of the Internet that incorporate intelligent agents to better understand and "interpret" content that can then be easily integrated and shared across applications. The "semantic web" (Berners-Lee et al. 2001) is part of this evolution in which artificial intelligence and human effort are integrated across the Web network. Early simple examples include tagging Flickr photos, Amazon's Mechanical Turk and smart webcams.

These social applications are important because as the Web progresses from a database to a guide that makes suggestions, marketers can regain some of the influence they are losing over consumer decisions. Web 2.0 applications will produce exponentially larger volumes of user-generated content, and the fraction of information practically useful to consumers will become smaller and smaller and more and more difficult to find. Just as modern search engines allowed users to navigate the steadily increasing volumes of Web 1.0 content and websites, consumers will turn to Web 3.0 semantic or knowledge agents as a way to gather practical nuanced recommendations and advice gleaned from otherwise unmanageable volumes of user- and firm-generated content.

WHAT IS THE SOCIAL WEB?

There are three key components to the social web: (1) social media applications like social networks, blogs and other Web 2.0 tools; (2) consumer motivations to use the social web; and (3) the user-generated content that people produce, depending on their motivations, using social media/Web 2.0 tools. Above we argued that social media enable and facilitate conversations among consumers. In our framework we define the social web as consumers interacting with each other through Web 2.0+ based social media applications. The currency of interaction is user-generated content. This allows us to expand our definition of social media as Web-based applications that permit creation, sharing, manipulation and consumption of user-generated content.

A number of attempts have been made to categorize or classify social web applications as the first step toward incorporating social media in marketing strategy. Such typologies may rely on a features-based approach (e.g. whether an application involves tags or widgets) while others focus on a services-based approach (e.g. whether an application involves blogging or multimedia sharing). Still another classification posits, only partly in jest, that the social web is a "state of mind" (Pigatto 2006).

There are undoubtedly many ways to organize the applications that make up the social web, but if we dig deeper into its underlying meaning we find that the social web embodies several very important concepts, including collaboration, sharing and community, where people are both the producers and consumers of content (McClure 2007) and that it enables markets as "conversations" (Levine et al 2001).

Our view is that the social web is the beginning of the realization of what the Internet was meant to be. The earliest visions of the commercial Internet foresaw the outcomes of this many-to-many model of interaction (e.g. Hoffman and Novak 1996), but it has taken over a decade for technology to advance to the point for this vision to be realized. The implications for marketers seem obvious: consumers are active, in control and influence each other. Marketers must be part of the conversation.

The Unique Characteristics of the Internet are Changing Customer Expectations

In our view, Internet marketing requires some differences in perspective compared to traditional marketing because the Internet itself is a unique phenomenon. Strong argu-

BOX 12.2 FUNDAMENTAL CHARACTERISTICS OF THE WEB

Decentralized, distributed network of computers – "network of networks"
Open structure – information can be accessed by any user
Any user can be a provider
Medium can be accessed anytime, anywhere
Digital information
Nonlinear presentation and access
Action is required of user
Many-to-many communication model
Asynchronous or synchronous communication
Machine interactivity required
Person interactivity is mediated
No limits on how much content there can be
Information immediately accessible
Content can be easily modified
Communications are persistent and endure over time
Addressable
Logging of all behavioral responses
Behavioral responses not necessarily linked to identity
Extendable to interface with external sources originally outside the Web

Source: Adapted from Hoffman and Novak (2005).

ments can be made that there is something fundamentally different about the Internet. Even though much of traditional marketing still applies, there are many ways where the Internet as a marketing medium diverges from the physical world. We have summarized these ways in Box 12.2. Interestingly, none of these characteristics has changed as the Web has evolved; nor do we believe they will they change as the Web evolves even further. What will change, however, is how advances in technology enable these characteristics to define powerful new applications. For example, Web 2.0 builds upon these fundamental characteristics of the Internet in important ways that enhance community, interactivity and individualization.

There are additional characteristics that differentiate the Web from the physical world. These higher-order characteristics displayed in Box 12.3 give insight into the opportunities and challenges that exist for marketers. For example, sources of information are often unknown. This has led to the development of reputation managers. Without ratings of buyer/seller reputations, eBay for example would not be successful. Other characteristics listed in Box 12.3 have revolutionized the music industry and allowed Apple, a company with its roots in the computer hardware industry, to find itself in the position of a major music and media retailer.

As we noted, the characteristics in Boxes 12.2 and 12.3 are just as true for Web 2.0 as they were for Web 1.0 – they are fundamental defining properties that taken together

---

BOX 12.3   HIGHER-ORDER ATTRIBUTES OF THE WEB

Range of content is anything that can be digitized (audio, video, text etc.)
Lack of physical constraints on content
Information is more easily accessed and readily available
Web is constantly changing
Digital copies are essentially free
Unbundled form from information
Environment approaches full information
Erases geographic distance between buyer and seller
Source of information is often unknown
Greater scalability compared to the physical world
Medium can be used for multiple and diverse communication purposes
Software agents can be developed to process content
Virtual communities form naturally as customers self-segment
Word of mouth role is magnified

Source: Adapted from Hoffman and Novak (2005).

---

make the Internet unique. We believe they will also hold true for Web 3.0 and beyond. Yet while the fundamental characteristics of the Internet may be the same for Web 1.0, Web 2.0 and Web 3.0, advances in technology define how these characteristics can be applied. Our argument is that while the basics of marketing and consumer behavior still apply, the Internet is different because it possesses unique characteristics compared to other media. It is also changing customer experience in several key ways (Raine 2006).

First, consumers are more mobile and the communication devices they use are no longer place bound. Second, consumers engage in more multitasking, slicing their attention among multiple devices and activities at the same time. Third, consumers are taking an active role in online content creation. This has led to perhaps the biggest change in customer experience: consumers' changing expectations. Consumer use of the Internet has led to different expectations about the availability of people and data as vast stores of material on the Internet and the ubiquity of e-mail, instant messaging and cellphones mean that consumers increasingly expect to immediately find online what – or who – they are looking for.

Technology Laws are Speeding up the Social Web's Evolution

Marketers should be aware that these broad impacts are likely to become more pronounced in the future because of the impact of four exponential growth curves: Moore's Law, Gilder's Law, Kryder's Law and Metcalfe's Law. Moore's Law, formulated by Gordon Moore of Intel in the early 1970s, states that the processing power of a microchip doubles every 18 months. The corollary to this law is that as computers become faster, the price of a given level of computing power halves every 18 months. Gilder's Law, proposed by George Gilder, suggests that the total bandwidth of communication systems grows at least three times faster than computing power, meaning that computing power doubles every six months. New technology developments seem to confirm that bandwidth availability will continue to expand at a rate that supports Gilder's Law. Kryder's Law, attributed to Seagate executive and Carnegie Mellon professor Mark Kryder, observes that the density of information hard drives can support is increasing exponentially and faster than Moore's Law for chips. In other words, hard drives are getting smaller and smaller and holding more and more bits. Finally Metcalfe's Law, ascribed to Robert Metcalfe, the originator of Ethernet and founder of 3COM, holds that the value of a network is proportional to the square of the number of nodes; so as a network grows, the value of being connected to it grows exponentially, while the cost per user remains the same or even reduces.

With exponential growth in computing power, communications power, storage power and network usefulness, it is difficult to predict precisely what the future will look like, but it is not hard to imagine that the impact of these technology laws in the next decade (on, e.g., search engines, Web browsers, online retail spaces and who and what consumers trust) will be profound.

CONSUMER MOTIVATIONS TO USE SOCIAL MEDIA DRIVE SOCIAL MEDIA STRATEGY

We have argued that social media are less about the different technological applications and more about what these applications let consumers *do*. This is an important distinction because it directs marketers' attention toward the fundamental motivations for consumers' behaviors in these media. By understanding the motivations underlying consumer behavior, managers are in a better position to develop more effective social media strategies.

In keeping with this motivational framework, social media are defined according to the "four Cs" (Hoffman and Novak 2010). Social media enable and facilitate conversations that connect people. These social media conversations occur through Web-based tools that consumers use to create and consume user-generated content. Social media significantly increase user control, which affects the balance of power between marketers and consumers. While marketers have discovered that they cannot control social media conversations, they can listen to, participate in and influence the conversations.

These four Cs – connect, create, consume and control – are not only the fundamental defining characteristics of social media, but also define the roles or behaviors that consumers adopt in pursuit of a given goal in connection with social media use. Any of these four roles could be adopted by a consumer whose goal for example was to "pass the time." A person may have the goal of wanting to pass the time and choose the role of connecting with friends through Facebook as a way to achieve the goal. Another consumer may express the same "pass the time" goal, but choose to adopt the role of consuming user-generated content on Twitter to pursue it. Still other consumers may pass the time by creating content in Second Life, or adding a layer of control to their large collection of Delicious bookmarks by tagging them.

Thus the consumer's role is not uniquely determined by the goal she is pursuing. To add to the complexity, the number of distinct social media goals that people pursue is quite large (e.g. finding information, interacting with friends, passing the time and many others). As the Internet evolves from a static mechanism for data access into a global operating system that seamlessly connects applications and people across space and time, the role a consumer adopts while pursuing a particular goal on the Internet is important for understanding the nature of behavior and has important implications for social media strategy.

Note that the role a consumer adopts in pursuit of a goal is not the same as the motivation for pursuing that role. To understand why consumers adopt some roles and not others, and what motivates that process, we recently proposed a general conceptual model (Hoffman and Novak 2010) in which user needs, motivations and dispositions influence goal choice, which in turn influences the social media behavioral roles defined by the four Cs. We argue that these four Cs represent roles that consumers adopt when engaged in social media in order to pursue a goal in connection with social media use. In our model, needs in turn also directly influence user role. Note that needs and motivations may either be chronic (individual differences) or goal specific.

Goal-specific characteristics explain differences in roles chosen for a specific goal and include the goal-specific needs for autonomy, competence, relatedness and self-esteem, and the goal-specific motivation of locus of causality. Chronic individual characteristics also explain differences in roles chosen for a specific goal and include the basic psychological needs of autonomy, competence, relatedness, self-esteem that parallel the goal-specific needs, along with dispositions of collective self-esteem, authenticity, self-construal and thinking style.

A series of multilevel models designed to determine the extent to which goal-specific and chronic needs, motivations and dispositions explain the variation of role within goal revealed several interesting results. First we found empirical support for our hypothesis that while a goal may influence which role is adopted, roles are not uniquely determined by goals, and that for a given goal there is considerable empirical variation in the user's role. Next we found that the different roles consumers adopted for a given behavioral goal are driven by the fundamental needs for autonomy, competence and relatedness. Finally, dispositional authenticity, conceptualized as a trio of traits including self-alienation, authentic living and accepting external influence (Wood et al. 2008), along with consumers' own evaluation of their social identity, including four constructs of collective self-esteem (Luhtanen and Crocker 1992), are important predictors of social media roles. In sum, our early results indicate that the roles people adopt when using social media relate to very personal needs, motivations and dispositions. How people behave when using social media tells us something about what matters to them.

THE CURRENCY OF ONLINE SOCIAL INTERACTION IS USER-GENERATED CONTENT

At its core the social web is about user-generated content (UGC). UGC, sometimes referred to as consumer-generated media, is gaining in importance as social networks become increasingly prevalent. This is because the influence of word of mouth is enhanced as consumers in the network have known reputations and are trusted by larger and larger numbers of other users. UGC includes media content, for example digital video, blogging, podcasting, mobile phone photography, wikis and so on, produced by end user consumers as opposed to traditional media producers, licensed broadcasters and production companies. From a marketing perspective, it is important to distinguish between unsolicited and solicited UGC. Unsolicited or organic UGC includes content produced by consumers on their own, without any involvement of a firm – for example a self-produced video review uploaded to YouTube. Solicited UGC on the other hand introduces a role for the firm, creating the possibility for some degree of influence of UGC. Solicited UGC may take the form of a firm-hosted product forum in which company representatives play an active role (e.g. Procter & Gamble's beinggirl.com site for the Always product line). Strategies for generating solicited UGC can be quite creative and highly participatory, including co-created products and crowd-sourced advertising.

Product reviews represent a particularly important category of UGC that has been the subject of considerable academic research. An important research question is the degree to which lessons learned about product reviews generalize to other forms of UGC. A Bazaarvoice/Keller Fay Group study (November 2007) analyzed online feedback for products and services written in the past month by US online consumers who posted at least one review over the three-month period of August–October 2007 and found that most consumers post positive reviews, with 87 percent of reviews positive most or every time and only 2 percent of reviews negative most or every time. This should not however be interpreted to mean that the impact of negative reviews is minimal.

Numerous industry studies have shown that reviewed products have higher conversion and retention rates, along with lower return rates. There is also some industry evidence that consumers who read reviews spend at least 5 percent more than consumers who do not. Further, it seems clear that product reviews impact sales. In short, the more reviews a product has and the higher the average rating, the higher the sales. Most online shoppers (77 percent, Jupiter 2007) use reviews, and shoppers who write reviews appear to buy more often, are more loyal and are more involved in the shopping process (Jupiter 2007). It is clear that this type of UGC is a key component of marketing strategy, with important implications for acquisition, retention and loyalty.

The academic literature supports and provides depth to industry observations about the importance of product reviews. In general, research has verified that the presence of reviews increases the perceived usefulness and social presence of a website (Kumar and Benbasat 2006). Additionally, reviews are overwhelmingly positive (Chevalier and Mayzlin 2006) and influence purchase behavior (Chevalier and Mayzlin 2006; Duan et al. 2005; Park et al. 2007; Senecal and Nantel 2004).

In terms of characteristics of reviews, review text is more influential than summary statistics (Chevalier and Mayzlin 2006) and negative reviews have more impact than positive reviews (Chavalier and Mayzlin 2006; Sen and Lerman 2007). Reviews with mixed subjective and objective information have a negative effect on sales, while reviews with only subjective or objective information have a positive effect on sales (Ghose and Ipeirotis 2008). Anonymous reviews are rated less helpful than reviews that disclose identity, but this effect is reduced when reviews are unequivocal (Forman et al. 2008). Reviews given high ratings by others are judged more useful (Korfiatis 2008) and moderate-length reviews with higher readability are judged more useful (Ghose and Ipeirotis 2008; Korfiatis 2008).

Positive reviews have more influence for hedonic products and negative reviews have more influence for utilitarian products (Sen and Lerman 2007). High-quality reviews have a stronger impact on high-involvement consumers, but high-quantity reviews have a stronger impact on low-involvement consumers (Park et al. 2007).

The Impact of Negative User-Generated Content

Research suggests that negative reviews have more impact than positive reviews. When reviews are negative and the company fails to act appropriately, the impact can be especially harmful to the bottom line. For example, in September 2004 a cyclist posted to a forum that he had discovered how to open his Kryptonite brand tubular cylinder bike lock using a Bic pen (Kahney 2004). The observation was reposted by bloggers, people posting in forums and the traditional media. Five business days after the original post, the company responded with a plan to exchange locks that they said would take another three days to implement. Eight business days later, details of a free "Lock Exchange Program" were announced and customers could register for a new lock in exchange for the defective one. The first exchanges did not occur until a few weeks after that. When the dust settled, the exchange program had cost the company $10 million and an inestimable amount of goodwill (Kirkpatrick 2005). Even worse, six years later Kryptonite is still paying the price as the incident lives on in Google searches (a search for "Kryptonite lock" returns the 17 September 2004 *Wired* article "Twist a Pen, Open a Lock" in the top ten list on the first page of results) along with several videos depicting step by step how to pick the lock with a Bic pen.

Strategically, negative reviews give managers an opportunity to diagnose product issues and problems, determine their severity and correct if necessary (see Varadarajan, Chapter 2 in this volume). If reviewers self-identify, they can be contacted directly for remedies. Marketers can use review content to inform promotions, ad copy and even use as "testimonials" in other contexts, such as direct e-mails, in-store promotions and so on. Analysis of negative reviews can suggest product or service improvements, merchandising opportunities and product mix adjustments and may even suggest latent or emerging needs.

The lessons for marketers are straightforward. Marketers should monitor online conversations carefully, engage in the discussions and work to fix any problems. For crisis-level feedback, it is critical to act quickly. At all times managers should not try to shut down or restrict negative content. Instead managers must learn how to respond calmly and creatively while avoiding "counter spin" with, say, fake posts about how great the product is. Marketers can treat negative word of mouth as one type of market research: study and learn from it, and rebut as appropriate. The Internet moves fast and companies may not always be able to keep up, but they need to do a better job of reacting in "Internet time."

Some firms seem more immune to the impact of negative reviews than others. For years Apple has been the target of negative reviews calling the sharp edges of the unibody MacBook Pro and MacBook Air lines of laptop computers a serious design flaw, with some viewers uploading photographs of cuts they have received from using the computer and showing how the sharp edge of the computer can be used to slice bread,[3] along with videos showing how to file down the edge of the computer to correct the problem.[4] A heated debate has emerged on discussion forums between Apple supporters and detractors, but Apple itself has been noticeably silent on the subject. The "Antennagate" case of the reception problems with the iPhone 4 issue presents a very similar story (Helft and Bilton 2010), this time with *Consumer Reports* and major news media joining unsolicited user reviews in criticizing Apple for signal loss experienced when the iPhone 4 is held in what for many people is a normal grip. Apple again appears to be going against the grain of how firms should respond to negative reviews, denying in a 16 July 2010 press conference that the problem is specific to the iPhone, and discounting the negative comments. Conventional wisdom suggests that these negative reviews have not seemed to hurt Apple sales, although without a careful econometric analysis of how demand for MacBook Pros and iPhones have been impacted by the negative publicity, we cannot assume that the current or future financial impact of these reviews is zero.

Solicited User-Generated Content

Participatory UGC, sometimes referred to as "crowdsourcing," involves parallel or joint collaborations among consumers working together to create useful content. The concept is that the "wisdom of the crowd" can generate more useful content than any one individual working on her own. Amazon's Mechanical Turk service is a novel approach to crowdsourcing. The service provides a framework for "outsourcing" digital tasks to online users. For example, users might be asked to post reviews to a website or tag photos in online catalogs. Popular social media sites that employ the participatory UGC model are Digg and StumbleUpon. Both of these sites are essentially peer recommendation systems in which the popularity of the content the sites display is determined by the social network of the users rating it. Managers can harness the fundamental idea underlying these concepts by actively creating compelling environments for consumers to create useful content. For example a number of companies including Apple and Dell have built company-controlled forums, blogs and wikis that allow their customers to provide technical support to each other and generate ideas for new products.

Co-creation takes this concept further by incorporating customers into the product development or advertising process. One of the most popular examples of co-creation is the Doritos Super Bowl TV commercial competitions where Doritos invites consumers to create brief ad spots and then vote on their favorite ads. The winner is shown during Super Bowl. The contests are wildly popular with consumers and the stakes are high: for the 2009 competition, each of six finalists won $25 000, one of the top three as determined by online voters saw their ad aired during Super Bowl 2010, and the top-ranked ad as determined by the *USA Today* ad meter won $1 million. The winning commercial, "Snack Attack Samurai," aired during the fourth quarter of the Super Bowl and was seen by an estimated 116.2 million viewers. In what is almost certain to be viewed with some irony by media experts, this user-generated content was the most watched television commercial of all time (McClellan 2010).

WHO CONTROLS THE SOCIAL MEDIA EXPERIENCE?

The increasing control consumers are experiencing online is leading to an interesting contradiction: consumers want to control their own online experiences, for example by finding things for themselves; yet the virtually limitless content afforded by the social web makes it increasingly hard to find what one is looking for. This presents marketers with opportunities to help consumers by doing these tasks for them. As we have suggested, the exponential growth in UGC from Web 2.0 social media will lead to Web 3.0 semantic Web solutions, in which consumers will relinquish some control in exchange for receiving answers to questions that would simply take too much time to find on their own.

The balance of control can be viewed as the distinction between customization, in which the consumer wants to do things for herself, and personalization, in which the consumer is content to have it done for her. We think an argument can be made that resolving this apparent contradiction for consumers will be increasingly important for marketers and represents important research opportunities for scholars.

Personalization and customization make consumers feel welcome online by providing them with relevant content based on their needs and interests. Both qualities foster customer loyalty, which vastly increases the chance of repeat site traffic. Repeat site traffic in turn has enormous potential for increasing advertising and sales revenue. Although personalization and customization are often used interchangeably, they have an important difference in terms of who is in control of the process.

Because the Web is addressable, content for consumers can be personalized. We define personalization as the firm-controlled process of providing relevant content for consumers based on knowledge of their individual preferences. This "do it for me" approach requires that firms obtain information about consumer wants and needs, either by implicitly tracking customer purchases or usage habits, or by explicitly gathering information through customer forms or questionnaires. Amazon.com, for example, uses both explicit and implicit personalization to attract and retain customers. A visitor who chooses to register with the site must submit personal information such as name and e-mail address. Amazon then uses that information to create personalized greetings throughout the site, such as "Hello, Donna." This is explicit personalization because the site creates tailored greetings using information obtained directly from the customer. Amazon also provides customers with personalized product recommendations based on their previous purchases and the purchases of customers with similar interests. This type of personalization is implicit because the site is tracking purchase information behind the scenes, without direct customer participation.

In contrast to personalization, customization is customer controlled and takes place when users are able to modify a website or application's look and feel, in effect an "I'll do it for myself" approach. Many sites provide both customization and personalization features. For example, after registering with the Excite and Yahoo! sites, users can create their own customized start pages by choosing their preferred layout, content and color scheme. Information such as customer names obtained through the registration process is also used to create personalized greetings within the customized start pages. Thus these sites combine customization and personalization features to provide users with the information they need, quickly and easily.

Personalization adds value to the marketing effort by making things easier for customers and reducing their effort. With too many choices and increasingly complex product/service options, customers may not always know what they want or how to choose it (Schwartz 2005). In that case personalization provides the opportunity to influence customers. However, customization (e.g. configurators that let customers design custom products or options to cosmetically customize websites by altering site layout and features) provides opportunities to learn from customers and give customers the opportunity to be in control. Customization can leverage the customer's need to "make it my own." Customization also generates customer-provided data, a source of revealed preferences, and is an excellent way of obtaining market research data.

Customization has a natural link with co-creation. It can be advantageous for customers and companies to cooperate to reshape existing business processes, products or services – and even create new ones. Instead of trying to read the consumer's mind and build the perfect customized site or product, firms can focus on co-creating websites or products with consumers. In these cases the firm provides the tools and the customer provides the necessary information inputs. There are significant advantages to setting up systems in which consumers provide the initial information investments in the application. Research has shown that consumers have a decreased propensity to search and switch after an initial investment (Zauberman 2003). Providing information about your product or music preferences or your friends to an application are initial investments that lock the customer in to the marketer's site and make switching less likely.

Marketers may wonder how these two types of tailored marketing – a "do it for me" personalization in which content is tailored to a particular consumer based on her previous online behavior, and an "I'll do it for myself" customization where consumers modify the content to suit their own tastes – are likely to play out as the Web continues to evolve. The presumptive advantage of personalization is reduced customer effort, but this comes at the cost of restricting consumers' options. Customization has the advantage of being easier for marketers to implement and benefits consumer control motives. We believe that personalization may play a strong role in the future as large amounts of information increasingly tax consumers' abilities to process and integrate it in meaningful ways. The four technology laws we reviewed earlier suggest strongly that technology will yield personalization methods that are more powerful and more effective and lead to personalization playing a more dominant role in the future.

SOCIAL MEDIA STRATEGY

Digital convergence is having an impact on social media strategy. Although many definitions abound, we think it can be highly productive for marketers to first consider digital convergence as the digitization of traditional media, as discussed by Hanson and Kalyanam (2007). Something is digital when all of its properties and information are stored as a string of zeroes and ones called bits. The falling cost of digital technology, driven by exponential growth curve laws, is one of the most powerful forces in the modern economy because it allows bits to substitute for atoms. This input substitution where atoms are translated into bits is one of the most obvious characteristics of the Internet, but less obvious is what this implies for marketers.

The immediate implication is that the marketing process itself responds well to digitization. Consider the digitized marketing process as composed of three parts: (1) archive; (2) substitute; and (3) redesign (Hanson and Kalyanam 2007). In the first step, archive, marketers retain and digitize existing materials, for example Google Book Search or Google Earth. Moving on to substitute, marketers begin to substitute digital materials into marketing process, for example pdf brochures and manuals, dynamic websites for product merchandizing and so on. In the third step, redesign, marketers change marketing processes to better capitalize on the digital features of the environment, for example online focus groups and surveys, virtual tours, e-ticketing, prediction markets and so on.

However, we can take this one step further beyond atoms to bits: we can translate the bits back to atoms. We call the full cycle ABBA (atoms to bits and back to atoms). While it may seem frivolous, and with apologies to the Swedish pop group, this idea is highly relevant for Internet marketing and social web strategy. ABBA refers to the idea that we can start with atoms, transform those atoms into bits through digitization and then transform them back to atoms again. The atoms-to-bits part of the sequence, the input substitution, has been around for a long time – it is the translation back to atoms that is new. One example of ABBA is that we can digitize a vinyl album and then put it back into a physical form, through for example an iPod. Now, unlike a Star Trek transporter where the crew of the star ship *Enterprise* is dematerialized into an energy pattern (atoms to bits) and then reconverted into physical matter (bits to atoms), we do not require a faithful reconstruction of the original atoms. Thus input substitution becomes "input translation."

How is this relevant to online consumption and social media? In ways we can only begin to imagine. Now that 3D printers or "fabbers" are in use for consumer applications, video game characters or Second Life avatars can literally come to life. Consider Second Life. Real consumers with real characters in real life (the atoms) create virtual characters representing some version of themselves as avatars in Second Life (atoms to bits) and then for $90 and up, create physical manifestations of their virtual characters (back to atoms) using a form of rapid prototyping called 3D microfabrication from a company called Fabjectory (Hansell 2007). Consumers can also "print" statuettes of their Nintendo Mii characters ($50) or reproduce their Google SketchUp designs as real-world objects. The consumer behavior implications of this phenomenon have yet to be researched.

As fabbers come into reach for ordinary consumers,[5] applications as mundane as a consumer recreating a new dishwasher part on her 3D home printer from manufacturer specifications, to "printing" foods like cheese or chocolate, or new products like athletic shoes or jewelry become possible. Rapid prototyping is expected to revolutionize manufacturing and could very well bring new opportunities to marketers seeking ways to help consumers link the real world and the online social world in exciting new ways.

Convergent Augmentation

Printing physical manifestations of virtual characters is a good example of how the Internet is augmentable. Marketers and researchers can explore the implications of augmentation through our notion of "convergent augmentation." To explain the marketing insights that can be derived from this concept, we start with the three broad classes of what can be augmented: (1) augmented products; (2) augmented consumers; and (3) augmented reality.

Augmented products enhance the physical product through online information and interaction (Mohammed et al 2002). So, for example, the iPod is augmented by the iTunes digital music service and, in a reverse case, the Skype online service is augmented by physical products like USB or Bluetooth phones or headsets. Augmented consumers can make themselves smarter and increase working memory through search engines, bookmarks, recommender systems and the like (Hoffman 2007). Augmented reality represents a field of computer science research that combines real-world and computer-generated data with applications in which computer graphics are blended into the real world (or into a live video stream), real-world objects are merged into virtual worlds, or in the broadest instance, where physical and digital objects coexist and interact in real time (e.g. Zhou et al. 2008). An early example is the virtual objects inserted into Disneyland's Haunted Mansion ride. Some current examples of augmented reality are the virtual first down, Google Maps street view, wearable maps for military and emergency applications, and the iPhone 3GS augmented reality New York City subway application. More recently, augmented reality applications leveraging laptop and smartphone cameras have included the recursive webcam and the GE Smart Grid and the USPS Priority Mail "virtual box simulator." Games are a popular category for augmented reality. For example, Cannonballz integrates motion capture technology, Flash and Facebook to let consumers dodge cannonballs while keeping their Facebook friends from being hit.

As applications of convergent augmentation accelerate, they will increasingly take advantage of the social web and increase the consumer's ability to connect, create, consume and control their interactions in the social web. An interesting example of one direction this is evolving is social retailing. A recent retailing experiment at Bloomingdale's in New York City gives insight into how retailers can combine social networking elements from the social web to improve customer experience and stimulate sales in store. Using an interactive mirror and touch display, shoppers can virtually try on clothes, view pictures of related clothes and accessories, and virtually try on clothes sent to the mirror by friends in their social network.

Social retailing combines all three elements of convergent augmentation. It augments the consumer decision process by providing suggestions and feedback from friends, it augments the reality of in-store shopping by allowing customers to virtually try on a multitude of clothes and accessories without having to search for pieces on the sales floor or physically try them on, and it augments the products because it shows suggestions of other products that complement the clothes. It is not difficult to predict that in the near future, marketers can expect to see further convergence as mobile devices, computers and the real world interact to augment customer experience among consumers who are increasingly connected to each other through social media. Researchers are just beginning to explore the consumer behavior issues underlying these augmented interactions.

How to Future-proof Digital Strategy in the Face of Rapid Change

The social media environment is rapidly evolving, yet marketers are still largely mass media focused. Social media efforts tend more toward passive advertising campaigns on Facebook instead of blogs, co-creation efforts or viral marketing campaigns launched on

YouTube. It is important that marketers avoid the temptation to treat the Web as just another channel for pushing their messages to consumers.

As marketers consider effective social media strategy, they should be careful to future-proof their strategies against exponential growth trends in technology that result in new applications and opportunities on an almost daily basis. It should be clear that we believe that the best way to manage the uncertainty is to first gain a firm understanding of the fundamentals of online consumer behavior and second, to adopt a meaningful toolkit, a kind of operating instructions or set of rules, for moving forward and navigating in this dynamic world.

The four Cs we discussed earlier are important because even as computing technology advances, consumers still have the fundamental need to connect, create, consume and control their online experiences. Because the social web gives more control to the consumer – and less to the marketer – marketers should focus on meeting the requirements of the four Cs as they develop social media strategy. This is a best-principles, not just best-practices, approach to developing social media strategy. New social media trends and applications are the marketer's window into what the future might look like. It is therefore important to keep up with these trends.

Although the social web is still in its early stages, there are tools and frameworks available to guide social media strategy. Marketers can improve their social web strategies by understanding consumer motivations to use social media and developing applications that take advantage of the different roles consumers adopt in pursuit of their goals when using social media. A practical implementation strategy is to listen to consumers by formally monitoring and analyzing brand-related user-generated content with the objective of enhancing customer experience, experiment with social web applications like social networking and participate in co-creation campaigns to actively engage customers in the marketing process, apply the lessons learned from the successful social media experiments into systematic practice and develop integrated marketing strategies that formally and fully incorporate appropriate social media elements into the marketing mix. Marketing scholars have much to contribute here as the consumer behaviors, along with the marketing models that can measure and predict consumer response in each of these phases, are largely unexplored.

NOTES

1. http://www.alexa.com/topsites/countries/US.
2. http://en.wikipedia.org/wiki/Social_media.
3. http://www.thewwwblog.com/macbook-air-sharp-enough-to-cut.html.
4. http://onemansblog.com/2010/03/11/video-rant-taking-the-sharp-edge-off-the-macbook-pro/.
5. As of this writing, a 3D printer can be purchased for less than $5000, the open source "fab at home" kit costs $2400 and the RepRap "self-replicating" 3D printing machine is free.

REFERENCES

American Marketing Association (2007), "AMA definition of marketing," retrieved from http://www.market-ingpower.com/Community/ARC/Pages/Additional/Definition/.

Berners-Lee, Tim, James Hendler and Ora Lassila (2001), "The semantic Web," *Scientific American*, **284**, 34–43.

Brand, Stewart (2001), "Founding father," *Wired 9.03*, retrieved from http://www.wired.com/wired/archive/9.03/baran.html.

Chevalier, Judith A. and Dina Mayzlin (2006), "The effect of word of mouth on sales: online book reviews," *Journal of Marketing Research*, **43** (August), 345–54.

Duan, Wenjing, Bin Gu and Andrew B. Whinston (2005), "Do online reviews matter? An empirical investigation of panel data," available at: http://ssrn.com/abstract=616262.

Forman, Chris, Anindya Ghose and Batia Wiesenfeld (2008), "Examining the relationship between reviews and sales: the role of reviewer identity disclosure in electronic markets," *Information Systems Research*, **19** (3), 291–313.

Ghose, Anindya and Panagiotis G. Ipeirotis (2008), "Estimating the socio-economic impact of product reviews: mining text and reviewer characteristics," available at: http://ssrn.com/abstract=1261751.

Hansell, Saul (2007), "Beam it down from the Web, Scotty," *New York Times*, May 7, retrieved from http://www.nytimes.com/2007/05/07/technology/07copy.html.

Hanson, Ward and Kirthi Kalyanam (2007), *Internet Marketing & e-Commerce*, Mason, OH: Thomson South-Western.

Helft, Miguel and Nick Bilton (2010), "Design flaw in iPhone 4, testers say," *New York Times*, July 12, retrieved from http://www.nytimes.com/2010/07/13/technology/13apple.html.

Hoffman, Donna L. (2007), "Cognitive augmentation: can the internet make you smarter and more creative?" Paper presented at the Sloan Center for Internet Retailing Research Networking Workshop, Riverside, CA, May 3–4.

Hoffman, Donna L. (2009), "Managing beyond Web 2.0," *McKinsey Quarterly*, July.

Hoffman, Donna L. and Marek Fodor (2010), "Can you measure the ROI of your social media marketing?" *Sloan Management Review*, **52** (1).

Hoffman, Donna L. and Thomas P. Novak (1996), "Marketing in hypermedia computer-mediated environments: conceptual foundations," *Journal of Marketing*, **60** (July), 50–68.

Hoffman, Donna L. and Thomas P. Novak (2005), "A conceptual framework for considering Web-based business models and potential revenue streams," *International Journal of Marketing Education*, **1** (1), 7–34.

Hoffman, Donna L. and Thomas P. Novak (2010), "Roles and goals: consumer motivations to use social media," paper presented at the 2010 INFORMS Marketing Science Conference, Cologne, Germany, June 16–19.

Jupiter (2007), "Web 2.0 retail technologies," August 29.

Kahney, Leander (2004), "Twist a pen, open a lock," *Wired*, September 17.

Kirkpatrick, David (2005), "Why there's no escaping the blog," *Fortune*, January 10.

Korfiatis, Nikolaos (2008), "Evaluating content quality and usefulness of online product reviews," available at: http://ssrn.com/abstract=1156321.

Kumar, Nanda and Izak Benbasat (2006), "The influence of recommendations and consumer reviews on evaluations of websites," *Information Systems Research*, **17** (4), 425–39.

Lavrusik, Vadim (2010), "Top 20 Mashable reader responses to 'What is social media?'" Retrieved from http://mashable.com/2010/06/11/top-20-mashable-reader-responses-to-what-is-social-media/.

Levine, Rick, Christopher Locke, Doc Searls and David Weinberger (2001), *The Cluetrain Manifesto*, New York: Da Capo.

Luhtanen, Rüa and Jennifer Crocker (1992), "A collective self-esteem scale: self evaluation of one's social identity," *Personality and Social Psychology Bulletin*, **18** (3), 302–18.

Markoff, John (2006), "Entrepreneurs see a Web guided by common sense," *New York Times*, Business Section, November 12.

McClellan, Steve (2010), "A Doritos SB spot becomes most-watched ad ever," *Brandweek*, February 10, accessed at http://www.brandweek.com/bw/content_display/news-and-features/packaged-goods/e3i6c8a99484479c6fe5f5718dc7a3ea72b.

McClure, Dave (2007), "Channeling crowds," *Release 2.0.2*, April.

Mohammed, Rafi A., Robert J. Fisher, Bernard J. Jaworski and Aileen M. Cahill (2002), *Internet Marketing: Building Advantage in a Networked Economy*, New York: McGraw-Hill.

O'Reilly, Tim and John Battelle (2009), "Web squared: Web 2.0 five years on," retrieved from http://assets.en.oreilly.com/1/event/28/web2009_websquared-whitepaper.pdf.

Park, Do-Hyung, Jumin Lee and Ingoo Han (2007), "The effect of on-line consumer reviews on consumer purchasing intention: the moderating role of involvement," *International Journal of Electronic Commerce*, **11**(4), 125–48.

Pigatto, Daniel F. (2006), "Photo: Web 2.0. *Web 2.0 não é uma coisa . . . É um estado de espírito.* Web 2.0 isn't a thing . . . It's a state of mind," Daniel F. Pigatto's Photostream, flickr, December 24, http://www.flickr.com/photos/pigatto/332193181/.

Raine, Lee (2006), "How the Internet is changing consumer behavior and expectations," Pew Internet & American Life Project, retrieved from http://www.pewinternet.org/~/media/Files/Presentations/2006/2006%20-%20 5.9.06%20SOCAP.pdf.pdf.

Schwartz, Barry (2005), *The Paradox of Choice: Why More is Less*, New York: HarperCollins.

Sen, Shahana and Dawn Lerman (2007), "Why are you telling me this? An examination into negative consumer reviews on the Web," *Journal of Interactive Marketing*, **21** (4), 76–94.

Senecal, Sylvain and Jacques Nantel (2004), "The influence of online product recommendations on consumers' online choices," *Journal of Retailing*, **80**, 159–69.

Wood, A.M., P. Linley, J. Maltby, M. Baliousis and S. Joseph (2008), "The authentic personality: a theoretical and empirical conceptualization and the development of the authenticity scale," *Journal of Counseling Psychology*, **55**, 385–99.

Zauberman, Gal (2003), "The intertemporal dynamics of consumer lock-in," *Journal of Consumer Research*, **30**, 405–19.

Zhou, Feng, Henry Been-Lirn Du and Mark Billinghurst (2008), "Trends in augmented reality tracking, interaction, and display: a review of ten years of ISMAR," *Proceedings of the 7th IEEE/ACM International Symposium on Mixed and Augmented Reality*, pp. 193–202.

13 Mobile marketing strategy
Venkatesh Shankar

INTRODUCTION

The use of mobile devices (e.g. cellphones, personal digital assistants [PDAs] and digital music players) and related services and applications (apps) is ubiquitous in the developed world and is growing rapidly in the developing world. Mobile marketing – the set of marketing initiatives that use mobile devices and media (vehicles of communication that involve mobile devices) – is growing in importance. Mobile advertising spending in the USA alone will likely reach $2.55 billion by 2014 (eMarketer 2010). Furthermore, e-mail use among US consumers aged 12–17 dropped by 59 percent in 2010 in favor of mobile text use (comScore 2011).

In response to the rapid growth in the use of mobile devices and applications, firms are viewing mobile marketing strategy with increased attention. About 49 percent of 200 merchants surveyed in a 2011 study indicated that mobile initiatives were important to achieving their strategic goals (10th Annual Merchant Survey 1st Quarter 2011). Many firms practicing mobile marketing are experiencing success. For example, in February 2011, Starbucks launched a branded mobile payment system through the Starbucks card mobile iPhone and Blackberry applications that can be used in 7000 of its US stores. Within about two months, approximately 3 million customers purchased coffee through this mobile service or application.

More formally, mobile marketing is "the two-way or multi-way communication and promotion of an offer between a firm and its customers[1] using a mobile medium, device, or technology" (Shankar and Balasubramanian 2009; Shankar et al. 2010). Mobile marketing is primarily interactive in nature and includes mobile advertising, promotion, customer support, and relationship-management initiatives (Ancarani and Shankar 2003).

Just as the use of mobile media and devices is expanding, research on mobile marketing is still evolving. Current research spans disciplines such as marketing, information systems, computer science and telecommunications. However, much research focuses on tactical aspects of mobile marketing such as mobile promotions and couponing. As mobile channel and media are increasingly becoming an integral part of a firm's overall marketing and channel strategies, mobile marketing is moving from a set of tactical activities to a set of both strategic and tactical activities. Strategic aspects of mobile marketing such as rearchitecting the firm's business model (Shankar et al. 2003), establishing mobile as an important channel (Verhoef, Chapter 8 in this volume), allocating significant resources to mobile marketing (Shankar, Chapter 9 in this volume) and managing mobile customer relationships (Arnold and Palmatier, Chapter 14 in this volume) need greater attention. Thus mobile marketing strategy is emerging as an important area for both researchers and managers.

The rest of the chapter is organized as follows. In the next section, we outline how mobile marketing strategy differs from traditional marketing strategy and present a

conceptual framework. In the subsequent three sections, we discuss the drivers, decision components and consequence of mobile marketing strategy. We then discuss the
implementation of mobile marketing strategy. We conclude by outlining the research
and managerial implications of mobile marketing strategy.

BASICS OF MOBILE MARKETING AND A CONCEPTUAL FRAMEWORK

To better understand mobile marketing, it is useful to briefly review the key
characteristics of mobile media and devices, and to compare mobile marketing with
traditional/mass marketing. The mobile channel – the marketing channel involving mobile devices and media – is growing rapidly in the multichannel environment
(Neslin and Shankar 2009). All mobile devices incorporate one or more of the following capabilities: audio, text/data and video (Shankar and Balasubramanian 2009).
The following properties of mobile devices that relate to these capabilities have key
marketing implications.

Location Specificity

Many mobile devices have global positioning system (GPS) capabilities to identify their
physical location. This property provides marketers with the opportunity to target
location-sensitive promotional offers to mobile device users, a practice referred to as
proximity marketing. Conventional marketing media such as billboards also allow
location-specific messages, but with mobile devices, such information can be targeted
to the location of the individual user based on their stated preferences and revealed
behaviors. Although such a practice needs to overcome privacy concerns, many customers have rapidly adopted location-based mobile services, with the number of users
of location-based services expected to touch 329 million worldwide in 2011 (eMarketer
2010).

Portability

An important benefit of a mobile device is its ultra small size and the ease with which
it can be carried. Because a mobile fits in a hand, it is a constant companion to the user
and is used on a continuous basis. This property enables marketers to instantaneously
communicate with the user at any point in time. However, the small screen size deters the
delivery of information-intensive messages.

Wireless Feature

Unlike other frequently used devices such as the desktop PC, the typical mobile device is
not connected by wires for much of its use. This property promotes its increased usage,
creating more opportunities for marketers to communicate with the user. At the same
time, however, the short duration of the typical usage occasion forces marketers to be
concise with their messages.

Table 13.1   Differences between traditional marketing and mobile marketing

Dimension	Traditional marketing	Mobile marketing
Scope of audience	All existing and potential users of the product	Existing and potential product users owning mobile devices who opt in to receive communication
Potential type of communication	Text, voice and video in rich formats	Text, voice and video in very limited visual space with limitations in transmission speed
Typical direction of communication	Marketer to consumer	Interactive between marketer and consumer
Ability to deliver message by target location	Low	High
Ability to measure and track response	Low	High
Consumer targetability	Low	Medium
Cost per target audience	High	Low

Source: Shankar and Balasubramanian (2009).

Based on these properties, there are key differences between mass marketing (typically conducted through mass media such as magazines and television) and mobile marketing. These differences appear in Table 13.1 (Shankar and Balasubramanian 2009). Mass marketing addresses a broad range of existing and potential customers. Mobile marketing, in contrast, is restricted to owners of mobile devices, and in many cases, to a subset of those owners who opt in to receive communications from marketers. Bandwidth capacity and tight screen size constraints related to mobile devices further restrict the types of communications possible in a mobile marketing context. However, the brevity of communication through a mobile device can also enable more frequent interactions between the marketer and the customer. Furthermore, with mobile marketing, the seller can more precisely target customers at a specific location and at a particular time, can better measure and track consumer response, and can have lower unit costs of communication with the target audience than those associated with mass marketing.

We can analyze mobile marketing strategy in terms of its antecedents/drivers, decision components and consequences. A conceptual framework linking these elements appears in Figure 13.1. The different types of antecedents include mobile characteristics (e.g. portability, location specificity), customer characteristics (e.g. demographics), firm characteristics (e.g. resources), competitor characteristics (e.g. size, number), and environment characteristics (e.g. technological, political). The mobile marketing strategy decision components range from overall mobile strategy to customer relationship management. The immediate consequences of mobile marketing strategy comprise customer attitudes (e.g. preferences) and actions (e.g. clicks, trials), which affect firm performance (e.g. sales, market share, profit).

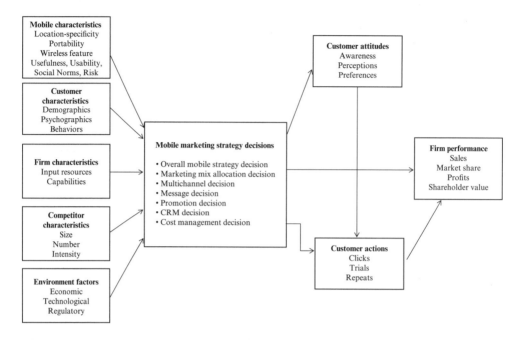

Figure 13.1   A framework of antecedents and consequences of mobile marketing strategy

DRIVERS OF MOBILE MARKETING STRATEGY

Mobile Characteristics

Consistent with the drivers of the adoption of any innovation, the key drivers of a consumer's decision to adopt a mobile device, application, service or offer include the relative advantage of the innovation, the innovation's fit with existing usage patterns, the perceived complexity of the innovation, the ability to try out the innovation, the perceived risk related to adoption, and the degree to which adoption and use of the innovation is observable by others (Rogers 1995). In addition, the technology adoption model (TAM, Davis 1989) posits that perceived usefulness and perceived ease of use or usability influence attitudes toward an innovation and, ultimately, its adoption. Furthermore, norms and pressures from a social group can induce customers within that group to adopt an innovation like mobile device or service, according to the TAM2 model.

An integration of scattered theoretical perspectives provides a better understanding of decisions to adopt a mobile device or service. Consistent with this notion, Nysveen et al. (2005) combine information systems theories from organizational contexts with theories that explain technology usage in everyday life to innovation adoption. The latter include uses and gratification theory, which focuses on non-utilitarian benefits from adoption such as expressiveness and enjoyment, and domestication theory (e.g. Silverstone and Hirsch 1992), which focuses on how customers "tame" technologies to fit them into their lives. Nysveen and colleagues demonstrate that the intention to use mobile devices can be driven by the perceived expressiveness of the mobile device (i.e. its ability to express fashion and style and to serve as a symbol), perceptions of enjoyment, usefulness and ease of use, normative pressure and behavioral controls.

However, some of these effects are mediated by the overall attitude toward the use of mobile services. The strengths of these influences vary across four mobile service areas: person-to-person interactive text messaging, contact services (which extend text messaging to a larger social network), payment services and gaming services. These services differ in terms of whether they are machine-interactive versus person-interactive, and whether they involve goal-directed versus experiential processes. Specifically, Nysveen et al. (2005) found that ease of use was a stronger motivation for using goal-directed mobile services whereas enjoyment and expressiveness were stronger motivators for experiential services. Normative pressures and the attitudes toward use were stronger motivators of adoption for person-interactive services compared to machine-interactive services, ostensibly reflecting the more pronounced role of social interactions in the former.

Pagani (2004) empirically examines the adoption determinants of third-generation mobile multimedia service in the Italian market. She finds that perceived usefulness, ease of use, price and speed of use, in that order, are the most important adoption determinants of multimedia mobile services.

Kleijnen et al. (2004) study the drivers of mobile gaming adoption using a survey of mobile game users in the Netherlands. They find that perceived risk, followed by complexity and compatibility were the most important drivers of mobile gaming adoption.

Significant adoption-related hurdles for mobile marketing exist. One such barrier is the penetration of video capability. In the USA, cellphones have a penetration of 86 percent with a user base of 260 million. Of these, about 60 percent use short message service (SMS). However, the number of video-capable mobile devices will likely reach only 8 percent of the population by 2011 (Shahnaz 2007).

Customer Characteristics

Customer demographics, psychographics and behaviors influence mobile marketing strategy. According to DMA (2008), responders to mobile marketing offers are more likely to be males, teens and young adults, individuals with higher incomes, and individuals with heavier usage of voice and data features. Given these insights, mobile marketing strategy could be targeted more toward the millennial generation (those born during 1977–95) – who constitute about one-fourth of the US population (US Census Bureau 2010) – than to the older generations.

In terms of psychographics, customer mindset regarding mobile marketing is important. About 79 percent of US consumers do not view a mobile advertisement (Nielsen Mobile 2008). Furthermore, about 18 percent of mobile device users in the USA do not trust SMS (Nielsen Mobile 2008). Trust is a key issue in online marketing (Bart et al. 2005) and could be important in mobile marketing as well.

The importance of determinants of third-generation multimedia services differ across segments based on age (Pagani 2004). The key drivers of mobile games also differ by consumer segments. For value seekers, compatibility is the critical driver; for risk avoiders, perceived risk is the key determinant; and for game players, navigation, communicability and payment options are the driving factors.

Firm Characteristics

A firm's resources and capabilities are directly relevant to its mobile marketing strategy. The greater the financial resources, the more the firm can invest in mobile marketing options and potentially lead other firms. Similarly, with more technological human power, a firm can invest in the development of advanced mobile solutions and services.

Aside from financial and human resources, firm capabilities also significantly influence mobile strategy. If a firm's R&D capabilities are high, then it is likely to produce leading-edge mobile services and solutions. If its marketing capabilities are strong, then it can develop highly customized offers and solutions for its customers.

Competitor Characteristics

Firms' mobile marketing strategies are shaped to a large extent by their competitors in their industry. A firm's mobile marketing activities are intense when competitors in its product category also follow mobile marketing practices. The use of mobile marketing is highest for the entertainment, music and video product category (44 percent), followed by food/beverage (21 percent), and beauty/personal care categories (15 percent) (DMA 2008). Furthermore, according to the study, the automotive/transportation, business services, consumer electronics, financial services and vacation/travel categories each accounted for 12 percent of the mobile offers.

Environment Factors

The external environment significantly influences firms' mobile marketing strategy. Advances in technology drive the development of new applications. Regulations relating to privacy and security determine the type and the delivery method of mobile marketing messages and their benefits to consumers.

MOBILE STRATEGY DECISIONS

The antecedents of mobile marketing strategy influence critical mobile strategy components. These include: What is the overall mobile strategy? How much resources should be allocated to mobile marketing from the overall marketing budget? How does mobile marketing fit in with the firm's multichannel strategy? What are the mobile marketing messages for the firm's brands? What promotional offers are made through mobile media? What customer relationship management initiatives are undertaken through the mobile media? How is mobile marketing used to manage costs or operational efficiency?

With a better understanding of the drivers of mobile marketing strategy, marketers can develop a more effective strategy. The framework of Shankar et al. (2003) (see Figure 13.2) is useful in formulating a firm's overall mobile strategy. According to this framework, mobile strategy can be viewed along two dimensions: (1) the degree of change it brings to the business model, and (2) the degree of organizational transformation required to execute the strategy. Depending on the combinations levels of these dimensions, a firm can adopt one of three overall mobile marketing strategies.

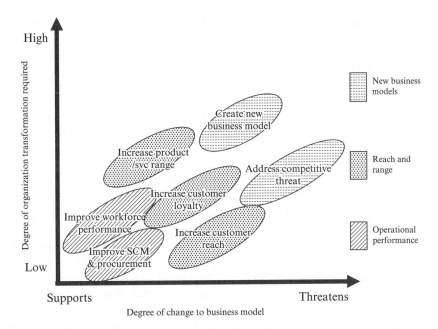

Source: Shankar et al. (2003).

Figure 13.2   A framework for developing mobile marketing strategy

Operational Performance Strategy

When both the need to change the business model and the need for organizational transformation are low, then the firm should follow the "operational performance" strategy. This strategy involves the use of mobile media and communications for supply chain and workforce productivity improvement.

Reach and Range Strategy

When both the need to change the business model and the need for organizational change are at moderate levels, then the recommended strategy is a "reach and range" strategy. Initiatives under this strategy include enhancing product/service range, improving loyalty and increasing customer reach.

New Business Model Strategy

When both the need to change the business model and the need for organizational transformation are high, then the firm should adopt a "new business model" strategy. Under this strategy, the firm fundamentally alters its structure and market strategy, or changes the way it does business to address competitive threats. Not all firms need to pursue this strategy because the need to change both the business model and the organization is not often very high.

A sound mobile marketing strategy pursued by appropriate methods may be a powerful complement to other marketing activities, but may only be a substitute for a limited set of those activities. Therefore the allocation of resources to the strategy depends on its marginal returns and its complementary effects with other activities, consistent with Shankar, Chapter 9 in this volume. If a new business model strategy is the overall mobile strategy, then resources allocated to mobile marketing will supplant resources allocated to erstwhile marketing methods. However, if a reach and range strategy is the overall mobile strategy, resources allocated to mobile marketing will likely complement resources allocated to other marketing activities. Finally, if operational performance strategy is the overall mobile strategy, then resources for mobile marketing will come from resources previously assigned to less effective marketing initiatives.

A broad question is: how should mobile marketing strategy complement or substitute elements of the firm's overall marketing strategy? Specifically, how should traditional advertising campaigns (Rucker, Chapter 11 in this volume) be redesigned to include a mobile element, and how should that element link to initiatives in the mass media or on the Internet? Mobile marketing may be associated with economies of scope in this context, increasing overall marketing efficiency and effectiveness. For example, customer response rates may improve significantly if mobile marketing campaigns are pursued in coordination with e-mail and/or direct mail campaigns than when these campaigns are uncoordinated. Furthermore, how should a firm's mobile marketing strategy evolve across (a) the product life cycle, and (b) the customer life cycle? The answers to these questions form important components of mobile marketing strategy.

With regard to mobile message, firms need to develop a message consistent with the overall marketing message, yet suited to the mobile medium. Text messages for products or services elicit the highest response rates (70 percent), followed by mobile survey participation (41 percent) (DMA 2008). According to the study, mobile e-mail, Web and coupons are less effective in eliciting response.

Mobile marketing can be used to lower costs and improve marketing efficiency. Consider the catalog marketing industry. Catalog marketers such as DwellStudio, Artful Home and Filson drive purchase via an iPad app that brings together multiple catalog titles in one mobile experience. In the past year, numerous catalogers have experimented with QR codes in their print books as well as dedicated iPad catalog apps. For example, Catalog Spree, an iPad app from Padopolis, aims to simplify shopping catalogs via the iPad by making multiple titles from a variety of sources available in one application. The launch of Catalog Spree follows Catalogs.com's iPad app, which was also designed for multiple catalogs. Featured catalogs in Catalogs.com's iPad app include Aeropostale and Coldwater Creek.

CONSEQUENCES OF MOBILE MARKETING STRATEGY

How does mobile marketing strategy influence customer attitudes and actions and firm outcomes such as sales, profit and shareholder value? There is scant academic research on this issue. However, industry reports offer an early glimpse into customer perceptions and behaviors in this context. Specifically, a survey by DMA (2008) of 800 US teenage and young adult users of mobile phone services reveals interesting findings.

Customer Attitudes and Actions

In general, consumers view mobile marketing as intrusive (Shankar and Hollinger 2007). Mobile marketing affects customer decision sequence through two stages (Shankar and Balasubramanian 2009). The first stage relates to mobile device or service adoption discussed earlier. This stage is important because, without such adoption, subsequent mobile marketing initiatives are irrelevant. The second stage comprises the well-known stages in the customer decision-making process – need recognition, information search, alternative evaluation, purchase and post-purchase (e.g. Balasubramanian et al. 2002). Researchers can examine how mobile marketing initiatives can affect each of these stages. There are two important issues: first, the economic, sociological and psychological influences that mobile marketing potentially exerts on customer attitudes and actions at each of these stages; second, the moderating roles of competition, product or service type, and the integration of mobile marketing with overall marketing strategy on these influences.

We need to better understand the effect of mobile marketing on each stage. For example, consider how mobile marketing may affect need creation/recognition. To be effective, advertising messages need to overcome the physical (sensory) and psychological (emotional) barriers erected by customers. In this regard, mobile advertising lacks the persuasive power of the print and TV media due to the highly constrained screen size and the sparseness of information that can be presented within the typical mobile interface. However, if mobile advertising is delivered through social media, it might be more influential than otherwise because of social media's credibility.

However, location-based advertising can provide timely and actionable information to customers. Drawing from the Elaboration Likelihood Model/ELM (Petty and Cacioppo 1986), it appears that mobile advertising is best suited for highlighting existing needs and possibly creating new needs in the context of products and services that call for low customer involvement levels. Specifically, in line with the ELM, mobile advertising can tap into consumers' peripheral route to persuasion that focuses on the presentation of timely and attention-catching information, rather than into the central route to persuasion that calls for intensive processing of detailed information.

Alternatively, mobile advertising can be used to supply specific pieces of information to facilitate a high-involvement purchase. For example, to encourage a quick transaction from a proximate customer, an electronics store could communicate a targeted price reduction coupon for a large-screen TV set to a customer who has asked to be informed about price promotions on that TV set. In particular, for high-involvement products and services, information-rich channels such as the Internet and print media would be required to build the case for the customer to choose the offer. However, more search-friendly and information-rich apps are being created for mobile devices. The mobile channel can then play its role at an appropriate stage of the purchase process. Similarly, we can analyze the other stages of the decision-making process.

Buyers of entertainment, music and video products are more responsive than consumers of other product categories, suggesting that mobile marketing works best for entertainment products and services (DMA 2008). Furthermore, brief messages elicit better response than do complex messages, consistent with the portability and untethered properties of a mobile device.

The effectiveness of mobile promotions depends on consumers' attitudes toward mobile marketing. A survey of 370 mobile phone users in Austria reveals that customers' attitudes toward and perceived control of mobile (m)-coupons affect their intention to redeem such coupons (Dickinger and Kleijnen 2008). Specifically, the study shows that the effort involved in redeeming m-coupons strongly affects customers' attitudes toward m-coupons and fear of mobile spam influences customers' perceived control in the context of mobile marketing.

From the firm's perspective, two desirable actions transpiring from customer attitudes are trials and repurchase. In the mobile marketing environment, conversions of screen views to clicks to purchases are critical for mobile marketing strategy to be effective.

Firm Performance

The aggregation of customer actions results in firm performance. Firm performance is typically measured by sales, market share, profits and, ultimately, shareholder value. While there is some evidence for effectiveness of mobile coupons in terms of sales lifts, the effect of mobile advertising on firm performance is largely unproven. Furthermore, there is scant research on long-term performance consequences such as changes in market share and in shareholder value. Furthermore, not much is known about whether a firm should be a pioneer or a follower in mobile marketing strategy in its industry (Shankar and Carpenter, Chapter 21 in this volume).

IMPLEMENTING A MOBILE MARKETING STRATEGY

Once a firm formulates a suitable mobile marketing strategy, it needs to select appropriate mobile marketing methods to implement the chosen strategy. Mobile marketing or mobile advertising methods include text messaging, integrated content, games, interactive voice response, wireless access protocol (WAP) sites, ring tones and ring-back tones, viral, geotargeting, mobile broadcast advertising, cellphone sponsorships and mobile telemarketing. Text messaging, the most popular mobile marketing method, is useful for sweepstakes, contest voting and instantly redeemable offers. The main advantages of text messaging are that it is simple for both the marketer and the consumer, it is measurable, and has high response and conversion rates. Mobile telemarketing also has favorable response rates among those who opt in, but if the wrong message is delivered to the wrong person at the wrong time, it can incur the wrath of consumers, the carrier and the government.

In selecting the mobile marketing methods to use for a campaign, mobile marketers need to (1) balance the pros and cons of each method, (2) consider the synergies among the methods, and (3) examine the methods used by competitors. Both business-to-consumer (B2C) and business-to-business (B2B) marketers are using these mobile marketing methods (Shankar and Hollinger 2007). For example, in the B2C space, Johnson & Johnson uses text messaging for its optical products. A poster asks optometry patients with mobile devices to type in "MYEYE" while they wait at the optician's or the optometrist's office. J&J then sends a reminder message or/and promotional message about its products when the patient is in the doctor's office (Cuno 2005). In the B2B space, Federal

Express (FedEx) uses the text messaging and geotargeting methods synergistically. It sends messages to business executives who have chosen to receive FedEx messages about document services when they are near a FedEx Kinko's location.

RESEARCH AND MANAGERIAL IMPLICATIONS

We have presented the conceptual underpinnings of mobile marketing strategy. Our synthesis offers some useful insights and several directions for future research on mobile marketing strategy.

Research Implications

Based on our review of the adoption of mobile devices and services, the following questions are worthy of exploration. What key factors inhibit greater use of mobile devices and services for information search and purchase of products and services? Are these inhibitors related to a lack of knowledge about these services, a lack of confidence in the customer's ability to use these services, an inability to project the cost of using these services, or technological limitations related to mobile browsing and/or communication bandwidth? What is the role of trust in the adoption of mobile devices and services? Answers to these questions will enhance our knowledge regarding the adoption of mobile devices and services and customer acceptance of mobile marketing offers.

Although we now have a good understanding of customer decision making in the context of mobile marketing, some unanswered questions are ripe for research. Customers differ in their response to mobile marketing initiatives and the use of mobile media to acquire products and services. How does customer decision making vary across the decision-making stages? Can a marketer use these differences as a basis for customer segmentation in the mobile marketing context? To what extent should such segmentation be guided by attitudes toward mobile marketing within the various stages of the decision-making process, relative to revealed behaviors at these stages?

With regard to post-purchase behavior, research shows that after controlling for selection, online customers are more loyal than offline customers, so migrating customers from offline to online could enhance customer loyalty (Shankar et al. 2003). In a similar vein, can mobile marketing be used to improve customer loyalty? User-generated content (UGC) or consumer-generated content is popular on the Internet through sites such as YouTube.com and MySpace.com. Such sites are being replicated in the mobile environment through services such as Cyworld in South Korea and SeeMeTV in the UK (Holdern 2007). Will the opportunity to create and consume content developed by other users through mobile devices enhance customer loyalty to a firm? These questions merit deep investigation.

At a high level, a number of questions remain unresolved in the context of a firm's mobile marketing strategy. A central issue relates to how the firm's mobile strategy meshes with its overall marketing strategy. The questions identified under mobile marketing strategy suggest that there are ample research opportunities related to the development and execution of a mobile marketing strategy.

In addition, several other issues deserve research attention. Researchers should examine how customers define the bounds of privacy in the mobile context, and under what conditions they are willing to allow companies to breach those bounds. Likewise, future research could examine how next-generation smart cards that can store information about customer needs and preferences will facilitate mobile marketing initiatives. Finally, the functionalities of multiple devices such as personal digital assistants (PDAs), cellphones, music players, cameras and video recorders are rapidly converging into single, multifunctional mobile devices. The relevance of such convergence for mobile marketing can be studied. Whereas a detailed discussion of these issues is beyond the scope of this chapter, they merit independent investigation.

The findings suggest that in the long run, mobile marketers will have to find creative ways to enhance customer receptiveness to mobile marketing in the broader population, and, in the short run, should focus on customers receptive to tactical initiatives. Furthermore, marketers will need to conduct further research to identify and pursue specific product categories and marketing activities that are amenable to mobile marketing initiatives. The ability to contact and send messages to customers on an anytime, anywhere basis offers a wealth of new opportunities, but also the temptation to overuse or misuse those opportunities. The challenge is to utilize interactive mobile technologies to disseminate marketing messages in a sophisticated manner that customizes the offering(s) to target customers.

Managerial Implications

Based on what is known about mobile marketing, Shankar and Balasubramanian (2009) offer the following implications for mobile marketing strategy development.

Use mobile marketing to learn about customer behavior

Customer behavior in the mobile environment is rapidly evolving. Firms could invest in mobile marketing initiatives with an experimental approach that allows them to probe and learn about how customers behave with respect to the mobile medium, and about what works and what does not work in that medium.

Make mobile marketing compelling for customers to opt in

A majority of customers do not appreciate unsolicited intrusions into their mobile space (Barwise and Strong 2002). Therefore it is important to get the users to opt in to receive mobile marketing communications through other media such as the TV, print and the Web. Users opt in when they experience significant benefits of receiving messages (Blum and McClellan 2006). Initially, the messages could deliver direct and tangible benefits such as a complimentary offer for a desired product or service, but in the long run, the messages have to be highly relevant to the customer to be successful (BusinessWeek.com 2007).

Make the mobile value proposition relevant to the context

A mobile device is not a standard personal computer. It is a frequently used, location-sensitive device with very limited visual space. A mobile message will be most effective if it is brief, memorable and well coordinated with time and the user's location. Simply transporting a company's Internet marketing strategy to mobile marketing strategy could be a recipe for failure. Rather, integrating mobile marketing strategy with current marketing strategy, as outlined earlier in the Starbucks example, could work well for the firm.

Blend with social media

The ability to network with friends and relatives is a major benefit for customers in an online environment. Indeed, social media have transformed customer interactions and business practices (Hoffman and Novak, Chapter 12, this volume). The mobile device's attractive properties make it ideal for social communications. Mobile marketers need to look for ways to creatively embed social networking opportunities within their mobile marketing strategy.

Leverage location-based benefits

In some sense, location specificity is the most important distinguishing feature of mobile marketing. Internet marketing is far superior to mobile marketing on dimensions such as the richness of information, access to a great deal of information, and applications of information that involve computations. But Internet-based marketing lacks location specificity. Therefore managers should focus on identifying mobile marketing opportunities that adequately leverage the customer's physical location. The location-based benefits may differ in different parts of the world as Internet features may differ across the world (Shankar and Meyer 2009).

Don't hound the customers

Managers must focus on targeting carefully customized messages to select customers rather than indiscriminately broadcasting messages to the entire mobile customer base. Developing a database of mobile customer profiles and preferences, using data often collected outside the mobile medium, is a crucial first step in this context. Mobile messages should be carefully customized to customers or, at a minimum, customer groups.

Offer creative mobile bundles

In addition, marketers may want to leverage the developments in digital convergence toward the emergence of a mobile wallet. A marketer may like to partner with a finance firm or a bank and complementary service providers to offer value-added bundles through mobile apps.

Mobile marketing is continuing to evolve and much remains to be learned about mobile marketing strategy. The growth in mobile devices and services adoption allows us to collect new data on customer behavior. Such data can help us explore the many important unresolved issues.

NOTE

1. For expositional ease, we use the terms consumer and customer interchangeably throughout the chapter.

REFERENCES

Ancarani, Fabio and Venkatesh Shankar (2003), "Symbian: customer interactions through collaboration and competition in a convergent industry," *Journal of Interactive Marketing*, **17** (1), 56–76.

Balasubramanian, Sridhar, Robert A. Peterson and Sirkka L. Jarvenpaa (2002), "Exploring the implications of M-commerce for markets and marketing," *Journal of Academy of Marketing Science*, **30** (4), 348–61.

Bart, Yakov, Venkatesh Shankar, Fareena Sultan and Glen L. Urban (2005), "Are the drivers and role of online trust the same for all web sites and consumers? A large-scale exploratory empirical study," *Journal of Marketing*, **69** (4), 133–52.

Barwise, Patrick and C. Strong (2002), "Permission-based mobile advertising, "*Journal of Interactive Marketing*, **16** (1), 14–24.

Blum, L. and S. McClellan (2006), "Mobile users welcome the ads they ask for," *Adweek*, September 11, 11.

BusinessWeek.com (2007), "Mobile ad biz comes of age," available at http://www.businessweek.com/glo balbiz/content/may2007/gb20070514_450138.htm?chan=innovation_branding_industry+trends, accessed August 16, 2007.

comScore (2011), *Mobile Lens Service Report*, March, Reston, VA.

Cuno, Alice Z. (2005), "Marketers get real serious about the third screen," *Advertising Age*, July 11.

Davis, Fred D. (1989), "Perceived usefulness, perceived ease of use and user acceptance of information technology," *MIS Quarterly*, **13**, 319–39.

Dickinger, Astrid and Mirella Kleijnen (2008), "Coupons going wireless: determinants of adoption of consumer intentions to redeem mobile coupons," *Journal of Interactive Marketing*, **22** (3), 23–39.

DMA (2008), "Mobile marketing: consumer perspectives," July, New York: Direct Marketing Association.

eMarketer (2010), *Mobile Marketing Report*, November, New York: eMarketer.

Holdern, Windsor (2007), "Mobile content from the masses," excerpted from *Mobile User-Generated Content: Dating, Social Networking, and Personal Content Delivery 2007–2012*, Hampshire, UK: Juniper Research, p. 122.

Kleijnen, Mirella, Ko De Ruyter and Martin Wetzels (2004), "Consumer adoption of wireless services: discovering the rules, while playing the game," *Journal of Interactive Marketing*, **18** (2), 51–61.

Neslin, Scott and Venkatesh Shankar (2009), "Key issues in multichannel management: current knowledge and future directions," Tenth Anniversary Special Issue, *Journal of Interactive Marketing*, **23** (1), 70–81.

Nielsen Mobile (2008), *Critical Mass: The Worldwide State of the Mobile Web*, New York: The Nielsen Company.

Nysveen, H., P.E. Pedersen and H. Thorbjørnsen (2005), "Intentions to use mobile services: antecedents and cross-service comparisons," *Journal of the Academy of Marketing Science*, **33** (3), 330–46.

Pagani, Margherita (2004), "Determination of adoption of third generation mobile multimedia services," *Journal of Interactive Marketing*, **18** (3), 46–59.

Petty, R.E. and J.T. Cacioppo (1986), "The elaboration likelihood model of persuasion," in L.Berkovitz (ed.), *Advances in Experimental Social Psychology*, 19, New York: Academic Press, pp. 123–205.

Rogers, Everett M. (1995), *Diffusion of Innovations*, 4th edn, New York: The Free Press.

Shahnaz, M. (2007), "What keeps putting mobile video on hold?" *Adweek*, **48** (35), 10.

Shankar, Venkatesh and Sridhar Balasubramanian (2009), "Mobile marketing: a synthesis and prognosis," Tenth Anniversary Special Issue, *Journal of Interactive Marketing*, **23** (2), 118–29.

Shankar, Venkatesh and Marie Hollinger (2007), "Online and mobile advertising: current scenario, emerging trends, and future directions," Marketing Science Institute Special Report, 07–206.

Shankar, Venkatesh and Jeff Meyer (2009), "Internet and international marketing," in Michael Kotabe and Kristiaan Helsen (eds), *Handbook of International Marketing*, New York: Sage, pp. 451–67.

Shankar, Venkatesh, Tony O'Driscoll and David Reibstein (2003), "Rational exuberance: the wireless industry's killer 'B,'" *Strategy + Business*, **31** (Summer), 68–77.

Shankar, Venkatesh, Amy Smith and Arvind Rangaswamy (2003), "Customer satisfaction and loyalty in online and offline environments," *International Journal of Research in Marketing*, **20** (2), 153–75.

Shankar, Venkatesh, Alladi Venkatesh, Charles Hofacker and Prasad Naik (2010), "Mobile marketing in the retailing environment: current insights and future research avenues," *Journal of Interactive Marketing*, **24** (2), 111–20.

Silverstone, Roger and Eric Hirsch (eds) (1992), *Consuming Technologies: Media and Information in Domestic Spaces*, London and New York: Routledge.

US Census Bureau (2010), *2010 U.S. Census*, Washington, DC.

14 Channel relationship strategy
Todd J. Arnold and Robert W. Palmatier

INTRODUCTION

Channels of distribution represent the specific routes followed by any product or service purchased by consumers and business buyers. By definition, a marketing channel is "a set of interdependent organizations involved in the process of making a product or service available for use or consumption" (Coughlan et al. 2006, p. 2). The key to this definition is the underlying notion that a channel consists of interdependent organizations. Each member of the channel must rely, at some level, on another member to accomplish a given strategic directive. As such, it is the management of relationships within the channel, or channel relationship strategy, which takes paramount importance. The management of channel relationships entails "the process of identifying, developing, maintaining, and terminating relational exchanges with the purpose of enhancing performance" (Palmatier 2008a, p. 5).

This process has been a research topic for decades, with a particular emphasis in the past 20 years. Several factors – the transition to service-based economies; advances in communication, logistics and computing technologies; increased global competition; and faster product commodization – have enhanced the importance of relationship-based interactions for both buyers and sellers within a channel. Sellers' motivation to engage in exchanges as a result of these trends seems obvious, but it also is important to note that customers increasingly value channel relationships to gain benefits such as reductions of their perceived risk, higher trust, enhanced cooperation and greater flexibility.

This chapter attempts to synthesize our knowledge of marketing channel relationships to give academics and managers a snapshot of what we know, as well as what the future may hold. We begin with a general discussion of relationship theory and antecedents to a relational channel exchange. This is followed by a section describing key drivers of channel relationships. We then discuss consequences of channel relationships and conclude with a discussion of current trends in channel research. In our discussion of key trends, we build upon illustrative channel research published during the past decade and detail three key channel trends. These trends and representative articles related to them appear in Table 14.1. Finally, the chapter concludes with a discussion of further research opportunities.

FOUNDATIONS OF RELATIONSHIPS WITHIN A CHANNEL

Managers who want to implement channel relationship strategies must build and maintain strong relationships, especially with downstream customers, and many empirical articles consider factors that might lead to such strong relationships. Palmatier et al. (2006) survey empirical research from 1987 to 2004 to identify 97 empirical investigations

Table 14.1   Illustrative channel research published in the last decade

Trend	Reference	Context	Key Findings
Retailer power			
	Corsten and Kumar (2005)	Retailer/ supplier	ECR has a positive impact upon supplier economic performance and capability development and can be most effective when retailers have heightened capabilities (relative to other retailers in the industry) and where supplier trust is high
	Raju and Zhang (2005)	Retailer/ manufacturer	Through reliance upon either quantity discounts or a menu of two-part tariffs, a manufacturer can enjoy heightened returns while still maintaining pricing fairness within the channel and keeping relationships viable
	Dukes et al. (2006)	Retailer/ manufacturer	Channel efficiencies exist when retailing costs are reduced; channel transactions based upon bilateral bargaining capture these efficiencies by transferring market share to the more efficient retailer, thereby increasing channel profits
	Geylani et al. (2007)	Retailer/ manufacturer	Through the increase of wholesale prices to weaker retailers within a channel, overall manufacturer margins can be enhanced while maintaining a positive relationship with both weak and strong retailers
Channel governance			
	Wathne and Heide (2004)	Apparel industry supply chain	A firm's ability to show flexibility toward a downstream customer is contingent upon the governance mechanisms that they have deployed in upstream supplier relationships
	Iyer and Villas-Boas (2003)	Retailer/ manufacturer	The bargaining process will affect the degree of coordination within a channel. The presence of a more powerful channel partner may promote channel coordination, thus working to the benefit of the entire channel
	Geyskens and Steenkamp (2000)	Alcoholic beverage channel	Both economic and social satisfaction must be accounted for when evaluating the effectiveness of a channel governance mechanism
	Heide et al. (2007)	Buyer/ supplier	Output monitoring decreases partner opportunism, while behavior monitoring increases partner opportunism
Multichannel route to market			
	Geyskens et al. (2002)	Newspaper industry	On average, investments made toward the addition of Internet channels have a positive net present value. Further, it appears that more powerful firms with a few direct channels to a target market are likely to have greater success than less powerful firms with a broader direct channel offering

Table 14.1 (continued)

Trend	Reference	Context	Key Findings
Multichannel route to market			
	Jindal et al. (2007)	Four consumer industries across three countries	Linkage between a firm's customer orientation and the number of different channels employed to reach customers. Weak linkage found between customer search behaviors and the number of routes used to reach customers
	Kabadayi et al. (2007)	Electronic component manufacturers	Multichannel strategy is most effective when it acts as a complement to a firm's current business-level strategy and serves as a match to environmental conditions. Further, more than one configuration of strategy, structure and environment can lead to superior performance when proper alignment occurs
	Konus et al. (2008)	Dutch consumers	Identification of three segments of consumer based upon attitudes toward multichannel shopping: multichannel enthusiasts, uninvolved shoppers, and store-focused. Covariates such as shopping enjoyment, loyalty and innovativeness predict segment membership. Identified segments seem to apply across multiple categories
	Kumar and Venkatesan (2005)	Cusomter database of multinational manufacturer	Customers who shop across multiple transaction channels provide higher revenues, higher share of wallet, have higher past customer value, and have a higher likelihood of being active than other customers
	Neslin et al. (2006)	None	Review article of major challenges and opportunities related to multichannel customer management. Five major challenges identified: data integration, understanding customer behavior, channel evaluation, allocation of scarce resources and coordination of strategies
	Neslin and Shankar (2009)	None	Review article of the key issues associated with multichannel marketing. Key areas of investigation include customer analysis, the development of multichannel strategy, channel design, strategy implementation and strategy evaluation

representing 38 077 different relationships. In their empirical meta-analysis, they combine investigations and correct for sample size and measurement errors; thus they are able to identify the most effective foundations for relationships, as well as relationship drivers and outcomes, without reference to researcher, industry or measurement method (see Figure 14.1 for an overview of the key interfirm relationship antecedents, drivers and outcomes, which will be discussed in this chapter).

Furthermore, evaluations of the relative impact of different relationship development

Relationship antecedents   **Relationship drivers**   **Relationship outcomes**

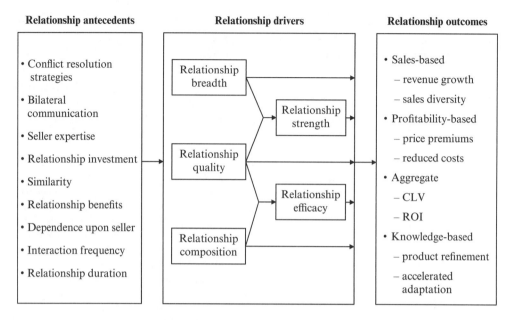

Figure 14.1   Overview of channel relationship development, drivers and outcomes

strategies suggest that conflict, or the overall level of disagreement between exchange partners (Gaski 1984), has the greatest impact on relational assets and destroys all aspects of relationship quality (e.g. trust, commitment) equally. Accordingly, prior research suggests that partners must resolve problems and disagreements to prevent potentially corrosive, relationship-damaging disagreements. Such conflict further minimizes customer confidence in the long-term orientation of the seller and willingness to invest in relationship building or maintenance; that is, conflict harms both trust and commitment toward the seller (Anderson and Weitz 1992; MacKenzie and Hardy 1996). Although functional conflict might lead to an amicable resolution of disagreements that increases trust (Morgan and Hunt 1994), especially among exchange partners with strong relationships, who should be able to cooperate and find a mutually acceptable solution, the greater effect of conflict appears to be negative. Without resolution, conflict festers and undermines even hard-won relationships, often because people naturally pay more attention to relationship negatives than positives (Fiske 1980; Shiv et al. 1997).

To resolve such conflict, the best option may be communication, which entails the amount, frequency and quality of shared information (Mohr et al. 1996). Bilateral communication (e.g. unilateral information exchanges, such as disclosure or openness) helps relationship partners resolve conflict, align goals and expectations, and uncover new value-creating opportunities, which increase relationship commitment (Morgan and Hunt 1994). The greater information and clarity that result from such communication also increase trust; both parties have confidence in the other's promises. Consistent with these roles, communication has significant positive effects on all aspects of relationship quality in the meta-analysis.

Furthermore, perceptions of the seller as more knowledgeable or credible (i.e. seller expertise) makes any information the seller provides seem more reliable, valuable and persuasive (Dholakia and Sternthal 1977). When a customer can interact with a competent seller, it gains value, finds the exchange relationship more important, and invests more relationship maintenance effort (Lagace et al. 1991). Vargo and Lusch (2004, p. 3) call "skills and knowledge . . . the fundamental unit of exchange," and thus seller expertise has the greatest positive impact across all forms of relationship quality (Palmatier et al. 2006). Because sellers' expertise (i.e. skill and knowledge in Vargo and Lusch's terms) creates value, firms absolutely must train their boundary spanners. Inexperienced, unskilled employees likely have seriously detrimental impacts.

Three other antecedents of strong relationships exert strong influences as well: relationship investment, similarity and relationship benefits. The first and last logically correlate: by investing time, effort and resources, sellers build stronger relationships, and these strong relationships generate the benefits of time savings, convenience, companionship and improved decision making. If relationship investments, such as preferential treatment or loyalty programs, are irrecoverable, psychological bonds and reciprocity expectations develop, which again makes the relationship stronger (Smith and Barclay 1997). Receiving benefits from their investments causes customers to perceive higher relationship value, welcome the seller's relational efforts, and invest their own resources to develop strong relational bonds.

Yet the effects of relationship investment and benefits differ. In particular, sellers' relationship investments do not necessarily generate customer relationship benefits, so this feature has the least impact on customer commitment. The seller might create a stronger relationship through investments (which could generate feelings of reciprocity), but its customer still might express relatively minimal commitment or desire to maintain the relationship. When faced with greater customer relationship benefits, in contrast, customers are far more likely to commit. These varying effects may reflect the actual value the customer receives; that is, relationship investments can generate debts of reciprocity but not customer value (De Wulf et al. 2001), in which case they likely cannot produce an enduring desire to maintain a valued relationship.

The second feature is distinct, in that similarity pertains to commonalities in appearance, lifestyle and status (individual level) or coordinating cultures, values and goals (organizational level) (Nicholson et al. 2001). A similar exchange partner might facilitate goal achievement and reduce uncertainty about the partner's actions because of their common perspectives, which should strengthen the exchange relationship. Similarity-inspired confidence, at both interpersonal and interorganizational levels, enhances trust, commitment and relationship quality (Nicholson et al. 2001).

Finally, the meta-analysis reveals three antecedents with weaker effects: dependence on seller, interaction frequency and relationship duration. Strategies that attempt to lock in customers, increase switching costs or increase customer dependence thus appear ineffective at best and harmful in the worst case. Dependence may increase commitment, in that customers prefer relationships with sellers on which they depend, but the actual influence of dependence on specific customer attitudes or actions varies, apparently according to the different relationship dimensions (commitment, trust). Relationship duration (i.e. length of the relationship between exchange partners) and interaction frequency (i.e. number of interactions per unit of time) can better predict confidence or trust in the exchange partner, because they both offer behavioral information in varied situations. But neither factor reveals customer relationships accurately; in the meta-analysis, they result in low correlations and negative signs at lower ranges, and the strongest correlation, between relationship duration and relational assets, appears to be due to a survival bias. Finally, interaction frequency exerts a relatively greater impact on trust compared with other measures. That is, frequent interactions may do nothing with regard to improving customer satisfaction or desire to maintain a relationship, but they give customers more information, reduce uncertainty about future behaviors and improve trust. A new salesperson brought into the exchange after a detrimental event (i.e. high commitment, low trust) therefore should engage in frequent sales calls, personalized follow-ups and customized mailings.

According to these findings, different channel relational strategies produce wide variations in the levels of effectiveness. The most effective strategies minimize conflict; improve seller expertise, bilateral communication, relationship investments and relationship benefits; and match the individual (boundary spanner) and organizational characteristics of the target customers. Generating customer relationship benefits and investing in customer relationships may strengthen some aspects, but increasing customer dependence and interaction frequency or just maintaining a customer relationship over time offer minimally effective relationship strategies.

DRIVERS OF CHANNEL RELATIONSHIPS

Any theory of channel relationships must acknowledge that relationships typically entail groups of employees on both sides of the exchange dyad. Thus firm-to-firm relationships involve multiple interactions among many people or, in effect, a network of relationships. Network theory as developed in sociology provides valuable insights into the impact of the structural characteristics of interactions among multiple entities (e.g. individuals, firms) within an overall network (Borgatti and Foster 2003; Houston et al. 2004; Van Den Bulte and Wuyts 2007); this network perspective recently has been applied to inter-firm relationships to show that relationship quality (e.g. trust, commitment), relationship breadth (network density) and relationship composition (network diversity/attractiveness) all influence exchange performance (Palmatier 2008b). A seller's relational activities influence these three fundamental drivers of relationship effectiveness, each of which captures a different and important aspect of channel relationships and has a positive impact on the seller's performance outcomes (see Figure 14.1 for an overview of antecedents, drivers and outcomes associated with channel relationships). These fundamental drivers appear to work synergistically to enhance relational outcomes, including channel relationship performance.

Relationship Quality

In parallel with the concept of tie strength (i.e. relational bonds among actors) from network theory, the caliber of relational bonds with an exchange partner represents the dyad's relationship quality. This measure captures the concepts of relational embeddedness, closeness and degree of reciprocity from social bond theory (e.g. Rindfleisch and Moorman 2001). The composite relationship quality construct therefore captures diverse elements required by a high-caliber relational bond, namely, commitment, trust, reciprocity norms and exchange efficiency (Crosby et al. 1990; Kumar et al. 1995).

Commitment represents the exchange partners' desire and motivation to maintain valued relationships; trust constitutes an evaluation of a partner's reliability and integrity and thus generates confidence in the partner's cooperative actions. Because they reflect internalized beliefs and expectations about the balance of obligations in an exchange, reciprocity norms have pervasive impacts on exchange behaviors, and they take longer to develop. Exchange efficiency – the assessment of time, effort and resources needed to maintain a relationship – improves exchange performance when "governance structures that have better cost economizing properties . . . eventually displace those that have worse, ceteris paribus" (Williamson 1981, p. 574). Relationship quality thus affects relationship performance positively (Palmatier 2008a).

Relationship Breadth

Relationship breadth entails the number of relational bonds with an exchange partner; it thus mirrors the concepts of network density (i.e. interconnectedness among network members) and degree centrality (i.e. number of direct ties between one member and other network members) from network theory (Houston et al. 2004). When channel relationships, such as that between a seller and a customer, include many interpersonal ties, they enjoy better access to key information, support the discovery of profit-enhancing opportunities, and suffer fewer disruptions to individual bonds from events such as staff turnover or reorganizations (Palmatier 2008b; Palmatier et al. 2007). When interorganizational relationships are broader, they can recover more easily from the departure of a key contact person (Bendapudi and Leone 2002), which in turn improves exchange performance. That is, network connections positively affect cooperation, knowledge transfer, communication efficiency and product development performance (Rowley 1997; Tsai 2001; Walker et al. 1997).

Relationship Composition

Relationship breadth often correlates positively with relationship composition, that is, the decision-making capability of relational contacts. If it has a diverse, authoritative portfolio, the seller can induce change among customers, and sellers with more contacts, *ceteris paribus*, should have more diverse contacts (horizontal and vertical diversification). However, breadth and composition also may diverge if sellers have many homogeneous contacts or only a few, very different contacts (Palmatier 2008b). In any case, greater diversity and authority mean the seller can cross-reference information it gathers from different perspectives and access critical decision makers in various stages of the sales cycle (Katrichis 1998). Imagine a seller with a new product to offer: the salesperson's strong relationship with a vice president of purchasing has little impact if the product is left sitting in quality control for months before it even gets to the purchasing department. Thus relationship composition recognizes the limits of relationship breadth, even if it features high-quality relationships, because if those relationships do not include key decision makers at various positions in the firm, they cannot effect change.

Interaction of Quality with Breadth and Composition

The relational drivers outlined previously capture different aspects of interfirm relationships, but also reinforce one another to achieve optimum relationship value.
Performance outcomes result when relationship quality exerts both a direct effect on the
seller's outcomes and a leveraging, positive effect through its meaningful interaction with
relationship breadth and composition (Palmatier 2008b). In connection with our recognition of the importance of these combinations, we highlight the synergies that occur
between relationship quality and both relationship breadth and composition.

Quality and breadth
When relationship quality interacts with relationship breadth, the result is relationship
strength, defined as a channel relationship's ability to withstand stress and conflict.
Multiple, high-quality relational bonds (great breadth, high quality) result in strong,
resilient relationships (Palmatier 2008a), marked by both relational motivation (commitment, norms of reciprocity) and confidence (trust), which leads to a supportive
environment during a service recovery. Multiple cursory contacts (greater breadth, low
quality) cannot effectively protect against the stress of a service failure though, because
the low-quality contacts refuse to support the seller (low relational motivation). A single
high-quality contact (high quality, less breadth) offers no good protection either, because
the contact likely cannot risk being the sole supporter or risk its reputation to influence
a decision-making group (Brown 2000). In indirect support of the idea that relationship
strength enhances seller outcomes by increasing the interfirm relationship's ability to
withstand problems and conflict but still function effectively (Palmatier 2008a), service
literature indicates that both relationship duration and breadth exert positive influences
on service recovery (Bejou and Palmer 1998; Hess et al. 2003).

Quality and composition
The interaction of relationship quality and relationship composition captures a channel
relationship's ability to achieve desired objectives in the form of relationship efficacy
(Palmatier 2008a). Formally, relationship composition reflects a latent ability to institute
change; only high-quality relationships can exploit this potential to enable the seller to
achieve its objectives (Anderson and Narus 1991; Morgan and Hunt 1994). Therefore
high-quality bonds in well-structured contact portfolios help sellers execute their selling
strategies, whereas high-quality relationships are virtually worthless if they entail only
one functional area with little decision-making ability (low composition) or fail to
provide access to divergent (nonredundant) information. In contrast, a seller's contact
portfolio could contain key decision makers (high composition) but weak interpersonal
bonds (low quality), in which case the contacts will not disclose information (Crosby
et al. 1990) or care much about the seller's needs (reciprocity). According to network
theory, "It is critical to separate the issues of tie strength from that of network diversity,"
because "the most desirable ties are both *strong* and *diverse*" (Li 2007, p. 239). When
both exist, performance can be maximized, so a "large network of strong ties to nonredundant actors is the best sort to have" (Rangan 2000, p. 826).

The resulting interfirm relationship framework, which relies largely on social network
theory, integrates two drivers (breadth and composition) with relationship quality as the

critical means for understanding the impact of interfirm relationships on performance (Palmatier 2008a) and also acknowledges the enhanced effects of interactions among these drivers. Despite the importance of realizing the drivers of overall relational performance within a channel, we note the need to adopt an applied perspective toward the fundamental building blocks of strong customer relationships within a channel.

CONSEQUENCES OF CHANNEL RELATIONSHIPS

Managers expend time and money on building channel relationships, believing that it ultimately leads to improved performance. Previous research (Palmatier 2008a) links relational behaviors to an influence upon four critical outcome categories: sales-based outcomes; profitability-based outcomes; aggregate outcomes; and knowledge-based outcomes. The most common of these, sales-based outcomes, recognize that relational behaviors (e.g. reciprocation, reduced search, last look) can increase, or minimize drops in, sales revenue. Sales-based outcome measures take many forms, including annual sales growth, sales diversity (number of different products and services sold to a customer), sales volatility (variability in sales over time) and share of wallet (sales penetration for a specific customer). Some sales-based metrics are relevant only for a portfolio of customers, such as the number of new customers generated or retention and churn rates (firm's ability to retain existing customers). Although some relational behaviors indirectly affect sales, they may have a more direct impact on the seller's profit levels with customers (e.g. price premium).

Profitability-based outcome measures include price premiums (e.g. percentage a customer will pay to deal with a seller with which it has a strong relationship) and reduced selling costs. The diverse mechanisms by which channel relationships can affect performance imply that aggregate measures of performance are best, because measuring sales alone probably provides an incomplete picture of the true effect of relational behaviors. For example, using customer lifetime value (CLV)-based measures captures the broad range of potential performance-enhancing relational behaviors because it discounts future cash flows and selling costs and thereby indicates the customer's present value (i.e. both sales and profit effects – see Kumar and Rajan, Chapter 7 in this volume). Many argue that CLV represents the best overall measure of customer value and should guide most marketing actions, but in practice, it is difficult to capture the required data to make such calculations and often is very sensitive to assumptions (margins, future growth rates, allocation of costs). Another aggregate outcome measure well suited for evaluating specific marketing programs, as compared with customers, is return on investment (ROI). Research evaluating ROI in social, structural and financial RM programs returns mixed results, in which social programs generate positive returns, structural programs break even in the first year, and financial programs fail to generate positive returns in the short term.

The final group of outcomes, knowledge-based outcomes, builds upon the premise that customer relational behaviors may provide sellers with insight into new markets, help them uncover new product opportunities, enable them to beta test and refine new product concepts, and accelerate adoption of new product launches; strong relationships also may influence sellers' financial performance in ways that typical outcome metrics cannot isolate (at least in the short run). These effects are especially difficult to capture because they occur displaced in both time and location from the customer's relational behaviors. For example, a customer may disclose critical information used by a seller to develop a proprietary new product, which generates profitable sales to different customers in different markets many years into the future. Linking relational investments in current customers to different future customers often represents an insurmountable problem. Instead, tracking an intermediate, knowledge-based outcome provides some indication of the ultimate effect of relational behaviors on future financial outcomes. Knowledge-based outcomes, such as number of patents, time to market and new product success rate, also may provide insights into some relational benefits not captured in financial measures. Measuring knowledge-based outcomes may be especially important for firms implementing innovation-based strategies.

KEY TRENDS IN CHANNEL RELATIONSHIP RESEARCH

The discussion of this chapter, to this point, has focused upon relationship theory and an overview of what we know about building relationships and evaluating relational outcomes. It is now time to examine how current research is moving forward in the development of our knowledge of channel relationships. Although multiple emerging trends are important for developing channel strategies (e.g. transition to service-based economies, advances in communication, logistics and computing technologies), topics related to three key areas seem to dominate recent research: retailer power, channel governance and multichannel routes to market.

Retailer Power

Power is seen as the ability of one channel member to get another channel member to do what the latter would not otherwise have done (see Reve and Stern 1979). Operationally, as Reve and Stern note (1979, p. 409), this implies that power is "the perceived or actual control one channel member exerts over the use of particular elements of another member's marketing strategies." As retailers have continued to gain such power, suppliers and manufacturers appear increasingly aware of the pitfalls of trying to compete simply on price to appease retailers (which can be a recipe for bankruptcy; see Lodish and Mela 2007; Rao, Chapter 6 in this volume). In addition, in the globally competitive modern retail environment, retailers are beginning to look beyond organizational boundaries to assess and integrate the resources and capabilities of their suppliers and customers to create superior value and thus a competitive advantage that they can sustain over time (Ganesan et al. 2009). In combination, these effects highlight the importance of effective and efficient channel relationships.

For example, Corsten and Kumar (2005) investigate the importance of developing retail channel relationships based on efficient consumer response (ECR), a concept characterized by the emergence of collaborative management across the supply chain. It is based on the understanding that companies can serve consumers far more effectively and at lower costs if they cooperate with channel partners. The rigid separation of "normative" roles for the supplier, manufacturer and retailer threatens to clutter the supply chain unnecessarily and fails to exploit synergies associated with recent informa- tion technologies and planning tools. In contrast, ECR helps companies seek a sustain- able competitive advantage by capitalizing on their superior ability to collaborate with trading partners and add value for the ultimate consumer. As Corsten and Kumar (2005) find, ECR has a positive impact on suppliers' economic performance and capability development, and can be most effective when retailers achieve heightened capabilities (relative to other retailers in the industry) and supplier trust is high.

Raju and Zhang (2005) investigate pricing mechanisms that work to benefit a given manufacturer, even in the presence of a dominant retailer. By relying on either quantity discounts or a menu of two-part tariffs (e.g. charging both a lump sum and per unit fee), a manufacturer can enjoy heightened returns while still maintaining pricing fair- ness within the channel (and keeping its relationships viable). Similarly, Geylani et al. (2007) demonstrate that by increasing the wholesale prices charged to weaker retailers in a channel, manufacturers can enhance their overall margins but still maintain a positive relationship with both weak and strong retailers. In short, dominant retailers are happy because wholesale prices are competitive for them; weaker retailers are happy because they benefit from joint promotions and advertising by the manufacturer, which wants to direct customers to higher margin customers. Dukes et al. (2006) demonstrate similar advantages from joint negotiations with dominant and weak retailers. Potential channel efficiencies emerge when retailing costs decline, and channel transactions based on bilateral bargaining capture efficiencies by transferring market share to the more efficient retailer, which increases total channel profits.

In summary, extant research demonstrates the importance of recognizing both dominant and weaker retailers when developing channel relationship strategies. It also shows that a manufacturer or supplier can use the retailer's strengths and weaknesses to its advantage but still maintain profitable and productive relationships with different retailer types. A channel assessment that incorporates evaluations of all relevant parties' capabilities and weaknesses (i.e. implementation of ECR) thus can work to create greater value for the ultimate consumer, which should be the end goal for any channel of distribution.

Channel Governance

As with power, governance relates to the interaction of independent entities. Formally defined, governance may be seen as "encompassing the initiation, termination and ongoing relationship maintenance between a set of parties" (Heide 1994, p. 72). Governance implies the creation of a structure that enables the assurance that individual channel member behaviors follow the desired rules for collective action. Research into retailer power certainly relates to channel governance, but this trend extends even further when it comes to managing channel relationships. For example, Heide et al. (2007) investigate whether monitoring, when used as a control mechanism for interfirm rela- tionships, may promote rather than reduce opportunistic behavior, depending on the use of outcome- versus behavior-based monitoring, as well as the context in which the moni- toring takes place. Output monitoring (i.e. measuring visible consequences of a partner's actions, such as delivery times or order) reduces partner opportunism; behavior moni- toring (i.e. evaluating the processes expected to produce the focal outcomes) actually increases partner opportunism. Context plays a key role in either regard, through the micro-level social contracts or agreements between buyers and sellers purposely designed for individual exchange relationships (beyond macro-level contracts at the societal level). Such micro-level contracts serve as buffers that both enhance the effects of output monitoring and suppress the opportunism affiliated with behavior monitoring. Such research thereby emphasizes the vast importance of informal relationships.

Work by Iyer and Villas-Boas (2003) addresses the importance of relative bargaining power within a channel relationship. Although power/dependence has been subject to investigation for decades, its importance persists. Iyer and Villas-Boas find that the bargaining process affects the degree of coordination in a channel, and the presence of a more powerful channel partner (e.g. a powerful retailer) may promote channel coordination, which benefits the entire channel (as the retailer power studies show). Thus the potentially positive effects of channel power once again emerge from this research.

Finally, Wathne and Heide (2004) investigate how relationships formed outside a focal dyad (but still related to the dyad) influence a firm's strategy in a downstream customer relationship. A firm's ability to exhibit flexibility toward a downstream customer is contingent on the governance mechanisms it has deployed in upstream supplier relationships. Specifically, the use of supplier qualification programs (e.g. to demonstrate firm values and norms to a potential supplier) and incentive designs formulated around a "hostage" (e.g. a manufacturer that requires a supplier to invest assets dedicated to their relationship) seems to influence a firm's ultimate downstream flexibility. In short, these authors find support for the notion that qualification programs enhance a manufacturer's ability to provide flexibility in downstream relationships in conditions of market uncertainty, but in scenarios with hostages, flexibility is more likely when both the manufacturer and supplier possess hostages (i.e. high mutual lock-in effects). As such, the nature of a relationship in one stage of the channel has a clear influence on relationships in other stages.

Multichannel Routes to Market

The emergence of the Internet in the 1990s and early 2000s has pushed many established companies to explore, at a minimum, the efficacy of reaching their target markets through more than one channel (see Verhoef, Chapter 8 in this volume). This practice has coincided with an upswing in academic research that investigates such "multichannel" routes to reaching a target market. In some early work in this domain, Geyskens et al. (2002) investigated the effect of adding an Internet channel on a firm's stock market return; on average, investments to add Internet channels appear to have positive net present value. Furthermore, and logically, it appears that more powerful firms with a few direct channels to market will have greater success than less powerful firms with a broader direct channel offering. Status as an early follower, as opposed to an innovator or late follower, also seems to have a positive effect, as does the execution of a publicity strategy to complement the development of the Internet channel. Because of the clear demonstration of a potentially positive effect of implementing a multichannel strategy, such research provides a solid foundation for ongoing work into the influence of such strategies.

For example, Kabadayi et al. (2007) build on this logic and apply configuration theory to investigate the importance of matching a multichannel strategy with the business-level strategy and environmental conditions. As might be expected, a multichannel strategy is most effective when it complements the firm's current business-level strategy and matches its environmental conditions. Furthermore, multiple configurations of strategy, structure and environment can lead to superior performance if proper alignment occurs. These authors also suggest specific application guidelines; for example, when firms face unpredictable and fast-changing (but lucrative) environments, managers should combine a differentiation strategy with an expansive multichannel system (i.e. high-quality, unique products that can be targeted widely through multiple, independently owned channels). Their research demonstrates the importance of not only self-assessment but also assessments of potential channel partners to understand which might be in a good position to help the firm complement its current strategy.

In further examination of multichannel routes to market, Jindal et al. (2007) examine whether the implementation of a multichannel strategy can be systematically explained. Specifically, the research examines how a firm's customer orientation (type and level) and target customer's search behaviors (type and depth) affect the development of multi-channel strategies. Findings indicate that a firm being more customer oriented does, indeed, predict the development of multichannel strategies, while customer search behavior has a limited effect upon such strategic development. This implies a potentially strong influence of organizational perspective upon the development of multichannel strategies.

Konus et al. (2008), as well as Kumar and Venkatesan (2005) investigate the identification and categorization of multichannel shoppers to understand the potential influence of customer characteristics upon the development of multichannel strategies. Specifically, Konus et al. (2008) identify three dominant forms of multichannel shoppers (multi-channel enthusiasts, uninvolved shoppers and store-focused consumers) that appear to exist across multiple categories of consumer products. That is, in most instances, over-riding customer characteristics appear to dominate an orientation toward multichannel usage tendencies, regardless of the product category being shopped. In complement to this, the importance of discovering and accurately identifying such shopper catego-ries among a firm's target customers is well illustrated by the findings of Kumar and Venkatesan (2005), who demonstrate that multichannel shoppers (i.e. multichannel enthusiasts) often provide a firm with higher revenues, higher share of wallet, higher past customer value, and are more likely to be active consumers. Such outcomes reinforce several of the important outcomes highlighted previously in this chapter (see Figure 14.1).

Finally, current work by Neslin and Shankar (2009), as well as by Neslin et al. (2006) discusses the challenges and potential benefits of simultaneously managing and operating multiple channel strategies. Neslin and Shankar (2009) build upon much of the previous research referenced earlier in this chapter to highlight several key issues associated with multichannel strategies, such as customer analysis across channels, effective segmenta-tion and competition assessments within and across channels, individual channel design strategies, implementation and evaluation issues that need to be addressed. Similarly, Neslin et al. (2006) highlight channel management challenges associated with such stra-tegic questions as those posed by Neslin and Shankar (2009). That is, Neslin et al. (2006) point out the importance of addressing data integration needs across channels, as well as understanding potential customer behaviors, evaluating each potential channel, allocat-ing resources across channels, and coordinating multiple channel strategies. In short, the authors effectively demonstrate that the implementation of a multichannel strategy is not something to be approached without proper investigation and forethought, which is demonstrated through the wealth of current research that has grown in relation to such strategic questions.

CONCLUSION AND FUTURE RESEARCH

This chapter highlights important elements associated with the study and application of relationship marketing within a channel of distribution (i.e. interfirm exchange). The key elements of relational foundations, drivers of relational maintenance and important outcomes have been presented both in relation to general relationship marketing knowledge (i.e. Figure 14.1), as well as in relation to current trends in channel research. Through identification of the key research trends, we have gained a general idea of future research directions. But, in addition to such important trends, it is important to highlight that there is still much more to investigate in association with channel relationship strategy. We conclude the chapter by highlighting several potential research questions associated with unique areas of channel relationship strategy.

Relational Antecedents

A relatively small set of antecedents affects the formation of relational assets, according to existing research; therefore additional research needs to expand the set. What relative importance does a selling firm's organizational design (e.g. leadership, strategy, culture, control and structure) have on its ability to execute relational strategies? Conflict clearly harms relational assets; how then can firms remedy conflict-laden relationships, especially those that demand service or relationship recovery strategies? Even communication, which affects both the level and growth of relational assets, requires more investigation if we are to gain a clear understanding of its role for a channel relationship strategy.

Recent findings expand the number of relational attributes (e.g. breadth, depth, reciprocity, efficacy, gratitude) available to represent a firm's relational assets; further research should isolate their relative efficacy across different relational constructs (Palmatier et al. 2009). Which relationship marketing programs tend to result in exchange inefficiencies? Which effective relational strategies work across relational drivers? For example, group social events, training seminars and telemarketing might expand the breadth or density of relational contacts by generating new prospects; one-on-one social programs and similarity across boundary spanners could build relationship quality; senior executives or experts may work best to improve relationship composition. In addition, some customers are less likely to develop relationships, which may imply that they dislike interpersonal relational development, which creates a reciprocity-based obligation to respond.

Relationship Dynamics

The antecedents require expansion not just in number but also over time. That is, channel relational drivers may affect exchange outcomes differently at different stages across the relationship life cycle. In early stages, the quality of the initial bonds seems critical, because they establish early interfirm norms. In the growth stage, sellers prefer greater sales penetration, requiring action by diverse decision makers, so relationship composition may be most critical. As relationships mature, sellers begin to focus on share protection, and relationship breadth may be crucial because it can create barriers to customer switching and competitive pressures. If "densely tied networks produce strong constraints," relationship breadth similarly may constrain customer actions (Rowley 1997, p. 897). Additional research should consider how suppliers might supplement weaknesses in relationship breadth or composition by leveraging channel members' contact portfolios. Certain underlying or mediating mechanisms also could clarify how relationship breadth and composition influence performance.

Relational Outcomes

Finally, if research fails to expand the range of performance outcomes it studies to identify the overall impact of relational strategies, it runs the risk of systematic underestimations. Additional outcomes that would complete the picture of sales-based relationship marketing outcomes include sales growth, diversity, volatility, share of wallet, retention, upselling and cross-buying. Research also should move beyond sales-based outcomes to consider profitability measures, such as price premiums, selling and acquisition costs, lifetime value and return on investments. By integrating innovation concepts, research could enter relational constructs into existing models to determine the potentially beneficial effects of relationship marketing on knowledge acquisition and new product development and launch. For example, knowledge-based measures such as patents, time to market and new product success could reveal ways in which high-quality relationships throughout a channel enable firms to innovate.

REFERENCES

Anderson, Erin and Baron A. Weitz (1992), "The use of pledges to build and sustain commitment in distribution channels," *Journal of Marketing Research*, **29** (February), 18–34.

Anderson, James C. and James A. Narus (1991), "Partnering as a focused market strategy," *California Management Review*, **33** (Spring), 95–113.

Bejou, David and Adrian Palmer (1998), "Service failure and loyalty: an exploratory empirical study of airline customers," *Journal of Services Marketing*, **12**, 7–22.

Bendapudi, Neeli and Robert P. Leone (2002), "Managing business-to-business customer relationships following key contact employee turnover in a vendor firm," *Journal of Marketing*, **66** (April), 83–101.

Borgatti, Stephen P. and Pacey C. Foster (2003), "The network paradigm in organizational research: a review and topology," *Journal of Management*, **29** (6), 991–1013.

Brown, Rupert (2000), *Group Processes: Dynamics Within and Between Groups*, Malden, MA: Blackwell Publishing.

Corsten, Daniel and Nirmalya Kumar (2005), "Do suppliers benefit from collaborative relationships with large retailers? An empirical investigation of efficient consumer response adoption," *Journal of Marketing*, **69** (July), 80–94.

Coughlan, Anne T., Erin Anderson, Louis W. Stern and Adel I. El-Ansary (2006), *Marketing Channels*, 7th edn, Upper Saddle River, NJ: Pearson, Prentice Hall.

Crosby, Lawrence A., Kenneth R. Evans and Deborah Cowles (1990), "Relationship quality in services selling: an interpersonal influence perspective," *Journal of Marketing*, **54** (July), 68–81.

De Wulf, Kristof, Gaby Odekerken-Schröder and Dawn Iacobucci (2001), "Investments in consumer relationships: a cross-country and cross-industry exploration," *Journal of Marketing*, **65** (October), 33–50.

Dholakia, Ruby Roy and Brian Sternthal (1977), "Highly credible source: persuasive facilitator of persuasive liabilities?," *Journal of Consumer Research*, **3** (March), 223–32.

Dukes, Anthony J., Esther Gal-Or and Kannan Srinivasan (2006), "Channel bargaining with retailer asymmetry," *Journal of Marketing Research*, **43** (February), 84–97.

Fiske, Susan T. (1980), "Attention and weight in person perception: the impact of negative and extreme behavior," *Journal of Personality and Social Psychology*, **38** (June), 889–906.

Ganesan, Shankar, George Morris, Sandy Jap, Robert W. Palmatier and Barton Weitz (2009), "Supply chain management and retailer performance: emerging trends, issues and implications for research and practice," *Journal of Retailing*, **85** (1), 84–94.

Gaski, John F. (1984), "The theory of power and conflict in channels of distribution," *Journal of Marketing*, **48** (Summer), 9–29.

Geylani, Tansev, Anthony J. Dukes and Kannan Srinivasan (2007), "Strategic manufacturer response to a dominant retailer," *Marketing Science*, **26** (2), 164–78.

Geyskens, Inge and Jan-Benedict E.M. Steenkamp (2000), "Economic and social satisfaction: measurement and relevance to marketing channel relationships," *Journal of Retailing*, **76** (1), 11–32.

Geyskens, Inge, Katrijn Gielens and Marnik G. Dekimpe (2002), "The market valuation of Internet channel additions," *Journal of Marketing*, **66** (April), 102–19.

Heide, Jan B. (1994), "Interorganizational governance in marketing channels," *Journal of Marketing*, **58** (1), 71–85.

Heide, Jan B., Kenneth H. Wathne and Aksel I. Rokkan (2007), "Interfirm monitoring, social contracts and relationship outcomes," *Journal of Marketing Research*, **44** (August), 425–33.

Hess, Ron L., Shankar Ganesan and Noreen M. Klein (2003), "Service failure and recovery: the impact of relationship factors on customer satisfaction," *Journal of the Academy Marketing Science*, **31** (2), 127–45.

Houston, Mark B., Michael D. Hutt, Christine Moorman, Peter H. Reingen, Aric Rindfleisch, Vanitha Swaminathan and Beth A. Walker (2004), "A network perspective on marketing strategy," in Christine Moorman and Donald R. Lehman (eds), *Assessing Marketing Strategy Performance*, Cambridge, MA: Marketing Science Institute, pp. 247–68.

Iyer, Ganesh and J. Miguel Villas-Boas (2003), "A bargaining theory of distribution channels," *Journal of Marketing Research*, **40** (February), 80–100.

Jindal, R., W. Reinartz, M. Krafft and W. Hoyer (2007), "Determinants of the variety of routes to market," *International Journal of Research in Marketing*, **24** (1), 17–29.

Kabadayi, Sertan, Nermin Eyuboglu and Gloria P. Thomas (2007), "The performance implications of designing multiple channels to fit with strategy and environment," *Journal of Marketing*, **71** (October), 195–211.

Katrichis, Jerome M. (1998), "Exploring departmental level interaction patterns in organizational purchasing decisions," *Industrial Marketing Management*, **27** (March), 135–46.

Konus, U., P.C. Verhoef and S.A. Neslin (2008), "Multi-channel customer segmentation," *Journal of Retailing*, **84** (4), 398–413.

Kumar, V. and R. Venkatesan (2005), "Who are the multichannel shoppers and how do they perform? Correlates of multichannel shopping behavior," *Journal of Interactive Marketing*, **19** (2), 44–62.

Kumar, Nirmalya, Lisa K. Scheer and Jan-Benedict E.M. Steenkamp (1995), "The effects of supplier fairness on vulnerable resellers," *Journal of Marketing Research*, **32** (February), 54–65.

Lagace, Rosemary R., Robert Dahlstrom and Jule B. Gassenheimer (1991), "The relevance of ethical salesperson behavior to relationship quality: the pharmaceutical industry," *Journal of Personal Selling and Sales Management*, **11** (Fall), 39–47.

Li, Peter Ping (2007), "Social tie, social capital and social behavior: toward an integrative model of informal exchange," *Asia Pacific Journal of Management*, **24** (2), 227–46.

Lodish, Leonard M. and Carl F. Mela (2007), "If brands are built over years, why are they managed over quarters?," *Harvard Business Review*, (July–August), 104–12.

MacKenzie, Herbert F. and Kenneth G. Hardy (1996), "Manage your offering or managing your relationship?," *Journal of Business & Industrial Marketing*, **11** (6), 20–37.

Mohr, Jakki J., Robert J. Fisher and John R. Nevin (1996), "Collaborative communication in interfirm relationships: moderating effects of integration and control," *Journal of Marketing*, **60** (July), 103–15.

Morgan, Robert M. and Shelby D. Hunt (1994), "The commitment-trust theory of relationship marketing," *Journal of Marketing*, **58** (July), 20–38.

Neslin, S.A. and V. Shankar (2009), "Key issues in multichannel customer management: current knowledge and future directions," *Journal of Interactive Marketing*, **23** (1), 70–81.

Neslin, S.A., D. Grewal, R. Leghorn, V. Shankar, M.L. Teerling, J.S. Thomas and P.C. Verhoef (2006), "Challenges and opportunities in multichannel customer management," *Journal of Services Research*, **9** (2), 95–112.

Nicholson, Carolyn Y., Larry D. Compeau and Rajesh Sethi (2001), "The role of interpersonal liking in building trust in long-term channel relationships," *Journal of the Academy of Marketing Science*, **29** (1), 3–15.

Palmatier, Robert W. (2008a), *Relationship Marketing*, Cambridge, MA: Marketing Science Institute.

Palmatier, Robert W. (2008b), "Interfirm relational drivers of customer value," *Journal of Marketing*, **72** (July), 76–89.

Palmatier, Robert W., Rajiv P. Dant and Dhruv Grewal (2007), "A comparative longitudinal analysis of theoretical perspectives of interorganizational relationship performance," *Journal of Marketing*, **71** (October), 172–94.

Palmatier, Robert W., Rajiv P. Dant, Dhruv Grewal and Kenneth R. Evans (2006), "Factors influencing the effectiveness of relationship marketing: a meta-analysis," *Journal of Marketing*, **70** (October), 136–53.

Palmatier, Robert W., Cheryl B. Jarvis, Jennifer R. Bechkoff and Frank R. Kardes (2009), "The role of customer gratitude in relationship marketing," *Journal of Marketing*, **73** (4), 1–18.

Raju, Jagmohan and Z. John Zhang (2005), "Channel coordination in the presence of a dominant retailer," *Marketing Science*, **24** (2), 254–62.

Rangan, Subramanian (2000), "The problem of search and deliberation in economic actions: when social networks really matter," *Academy of Management Review*, **25** (4), 813–28.

Reve, Torger and Louis W. Stem (1979), "Interorganization relations in marketing channels," *Academy of Management Journal*, **4** (3), 405–16.

Rindfleisch, Aric and Christine Moorman (2001), "The acquisition and utilization of information in new product alliances: a strength-of-ties perspective," *Journal of Marketing*, **65** (April), 1–18.

Rowley, Timothy J. (1997), "Moving beyond dyadic ties: a network theory of stakeholder influences," *Academy of Management Review*, **22** (4), 887–910.

Shiv, Baba, Julie A. Edell and John W. Payne (1997), "Factors affecting the impact of negatively and positively framed ad messages," *Journal of Consumer Research*, **24** (December), 285–94.

Smith, J. Brock and Donald W. Barclay (1997), "The effects of organizational differences and trust on the effectiveness of selling partner relationships," *Journal of Marketing*, **61** (January), 3–21.

Tsai, Wenpin (2001), "Knowledge transfer in interorganizational networks: effects of network position and absorptive capacity on business unit innovation and performance," *Academy of Management Journal*, **44** (October), 996–1001.

Van Den Bulte, Christophe and Stefan Wuyts (2007), *Social Networks and Marketing*, Cambridge, MA: Marketing Science Institute.

Vargo, Stephen L. and Robert F. Lusch (2004), "Evolving to a new dominant logic for marketing," *Journal of Marketing*, **68** (January), 1–17.

Walker, Gordon, Bruce Kogut and Weijan Shan (1997), "Social capital, structural holes and the formation of industry networks," *Organization Science*, **8** (March–April), 109–25.

Wathne, Kenneth and Jan B. Heide (2004), "Relationship governance in a supply chain network," *Journal of Marketing*, **68** (January), 73–89.

Williamson, Oliver E. (1981), "The economics of organization: the transaction cost approach," *American Journal of Sociology*, **87** (November), 548–77.

15 Behavioral perspectives on pricing strategy
Russell S. Winer

INTRODUCTION

Because it is the only decision made by the manager that directly generates revenues, price is often thought to be the most important element of the set of decision variables at the manager's discretion. While other decision variables such as advertising and channels of distribution certainly impact a brand's performance, no decision compares to price in terms of its impact on the customer and the bottom line. Price is an observable component of the product that results in customers purchasing or not purchasing it while simultaneously affecting the profit margin per unit sold.

Price is also a communications decision. The price set signals to the customer the value and quality that the product contains relative to competing products. Customers interpret relative price the way they interpret advertisements in that they mentally process the information content represented by the numbers (versus processing the copy in an ad). A price set higher than a competitor's implies that the manager feels his or her brand delivers greater value to the customer. A price set at $3.99 may be interpreted differently than a price set at $4.00. A brand positioned as a luxury or high-quality brand but priced lower than the customer expects may confuse its image. Price positions the product in the customer's mind similarly to how a television ad delivers a message.

Thus customers actively process the information conveyed in prices. That is, they are not just price "takers" (to use the conventional term from microeconomics). Customers continually assess the prices charged for products based on prior purchasing experience, formal communications (e.g. advertising) and informal communications (e.g. friends and neighbors), and point-of-purchase or Web-derived listings of prices and use those assessments in the ultimate purchase decision. The term "behavioral pricing" has been used to describe the customer side of pricing strategy – how to incorporate this price information processing into the pricing decision.

Research on the behavioral aspects of price has been conducted for many years and there have been occasional reviews of the literature (e.g. Ofir and Winer 2002; Winer 2006). The purpose of this chapter is to describe some of the recent research that has been done on the variety of topics that fall under this umbrella of behavioral pricing.

Some key concepts relating to the psychological aspects of pricing that have been the subject of recent research in marketing are the following:

- Price knowledge
- Price thresholds
- Processing prices
- Reference price
- Fairness

- Price–quality perceptions
- Context effects in price perceptions.

The rest of this chapter focuses on these topics and finishes with some directions for future research.

PRICE KNOWLEDGE

Marketing researchers have attempted to assess the degree to which consumers remember prices of recently purchased products. A well-known paper (Dickson and Sawyer 1990) found that a relatively low percentage of consumers can recall prices accurately. This finding is opposed to neoclassical economic thinking according to which consumers have complete knowledge of product prices and may suggest that consumers do not pay attention to prices they pay. Estalami et al. (2000) investigated the effects of macro-economic factors on consumer price knowledge. They found that a simple task characteristic might have significantly biased the results. Using meta-analysis, they examined more than 200 studies and found that not allowing respondents to provide the requested price estimate accounted for a significant reduction in percentage average deviations from actual prices. Removing these consumers reduces the relative deviation from actual prices by more than 50 percent. Thus attention to a seemingly trivial measurement format may bias the results and change the scope of the conclusions. Vanhuele and Drèze (2002) also challenge the Dickson–Sawyer result by showing that price-recall studies only focus on recall and short-term memory, which significantly underestimate price knowledge. By developing a method that taps into long-term price memory, the authors show that while customers may not recall exact prices, they possess a working knowledge of prices that is sufficiently accurate for good decision making.

An important contribution to this area of research is the paper by Vanhuele et al. (2006). While the Dickson–Sawyer and related papers studied price accuracy, Vanhuele and his colleagues focus on the cognitive processes involved in the encoding, storage and retrieval of prices. They find a relationship between the time needed to pronounce a price and its likelihood of recall. For example, each extra syllable in a price reduces its chance of being recalled by 20 percent. In addition, they find that good "visual" coders, people who process numbers quickly, perform better on price-recall tests. Overall, the researchers find considerable heterogeneity in individuals' capabilities for recalling prices.

PRICE THRESHOLDS

An idea emerging from early work on behavioral pricing is that consumers have lower and upper thresholds for price: a lower threshold below which prices may signal suspected product quality and are therefore unacceptable, and an upper price threshold above which prices of a product are too expensive and not worth the product. It should be noted that economists only refer to an upper price threshold (referred to as reservation price), since it is assumed that "cheaper is better" and, therefore, no lower price limit is assumed. Reservation price is a managerially important construct as it informs marketing managers of the most they can charge for their products. Reservation prices are usually estimated using some form of judgment method where the reservation price is measured using a variety of survey-based methods. There is also a stream of research that attempts to estimate reservation prices using actual customer purchase data.

Two recent papers have continued to explore the reservation price concept. Krishna et al. (2006) study how malleable reservation price can be by studying the impact of placing a high-priced alternative in a set of more moderately priced products. Using experimental studies where respondents were exposed to products in a catalog, the authors show that extreme-priced products can influence the maximum amount consumers are willing to pay for a product category and for specific products, and the more related the extreme-priced product is to the other products in the set, the greater the impact. Wang et al. (2007) introduce the notion that reservation price is a range, not a single point estimate. One foundation for their argument is that there is a variety of definitions of reservation price in the literature, resulting in the possibility of multiple reservation prices for any individual consumer. A second basis is that there is always uncertainty around a particular point estimate, particularly when considering the maximum a consumer would be willing to pay for a good or service. The authors develop a method called ICERANGE to estimate the range of reservation prices for a consumer.

PROCESSING PRICES

An interesting area of research involving price judgments is how consumers process the numerical aspects of price. While some of this research has focused specifically on the digits of prices, a number of studies have examined prices in the context of money and how consumers value different denominations. In addition, the idea of "free," that is, a zero price, has taken hold in many business contexts such as iPhone applications.

Price Digit Research

A large number of studies have documented that certain price endings (0, 5, 9) occur much more often than others. In particular, interest has centered around endings in 9, often called "odd" prices. In an effort to explain the frequent use of odd prices, academics often propose that consumers round prices down, essentially ignoring the right-hand digits. Other potential explanations are that consumers discern meaning from prices that end in 9 (e.g. good value) and that consumers compare prices from left to right. The main point of this work is that consumers do not necessarily process price holistically but, instead, use some heuristic to process the digits separately. Almost all work in price assumes holistic processing.

This research area has been attacked from three perspectives. Work by Schindler and his co-authors (see, e.g. Schindler and Kirby, 1997) has used field experimental methods to infer why certain digits occur more often than others. They have found support for the argument that the reason the numbers 0 and 5 occur more frequently is due to the high cognitive accessibility of those numbers as the use of these "round-number" endings makes price information easier for consumers to perceive, compare and remember. Endings with 9 occur most frequently with high potential underestimation prices, that is, those where the 9s represent a large psychological drop in price from the price with one penny added (e.g. $49.99 versus $50.00). A more recent study by Anderson and Simester (2003) described three field experiments manipulating catalog prices with some prices ending in $9. They found that the use of the $9 ending consistently increased demand across all three experiments, with the increase being the strongest for new items in the catalogue.

A second approach has been to better understand the psychological underpinnings of the phenomenon. Although there has been a considerable amount of literature in this area, Thomas and Morwitz (2005) develop a conceptual framework based on the analog model of numerical cognition to explain why, say, $2.99 is perceived to be significantly cheaper than $3.00. The theory suggests that when two multi-digit numbers are compared, the quantitative meaning of the numbers is assessed by mapping then onto an internal analog magnitude scale. When this mapping occurs, left-to-right processing of the numbers distorts the price magnitude towards the leftmost digit. While this is an important theoretical finding, the practical implications of the Thomas and Morwitz work were explored in a paper by Manning and Sprott (2009). These authors found that the choice share of a lower-priced alternative was maximized when it had a just-below price (e.g. $1.99) and the higher-priced alternative had a round price (e.g. $3.00). In addition, they found that just-below pricing can lead to greater choice share for lower-priced goods than round pricing. Coulter and Coulter (2007) find experimental evidence supporting a "right-digit" effect, that is, when the left digits are identical, consumers compare the right digits in relative terms. In addition, the experimental subjects perceived larger discounts when the rightmost digits were small rather than large. Finally, Thomas et al. (2010) examine buyers' reactions to "precise" prices (e.g. $364 578) to round prices (e.g. $350 000). Based on both experimental and actual real-estate purchase data, they discover two interesting findings. First, consumers judge precise prices to be smaller than comparable round prices, even when the precise price is higher. Second, they find some evidence that precise prices positively affect willingness to pay.

The third perspective estimates empirical choice models with alternative formulations to capture different price processing heuristics (Stiving and Winer 1997). Using two different frequently purchased product categories, the authors found consistent support for left-to-right price processing rather than holistic or rounding. These empirical results are consistent with those of Schindler and Kirby's (1997) findings with respect to the endings in 9 since a large psychological drop in price using a 9 would occur if left-to-right processing were being used.

The Value of Money

Obviously, the role of money is important in marketing as it is the medium of exchange, a key concept underlying the definition of marketing. As noted above, an emerging research area is the value of money and how different denominations of currency affect consumer behavior. A paper by Mishra et al. (2006) tested whether consumers' willingness to spend varies depending upon whether their money is in the form of a whole amount such as a $100 or $50 bill or in the form of parts (e.g. ten $10 bills). They found a "bias for the whole," that is, a preference for the whole amounts in that people preferred to hold on to whole amounts as opposed to a preference to spending the parts. The authors attributed this finding to greater processing fluency experienced in processing the whole as opposed to the parts, that is, the whole is coded more efficiently and economically. This "bias for the whole" was further investigated by Raghubir and Srivastava (2009). In this paper, the authors were interested in whether spending decisions (actual purchases with real money versus purchase intentions) and decisions to receive money were affected by identical sums in different denominations. As with the Mishra et al. findings, Raghubir and Srivastava again found that people are less willing to spend large denominations of equivalent amounts to smaller denominations. They found that the demand for denominations (i.e. receiving money) varied depending upon the need to exert self-control. Subjects preferred to be paid in a single large denomination when the need to exert self-control and save money was high; the reverse was true when the need for self-control was low.

Other research in this area has focused on what has been termed "money illusion", where the face value of an amount of money affects people's preferences to a greater extent than the purchasing power of that amount. Raghubir and Srivastava (2002) found that when the nominal value of a foreign currency is a multiple of the home currency (e.g. for a US consumer considering a purchase in Indian rupees, US$1 = Rs47), consumers are likely to spend less when buying in the foreign than in the home currency. However, when the nominal value of the foreign currency is a fraction of the home currency (e.g. US$1 = 0.77 euros), they are likely to spend more. Wertenbroch et al. (2007) extended this research by considering money illusion with budget constraints and prices of competing options.

Free

Interestingly, the concept of a zero price has not been studied extensively. A recent paper by Shampanier et al. (2007) examines whether or not consumers overvalue free items (e.g. standing in a long line to get a free sample). They ran a very interesting experiment. The researchers set up a table in a cafeteria and offered normally high-priced Lindt chocolate truffles for 15 cents and ordinary Hershey Kisses for a penny. A total of 73 percent went for the truffles. When prices were cut to 14 cents for the chocolate and zero for the Kisses, 69 percent went for the Kisses even though the truffles were an even better deal than before. The researchers concluded that a zero price not only reduces its cost but also adds to its perceived value.

"Free" has also been examined in the context of product bundles. Raghubir (2004) found that when a free product is bundled together with another product and offered at one price, consumers are willing to pay less for the free product when it is sold alone at another time or place. This work was extended by Kamins et al. (2009), who show that a "freebie" promotion can have a negative effect on a consumer's valuation of the overall bundle and on the focal "free" product compared to when the same type of bundled promotion lacks a freebie designation.

REFERENCE PRICES

A particular form of a price judgment is a reference price. A reference price is any standard of comparison against which an observed price is compared. A number of psychological theories provide the conceptual underpinnings for the concept of the comparison of observed price to a reference price. There are two kinds of reference prices: internal and external, also sometimes referred to as "temporal" and "contextual" respectively (Rajendran and Tellis 1994). External reference prices are usually observed prices that, in a retailing setting, are typically posted at the point of purchase as the "regular retail price." Internal reference prices are mental prices used to assess an observed price. Some empirical work has found that different market segments use the internal and external reference prices (Mazumdar and Papatla 2000). Since the product manager cannot easily manipulate internal reference prices yet they have a strong effect on buying behavior, we discuss them in more detail.

A large number of internal reference prices have been proposed, including:

- The "fair" price, or what the product ought to cost the customer
- The price frequently charged
- The last price paid
- The upper amount someone would pay (reservation price)
- The lower threshold or lowest amount a customer would pay
- The price of the brand usually bought
- The average price charged for similar products
- The expected future price
- The typical discounted price.

Many of these considerations contribute to the concept we call the "perceived" price, the price the customer thinks is the current actual price of the product.

The research literature has generally found that reference price has a significant impact on brand choice of both durable and nondurable goods (see Mazumdar et al. 2005, for a recent review) and that it can have important normative implications. In particular, when the observed price is higher than the reference price, it can negatively affect purchasing because the consumer perceives this situation as an unpleasant surprise or a bad deal. For example, the large price increases for cars in the 1970s created what became known as a "sticker shock" effect when consumer reference or perceived prices for cars were significantly lower than the prices they saw in the showroom. A happier situation occurs when the observed price is either at or below the reference price. This happens when a brand a consumer might buy anyway is being promoted at a lower price.

In the normal implementation of reference price in choice models, a point estimate of reference price is used. This point estimate is usually determined by assuming a reference price formation process and using scanner panel data to infer the reference prices from observed prices paid by consumers and actual prices on the shelf on the day a purchase in a category was made. A paper by Niedrich et al. (2009) expanded the point reference price to include other moments of the reference price distribution such as range, modality and skewness.

A concept that has been borrowed from psychology and adapted to reference price research is loss aversion. Popularized by the work of Kahneman and Tversky and others, the basic idea is that individuals weight losses more than gains relative to a reference point. Some empirical work has demonstrated the existence of reference price segments with respect to loss aversion. Mazumdar and Papatla (2000) found that consumers relying more on internal than external reference prices were more sensitive to gains than losses, while those using external reference prices had the opposite behavior. In an extensive analysis across multiple product categories, Erdem et al. (2001) discovered that loss-sensitive shoppers are less affected by past brand use and react more strongly to price, display and newspaper feature advertising than the average consumer. Loss-sensitive households are also larger with employed heads of household. Gain-sensitive consumers have similar responses to brand use, price, display and feature advertising but to a lesser degree than the loss-sensitive households, and they have no clear demographic descriptors.

A second important concept of reference price is expected future price. This is a particularly important concept for any product category that experiences significant price changes over time. For example, new consumer durables are subject to this phenomenon. The prices of personal computers, camcorders, DVD players and so on are falling so rapidly that customers are worried they will overpay. Discretionary purchasers can simply wait until the prices decrease further as they are willing to forgo the utility from owning the product sooner. This reference price concept has been studied much less in the literature, an exception being Winer (1985).

Other than durable goods, a context in which future price expectations matter is sales promotion. A current low promoted price could influence consumers' expectations of what the price will be in the future. As promotion depth increases, consumers might lower their expectations of future price, which might have a negative impact on choice when prices return to more normal levels. DelVecchio et al. (2007) examine this issue from a promotion-framing perspective: What is the different impact of framing the promotion in terms of cents-off versus percentage-off? The authors find that managers can protect future choice by framing the promotion in percentage terms rather than in terms of cents-off. Tsiros and Hardesty (2010) look at a similar issue in the context of Hi–Lo pricing, that is, a store pricing strategy of normal prices paired with periodic significant discounts. After one of the discounts, the authors propose a policy called "steadily decreasing discounting," or SDD, where instead of immediately returning to a normal price which is perceived to be a substantial price increase following the promotion, the normal price is reached after a few intervening decreases in the discount or steps. The authors show, using both experimental and field research, that this pricing strategy accounting for future price expectations has some potential.

As noted above, reference prices can be both internal and external. While both have been found to significantly affect consumer choice, the empirical research about which of the two types of references prices is more significant is mixed and seems to depend upon the product category analyzed. The most comprehensive study was performed by Briesch et al. (1997), who estimated brand choice models using four different frequently purchased product categories and found that internal reference price provides a better fit than external reference price.

There are also measurement issues in the reference price area. Most of the prior work has estimated references prices from scanner panel data or other observed behavior. Thomas and Menon (2007) consider the topic of measurement of internal reference prices in the context of comparing the internal reference price to observed prices. Results from their experiments suggest that consumers with less confidence about prices in a product category (perhaps due to less experience) have higher internal reference prices than more confident consumers.

FAIRNESS

As noted above, one of the reference prices customers form in their minds is the fair price. Perceptions of price unfairness can have a significant negative impact on a firm. These include not purchasing, thus significantly reducing lifetime customer value, spreading negative word of mouth, and possible engaging in other negative actions (Campbell 1999).

Research has shown that there are two main sources of perceived unfairness: (1) the perceived profit being made by the vendor; and (2) customers' inferences about the motives for the price perceived to be unfair (Campbell 1999). Thus a customer can perceive a price as being unfair in a number of different contexts. A sports team charging $5 for a small beer at a baseball game would fall into the first source of unfairness, excess profits. Similarly, drug companies have been criticized for generating high profits from prescription drugs. A hardware store raising the price of an existing inventory of snow shovels during a snowstorm would be characterized as being unfair due to the motive of price gouging or taking advantage of the misfortunes of its customers. Note that rational explanations for such increased prices such as supply–demand conditions are irrelevant as the concept of fairness is based on the perception of the customer.

Bolton et al. (2003) show in a series of experiments that respondents consistently believe that selling prices are higher than fair prices. This emanates from their knowledge of prices, costs and estimates of profits in the marketplace. Interestingly, consumers systematically underestimate the impact of inflation on prices. Price differences are perceived to be the fairest only if they can be attributed to differences in quality. Also, when considering costs, only those costs associated with cost of goods sold are considered.

Xia et al. (2004) developed a complete conceptual model of how customers form perceptions of price unfairness. The central part of the price fairness process begins with a price comparison. The comparison can be to an external price (e.g. a competitor) or an internal standard (e.g. normal price paid). The output of this comparison is a judgment of the fairness of the price, both cognitive and affective. The former is the basic assessment of the fairness (thoughts, beliefs); the latter is an emotional response (e.g. anger) that could result. A number of variables potentially mediate the relationship between the price comparison and the perceived price fairness, such as the distribution of cost and profit, the historical relationship between the customer and the seller, and others. The perceived fairness then creates an assessment of the perceived value of the seller's offering. Finally, some kind of action results such as spreading negative word of mouth.

Recent work has extended the notion of fairness in several directions. Bolton and Alba (2006) examine the role of vendor costs in perceptions of fairness of price increases. The authors break down vendor costs into those that are alignable (directly related to the cost of making the product, such as milk in ice cream) and those that are non-alignable (such as rent or debt interest rates). The authors find that alignable costs are more acceptable as justifications for price increases than those that are non-alignable. Haws and Bearden (2006) examine fairness in the context of dynamic pricing. It is common today, particularly on the Internet, for retailers to offer different prices to different customers and at varying points in time. Their studies show that consumers feel that pricing differences between consumers are the most unfair and produce the lowest levels of satisfaction. Timing differences also produce feeling of unfairness, particularly if the price changes occur within very short time periods. Bolton et al. (2010) extend fairness research into the cross-cultural arena. The authors hypothesize that collectivist societies (e.g. China) care more about loss of face that could occur if one pays a higher price than someone else for the same good than do consumers from more individualistic societies (e.g. the USA). This central hypothesis was supported by their data. Do customers of larger sizes of clothing expect to pay the same prices for identical smaller sized items? Apparently they do not. Anderson and Simester (2008) conducted a large-scale field study of a catalogue retailer and found that customers of the larger sizes reacted unfavorably in terms of sales to paying a higher price than customers for small sizes.

Two new pricing mechanisms feature customer participation in the price. One version of this is Name Your Own Price (NYOP), which is employed by the Web retailer Priceline. In this case, a customer inputs a reservation price and vendors (e.g. hotels) indicate whether they will meet that price. However, if the price is set too low by the customer, no company may meet the price. An interesting version that incorporates fairness is called Pay What You Want (PWYW). This is an unusual pricing strategy in that in its strictest form, a vendor (e.g. restaurant) simply asks customers to pay what they wish for a meal with no lower bound. PWYW was studied by Kim et al. (2009). They ran field experiments in three contexts: buffet lunches at a restaurant, movie tickets at a theater; and hot beverages at a delicatessen. In the cases of the lunches and tickets, the prices offered were below the regular prices, although in the case of buffet lunches, total revenues increased due to attracting more customers. In the case of the hot beverages, the NYOP was actually higher than the regular price. Across the three studies, people who reported having paid a fair price offered higher prices to the seller.

PRICE/QUALITY

In some situations, contrary to standard microeconomic theory, a higher price can lead to higher rather than lower demand. This occurs when price is used to signal that the product is of high quality. It often occurs under a condition of asymmetric information, that is, when the seller has more information about the true quality of the product or service than the buyer (Kirmani and Rao 2000). Thus many instances of a strong price–perceived quality relationship occur when a product's quality is difficult to assess before purchasing or difficult to assess at all. These products are often called experience goods (if you have to try the product before assessing its quality) or credence goods (if even after you have purchased and used the product or service, the quality is hard to evaluate). Examples of the former are most services, such as haircuts and legal advice. Examples of credence goods are car repairs, such as brake servicing (the customer cannot actually see what happened) and wine (only experts can distinguish between different levels of quality). Marketers also use price to signal exclusivity or prestige. A high price means that fewer customers can afford it. Rolex could charge substantially less for its watches and still make a profit. However, because few customers can afford thousands of dollars for a watch, few will own a Rolex, which is how their owners want it.

There is a long tradition of academic research on this topic. Integrative reviews have generally found that there is a statistically significant relationship between price and perceived quality. More recent work has focused on mediating factors that might attenuate the relationship. For example, Kardes et al. (2004) showed in an experimental context that the relationship between price and perceived quality is reduced the greater the quantity of information presented to respondents, if that information is presented in a random order, and when concern for closure is low (when respondents could take as much time as needed to make their judgments). Cronley et al. (2005) show that quality inferences from price are more likely when individuals have a high need for cognitive closure (i.e. desire to reach a definite opinion), when the amount of information presented is high, and when the information presented is rank ordered in terms of quality rather than presented randomly.

Shiv et el. (2005) present the results of several interesting studies showing that, in fact, price can not only affect perceived quality but actual quality as well. They liken their results to the well-known placebo effect sometimes found in the medical field. For example, the authors studied a number of people who regularly exercised at a fitness club. The subjects were given an energy drink to consume prior and during a workout. One group was told that the energy drink was purchased for them at the regular price of $2.89. The other group was told that the regular price was $2.89 but because the authors bought it in bulk, it only cost $0.89. All subjects then completed a survey rating the intensity of their workout and how fatigued they felt. The participants who received the reduced-price drink rated both the workout intensity as lower and feeling more fatigued. In a debriefing, no one felt that the price of the drink affected their evaluations. Other studies confirmed this finding.

CONTEXT EFFECTS IN PRICE JUDGMENTS

Research has found that customer decision making can vary greatly in different purchasing contexts. For example, in an experiment simulating purchasing decisions, asking someone if they would purchase an expensive watch will depend upon how much income is endowed upon them. An alternative context would be the difference in behavior between purchasing a product for yourself or as a gift. A classic study by Huber et al. (1982) showed that the introduction of a new product can affect the sales of the incumbent products in an interesting way. For instance, using an example from their study:

> A store owner has two camel hair jackets priced at $100 and $150 and finds that the more expensive jacket is not selling. A new camel hair jacket is added and displayed for $250; the new jacket does not sell, but sales of the $150 jacket increase.

Thus the different choice contexts produce the surprising result that a product's value to customers can be enhanced by introducing a more expensive option.

Another famous example is from Thaler (1985). This is the well-known "beer on the beach" example of context effects:

You are lying on the beach on a hot day. All you have to drink is ice water. For the last hour you have been thinking about how much you would enjoy a nice cold bottle of your favorite brand of beer. A companion gets up to go make a phone call and offers to bring back a beer from the only nearby place where beer is sold [a fancy resort hotel] [a small, run-down grocery store]. He says that the beer might be expensive and so asks how much you are willing to pay for the beer. He says that he will buy the beer if it costs as much or less than the price you state. But if it costs more than the price you state he will not buy it. You trust your friend and there is no possibility of bargaining with the [bartender] [store owner]. What price do you tell him?

In both of these cases, the context in which a price judgment is being made has a significant impact on the decision. A considerable amount of research has been conducted on context-dependent price judgments.

An example of a context that can affect price judgments is price "partitions." The context is whether a product or service with two parts has one price for both parts or separate (partitioned) prices. Partitioned prices are common. When ordering from an online bookseller, for example, the price of the book is unbundled from the shipping cost. Previous research by Morwitz et al. (1998) showed that in these cases, consumers may process one component (perhaps the base price) more thoroughly than the other component (the shipping cost) and thus underestimate the total cost compared to when prices are not partitioned. More recent research by Hamilton and Srivastava (2008) does not directly compare partitioned with non-partitioned prices. Instead, the authors find that consumers' reactions to price partitioning are moderated by the perceived consumption benefit of the components in that they are more sensitive to the price of components that provide low consumption benefits than to the price of components that provide relatively high consumption benefits. As a result, consumers prefer partitions in which the price of the low-benefit component is lower and the price of the high-benefit component is higher.

FUTURE RESEARCH DIRECTIONS

Fortunately, a substantial body of knowledge has been accumulated in some behavioral areas. We have developed a fairly good idea of how much knowledge consumers have about prices, and the literature on reference price is expansive and comprehensive. There continues to be some work in the area of price thresholds, particularly measurement issues. For example, there has been a considerable amount of recent work on incentive compatible methods for eliciting willingness-to-pay (i.e. reservation prices) estimates from consumers using conjoint analysis (e.g. Dong et al. 2010). However, more work is needed to better understand customers' reactions to and processing of price information, particularly in this era of dynamic prices with an increasing number of price tactics. New methods of measuring consumer response to stimuli developed in neuroscience could provide some exciting insights (Camerer et al. 2005). More work in the area of how consumers process price digits would be welcome. We still know little about the power of "odd" prices and why they are effective in a variety of circumstances. In addition, this research could be extended cross-culturally, particularly to countries and regions of the world that have currencies with many zeroes and, therefore, few odd endings. The literature on context effects is increasing, but given the many contexts in which price information is processed, there is room for more work in this area. For example, we still do not know much about how people process price information on the Internet. In fact, given the proliferation of channels of distribution due to improvements in technology (e.g. wireless), price information and reactions to those prices create new opportunities for research across all the areas noted in this chapter.

Overall, given the importance of price, I expect to see behavioral pricing research to continue to be an exciting area for marketing scholars.

REFERENCES

Anderson, Eric T. and Duncan I. Simester (2003), "Effect of $9 price endings on retail sales: evidence from field experiments," *Quantitative Marketing and Economics*, **1** (March), 93–110.

Anderson, Eric T. and Duncan I. Simester (2008), "Does demand fall when customers perceive that prices are unfair? The case of premium pricing for large sizes," *Marketing Science*, **27** (May–June), 492–500.

Bolton, Lisa E. and Joseph W. Alba (2006), "Price fairness: good and service differences and the role of vendor costs," *Journal of Consumer Research*, **33** (September), 258–65.

Bolton, Lisa E., Hean Tat Keh and Joseph W. Alba (2010), "How do price fairness perceptions differ across culture?", *Journal of Marketing Research*, **47** (June), 564–76.

Bolton, Lisa E., Luk Warlop and Joseph W. Alba (2003), "Consumer perceptions of price (un)fairness," *Journal of Consumer Research*, **29** (March), 474–91.

Briesch, Richard A., Lakshman Krishnamurthi, Tridib Mazumdar and S.P. Raj (1997), "A comparative analysis of reference price models," *Journal of Consumer Research*, **24** (September), 202–14.

Camerer, Colin, George Loewenstein and Drazen Prelec (2005), "Neuroeconomics: how neuroscience can inform economics." *Journal of Economic Literature*, **43** (March), 9–64.

Campbell, Margaret C. (1999), "Perceptions of price unfairness: antecedents and consequences," *Journal of Marketing Research*, **36** (May), 187–99.

Coulter, Keith S. and Robin A. Coulter (2007), "Distortion of price discount perceptions: the right digit effect," *Journal of Consumer Research*, **34** (August), 162–73.

Cronley, Maria L., Steven S. Posavac, Tracy Meyer, Frank R. Kardes and James J. Kellanis (2005), "A selective hypothesis testing perspective on price–quality inference and inference-based choice," *Journal of Consumer Psychology*, **15** (2), 159–6.

DelVecchio, Devon, H. Shanker Krishnan and Daniel C. Smith (2007), "Cents or percent? The effects of promotion framing on price expectations and choice," *Journal of Marketing*, **71** (July), 158–70.

Dickson, Peter R. and Alan G. Sawyer (1990), "The price knowledge and search of supermarket shoppers," *Journal of Marketing*, **54** (July), 42–53.

Dong, S., Min Ding and Joel Huber (2010), "A simple mechanism to incentive align conjoint experiments," *International Journal of Research in Marketing*, **27**, 25–32.

Erdem, Tülin, Glenn Mayhew and Baohong Sun (2001), "Understanding reference-price shoppers: a within- and cross-category analysis," *Journal of Marketing Research*, **38** (November), 445–57.

Estalami, Hooman, Alfred Holden and Donald R. Lehmann (2000), "Exploring the macro-economic determinants of price knowledge: a meta-analysis of four decades of research," unpublished working paper, Columbia University.

Hamilton, Rebecca W. and Joydeep Srivastava (2008), "When 2+2 is not the same as 1+3: variations in price sensitivity across components of partitioned prices," *Journal of Marketing Research*, **45** (August), 450–61.

Haws, Kelly L. and William O. Bearden (2006), "Dynamic pricing and consumer fairness perceptions," *Journal of Consumer Research*, **33** (December), 304–11.

Huber, Joel, John W. Payne and Christopher Puto (1982), "Adding asymmetrically dominated alternatives: violations of regularity and the similarity hypothesis," *Journal of Consumer Research*, **9** (June), 90–98.

Kamins, Michael A., Valerie S. Folkes and Alexander Fedorikhin (2009), "Promotional bundles and consumers' price judgments: when the best things in life are not free," *Journal of Consumer Research*, **36** (December), 660–70.

Kardes, Frank R., Maria L. Cronley, James J. Kellaris and Steven S. Posavac (2004), "The role of selective information processing in price–quality inference," *Journal of Consumer Research*, **31** (September), 368–74.

Kim, Ju-Young, Martin Natter and Martin Spann (2009), "Pay what you want: a new participative pricing mechanism," *Journal of Marketing*, **73** (January), 44–58.

Kirmani, Amna and Akshay R. Rao (2000), "No pain, no gain: a critical review of the literature on signaling unobservable product quality," *Journal of Marketing*, **64** (April), 66–79.

Krishna, Aradhna, Mary Wagner, Carolyn Yoon and Rashmi Adaval (2006), "Effects of extreme-priced products on consumer reservation prices," *Journal of Consumer Psychology*, **16** (2), 176–90.

Manning, Kenneth C. and David E. Sprott (2009), "Price endings, left-digit effects, and choice," *Journal of Consumer Research*, **36** (August), 328–35.

Mazumdar, Tridib and Purushottam Papatla (2000), "An investigation of reference price segments," *Journal of Marketing Research*, **37** (May), 246–58.

Mazumdar, Tridib, S.P. Raj and Indrajit Sinha (2005), "Reference price research: review and propositions," *Journal of Marketing*, **69** (October), 84–102.

Mishra, Himanshu, Arul Mishra and Dhananjay Nayakankuppam (2006), "Money: a bias for the whole," *Journal of Consumer Research*, **32** (March), 541–9.

Morwitz, Vicki, Eric A. Greenleaf and Eric J. Johnson (1998), "Divide and prosper: consumers' reactions to partitioned prices," *Journal of Marketing Research*, **35** (November), 453–63.

Niedrich, Ronald W., Danny Weathers, R. Carter Hill and David R. Bell (2009), "Specifying price judgments with range-frequency theory in models of brand choice," *Journal of Marketing Research*, **46** (October), 693–702.

Ofir, Chezy and Russell S. Winer (2002), "Pricing: economic and behavioral models," in B. Weitz and R. Wensley (eds), *Handbook of Marketing*, London: Sage Publications, pp. 267–81.

Raghubir, Priya (2004), "Free gift with purchase: promoting or discounting the brand?", *Journal of Consumer Psychology*, **14** (1–2), 181–6.

Raghubir, Priya and Joydeep Srivastava (2002), "The effect of face value on product valuation in foreign currencies," *Journal of Consumer Research*, **29** (December), 335–47.

Raghubir, Priya and Joydeep Srivastava (2009), "The denomination effect," *Journal of Consumer Research*, **36** (December), 701–13.

Rajendran, K.N. and Gerard J. Tellis (1994), "Contextual and temporal components of reference price," *Journal of Marketing*, **58** (January), 22–34.

Schindler, Robert M. and Patrick N. Kirby (1997), "Patterns of rightmost digits used in advertised prices: implications for nine-ending effects," *Journal of Consumer Research*, **24** (September), 192–201.

Shampanier, Kristina, Nina Mazar and Dan Ariely (2007), "Zero as a special price: the true value of free products," *Marketing Science*, **26** (November–December), 742–57.

Shiv, Baba, Ziv Carmon and Dan Ariely (2005), "Placebo effects of marketing actions: consumers may get what they pay for," *Journal of Marketing Research*, **42**, 383–93.

Stiving, Mark and Russell S. Winer (1997), "An empirical analysis of price endings with scanner data," *Journal of Consumer Research*, **24** (June), 57–68.

Thaler, Richard (1985), "Mental accounting and consumer choice," *Marketing Science*, **4** (Summer), 199–214.

Thomas, Manoj and Geeta Menon (2007), "When internal reference prices and price expectations diverge: the role of confidence," *Journal of Marketing Research*, **44** (August), 401–9.

Thomas, Manoj and Vicki Morwitz (2005), "Penny wise and pound foolish: the left-digit effect in price cognition," *Journal of Consumer Research*, **32** (June), 54–64.

Thomas, Manoj, Daniel H. Simon and Vrinda Kadiyali (2010), "The price precision effect: evidence from laboratory and market data," *Marketing Science*, **29** (January–February), 175–90.

Tsiros, Michael and David M. Hardesty (2010), "Ending a price promotion: retracting it in one step or phasing it out gradually," *Journal of Marketing*, **74** (January), 49–64.

Vanhuele, Marc and Xavier Drèze (2002), "Measuring the price knowledge shoppers bring to the store," *Journal of Marketing*, **66** (October), 72–85.

Vanhuele, Marc, Gilles Laurent and Xavier Drèze (2006), "Consumers' immediate memory for prices," *Journal of Consumer Research*, **33** (September), 163–72.

Wang, Tuo, R. Venkatesh and Rabikar Chatterjee (2007), "Reservation price as a range: an incentive-compatible measurement approach," *Journal of Marketing Research*, **44** (May), 200–213.

Wertenbroch, Klaus, Dilip Soman and Amitava Chattopadhyay (2007), "On the perceived value of money: the reference dependence of currency numerosity effects," *Journal of Consumer Research*, **34** (June), 1–10.

Winer, Russell S. (1985), "A price vector model of demand for consumer durables: preliminary evidence," *Marketing Science*, **4** (Winter), 74–90.

Winer, Russell S. (2006), *Pricing*, Cambridge, MA: Marketing Science Institute.

Xia, L., K.B. Monroe and J.L. Cox (2004), "The price is unfair! A conceptual framework for price fairness perceptions," *Journal of Marketing*, **68**, 1–15.

16 Managing customer satisfaction
Vikas Mittal and Carly Frennea

Firms invest in customer satisfaction (CS) because customers are the biggest source of cash flow for a company (Gruca and Rego 2005). A customer base with high levels of satisfaction provides many long-term benefits for the firm. Satisfied customers are likely to continue repurchasing a firm's offerings (Bolton 1998), purchase more from the firm (Anderson 1994), engage in more cross-buying (Verhoef et al. 2001), and have lower service and retention costs (Borle et al. 2007). Satisfied customers help a firm to lower the cost of customer acquisition through positive word of mouth and recommendations to friends and family (Anderson 1998). They also have lower price elasticity (Anderson 1994), that is, are less likely to defect when competitors offer lower prices. Finally, they are also more forgiving: when there is an occasional good or service failure, highly satisfied customers may attribute it to external causes and stay loyal to the firm (Tsiros et al. 2004). No wonder smart firms incorporate customer satisfaction within their overall strategic framework.

WHAT IS CUSTOMER SATISFACTION?

CS is customers' post-consumption/purchase evaluation of a good or service based on a single experience (i.e. transactional CS) or a series of experiences (i.e. cumulative CS). They may also form CS judgments about a firm that markets one or more products or for purchases or experiences in online/offline environments (Shankar and Rangaswamy 2003). Two decades of academic research starting from the 1970s were devoted to understanding factors that influence overall satisfaction evaluations (see Oliver 2010 for a detailed review). For example, CS ratings can be influenced by factors such as: expectations about product performance (Anderson and Sullivan 1993), absolute product performance (Churchill and Surprenant 1982), performance relative to expectations or disconfirmation level (Oliver 1980), performance level experienced during previous consumption episodes (Mittal et al. 1999), and performance levels of and expectations about competitive offerings (Anderson and Salisbury 2003; Johnson et al. 1995). To implement CS strategically, it is useful to understand the macro-, meso- and micro-implications of CS measurement and comparisons for firms.

A STRATEGIC OVERVIEW OF CUSTOMER SATISFACTION

CS can be examined from three perspectives, each providing different insights: comparing a firm to other firms cross-sectionally and over time (macro); understanding how CS affects the firm's entire customer base (meso); and examining the antecedents of overall CS (micro).

Macro-level

At the macro-level, researchers are interested not only in benchmarking firms against other firms but also understanding if CS is related to shareholder wealth. This is a "bird's-eye" view with a single firm as the unit of analysis. Senior managers may ask strategic questions such as: How does a firm compare to other firms in the same industry and across industries on CS? Is there an association between CS and financial performance of firms? Answers to these strategic questions can enable marketing executives to make a credible case to CEOs and CFOs about the importance of making CS investments. Academically, this perspective helps link key marketing constructs such as customer satisfaction to shareholder value.[1]

Marketing scholars have developed a strong body of research showing how the American Customer Satisfaction Index (ACSI) is associated with various firm performance metrics (see Table 16.1 for a review). The ACSI was developed by the National Quality Research Center at the University of Michigan to obtain a customer-based measure of firms' ability to satisfy customers (Fornell et al. 1996; Grewal et al. 2010). A representative sample of approximately 250 current customers from each firm is interviewed each year using computer-assisted telephone interviews. A different sample of customers is contacted each year. All respondents have purchased and used goods or services from the firm in a defined period of time. For a given year, the database contains over 200000 customer surveys. Approximately 25 industries from the retail, finance/real-estate/insurance, durable manufacturing, non-durable manufacturing, basic services and transportation/communications/utilities sectors are included in the ACSI dataset. Examples include: apparel (Liz Claiborne, Levi Strauss); athletic shoes (Nike); automobiles (Honda); banks (Wells Fargo); department stores (Federated, May); discount stores (Wal-Mart); fast food (McDonald's, Wendy's); food processing (Dole Foods, Heinz, Kellogg, Quaker Oats); household appliances (Maytag, Whirlpool); soft drinks (Coca-Cola); personal care (Colgate–Palmolive); personal computing (Dell); pet foods (Ralston); service stations (Mobil); supermarkets (Kroger); and tobacco (Phillip Morris).

Each firm in the ACSI has a customer satisfaction index that can range from 0 to 100, with 100 as the highest level of satisfaction. The ACSI is methodologically consistent across all firms and over time. Thus a firm's CS level can be benchmarked against competitors in the same industry as well as used to monitor performance relative to other industries – cross-sectionally and over time (see Fornell et al. 1996 for details).

Table 16.1 lists key academic studies investigating the association between the ACSI and a firm's financial performance using measures such as long-term shareholder value or Tobin's q (Anderson et al. 2004), ROI (Anderson et al. 1997), portfolio returns (Aksoy et al. 2008), cash flow (Gruca and Rego 2005; Morgan and Rego 2006) and risk (Tuli and Bharadwaj 2009). The conclusion from these and other similar studies is clear: CS (as measured by the ACSI) is strongly associated with a firm's financial performance measured with many different indicators. For senior executives, the strategic implication is that managing overall CS is an important element of firms' responsibility to Wall Street (shareholders, bondholders, analysts etc.). Building on this macro-level evidence, firms can begin to understand the strategic importance of CS and make CS investments. Importantly, resources spent on CS improvements are correctly viewed as investments, and not expenses.[2]

Table 16.1 Macro-level customer satisfaction: strategic impact of CS on financial performance (key studies)

Study	Sample	CS & firm financial performance	Potential moderators
Return on investment			
Anderson et al. (1994)	ACSI, 1989–94	A one-point increase in ACSI associated with 11.4% increase in ROI over 5 years	
Anderson et al. (1997)	ACSI, 1989–92	A one-unit increase in ACSI associated with 0.37% increase in ROI for a goods firm and 0.22% increase for service firms that simultaneously increase CS and productivity	
Anderson and Mittal (2000)	Swedish Customer Satisfaction Barometer (SCSB)	A 1% increase in CS associated with 2.37 unit increase in ROI, while a 1% decrease in CS associated with a 5.08% decrease in ROI	
Cash flow			
Gruca and Rego (2005)	ACSI, 1994–2002	A one-unit increase in ACSI associated with $1.01 increase in cash flow (for over $1000 in assets), which translates to $55 M increase in cash flow for average firm in dataset, accompanied by a 4% decrease in cash flow variability	• The association between satisfaction and cash flow growth was stronger when market share and advertising intensity were high • The association between satisfaction and cash flow growth was weaker when industry demand increased
Morgan and Rego (2006)	ACSI, 1994–2000	A one-unit increase in ACSI associated with a 0.10-unit increase in net operating cash flow	
Short-term financial performance			
Morgan and Rego (2006)	ACSI, 1994–2000	• A one-unit increase in ASCI associated with: – 0.19-unit increase in sales growth – 0.05-unit increase in gross margin – 0.10-unit increase in market share	

Table 16.1 (continued)

Study	Sample	CS & firm financial performance	Potential moderators
Long-term financial performance and shareholder value			
Anderson et al. (2004)	ACSI, 1994–97	A one-point increase in ACSI associated with a 1.02% increase in Tobin's q, which translated to an increase in firm value of $275 M for an average firm in the dataset	• The association between satisfaction and shareholder value was weaker when industries were fragmented and concentration was low • The association between satisfaction and shareholder value was strongest for department stores, supermarkets and appliances, and weakest for the apparel and automotive industries
Mittal et al. (2005)	ACSI, 1994–2000	A 1% increase in customer satisfaction associated with a $1.61 B increase in market value for average firm in dataset that successfully achieved a dual emphasis, i.e. were also efficient	Efficiency moderated the relationship between satisfaction and Tobin's q (i.e. only by having high satisfaction and high efficiency did firms achieve the greatest long-run financial performance)
Morgan and Rego (2006)	ACSI, 1994–2000	• A one-unit increase in ASCI associated with: – 0.26-unit increase in Tobin's q – 0.17-unit increase in total shareholder returns	
Luo and Bhattacharya (2006)	ACSI, 2001–04	A one-point increase in ACSI associated with a 0.25-unit increase in Tobin's q and a 0.2-unit increase in stock returns	CSR impacted market value partially through CS and product quality and innovativeness capability moderated this relationship
Fornell et al. (2006)	ACSI, 1994–2002	• A one-point increase in ACSI associated with a 4.6% increase in market value of equity • Hypothetical and actual portfolios composed of firms in top 20% of ACSI outperformed the Dow Jones, NASDAQ and S&P 500	

Study	Data	Findings	Moderators
Aksoy et al. (2008)	ACSI, 1996–2006	Portfolio composed of firms with high levels of and increasing ACSI outperformed alternative portfolios and S&P 500	
Luo and Homburg (2008)	ACSI (airline industry only) 1999–2006	A one-unit increase in ACSI associated with a 5-unit decrease in the stock value gap (the difference between a firm's actual and optimal market value)	The association between satisfaction and the stock value gap was stronger when: – A firm's working capital was high – A firm had a high degree of specialization
Jacobson and Mizik (2009)	ACSI, 1996–2006	ACSI announcements associated with short-term abnormal returns, but do not predict long-run abnormal returns for most firms	
Debt financing Anderson and Mansi (2009)	ACSI, 1994–2004	A one-point increase in ACSI associated with: – 6% increase in credit ratings – 2% decrease in cost of debt financing	The association between satisfaction and cost of debt was weaker when the firm's level of risk was high
Risk Tuli and Bharadwaj (2009)	ACSI, 1994–2006	A one-unit increase in ACSI associated with: – 1.88-unit decrease in systematic risk – 3.76-unit decrease in downside systematic risk – 3.42-unit decrease in idiosyncratic risk – 2.31-unit decrease in downside idiosyncratic risk	

Table 16.1 (continued)

Study	Sample	CS & firm financial performance	Potential moderators
Other Metrics			
Luo and Homburg (2007)	ACSI, 2002–03	• A one-point increase in ACSI associated with: – 0.29-unit increase in advertising and promotion efficiency – 0.33-unit increase in human capital performance	• The association between satisfaction and future advertising and promotion efficiency was stronger when market concentration was high • The association between satisfaction and future human capital performance was stronger when market concentration was low
Luo et al. (2010)	ACSI, 1995–2006	• A one-point increase in ACSI associated with more positive analyst stock recommendations for a firm and smaller dispersion among analyst recommendations	• The association between customer satisfaction and analyst recommendations was stronger when: – competition in product markets was high – financial market uncertainty was high • The association between customer satisfaction and recommendation dispersion was stronger when product market competition was high

Note: For each coefficient reported, the statistical significance is 5% ($p < 0.05$) unless otherwise noted.

Meso-level

At this level, managers are interested in examining the firm's customer base to understand the behavioral consequences of CS. Thus managers may ask questions such as the following: Do improvements in CS translate into higher sales (Gómez et al. 2004), greater word of mouth (Anderson 1998), or cross-sales (Verhoef et al. 2001)? What is the impact of CS on customer retention (Bolton 1998; Mittal and Kamakura 2001) and share of wallet (Cooil et al. 2007; Keiningham et al. 2003)? To answer these questions, firms measure overall CS for their customers and relate it to specific customer behaviors. These studies provide a more nuanced view of how a firm's CS efforts translate into improved revenues through customer behaviors associated with retention, sales, word of mouth, share of wallet and cross-selling. Here the goal is not so much to compare the focal firm with other firms, but to look "inside" a firm's customer base.

The last decade has seen a steady accumulation of studies addressing this question, that is, to ascertain the association between overall CS scores of a customer and subsequent behavioral outcomes. Key studies are summarized in Table 16.2. They span industries such as insurance (Verhoef et al. 2001), retailing (Seiders et al. 2005), banking (Cooil et al. 2007), telecommunications (Bolton 1998), automotive (Kamakura et al. 2002), B2B (Bolton et al. 2008) and so forth. These studies clearly support one conclusion: for a given firm, CS is strongly associated with beneficial customer behaviors such as retention, recommendations to friends and family, increased share of wallet and repurchase behavior.

Strategically, these results show that a satisfied customer base will engage in behaviors that should benefit the firm in both the short and long run. More importantly, firms can monetize the different behavioral outcomes of CS to calculate a return on CS investments for their own firm. There are established models to do that, such as the return on quality model (Rust et al. 1995) and the satisfaction–profit chain model (Kamakura et al. 2002). A key implication of these models is that firms should view CS as a strategic lever that can enable them to accomplish goals related to customer behaviors and financial outcomes. Thus firms should not attempt to simply maximize CS – rather their goal should be to optimize CS in a way that is profit maximizing.

Micro-level

In addition to understanding the macro- and meso-level perspectives, managers are also interested in improving overall CS. Thus the micro-level perspective engages the managers' attention to an attribute-level model of overall CS. Overall CS is a function of attribute-level evaluations (LaTour and Peat 1979; Wilkie and Pessemier 1973), which may be based on performance and/or disconfirmation at the attribute level. For example, overall satisfaction with a retailer may be based on a customer's satisfaction with the store, sales staff, value provided and merchandise. Research shows that when describing their experiences with brands, consumers are twice as likely to use attributes than the overall product (Gardial et al. 1994).

Table 16.3 lists a few studies examining the relative importance of attributes (i.e. the association of performance on an attribute with overall satisfaction) in determining overall CS. These studies span many industries and customer types. The key conclusion

Table 16.2 Meso-level customer satisfaction studies: the association of CS with customer behaviors in various industries

Study	Industry and sample size	Method	Customer behavior	How CS impacts customer behavior
Loveman (1998)	Banking (*n* = 955)	Linear regression	• Percentage of investable assets held at bank (SOW) • Retention of checking accounts • Cross-sell (number of services purchased per household)	A one-unit increase in average CS associated with: • 0.02 unit increase in share of wallet • 0.03 unit increase in retention • 0.13 unit increase in number of services purchased per household
Bolton (1998)	Telecommunications (*n* = 650)	Proportional hazards regression	Relationship duration	• A one-unit change in CS was associated with a 1.7-unit increase in relationship duration • The relationship between CS and relationship duration was stronger for customers who have more experience with the organization
Bolton and Lemon (1999)	Television entertainment service (*n* = 184) Cellular communications (*n* not reported)	Tobit model	Service usage	A one-unit increase in CS was associated with a 310.5-unit increase in future service usage for entertainment service customers and 34.6-unit increase for telecommunications customers
Mittal and Kamakura (2001)	Automotive (*n* = 100 400)	Logit model	Repurchase behavior	• The relationship between CS and repurchase behavior was non-linear and exhibited increasing returns (while CS-repurchase intention relationship exhibited decreasing returns) • Differences in customer characteristics can cause variability in the satisfaction-retention link via variation in satisfaction thresholds, response bias, and functional form of the relationship

Study	Sample	Method	Dependent variables	Findings
Kamakura et al. (2002)	Banking (n = 5055)	Structural equation modeling	• Share of wallet (% of funds held at bank) • Customer tenure • Number of transactions per month	• A one-unit increase in intent to recommend associated with 0.27-unit increase in customer behaviors (share of wallet, relationship tenure and number of transactions per month) • The indirect effect of intent to recommend on profit (through customer behaviors) was 0.04
Keiningham et al. (2003)	B2B financial institution (n = 348)	Linear and cubic regression models	Share of wallet	The relationship between CS and share of wallet was nonlinear and exhibited increasing returns
Bowman and Narayandas (2004)	Processed metal (n = 374)	Regression (linear and nonlinear models)	Share of wallet	The relationship between CS and share of wallet exhibited increasing returns and was contingent on context (customer size, tenure and satisfaction with closest competitor)
Gómez et al. (2004)	Grocery stores (n = 250)	Regression	Sales performance	• A one-unit change in CS was associated with a 54.2-unit change in sales performance (sales per square foot) • Sales performance was more sensitive to negative than positive changes in CS
Lam et al. (2004)	B2B courier service (n = 234)	Structural equation modeling	• Recommendation • Patronage	• CS positively impacted recommendations (γ = 0.36) • CS positively impacted patronage (γ = 0.31)
Keiningham et al. (2005)	Institutional securities (n = 81)	Regression	• Share of wallet • Customer revenue	• Increase in CS associated with an increase in share of wallet (b = 0.47) • Increase in CS associated with a 0.25¢ increase in customer revenue
Perkins-Munn et al. (2005)	• Fleet trucking (n = 267) • Pharmaceuticals (n = 176)	Linear and logistic regression	• Share of wallet • Repurchase	• Increase in CS was associated with an increase in share of wallet (b = 0.13, b = 0.14, for trucking and pharmaceutical datasets respectively) • Increase in CS associated with an increase in actual repurchase (b = 0.62, b = 0.61)

Table 16.2 (continued)

Study	Industry and sample size	Method	Customer behavior	How CS impacts customer behavior
Seiders et al. (2005)	Retail (*n* = 945)	Regression	Repurchase	• Relationship between CS and repurchase frequency moderated by income and convenience with competitive intensity attenuating the moderating effect of convenience • Effect of CS on repurchase spending moderated by involvement, income and convenience with competitive intensity attenuating the moderating effect on convenience
Cooil et al. (2007)	Banking (*n* = 4319)	Latent class regression	Share of wallet	• Changes in CS were positively and nonlinearly related to share of wallet • The association between satisfaction and share of wallet was weaker when income and tenure were high
Larivière (2008)	Financial services (*n* = 522)	• Proportional hazard model • Ordered logit model • Mixed model	• Retention • Share of wallet • Customer profitability	• A one-point increase in loyalty intentions was associated with a 17% higher likelihood of repurchase • High share of wallet customers had higher loyalty intentions and the best profitability trajectory
Bolton et al. (2008)	Computing support systems (*n* = 2076)	Logit model	Contract upgrades	Satisfaction influenced the decision to upgrade to a higher margin product/service

Note: For each coefficient reported, the statistical significant is 5% (*p* < 0.05) unless otherwise noted.

Table 16.3 Micro-level customer satisfaction studies: attribute-level antecedents of overall CS (examples)

Study and industry	Industry and sample size	Method	Attribute performance and overall satisfaction	Strategic implications
Kekre et al. (1995)	Software (*n* = 2026)	Ordered probit	• Seven drivers of overall satisfaction were identified, with capability found to be the most important • Driver importance varied across customer groups, as did the stringency with which satisfaction was judged	Improvement of satisfaction drivers substantially impacts customer satisfaction
Levesque and McDougall (1996)	Retail banking (*n* not reported)	Regression	• The most important drivers of CS were core and relational performance, problem encountered and satisfaction with problem recovery • Core performance and problems encountered were determinants of switching intentions	An unresolved service problem substantially impacts a customer's attitude toward the provider, highlighting the importance of failure recovery in maintaining satisfaction
Danaher (1998)	Airline (*n* = 260)	Latent class regression	• Segments varied in their valuation of service attributes (flight crew, meals/drinks and flight comfort) • Segments characterized by different demographics (gender, age and occupation) and travel behaviors (travel purpose, flight duration, flight class and frequency of international travel)	• Focus on easily identifiable customer segments to deliver service they value most • Prioritize segments most extreme in their attribute preferences over those who are relatively satisfied and less demanding of service performance • Consider self-selection as a means to provide segments with what they value

271

Table 16.3 (continued)

Study and industry	Industry and sample size	Method	Attribute performance and overall satisfaction	Strategic implications
	Telephone directory service (n = 166)		• Operator performance most important to segment 1 • Successful communication with operator most important to segment 2 and 3, but 3 was more satisfied if they repeated information to operator • Segments varied in their overall satisfaction, proportion of phone numbers found, percentage of correct numbers given and attribution of blame for incorrect numbers	Cues provided by the customer should be used by employees to adjust the service interaction and meet customer's particular needs
Mittal et al. (1998)	Healthcare (n = 4517)	OLS and logistic regression	Negative attribute performance had a greater impact on CS and switching intentions than positive performance on same attribute	• Positive and negative attribute performance asymmetrically impact CS and behavioral intentions • Prioritize eliminating negative performance, then aim to increase positive performance
	Automotive (n = 9359)		Overall satisfaction exhibited diminishing sensitivity to each additional instance of positive performance, but not negative performance	
	Automotive (n = 13759)		Negative disconfirmation on attributes such as comfort, quality of vehicle and maneuverability/handing had a greater impact on CS than positive disconfirmation on same attributes	

272

Study	Context (sample)	Method	Findings
Garbarino and Johnson (1999)	Performing arts (n = 401)	Structural equation modeling	• Overall satisfaction mediated the relationship between satisfaction component attitudes and future intentions for low relational customers (occasional subscribers and individual ticket buyers) • Trust and commitment mediated the relationship between component attitudes and future intentions for high relational customers (subscribers) • For low relational customers, transactional marketing focused on improving satisfaction is recommended • Relationship marketing should target high relationship customers and focus on maintaining and building trust and commitment, not satisfaction
Krishnan et al. (1999)	Financial services (n = 1280)	Bayesian analysis	• A one-unit improvement in product line shifted 12% of customers from not very satisfied to very satisfied • A one-unit improvement in financial reports shifted 5% of customers to very satisfied • A one-unit improvement in branch service shifted 5% of customers to very satisfied • A one-unit improvement in automated telephone service shifted 3% of customers to very satisfied • Satisfaction with product offerings was the primary driver of overall satisfaction • Identify customer segments to target the drivers and enhance overall satisfaction
Mittal and Katrichis (2000)	Credit card customers (n = 573)	Regression	Credit card statement and customer service were more important for new customers while loyal customers placed more emphasis on promotional benefits and adequacy of the credit limit To attract customers, marketing should focus on quality of customer service and the user-friendliness of the credit card statement. To maintain the relationship, managers should assess the benefits and credit limit of their customers
	Mutual fund investors (n = 1272)		• Trust, confidence and courtesy were most important at the beginning of the relationship between customer and mutual fund advisor, while loyal customers were most concerned with efficiency Trust and rapport were a necessary precondition to cultivate a long-term relationship between advisor and customers. Once achieved, the focus should turn to efficiency

Table 16.3 (continued)

Study and industry	Industry and sample size	Method	Attribute performance and overall satisfaction	Strategic implications
	Automotive (*n* = 5250)		• Service was most important at the beginning of car ownership with the vehicle itself becoming most important as the relationship progresses	Manufacturers should focus on service at the beginning of the relationship and then the actual product at later stages of the relationship
Slotegraaf and Inman (2004)	Automotive (*n* = 17 000)	Sequential hierarchical regression model	• Overall attribute satisfaction declined over time • Satisfaction declined at a greater rate for resolvable compared to irresolvable attributes • The effect of attribute satisfaction on CS with product quality increased over time for resolvable attributes but decreased for irresolvable attributes	• Attribute satisfaction declines over time, but the rate depends on attribute resolvability • It is important to understand how product quality assessments evolve over the long term
Driver and Johnston (2001)	Banking (*n* = 259)	Factor analysis, ANOVA	Customers differed in their valuation of soft/interpersonal and hard/noninterpersonal attributes – "Relaters" valued soft attributes – slightly skewed female, young (<35 years) – "Nonrelaters" valued hard attributes – majority male – "Demanders" found every attribute important – majority female, almost half age 45–54	• Prioritize most important quality in service delivery • For each customer group, management should strive to increase importance of attributes (hard or soft) on which they perform best • Use demographic information to target three groups and develop quality related messaging to each

| Dagger and Sweeney (2007) | Healthcare ($n = 635$) | Structural equation modeling (invariance testing) | Salience of service attributes differed by length of customer relationship, such that:
– Novice customers (visiting clinic for less than 6 months) perceived tangible aspects of service and operation to be more important to service quality
– Long-tem customers (visiting for more than 3 years) perceived atmosphere and outcome to be more important to service quality
– Expertise was the most important attribute to both groups, but significantly more so for long-term customers
Drivers of behavioral intentions:
– Service quality was most important driver for novice customers
– Service satisfaction was most important driver for long-term customers | • Attribute importance changes over the length of a customer's experience with a firm
• Service firms can use customer experience as a behavioral-segmentation variable |

is that attribute performance is strongly associated with overall satisfaction, which in turn is associated with customer intentions and behaviors. We can also calculate attribute-importance by customer sub-group. For example, the importance of attributes in airlines varies depending on business-class or economy-class customers (Danaher 1998). Similarly, as the relationship between a customer and a firm evolves over time, the relative importance of attributes changes (Mittal and Katrichis 2000). In general, identifying the important attributes can help firms to set resource allocation priorities for different customer segments. Finally, consistent with loss aversion, research shows that the deleterious impact of failing to meet expectations on an attribute is greater than the beneficial impact of meeting expectations on the same attribute (Mittal et al. 1998).

CUSTOMER SATISFACTION SURVEYS

At the heart of CS satisfaction research lies a carefully designed CS survey instrument. Although researchers have used experimental (Rust, Inman et al. 1999) and ethnographic (Oliver 1999) methods to understand CS, the majority of research in this area has relied on customer surveys. Importantly, CS is one of the few areas where close collaboration among academics and firms has produced rich findings (e.g. Rust, Keiningham et al. 1999).

Satisfaction Survey: Design and Content

A CS survey typically consists of four parts, each measuring a key set of constructs.

1. Overall customer satisfaction: A customer's overall satisfaction may be measured using a variety of scales such as:
    (a) "Overall, how satisfied are you with . . .?" (1 = extremely dissatisfied, 5 = extremely satisfied)
    (b) "Please rate your agreement with the following item: I am very satisfied with . . ." (1 = strongly disagree, 10 = strongly agree)
    (c) "How would you rate your experience with . . .?" (1 = poor, 7 = excellent)

    While there are scores of overall satisfaction scales, each with its own advantages and disadvantages, most of them perform adequately (see Oliver 2010 for a detailed discussion). In addition to being valid and reliable (Drolet and Morrison 2001), the research should also ensure the context appropriateness of the scale, modifying it to the specific situation (Morgan et al. 2005).
2. Behavioral intentions: These include measures such as likelihood to repurchase, likelihood to recommend and likelihood to complain. They can be worded in many different ways:
    (a) "How likely are you to repurchase brand XXX in the next six months?" (1 = not at all likely, 10 = completely likely)
    (b) "Would you be likely to repurchase . . .?" (1 = definitely not, 5 = most definitely)
    (c) "Would you recommend this brand to your friends and family?" (1 = definitely will not recommend, 7 = will definitely recommend)

Researchers can also obtain retrospective self-reports of behavior to ascertain the actual level of word-of-mouth activity, recommendations, spending and share of wallet for their own brand relative to competitors (Agustin and Singh 2005; Anderson 1998; Richins 1983; Westbrook 1987). More recently, researchers have merged CS surveys with actual behavioral data such as repurchase (Bolton 1998; Mittal and Kamakura 2001), share of wallet (Keiningham et al. 2003), and sales (Gómez et al. 2004), to provide richer insights into the association between CS and customer behaviors.

3. Attribute-level perceptions: Typically, CS surveys measure customer perceptions of performance on various attributes. Performance ratings on each attribute can be obtained using a variety of scales:
    (a) "Rate the performance of each attribute as excellent = 5, very good = 4, good = 3, fair = 2, poor = 1."
    (b) "How did the product perform relative to your expectations?" Responses are obtained as: (above my expectations, met my expectations, below my expectations).
4. Customer background variables: In addition to demographics such as gender, age and income, firms may also measure ownership of competitive brands (e.g. as in an automotive study) or share of wallet (e.g. as in a banking study). Managerially, these measures enable a firm to engage in competitive assessment. From a research perspective, we can develop a context specific and contingent approach to understanding the antecedents and consequences of CS.

Survey Sample

A typical sample for a CS study includes customers who have purchased and/or used the firm's offering during a prespecified period of time. However, there is an increasing need to measure CS among several other customer groups in addition to current customers such as:

- Past customers who no longer use the firm's offerings. These are also termed "lapsed customers," "former customers" or "defectors."
- Potential customers who currently use competitive offerings but not the focal firm's brand. In many cases, potential customers may have been past customers of the firm.
- Finally, for many services (e.g. banking and insurance) and goods (e.g. automobile), it is possible for customers to simultaneously use multiple brands. In such cases, firms should measure overall satisfaction with all the relevant brands.

Broadening the sample in this way is strategically and theoretically useful. A comparison of CS scores and intentions among current and potential customers provides competitive benchmarking for overall satisfaction scores and attribute performance scores. Comparing current and past customers can provide insights into why some customers may have left the firm. Comparing CS based on how long a current customer has been with a firm helps identify CS improvement efforts as the customer relationship with a firm evolves. From a theoretical perspective, broadening the scope of CS surveys beyond current customers enables us to gain useful insights into firm behaviors rooted in a competitive context.

Analysis of Customer Satisfaction Surveys

From a managerial perspective, the analysis of a CS survey can take many forms, ranging from basic univariate analysis to advanced multivariate analysis (Morgan et al. 2005). Examples include:

1. Either the average score or some variation of the "top box score" (e.g. top-2 or top-3 box) is used to describe customer responses to each item in the survey. This allows managers to get a snapshot of how the firm is rated by the customer base on overall satisfaction, attribute performance and behavioral intentions. Thus managers can determine the relative attribute performance on each attribute. The scores could be broken down by customer characteristics deemed relevant (e.g. by gender, age, brand ownership, number of years with the firm and so forth).
2. Managers may also want to know the association between (1) attribute performance and overall CS and (2) CS and behavioral intentions. Using multivariate techniques such as regression analysis, one can ascertain the relative attribute importance of each attribute as a determinant of overall CS.[3] The stronger the relative association of performance on an attribute with CS, the more important it is deemed as a driver of CS.
3. The importance and performance on each attribute is used to classify attributes into four groups.

    *   Attributes that have high importance and on which the firm is performing high represent strengths of the firm.
    *   Attributes that have high importance but on which the firm has low performance represent weaknesses that should be immediately addressed.
    *   If an attribute is not important but the firm has very high performance, then the firm may be overinvesting in that attribute. Another strategy may be to increase the perceived importance of the attribute.
    *   For attributes having low importance and performance, continuous monitoring is warranted lest either changes dramatically.

An importance–performance analysis results in a 2 × 2 map where the Y axis shows the relative performance and the X axis shows the relative importance of each attribute. While different terms like "quadrant analysis" or "strategic attribute mapping" are used, the basic logic remains the same. Sometimes, it is useful to also plot the relative performance of a "best in class" competitor for benchmarking purposes on the same map. An example of such a map is shown in Figure 16.1, which we discuss at the end of the following section.

Academically, the analysis of CS surveys has evolved over time. Earlier studies used covariance-based analyses such as multiple regression (Churchill and Surprenant 1982; Oliver 1993) and structural equation modeling (Fornell and Westbrook 1984; Mano and Oliver 1993) to link theoretically specified models. More recently, the trend has been to

Comparative benchmarking

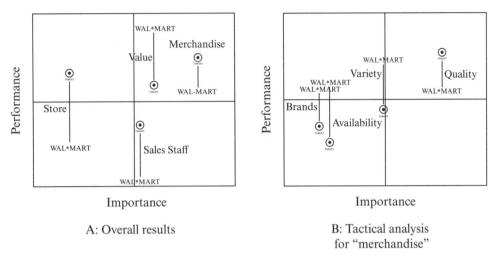

A: Overall results

B: Tactical analysis
for "merchandise"

Figure 16.1 Importance performance chart for two retailers

incorporate econometric approaches to address both cross-sectional and longitudinal variation in data (Gruca and Rego 2005; Jacobson and Mizik 2009; Luo and Homburg 2008). This latter trend is reflective of the fact that CS satisfaction research – at least at the macro-level – has borrowed heavily from literatures in finance and accounting to examine the impact of CS on the financial performance of a firm (Kimbrough and McAlister 2009; Mittal and Frennea 2010) using large-scale datasets that link CS to firm attributes and financial performance.

CUSTOMER SATISFACTION STRATEGY MAPS

Managerially, one of the most important uses of a CS study for a firm is to develop a CSSM – customer satisfaction strategy map. As shown in Figure 16.2, a CSSM provides a visual representation of the key elements of a firm's marketing strategy designed to quantify the implicit linkages based on data. The quantification provides guidance that is strategic (meso-level) as well as tactical (micro-level) for implementing a CS strategy. Managers can quantify the association between its CS investments and key customer behaviors as well as financial outcomes. More importantly, a CSSM is a blueprint for action for front-line managers and employees. They can map out all the inputs, that is, the attributes that affect overall satisfaction, and key firm behaviors that should be changed to affect perceptions on those attributes (Rust et al. 1995; Rust, Keiningham et al. 1999).

A key element of the CSSM is a firm's ability to link data from a CS survey to operational inputs and behavioral outcomes (Loveman 1998; Rust et al. 1995). For example, a bank tracked each customer who filled out its CS survey and linked the survey data to account balance, number of accounts, sales, ATM usage and profitability. The bank was

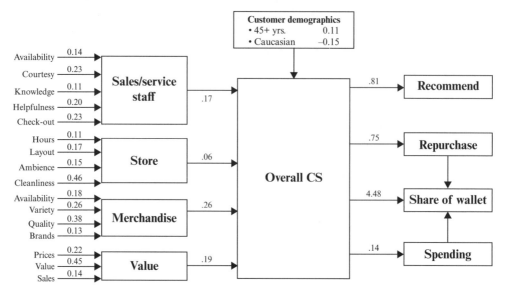

Note: All relationships shown here are statistically significant (p < 0.05).

Figure 16.2   Customer satisfaction strategy map for a retailer

also able to determine the branch at which each customer banked most often, and link the job satisfaction of those employees to customer satisfaction. Using such a dataset combined with advanced multivariate techniques, a CSSM was developed. Satisfaction strategy maps have been developed and implemented in a number of industries like banking (Kamakura et al. 2002; Larivière 2008; Loveman 1998), B2B services (Bowman and Narayandas 2004) and tourism (Homburg et al. 2009).

As an example, we discuss a CSSM developed for the retailing industry, focused on Wal-Mart and Target. This map was based on a satisfaction survey of 855 retail customers of firms such as Wal-Mart, Target, Home Depot, Lowes, Macy's, Sam's Club, Costco and Kohl's. Using this map, we show how Wal-Mart can examine its satisfaction strategy relative to Target. In the CSSM shown in Figure 16.2, all the key elements of retail strategy are visually represented in a causal manner, with the causal linkages quantified.[4] To improve sales and profitability, a retailer should consider improving customers' recommendation, repurchase and patronage, as well as customer spending and share of wallet. These customer intentions and behaviors are driven by overall satisfaction. The tactical part of the strategy map depicts all the component areas – sales staff, store, merchandise and value – that must be managed to optimize overall satisfaction. Within each component area, specific action levers are mapped. For instance, the component area store comprises action levers such as layout, hours, ambience and cleanliness.

Statistical analysis[5] quantifies each linkage. Among the component areas, merchandise (0.26) has the largest association with overall satisfaction, followed by value (0.19), sales staff (0.17) and store (0.06). Thus improving "merchandise" by one unit improves overall satisfaction by 0.26 units, which in turn improves repurchase intentions (by 0.75 units), likelihood to recommend (by 0.81 units), as well as share of wallet (by 4.48 percent).

How can a retailer improve its overall score on merchandise? The key levers, in order of importance, are: quality of merchandise (0.38), variety (0.26), availability (0.15) and brands (0.13).

A store manager can easily understand the relative association between merchandising, sales/service staff and value on overall CS. More important, within each area, the CSSM can help management understand the specific tasks that need to be accomplished for improving overall CS. For instance, in Figure 16.2, a one-unit change in quality is associated with a 0.38-unit change in overall merchandising, which then is associated with a 0.26-unit change in overall CS. In turn, CS is strongly associated with behaviors such as recommendations, repurchase and share of wallet. Such a comprehensive overview can also help the CMO to explain the "satisfaction logic" to CEOs to gain their support.

Firms can also assess what needs to be done internally to make improvements, and what needs to be done to match or stay ahead of the competition. For example, panel A of Figure 16.1 shows that to improve its overall performance Wal-Mart should focus on merchandise, which is not only the most important attribute, but where it lags Target. Wal-Mart performs highest on value, the second most important attribute, and should monitor its efforts there to ensure performance remains high. Panel B of Figure 16.1 details how customers perceive the retailers' performance on the specific attributes of merchandising. Quality is the most important lever and is also the only one in which Target outperforms Wal-Mart. To improve its performance on merchandise, Wal-Mart should focus its efforts on improving the quality of merchandise offered. In other situations, firms may work on attributes that were important to close a competitive gap, even if diagnostically speaking they were not that important from an internal perspective. Thus inward–outward focus on strategy is critical to ensure that marketing provides feedback internally, while helping the firm improve and stay ahead of the competition.

A CSSM can also enable organizations to become more financially responsible. We linked overall satisfaction to year-on-year change in monthly sales for the retailers in this sample: a one-unit change in overall satisfaction is associated with a 21 percent improvement in monthly sales. Thus, for a large retailer with about $1 billion in monthly sales, this improvement translates to a sales increase of $210 million! Assuming a conservative profit margin of 2 percent, the improvement amounts to $4.2 million in extra profit per month. Using this thinking, a financially responsible CS strategy can be developed. Over time, as additional data become available, the statistical estimation models underlying the CSSM can be refined to make more robust predictions. Managers can use the CSSM as a starting point to drive the strategic process within their firms and embrace strategic marketing initiatives that are financially accountable.

CONCLUDING COMMENTS

About a decade ago, CS was used primarily for benchmarking. Firms compared their levels of satisfaction over time and with other firms, assuming that higher CS scores translated to superior performance. Today, we have robust evidence that CS improvements help firms improve shareholder value (see Table 16.1), as well as benefit their customers (see Table 16.2). More importantly, our understanding of how CS can be improved by focusing on attribute-level performance has also been enhanced (see Table 16.3). A strategic approach to accomplish this is the use of CSSM (see Figures 16.1 and 16.2). Together, these developments have elevated CS efforts within firms from a benchmarking exercise to a strategic imperative.

So that firms can better understand and use CS studies in the future, several issues need to be addressed in academic research. First, most published studies on CS at the meso- or micro-level focus on data from a single, focal firm. For instance, when estimating attribute importance, we link attribute perceptions to overall CS of the customer base of a single firm. This is mainly due to constraints on data availability. Data are typically available for a single firm. However, CS is partly based on relative performance by competitive offerings and should have a clear competitive dimension. Thus examining perceptions of and incorporating competitors' attribute performance and overall CS performance is a clear direction for research. For example, does the importance of an attribute depend on how customers of a focal firm perceive competitor performance to be? Second, CS needs to be viewed in the larger context of constructs such as brand equity (BE), corporate social responsibility (CSR) and sustainability. In particular, what is the joint effect of CS and CSR on customer repurchase intentions and behaviors? If customers are highly satisfied, then are they willing to forgive a company's CSR transgressions? Conversely, are customers tolerant of lower CS from companies having high CSR? These are fascinating issues requiring research attention (for a recent example, see Luo and Bhattacharya 2006). A third issue in need of further research is a deeper understanding of the firm's customer base. Most CS studies segment the firm's customers based on observable characteristics, that is, demographics (e.g. males typically have lower satisfaction ratings than females). What is the theoretical basis for such systematic differences? Could it be that males have a different social identity (He et al. 2008), and the identity somehow drives the differences in perceived attribute importance? Similarly, differences based on age, culture, education, relationship duration and switching propensity need to be theoretically explored. Fourth, there is also a need to broaden the scope of CS research to understand cross-cultural and cross-national issues. For example, is it the case that Asian customers – because of their interdependent identity (Zhang et al. 2006) – have higher levels of commitment to a brand? Because of this, are Asian customers more tolerant of lower CS than their Western counterparts? Naturally, large-scale global studies are needed to address these issues. In general, research needs to focus on studies that encompass both firm-level differences (e.g. examine the focal firm and its competitors) and customer-level differences (cross-cultural samples, theoretically examine customer differences). Finally, there is a need to test theories that closely integrate related concepts such as emotions (Oliver 1993; Westbrook and Oliver 1991) and commitment (Garbarino and Johnson 1999; Verhoef 2003) within CS research. For example, how do different forms of commitment influence overall satisfaction and what roles do emotions play in driving the commitment–satisfaction relationship? As product offerings from firms become more and more similar, it is critical to examine how firms can leverage customer emotions and commitment to build overall satisfaction. Moreover, such theories need to be tested using broader samples – that go beyond the USA and Europe alone – to ensure the universality of CS as a relevant and critical construct.

CS research has matured in its own right – academically and managerially – as a construct and as a body of research (Gupta and Zeithaml 2006; Mittal and Frennea 2010). Although important questions have been answered, many more issues that are increasingly important and interesting have emerged. We hope that the next decade of academic research will seize this opportunity so that firms can not only evaluate their current practices, but also improve them in the near future.

NOTES

1. For further discussion, see Shankar, Chapter 24 in this volume.
2. See Shankar, Chapter 24 in this volume.
3. This is typically the regression coefficient of each attribute in a regression equation with overall satisfaction as the dependent variable. The regression coefficient represents how a one-unit change in attribute performance is associated with overall satisfaction. The stronger this association, the more important an attribute. For further discussion, see Hanson (1992) and Wittink and Bayer (1994).
4. Note that the causality implied here is simply based on a manager's interpretation of the causal sequence of the variables involved. A randomized experiment would be necessary to isolate true "cause and effect" among variables.
5. Various techniques such as structural equation modeling (SEM) and regression can be used. For a discussion see Kamakura et al. (2002). The linkages shown here were estimated using multiple regression analysis and also verified with SEM. For each equation the VIF was less than 5 for all predictors, indicating multicollinearity was not an issue.

REFERENCES

Agustin, Clara and Jagdip Singh (2005), "Curvilinear effects of consumer loyalty determinants in relational exchanges," *Journal of Marketing Research*, **42** (February), 96–108.
Aksoy, Lerzan, Bruce Cooil, Christopher Groening, Timothy L. Keiningham and Atakan Yalçin (2008), "The long-term stock marketing valuation of customer satisfaction," *Journal of Marketing*, **72** (July), 105–22.
Anderson, Eugene W. (1994), "Cross-category variation in customer satisfaction and retention," *Marketing Letters*, **5** (1), 19–30.
Anderson, Eugene W. (1998), "Customer satisfaction and word of mouth," *Journal of Service Research*, **1** (1), 15–17.
Anderson, Eugene W. and Sattar A. Mansi (2009), "Does customer satisfaction matter to investors? Findings from the market," *Journal of Marketing Research*, **46** (October), 403–14.
Anderson, Eugene W. and Vikas Mittal (2000), "Strengthening the satisfaction–profit chain," *Journal of Service Research*, **3** (2), 107–20.
Anderson, Eugene W. and Linda Court Salisbury (2003), "The formation of market level expectations and its covariates," *Journal of Consumer Research*, **30** (June), 115–24.
Anderson, Eugene W. and Mary W. Sullivan (1993), "The antecedents and consequences of customer satisfaction for firms," *Marketing Science*, **12** (2), 125–43.
Anderson, Eugene W., Claes Fornell and Donald R. Lehmann (1994), "Customer satisfaction, marketing share, and profitability: findings from Sweden," *Journal of Marketing*, **58** (July), 53–66.
Anderson, Eugene W., Claes Fornell and Sanal K. Mazvancheryl (2004), "Customer satisfaction and shareholder value," *Journal of Marketing*, **68** (October), 172–85.
Anderson, Eugene W., Claes Fornell and Roland T. Rust (1997), "Customer satisfaction, productivity, and profitability: differences between goods and services," *Marketing Science*, **16** (2), 129–45.
Bolton, Ruth N. (1998), "A dynamic model of the duration of the customer's relationship with a continuous service provider: the role of satisfaction," *Marketing Science*, **17** (1), 45–65.
Bolton, Ruth N. and Katherine N. Lemon (1999), "A dynamic model of customers' usage of services: usage as an antecedent and consequence of satisfaction," *Journal of Marketing Research*, **36** (May), 171–86.
Bolton, Ruth N., Katherine N. Lemon and Peter C. Verhoef (2008) "Expanding business-to-business customer relationships: modeling the customer upgrade decision," *Journal of Marketing*, **12** (January), 46–64.

Borle, Sharad, Utpal M. Dholakia, Siddharth S. Singh and Robert A. Westbrook (2007), "The impact of survey participation on subsequent customer behavior: an emiprical investigation," *Marketing Science*, **25** (5), 711–26.

Bowman, Douglas and Das Narayandas (2004), "Linking customer management effort to customer profitability in business markets," *Journal of Marketing Research*, **39**, 433–47.

Churchill, Gilbert A. Jr and Carol Surprenant (1982), "An investigation into the determinants of customer satisfaction," *Journal of Marketing Research*, **19** (4), 491–504.

Cooil, Bruce, Timothy L. Keiningham, Lerzan Aksoy and Michael Hsu (2007), "A longitudinal analysis of customer satisfaction and share of wallet: investigating the moderating effect of customer characteristics," *Journal of Marketing*, **71** (January), 67–83.

Dagger, Tracey S. and Jillian C. Sweeney (2007), "Service quality attribute weights: how do novice and longer-term customers construct service quality perceptions?," *Journal of Service Research*, **10** (1), 22–42.

Danaher, Peter J. (1998), "Customer heterogeneity in service management," *Journal of Service Research*, **1** (2), 129–39.

Driver, Carole and Robert Johnston (2001), "Understanding service customers: the value of hard and soft attributes," *Journal of Service Research*, **4** (2), 130–39.

Drolet, Aimee L. and Donald G. Morrison (2001), "Do we really need multiple-item measures in service research?," *Journal of Service Research*, **3** (3), 196–204.

Fornell, Claes and Robert Westbrook (1984), "The vicious circle of consumer complaints," *Journal of Marketing*, **48** (3), 68–78.

Fornell, Claes, Michael D. Johnson, Eugene W. Anderson, Jaesung Cha and Barbara Everitt Bryant (1996), "The American Customer Satisfaction Index: nature, purpose, and findings," *Journal of Marketing*, **60** (October), 7–18.

Fornell, Claes, Sunil Mithas, Forrest V. Morgeson III and M.S. Krishnan (2006), "Customer satisfaction and stock prices: high returns, low risk," *Journal of Marketing*, **70** (January), 3–14.

Garbarino, Ellen and Mark S. Johnson (1999), "The different roles of satisfaction, trust, and commitment in customer relationships," *Journal of Marketing*, **63** (April), 70–87.

Gardial, Sarah Fisher, D. Scott Clemons, Robert B. Woodruff, David W. Schumann and Mary Jane Burns (1994), "Comparing consumers' recall of prepurchase and postpurchase product evaluation experiences," *Journal of Consumer Research*, **20** (4), 548–60.

Gómez, Miguel I., Edward W. McLaughlin and Dick R. Wittink (2004), "Customer satisfaction and retail sales performance: an empirical investigation," *Journal of Retailing*, **80** (4), 265–78.

Grewal, Rajdeep, Murali Chandrashekaran and Alka V. Citrin (2010), "Customer satisfaction heterogeneity and shareholder value," *Journal of Marketing Research*, **47** (August), 612–26.

Gruca, Thomas S. and Lopo L. Rego (2005), "Customer satisfaction, cash flow, and shareholder value," *Journal of Marketing*, **69** (July), 115–30.

Gupta, Sunil and Valarie Zeithaml (2006), "Customer metrics and their impact on financial performance," *Marketing Science*, **25** (6), 718–39.

Hanson, Randy (1992), "Determining attribute importance," *Quirk's Marketing Research Review*, **6** (October), 16–18.

He, Xin, J. Jeffrey Inman and Vikas Mittal (2008), "Gender jeopardy in financial risk taking," *Journal of Marketing Research*, **45** (4), 414–24.

Homburg, Christian, Jan Wieseke and Wayne D. Hoyer (2009), "Social identity and the service–profit chain," *Journal of Marketing*, **73** (2), 38–54.

Jacobson, Robert and Natalie Mizik (2009), "The financial markets and customer satisfaction: reexamining possible financial market mispricing of customer satisfaction," *Marketing Science*, **28** (5), 809–18.

Johnson, Michael D., Eugene W. Anderson and Claes Fornell (1995), "Rational and adaptive performance expectations in a customer satisfaction framework," *Journal of Consumer Research*, **21** (March), 695–707.

Kamakura, Wagner A., Vikas Mittal, Fernando de Rosa and José Afonso Mazzon (2002), "Assessing the service–profit chain," *Marketing Science*, **21** (3), 294–317.

Keiningham, Timothy L., Tiffany Perkins-Munn and Heather Evans (2003), "The impact of customer satisfaction on share-of-wallet in a business-to-business environment," *Journal of Service Research*, **6** (1), 37–50.

Keiningham, Timothy L., Tiffany Perkins-Munn, Lerzan Aksoy and Demitry Estrin (2005), "Does customer satisfaction lead to profitability?" *Managing Service Quality*, **15** (2), 172–81.

Kekre, Sunder, Mayuram S. Krishnan and Kannan Srinivasan (1995), "Drivers of customer satisfaction for software products: implications for design and service support," *Management Science*, **41** (9), 1456–70.

Kimbrough, Michael D. and Leigh M. McAlister (2009), "Linking marketing actions to value creation and firm value: insights from accounting research," *Journal of Marketing Research*, **46** (June), 313–19.

Krishnan, M.S., Venkatram Ramaswamy, Mary C. Meyer and Paul Damien (1999), "Customer satisfaction for financial services: the role of products, services, and information technology," *Management Science*, **45** (9), 1194–209.

Lam, Shun Yin, Venkatesh Shankar, Krishna Erramilli and Bvsan Murthy (2004), "Customer value, satisfaction, loyalty, and switching costs: an illustration from a business-to-business service context," *Journal of the Academy of Marketing Science*, **32** (3), 293–311.

Larivière, Bart (2008), "Linking perceptual and behavioral customer metrics to multiperiod customer profitability: a comprehensive service–profit chain application," *Journal of Service Research*, **11** (3), 3–21.

LaTour, Stephen A. and Nancy C. Peat (1979), "Conceptual and methodological issues in consumer satisfaction research," in William L. Wilkie (ed.), *Advances in Consumer Research Volume 6*, Ann Abor, MI: Association for Consumer Research, pp. 431–47.

Levesque, Terrence and Gordon H.G. McDougall (1996), "Determinants of customer satisfaction in retail banking," *International Journal of Bank Marketing*, **14** (7), 12–20.

Loveman, Gary W. (1998), "Employee satisfaction, customer loyalty, and financial performance: an empirical examination of the service profit chain in retail banking," *Journal of Service Research*, **1** (1), 18–31.

Luo, Xueming and C.B. Bhattacharya (2006), "Corporate social responsibility, customer satisfaction, and market value," *Journal of Marketing*, **70** (October), 1–18.

Luo, Xueming and Christian Homburg (2007), "Neglected outcomes of customer satisfaction," *Journal of Marketing*, **71** (April), 133–49.

Luo, Xueming and Christian Homburg (2008), "Satisfaction, complaint, and the stock value gap," *Journal of Marketing*, **72** (July), 29–43.

Luo, Xueming, Christian Homburg and Jan Wieseke (2010), "Customer satisfaction, analyst stock recommendations, and firm value," *Journal of Marketing Research*, **47** (December), 1041–58.

Mano, Haim and Richard L. Oliver (1993), "Assessing the dimensionality and structure of the consumption experience: evaluation, feeling, and satisfaction," *Journal of Consumer Research*, **20** (December), 451–66.

Mittal, Vikas and Carly M. Frennea (2010), "Customer satisfaction: a strategic review and guidelines for managers," MSI Fast Forward Series (Report 10-701), Cambridge, MA: Marketing Science Institute.

Mittal, Vikas and Wagner A. Kamakura (2001), "Satisfaction, repurchase intent, and repurchase behavior: investigating the moderating effect of customer characteristics," *Journal of Marketing Research*, **38** (February), 131–42.

Mittal, Vikas and Jerome M. Katrichis (2000), "Distinctions between new and loyal customers," *Marketing Research*, **12** (Spring), 26–32.

Mittal, Vikas, Pankaj Kumar and Michael Tsiros (1999), "Attribute-level performance, satisfaction, and behavioral intentions over time: a consumption-system approach," *Journal of Marketing*, **63** (April), 88–101.

Mittal, Vikas, William T. Ross and Patrick M. Baldasare (1998), "The asymmetric impact of negative and positive attribute-level performance on overall satisfaction and repurchase intentions," *Journal of Marketing*, **62** (January), 33–47.

Mittal, Vikas, Eugene W. Anderson, Akin Sayrak and Pandu Tadikamalla (2005), "Dual emphasis and the long-term financial impact of customer satisfaction," *Marketing Science*, **24** (4), 544–55.

Morgan, Neil A. and Lopo Leotte Rego (2006), "The value of different customer satisfaction and loyalty metrics in predicting business performance," *Marketing Science*, **25** (5), 426–39.

Morgan, Neil A., Eugene W. Anderson and Vikas Mittal (2005), "Understanding firms' customer satisfaction information usage," *Journal of Marketing*, **69** (July), 131–51.

Oliver, Richard L. (1980), "A cognitive model of the antecedents and consequences of satisfaction decisions," *Journal of Marketing Research*, **17** (4), 460–69.

Oliver, Richard L. (1993), "Cognitive, affective, and attribute bases of the satisfaction response," *Journal of Consumer Research*, **20** (3), 418–30.

Oliver, Richard L. (1999), "Whence consumer loyalty?," *Journal of Marketing*, **63** (Special Issue), 33–44.

Oliver, Richard L. (2010), *Satisfaction: A Behavioral Perspective on the Consumer*, Armonk, NY: M.E. Sharpe, Inc.

Perkins-Munn, Tiffany, Lerzan Aksoy, Timothy L. Keiningham and Demitry Estrin (2005), "Actual purchase as a proxy for share of wallet," *Journal of Service Research*, **7** (3), 245–56.

Richins, Marsha (1983), "Negative word-of-mouth by dissatisfied consumers: a pilot study," *Journal of Marketing*, **47** (1), 68–78.

Rust, Roland T., Anthony J. Zahorik and Timothy L. Keiningham (1995), "Return on quality (ROQ): making service quality financially accountable," *Journal of Marketing*, **59** (April), 58–70.

Rust, Roland T., J. Jeffery Inman, Jianmin Jia and Anthony Zahorik (1999), "What you don't know about customer-perceived quality: the role of customer expectation distributions," *Marketing Science*, **18** (1), 77–92.

Rust, Roland T., Timothy Keiningham, Stephen Clemens and Anthony Zahorik (1999), "Return on quality at Chase Manhattan Bank," *Interfaces*, **29** (March–April), 62–72.

Seiders, Kathleen, Glen B. Ross, Dhruv Grewal and Andrea L. Godfrey (2005), "Do satisfied customers buy more? Examining moderating influences in a retailing context," *Journal of Marketing*, **69** (October), 26–43.

Shankar, Venkatesh, Amy Smith and Arvind Rangaswamy (2003), "Customer satisfaction and loyalty in online and offline environments," *International Journal of Research in Marketing*, **20** (2), 153–75.

Slotegraaf, Rebecca J. and J. Jeffrey Inman (2004), "Longitudinal shifts in the drivers of satisfaction with product quality: the role of attribute resolvability," *Journal of Marketing Research*, **41** (August), 269–80.

Tsiros, Michael, Vikas Mittal and William T. Ross Jr (2004), "The role of attributions in customer satisfaction: a reexamination," *Journal of Consumer Research*, **31** (2), 476–83.

Tuli, Kapil R. and Sundar G. Bharadwaj (2009), "Customer satisfaction and stock returns risk," *Journal of Marketing*, **73** (November), 184–97.

Verhoef, Peter C. (2003), "Understanding the effect of customer relationship management efforts on customer retention and customer share development," *Journal of Marketing*, **67** (October), 30–45.

Verhoef, Peter C., Philip Hans Franses and Janny C. Hoekstra (2001), "The impact of satisfaction and payment equity on cross-buying: a dynamic model for a multi-service provider," *Journal of Retailing*, **77** (2), 359–78.

Westbrook, Robert A. (1987), "Product/consumption-based affective responses and postpurchase processes," *Journal of Marketing Research*, **24** (August), 258–70.

Westbrook, Robert A. and Richard Oliver (1991), "The dimensionality of consumption emotion patterns and consumer satisfaction," *Journal of Consumer Research*, **18** (June), 84–91.

Wilkie, William L. and Edgar A. Pessemier (1973), "Issues in marketing's use of multi-attribute attitude models," *Journal of Marketing Research*, **10** (November), 428–41.

Wittink, Dick R. and Leonard R. Bayer (1994), "The measurement imperative," *Marketing Research*, **6** (Winter), 14–23.

Zhang, Yinlong, Lawrence Feick and Lydia J. Price (2006), "The impact of self-construal on aesthetic preference for angular versus rounded shapes," *Personality and Social Psychology Bulletin*, **32** (6), 794–805.

PART V

BRANDING AND BRAND STRATEGIES

17 Brand strategy
Kevin Lane Keller

INTRODUCTION

Branding has been around for centuries as a means to distinguish the goods of one producer from those of another. According to the American Marketing Association, a brand is a "name, term, sign, symbol, or design, or a combination of them intended to identify the goods and services of one seller or group of sellers and to differentiate them from those of competition." By virtue of their ability to identifiy and differentiate, brands can create value to consumers and organizations.

Given the importance of brands as intangible assets for organizations, the ability to strategically manage those brands is critical (Aaker 1991, 1996; Aaker and Joachimsthaler 2000; Kapferer 2008; Levy 1999). An effective branding strategy can provide a product roadmap to the future for a brand, clarifying where it can go and how it can get there. It is virtually impossible to manage and maximize the value and equity of a brand without a clear, compelling brand strategy, whether explicitly written down or not.

In this chapter, we consider how brands can and should manage their brand strategies. After briefly reviewing the role of branding and brand strategies, we introduce the concept of brand architecture and outline a three-step process by which a firm can design and implement their brand architecture strategy. Throughout our discussion, we introduce key concepts, provide insights and guidelines, and offer illustrative examples. We also suggest areas worthy of future research attention. Keller (2002) and Keller and Lehmann (2006) offer some additional academic perspectives on branding in general and brand architecture in particular.

THE ROLE OF BRANDING AND BRANDING STRATEGIES

In this first section, we describe the role of branding from a consumer and company perspective and how brand strategies can be developed through the concept of brand architecture.

Role of Branding

Branding benefits both consumers and firms (Hoeffler and Keller 2003; Keller 2008).

Role of Brands to Consumers

To consumers, brands provide important functions. Brands identify the source or maker of a product and allow consumers to assign responsibility as to which particular manufacturer, distributor or provider should be held accountable. More importantly, brands can take on special meaning to consumers. Because of past experiences with the product and its marketing program over the years, consumers learn about brands. They find out which brands satisfy their needs and which do not. As a result, brands provide a shorthand device or means of simplification for their product decisions. Brands may become particularly important signals of quality and other characteristics to consumers (e.g. with durable goods) (Erdem 1998). In these ways, brands can reduce the risks in product decisions.

The meaning imbued in brands can be quite profound (Keller 2001). The relationship between a brand and the consumer can be seen as a type of "bond" or "pact." Consumers offer their trust and loyalty with the implicit understanding that the brand will "behave" in certain ways and provide them utility through consistent product performance and appropriate marketing programs and activities. To the extent that consumers realize advantages and benefits from purchasing the brand, and as long as they derive satisfaction from product consumption, they are likely to continue to buy the brand. These benefits may not be purely functional in nature (Holt, Chapter 18 in this volume). Brands can serve as symbolic devices, allowing consumers to project their self-image. Certain brands are associated with being used by certain types of people and thus reflect different values or traits. Consuming such products is a means by which consumers can communicate to others – or even to themselves – the type of person they are or would like to be.

Role of Brands to Firms

Brands take on unique, personal meanings to consumers that facilitate their day-to-day activities and enrich their lives. Brands also provide a number of valuable functions to firms. Fundamentally, they serve an identification purpose to simplify product handling or tracing for the firm. Operationally, brands help to organize inventory and accounting records and so on.

A brand also offers the firm legal protection for unique features or aspects of the product. The brand name can be protected through registered trademarks; manufacturing processes can be protected through patents; and packaging can be protected through copyrights and designs. These intellectual property rights ensure that the firm can safely invest in the brand and reap the benefits of a valuable asset.

Brands can signal a certain level of quality so that satisfied buyers can easily choose the product again. This brand loyalty provides predictability and security of demand for the firm and creates barriers to entry that make it difficult for other firms to enter the market. Although manufacturing processes and product designs may be easily duplicated, lasting impressions in the minds of consumers from years of marketing activity and product experience may not be so easily reproduced (Kumar and Rajan, Chapter 7 in this volume). In this sense, branding can be seen as a powerful means to secure a competitive advantage (Sabnis and Grewal, Chapter 5 in this volume).

In short, to firms, brands represent enormously valuable pieces of legal property, capable of influencing consumer behavior, being bought and sold, and providing the security of sustained future revenues to their owner (Shankar, Chapter 24 in this

---

BOX 17.1   A THREE-STEP MODEL FOR DEVELOPING BRAND ARCHITECTURE

1. Defining brand potential
- What is the brand vision?
- How should the brand be competitively positioned?
- What are the brand boundaries?

2. Identifying extension opportunities
- What products or services will help to achieve that potential?

3. Branding new products and services
- How should products and services be branded so that they achieve their maximum sales and equity potential?

---

volume). For these reasons, large earning multiples continue to be paid for established brands in mergers or acquisitions.

Role of Branding Strategies

Brands are clearly important and must be managed carefully as a valuable corporate asset. An important aspect of that brand management is the branding strategies the firm adopts. Branding strategies can be defined broadly in terms of how the products or services offered by a firm are branded both in terms of literally the brand elements (names, logos, symbols, packaging, signage etc.) involved as well as how those different products or services are given meaning in terms of how they are positioned (Aaker 2004).

Branding strategies are often described in terms of the concept of brand architecture. Formally, brand architecture refers to the number and nature of common or distinctive brand elements applied to the different products sold by the firm. Brand architecture involves defining both brand boundaries and brand relationships across products and services.

A good brand architecture performs two key functions: (1) it boosts brand awareness by communicating similarities and differences between products in a brand family; and (2) it enhances brand image by maximizing the transfer of equity to/from the parent brand. In other words, a good brand architecture improves consumer understanding and increases consumer trial and repeat loyalty for the products and services a company sells.

Three key dimensions of brand architecture are: (1) brand assortment in terms of brand portfolios and the number of distinctive brands a company sells; (2) brand depth in terms of line extensions associated with any one brand in a category that a company sells; and (3) brand breadth in terms of category extensions and the number of different categories associated with any one brand a company sells. We consider these dimensions in the context of a three-step process that can be used to develop a brand architecture strategy, as displayed in Box 17.1. We next outline considerations for each of these three steps.

BRAND ARCHITECTURE DECISIONS

Step 1: Defining Brand Potential

The first step in developing an architecture strategy is defining the brand potential. There are three key considerations in defining the potential of the brand: (1) articulating the brand vision; (2) crafting the brand positioning; and (3) defining the brand boundaries.

Articulating the brand vision

Brand vision is a point of view on the long-term potential of a brand. It is impacted by how well the firm is able to recognize the current equity of the brand, as well as its possible future brand equity. Many brands have latent brand equity that is never realized because of the inability or unwillingness of a firm to consider what the brand could and should become (Keller and Lehmann 2009).

There are numerous examples of brands that have transcended their initial market boundaries to become much more. Consider Crayola, which had a long history as a maker of crayons. After the successful introduction of markers as a brand extension, the firm was subsequently able to introduce a series of other brand extensions that redefined the brand as "colorful arts and crafts for children."

Without a clear understanding of the current equity of a brand, however, it is difficult to understand what the brand could be built on. A good brand vision has both a "foot in the present" and a "foot in the future." Brand vision obviously needs to be aspirational so that the brand has room to grow and improve in the future. Yet, at the same time, the vision cannot be so removed from the current brand reality that it is essentially unobtainable. The trick in developing a brand vision is to strike the right balance between what the brand is and what it could become and to define the right series of steps to get it there.

Fundamentally, brand vision relates to the "higher-order purpose" of the brand based on keen consumer and customer understanding. Anchored in consumer aspirations and brand truths, the vision of a brand transcends its physical product category descriptions and boundaries.

Crafting the brand positioning

A brand positioning puts some specificity into a brand vision. Positioning is the act of designing the company's product or service offering and image to occupy a distinctive place in the minds of the target market (Keller et al. 2002). A good brand positioning helps guide marketing strategy by clarifying the brand's essence, what goals it helps the consumer achieve, and how it does so in a unique way. Everyone in the organization should understand the brand positioning and use it as a context for making decisions.

Positioning requires that similarities and differences between brands be defined and communicated. Specifically, there are four key components to a superior competitive positioning:

1. Competitive frame of reference in terms of the target market and nature of competition
2. Points of difference in terms of brand associations that establish the potential advantages of the brand

3. Points of parity in terms of brand associations that negate any potential deficiencies of the brand
4. Brand mantra in terms of a three–five-word summary of the essence of the brand and key points of difference.

We next elaborate on the theory and practice involved with each of these four components.

Competitive frame of reference The competitive frame of reference identifies who the brand is targeting and which other brands a brand competes with as a result (Czepiel and Kerin, Chapter 4 in this volume). Formally, the competitive frame of reference is defined in terms of two components – the brand target and the nature of competition.

Target market decisions are closely linked to decisions about the nature of competition. Deciding to target a certain type of consumer can define the nature of competition because certain firms have decided to target that segment in the past (or plan to do so in the future), or because consumers in that segment may already look to certain products or brands in their purchase decisions.

A good starting point in defining a competitive frame of reference is to understand consumer behavior and the consideration sets that consumers use in making brand choices. For a brand with explicit growth intentions to enter new markets, a broader or maybe even more aspirational competitive frame may be necessary to reflect possible future competitors.

It is not uncommon for a brand to identify more than one possible frame of reference as the result of broader category competition or the intended future growth of a brand. For example, Starbucks competes with quick-serve restaurants and convenience shops (e.g. McDonald's and Dunkin Doughnuts), supermarket brands for home consumption (e.g. Nescafé and Folger's), other coffee chains (e.g. Caribou Coffee and Tim Horton's) and local cafés all over the world. These very distinct sets of competitors would suggest different points of difference (PODs) and points of parity (POPs) as a result, as developed below.

With multiple frames of reference, there are two main options. Ideally, a robust positioning could be developed that would be effective across multiple frames. If not, then it is necessary to prioritize and choose the most relevant set of competitors to serve as the competitive frame. It is crucial, though, to be careful to try not to be "all things to all people" – that can lead to an undesirable "lowest common denominator" positioning.

Once marketers have fixed the competitive frames of reference by defining the customer target markets and the nature of competition associated with each target, they can define the appropriate PODs and POPs for positioning.

Points of difference Points of difference (PODs) are attributes or benefits consumers strongly associate with a brand, positively evaluate, and believe they could not find to the same extent with a competitive brand. They are key drivers of brand equity that create relevant differentiation. There are three key criteria that determine whether or not a brand association can truly function as a POD:

- *Desirable to consumers*   The brand association must be seen as personally relevant to consumers as well as believable and credible.
- *Deliverable by the company*   The company must have the internal resources and commitment to be able to actually feasibly and profitably create and maintain the brand association in the minds of consumers. Ideally, the brand association would be pre-emptive, defensible and difficult to attack.
- *Differentiating from competitors*   Finally, the brand association must be seen by consumers as distinctive and superior compared to relevant competitors.

Any attribute or benefit associated with a product or service can function as a POD for a brand as long as it is sufficiently desirable, deliverable and differentiating. PODs, as well as POPs, ideally would have rational and emotional components, appealing both to the "head" and the "heart." Regardless of its specific nature, the brand must demonstrate clear superiority on the attribute or benefit, however, for an association to function as a true POD. Consumers must be convinced, for example, that Louis Vuitton has the most stylish handbags, Energizer is the longest-lasting battery, and Fidelity Investments offers the best financial advice and planning.

Points of parity   Points of parity (POPs), on the other hand, are associations that are not necessarily unique to the brand but may in fact be shared with other brands. If, in the eyes of consumers, a brand can "break even" in those areas where the competitors are trying to find an advantage and achieve advantages in other areas, the brand should be in a strong – and perhaps unbeatable – competitive position. In other words, POPs allow PODs to matter. POPs come in three basic forms: category, competitive and correlational.

Category POPs are associations that consumers view as essential to be a legitimate and credible offering in a certain product or service category. In other words, they represent necessary – but not sufficient – conditions for brand choice. Consumers might not consider a rental car agency truly a rental car agency unless it is able to offer a fleet of different types of car, different payment methods and so on. Category POPs may change over time due to technological advances, legal developments or consumer trends, but they are the "greens fees" to play the branding game.

Competitive POPs are associations designed to negate competitors' PODs. For an offering to achieve a POP on a particular attribute or benefit, a sufficient number of consumers just must believe that the brand is "good enough" on that dimension. POPs are not points of equality – there is a zone or range of indifference or tolerance. The brand does not literally have to be seen as equal to competitors, but consumers must feel that the brand does well enough on that particular attribute or benefit. If they do, they may be willing to base their evaluations and decisions on other factors potentially more favorable and valuable to the brand.

Correlational POPs are those areas where the strengths of a brand and its PODs may suggest a weakness. Inverse product relationships in the minds of consumers are pervasive across many categories, that is, "if you are good at one thing, you must *not* be good at something else." For example, if a food or beverage brand emphasizes that it has low calories, consumers may also infer that it must not taste good. The key to Miller Lite's success in launching and establishing the light beer market in North America was its ability to overcome such perceived negative product correlations by convincing consumers that Miller Lite could have both fewer calories *and* great taste.

Brand mantras   To provide further focus as to the intent of the brand positioning and how firms would like consumers to think about the brand, it is often useful to define a brand mantra. A brand mantra is an articulation of the "heart and soul" of the brand. Brand mantras are short, three-to-five-word phrases that capture the irrefutable essence or spirit of the brand positioning. Their purpose is to ensure that all employees within the organization and all external marketing partners understand what the brand most fundamentally represents so that they can adjust their actions accordingly. In effect, brand mantras are designed to create a mental filter to screen out brand-inappropriate marketing activities or actions of any type that may have a negative bearing on customers' impressions of a brand.

What makes for a good brand mantra? Brand mantras must clearly delineate what the brand is supposed to represent and therefore, at least implicitly, what it is not. Disney's brand mantra of "Fun Family Entertainment" has ensured that the brand did not stray from their children fantasy roots. When they wanted to venture into more adult fare in their films, they did so with their Touchstone Pictures.

Brand mantras are designed with internal purposes in mind. A brand slogan is an external translation that attempt to creatively engage consumers. So although Nike's internal mantra was "Authentic Athletic Performance," its external slogan was "Just Do It." Here are the three key criteria for a brand mantra.

- *Communicate*   A good brand mantra should clarify what is unique about the brand. It may also need to define the category (or categories) of business for the brand and set the brand boundaries.
- *Simplify*   An effective brand mantra should be memorable. As a result, it should be short, crisp and vivid in meaning.
- *Inspire*   The brand mantra should also stake out ground that is personally meaningful and relevant to as many consumers and employees as possible.

Brand mantras typically are designed to capture the brand's PODs and what is unique about the brand. McDonald's brand philosophy of "Food, Folks, and Fun" captures their brand essence and core brand promise. Other aspects of the brand positioning – especially the brand's POPs – may also be important, however, and may need to be reinforced in other ways.

Defining the brand boundaries
Defining brand boundaries involves deciding, based on the brand vision and positioning, the products or services the brand should offer, the benefits it should supply and the needs it should satisfy. Some of the world's strongest brands have been stretched across multiple categories, for example GE, Virgin and Apple. Although many product categories may seem to be good candidates for extension for a brand, as will be developed in greater detail below, marketers would be wise to heed the "Spandex Rule" espoused by Scott Bedbury, former VP-Advertising for Nike and VP-Marketing for Starbucks: "Just Because You Can . . . Doesn't Mean You Should!"

A "broad" brand is one with an abstract positioning that is able to support a higher-order promise. It often has a transferable POD due to a widely relevant benefit supported by multiple reasons to believe or supporting attributes. For example, Nivea's core brand associations are "gentle," "mild," "caring" and "protective," which are relevant in many categories. Through skillful product development and marketing, the Nivea brand has been successfully expanded across a wide variety of skin care and personal care product categories.

Nevertheless, all brands have boundaries. Nivea would find it very difficult to introduce a car, tennis racquet or lawnmower. Japanese car makers Honda, Nissan and Toyota chose to introduce their luxury brands in North America under new brand names, Acura, Infiniti and Lexus respectively. Even for all its growth, Nike chose to purchase Cole Haan to sell into the dressier, more formal shoe market. The brand portfolio is the set of all brands and brand lines a particular firm offers for sale in a particular category or market segment. Multiple brands are employed in a category to improve market coverage by targeting different market segments.

Companies have to be careful to not overbrand, however, and attempt to support too many brands. The trend in recent years by many top branding companies is to focus on fewer, stronger brands. The basic principle in designing a brand portfolio is to maximize market coverage so that no potential customers are ignored, but to minimize brand overlap so that brands are not competing for customer approval. Each brand should be clearly differentiated and appealing to a sizable enough marketing segment to justify its marketing and production costs.

In some special cases, brands can also play a specific role as part of a portfolio. Flanker or fighter brands are positioned with respect to competitors' brands so that more important (and more profitable) flagship brands can retain their desired positioning (Ritson 2009). Cash cow brands may be kept around despite dwindling sales because they manage to maintain their profitability with virtually no marketing support. The role of a relatively low-priced entry in the brand portfolio may be to attract customers to the brand franchise. Retailers like to feature these "traffic builders" because they are able to "trade up" customers to a higher-priced brand. Finally, the role of a relatively high-priced entry in a brand line may be to add prestige and credibility to the entire portfolio.

Step 2: Identifying Brand Extension Opportunities

Determining the brand vision, positioning and boundaries in Step 1 helps to define the brand potential and provides a clear sense of direction for the brand. Step 2 is to identify new products and services to achieve that potential through a well-designed and implemented brand extension strategy. A brand extension is a new product introduced under an existing brand name. Extensions can be distinguished between line extensions, new product introductions within existing categories, and category extensions, new product introductions outside existing categories.

Launching a brand extension is harder than it might seem. Given that the vast majority of new products are extensions and the vast majority of new products fail, the clear implication is that too many brand extensions fail. Some of the world's most successful brands have introduced unsuccessful brand extensions, for example Campbell's tomato sauce, Bic perfumes, Levi's Tailored Classic suits and Coke C2 cola, to name just a few.

Where did these companies go wrong? Although many factors may come into play, one common problem with failed extensions is that marketers mistakenly focus on one or perhaps a few brand associations as a potential basis of extension fit and ignore other, possibly more important, brand associations in the process. All of consumers' brand knowledge structures must be taken into account in judging the viability of an extension. Bic perfumes failed because whether or not the brand extension had a sufficiently compelling POD (small and disposable) was largely irrelevant given that it badly lacked a key POP (image).

Extensions fail when they do not create sufficient relevance and differentiation in their new product or service categories. An increasingly competitive marketplace will be even more unforgiving to poorly positioned and marketed extensions in the years to come. To increase the likelihood of success, marketers must be rigorous and disciplined in their analysis and development of brand extensions.

Extension guidelines

Much academic research has focused on brand extensions (see Völckner and Sattler 2006 for a review). Box 17.2 highlights some key findings that have emerged from those studies. Based on this and other research, the following checklist highlights six key considerations for extension success.

- *Does the parent brand have strong equity?* If the parent brand does not have sufficiently strong, favorable and unique PODs and POPs, then those should be addressed first.
- *Is there a strong basis of fit?* There are many bases of fit – product similarity, common users or usage situations, consistent imagery and so on. Consumers must feel the extension is logical in some way and makes sense.
- *Will the extension have necessary POPs and PODs?* The farther removed the extension category is from existing parent brand categories, the more likely it is that PODs and POPs will not be seen as sufficiently strong, favorable or unique enough to function properly.
- *How can marketing programs enhance extension equity?* One common mistake with extensions is to fail to devise sufficiently effective, sustained marketing programs. Although brand extensions are designed to leverage parent brand equity, supporting marketing activities are still necessary to establish the right image and positioning in the extension category. Extensions require adequate investment.
- *What implications will the extension have for parent brand equity and profitability?* The closer the brand is seen to "fit" with the parent brand, the more the parent brand equity affects perceptions of extensions and vice versa. Dilution of parent brand equity is typically limited only to when the extension has fundamental performance problems and the extension category is seen as highly related to the parent brand category.
- *How should feedback effects best be managed?* As will be shown below, extension feedback effects can be managed, in part, by the particular branding strategy that is adopted.

BOX 17.2   BRAND EXTENSION GUIDELINES BASED ON ACADEMIC RESEARCH

1. Successful brand extensions occur when the parent brand is seen as having favorable associations and there is a perception of fit between the parent brand and the extension product.
2. There are many bases of fit: product-related attributes and benefits as well as non-product-related attributes and benefits related to common usage situations or user types.
3. Depending on consumer knowledge of the product categories, perceptions of fit may be based on technical or manufacturing commonalities or more surface considerations such as necessary or situational complementarity.
4. High-quality brands stretch farther than average-quality brands, although both types of brands have boundaries.
5. A brand that is seen as prototypical of a product category can be difficult to extend outside the category.
6. Concrete attribute associations tend to be more difficult to extend than abstract benefit associations.
7. Consumers may transfer associations that are positive in the original product class but become negative in the extension context.
8. Consumers may infer negative associations about an extension, perhaps even based on other inferred positive associations.
9. It can be difficult to extend into a product class that is seen as easy to make.
10. A successful extension can not only contribute to the parent brand image but also enable a brand to be extended even farther.
11. An unsuccessful extension hurts the parent brand only when there is a strong basis of fit between the two.
12. An unsuccessful extension does not prevent a firm from backtracking and introducing a more similar extension.

Source: Keller (2008).

Based on this research and other inputs, Box 17.3 contains a scorecard that identifies a set of possible criteria for evaluating a proposed brand extension. The specifications in this scorecard are intended to offer a starting point; particular items or the weights applied to these items can be adjusted based on the specific marketing context or marketer's personal point of view or preferences. The key point is that, by adopting some type of formal model or scorecard, systematic thinking can be applied to judge the merits of a proposed extension to increase its likelihood of success.

Extension dynamics

It is important to plan the optimal sequence of new product introductions to achieve brand potential. Marketers grow brands through "little steps." The key is to understand

---

BOX 17.3   BRAND EXTENDIBILITY SCORECARD

Allocate points according to how well the new product concept rates on the specific dimensions in the following areas:

Consumer perspectives: desirability
10 pts _____ Product category appeal (size, growth potential)
10 pts _____ Equity transfer (perceived brand fit)
 5 pts _____ Perceived consumer target fit

Company perspectives: deliverability
10 pts _____ Asset leverage (product technology, organizational skills, marketing effectiveness via channels and communications)
10 pts _____ Profit potential
 5 pts _____ Launch feasibility

Competitive perspectives: differentiability
10 pts _____ Comparative appeal (many advantages; few disadvantages)
10 pts _____ Competitive response (likelihood; immunity or invulnerability from)
 5 pts _____ Legal/regulatory/institutional barriers

Brand perspectives: equity feedback
10 pts _____ Strengthens parent brand equity
10 pts _____ Facilitates additional brand extension opportunities
 5 pts _____ Improves asset base

TOTAL _____ pts

---

equity implications of each extension in terms of POPs and PODs. By adhering to the brand promise and growing the brand carefully through "little steps," brands can cover a lot of ground. For example, through a well-planned and -executed series of product introductions over a 25-year period, Nike evolved from a company selling mostly running, tennis and basketball shoes to 12–29-year-old males in North America in the mid-1980s to a company now selling athletic shoes, clothing and equipment across a range of sports to men and women of all ages in virtually all countries.

Step 3: Branding New Products and Services

The final step in developing the brand architecture is to decide on the specific brand elements to use for any particular new product or service. New products and services must be branded so as to maximize the brand's overall clarity and understanding to consumers and customers. What names, looks and other branding elements will be applied to new products?

It is useful to think of a brand family in terms of a brand hierarchy. Figure 17.1

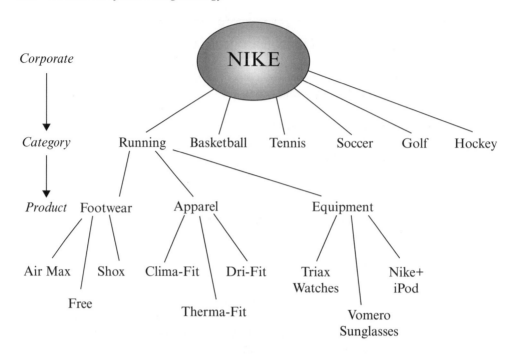

Figure 17.1   Partial depiction of a sample Nike brand hierarchy

displays a partial depiction of a sample Nike brand hierarchy. As the figure shows, a brand hierarchy can involve multiple levels. Box 17.4 summarizes a set of principles concerning how to manage a brand hierarchy. Although all are important, perhaps the most critical ones relate to relevance and differentiation: put equity at the highest level of the hierarchy as possible but ensure that brands at lower levels are well differentiated.

Role of sub-brands
Sub-brands are an extremely popular form of brand extension where a new product is given both the parent brand name and a new name (e.g. Apple iPad, Ford Fusion and American Express Blue card). Sub-brands play an important brand architecture role by signaling to consumers to expect similarities and differences in a new product. A good sub-branding strategy can facilitate access to associations and attitudes to the company or family brand as a whole, while also allowing for the creation of new brand beliefs to position the extension in the new category.

Sub-branding offers many other benefits. It can also help to protect or shield the parent brand from any potentially negative feedback that might be associated with an extension (Sood and Keller 2012). In a carefully researched study, the sudden acceleration problems experienced by the Audi 5000 a number of years ago were found to significantly hurt the sales of its sibling Audi 4000, but had a much less pronounced effect on sales of the Audi Quattro in part because of its more distinctive sub-branding (Sullivan 1998).

To realize these benefits, however, sub-branding typically requires significant investments and disciplined and consistent marketing to establish the proper brand meanings

---

BOX 17.4   GUIDELINES FOR BRAND HIERARCHY DECISIONS

1. **Decide on the number of levels**
   - *Principle of simplicity*   Employ as few levels as possible.
   - *Principle of clarity*   Logic and relationship of all brand elements employed must be obvious and transparent.

2. **Decide on the levels of awareness and types of associations to be created at each level**
   - *Principle of relevance*   Create abstract associations that are relevant across as many individual items as possible.
   - *Principle of differentiation*   Differentiate individual items and brands.

3. **Decide on which products to be introduced**
   - *Principle of growth*   Investments in market penetration or expansion versus product development should be made according to ROI opportunities.
   - *Principle of survival*   Brand extensions must achieve brand equity in their categories.
   - *Principle of synergy*   Brand extensions should enhance the equity of the parent brand.

4. **Decide on how to link brands from different levels for a product**
   - *Principle of prominence*   The relative prominence of brand elements affects perceptions of product distance and the type of image created for new products.

5. **Decide on how to link a brand across products**
   - *Principle of commonality*   The more common elements shared by products, the stronger the linkages.

Source: Keller (2008).

---

with consumers. In the absence of such financial commitments, marketers may be well advised to adopt the simplest brand hierarchy possible, for example using the company or family brand name with product descriptors. Sub-branding should only be introduced when there is a distinctive, complementary benefit; otherwise, marketers should just use a product descriptor to designate the new product or service.

Developing the sub-brands
Marketers can employ a whole host of brand elements as part of a sub-brand. Nomenclature, product form, shape, graphics, color and versioning are all some of the means to help develop the sub-brand. By skillfully combining new brand elements

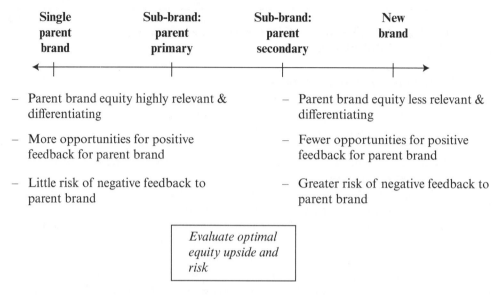

Single parent brand	Sub-brand: parent primary	Sub-brand: parent secondary	New brand

– Parent brand equity highly relevant & differentiating

– More opportunities for positive feedback for parent brand

– Little risk of negative feedback to parent brand

– Parent brand equity less relevant & differentiating

– Fewer opportunities for positive feedback for parent brand

– Greater risk of negative feedback to parent brand

Evaluate optimal equity upside and risk

Figure 17.2   Branding strategy screen

with existing parent brand elements, sub-branding can be an effective way to signal the intended similarity or fit of a new extension with its parent brand.

According to the principle of prominence, the more prominent a brand element, the more emphasis it will receive from consumers in forming their brand opinions. Consumers are very literal. For example, putting the parent brand name before a new, individual name – as compared to putting the parent brand second – makes a sub-brand extension more like the parent brand. In other words, Marriott's Courtyard would be seen as much more of a Marriott hotel than Courtyard by Marriott by virtue of having the corporate name first.

Marketers can use the branding strategy screen displayed in Figure 17.2 to "dial up" or "dial down" different brand elements. If a potential new product or service is strongly related to the parent brand so that there is a high likelihood of parent brand equity carryover and if there is little equity risk, a product descriptor or parent-brand-first sub-brand may make sense. On the other hand, if a potential new product or service is more removed from the parent brand so that there is a lower likelihood of parent brand equity carryover or if there is higher equity risk, then a parent-brand-second sub-brand or even a new brand may be more appropriate. In these latter cases, the parent brand may be just used as an endorser, as with General Mills and their "Big G" logo, which links their different cereal brands such as Cheerios, Wheaties and Lucky Charms.

In creating sub-brands, it is important to recognize what consumers know about and want from the brand and appreciate how they will actually use the sub-brand. Although using multiple sub-brands as part of a detailed brand family may seem to provide more descriptive details, it can easily backfire. For example, when one-time technology hotshot Silicon Graphics named their new 3D work station "Indigo^2 Solid Impact," their customers chose to simplify the name by calling it simply "Solid." Creating equity for a

---

BOX 17.5   SUMMARY BRAND ARCHITECTURE GUIDELINES

1. Must adopt strong customer focus: recognize what they know and want; appreciate how they will behave
2. Must avoid overbranding: fewer brands are better than more brands
3. Must establish rules and conventions
4. Must be disciplined: consistency is key, but flexibility may be needed as pure models are rare
5. Must create broad robust brand platforms: strong umbrella family brands are highly desirable
6. Maximize synergies and equity flow
7. Must employ sub-brands as means of complementing and strengthening brands: sub-brands must be consistent with parent brand but have clear differentiation
8. Vertical extensions are difficult and are only possible with a sub-brand and strong point of differentiation
9. Must selectively extend brands to establish new equity and enhance brand equity: any offering must live up to the brand promise and reinforce brand mantra
10. In updating a brand hierarchy, must preserve as much brand equity as possible

---

low-level brand modifier (Solid) would certainly not be called good branding practice. Brand equity ideally resides at the highest level of the branding hierarchy possible where it can benefit more products and services.

DISCUSSION

Summary and Implications

The focus on creating fewer, stronger brands has put pressure on marketers to assemble the right brand architectures to ensure that brands reach their marketplace potential. A good brand architecture defines brand "boundaries" – what products or services the brand could represent, what benefits it could supply, and what needs it could satisfy. It provides "guardrails" as to appropriate – and inappropriate – line and category exten-sions. It clarifies the meaning and promise of the brand to consumers and helps consum-ers choose the right version of the product or service for themselves.

Three key steps in developing a good brand architecture are: (1) assessing brand potential; (2) identifying product and service extension opportunities to achieve brand potential; and (3) defining a brand extension roadmap. A structured approach must be adopted that incorporates academic and industry guidelines for understand-ing brand potential, launching brand extensions, and naming new products to create the optimal brand stretch. Marketers must be disciplined, but creative in their brand architecture strategies – a classic blend of "art and science." Box 17.5 summarizes a set of brand architecture guidelines that have emerged from this analysis.

Future Research Opportunities and Challenges

As one of the most important topics in branding and brand management, it is not surprising that brand architecture has many potentially promising future research directions. Although extensively reviewing those areas is beyond the scope of this chapter, in this final section we suggest one key issue for each of the three steps involved in developing a good brand architecture.

In terms of assessing brand potential, the first step in developing a good brand architecture, one of the fascinating questions is how consumers choose to give "permission" to brands to expand into new products or services. The rules of the branding game have undoubtedly evolved as consumers have experienced, either directly or indirectly, a wide variety of branding strategies in recent years. Given the aggressive expansion strategies adopted by many brands, consumers have had to constantly evaluate the boundaries of brands. What is the process by which that calculation is made and what factors influence it?

Without question, the research area that has already received the most academic attention is brand extensions, the second step in developing a good brand architecture. Even there, some key issues remain. Perhaps one of the more critical areas deserving more study is the dynamics of brand extensions and how one extension impacts the acceptance of subsequent extensions. The vast majority of brand extension research adopts a static view of factors affecting brand extension acceptance at one point in time. A better conceptual and methodological understanding of the dynamics of extensions will undoubtedly help marketers better map the potential growth of their brands.

Finally, the third step in developing a brand strategy, the actual branding involved, would benefit from a comprehensive examination of the myriad of design factors that can be employed to create similarities and differences across products and services. Much lay wisdom exists about how consumers interpret and evaluate branding strategies related to product versioning, the use of prepositions such as "by," "with," "from" and so on. A well-thought-out research program that explores how words, numbers, colors and other brand design elements can be used to convey the right information to consumers about brand extensions would be enormously helpful.

Two broad themes cut across these three research questions. One is the need, as always, to infuse a deeper, richer understanding of consumer behavior into branding and brand architecture in particular. A more complete picture of how consumers interpret and judge various branding decision variables will go a long way towards developing better brand management guidelines. The second is the critical importance of adopting a more dynamic perspective in the study of brand architecture. Brands never stay still and branding academics must be sure to adopt concepts, theories and methodological tools reflecting that reality.

REFERENCES

Aaker, David A. (1991), *Managing Brand Equity*, New York: Free Press.

Aaker, David A. (1996), *Building Strong Brands*, New York: Free Press.

Aaker, David A. (2004), *Brand Portfolio Strategy: Creating Relevance, Differentiation, Energy, Leverage, and Clarity*, New York: Free Press.

Aaker, David A. and Erich Joachimsthaler (2000), *Brand Leadership*, New York: Free Press.

Erdem, Tulin (1998), "Brand equity as a signaling phenomenon," *Journal of Consumer Psychology*, **7** (2), 131–57.

Hoeffler, Steve and Kevin Lane Keller (2003), "The marketing advantages of strong brands," *Journal of Brand Management*, **10** (6), 421–45.

Kapferer, Jean-Noel (2008), *The New Strategic Brand Management*, 4th edn, London: Kogan Page.

Keller, Kevin Lane (2001), "Building customer-based brand equity: a blueprint for creating strong brands," *Marketing Management*, July/August, 15–19.

Keller, Kevin Lane (2002), "Branding and brand equity," in Bart Weitz and Robin Wensley (eds), *Handbook of Marketing*, London: Sage Publications, pp. 151–78.

Keller, Kevin Lane (2008), *Strategic Brand Management: Building, Measuring, and Managing Brand Equity*, 3rd edn, Upper Saddle River, NJ: Prentice-Hall.

Keller, Kevin Lane and Don Lehmann (2006), "Brands and branding: research findings and future priorities," *Marketing Science*, **25** (November–December), 740–59.

Keller, Kevin Lane and Don Lehmann (2009), "Assessing brand potential," in special issue, "Brand Value and Valuation," of *Journal of Brand Management*, special issue editors Randall Raggio and Robert P. Leone, **17** (1), 6–7.

Keller, Kevin Lane, Brian Sternthal and Alice Tybout (2002), "Three questions you need to ask about your brand," *Harvard Business Review*, **80** (9), 80–89.

Levy, Sydney J. (1999), *Brands, Consumers, Symbols, and Research: Sydney J. Levy on Marketing*, Thousand Oaks, CA: Sage Publications.

Ritson, Mark (2009), "Should you launch a fighter brand?," *Harvard Business Review*, October, 87–94.

Sood, Sanjay and Kevin Lane Keller (2012), "The effects of product experience and branding strategies on parent brand evaluations and brand equity dilution," *Journal of Marketing Research*, in press.

Sullivan, Mary W. (1998), "How brand names affect the demand for twin automobiles," *Journal of Marketing Research*, **35** (May), 154–65.

Völckner, Franziska and Henrik Sattler (2006), "Drivers of brand extension success," *Journal of Marketing*, **70** (April), 1–17.

18 Cultural brand strategy
Douglas B. Holt

Cultural brand strategy is – as the term implies – a distinctive approach to strategy, informed by theories of culture, society and politics. The aim of this approach is to propel branding as a distinctive and value-added framework for managing the "big picture" marketplace challenges that firms face, particularly with respect to innovation. The most influential work in this area has been dominated by faculty in strategy and innovation for several decades now. In marketing, brand strategy has generally focused on the tactical issues of day-to-day stewardship of ongoing businesses, and on providing direction for leveraging the equities of ongoing businesses (e.g. line-extension strategies) (see Keller, Chapter 17 in this volume for a detailed review of this approach). I shall argue that cultural branding adds a crucial strategic perspective for the most important marketplace goals: developing new businesses and resurrecting moribund ones. In this chapter, I first define this gap in the innovation and strategy literature, and then I overview how cultural brand strategy addresses this gap, using Jack Daniel's as a case to demonstrate how the theory works.

BETTER-MOUSETRAPS INNOVATION

Theories of innovation in the strategy literature have long been dominated by the worldview of engineers and economists – build a better mousetrap and the world will take notice. This worldview leaves no room for branding. It assumes that the superior value of the product or service "speaks" for itself. And then branding proceeds in the straightforward manner often noted by economists, as the process of accumulating a reputation over time. This functional point of view certainly has merit. But, because it is the only way that academics have approached innovation, the better-mousetraps approach has had the effect of eclipsing a very different innovation worldview – champion a better ideology and the world will take notice as well. This is what I call "cultural innovation", the point of departure for cultural brand strategy (Holt and Cameron 2010).

Cultural innovation has been ignored by the strategy and innovation literature, despite its pivotal role in launching and reinvigorating any number of billion-dollar businesses. The list of cultural innovations that have launched or reinvigorated businesses worth billions goes on and on: Marlboro, Coca-Cola, Levi's, Diesel, Dove, Axe/Lynx, American Express, American Apparel, The Body Shop, Target, Virgin, Pepsi-Cola, Polo, Harley-Davidson, Seventh Generation, Method, Burt's Bees, Brita, Whole Foods, Patagonia, Jack Daniel's, Mountain Dew, Absolut, Starbucks, Volkswagen. Just as important, cultural innovation often serves to turbo-charge better-mousetraps innovation: witness Apple, Google, MINI, Red Bull, JetBlue and Wikipedia.

When these enterprises advanced a more compelling ideology – leapfrogging the staid cultural orthodoxies of their categories – consumers beat a path to their doors. These businesses have been every bit as innovative as the technological and mix-and-match businesses celebrated by innovation experts. But what was radical about them was what the product stands for – its ideology, which, when staged through myth and cultural codes, becomes a distinctive cultural expression.

Cultural brand strategy is an approach to strategy that directs organizations how to build brands with innovative ideologies. I developed this theory with my collaborators over a decade of academic research, conducting detailed comparative-historical analyses of more than 30 important cultural innovations (Holt 2003, 2004, 2006a, 2006b; Holt and Cameron 2010). So this is necessarily an egocentric chapter. In particular, this chapter draws extensively from my book *Cultural Strategy: How Innovative Ideologies Build Breakthrough Brands*, written with Douglas Cameron. Our framework draws extensively from the sociocultural theoretical foundations (e.g. Holt 2002; Thompson 2004; Thompson and Arsel 2004) established in the subdiscipline of consumer culture theory (Arnould and Thompson 2005). As space requirements do not allow a discussion of these theoretical linkages, I encourage the interested reader to explore them on his or her own.

RETHINKING BLUE OCEANS

Crafting "the next big brand" – the innovative idea that resonates powerfully with con-sumers and takes off to establish a profitable new business – is the holy grail of managers and entrepreneurs alike. Strategy experts have built models to identify and exploit such opportunities for decades. In the early 1990s, Gary Hamel and C.K. Prahalad (1994) offered a pioneering call to arms: to "create the markets of tomorrow," they urged managers to focus on industry foresight and strategic intent. To avoid getting bogged down in an established market's internecine tactical battles, they encouraged managers to stake out new market space – what they famously termed "white space" – in order to create and dominate emerging opportunities. More than a decade later, W. Chan Kim and Renée Mauborgne (2005) introduced a new metaphor, "blue ocean", to dramatize a very similar idea. They characterize existing markets as dog-eat-dog fights to outdo competitors on a conventional set of benefits. Incumbents rely on incremental changes in product and tactical marketing to fight over thin margins. This is "a red ocean". In order to develop future-leading businesses, companies must reject the conventions of the category to craft "value innovations" that have no direct competition – blue oceans. These marching orders have inspired many managers and entrepreneurs. But what kinds of future opportunities should we be looking for? And how does one actually go about spotting these opportunities and designing new concepts that will take advantage of the blue oceans? Innovation experts have offered us two paths.

Technological Innovation

For most innovation experts, future opportunities mean one thing – the commercializa-tion of new technologies. Technology-driven innovations are the stars of business. From historic innovations such as the light bulb, the telephone, the television, the Model T and the personal computer to recent stars like the iPod, Amazon.com, Blackberry, Viagra and Facebook, the commercialization of breakthrough technologies has clearly had a huge impact on business and society. In *The Innovator's Dilemma* and subsequent books, Clayton Christensen (2003; Christensen and Raynor 2004) argues that new technologies allow companies to design "disruptive innovations" that transform their categories. Disruptive innovations are products and services that trump the value delivered by existing category offerings because they are cheaper, more useful, more reliable or more convenient. Disruptive innovations dramatically alter the conventional value proposition of an existing category, often attracting new or underserved customers, or even inventing a new category.

Mix-and-Match Innovation

In recent years, a "mix-and-match" approach to innovation has become influential. In the view of Kim and Mauborgne, blue oceans are untapped opportunities that can be exploited through unique value combinations that have not yet been formulated. In order for companies to offer customers a significantly better value proposition, they must methodically break the rules of their existing category: subtracting and enhancing conventional benefits, as well as importing new ones from other categories. For instance, in *Blue Ocean Strategy*'s lead example, the authors describe how Cirque du Soleil created a blue ocean by borrowing from theater and Broadway musicals to reinvent the circus. Andrew Hargadon's (2003) *How Breakthroughs Happen* and *The Medici Effect* by Frans Johansson (2004) both advocate a similar idea – the unexpected mixing and matching of existing features and technologies across different categories, leading to a unique constellation of benefits for the consumer.

Despite the considerable differences between these two models, they rely upon a common notion of what constitutes an innovation. Innovation boils down to providing a step change in the value proposition. Innovations beat out existing competition on the tangible benefits that count in the category: medical instruments that save more lives, cars that run longer with higher miles per gallon and less carbon emissions, cellphones that have more applications, hard drives that hold more data and are cheaper and smaller and more reliable. In other words, these two better-mousetraps innovation models are based upon the worldview of the economist and the engineer – a world in which it is only the material properties of what we buy that is important. Blue oceans exist where there is latent demand for products and services with truly novel whiz-bang features.

CULTURAL INNOVATION

Curiously, this is not how consumers see it. Consumers – the ultimate arbiters of market innovation efforts – often find offerings to be innovative even though they seem quite pedestrian from a product-design standpoint. It turns out that blockbuster new businesses do not necessarily require radically new features that fundamentally alter the value proposition.

Consider beer. From a better-mousetraps perspective, the American beer market has long been a mature category – a notoriously red ocean that resists innovation. Many product innovation efforts have been tried, and the vast majority have failed despite their seeming combinatorial creativity. Brewers have tried to follow blue ocean strategy for many years. Combining concepts across categories, they have launched beer + energy drinks (Sparks, Be), beer + tequila (Tequiza), beer + soft drinks (Zima) and so on. All of these supposed innovations were failures in the mass market.

Now let us look at the beer category from an ideological viewpoint. While the product – the beer itself – has seen only minor changes over the past 30 years, the category has been very dynamic in terms of the cultural expressions that consumers value. Incumbents have been pushed aside by new entrants with better ideology. In the popular price tier, Budweiser took off in the 1980s with branding that showcased men working cheerfully and industriously in artisanal trades, men whom Budweiser beer saluted with a baritone-voiced announcer proclaiming "This Bud's for you!" The results were startling. The beer brand quickly became the go-to choice for working-class American men. By the middle of the decade, Budweiser was unchallenged as the most desirable beer in the country.

By the early 1990s Bud's ideology had lost resonance and the business sank, to be replaced by its stablemate. Bud Light took off in the 1990s to become by far the dominant American beer brand, speeding by the brand that had pioneered light beer as a product innovation, Miller Lite. Bud Light tastes little different from Miller Lite. Rather what was different was a decade's worth of silly Peter Pan stories of men who engage in all sorts of juvenile high jinks, which conjured up a new kind of rebellious masculinity for adult men.

At the same time, Corona became the leading import brand, rocketing ahead of the long-dominant Heineken, by offering a new way of thinking about how to relax with a beer – escaping the American white-collar sweatshop to do absolutely nothing on a Mexican beach. These beers were me-too product offerings, not original at all as mouse-traps. But, as brands, they offered very innovative cultural expressions that resonated perfectly with the ideological needs of their target.

Or consider soft drinks – a category that would seem to be one of the most masochistic red oceans around. The two leading soft-drinks marketers in the world, PepsiCo and The Coca-Cola Company, have invested hundreds of millions to innovate their way out of this mature category. Both companies have aggressively pursued mix-and-match concepts to create new value propositions. The Coca-Cola Company has placed big bets on Coke Blak (coca-cola + coffee) and Enviga (a "calorie-burning" green tea). Both of these ambitious efforts – supposedly targeting distinctive consumer "need states" – have failed to break through.

Likewise, many drinks entrepreneurs have tried their hand at mix-and-match strategies, and also with little evidence of success. A basic problem with undertaking blue-ocean-styled product innovation in mature categories is that it forces the innovator to pursue ever smaller niches – aimed at ever narrower "need states" – to carve out a truly new offering. For example, recently some British entrepreneurs got their food engineers to concoct Alibi – billed as "the world's first pretox drink" – to serve a very focused niche of young partiers who might be interested in downing a prophylactic drink to prepare them for a weekend binge. A blue puddle does not an ocean make.

While the food scientists were struggling to make oddball mix-and-match drinks combinations, cultural entrepreneurs were playing an entirely different game. They pursued radical innovations in culture, not product. Consider Innocent Drinks in the UK. The market for alternative natural fruit smoothies had long been established in the USA, pioneered by Odwalla (est. 1980) and Fresh Samantha (est. 1992). The big UK grocers such as Marks & Spencer, Sainsbury's and Tesco imported the concept and developed their own versions. Innocent grabbed hold of this well-established mousetrap and added a heavy dose of leading-edge ideology that was beginning to resonate widely amongst British middle-class consumers. Innocent asserted through its package design – featuring a childlike anthropomorphized apple sporting a halo, and a stripped-down transparent listing of ingredients such as "ingredients = 3 apples + 1 banana + 16 raspberries + 43 blueberries" – that their smoothies were the antithesis of the scientific–industrial foods that big corporations marketed. Innocent easily won over consumers worried about health issues by making a cultural assertion – championing the pre-industrial purity of "only fruit" against drinks full of preservatives and synthetic ingredients. Further, Innocent turned the personal act of drinking a smoothie into a broad environmental statement through a diverse range of provocative guerrilla communications efforts, all of which suggested that Innocent was an anti-corporate green company wishing to transform the drinks marketplace toward sustainability. The Coca-Cola Company, which had paid $180 million to buy out the ideologically innovative Odwalla in 2001, followed suit by paying $50 million for about 15 percent of Innocent in 2009 – a $333 million valuation. Failing at its better-mousetraps innovation strategy, the company has had no choice but to acquire ideologically innovative brands at very steep prices.

PRINCIPLES OF CULTURAL BRAND STRATEGY

To understand how cultural brand strategy can drive innovation, one must conceptualize key strategy constructs in a new way: markets, competition, opportunities and innovation itself get turned upside down. A cultural innovation is a brand that delivers an innovative cultural expression. Some of the most powerful and valued brands in the world have become so by offering an innovative cultural expression. So, to develop a strategic model for cultural innovation, one needs first to conceptualize the central role of cultural expressions in creating customer value. And then one needs to understand how particular cultural expressions target a new kind of blue ocean – what we call ideological opportunities – to leapfrog competitors pursuing more conventional product-innovation and marketing strategies. Figure 18.1 shows the resulting conceptual framework. I shall use the spectacular rise of Jack Daniel's Tennessee Whiskey from a tiny regional distillery to one of the top 100 most valuable brands in the world as an example.

CULTURAL EXPRESSIONS AND INNOVATION

Throughout history, people have valued the "right" cultural expressions because they play such an important role in organizing their lives within societies. Cultural expressions serve as compass points, organizing how we understand the world and our place in it, what is meaningful, what is moral, what is human, what is inhuman, what we should strive for, and what we should despise. And cultural expressions serve as linchpins of identity: they are the foundational materials for belonging, recognition and status. Cultural expressions permeate society, providing us with the building blocks with which

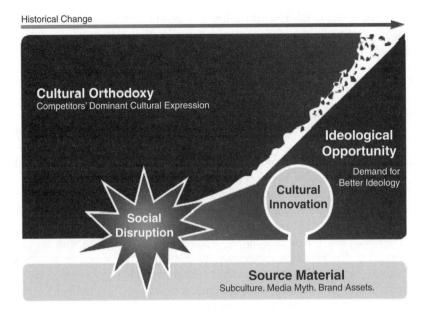

Figure 18.1   Conceptual framework

we construct meaningful lives. They give guidance on all of the key social, political and existential constructs: from the nation, social class, gender, race, sexuality and ethnicity, to constructs like beauty, health, religion, nature, compassion, generosity, ethics, the body, work, competition, the market and success.

In modern society, traditional sources of cultural expression – religion, the state, the arts, education and other social institutions – have been superseded in large measure by the mass media and commerce. Since the beginning of the twentieth century, companies in the West have competed to monetize this rich source of economic value. And brands have become the prime commercial vehicles for marketing cultural expression. Hence markets for cultural expression are, by definition, much broader than typical product markets. Rather than view brands as located within market "spaces," instead we need to understand that all brands are embedded in these broader cultural marketplaces. Fortunately for strategists, only a small subset of these constructs will be "in play" for any given brand. Brands can only engage topics that are credible from the consumers' viewpoint, which usually depends on how the product, benefits, uses and its consumers are represented in the mass media.

CULTURAL EXPRESSIONS CONSIST OF IDEOLOGY, MYTH AND CULTURAL CODES

Cultural expressions consist of an ideology, which is "brought to life" with the right myth and cultural codes, so we need to examine how innovation works across these three core components. Consider Jack Daniel's Tennessee Whiskey. Whiskeys have both long competed to champion the best cultural expression of one particularly important construct – masculinity. Jack Daniel's offered an innovative cultural expression of masculinity, by which I mean that the brand significantly surpassed its competitors in terms of ideology, myth and cultural codes.

Ideology

An ideology is a point of view on one of these important cultural constructs, which has become widely shared and taken for granted, naturalized by a segment of society as a "truth." Ideologies profoundly shape our everyday evaluations and actions. We all hold dear many ideologies, which allow us to function consistently, coherently and effectively in our social lives. Ideologies also serve as the foundation of consumer markets. Strong brands sustain ideologies – a particular point of view on a cultural construct that is central to the product. Jack Daniel's advocated the revival of frontier masculinity, a particular point of view that incited American men to embrace the country's historic tough plain-spoken self-reliant masculinity before it became overrun with soft, sedentary organization men. Yet ideologies are concepts, not expressions; and an ideology can be expressed in any number of ways. Consumers experience ideology through layers of cultural expression, not as a declarative intellectual proposition. So ideologies enter culture when they are conveyed via myth and cultural codes.

Myth

Myths are instructive stories that impart ideology. In American commerce during the 1950s and 1960s, the revitalization of the country's historic rugged individualist masculinity was dramatized using two different myths, each of which spun off major cultural innovations. Jack Daniel's proffered a myth, which was drawn from America's hillbilly subculture, romanticizing a small distillery in the Tennessee backwoods that had survived untouched by industrialization and the postwar ideology of the organization man. Jack Daniel's men, proudly and stubbornly, continued to uphold time-honored, frontier ideals of masculinity with their whiskey making. Marlboro finally struck gold when it hit upon the ranch subculture of the America West to convey a myth about hard-working cowboys herding their cattle with determination and skill on the desolate, weather-threatening range. In each case, the ideology became comprehensible, viscerally felt, and resonant only because it was embedded in myth; it would have made little sense as a conceptual statement.

Cultural Codes

For a myth to resonate with consumers, it must be composed using the most appropriate and compelling cultural content – what cultural theorists often call cultural codes. All mass-cultural expressions – whether a film or a retail store design or packaging graphics – rely on elements for which the meaning has been well established historically in the culture. It would be impossible to compose an expression from scratch, because, with no historic conventions to fall back upon, each and every element in the composition would have to be defined for the audience in a way that would allow them to interpret it properly. Cultural codes provide a shorthand for the consumer, allowing them easily to understand and experience the intended meanings. (What usually differentiates more "artistic" and avant-garde expressions is that they ignore, challenge, play with, or purposely mangle cultural codes.)

The most apt ideology embedded in a potentially powerful myth will backfire if it is composed with culturally illiterate, clunky, off-strategy codes. An adroit and precise use of codes is essential. To signify a preference for old-world craft over modern machines, Jack Daniel's advertising romanticized the process of assembling the staves of the oak barrels and charcoaling their insides. To signify the old-time frontiersman, the antithesis of the organization man, the advertising showcased hefty, rural, Southern men in old-fashioned denim overalls. To signify the celebration of active outdoor labor over sedentary office work, the advertising showed men burning huge ricks of maple for the charcoal filtering. To celebrate the "tell-it-like-it-is" plain-speaker over the glib city-slicker, the advertising used folksy, parochial, phrases like "welcome to the holler." All of these codes worked together in a redundant manner to create the intended meaning.

Cultural competition spans all three elements of cultural expression. Since cultural expression is such a potent driver of customer value, it should be no surprise that innovating in cultural expression is a powerful tool for building new businesses and reviving failing ones. Cultural innovations break through when they bear the right ideology, which is dramatized through the right myth, expressed with the right cultural codes. As we continue to build the cultural brand strategy model, let us consider how Jack Daniel's cultural expression broke through in the 1950s.

AVOIDING RED OCEANS: BREAKING OUT OF THE CULTURAL ORTHODOXY

In the better-mousetraps paradigm, competitive red oceans are understood as spaces where there is a great deal of overlapping functionality across current offerings and, therefore, little opportunity to innovate. Innovators need to look for blue oceans (or white spaces) that provide significantly improved value propositions for a brand, whether they are created by new technology or by mixing-and-matching value propositions across categories.

Few businesses – whatever the physical product or service they sell – understand that their offering is understood, experienced and valued by consumers as a cultural expression. Few businesses, therefore, are managing their cultural expressions. As a result, incumbents in a category tend to arrive at a conventional idea of what is good cultural expression and then copy one another. This is a common phenomenon in business and other types of institutions, well documented by neo-institutional organization theorists, who call it mimesis (DiMaggio and Powell 1983). While businesses compete to outdo each other in providing different benefits, at the cultural level they imitate each other, developing their marketing initiatives as minor variations of the same ideology, myth and cultural codes. As certain cultural expressions become dominant, businesses come to treat these conventions as durable taken-for-granted "facts" of the marketplace.

This is exactly what happened in the 1950s whiskey market. The major whiskey-makers all assumed that middle-class American men desired that their whiskeys express the "classy" modern lifestyle of the well-to-do organization man. Competition between whiskey brands was largely based upon which brand could represent the organization man's lifestyle in a more interesting and credible way. I call these taken-for-granted cultural expressions that are widely imitated the category's "cultural orthodoxy."

The fact that incumbents tend to market their wares using the same well-worn cultural expressions creates a great opportunity for agile cultural entrepreneurs. Categories that are red oceans from a better-mousetraps perspective are often blue oceans from a cultural perspective precisely because the most powerful competitors are focused on fierce product-level competition, ignoring the cultural aspects of their businesses.

SOCIAL DISRUPTIONS CREATE IDEOLOGICAL OPPORTUNITIES

Cultural blue oceans are fundamentally different. The engine of cultural innovation is historical change in society that is significant enough to destabilize the category's cultural orthodoxy, creating latent demand for new cultural expressions. Markets often sustain these orthodoxies for years at a time, occasionally a decade or longer. But at some point, as history unfolds and social structures shift, one or more of these shifts will be disruptive, challenging the taken-for-granted cultural expressions offered by category incumbents, and creating emergent demand for new cultural expressions. These are moments when once-dominant brands lose their resonance and new historical conditions arise, creating opportunities for innovative brands to take off.

These social disruptions create ideological opportunities. The category's cultural orthodoxy no longer adequately delivers the cultural expressions that consumers demand. Consumers yearn for brands that champion new ideology, brought to life by new myths and cultural codes. For Jack Daniel's, the organization-man myth propagated by the mass media and political elites rubbed against the country's historically dominant myth of the gunfighter on the frontier. The success of the organization man created a backlash: a widely shared belief that the organization man was too wimpy and effeminate to serve as a model for American men, especially in the midst of the cold war, and a yearning to resuscitate what the gunfighter stood for. In our terms, a massive ideological opportunity was created. Yet, because the major whiskey brands were locked into the category's cultural orthodoxy, they could not imagine giving up their "modern" "aspirational" positioning to return to whiskey's rough-and-tumble rural heritage.

This way of thinking about blue oceans is radically different from the better-mousetrap models. According to technological and mix-and-match models, opportunities are always out there in the world, lying dormant, until the right new technology or creative mix-and-match offering comes along. People always want better functionality. Ideological opportunities, in contrast, are produced by major historical changes that shake up cultural conventions of the category. These shifts unmoor consumers from the goods that they have relied on to produce the symbolism they demand and drive them to seek out new alternatives. It is an emergent kind of opportunity that is specific to a historical moment and a particular group of people.

Ideological opportunities provide one of the most fertile grounds for market innovation. Yet these opportunities have gone unrecognized because of the extraordinary influence of economics and engineering on how managers view innovation. These disciplines share an assumption – in order to simplify the world, they purposely ignore cultural context and historical change. These theories remove all of the messy bits of human life in order to present a tidy view of consumption that allows for corporations to function in a streamlined fashion. But it is in these untidy parts that innovation opportunities lurk.

CULTURAL INNOVATIONS REPURPOSE SOURCE MATERIAL

Cultural innovations adapt and repurpose what we call "source material" in order to take advantage of the ideological opportunity. This source material comes in three types: subcultures, media myths and brand assets.

Subcultures

Innovations adapt alternative ideologies, myths and cultural codes that are lurking in subcultures and social movements (which we shall refer to jointly as subcultures to simplify). For our purposes, subcultures are groups or places that cohere around an ideology that is antithetic to the category's cultural orthodoxy. Social movements are the same, except that they have an explicit agenda to change society, and so often seek to challenge dominant ideologies directly. The organic foods, slow food and fair-trade movements are all good examples. Subcultures provide great credibility as foundations for brand expressions because they "prove" that the ideology actually exists in the world as a viable worldview that has value for its participants.

Media Myths

Often the mass media are quicker than other forms of commerce to borrow from subcultures in order to promulgate new cultural expressions. Media myths come packaged in all types of popular culture products: in films, television programs, music, books, magazines, newspapers, sports, politics, even in the news. In addition to the direct appropriation of subcultures, cultural innovations often draw inspiration from the media's mythic treatments of these subcultures.

Brand Assets

Businesses usually have cultural assets that can be leveraged as well. These assets include both the company's business practices that have significant cultural potential, as well as the brand's historic cultural expressions that people still remember. One of the central objectives of *How Brands Become Icons* was to document these equities and to show how they are reworked as the brand evolves historically.

The Jack Daniel's innovation was sourced from the rural hillbilly subculture: denigrated in American culture at the time as backwards, parochial, unmannered and lower class, the antithesis of the organization man. That the Jack Daniel's distillery had been located in the heart of hillbilly country in Lynchburg, Tennessee, since the region was part of the country's frontier, and that distilling whiskey had remained since the frontier days a backwoods hobby in this subculture, made Jack Daniel's a particularly credible brand to champion this ideology. The mass media performed the inversion of the myth of the hillbilly whiskey-maker – from backwoods bumpkin to recalcitrant frontiersman. The fact that the brand had a storied existence among insiders as a tiny regional distillery cranking out the same quality whiskey year in and year out gave tremendous credibility to the brand's anachronistic ideology. The subculture, media myth and brand assets were all crucial sources for the Jack Daniel's innovation. Without these components, the innovation would have never occurred.

Consider other extraordinary cultural innovations, all of which advocated frontier masculinity: cigarettes (Marlboro), whiskey (Jack Daniel's), motorcycles (Harley-Davidson), jeans (Levi's, Lee), and SUVs (Jeep). The historic uses of these products within a particular subculture – frontiersmen drank whiskey, wore denim and liked to smoke; soldiers, the modern frontiersmen, drove Harleys and Jeeps in the Second World War, and liked to smoke and drink whiskey as well – gave these brands their credibility. And then the mass media turned these subcultural ideologies into myth – the rebel films with Marlon Brando and James Dean, and the Western films and television programs – providing valuable fodder for brands to repurpose.

DESIGNING THE CULTURAL INNOVATION

The final stage of cultural brand strategy involves designing a concept that responds to the ideological opportunity in a compelling and original manner, drawing upon appropriate source materials. Executing the design requires that each important consumer-facing element of the brand convey the cultural expression in an original and artful manner. This transformation of source material into design is the "creative" aspect of cultural innovation, but it is a creative act that is far more directed and constrained than typical "out-of-the-box" tabula-rasa creative projects typical in marketing today. Once the prospective innovator has understood the right ideology, myth and cultural codes, instilling these elements into the offering across the marketing mix is usually a straightforward task that is much more susceptible to constructive management than typical creative assignments.

Brands that deliver innovative cultural expressions become powerful cultural symbols – what I call iconic brands. What makes these brands so powerful is that they become collectively valued in society as a widely shared symbol of a particular ideology for a segment of the population. People use the brand in their everyday lives to experience and express this ideology. The brand's cultural role in social life becomes conventional, and so is continually reinforced. Cultural innovations generate three kinds of value, all interrelated:

- *Symbolic value* Cultural expressions sort out the most important aspects of human life and provide concrete direction and motivation, acting as symbolic anchors for questions of identity, purpose, aspiration and value. Consumers of branded cultural expressions are able viscerally to experience these desirable ideas and values in everyday life (what anthropologists call "ritual action").

- *Social value* Cultural expressions stake out social identities, often based upon key social categories such as social class, gender, race and ethnicity. They can buttress important political identities as well – for instance, ideals concerning environmentalism, nationalism and social justice. These social and political identities are used to convey status – demonstrating one's superiority to others, and building solidarity and community with others.
- *Functional halo* When people find symbolic and social value in a brand's cultural expression, they tend to perceive that the brand provides better functionality, is higher quality, and is more trustworthy. Foods and drinks taste better. Companies are trusted. Services are performed with more consistency. Durable goods are more reliable. When consumers resonate with a brand's cultural expression, they want to believe the branded products and services are excellent, and so the expression strongly influences their perceptions of seemingly functional qualities. Functional benefits are social constructs, not objective facts as assumed by economists and engineers.

REFERENCES

Arnould, Eric J. and Craig J. Thompson (2005), "Consumer culture theory (CCT): twenty years of research," *Journal of Consumer Research*, **31** (4), 868–82.

Christensen, Clayton M. (2003), *The Innovator's Dilemma*, New York: Collins Business.

Christensen, Clayton M. and Michael E. Raynor (2004), *The Innovator's Solution: Creating and Sustaining Successful Growth*, Boston, MA: Harvard Business School Press.

DiMaggio, Paul and Walter W. Powell (1983), "The iron cage revisited: institutional isomorphism and collective rationality in organizational fields," *American Sociological Review*, **48** (April), 147–60.

Hamel, Gary and C.K. Prahalad (1994), *Competing for the Future*, Boston, MA: Harvard Business School Press.

Hargadon, Andrew (2003), *How Breakthroughs Happen: The Surprising Truth about How Companies Innovate*, Boston, MA: Harvard Business School Press.

Holt, Douglas B. (2002), "Why do brands cause trouble? A dialectical theory of consumer culture and branding," *Journal of Consumer Research*, **29** (2), 70–90.

Holt, Douglas B. (2003), "What becomes an icon most?," *Harvard Business Review*, **81** (3), 43–9.

Holt, Douglas B. (2004), *How Brands Become Icons: The Principles of Cultural Branding*, Boston, MA: Harvard Business School Press.

Holt, Douglas B. (2006a), "Jack Daniel's America: iconic brands as ideological parasites and proselytizers," *Journal of Consumer Culture*, **6** (3), 355–77.

Holt, Douglas B. (2006b), "How societies desire brands: using cultural theory to explain brand symbolism," in Mick and S. Ratneshwar (eds), *Inside Consumption: Consumer Motives, Goals, and Desires*, London: Routledge, pp. 273–92.

Holt, Douglas B. and Douglas Cameron (2010), *Cultural Strategy: How Innovative Ideologies Build Breakthrough Brands*, New York: Oxford University Press.

Johansson, Frans (2004), *The Medici Effect: What Elephants and Epidemics can Teach Us about Innovation*, Boston, MA: Harvard Business School Press.

Kim, W. Chan and Renée Mauborgne (2005), *Blue Ocean Strategy*, Boston, MA: Harvard Business School Press.

Thompson, Craig J. (2004), "Marketplace mythology and discourses of power," *Journal of Consumer Research*, **31** (1), 162–80.

Thompson, Craig J. and Zeynep Arsel (2004), "The Starbucks brandscape and consumers' (anticorporate) experiences of glocalization," *Journal of Consumer Research*, **31** (Dec.), 631–42.

19 Private label strategies – myths and realities
Raj Sethuraman and Jagmohan S. Raju

It is believed that the oldest profession in the world is trading. When traders traveled around the globe selling their wares in exchange for money, goods or services, the operative phrase was "Caveat emptor" – "Buyer beware!" If the product did not meet expectations, the buyer bore all the consequences once the transaction was completed. Since the identity or origin of the good was seldom known, buyers placed a lot of trust in the trader selling the good. Essentially, the traders were extending their names and reputations to the goods they were selling. It was the era of implicit traders' brands – a precursor to modern-day store brands! The evolution from traders to trading places or small stores, where goods could be purchased for money, saw the emergence of products with manufacturers' names attached, like the Remington revolver, as well as goods with no names, such as a bag of flour or sugar. Manufacturers' brands and traders' brands coexisted, but in distinct categories. As small stores grew into superstores, the concept of national brands grew with them.

Branding means burning, a practice dating back to the seventeenth century and associated with the process of marking an animal with a unique symbol so that the owner could identify it. With hundreds of product categories and dozens of items within a category, branding performs the basic identification function for a large retailer. When the doctrine of "Caveat emptor" gave way to "Caveat venditor" ("Seller beware"), forcing sellers to take responsibility for products and discouraging them from selling products of dubious quality, brands began to perform the role of providing implicit warranty. Now, thanks to mass media channels and sophisticated marketing, national brands have established themselves as the primary goods of transaction in frequently purchased consumer goods. Brands like Coca-Cola and Starbucks represent not just identity and quality but status, image, emotion – a rich collection of tangible and intangible benefits.

While the traders' brands pre-date the national brands, modern-day store brands or private labels – brands generally owned, controlled and marketed exclusively by a retailer – are a relatively recent phenomenon. They were introduced more than 100 years ago in some limited items such as tea, and they are now prevalent in over 60 percent of product categories in the USA (Fitzell 1992; Quelch and Harding 1996). According to the Private Label Manufacturers Association (www.plma.com), nearly one out of four products bought in US supermarkets in 2009 was a store brand; market share rose to all-time record highs of 18.7 percent dollar share and 23.7 percent unit share. In fact, store brands accounted for almost 90 percent of all new revenue in the supermarket channel. In Europe, private label share is even higher at 30 percent and may even reach 40–50 percent over the next two decades, according to Kumar and Steenkamp (2007). Private labels are also beginning to take root in developing economies such as Asia and Latin America.

Despite the significant growth of private labels, the strategy formulation for store

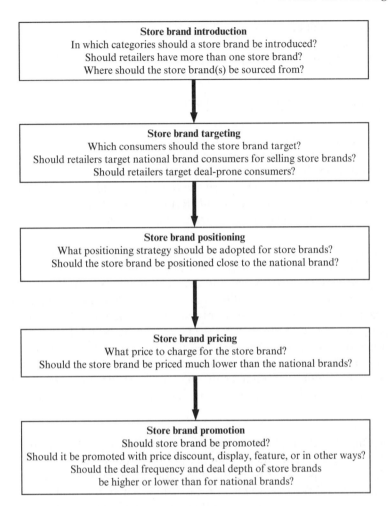

Figure 19.1   Private label (store brand) strategies

brands or private labels has been reactive for the most part – that is, store brand strategies are determined in relation to existing national brands. In this chapter, we adopt a similar stance and consider store brands as a means of increasing profits (or achieving other objectives) for the retailer, given a set of national brands that s/he carries or can carry in the product category. Store brands are thus an integral part of category management.

In particular, we address five broad strategies related to private label or store brand marketing: (1) introduction; (2) targeting; (3) positioning; (4) pricing; and (5) promotion. Pertinent decisions related to these strategies are shown in Figure 19.1. Keller (Chapter 17 in this volume) and Holt (Chapter 18 in this volume) discuss brand and marketing strategies primarily for national brands. We draw on conceptual, analytical and empirical works from the academic literature, as well as anecdotes and opinions from the managerial literature, to provide insights into store brand or private label strategies.

In the process, we highlight some realities and dispel some myths about private label marketing. We conclude by summarizing key insights and providing some predictions and research directions for the future.

CONCEPTUAL BACKGROUND

We focus on a retailer who carries or has the potential to carry both the national brands and its own store brand or private label. The focal retailer purchases the national brand from the manufacturers at wholesale price and sells it to the consumers at retail price. The difference between the retail price and the wholesale price is the retailer's margin from the national brand. Retailer's profits from the national brand are calculated as the national brand margin (times) quantity of national brand sold by the retailer.

The retailer can also sell a store brand that is produced by the retailer or supplied by an independent manufacturer or the national brand manufacturer. The difference between the cost of procuring the store brand and the retail selling price is the retailer's margin from the store brand. Retailer's profits from the store brand are calculated as the store brand margin (times) quantity of store brand sold by the retailer. Retailer's total category profits are the sum of profits from the national brands and the store brand.

The nature of competition between national brands and store brands is distinct from the nature of competition among national brands analyzed in Czepiel and Kerin, Chapter 4 in this volume. A number of unique factors characterize the competition between national brands and store brands and thus the retailer's decision-making scenario:

1.   Retailer has the potential to carry both national brands and its own competing store brand and can set prices and in-store promotion of both these brands.
2.   Retailer has the potential to source the national brand from the national brand manufacturer, third-party supplier or through own manufacturing.
3.   Category profits are more important than individual brand profits.
4.   However, in some categories the retailer may choose to forgo profits for building store traffic.
5.   The fixed cost for the retailer is not only related to cost of salaries, utilities and so on, but also opportunity cost of shelf space.
6.   Competing retailers typically carry the same national brands and may have a store brand of their own.

These factors play a role in the determination of private label strategies, which are discussed next.

STORE BRAND INTRODUCTION

The general premise is that the retailer will introduce a store brand if doing so increases category profits. In other words, the profits obtainable from the store brand should be large enough to offset possible loss in profits from the national brands. Using this condition, academics have identified a number of factors that could influence the decision to introduce store brand: (1) price substitutability; (2) store brand quality; (3) number of national brands; (4) category volume and margin; (5) economies of scale; and others. Results related to some key characteristics are discussed below in the form of myth or reality points.

Myth or reality 1 – Introduce store brands in commodity products

A major selling point for a store brand is its lower price relative to national brands. Therefore it would seem obvious that store brands should be introduced in "commodity" products, where consumers have a high propensity to switch brands on the basis of price (Stern 1966). It is true that high price substitutability is conducive to increasing private label market share, as more consumers would switch from national brand to store brand for a given price differential. But is it profitable for the retailer to introduce a store brand in that market? The answer is not obvious.

Researchers have shown that higher price substitutability between national brand and store brand increases the retailer's category profits from store brand introduction. There are two explanations for this result. One rationale, offered by Raju et al. (1995a) and others, points to the high margins obtained from store brands. In their model, in equilibrium, the retail margin on the store brand is greater than the corresponding margin on the national brand. High price substitutability between national brand and store brand increases the quantity of private labels sold. Therefore switching consumers to higher-margin private labels increases retailer profits.

A second explanation, forwarded by Mills (1995) and Scott-Morton and Zettelmeyer (2004), states that high price substitutability makes national brands less indispensable; that is, reduces the incremental contribution of national brand to channel profits, thus eroding manufacturers' bargaining power. Hence retailers are able to extract higher profits and share of channel profit if there is a store brand that resembles the national brand.

While high price subsitutability between national brand and store brand favor introduction, high price substitutability (price competition) among national brands deters store brand entry (Raju et al. 1995a). When price competition among national brands is high, the average national brand retail price decreases. The reduced national brand price, in turn, depresses the price and retail margins for the store brand, resulting in lower category profits for the retailer. For example, if Coke and Pepsi compete with each other aggressively on price, there may be little room for a store brand to enter the market and be profitable.

Thus commodity products, characterized by price subsitutability, can be a double-edged sword when it comes to store brand introduction. The category is high on both price substitutability between national brands and store brands, and among national brands – the former favors store brand introduction while the latter deters it. One strategy for the retailer is to reduce the number of national brands, and thus national brand price competition, in undifferentiated categories (simplify assortment without loss of variety) and introduce the store brand. An alternate strategy is to reap the benefits of the competing national brands and not introduce a store brand.

Myth or reality 2 – Quality is important for a successful private label program

It is true that a store brand comparable in quality to that of national brands will increase price substitutability and lead to more store brand sales. Hoch and Banerji (1993) show a strong result, across 180 categories, that store brand quality is the most important determinant of private label share – even more important than price. Our discussion considers the role of quality beyond its ability to influence price substitutability. Raju et al. (1995a) and related studies capture this role through brand strength or store brand loyalty – that is, high quality can reduce the need for a store brand to be priced much lower than national brands. Corstjens and Lal (2000) operationalize quality of store brand in terms of the fraction of consumers who try the store brand and find it "acceptable." They show that total retailer profits are increasing in store brand quality, even if the store brand does not have a cost or margin advantage. The basic intuition is that a high-quality store brand differentiates stores from each other and increases store loyalty. Hence, even when a high-quality store brand is not profitable, the optimal strategy might be to introduce the high-quality brand because ancillary benefits derived through the purchase of goods elsewhere in the store by the loyal consumer may be greater. In our interviews (Sethuraman 2008), managers concurred. One even commented, "Exactly! For a store brand positioned as offering quality, it makes more business sense to focus on promoting store loyalty than simply go after national brands." Thus we state what managers perhaps already know: emphasize quality store brands in order to enhance store brand share and store image.

Myth or reality 3 – There is no place for a store brand when there are already many national brands

Schmalensee (1978) argues that preemptive product differentiation and proliferation by national brands in a market can deter a store brand entrant. He points to cereals as a category where numerous national brand varieties leave little room for store brands. Contrary to this common belief, Raju et al. (1995a) show analytically that retailers would find it more profitable to introduce a store brand in categories with a large number of national brands. They reason that it is easy to "sneak in" a store brand without affecting the profits of the existing brands when the number of existing national brands is large. While not explicitly modeling the number of national brands, Scott-Morton and Zettelmeyer (2004) argue that more manufacturers actively producing national brands indicates fewer barriers to entry; hence the retailer can easily find a supplier for its store brand. Managers tended to agree with the latter view and offered an additional supporting argument: when there are many national brands, each one, on average, tends not to be very strong. This lack of national brand strength provides an opportunity for store brands to enter (Sethuraman 2008). So, when it comes to store brand entry in a fairly well-differentiated category, the more national brands the merrier, even if it means smaller private label share. It may also be pointed out that in the cereal category, the example used in Schmalensee (1978), private labels have witnessed reasonable growth; in January 2010, private label share exceeded 10 percent, according to Information Resources, Inc. (http://www.privatelabelmag.com/issues/pl-march-2010/breakfast.cfm).

Myth or reality 4 – Retailers eye the high-dollar-volume categories for store brand introduction

The profits for store brand can be written as: store brand margin (times) store brand volume – fixed costs = Store brand margin (times) [category volume * store brand share] – fixed costs. In high-dollar-volume categories, for a given share, store brand volume will be higher. So store brand profits will be higher in categories with large dollar sales, other things equal. However, the effect on total retailer profits is not clear. In the same high-volume categories, the retailer will stand to lose a greater amount from the national brands because of consumers switching to store brands. So perhaps a necessary condition for a retailer to introduce a store brand in high-volume mature categories is that the retailer's margin on the store brand should be higher than that for the national brand. (We discuss this idea in the following section.)

In a survey by Sethuraman (2008), managers looked beyond margins and viewed category volume in terms of its components: household penetration (times) purchase frequency (times) price per purchase. All three components favor store branding. Higher household penetration provides visibility of store name and brand to a larger group of consumers; higher frequency provides the retailer with greater velocity and greater opportunity to be in the market baskets and the minds of consumers; higher price per purchase enables retailers to highlight the large price differential. (It is easier to showcase price differential in a five-dollar item than in a 50-cent item.) Sethuraman (2009, Table 1, R5) finds the results on positive relationship between store brand introduction and category volume to be sufficiently robust analytically, empirically and managerially that we can deem it as a reality.

Myth or reality 5 – Higher margin is the prime reason for store brand introduction

In a survey in the 1990s, retailers stated that the most important reason for carrying a store brand is better profit margins (Discount Merchandiser 1996). An argument for store brand introduction based on switching consumers from national brands must be predicated on the belief that retailers will gain higher margins from store brands than from the national brand that it is switching consumers from. Two explanations have been put forward for the higher margins from store brands (Sayman and Raju 2007). First, on the supply (cost) side, retailers can procure store brands at a relatively low cost from suppliers who do not have much marketing power. Thus retailers avoid the double marginalization problem when it comes to store brands. Second, on the demand (price) side, retailers compete vigorously on price of national brands, driving prices and margins down. On the other hand, the store brand is proprietary to the retailer; consumers can not make direct price comparisons across retailers. And so retailers have room to increase margins from store brands, thereby raising profits (Steiner 2004).

While it is generally true that percentage margins for store brands are higher, empirical evidence is mixed on absolute dollar margins (see Sethuraman 2009, Table 1, R10). For example, Corstjens and Lal's (2000) illustration of a beverage category (from a Canadian retailer) indicates that, in fact, when all factors (deal allowances, warehousing, in-store labor etc.) are taken into account, even net percentage margins from store brands may be lower than margins from national brands. It is generally true that retailers' cost of acquisition of store brands is less than the cost (wholesale price) of national brands; it is also true that price of store brands is generally lower than price of national brands. But the retailer's store brand margin is higher than national brand margin only if the cost differential between the two brands is greater than the price differential.

In summary, higher margin on store brands is neither a myth nor a reality. Retail margin depends on a number of factors, including whether the brand is positioned as a generic brand (low margin) or a premium brand (high margin). However, retailers whose private label programs hinge on higher store brand margin must institute proper accounting procedures to include all relevant costs in determining the relative margins. At the same time, theoretical and empirical researchers should shed light on whether and when retail margins on store brands are higher than those for national brands, along the lines of Ailawadi and Harlam (2004).

If margins from store brands are higher than from national brands, retailers would be better off by diverting consumers to store brands. Otherwise, there should be other benefits or expectations from store brands. One such benefit is store patronage, which is discussed below.

Myth or reality 6 – Store brands increase store's share of consumer wallet

Retailer-level data from the UK (Corstjens and Lal 2000) suggest that store brand penetration is positively related to store loyalty and store sales. Similarly, household-level data from the USA and Canada provide evidence that loyalty (as measured by share of expenditures from the store) increases with increasing household-level store brand penetration. Sudhir and Talukdar (2004) analyze household expenditures in 44 product categories from a large retailer and find that a household buying store brands in more categories is likely to spend more on any particular category. They suggest that a broader store brand line may be necessary for creating loyalty and differentiation. This "umbrella" effect is also supported by Sayman and Raju (2004a). Using data from 13 food categories and 122 US retailers, they offer evidence that sales and number of store brands in other product categories increase the sales of the store brand in the target category. Hence propensity to buy store brands increases the store's share of wallet.

In a recent article, Ailawadi et al. (2008) find an inverted-U-shaped relationship between private label use and store loyalty. The authors estimate the model for two retail chains in the Netherlands and find that private label share significantly affects all three measures of behavioral loyalty in the study: share of wallet, share of items purchased and share of shopping trips. In addition, behavioral loyalty has a significant effect on private label share. The virtuous cycle, where private label share increases store loyalty and store loyalty increases private label share, operates up to a certain level – private label share below 40 percent or so. After that, there may be reduction in store loyalty because heavy store brand buyers are often price-sensitive store hoppers (cherry pickers).

Overall, there appears to be evidence of a positive relationship between private label share and store's share of wallet and, up to a point, store loyalty and store brand share may reinforce each other.

STORE BRAND SEGMENTATION AND TARGETING

Which types of consumers should the store brand target? To begin with, retailers should aim for those consumers who would be most willing to purchase store brands. This leads one to ask: which consumers are those? Below, we discuss some myths and realities related to the nature of store-brand-prone consumers.

Myth or reality 7 – Target the store brands at the high-price-sensitive, low-quality-sensitive consumers

Store brands have traditionally been viewed as lower-priced, lower-quality alternatives to national brands (Stern 1966). Hence store brand consumers are deemed to be very price sensitive (or more price sensitive than national brand consumers) and not quality sensitive. Sayman and Raju (2007) and Sethuraman (2006) have conducted extensive reviews of the consumer literature and find mixed evidence. In 18 of 19 studies reviewed by Sethuraman (2006, Table 1), consumers stated that price is an important component in private label purchase. However, contrary to the traditional view, private label consumers are, in fact, quality sensitive. Fourteen out of 16 studies in Sethuraman (2006) find a strong positive relationship between quality or quality consistency of store brands and private label proneness or private label purchases. In fact, there is reasonable evidence indicating that quality may be of equal or greater importance than price in influencing private label purchase. For example, in a 1990 Gallup survey, 83 percent of consumers interviewed cited quality as a very important factor in private label purchase, while only 74 percent stated that price was important (Fitzell 1992). Similarly, in a comprehensive study of store brand proneness Richardson et al. (1996) find that perceived quality is more important than perceived value for money in influencing consumers' propensity to purchase store brands. Erdem et al. (2004) find that quality uncertainty is the key determinant of differences in store brand market share across countries, more important than price sensitivity.

   Of course, many private label marketers have realized the importance of quality in selling their brands and have taken steps to raise the quality of their store brands to be on par with that of national brands. For instance, the Private Label Manufacturers Association's (PLMA) official website claims that in an independent study conducted in 2010 nearly all of the shoppers who did switch (from national brand to store brand) were pleased with their decision (http://plma.com/storeBrands/sbt10.html). An August 2005 *Consumer Reports* study that tested 65 products finds that many store brands are at least as good as national brands.

   In summary, the notion that store brands are targeted at consumers who do not care that much about quality but primarily care about price is unfounded. Quality is an important consideration when purchasing store brands but these consumers desire value (good quality brands at low prices) over brand image.

Myth or reality 8 – Target the store brands at the low-income, less-educated, large families

Because store brands are viewed as lower-priced, lower-quality alternatives to national brands, it is a logical next step to believe that store brands are intended to serve the needs of a relatively lower-income segment of the population who are generally less educated and have large families (Fitzell 1992). Only six out of 18 studies in Sethuraman (2006) supported this economic view, and four studies actually showed the opposite – that is, low-income consumers are less likely to purchase private labels than middle-income consumers. Fitzell (1992) also laments that the very consumers for whom private labels would make the most sense are more loyal to national brands because of their lack of knowledge about store brands and the imagery associated with name brands.

A review by Sayman and Raju (2007) indicates that, by and large, private label consumers tend to be middle-income, educated, older consumers with large families. However, these socio-economic variables account for only 4–5 percent of the variation in private label purchases (Dhar and Hoch 1997). The modest explanatory power of demographic variables has led some researchers to conclude that private and national brands are consumed by households with virtually the same demographic characteristics. The dilemma, then, for the store brand marketer is whether demographic variables can be used as the bases for segmentation and targeting. Our view is that, while they cannot form the primary basis for segmenting the market, the collective knowledge gained from past research can be exploited for developing targeting strategies. First, store brand managers should target the middle-income, educated consumers, since those consumers appear more prone to purchasing private labels. Second, store brand marketers may also consider attracting low-income consumers by educating them about store brand quality and making them aware of the price differentials. This targeting would not only increase private label market share but could also increase overall consumer welfare.

Myth or reality 9 – Target the store brands at national brand-deal-prone consumers

If demographics do not explain store brand propensity, does deal proneness explain it? One question of interest is whether users of national brand promotions and store brands are the same consumers. Ailawadi et al. (2001) find that national brand deal users and store brand buyers entail different psychographics. In particular, out-of-store promotions (coupons, flyers etc., which involve active consideration and planning) are associated with hedonic benefits such as enjoying shopping, while store brand usage is related with economic benefits and cost-related characteristics. The authors also find that there are four distinct segments: deal-focused, store-brand-focused, deal and store brand users, and non-users. Summarizing the findings in the literature, Sayman and Raju (2007) assert that deal proneness is not an intrinsic characteristic of store brand purchasers.

STORE BRAND POSITIONING

In the context of competition between national brands and store brands, store brand positioning is conceptualized as the extent of similarity to the national brand. Retailers attempt to position their store brand close to the national brand in at least four ways: by reducing the perceived quality gap between the national brand and the store brand; by imitating national brand packaging; by placing the store brand on the shelf next to the national brand; and by using shelf talkers with "compare and save" or similar slogans.

The central question for retailers is: should the store brand be positioned close to the national brand or not?

Myth or reality 10 – Position the store brand close to the national brand

There is a tendency among grocery retailers to increase the sales of private labels at the expense of national brands by positioning the store brand close to the national brand. Academic research supports this conventional wisdom. Several researchers (e.g. Mills 1995; Scott-Morton and Zettelmeyer 2004; Raju et al. 1995a) unanimously suggest that retailers would be better off (obtain higher category profits) if they positioned their store brands close to the national brands. Sayman et al. (2002), in particular, further strengthen this assertion. They show that if there are two symmetric national brands, it is better to position the store brand close to one of them than to stay in the middle. If the national brands are not symmetric (i.e. they have different market shares), then it is profitable for the store brand to go after the national brand with the larger share. In fact, the larger the share of the national brand, the more profitable it is for the store brand to mimic it.

Empirical findings from Sayman et al. (2002), and from Sethuraman (2004), indicate that many retailers' behavior tends to be consistent with this prediction. In particular, when store brands do target a particular national brand, the targeted brand is the leading brand in 80 percent of the cases. The authors also find that the likelihood of targeting a national brand is greater when the national brand has higher market share. However, interestingly, in both these studies, store brands targeted a particular national brand in only about 30 percent of the categories. Why might retailers fail to target a particular national brand? Some reasons may be cost of imitating and/or not wanting to alienate the national brand manufacturer.

Sethuraman (2004) offers a market-driven reasoning and shows that positioning a store brand close to the national brand may not be profitable for the retailer if the national brand manufacturer can significantly expand category demand through investments in non-price marketing activities such as advertising, and/or if the store brand can garner a significant portion of the market with low-reservation-price consumers who cannot afford the national brand. In a similar vein, Choi and Coughlan (2006) show that, when two national brands are undifferentiated in features, it is better for the private label to position itself away from them by offering a different feature (e.g. private label pasta in large package sizes or fat-free sour cream).

Thus positioning the store brand closer to the national brand is optimal (i) in mature products with limited category expansion and (ii) if retailers' store brand margins are greater than their margins on the national brands. However, there are many situations in which close store brand positioning may not be optimal.

STORE BRAND PRICING

What price should a retailer charge for the store brand? Because the store brand is generally a follower, pricing decisions have focused on what price differential to maintain between national brands and the store brand.

Myth or reality 11 – Keep store brand price as low as possible relative to competing national brand

The private label sales maximization objective and the notion that the purpose of private labels is to wean consumers away from the national brands leads to the belief that it is good to charge a low price for the store brand and to maintain a large price differential between national brands and the store brand. Empirical evidence supports the existence of this pricing behavior. Using extensive in-store experiments in analgesics and other product categories, Hoch and Lodish (2001) found that store brand analgesics were priced 45 percent lower than national brands when a 30 percent price differential appeared to yield more category profits. Pauwels and Srinivasan (2004) observe that retailers tend to increase the price of the national brand and maintain a high price differential between that brand and their own store brand. The reason for this overpricing of the national brand may be the retailers' focus on increasing private label share as opposed to profits (Chintagunta et al. 2002).

A recurring theme in most academic research based on category profitability considerations is to point out that a large price gap between national brands and the store brand is not necessarily desirable. In addition, a number of theoretical studies have shown that when retailers close the quality gap between national brands and the store brand, as they have attempted to do in recent times, they can obtain higher profits by also reducing the price gap (Mills 1995; Raju et al. 1995b; Sayman et al. 2002).

Does this mean that when consumers perceive very little quality differential between national brands and the store brand, the price differential can be reduced to near zero? Managerial literature has opined that if the price differential is small, then consumers will not purchase the store brand because they will not see its value (e.g. Donegan 1989). Recent empirical evidence supports this viewpoint. Sethuraman (2003) and Applebaum et al. (2003) have found that, even if consumers perceive that national and store brands are physically identical, they are willing to pay, on average, about a 20–30 percent price premium for national brands. This reputation economy has also been documented in the economics literature (Steiner 2004). Pricing of store brands *vis-à-vis* national brands is complex (see Pauwels and Srinivasan 2007 for a detailed discussion). When a store brand is positioned to be similar to national brands, it is profitable for the retailer to reduce the price differential between it and the national brands. However, the price differential cannot be too low, as consumers will pay a premium for national brand image, even if they perceive the store brand to be equivalent.

STORE BRAND PROMOTIONS

Allocating resources across various elements of the marketing mix is an important aspect of brand management (Shankar, Chapter 9 in this volume). In the case of store brands, resources are typically allocated to product development and in-store promotions. Store brands generally do not promote through media advertising. The promotion options for these brands are primarily price promotions (shelf price discounts), coupons and features/displays. Of these, price promotion is most common.

Myth or reality 12 – Store brands should not price-promote

There are two aspects to price promotions: discount frequency and discount depth. Theoretical assertions and empirical evidence are mixed for discount frequency. A number of analytical models (Lal 1990; Narasimhan 1988; Rao 1991) recommend that private labels not promote in equilibrium. The general intuition for the above result is as follows. The incentive for national brands to price-promote stems from having to charge a regular price to cater to its loyal customer base and occasionally make forays into the switcher segment through price cuts. Because store brands are primarily viewed as brands with little loyalty and catering mainly to the price-sensitive (switcher) segment, this incentive does not arise. The pricing role of store brands is to simply protect its switcher segment from encroachment. In this situation, store brands do not price-promote unless their switcher base is significantly threatened. Tellis and Zufryden (1995) develop an optimization model for retailer discounts and conduct extensive analysis to understand how optimal discounts vary with brand characteristics. They find that in none of their sensitivity analyses were promotions for private labels recommended because consumers' response to price promotions is so low. The low sales response is also supported by the asymmetric price tier effect proposed by Blattberg and Wisniewski (1989), which states that low-priced private labels do not gain much sales through price discounting.

The exception to the above theoretical result comes from Raju et al. (1990), who state that the weak store brand (with lower loyalty) should promote more often because the retailer can offer smaller discounts than the strong national brand. These authors also find empirical evidence supporting their proposition. The same argument is also made by Shankar and Krishnamurthi (2007), who find from their decision-support model that the optimal discount frequency of private labels is greater than the optimal discount frequency for large national brands. The reason for this is that the optimal deal depth is lower for store brands than for national brands.

There is greater consensus on discount depth. All four game-theory models (Lal 1990; Rao 1991; Narasimhan 1988; Raju et al. 1990) directly or indirectly state that the average discount of higher-priced national brands is greater than the average discount of lower-priced private labels. This assertion is supported by the decision models of Tellis and Zufryden (1995) and Shankar and Krishnamurthi (2007); the asymmetric price-tier effect theory of Blattberg and Wisniewski (1989); and has strong external validity – Sethuraman (2009, Table 2, M15).

In summary, private labels discount fairly frequently. Managers and researchers need to better understand the profitability of private label discounts. However, private labels do (rightly) offer shallower discount than national brands in both absolute and percentage (of price) terms.

TRENDS, FUTURE RESEARCH AND CONCLUSION

In this section, we provide some predictions and future research directions and summarize the key strategies for private label marketing.

Trends and Predictions

We offer some predictions related to private label sales and marketing based on our reading of the literature and understanding of the groceries market.

Private label share
It is well known that private label sales and market share in grocery products have grown globally in the last ten years. Recent growth has been partly attributed to recession. Will the growth trend continue post-recession? We think it will, up to a point. When retailers are establishing a foothold with their private labels, they are doing so increasingly with quality products at value prices. Thus there is some inertia once consumers have switched to store brands. At least we do not expect to see a significant drop in private label share post-recession. But will private labels account for 40–50 percent of category volume, on average, as some are predicting? We think this situation is unlikely because of consumers' need for variety (a case in point is consumers' reduced patronage of Sears in the 1970s when it overemphasized private labels), retailers' profitability and inability to manage private label at that volume, and retail competition (dollar stores and other discount stores may offer the national brands at value prices and draw away consumers). It is worth noting that even Aldi's, an exclusive private label seller, is planning to add some national brands to improve variety and counter competition.

Private label offerings
There is clearly a general trend towards quality equivalence between private labels and national brands, although the quality differential may vary across products and retail outlets. We believe, at least in the case of retailers with strong private label programs, that product quality will cease to be a differentiator between national and store brands. Competition will be based on value and store image for store brand and status and brand image for the national brands. We will also see emergence of premium private labels in some limited categories, like pasta and chocolates, and niche private labels in some other categories like nutrition or diet products, but we do not think they will be a force to reckon with. Traditional (standard) private labels will continue to dominate the market.

Private label sourcing
We believe there will be increasing use of national brand manufacturers as suppliers of private labels. Both retailers and manufacturers are recognizing the potential mutual benefits. Private labels are here to stay. Manufacturers believe, "If you can't beat 'em, join 'em!" Competition from other manufacturers, excess capacity and reduced demand during tough economic times have forced national brand manufacturers to rethink their supply strategies. It is also in the interest of retailers to obtain private labels from national brand manufacturers for quality assurance and better category management.

Private label marketing
As the quality gap between national brands and store brands closes, we should see a general reduction in the price gap. But at the same time, national brands will continue to

command a price premium above the "just noticeable difference" threshold of about 15 percent. As quality becomes less of a differentiator and national brands compete on the basis of image and coupons, retailers will increase their in-store non-price promotions of store brands through displays and features. At the same time, both retailers and leading manufacturers will develop some cooperative marketing arrangements for increasing category profits.

Future Research

Based on our review, we believe the following research topics are important and germane for future analytical and empirical research.

Private label sourcing

When selecting a store brand supplier, the retailer has three options: (1) procure from an independent (fringe) manufacturer; (2) obtain from a national brand manufacturer (dual branding); or (3) produce its own store brands. Broadly, there are two considerations for both the retailer and the manufacturer to participate in dual branding: cost consideration and strategic consideration. Cost consideration relates to the cost advantage that a national brand manufacturer may have compared to other potential suppliers. Strategic considerations include (a) quality assurance and (b) increased cooperation from the national brand manufacturer, especially in a market where there are many store switchers. It is difficult to obtain data on dual branding because of the desire for manufacturers not to divulge the information. Nevertheless, we need better understanding of why a manufacturer would supply private labels and why a retailer would accept the same (see Kumar et al. 2010 for some analytical work and Chen et al. 2010 for some empirical work on this topic).

Premium private labels

While most of the analysis is based on one store brand per category, some retailers may follow a two-tier or three-tier store brand strategy (Steiner 2004). For example, Wal-Mart has two apple juices, the low-priced Great Value and the premium Sam's American Choice. Some retailers may introduce multiple store brands that target different national brands – possibly for better trade terms from both brands (Sayman and Raju 2004b). In particular, Kumar and Steenkamp (2007) say premium private labels is perhaps the hottest trend in private label retailing. However, we have little understanding of what such private labels represent, what the right conditions are for introducing premium labels, or their profitability. Geyskens et al. (2010) explore the effect of introducing economy and premium private labels on the sales of national brands and standard private labels. More work is needed in this area.

National brand competition

Managers believe that the manner in which private labels react to national brands and the manner in which national brands strategize against private labels depend on the nature of #1, #2 and #3 national brands. Hence incorporating multiple, asymmetric national brands would better reflect real-world market conditions. Some researchers (e.g. Sayman et al. 2002) have studied private label strategies in the presence of multiple non-equivalent national brands, but more work is needed.

Table 19.1   Summary of myths and realities on private label strategies

No.	Myth or reality	Finding	Insights and implications
1	Introduce store brands in commodity products	Part myth and part reality!	Undifferentiated commodity products are likely to be characterized by high price substitutability between national brand and store brand and high price substitutability among national brands. The former favors store brand reduction; the latter deters it. In categories with high price competition among national brands, retailer can reduce the number of national brands (reduce competition) and introduce the store brand, or reap the benefits of the competing national brands and not introduce a store brand.
2	Quality is important for successful private label program	Reality	Most research evidence points to quality being an important determinant of private label share and profitability. Focusing on private label quality, even if it means slightly higher cost and lower store brand margin, is likely to pay off for the retailer in the long run.
3	There is no place for a store brand when there are already many national brands	Not necessarily true	Retailer can introduce a store brand even when there are many national brands, especially when brands are differentiated, store brand can get incremental volume, and store brand margins are higher.
4	Retailers eye the high-dollar-volume categories for store brand	Reality	High-dollar-volume categories are characterized by high household penetration and/or high purchase frequency and/or high price per purchase, all of which are conducive to store brand introduction. Retailer can introduce a store brand in high-volume categories, especially when the store brand margins are higher than those from national brands.
5	Higher margin is the prime reason for store brand introduction	Partly true	Retailer's percent margin on store brand is generally higher than that for national brands but absolute dollar margin may not be higher. Higher margin is often a stated reason for store brand introduction but even if margins are not higher, building store loyalty is a viable reason for store brand introduction.
6	Store brands increase store's share of consumer wallet	Generally true	Most evidence points to a positive relationship between private label share and store's share of wallet. Both may reinforce each other – store brand loyalty promotes store loyalty and vice versa.
7	Target store brands at high-price-sensitive/low-quality-sensitive consumers	Myth	Store brand consumers do care about quality as much as or more than price. Good (acceptable) quality store brand is essential for strong, successful private label program.

Table 19.1   (continued)

No.	Myth or reality	Finding	Insights and implications
8	Target store brands at low-income, less-educated, large families	Myth	Demographics are not significant influencers of private label purchase. In general, middle-income, educated consumers are more prone to purchasing store brands and should be the primary target. Retailers can also educate and offer trials to low-income consumers to attract them to their brands.
9	Target the store brands at national brand deal-prone consumers	Myth	People who purchase national brands on deal are distinct from typical store brand consumers. In general, deal proneness is not a defining characteristic of store brand consumers.
10	Position store brand close to the national brands	Part myth and part reality	Positioning the store brand closer to the national brand is optimal (a) in mature products with limited category expansion and (b) if retailers' store brand margins are greater than their margins on the national brands. However, there are many situations in which close store brand positioning may not be optimal.
11	Keep store brand price as low as possible relative to competing national brand	Myth	When a store brand is positioned close to the national brand, retailer should actually reduce the price differential between the two brands and not price the store brand much lower than national brand. However, the price differential can not be too low – consumers will buy the national brand if they believe the price is only slightly above that of the store brand.
12	Store brands should not price-promote	Mixed results	Store brands do price-promote for various reasons. In fact, deal (price promotion) frequency of store brand is higher than that for leading national brands in many categories. However, deal depth (dollar discount) is generally less for private labels than for national brands.

Private label price promotion
While conventional wisdom suggests that retailers should not price-promote their private labels, they do in fact promote. The reasons for promoting private labels, as stated by retailers, include: (a) the need to protect store brand turf; (b) the need to generate trial and repeat of store brand; and (c) the desire to simply promote what customers want (Sethuraman 2008). We need better understanding of these motivations and more detailed analysis of the profitability of private label discounts.

Private label non-price promotions
Non-price promotions include in-store promotions such as displays and features, as well as coupons, free samples and gifts. There is mixed evidence on the effect of non-price

promotions on private label sales. However, the research on non-price promotions is too limited to draw any meaningful recommendations.

Non-grocery products

The analytical models and empirical work have predominantly focused on grocery products. Would the results be different for non-grocery products, such as appliances and apparel? Future research should incorporate the institutional and market structures pertinent to the non-grocery product markets.

In conclusion, academic literature combined with managerial wisdom have dispelled some myths, highlighted some realities, and provided insights into private label strategies. These myths and realities and their implications are summarized in Table 19.1. However, more theoretical and empirical research is needed to address several issues related to store brand strategy in grocery and non-grocery products.

REFERENCES

Ailawadi, Kusum L. and Bari Harlam (2004), "An empirical analysis of the determinants of retail margins: the role of store brand share," *Journal of Marketing*, **68** (January), 147–65.

Ailawadi, Kusum L., Scott A. Neslin and Karen Gedenk (2001), "Pursuing the value-conscious consumer: store brands versus national brand promotions," *Journal of Marketing*, **65** (January), 71–89.

Ailawadi, Kusum L., Koen L. Pauwels and J.B. Steenkamp (2008), "Private-label use and store loyalty," *Journal of Marketing*, **72** (November), 19–30.

Applebaum, Eidan, Eitan Gerstner and Prasad Naik (2003), "The effects of expert quality evaluations vs. brand name on price premiums," *Journal of Product and Brand Management*, **12** (3), 154–65.

Blattberg, Robert C. and Kenneth J. Wisniewski (1989), "Price induced patterns of competition," *Marketing Science*, **8** (Fall), 291–309.

Chen, Xinlei, Om Narasimhan, George John and Tirtha Dhar (2010), "An empirical investigation of private label supply by national label producers," *Marketing Science*, **29** (July–August), 738–55.

Chintagunta, Pradeep K., Andre Bonfrer and Inseong Song (2002), "Investigating the effects of store brand introduction on retailer demand and pricing behavior," *Management Science*, **48** (10), 1242–67.

Choi, Chan S. and Anne T. Coughlan (2006), "Private label positioning: quality versus feature differentiation from national brand," *Journal of Retailing*, **82** (2), 79–93.

Corstjens, Marcel and Rajiv Lal (2000), "Building store loyalty through store brands," *Journal of Marketing Research*, **37** (August), 281–91.

Dhar, Sanjay K. and Stephen J. Hoch (1997), "Why store brand penetration varies by retailer," *Marketing Science*, **16** (Summer), 208–27.

Discount Merchandiser (1996), "Revealing private thoughts," **36** (11), 58–60.

Donegan, Priscilla (1989), "Private label is alive and well," *Progressive Grocer*, February, 61–7.

Erdem, Tülin, Ying Zhao and Ala Valenzuela (2004), "Performance of store brands: a cross-country analysis of consumer store brand preferences, perceptions, and risk," *Journal of Marketing Research*, **41** (1), 86–100.

Fitzell, Phillip B. (1992), *Private Label Marketing in the 1990s: The Evolution of Price Labels into Global Brands*, New York: Global Book Productions.

Geyskens, Inge, Katrijn Gielens and Els Gijsbrechts (2010), "Proliferating private-label portfolios: how introducing economy and premium private labels influences brand choice," *Journal of Marketing Research*, **42** (October), 791–807.

Hoch, Stephen J. and Shumeet Banerji (1993), "When do private labels succeed?," *Sloan Management Review*, Summer, 57–67.

Hoch, Stephen J. and L.M. Lodish (2001), "Store brands and category management," Working Paper, Wharton School, University of Pennsylvania.

Kumar, Nanda, Suresh Radhakrishnan and Ram C. Rao (2010), "Private label vendor selection in a supply chain: quality and clientele effects," *Journal of Retailing*, **86** (2), 148–58.

Kumar, Nirmalya and Jan-Benedict E. M. Steenkamp (2007), *Private Labels Strategy*, Boston, MA: Harvard Business School Press.

Lal, Rajiv (1990), "Manufacturer trade deals and retail price promotions," *Journal of Marketing Research*, **27**, 428–44.

Mills, David E. (1995), "Why retailers sell private labels," *Journal of Economics and Management Strategy*, **4** (3), 509–28.

Narasimhan, Chakravarthi (1988), "Competitive promotional strategies," *Journal of Business*, **61** (October), 427–50.

Pauwels, Koen and Shuba Srinivasan (2004), "Who benefits from store brand entry?," *Marketing Science*, **23** (Summer), 364–90.

Pauwels, Koen and Shuba Srinivasan (2007), "Pricing of national brands versus store brands: market power components, findings and research opportunities," in Vithala Rao (ed.) *Handbook of Pricing Research in Marketing*, Cheltenham, UK and Northampton, MA, USA: Edward Elgar, pp. 258–82.

Quelch, John A. and David Harding (1996), "Brands versus private labels: fighting to win," *Harvard Business Review* (January–February), 99–109.

Raju, Jagmohan S., Raj Sethuraman and Sanjay K. Dhar (1995a), "The introduction and performance of store brands," *Management Science*, **41** (6), 957–78.

Raju, Jagmohan S., Raj Sethuraman and Sanjay K. Dhar (1995b), "National brand-store brand price differential and store brand market share," *Pricing Strategy and Practice*, **3** (2), 17–24.

Raju, Jagmohan S., V. Srinivasan and Rajiv Lal (1990), "The effects of brand loyalty on competitive price promotional strategies," *Management Science*, **36** (3), 276–304.

Rao, Ram C. (1991), "Pricing and promotions in asymmetric duopolies," *Marketing Science*, **10** (2), 131–44.

Richardson, Paul S., Arun K. Jain and Alan Dick (1996), "Household store brand proneness: a framework," *Journal of Retailing*, **72** (2), 159–85.

Sayman, Serdar and Jagmohan S. Raju (2004a), "Investigating the cross-category effects of store brands," *Review of Industrial Organization*, **24** (2), 129–41.

Sayman, Serdar and Jagmohan S. Raju (2004b), "How category characteristics affect the number of store brands offered by the retailer: a model and empirical analysis," *Journal of Retailing*, **80**, 279–87.

Sayman, Serdar and Jagmohan S. Raju (2007), "Store brands: from back to the future," in N.K. Malhotra (ed.), *Review of Marketing Research*, Volume 3, Armonle, NY: M.E. Sharpe Inc.

Sayman, Serdar, Stephen J. Hoch and Jagmohan S. Raju (2002), "Positioning store brands," *Marketing Science*, **21** (Fall), 378–97.

Schmalensee, Richard (1978), "Entry deterrence in the ready-to-eat breakfast cereal industry," *Bell Journal of Economics*, **9**, 305–27.

Scott-Morton, Fiona and Florian Zettelmeyer (2004), "The strategic positioning of store brands in retailer–manufacturer negotiations," *Review of Industrial Organization*, **24**, 161–94.

Sethuraman, Raj (2003), "Measuring national brands' equity over store brands," *Review of Marketing Science*, **1** (2), 1–26.

Sethuraman, Raj (2004), "Positioning store brands against national brands: get close or keep a distance?" Working Paper, SMU–Cox School of Business.

Sethuraman, Raj (2006), "Private label marketing strategies in packaged goods; management beliefs and research insights," Marketing Science Institute Working Paper No. 06–108 (June).

Sethuraman, Raj (2008), "There is nothing more practical than the practice of theory: what practitioners think about theoretical results on national brand–store brand competition," Marketing Science Institute Special Report No. 08–209 (November).

Sethuraman, Raj (2009), "Assessing the external validity of analytical results from national brand and store brand competition models," *Marketing Science*, **28** (4), 759–81.

Shankar, Venkatesh and Lakshman Krishnamurthi (2007), "RETPRICE: a retailer pricing and promotions decision support model," Working Paper, Texas A & M University.

Steiner, Robert L. (2004), "The nature and benefits of national brand/private label competition," *Review of Industrial Organization*, **24** (2), 105–27.

Stern, Louis W. (1966), "The new world of private brands," *California Management Review*, **8** (3), 43–50.

Sudhir, K. and Debrata Talukdar (2004), "Does store brand patronage improve store patronage?," *Review of Industrial Organization*, **24** (2), 143–60.

Tellis, Gerard and Fred Zufryden (1995), "Tackling the retailer decision maze: which brand to discount, how much, when and why?," *Marketing Science*, **14** (3), 271–99.

PART VI

MARKETING STRATEGY DYNAMICS

20 First-mover/pioneer strategies

Marvin B. Lieberman and David B. Montgomery

The issue of first-mover/pioneer advantages and disadvantages is more complex and nuanced than often portrayed in journalistic popular press writings, commentaries by consultants and even academic articles. This literature sometimes gives the impression that first-mover advantages are essentially automatic, a birthright in effect.

This chapter explores many of the ambiguities, misperceptions and some myths concerning the advantages of being a first mover or pioneer, hereafter termed FMAs. This discussion is followed by a brief review of the antecedents of performance and how these relate to FMAs. The third section presents the fundamental mechanisms that may create or inhibit FMAs. (It is our contention that suspicion should be aroused whenever FMAs are cited in a discussion without identifying plausible mechanisms that might underlie such effects in the specific case at hand.) The fourth section provides an overview of the empirical evidence relating to FMAs. The fifth section outlines strategy considerations that might be used by potential first movers and fast followers. Fundamentally, the first-mover/pioneer should determine if a first-mover strategy is likely to be optimal for its firm; if so, it should seek to develop its resources to support advantages and seek to eliminate and/or counter its disadvantages. How this applies to fast followers will also be considered. Finally, the chapter is summarized and suggestions are made for further research.

1. AMBIGUITIES, MISCONCEPTIONS AND MYTHS

First-mover Advantage: What Is It?

"First-mover advantage" (FMA) is the benefit enjoyed by a firm as the consequence of its early entry into a new market. This benefit can arise along several dimensions of corporate performance, including profit, market share and business survival. Although economic profit represents the ultimate and perhaps most meaningful reward for market pioneering, most empirical studies focus on market share because this dimension is easiest to measure.

Ambiguities

The research landscape as well as popular press discussions are littered with confusion (usually not recognized) over inconsistent use of definitions of the "who, what, when and where" of FMAs. (See Box 20.1.) The popular press often naively discusses FMAs as though they are inevitable outcomes of first movership *per se*. FMAs are by no means inevitable. They are generated by a combination of mechanisms that interact with the first mover's actions and reactions, competitor actions and reactions and dynamics of the external environment. This combination of forces will impact performance on whatever dimension of advantage is in question.

BOX 20.1   AMBIGUITIES

What?   First in what? Technology? Product introduction? Market development?

Fundamentally new product? New product generation? New geographic market?

When?   Short term or long term? Latency or speed of competitive response?

Who?   First- mover? Pioneer? Early or fast follower? Late follower? Laggard?

Where?   Market definition? How broad or narrow?

To resolve the ambiguities in FMAs, one must initially ask: first mover in what? First to generate the appropriate technology? First to actually introduce a new type of product? Or first to actively develop the market? Surely one might expect different results depending upon the answer to these questions. Although order of entry can be defined in many contexts, the standard definition is based on the timing of product introduction, where "first mover" refers to the initial firm(s) to enter a new market with a commercial product.

This raises a related issue: what type of new market is being considered? Is it a new product or service that is being introduced to the world for the first time? Or is the market a new geographic location for a product previously sold elsewhere (e.g. introduction of a product into a new national market, such as China)? Furthermore, technological progress often takes the form where new products are introduced in discrete "generations" of improvement over the existing technology. This pattern can be observed, for example, in successive generations of computer hard disk drives, game consoles and semiconductor memory (DRAM). In such cases, the "what" may be a specific new generation of product, rather than the first appearance of the product category *per se*.

Another "what" issue relates to the type of advantage being considered. Advantage in market share? Profits? Survival? Market pioneers may value these objectives in dissimilar ways. For example, some market pioneers value long-term survival, whereas others aim to sell their business to larger firms that enter as followers.

There are also at least two issues of potential ambiguity with respect to the when or time frame one has in mind when referring to FMAs. Are short-term results only being considered? Long-term? What is the definition of short and long term? Sometimes the when is even taken as the time since some major event, such as the opening of China for foreign direct investment in January 1979 (Luo and Peng, 1998). Boulding and Christen (2003) demonstrated in the Profit Impact of Market Strategy (PIMS) sample that pioneers are more profitable for the first 12 to 14 years, but thereafter followers tend to be more profitable, on average. This implies that the answer one achieves for FMAs related to profits may depend upon the time frame used. Time also relates to how quickly competitors respond to the introduction of the pioneer. The evidence discussed in Section 4 indicates that competitor reaction both in terms of imitation and substitution seems to be coming more quickly than in an earlier era.

Studies of pioneering advantage also differ in the way they define the term "first mover", the who in Box 20.1. Strictly speaking, a market has only one "first mover," but in practice, multiple firms are often identified as "first movers" or "pioneers." Such classification is not unreasonable, given that firms may enter the market more or less simultaneously and in many cases the exact date of entry is not precisely defined. Firms that enter later in the evolution of the market are characterized as "followers" and may be further distinguished as "fast followers," "late followers" and so on, although these labels are often somewhat arbitrary.

The where issue encompasses the appropriate definition of market breadth, the location of the market in geographic or customer space and whether the FMAs are empirically true or simply exist in the manager's mind. Disagreements over market breadth may lead one observer to classify a given firm as the first mover, whereas another may view that same firm as a follower within a more broadly defined, existing market – or alternatively, as a pioneering firm in a separate, precursor market whose characteristics arguably differ from the new market under consideration. For example, the authors contend that the Golder and Tellis (1993) definition of Xerox as a follower in the copier business instead of as the pioneer in the plain paper copier business is inappropriate. (We disagree with their definition of market breadth.) Customer segments can also give rise to ambiguity in market definition. In geographic or regional or country markets, a firm might well be a laggard in one such market and yet a pioneer in another. Some research deals with the beliefs of managers in different industries such as manufacturing versus service, or managers from different countries or regions (Song et al. 1999).

A further complication (relating also to the "what" issue described above) is that multiple categories of new markets can arise, including fundamentally new products, new "generations" of existing products and new geographic markets for products previously introduced elsewhere. Some of these markets emerge through radical innovation, whereas others emerge incrementally in a more predictable way. Moreover, sampling biases can lead to the omission of important firms. For example, available data sources may go back only as far as the initial firm that achieved market success, omitting the true pioneer(s) that failed to survive.

Common Misperceptions and Myths

Reflection on how the idea of first-mover advantages was naively applied during the dot. com era reveals the need for a more holistic, complex and nuanced view of first-mover (dis)advantages. As Internet-related markets began to develop in the 1990s, companies and venture capitalists raced ahead to be first without giving careful thought to what mechanism(s) would support FMAs in a given instance and how durable such FMAs might be, given the likely competitive and environmental situation. In retrospect, the excesses of the era are apparent.

One common managerial misperception is the belief that first-mover advantages are ubiquitous, virtually inevitable and should normally be pursued. Although the term "first-mover advantage" seems to suggest that early entry is desirable, market pioneering is a high-risk strategy. The advantages of pioneering a new market are often offset by disadvantages. The question of whether on balance a "first-mover advantage" exists in any specific context depends on characteristics of the emerging market and the entering firm as well as potential and current competitors and the overall environment. As we argue below, first-mover advantage must be thought of as a contingent property, rather than one that exists in any absolute, inevitable sense.

A related misconception arises from failure to recognize interdependence of cause and effect (commonly referred to in the economics literature as "endogeneity"). A pioneering firm may prove successful not because it chose to pursue a first-mover strategy, but rather because of underlying skills that enabled the firm to implement such a strategy effectively. Indeed, it may be difficult to separate the benefits of a firm's distinctive capabilities from those attributable to the timing of entry.

To the myth of inevitable FMAs must be added the notion that the advantages will persist forever (or at least for a very long time). Ultimately, all advantages erode. To maintain advantage, the first mover/pioneer must continue to be active and vigilant and adjust appropriately to changing conditions, both competitive and environmental. And for pioneers fortunate to enjoy an initial advantage in market share and/or profitability, there may come a point where the optimal strategy is sell out or otherwise beat a graceful retreat.

2.   FIRM PERFORMANCE AND ENTRY ORDER

Before exploring the specific mechanisms that give support to FMAs, it is well to be reminded of the spectrum of determinants that impact a firm's performance (be the firm a pioneer, an early entrant, a late entrant or a laggard). Any empirical result on entry order (see Section 4) reflects the convergence of multiple influences. Firm performance is the consequence of a firm's actions and inactions, potential and actual competitor actions and inactions and the environment (including governments, markets and the economy, customers, technology evolution and even luck, which may be embedded in all of the foregoing factors). In any given case these multiple forces converge in creating the end result: failure or degree of success on any given performance attribute. A potential pioneer should carefully consider all of these forces in deciding whether and when to enter a market.

It has been suggested by Lieberman and Montgomery (1998) and others that the conceptual framework of the resource-based view of the firm (RBV) may fruitfully be paired with the more empirical perspective of FMA. The RBV suggests that a firm's performance flows to a substantial degree from its resources and capabilities. The FMA perspective shows how the order and timing of entry can define the firm's potential to realize competitive advantages. This potential, within a context of competitor actions and environmental shifts, shapes the manner and extent to which the firm can apply its existing stock of resources and capabilities and accumulate additional resources over time. Conversely, the firm's evolving resource stock is likely to influence the duration of any FMAs. The specific mechanisms for generating advantage from pioneering and the concomitant risks, are discussed in Section 3.

A case can also be made that order of entry, especially for pioneers, may be endogenously determined. That is, firms having specific preconditions of resources and capabilities may be more likely or willing to pioneer. Further, if FMAs exist, they may contribute further to the pioneering firm's resources and capabilities over time. This, in turn, may support early entry by the firm into new product generations or new geographic markets. For example, Samsung built up a set of strong technical capabilities that enabled it to enter as the pioneer in successive generations of DRAMs. While the initial development of these capabilities required a large allocation of outside resources, Samsung was ultimately able to sustain its leadership across generations by reinvesting the high profits earned at the start of each product generation, when it enjoyed a dominant market share and limited price competition (Shin and Jang 2005). Consequently, the conditions exist for potential bidirectional causality between firm performance and the timing of market entry.

It has also been suggested that FMAs may be impacted by a number of contingent effects that may enhance or detract from the magnitude of the first-mover effect. This implies variations in FMAs depending upon the nature and magnitude of these contingent effects. These can be identified in an empirical context by testing models that include an interaction of the order of entry variable with the identified contingent variable(s). Potentially, the impact might differ across the performance variables such as market share, profits, survival and so on.

One contingent situation that has been considered is the instance of service versus manufacturing industries. Service industries are sometimes thought of as having low entry barriers, thus making services easier to imitate. This would make it difficult for a pioneering firm to maintain its FMAs for very long. However, capabilities embedded in know-how and networks in service industries may be sustainable and many successful pioneers, such as FedEx, Amazon and eBay, are service providers.

Geographical markets may also offer contingent benefits or costs that will impact FMAs. A firm that is a laggard in one geographic market may become a pioneer in another and reap FMAs. In the premium gin market Beefeaters was the first to establish a premium segment in the US market, whereas Gordon's occupied the pioneer position in the UK, the original home of gin. The conditions supporting FMA in a new international market may be quite different from those that prevail in the original market. An international market may offer reduced uncertainty about some aspects of market and technology, yet contain hidden dangers with respect to lack of knowledge of culture and customs as well as governmental and political uncertainties that may well offset the FMAs.

Dynamic technology and markets raise the further specter of competitive substitution rather than imitation being a danger to the original pioneer. Superior products introduced by competitors may render the original basis (or mechanism) for FMA of lesser or no value. With respect to technology, this is reflected in the evolution over time of multiple generations of technologies and products. Each new technology generation poses a threat to leaders in the previous generation. For example, Digital Equipment Corporation (DEC) was a highly successful pioneer when the minicomputer segment emerged in the computer industry, but the firm failed dramatically when the market for minicomputers was "disrupted" by the new generation of personal computers.

In general, these contingent factors relate to features of the new market or characteristics of the entering firm. We consider the nature of these contingencies in greater detail in Sections 3 and 4 below and in Section 5 we discuss how they shape the firm's optimal strategy.

Counterbalancing these potential opportunities are potential disadvantages of early entry. Competitors may imitate, perhaps doing better than the pioneer with respect to customer preferences. Pioneers may become complacent, slow to perceive and act upon new conditions and thereby lose FMAs to later entrants. Technology and market changes may nullify the pioneer's original advantages and require adaptation by the original pioneer for continued success. Thus order of entry advantages are not inevitably positive (or negative). It depends.

3.   MECHANISMS BY WHICH FMAs MAY BE CREATED AND SUSTAINED

First-mover advantages, when they exist, are the result of specific mechanisms. These mechanisms are typically shaped by a wide range of factors: market characteristics, potential resource advantages of the first mover (including those that existed prior to entry and others developed by design or luck after entry), strategic actions pursued by the first mover/pioneer, strategies of potential and actual competitors and factors in the broader market environment (customer response and actions, governments, technology and market evolution). In our early paper on FMA (Lieberman and Montgomery 1988) we argued based on theory and empirical observation that FMAs depend upon one of three generic sources: (1) leadership in product or process technology; (2) preemption of scarce assets; and/or (3) buyer switching costs. Subsequently, we recognized that network effects should be considered a fourth generic mechanism for first-mover advantages (Lieberman and Montgomery 1998). Note that our position is that FMAs result from some specific mechanism(s) which offers a potential but by no means guaranteed advantage to the first mover/pioneer.

Market and Firm Characteristics and the Sustainability of First-mover Advantage

Although "luck" plays an important role in determining whether a first mover will ultimately be successful, an astute entrant must consider characteristics of the market and the firm itself in deciding the optimal timing of entry. Informed notions of competitor actions and reactions are also vital. What specific mechanisms are likely to support a strategy of market pioneering? Moreover, can the benefits be sustained over time?

An FMA will not exist or be sustainable unless some of the following market characteristics are present: (1) appropriable technology; (2) preemptible resources; (3) customer switching costs; (4) network effects. To be successful, a first mover must exploit these characteristics to defend against competition from follower firms.

Appropriable technology
A market pioneer that develops unique technology must find a way to keep that technology proprietary. Patents are a common mechanism, but their effectiveness varies greatly across industries. Secrecy and aggressive movement down a "learning curve" can allow a firm to maintain technological leadership. Even so, such an advantage is difficult

to maintain in industries where technological progress is rapid, as rivals have greater opportunity to leapfrog the pioneer's technology. Levin et al. (1984) found substantial differences between industries in appropriability mechanisms, with learning-curve and lead-time advantages being relatively important in many industries and with patents being important in relatively fewer.

Preemptible resources

In some markets, superior resources can be acquired preemptively by the initial entrant. These include raw material inputs, geographic locations and, potentially most important, positions in consumers' perceptual spaces. As markets globalize there are increasing opportunities for companies to become pioneers in customers' perceptual spaces in emerging and transitional markets, even if those companies may have been followers in more advanced markets.

Customer switching costs

The initial entrant in the market may have the ability to develop buyer switching costs or "lock in." Once these mechanisms are in place, later entrants must invest greater resources to attract customers away from the pioneer. Switching costs include initial time and financial investments made by the buyer in adapting to the seller's product (e.g. employee training costs, costs of ancillary products such as software, supplier qualification etc.), product-specific learning by the buyer over time and contractual switching costs intentionally created by the seller (as with the airlines' frequent flyer programs).

Network effects

In situations where customers seek a common standard or the ability to interact with other users, the pioneering firm has the first opportunity to develop "network effects." In this case the value of the product or service increases with the number of users. Thus advantage goes to the company with the largest user base. Such effects, which are most common in the information technology sector, create a preference among buyers for the product that has emerged as the standard. In addition, network effects may attract valuable alliance partners to the leading firm.

First-mover Disadvantages

In addition to the mechanisms described above that offer potential benefits to the first-mover, other mechanisms favor market followers. Often, these benefits to followers are relatively more potent. Hence it is true in many situations that market pioneering is, on balance, an unattractive strategy.

Spillover and free-rider effects

Followers typically benefit from investments made by early entrants and from the resolution of uncertainty. (Such benefits to followers are, in effect, "first-mover disadvantages.") More specifically, early entrants often must invest in buyer education and infrastructure in order to develop the new market. To some extent, followers can "free-ride" on these investments and on the R&D of pioneering firms, which may resolve key uncertainties about the best technological approaches and salient customer needs. There is evidence of such effects in Mansfield's (1981) early studies, which found that imitators could duplicate patented innovations for about 65 percent of the pioneer's costs. Mansfield also found that this often occurs quite rapidly as 60 percent of patented innovations were successfully duplicated within four years of introduction.

The "free-rider" disadvantage of pioneers depends upon leakage of information and know-how underlying the original pioneering advantage. Many mechanisms exist for the possible spillover of proprietary knowledge: workforce mobility, research publications, informal technical communications (perhaps by customers), reverse engineering, plant tours and so on. Process technology tends to leak more slowly, but Mansfield (1985) found that both product and process technology tended to leak in detail within a year of original product introduction. Lieberman (1989) found that diffusion of process technology allowed late entry by followers in 39 chemical processing industries, despite strong industry learning-curve effects.

In many industries, resolution of the best technical approach occurs through convergence on a "dominant design" or product format that meets the needs of the majority of customers in a relatively low-cost way. If an astute follower is able to time its entry to coincide with the emergence of the dominant design, it can avoid the costly experimentation and potential mistakes committed by early entrants prior to this stage.

Technology and/or market shifts

The previous discussion has essentially focused upon disadvantage to the pioneer due to competitor imitation. But competitor substitution may also lead to pioneer disadvantage. Schumpeter (1961) viewed technological progress as a process of "creative destruction." Thus new technologies may come to eclipse earlier dominant technologies. Often, the new technology is developed even while the original technology is still experiencing substantial growth. This can render it difficult for the first mover/pioneer to perceive the threat. Witness American Viscose's failure to recognize the potential of polyester to replace rayon and Transitron's inattention to the substitution of silicon for the much more rare germanium in semiconductor fabrication (Foster 1986). Market shifts, such as an emerging need for electronic funds transfer, substituted computer systems for the original automatic teller machines of Docutel, which was reduced to a bystander in the market. This inattention of a pioneer to substitution danger is related to incumbent inertia, which is discussed next.

Incumbent inertia

Incumbent pioneers may not just be inattentive; they may also suffer from what may be termed incumbent inertia. Incumbent pioneers may be locked in to fixed assets, which make it very difficult for them to adapt, they may be reluctant to launch improved products or processes for fear of cannibalization of current products or production technologies (a reluctance not shared by eager new entrants) and/or they may suffer from organizational inflexibility. Similarly, they may not understand the potential of a "disruptive technology" that is initially viewed as inferior (Christensen 1997). All of these sources of inertia may contribute to an incumbent pioneer being slow to respond to either radical or even more gradual improvement offered by later entrants (who might themselves be the pioneers of the new product or service generation).

Generalizations relating to industry/market characteristics

A number of authors have generalized about how industry characteristics affect the possibility for first-mover advantages versus disadvantages. One set of generalizations relates to horizontal versus vertical product differentiation and the speed of technical change (Bohlmann et al. 2002; Suarez and Lanzolla 2007). The threat of substitution is particularly salient when technological change is rapid or abrupt and when product differentiation is primarily vertical (consumers have similar rank ordering of quality) rather than horizontal (consumer preferences differ, leading to the existence of comparatively stable segments and niches). With rapid product improvement and fairly homogeneous customer tastes, a pioneering firm can be easily leapfrogged over time by entrants offering newer, superior products.

4. EMPIRICAL EVIDENCE: AN OVERVIEW FOR FIRST-MOVER ADVANTAGES

The purpose of this section is to summarize empirical issues related to the subject of first-mover/pioneer advantages. This discussion will cover most of the important issues, including the contexts where FMAs may arise, contextual effects or contingencies that determine the importance of FMAs and the dynamics of FMAs over time. These will be summarized as statements of what is known, often being illustrated by examples and studies that illuminate the summary statements. (For more summary information on empirical issues in FMA see Lieberman and Montgomery 1998, especially Table 1.)

Empirical issue 1: first-mover/pioneer advantages exist empirically in a wide variety of contexts and for various performance criteria

FMAs have been identified for various types of markets. These include fundamentally new products being introduced to the world for the first time, as well as new generations of existing products and new geographic markets for products previously introduced elsewhere. Although FMAs are often considered to be a general phenomenon, the specific drivers of FMA in any given situation depend on the exact market context and other contingencies that we consider in the next subsection. We start, however, with a broad perspective on the empirical evidence.

FMAs have been found empirically for market share, profit and survivorship, although results for market share are far more common. In their study of empirical generalizations relating to order of entry and performance, Kalyanaram et al. (1995) focus on market share results, having found substantially more evidence relating to market share advantages. Their first generalization, based upon a wide variety of empirical research, was that "For mature consumer and industrial goods, there is a negative relationship between order of market entry and market share." That is, they find that, on average, first movers/pioneers have an advantage in market share, at least for some period of time. Even for markets with very low barriers to entry/imitation – e.g. money market mutual funds – moderately sustainable market share advantages have been found for first movers/pioneers (Makadok 1998). In the case of money market funds, average market share was found to be 29.2 percent for first movers, dropping to 19.2 percent for second movers, 5.7 percent for third movers and continuing monotonically down thereafter. More recently, a study of 379 subsidiaries of multinational advertising agencies in 43 developing markets found market share performance related inversely to entry order lag, thereby reinforcing the evidence of market share advantage on average to pioneers in service markets as well as in manufacturing contexts (Magnusson et al. 2009). It also supports the notion that first-mover share advantages exist in emerging markets as well as in the more advanced ones, thus greatly broadening the scope of empirical support for FMAs in market share. The international applicability of FMAs is further reinforced by Cui and Lui's (2005) study of foreign investors in China, which also found small but significant FMAs in market share.

First-mover advantage is also found for profit, but evidence for this is less extensive and more mixed. Cui and Lui (2005) in their study of foreign investment in China found little evidence for FMA in profit, in contrast to their results for market share. In a study using the PIMS data and accounting for potential endogeneity, Boulding and Christen (2003) found that first to market yields an initial profit advantage which lasts for about 12 to 14 years. Luo and Peng (1998) found that return on sales and return on equity were both substantially inversely related to entry timing for foreign invested manufacturing firms in China. However, in a separate test they found that during the first three years of operations early entrants had a bit over half the ROI of late entrants.

Findings for survival in the context of FMA depend heavily on the market context and definitions applied. Golder and Tellis (1993) performed a historical analysis of 36 product categories in which they found that market pioneers suffered a 47 percent failure rate, in contrast to early market leaders, which experienced only 8 percent. (Recall, however, the question raised earlier about market definitions; Golder and Tellis categorized Xerox as a later entrant in the copier market instead of the pioneer in plain paper copying.) In contrast, Luo and Peng (1998) found an advantage to early China investors in terms of reducing operational risk. Wang et al. (2010) found both pioneering and network effects provided survival advantage in markets with network effects. In their presentation of empirical generalizations relating to order of market entry effects, Kalyanaram et al. (1995, p. G218) stated that based upon their analysis, "Order of market entry is not related to long-term survival rates." So the literature is very mixed when it comes to survival and order of entry, from the large disadvantage suggested by Golder and Tellis to the no-effects conclusion of Kalyanaram et al. to the positive effects found in China studies. Such variation seems consistent with the fact that survival is not always a primary objective of market pioneers, who may aim to be acquired at an attractive price as the market develops over time. For example, acquisition is often the goal of technology startups, but not of multinational corporations attempting to extend their businesses to emerging markets such as China.

In summary, first-mover advantages are fairly common, particularly in terms of market share. But the empirical results represent what has played out in the marketplace as a result of the multiple factors impacting performance, as noted in Section 2. A final message, developed further below, is that first movers/pioneers often achieve advantage, but such results typically must be earned by vigilance and continuous attention. They are by no means guaranteed.

Table 20.1   China contingent factors: hypotheses and support

Hypothesis	Support for market share?	Support for profit?
Pioneers in high-growth industries achieve better performance	Supported	Not supported
Pioneers in less competitive industries achieve better performance	Significant sign reversal, i.e. competition had a positive effect	Not supported
Larger pioneers achieve better performance	Supported	Supported
Pioneers entering with joint ventures achieve better performance than those entering with wholly owned subsidiaries	Supported	Supported
Pioneers making large resource commitments perform better	Supported	Supported
Followers making large resource commitments perform better	Not supported	Supported
Pioneers adopting high marketing intensity achieve better performance	Not supported	Supported
Followers adopting high marketing intensity achieve better performance	Supported	Supported

Source: Based on Cui and Lui (2005).

Empirical issue 2: FMAs are best considered including contextual or contingency factors

A broad theme of this chapter is that FMAs are not automatic; they depend upon characteristics of both the market and the firm, as well as implementation of a first-mover strategy in a competitive context. Thus one would expect that empirical studies that consider such contingencies would provide greater explanatory power and insight than studies that simply examine whether dimensions of performance are correlated with entry order (Kerin et al. 1992).

Using PIMS data, Szymanski et al. (1995) demonstrated that a contingency perspective, implemented by including interaction terms in the empirical model, not only provides further evidence of the market share benefit of first-mover/pioneer entry, but fits the data better and adds insights relating to the interaction of entry order with the contingent variables. Positive contingent effects indicating that pioneer market share would be enhanced by the contingent factor were found to be significant for order of entry and the firm variables of service quality, vertical integration, R&D expenditures, shared facilities and shared customers. Positive interactions were also found for the marketplace factors of market growth rate and immediate customer purchase frequency. A negative impact on market share was found for pioneers using shared marketing programs.

Further insights into contingent effects and FMAs were found for both market share and profit in Cui and Lui's (2005) study of contingent resources and strategies for 4480 Chinese firms in some 80 industries at the four-digit level of the International Industry Standards of Industry Classification. The results are summarized in Table 20.1. As in the Szymanski et al. (1995) study, the contingent model provided a better fit to the data. Much like the Szymanski et al. (1995) results discussed above, Cui and Lui found that pioneers in high-growth industries achieved a better market share (but not higher profit). The competitiveness of the marketplace had an unexpected significant positive impact on pioneer market share, but again had no significant effect on profits. Positive impacts on both market share and profit were found for larger pioneers, those choosing to enter with joint ventures as opposed to wholly owned subsidiaries and when the pioneer opted to make a large resource commitment. The first two of these contingent results were echoed in a study of over 220 Sino-Japanese joint ventures in China (Isobe et al. 2000). Pioneers adopting high marketing intensity benefited from a boost in profit, but not in market share. The study also found that followers adopting high marketing intensity benefited in both market share and profit performance; large resource commitments enhanced profits, but not market share for a follower. Again this study demonstrates FMAs in the transition economy of China as well as the importance and usefulness of contingent factors.

The Luo and Peng (1998) study of 96 foreign invested enterprises in China found profitability (measured as ROS and ROE) significantly positively impacted by industry growth rate and R&D intensity (measured as R&D expenditures divided by sales). Neither firm size nor equity percentage owned by the foreign firm were found to impact either profit measure. This contrasts to the Cui and Lui result discussed above, where size positively impacted profits. This serves to remind us that the results of FMA studies exhibit variance, which suggests that further work continues to be worthwhile, perhaps especially in an international context.

Empirical issue 3: network externalities impact pioneer survival

Our 1988 paper argued that FMAs are contingent on the first three market mechanisms described in Section 3 above. Moreover, we showed that the empirical evidence is consistent with this prediction. Over the decades since our 1988 publication, considerable research attention has been devoted to understanding the fourth mechanism, network effects, which have become increasingly important as the information economy has expanded dramatically.

Network externalities reflect the condition where the value of a product or service to a customer increases with the number of users, often reflected in the installed base. In a study of 45 office products and consumer durables, Srinivasan et al. (2004) found that network externalities exhibited a negative main effect on the survival duration of pioneers. However, there were circumstances in which network effects actually contributed to longer pioneer survival, notably for more technologically intense and more radical products. Another contingent finding was that the larger the pioneer, the more network effects would enhance the pioneer's survival duration. If a pioneer was an incumbent, in the sense that it marketed a previous generation product which satisfied the same customer need, its survival duration was found to be reduced relative to what would be achieved by a pioneer that was not an incumbent in the previous generation.

The impact of network effects on pioneer survival has been found to be contingent upon product compatibility both between and within product generations (Wang et al. 2010). Wang et al. found that the impact of network effects on survival of pioneers relative to followers could be positive or negative depending on these two compatibility issues. "Between-product compatibility" reflects compatibility between product generations. An example of incompatibility would be the original CBS color TV system that was incompatible with the original black and white systems in that the CBS color system could not receive the ongoing black and white programming and the original black and white TV sets could not receive the CBS color broadcasts. CBS's system failed due in large measure to this incompatibility. Color TV took off only after the introduction of the RCA compatible color television. Within-generation product incompatibility is illustrated by the fact that HP and Canon copier and printer cartridges cannot be interchanged. Under the condition that products are compatible across generations but incompatible within generation, empirical support was found that pioneer survival advantage increases with the strength of the network effects, is negative in markets with extremely weak network effects and is positive in markets with strong network effects. When products are cross-generation incompatible but within-generation compatible, pioneers' survival advantage was found to decrease with the strength of network effects in the market. Thus network effects and product compatibility interact empirically in pioneer survival advantage.

Related to the issue of network effects is the idea that new products may require support by an ecosystem of complementary products and services. If these complements remain underdeveloped, a market pioneer may be at a disadvantage and ultimately fail. In a study of multiple product generations in the semiconductor photolithography industry, Adner and Kapoor (2010) found that the success of an early entry strategy by makers of lithographic tools depended upon the availability of technological complements. Firms that pioneered into a new product generation were unsuccessful when the necessary complements for their product (mask and resist), developed and sold by external parties, were still facing technical challenges at the time of the firm's entry.

Empirical issue 4: customer perceptual space may evolve in a manner that favors a pioneer

First movers/pioneers may benefit from the formation and evolution of customer perceptual spaces in their favor. Attitudes, brand retrieval, preferences and purchase intentions may evolve in a manner that favors a pioneer. Carpenter and Nakamoto (1989) demonstrated this in a controlled experimental context and additional studies have rendered this a very plausible source of first-mover/pioneer advantage. For example, Kardes et al. (1993), also in an experimental context, found that brand retrieval and consideration processes contribute to pioneering advantage. Using survey methods, Alpert and Kamins (1995) found that pioneers generate positive attitudes and purchase intentions, as well as pioneer advantage in retrieval and recall, although the latter two were not as favorable to the pioneers. A study of food distribution in China (Gao and Knight 2007) found that the Chinese have strong preferences for the pioneer product, which they view as the "authentic" product, perceived to be of better quality and higher status. This seems likely to be due to the long-term Chinese cultural orientation that respects tradition and history. The prevalence of counterfeit products in the experience of Chinese consumers seems likely to augment this pioneer preference by generating mistrust of non-authentic products. That these customer perceptual space advantages are actually due to perceptions by customers and not due to objective performance-based characteristics of first movers/pioneers was established in a field study of the discount retail grocery industry in Trondheim, Norway (Denstadli et al. 2005). The study found persistent first-mover/pioneer advantages even when store attributes were documented to be essentially similar across chains. It would seem that advantages driven by position in customer perceptual space would be particularly difficult for later entrants to dislodge.

Empirical issue 5: competitor response has speeded up over time

Historically, the duration of the time period between the commercial introduction of a new product and the time of competitor entry has substantially contracted. A study of 46 major product innovation introductions found that the average time lapse before competitive entry was nearly 33 years at the turn of the twentieth century but had shrunk to an average of 3.4 years for innovations in the 1967–86 time frame (Agarwal and Gort 2001). This trend appears to continue, as Vakratsas et al. (2003) in their study of follow-ers' response to pioneers found that followers enter more rapidly in more recent product categories. However, they found that this more rapid response did not totally overcome the pioneer's advantage. In general, evidence indicates that a longer lead time for com-petitive entry increases a pioneer's FMA in terms of market share (Huff and Robinson 1994). The trend toward speeded-up follower response via either imitation or substitu-tion, of course, places a premium on competitor analysis, competitor anticipation and competitor surveillance in today's world.

Empirical issue 6: first-mover/pioneer advantages typically decay over time

The duration of first-mover advantages is not perpetual, as argued in Section 1. This earlier assertion is supported by empirical evidence. For first-mover/pioneer market share advantages, Brown and Lattin (1994) and Huff and Robinson (1994) found that the advantage dissipates over time, particularly with competition. These results were at the brand level. Similarly, declines were found at the business unit level using the PIMS data as reported in Robinson and Fornell (1985) and Robinson (1988). In their study of empirical generalizations relating to market share advantages and order of entry into markets, Kalyanaram et al. (1995, p. G-214) offer as their third empirical generalization that "In mature consumer and industrial goods markets, market pioneer share advan-tages slowly decline over time." First-mover/pioneer advantages in profits have also been found to dissipate or decay over time. Boulding and Christen (2003) found using the PIMS data that although first movers/pioneers enjoyed a profit advantage over about 12 to 14 years, in the longer term they suffered a profit disadvantage. Evidently, the market share advantage persisted, but the pioneer's initial profit advantage was dissipated by long-term cost disadvantages. (See the Boulding and Christen paper for details.)

Empirical issue 7: FMAs are generally weaker in relation to marketing mix effects on per-formance

Entry order or first-mover effects are generally weaker than marketing mix effects relating to price and advertising in their impact on performance (Lieberman and Montgomery 1998). This, of course, offers later entrants, perhaps with deeper pockets, the potential opportunity to overcome FMAs and to catch up with and surpass first movers. This raises a variety of strategic issues for first movers and fast followers, which we discuss in the next section.

Summary of Empirical Evidence

In summary, empirical studies show that FMAs are fairly common when assessed in terms of market share. The evidence in terms of profit and survival is mixed. While the pattern for market share might appear to reflect a general phenomenon with a simple explanation, studies show that the exact reasons for FMA are often complicated and they vary by context. Various contingencies have been shown to affect the existence and duration of FMA, including the mechanisms discussed in Section 3 and the entry strategy and resources of the pioneer. FMAs have been shown to decay over time. There is some evidence that the rate of decay has been increasing, reflecting global trends toward greater competitive intensity and speed of change in technology.

5. FIRST-MOVER/PIONEER STRATEGIES

If a firm has the opportunity to be an early mover in an emerging market, its managers face two main strategic questions. The first is whether to attempt market entry at all. If entry in general is judged to offer a sufficient chance of success, the second question relates to the optimal timing of entry – should the firm attempt to pioneer, or should it delay entry until later in the evolution of the market, after some of the initial uncertainties have been resolved?

In deciding whether to enter the new market at all, managers need to assess their firm's resources and capabilities against those of other likely entrants. Does the firm possess the full repertoire of skills needed to enter and compete effectively? If the firm is lacking in key areas, can these deficiencies be overcome within a reasonable period of time by developing or acquiring the necessary capabilities? These assessments should be made as objectively as possible. Managers must be wary of overconfidence and other cognitive biases that often distort the judgment of market entrants (Horn et al. 2005). Entrepreneurs in particular tend to vastly overestimate their odds of success. Indeed, numerous studies have shown that the majority of market entrants ultimately fail (Dunne et al. 1988; Audretsch 1995).

Entry Timing Strategies

If entry into the market can be justified, the second strategic question relates to the optimal timing of entry. Among the entry timing strategies often considered are the following:

- first mover/pioneer
- fast follower
- late follower into primary market
- late follower into niche market (potential first mover into niche).

The discussion below focuses primarily on choice between the first two of these strategies: first mover/pioneer versus fast follower. A fast follower (sometimes called "fast second") enters once the pioneer has demonstrated the viability of the market, but before the pioneer has had an opportunity to scale up and consolidate its position. These are the two strategies most commonly recommended for market entrants. Nevertheless, a late-follower strategy can sometimes prove optimal. For example, Google entered the Internet search space several years after the market pioneers and early followers, but has grown to dominate that market. As in Google's case, a late entrant may introduce a superior technology that displaces earlier entrants. Often in new industries, many years elapse before uncertainties are resolved through the introduction of a "dominant design" (Abernathy and Utterback 1986); by embracing that design, late entrants may be able to avoid the early period of market ferment and introduce a viable product (Christensen et al. 1998). Moreover, once the direction of the technology and market become clear, stable market niches may emerge, which provide opportunities for late entry. Chapter 21 of this handbook (Shankar and Carpenter) discusses strategies for late entry.

The primary trade-off in comparing pioneer versus follower strategies is between breadth of opportunity and degree of risk. Uncertainties relating to technology and customer preferences normally diminish as the new market evolves, reducing elements of entry risk. Nevertheless, early entrants may be able to establish strong market positions that are difficult for later entrants to overcome. Although pioneering is a risky strategy, an early entrant that is both capable and lucky can establish "mechanisms" that defend against attack, as described in Section 3. If a pioneer fails to establish a dominant position, fast followers have an opportunity to do so at lower risk and potentially lower cost. The several mechanisms relating to first-mover/pioneer disadvantages need to also be borne in mind by managers in assessing the optimal entry strategy for their firm. This trade-off between risk and opportunity implies that early entry is likely to be optimal for some firms, but not for others. Unfortunately, there are no simple strategic prescriptions. The optimal strategy for a given firm depends on characteristics specific to the market and technology (particularly the pace of change in both) as well as the firm's characteristics, the characteristics of competitors and customers and the general environment.

Choice between First Mover versus Follower Strategy Depends on Characteristics of the Market and Technology

Not all markets offer the potential for first-mover advantage. As argued in Section 3, acting as a first mover is likely to be optimal only in markets characterized by at least one of the four "mechanisms" that provide defenses against imitation. The early mover must be able to: protect a proprietary technology; preempt key resources (including customer based phenomena, such as top of mind awareness, recall etc.); develop customer switching costs and/or establish a significant network effect. New markets that lack all of these mechanisms are unlikely to offer any potential advantage to a pioneering firm.

Moreover, even if one or more of these mechanisms is present, the pace of technological change affects the desirability of early entry. In markets where technology improves very rapidly or customer needs shift abruptly, it is unlikely that an early entrant can maintain an initial lead (Suarez and Lanzolla 2005). In such environments, the main threat to the firm is not imitation; it is substitution. Managers need to think very carefully about whether and how the firm can defend against superior products introduced by rivals over time. While the four mechanisms provide some degree of defense, the firm will fail if it cannot keep up with changes in product features or best-practice technology.

Table 20.2   Pace of market and technology evolution

		Pace of market evolution	
		Slow	Fast

Pace of technology evolution	Slow	CALM WATERS
		Scotch tape
		Need: one or more
		  mechanisms for FMA
			MARKET LEADS
			Sewing machines
			Need: strong marketing &
			  distribution, production capacity

	Fast	TECHNOLOGY LEADS
		Digital cameras
		Need: strong R&D and
		  NPD and deep pockets
			ROUGH WATERS
			Personal computers
			Need: strong marketing, distribution,
			  production and deep pockets

Source: Based on Suarez and Lanzolla (2005).

Indeed, as a market evolves over time, the pace of technological change often diminishes and its direction becomes more predictable, making competitive advantages relatively more sustainable for later entrants. Thus, if the new market is judged to have an "excessively" rapid or discontinuous rate of change or to lack mechanisms to defend a pioneering firm from imitation, early entry is unlikely to prove a superior strategy.

Typically, markets in which technological change is very rapid or abrupt are for products that are fundamentally new. By comparison, the pace and direction of technical change are likely to be more predictable for new generations of existing products or new geographic/international locations. These types of new markets are often characterized by much lower levels of uncertainty than markets for fundamentally new products or services. Hence the risk associated with early entry tends to be lower, particularly for established firms that participate in a previous generation or market location. In this type of new market context, established firms are often the early movers (whereas they tend to be followers in markets where change is more radical).

Suarez and Lanzolla (2005, 2007) have suggested a framework relating to the potential to realize an FMA and the combined pace of market and technology evolution. Their framework is outlined in Table 20.2 along with exemplars and key resource requirements. To be sure, slow and fast evolution are loosely defined, yet conceptually useful. The Calm Waters quadrant reflects slow evolution in both the market and the technology. Durable FMAs are envisioned here, provided, of course that they exist (as a result of one or more of the mechanisms discussed in Section 4). In the Market Leads quadrant, the market is evolving fast, but the pace of technology evolution is slow. This gives a first mover/pioneer an excellent opportunity to reap FMAs on a durable basis, provided, of course, that the pioneer has the resources and the foresight to address all important market segments that emerge. The key resources are strength in marketing and distribution as well as production capacity. At the opposite extreme, when technology changes rapidly (or discontinuously) and markets evolve more slowly, first-movers/pioneers are unlikely to achieve advantage in either the short or the longer term, as rapid technology change offers late entrants ample opportunity to compete away any short- or long-term gains. Resource requirements relate to strong R&D and product development as well as deep pockets in order to sustain the necessary R&D investments. Finally, the Rough

Waters quadrant holds little promise of long-term FMAs, although there may be value in a quick in and out strategy when the opportunity presents itself. The resource requirements of this quadrant are awesome, as strong marketing and distribution, R&D and product development, production capacity (and flexibility) and very deep pockets are all simultaneous requirements. This framework, although very qualitative, should be a helpful guide to managers in developing self-assessment questions before pursuing a first-mover/pioneer opportunity in any given instance.

We now consider how firm-specific characteristics must be considered along with market characteristics to define the optimal entry timing strategy.

Choice between First-Mover/Follower Strategy Depends on Characteristics of the Firm

Even when the new market contains features that may allow a first mover to defend against competition, a follower strategy is often superior for many firms. Most new markets have two broad categories of entrants: *de novo* startups that are born to embrace the new market opportunity and existing firms that hold established positions in other markets (potentially including participation in prior generations or geographic locations for the focal product). We now consider how strategic prescriptions regarding the timing of market entry are likely to differ between these two major categories of firms.

Strategy for established firms

For established firms, a "fast follower" strategy is often advocated as being superior to pioneering (e.g. Markides and Geroski 2005). Established firms are likely to have complementary assets and skills in marketing, distribution and manufacturing that allow production be scaled up quickly and efficiently to serve a mass market. Rather than commit these assets early in a highly uncertain environment and risk significant loss, it may be optimal for an established firm to track the initial evolution of the market and prepare to enter just prior to the start of the rapid growth phase. Moreover, established firms often lack the perspectives and skills needed for radical innovation and hence may be relatively ineffective in the initial phase of the industry.

One major risk facing a firm that attempts a fast follower strategy is that it misses the entry window. By the time the firm introduces its product to the market, the pioneer may be entrenched or the market may be crowded with other strong challengers. To be an effective fast follower, a firm must invest in "absorptive capacity," that is, the "ability to recognize the value of new information, assimilate it and apply it to commercial ends" (Cohen and Levinthal 1990). This requires early investment in R&D, close tracking of market evolution and the development of organizational capabilities for the new product well in advance of its planned introduction.

The generalization that established firms should aim to be "fast followers" applies to markets for products that are fundamentally new. When markets emerge more incrementally, in the form of new product generations or geographic/international locations, uncertainty is lower and the firm may have resources from the existing market that can be effectively leveraged into the new one. Hence the risk that the firm will damage its complementary assets through early entry is often comparatively modest, while the value of these assets may be high in providing a strong beachhead for the firm in the new market.

Thus, for established firms that participate in a previous product generation or market location, early entry into the new market is likely to be a superior strategy. One such example is Samsung: once it built strong capabilities in DRAMs and became the market leader, Samsung chose to enter before its rivals into each new product generation. Limited competition at the start of each generation ensured that Samsung enjoyed high prices during the early period, making this first-mover strategy highly successful for Samsung (Shin and Jang 2005).

Nevertheless, there are some important exceptions to this rule that incumbents from a previous generation or location should enter early. Adner and Kapoor's (2010) study of multiple product generations in the semiconductor photolithography industry shows that the success of an early entry strategy depends on the availability of technological complements. Their findings imply that if these complements are not yet ready, the firm should delay its entry even if this means giving up the position of first mover. (Note that this argument also applies outside of the new product generation context.)

Another exception is when the firm lacks strong technological capabilities for the new generation. (For example, the firm's competitive strength may be in marketing or distribution rather than technology.) In a study of product generations in the disk drive industry, Franco et al. (2009) found that FMAs were contingent on the pioneer having strong technological capabilities. Hence firms that are active in the prior generation, but whose strengths lie outside of technology *per se*, may find it preferable to act as followers.

Strategy for startup firms

New companies typically lack the resources of established firms and hence a superior strategy for many startups is to attempt entry as a market pioneer. For startups, pioneering is a high-risk strategy that offers the possibility of high returns.

Prior to any attempt at pioneering, startup companies must determine if the market offers a potential for FMA. Pioneering can be justified only if managers see a clear path to exploit at least one of the four sustainability mechanisms described in Section 3. Moreover, managers must recognize that rapid technological change reduces the firm's likelihood of long-term viability, even though it may offer a richer set of channels for entry. Only if the startup meets with initial success and is also able to defend against the twin threats of imitation and substitution can it thrive as a first mover.

A pioneering strategy can sometimes be justified on a more limited basis. A fundamental question for startup managers and founders is their long-term objectives: are they building their firm for survival or to sell out? Startups that achieve competitive advantage in the early stage of a market often lack the resources and capabilities to sustain their advantage over the long term. At the same time, follower firms often bring such capabilities to the market and may find it advantageous to link these with the complementary skills of (initially) successful pioneers. Acquisitions, therefore, may serve the interests of both parties.

A pioneering startup that meets with initial success and whose managers aim for long-term survival, must build capabilities to sustain their competitive advantages over time. Consider, as an example, Amazon, the successful pioneer of Internet retailing. Since its founding in 1994, Amazon has invested heavily in technology, infrastructure, internal organization and external partnerships. These have broadened and deepened Amazon's competitive advantages and have enabled the company to extend its dominance from the initial market of books into many other retail categories where the firm was not the Internet pioneer.

Although this chapter focuses on strategies for market pioneering, it should be recognized that many successful startups enter comparatively late in the process of market evolution, when stable niches become more evident. Such niche strategies are often viable and well suited for startup companies. A more general discussion of late entry strategies is provided in Chapter 21 of this volume (Shankar and Carpenter).

Smart Movers/Dumb Movers

In the aftermath of the turn-of-the-century dot.com fiasco, Hamel (2001) made the provocative observation that most Internet companies failed due to being dumb movers rather than due to being pioneers. By dumb movers he meant those whose business model was defective from the start (due to misreading customers or unsound economics) and entrants that got the timing wrong. In the latter case he suggests that once a company overdrives an opportunity, it is more likely to underdrive a later opportunity, thereby compounding the firm's longer-term strategic problems. Overdriving opportunities can lead to expensive failures.

In relation to the timing issue, he uses the analogy of a sprint versus a marathon. If a company sprints when it actually faces a marathon situation, it may exhaust itself prematurely. He suggests several questions that a potential entrant considering being a pioneer should ask itself: "Are there difficult technical hurdles? Does market takeoff depend on the development of complementary products or services? Will a new infrastructure be required? Will customers need to learn new skills or adopt new behaviors? Are there high switching costs for customers? Will competing standards confuse customers? Are there powerful competitors that will seek to delay or derail us?" He suggests that if the answer to any of these questions is "yes," the potential pioneer must be careful not to pour in resources too soon, as the race is likely to be a long one.

But this doesn't mean that companies should generally set out to be followers. They should be careful not to miss the strategic window of opportunity. If a firm believes that the anticipated first mover will be a slow learner, that market penetration will remain in single digits for some time (thus giving a follower an opportunity to acquire customers later on), that rapid technological change will yield opportunities to supplant the pioneer and that the pioneer will be unable to acquire the most valuable partners, then being a fast follower or even a late mover may prove to be a viable, perhaps optimal, strategy.

Hamel notes that smart movers, be they pioneers, fast followers or later followers, continuously reevaluate and update their assumptions and business model, watch out for narrow market definitions that grant late movers entry opportunity, move quickly to collaborate with partners even if they are competitors and outsource to maintain flexibility in responding to evolving market and competitive conditions. All these caveats are useful, but are easier to foresee with hindsight than *ex ante*. That is why some entrepreneurs and managers make the big bucks.

6 CONCLUSION AND FUTURE RESEARCH

First movership/pioneering is a risky, yet often rewarded strategy, but it is by no means a universally dominant strategy. It works best when a large number of mechanisms (or perhaps a few particularly potent ones) yield barriers to imitation that followers find difficult to supplant. The overall magnitude of advantage that these barriers contribute to a first mover/pioneer is dependent upon the market context as well as the firm's managerial capabilities and resourcefulness. Some contexts, such as those with strong intellectual property protection, customer switching costs or network effects, may present a first mover/pioneer with a rich array of supporting mechanisms, whereas other contexts may offer far less potential for FMAs. The nature of competitors and their actions and reactions also affects the availability of FMAs and their magnitude. Deep pocketed, fast reacting, capable competitors can substantially diminish first-mover opportunities for advantage. These contextual attributes also determine the potential duration of FMAs.

Wise firms will carefully assess the likely existence and potential duration of any mechanisms that might support FMA. As well, they should be especially mindful of mechanisms such as incumbent inertia that might create problems. In deciding to enter a new business or market, the firm must be clear about its objectives: is it seeking short- or long-term profits? Market share or position? Is the entry actually a cross-parry designed to keep tabs on a competitor or limit its access to resources and position?

Thus, is being a first mover/pioneer a good strategy? It depends. It depends upon characteristics of the emerging market. It depends upon the resources and capabilities of the potential first mover/pioneer and those of its competitors. It depends upon the broader environment – what will be the response of customers, the state of the economy, short- and long-term government issues and so on? It is a strategy that can be richly rewarded, at least for a time, but that requires the utmost of due diligence and realism on the part of the managers making the entry decision. Would it be well to wait? What are the risks of waiting? And when should the firm get out, perhaps by selling out to more deep pocketed rivals once the technology and the market itself have matured?

Future Research

There remains much room for further research in this area despite the volume of papers that have been spawned in the past few decades. While a good start has been made, as discussed in Section 4, more empirical knowledge relating to services, retailers and emerging markets would still seem worthwhile (Kalyanaram et al. 1995). Magnusson et al. (2009) make the interesting observation that the first-mover/order of entry strategy studies have rarely taken a resource-seeking perspective such as global sourcing. Might there be opportunity to extend the first-mover ideas to this new dimension and how it relates to global supply chain management? They also suggest that additional contingencies such as firm innovativeness and culture and global strategic posture, might impact the performance consequences of entry order. Some support for the impact of innovativeness is found in Shankar et al. (1998), who found for two prescription drug markets that innovative followers were able to grow faster than the pioneers, slowing the growth of the pioneers and reducing the effectiveness of marketing by the pioneers (for further details on late-mover strategies, see Shankar and Carpenter, Chapter 21 in this volume).

Efforts to link first movership/pioneering to stock market returns would also seem worthwhile. Early movers have been found to receive better stock market reactions to new product announcements, but later imitative announcements have the expected negative stock market impact on the early movers (Lee et al. 2000). Further, do established behavioral notions such as consumer risk aversion, consideration set advantages and prototypicality benefit the pioneer in industrial, service and emerging markets? Finally, Ketchen et al. (2004) suggest the potential for building bridges between FMA research and the research streams of strategic groups and regional clusters.

REFERENCES

Abernathy, W.J. and Utterback, J.M. (1986), "Patterns of innovation in technology," *Technology Review*, **80**(7): 40–47.
Adner, R. and Kapoor, R. (2010), "Value creation in innovation ecosystems: how the structure of technological interdependence affects firm performance in new technology generations," *Strategic Management Journal*, **31**(3): 306–33.
Agarwal, R. and Gort, M. (2001), "First-mover advantage and the speed of competitive entry, 1887–1986," *Journal of Law and Economics*, **44**(1): 161–77.
Alpert, F.H. and Kamins, M.A. (1995), "An empirical investigation of consumer memory, attitude and perceptions toward pioneer and follower brands," *The Journal of Marketing*, **59**(4): 34–45.
Audretsch, D.B. (1995), "Innovation, growth and survival," *International Journal of Industrial Organization*, **13**(4): 441–57.
Bohlmann, J.D. Golder, P.N. and Mitra, D. (2002), "Deconstructing the pioneer's advantage: examining vintage effects and consumer valuations of quality and variety," *Management Science*, **48**(9): 1175–95.
Boulding, W. and Christen, M. (2003), "Sustainable pioneering advantage? Profit implications of market entry order," *Marketing Science*, **22**(3): 371–92.
Brown, C.L. and Lattin, J.M. (1994), "Investigating the relationship between time in market and pioneering advantage," *Management Science*, **40**(10): 1361–69.
Carpenter, G.S. and Nakamoto, K. (1989), "Consumer preference formation and pioneering advantage," *Journal of Marketing Research*, **26**(3): 285–98.
Christensen, C. (1997), *The Innovator's Dilemma: When New Technologies Cause Great Firms to Fail*, Boston, MA: Harvard University Press.
Christensen, C.M., Suárez, F.F. and Utterback, J.M. (1998), "Strategies for survival in fast-changing industries," *Management Science*, **44**(12): S207–S220.
Cohen, W.M. and Levinthal, D.A. (1990), "Absorptive capacity: a new perspective on learning and innovation," *Administrative Science Quarterly*, **35**(1): 128–152.
Cui, G. and Lui, H.-K. (2005), "Order of entry and performance of multinational corporations in an emerging market: a contingent resource perspective," *Journal of International Marketing*, **13**(4): 28–56.
Denstadli, J.M., Lines, R. and Grønhaug, K. (2005), "First mover advantages in the discount grocery industry," *European Journal of Marketing*, **39**(7/8): 872–84.
Dunne, T., Roberts, M.J. and Samuelson, L. (1988), "Patterns of firm entry and exit in U.S. manufacturing industries," *Rand Journal of Economics*, **19**(4): 495–515.
Foster, R.N. (1986), *Innovation: The Attacker's Advantage*, New York: Summit Books.
Franco, A.M., Sarkar, M., Agarwal, R. and Echambadi, R. (2009), "Swift and smart: the moderating effects of technological capabilities on the market pioneering–firm survival relationship," *Management Science*, **55**(11): 1842–60.
Gao, H. and Knight, J. (2007), "Pioneering advantage and product-country image: evidence from an exploratory study in China," *Journal of Marketing Management*, **23**(3): 367–85.
Golder, P.N. and Tellis, G.J. (1993), "Pioneer advantage: marketing logic or marketing legend?" *Journal of Marketing Research*, **30**(2): 158–70.
Hamel, G. (2001), "Smart mover, dumb mover," *Fortune*, **144**(4): 191–3.
Horn, J.T., Lovallo, D.P. and Viguerie, S.P. (2005), "Beating the odds in market entry: how to avoid the cognitive biases that undermine market entry decisions," *McKinsey Quarterly*, **2005**(4): 34–45.
Huff, L.C. and Robinson, W.T. (1994), "The impact of leadtime and years of competitive rivalry on pioneer market share advantages," *Management Science*, **40**(10): 1370–77.
Isobe, T., Makino, S. and Montgomery, D.B. (2000), "Resource commitment, entry timing and market

performance of foreign direct investments in emerging economies: the case of Japanese international joint ventures in China," *The Academy of Management Journal*, **43**(3): 468–84.

Kalyanaram, G., Robinson, W.T. and Urban, G.L. (1995), "Order of market entry: established empirical generalizations, emerging empirical generalizations and future research," *Marketing Science*, **14**(3, supplement): G212–221.

Kardes, F.R., Kalyanaram, G., Chandrashekaran, M. and Dornoff, R.J. (1993), "Brand retrieval, consideration set composition, consumer choice and the pioneering advantage," *The Journal of Consumer Research*, **20**(1): 62–75.

Kerin, R.A., Varadarajan, P.R. and Peterson, R.A. (1992), "First-mover advantage: a synthesis, conceptual framework and research propositions," *The Journal of Marketing*, **56**(4): 33–52.

Ketchen, D.J., Snow, C.C. and Hoover, V.L. (2004), "Research on competitive dynamics: recent accomplishments and future challenges," *Journal of Management*, **30**(6): 779–804.

Lee, H., Smith, K.G., Grimm, C.M. and Schomburg, A. (2000), "Timing, order and durability of new product advantages with imitation," *Strategic Management Journal*, **21**(1): 23–30.

Levin, R.C., Klevorick, A.K., Nelson, R.R. and Winter, S.G. (1984), *Survey Research on R&D Appropriability and Technological Opportunity*, New Haven, CT: Yale University Press.

Lieberman, M.B. (1989), "The learning curve, technology barriers to entry and competitive survival in the chemical processing industries," *Strategic Management Journal*, **10**: 431–47.

Lieberman, M.B. and Montgomery, D.B. (1988), "First-mover advantages," *Strategic Management Journal*, **9**(Summer): 41–58.

Lieberman, M.B. and Montgomery, D.B. (1998), "First-mover (dis)advantages: retrospective and link with the resource-based view," *Strategic Management Journal*, **19**(12): 1111–25.

Luo, Y. and Peng, M.W. (1998), "First mover advantages in investing in transitional economies," *Thunderbird International Business Review*, **40**(2): 141–63.

Magnusson, P., Westjohn, S.A. and Boggs, D.J. (2009), "Order-of-entry effects for service firms in developing markets: an examination of multinational advertising agencies," *Journal of International Marketing*, **17**(2): 23–41.

Makadok, R. (1998), "Can first-mover and early-mover advantages be sustained in an industry with low barriers to entry/imitation?" *Strategic Management Journal*, **19**(7): 683–96.

Mansfield, E. (1981), "Composition of R and D expenditures: relationship to size of firm, concentration, and innovative output," *The Review of Economics and Statistics*, **63**(4): 610–15.

Mansfield, E. (1985), "How rapidly does new industrial technology leak out?" *The Journal of Industrial Economics*, **34**(2): 217–23.

Markides, C.C. and Geroski, P.A. (2005), *Fast Second: How Smart Companies Bypass Radical Innovation to Enter and Dominate New Markets*, San Francisco, CA: Wiley.

Robinson, W.T. (1988), "Sources of market pioneer advantages: the case of industrial goods industries," *Journal of Marketing Research*, **25**(1): 87–94.

Robinson, W.T. and Fornell, C. (1985), "Sources of market pioneer advantages in consumer goods industries," *Journal of Marketing Research*, **22**(3): 305–17.

Schumpeter, J.A. (1961), *Theory of Economic Development*, New York: Oxford University Press.

Shankar, V., Carpenter, G.S. and Krishnamurthi, L. (1998), "Late mover advantage: how innovative late entrants outsell pioneers," *Journal of Marketing Research*, **35**(1): 54–70.

Shin, J.-S. and Jang, S.-W. (2005), "Creating first-mover advantages: the case of Samsung Electronics," in SCAPE Policy Research Working Paper Series, National University of Singapore, Department of Economics.

Song, X.M., Benedetto, C.A.D. and Zhao, Y.L. (1999), "Pioneering advantages in manufacturing and service industries: empirical evidence from nine countries," *Strategic Management Journal*, **20**(9): 811–35.

Srinivasan, R., Lilien, G.L. and Rangaswamy, A. (2004), "First in, first out? The effects of network externalities on pioneer survival," *The Journal of Marketing*, **68**(1): 41–58.

Suarez, F.F. and Lanzolla, G. (2005), "The half-truth of first-mover advantage," *Harvard Business Review*, **83**(4): 121–7.

Suarez, F.F. and Lanzolla, G. (2007), "The role of environmental dynamics in building a first mover advantage theory," *Academy of Management Review*, **32**(2): 377–92.

Szymanski, D.M., Troy, L.C. and Bharadwaj, S.G. (1995), "Order of entry and business performance: an empirical synthesis and reexamination," *The Journal of Marketing*, **59**(4): 17–33.

Vakratsas, D., Rao, R.C. and Kalyanaram, G. (2003), "An empirical analysis of follower entry timing decisions," *Marketing Letters*, **14**(3): 203–16.

Wang, Q., Chen, Y. and Xie, J. (2010), "Survival in markets with network effects: product compatibility and order-of-entry effects," *Journal of Marketing*, **74**(4): 1–14.

21 Late-mover strategies
Venkatesh Shankar and Gregory S. Carpenter

INTRODUCTION

Be the first to market. Many successful firms (e.g. Coca-Cola, Levi's and De Beers) have followed this conventional wisdom by pioneering markets. For these pioneers, the rewards have been fruitful and enduring. Coca-Cola, created in 1886, earned over $10 billion in 2010; at its peak, sales of Levi's blue jeans reached $7 billion; and diamond sales, in the market created and dominated by De Beers for decades, reached $50 billion in 2000. Although these companies all have aggressive competitors, including De Beers, they continue to dominate their markets.

Are later entrants doomed to lower sales and poorer profits? Consider the following examples. Karl Benz invented the automobile in the latter half of the 1800s, but it was Henry Ford who created the mass market for cars that, today, Toyota dominates. Toyota did not even enter the US market in a meaningful way until the mid-1970s, about 90 years after Benz created the car. Smith Kline Beecham's Tagamet, the first mover in the anti-ulcer prescription drug market, was eclipsed in sales by Glaxo's Zantac, which entered six years after Tagamet. The world's most successful pharmaceutical product, Lipitor, was fifth to its market (among cholesterol-lowering statins).

Indeed, a study of 50 product categories shows that pioneers were more successful than later entrants in only 30 percent of the categories (Golder and Tellis 1993). And, among the firms in the first-published *Fortune 500* list of largest firms, many of whom were pioneers in their markets, only 16 percent of these firms were still on the list in 2010 (Vadakkepatt et al. 2010). These examples and results suggest that there could be certain strategic advantages of being a later entrant in new markets. If so, what are these advantages? How should firms plan their entry strategy in new markets? Should they be pioneers or later entrants? When does it pay to be a pioneer? When is it advantageous to be a late entrant? What strategies are available for later entrants? This chapter addresses these important questions.

The rest of the chapter is organized as follows. In the next section, we briefly discuss pioneering advantage. We then present fast-following and differentiation strategies for late movers. In the subsequent sections, we discuss innovative late-mover strategy and present a summary of late-mover advantage. We discuss a framework that enables managers to decide whether to pioneer a market or enter later. We outline how firms can develop a late-mover strategy and close by highlighting underexplored questions and future research directions.

PIONEERING ADVANTAGE

Pioneers face a difficult challenge. Buyers have no knowledge of the dimensions on which brands differ, the value of those differences, or how to choose among different brands.

The technology associated with the pioneer can be risky. It remains unclear to buyers whether the product will actually work. Successfully pioneering a market requires overcoming these obstacles. If pioneers successfully educate buyers, if they make the right, perhaps lucky, technology choice, and if they have sufficient funding, they may survive, earning a meaningful competitive advantage.

Preference Formation

One of the most powerful advantages the pioneer enjoys is derived from its impact on how buyers value brand attributes. By establishing the category, the pioneer gains a very important advantage. It can help influence the relative importance of certain product attributes. As the pioneer educates buyers, buyers develop a naive theory relating brand features to value, which advertising and repeat purchase reinforce. Thus buyers learn how to value attribute combinations through trial, but trial favors the pioneer, so buyers learn to like the pioneer and the combination of attributes it offers (Carpenter and Nakamoto 1989).

Category Association

By establishing the category and being seen as very close to the ideal product, a pioneer can become the standard against which later entrants are judged. Standards in markets take at least two forms—psychological standards and technological standards. Technological standards, such as the qwerty keyboard, Microsoft Windows and Lego children's building blocks, create architectural standards. In most product categories, buyers consider only a subset of all brands in the market; this so-called consideration set is typically a reasonably small number of brands, around three to five. A brand that is the psychological standard will, for most buyers, be considered more often, gaining an advantage over other brands (Carpenter and Nakamoto 1989).

Awareness and Recall

Pioneering affects the buyers' memory in other ways. Buyers do not recall all brands equally often or with equal ease. We know more about some brands than others and we recall those better-known brands more easily and more often. A pioneer can be uniquely distinctive among brands. Being the category standard, it is often recalled first and/or more often than rivals. For example, in one study, subjects recalled the pioneer most, and they recalled the most positive elements about it, even adjusting for differences in the actual product (Kardes et al. 1993).

Preemptive Positioning

As a standard, the pioneer can become strongly associated with one perceived position in the market. Coca-Cola offers a unique mix of sweetness and carbonation and Levi's offers a particular cut. Preemptive positioning in the category translates into an important competitive advantage for the pioneer. In essence, it makes the pioneer's position very difficult to assail. A me-too product (just like the pioneer but with a lower price) will suffer in comparisons despite its similarity to the pioneer. The more similar the me-too and the pioneer, the greater is the relative prominence of the pioneer. This is because the me-too brand derives its identity from the pioneer, and greater similarity reduces the distinctiveness of the me-too brand (Carpenter and Nakamoto 1989). Thus the pioneer derives some of its unique advantage by becoming uniquely associated with the category, creating a perceptual advantage that is not easily duplicated.

In addition to impacting consumer perceptions, pioneers can preempt rivals through the products they launch. One advantage of a strong association with the category is a low cost of launching new, adjacent products. Through a broader product line, a pioneer can effectively occupy market positions before rivals are able to occupy them. By creating variety from the original standard, the pioneer can enjoy greater market shares and profits (Boulding and Christen 2009).

Risk

The knowledge that buyers gain through trial can contribute to a pioneer's advantage. Imagine a new product, an experience good, such as a razor blade. The pioneer offers it, buyers try it, and they learn that it either works well or does not. If it does work well, consumers now have valuable information. When they return to the store, they may find the pioneer's brand alongside other new rivals. The choice between the pioneer and the new rivals is, however, not on the same level playing field. The buyer has more information about the pioneer. The product works. The other brands remain untested. That doubt makes the untried alternative risky, and thus buyers will favor the known alternatives, even paying a premium for them. Essentially buyers are paying a premium to avoid risky alternatives (Schmalensee 1982).

FAST FOLLOWING AND DIFFERENTIATION AS LATE-MOVER STRATEGIES

Pioneers enjoy significant advantages, to be sure, but these advantages are surmountable through well-crafted competitive strategies.

Fast Following

One such strategy is fast following. Fast followers typically enter the market soon after its emergence, on a large scale, but without dramatic innovation. Such imitation has proven to be a successful strategy in many markets. For example, Yahoo pioneered Internet search engines only to be overtaken by Google, de Havilland Comet created the commercial aircraft market that Boeing soon led, and later entrants overtook pioneers Raytheon and Sperry-Univac in microwave ovens and mainframe computers, respectively.

What advantages arise from fast or early following? One study offers some potential insights (Shankar et al. 1999). The study examines the impact of marketing activity, order of entry, sales diffusion and the timing of entry (pioneer, growth-stage or maturity-stage entry) on the sales of 29 pharmaceutical brands. In six markets, fast followers grew

Advantage of pioneer / Differentiation of later entrant	Low	High
High	**Me-too** Low price Low advertising	**Differentiated** High price High advertising
Low	**Challenger** High price High advertising	**Fringe** Low price Low advertising

Source: Carpenter and Nakamoto (1990).

Figure 21.1 Differentiation options for later entry

faster than the pioneers, buyers were more responsive to their product quality, and fast followers were less vulnerable to the success of competitors.

These findings suggest that entry at the right moment in the evolution of a market can facilitate growth and provide significant insulation from competitors. By entering soon after the pioneer, the fast follower can become the brand with which many consumers first gain experience. As a result, fast followers can be seen as lower risk, better known and distinctively positioned, so they can establish the standard in a market. Fast followers can enjoy many of the advantages associated with pioneering. Fast following, however, requires scale, resources and nimbleness—characteristics that may not be commonly found in all organizations.

Differentiation

Differentiation is a classic competitive strategy. The goal of differentiation is to create a meaningful difference between the pioneer and later entrant without dramatic innovation. Differentiation relative to the pioneer presents a unique challenge. If the pioneer defines the standard in the market and becomes strongly associated with it, then research shows that copying its positioning can actually improve the performance of the pioneer rather than the later entrant (Carpenter and Nakamoto 1989). One analysis identifies four different options depending on the strength of the pioneer's advantage (Carpenter and Nakamoto 1990), as illustrated in Figure 21.1.

As shown in Figure 21.1, the analysis reveals that when entering later in a market with an established pioneer, four options are possible. If the pioneer has a powerful advantage (is strongly associated with the category etc., as in the case of Coca-Cola), then two options are possible: a me-too strategy in which the later entrant positions close to the pioneer with a lower price and a smaller advertising budget. The other option is to differentiate, that is, position further from the pioneer, price above the me-too brand and advertise more as well. If the pioneer is weaker (that is, less strongly associated with the category), then two other options exist: one is to become a fringe brand by positioning far from the pioneer with a low advertising budget and low price. The other option is to challenge the pioneer by positioning close to it, pricing above the fringe brand and advertising at a higher level.

Analysis of these four options shows that two are optimal. When the pioneer is strong, positioning close to it with a me-too strategy means that the pioneer overshadows the later entrant. The me-too brand derives its identity from the pioneer but the pioneer is very strong, so the me-too brand has a difficult time creating a unique identity. It suffers as a result. The differentiated brand, on the other hand, can create a more distinct identity by positioning further from the pioneer; a greater advertising spending and a higher price contribute to its distinct position apart from the pioneer. When the pioneer is weaker, adopting a more differentiated position using a fringe strategy is not optimal. The pioneer is weak but the later entrant positions a long distance from it; establishing a distinct identity with a low price and small advertising budget is difficult. Challenging the pioneer more directly with a more similar position, a high price and a more substantial advertising budget is more effective than the fringe strategy.

INNOVATIVE LATE-MOVER STRATEGY

One avenue for later entrants is innovation. In overtaking Karl Benz's initial lead in automobiles, Henry Ford exploited the new technology of mass production. In becoming a successful mobile device maker in a market pioneered by Motorola, Apple relied on innovation, and in transforming the 1500-year-old coffee market, Starbucks created innovation of another form. While managing the process of innovations has been extensively studied, as have methods for developing new products, the role of innovation in overtaking pioneers has received less attention. One study did examine the issue in the context of pharmaceuticals (Shankar et al. 1998).

The study examined 13 brands in two categories. In both the categories, a pioneer created the market, and the pioneer's success drew competitor entry. Late entrants included brands pursuing a range of strategies. In both the categories, an innovative later entrant overtook the successful pioneer. The question is, how? To explore that question the authors examined how different strategies affected the evolving potential of the market, the growth of brands, effectiveness of their marketing spending, their vulnerability to competitors and the rate of repeat purchase. From this analysis, one important difference emerged: the role of innovation in the success of late entry.

Non-innovative Later Entrant

Compared to pioneers, non-innovative later entrants tend to suffer. The analysis shows that pioneers have higher rates of repeat purchase and more effective marketing spending than non-innovative later entrants. In addition, pioneers create larger potential markets compared to their non-innovative later entrants, pioneers' sales tend to grow faster than those of non-innovative later entrants, and pioneers are insulated from competitors' marketing activities. Combined with the traditional sources of pioneering advantage (fast and easy brand recall, low risk, strong association with the category and an influence on buyer preferences), pioneers enjoy substantial advantages over this class of later entrants.

Innovative Later Entrant

In contrast to non-innovative later entrants and the pioneer, innovative later entrants enjoy many advantages. First, innovative later entrants grow faster than the pioneer; their sales diffuse more quickly, creating an installed base of buyers more quickly than even the pioneer. In addition, growth of the innovative later entrant can slow the growth of the pioneer. Second, innovative later entrants create larger potential markets and their rates of repeat purchase are higher compared to pioneers. Third, innovative later entrants' marketing spending reduces the effectiveness of the pioneer's marketing efforts. Thus, compared to the pioneer, innovative later entrants create larger markets, grow faster, and can actually impose additional costs on the pioneer by slowing its growth rate and reducing its marketing effectiveness.

These results suggest that innovation is a powerful strategy for late movers. But in a somewhat unexpected twist, the analysis also suggests that many of the advantages of being an innovative late mover arise from the same sources as pioneering advantage. By being innovative, the late mover essentially redefines the category. When General Motors entered after Henry Ford's great success, it redefined automobiles not in terms of lower cost, but in terms of brands and the image they projected. Through this process of redefinition, a successful innovative late mover can restart the consumer learning process, become well known, redefine brand preferences and become the safe choice for many, capturing the sources of the pioneer's success, leaving them is a weak position competitively.

LATE-MOVER ADVANTAGE

What are some of the other advantages of later entry? One major advantage of entering later is that later entrants can free-ride on the pioneer's efforts to build a new category (Lieberman and Montgomery, Chapter 20 in this volume). A later entrant can also learn from the pioneer's mistakes and potentially enjoy a greater response to perceived product quality (Shankar et al. 1999). For those later entrants with innovative products, the benefits of later entry are even better. They can grow faster than pioneers, make pioneers' marketing efforts less effective, and enjoy greater repeat purchase rates (Shankar et al. 1998). Moreover, even in markets with network externalities such as those for videogames and telephones, innovative late entrants can successfully overtake the pioneer (Shankar and Bayus 2003).

There are cost disadvantages of being a pioneer that confer advantages on late entrants (Boulding and Christen 2003, 2008, 2009). In a study of business units in the Profit Impact of Market Strategy (PIMS) database, pioneers in both consumer and industrial markets enjoyed initial cost advantage, but after 12–14 years the advantage turned into a cost disadvantage (Boulding and Christen 2003). Although pioneers typically enjoy a cost advantage in purchasing, later entrants have lower production and selling and administrative costs than do pioneers (Boulding and Christen 2008). And if the pioneer creates a large variety of products through customization of products to different consumer microsegments, then it suffers a cost disadvantage relative to later entrants (Boulding and Christen 2009). The cost disadvantage for the pioneer suggests opportunities for later entrants.

In the international arena, there may be certain advantages of entering different countries. Brands that enter countries as a later entrant benefit from cross-national diffusion and a greater response to marketing mix than if they enter as a pioneer (Fischer et al. 2005). In an Internet-enabled environment, there are limitations to first-mover advantage and late movers can enjoy certain benefits as well. Later entrants can imitate pioneers faster and offer superior experience on the Web (Varadarajan et al. 2008). For example, Prodigy was the pioneer among Internet content service providers or Web portals. Since then, a succession of late movers have become market leaders – Compuserve, AOL and Yahoo.

TO PIONEER OR TO ENTER LATER

A firm should base its decision to pioneer or enter later based on an analysis of the benefits of pioneering with the advantages of being a later entrant in the market which it plans to enter. A firm's decision to pioneer or enter later is thus based on a contingency framework comprising critical questions. Table 21.1 presents an adapted version of the framework by Krishnamurthi and Shankar (1998).

Table 21.1   Pioneering versus late entry

Question	Answer	Decision
What is the likely life of the product category?	Long	Enter later
	Short	Pioneer
Is consumer's perception of value based on objective or subjective attributes?	Objective	Enter later
	Subjective	Pioneer
What are the expected costs of imitation?	High	Pioneer
	Low	Enter later
What are my resources?	High	Enter later
	Low	Pioneer
What are the expected switching costs in this market?	High	Pioneer
	Low	Enter later
How important is brand equity in customer choice?	High	Pioneer
	Low	Enter later
What are the likely costs of market education?	High	Enter later
	Low	Pioneer
Does the product category exhibit network externalities?	High	Pioneer
	Low	Enter later

Source: Adapted from Krishnamurthi and Shankar (1998).

What is the Likely Life of the Product Category?

One benefit of pioneering is the potential for profits during the monopoly period (Schmalensee 1982). The monopoly period is relatively longer when the life of the category itself is shorter. In product categories with short life cycles, it pays to be the first mover rather than a later entrant. Certain software products fall under this classification. One such example is Y2K or Year 2000 software that had a short business horizon.

Is Value Objective or Subjective?

In many cases, the value buyers derive from one product versus another is objective, but in other cases it is highly subjective. In the case of buying a car, for example, value has subjective components to be sure (e.g. styling and driving excitement) but has many objective dimensions as well (price, fuel economy, operating cost etc.). In comparison, consider champagne, in which the value derived is highly subjective. When value is highly subjective, the benefits of pioneering increase (Carpenter and Nakamoto 1989). If one can establish the standard, then other perfectly fine products suffer by comparison. If you are not Dom Perignon, the alleged champagne pioneer, you simply cannot ever be judged as an equal by some. If value is more objective, later entry is more attractive. Even though Karl Benz invented the auto, Toyota was remarkably successful launching Lexus in North America, overtaking Mercedes-Benz in sales in less than five years.

What are the Expected Costs of Imitation?

In many product categories, the cost of imitation may be quite low relative to the pioneer's cost of development. For example, a study of chemical, ethical drug, electronics and machinery industries shows that, on average, imitation costs are only 65 percent of the pioneer's product development costs (Lilien and Yoon 1990). Pioneers suffer from substantial cost disadvantages relative to later entrants due to imitation (Boulding and Christen 2008). If this is likely to be the case, it is better to enter later than pioneer the new market (Lieberman and Montgomery 1988). On the other hand, in some cases, pioneering may confer valuable patents that would make the cost of imitation substantially high. For instance, Polaroid benefited from substantial margins on its pioneering instant cameras, thanks to the long-running patent that it enjoyed. In these cases, pioneering is a better option.

What are my Resources?

Firms with large resources do not have to pioneer a market (Kerin et al. 1992). It may be better for them to let some other firm undertake the risk of pioneering a new market. In fact, by waiting and entering later, they can cash in on the pioneer's efforts in creating the market, and out-muscle them. Corporate history is replete with examples of large firms outsmarting small pioneers. Minnctonka, Inc. was the first dispenser soap in the market, but Procter & Gamble ousted it as the leader with its Ivory brand of dispenser soap. Microsoft is another firm that has succeeded in many markets by entering later with its stronger resources.

Are Radical Product Innovations Possible in the Category?

In some product categories, radical innovations are possible due to technological advancements. In other categories, technology may only allow for gradual and continuous improvements. In the latter case, a firm should enter the market as early as possible. The pioneer has a clear advantage. By being in the market for a longer period, it can learn faster and be constantly ahead of later entrants in offering the best-quality products. In categories such as computer software and pharmaceutical drugs, radical innovations are possible. In these cases, later entrants with innovative brands can overtake pioneers (Shankar et al. 1998).

What are the Expected Switching Costs in this Market?

In some markets, it is highly expensive for customers to switch from one brand to another. A pioneer can lock in customers earlier than can later entrants. This lock-in creates an uphill task for later entrants, which are often reduced to competing only for new customers to the market. This phenomenon is particularly common in many industrial and business-to-business markets. If switching costs are high, then pioneering is a better option.

How Important is Brand Equity in Customer Choice?

The role of the brand varies in different markets. In some markets, brands signal quality, convey images with which customers want to associate, or minimize risks (Schmalensee 1982). In such markets, brand equity can be critical. However, in many markets, consumers can easily compare features of alternative offerings and choose based on the desired features. In those markets, brands may not be that important in customer choice. Consider the personal digital assistant (PDA) market. Palm Pilot was a late entrant, following earlier entrants such as Apple's Newton and Motorola's Envoy. Apple and Motorola are better known and have greater brand equity. However, these earlier brands lacked quality handwriting-recognition software that is critical for the functioning of a PDA. Palm Pilot innovated this software and improved on other features as well. Thus, by producing a better-quality product, it overcame the handicap in brand equity (Bayus et al. 1997). However, brand equity, matched with reasonable product quality, does favor the pioneer (Shankar 2006). Hewlett Packard (HP) pioneered laser printing in the desktop market. The power of the HP name along with high product quality has made the HP LaserJet the technical and the psychological standard in the market. Similarly, Apple's brand equity together with the first touch-screen mobile device made iPhone an instant success.

What are the Likely Costs of Market Education?

If it costs a substantial amount to educate the customers of a new market, the chances are that it will allow later entrants to free-ride on the pioneer (Lieberman and Montgomery 1988). If later entrants can seize the opportunity, later entry may be a preferable option. Pravachol educated physicians about lowering cholesterol through a new class of drugs called statins. Zocor and Lipitor, later entrants, did not have to educate the market about statins but focused on communicating how superior they were. They overtook the pioneer by capitalizing on the market knowledge created by Pravachol.

Does the Product Category/Market Exhibit Network Externalities?

Product categories such as video games, automated teller machines (ATMs) and tele-communication services exhibit network externalities – a phenomenon in which the benefits to a customer of a brand increase when more customers adopt the brand. For example, a video game consumer's value for a video game brand like Nintendo will be higher if more consumers use the same brand so that more game software titles are available for consumers to play. In this case, the pioneer has an opportunity to create an installed base earlier than do later entrants and free-ride on them. However, later entrants can overcome such installed base with innovative offerings and by bringing related benefits (Shankar and Bayus 2003). Indeed, the first firm to market could be the first to fail in such product categories if the right benefits are not provided (Srinivasan et al. 2004).

The answers to these questions may not always point to one clear path. Firms will have to weigh these questions and make an overall decision. Successful firms will be those that are able to clearly think through all these issues before making a final decision.

DEVELOPING A LATE-MOVER STRATEGY

For many firms, however, pioneering is not an option. In many markets, some firm always beats others to the market to become a pioneer. If so, what can later entrants do to compete with the pioneer or, more generally, the dominant incumbent? A later entrant should consider different strategies (Carpenter and Nakamoto 1990).

A later entrant should ask five questions: (1) How many financial resources do I have? (2) What is my ability to come up with an innovative product? (3) What is the perceived quality of the dominant incumbent's product? (4) What are the expected reactions of the dominant incumbent, in particular the pioneer? (5) What is the source of the pioneer's advantage? The late mover's strategy will depend on the answers to these questions. Krishnamurthi and Shankar (1998) provide evidence for the importance of the first three questions.

A firm's financial resources are typically reflected by capital, free cash flow and other assets. The ability to innovate depends on its R&D unit's expertise. A pioneer's perceived quality is driven by consumer perceptions, and the pioneer's marketing efforts to influence those perceptions. The dominant incumbent, including the pioneer, can retaliate or accommodate the late mover's entry (Shankar 1997). The source of the pioneer's advantage can be brand consumer perception, risk or preemptive positioning.

Depending on the combination of these factors, a late mover has many strategic options. Based on the answers to the first three questions alone, later entrants can follow one of the strategies presented in Table 21.2 (Krishnamurthi and Shankar 1998).

A later entrant with high resources and a high innovative ability that faces a dominant brand with a low perceived quality has the easiest challenge. The best strategy would be to

Table 21.2   Later entrant strategies for competing with dominant incumbents

Dominant incumbent's perceived product quality	Financial resources			
	Low		High	
	Ability to innovate		Ability to innovate	
	Low	High	Low	High
Low	Be an early follower (e.g. Google search engine)	Innovate product (e.g. US Robotics' Palm Pilot PDA)	Outspend or/and underprice the incumbents (e.g. Microsoft Office suite)	Innovate product (e.g. Gillette razor)
High	Be a niche marketer (e.g. Hon Industries office furniture)	Differentiate product (e.g. Amazon.com super bookstore)	Be an early follower and outspend or/and underprice the incumbents (e.g. Microsoft Excel spreadsheet, Microsoft Explorer)	Innovate product and outspend or/and underprice the incumbents (e.g. Zantac anti-ulcer drug)

Source: Adapted from Krishnamurthi and Shankar (1998).

develop an innovative product relative to the incumbents. A good example of this strategy is Gillette in the shaving razor market. Gillette has built a powerful position in the razor market through a process of continuing innovation. Through these innovations, it has overtaken the pioneer, Star, and many others. Similarly, Boeing surpassed deHavilland Comet 1, the pioneer in commercial jet aircraft, through product innovation—by building a safer, larger and more powerful jet. The role of innovation is particularly vivid in evolving or so-called "high-technology" markets such as the video cassette recorder market in which the pioneer Ampex was overtaken by Matsushita, and the microwave market in which the pioneer Amana was eclipsed by Samsung. Innovation also plays a role in so-called "low-technology" markets as well: Tide dominates the liquid laundry detergent market pioneered by Whisk, and Eveready leads the flashlight battery market launched by Bright Star.

At the other end of the spectrum, a late mover with scarce resources and a low R&D capability that faces a dominant incumbent with a high perceived quality has the most daunting task. Such a late mover may have to settle for a lower market share, but could remain very profitable, sometimes more than the dominant player by focusing on market niches. Hon Industries is a good example of a successful niche marketer in the office furniture market dominated in market share by the "high-quality" Steelcase. Although it is only the fourth-largest office furniture manufacturer in the USA, Hon is the leader in the $4 billion "medium-priced" office furniture niche with a share of over 20 percent. What is interesting is that Hon generates about twice the rate of return of Steelcase, which is three times as large as Hon. How did Hon achieve this position? Hon has developed an excellent reputation for offering value products at attractive price points, backing this with a broad product line in its market niche. Also, by focusing on distribution through office products wholesalers, it is able to offer quick delivery to its customers from its US network of 135 wholesalers.

Many later entrants are small firms with a limited ability to innovate at the beginning but face markets in which the dominant brand's perceived quality is low. These firms are better off entering early after the pioneer when the market is in the growth stage. One such firm is Google, which entered the market for Web search engines much later than Yahoo, the pioneer. Today, Google is the dominant search engine.

Some later entrants have the ability to produce a superior product, but may lack resources and could face a dominant incumbent with a low perceived product quality. The best strategy for such firms is to innovate. One example is computerized ticketing service for events. Ticketron, a subsidiary of Control Data Corporation, pioneered this service. Ticketmaster, an upstart firm, innovated the product by helping customers promote shows, doing demand analysis for them, and offering superior customer service. Ticketmaster also stressed continual product improvements. It kept innovating its ticketing software by increasing the speed of processing and including features such as language translations to serve foreign markets. With all these, Ticketmaster overtook Ticketron. It took only five years for Ticketmaster to dethrone a pioneer that was a market leader for over ten years.

By better understanding consumer preferences, even a later entrant with limited resources can identify a superior, but overlooked, product position and differentiate itself. Consider the super bookstore market. Amazon.com was a startup firm with few resources. It successfully differentiated its product (selection of books) from the highly rated dominant incumbent, Barnes and Noble. It accomplished this by offering its products on the Internet, allowing potential customers to electronically browse its selection, and customizing book suggestions for potential customers on its website. Today, with a market capitalization of over $75 billion, it is one of the biggest success stories of a startup firm.

When a later entrant has high resources, but is less known for its innovation, it should try to beat the dominant incumbent at the latter's own game by out-advertising or out-distributing that incumbent. When the dominant brand's perceived quality is low, the late mover simply has to outspend or underprice the dominant brand (Shankar 1999), but when the dominant brand's perceived quality is high, it should enter early as well. Microsoft has successfully pursued this strategy. In the market for software suites, it eclipsed the "not-so-high" quality Corel Suite by out-advertising and out-distributing Corel. In the market for spreadsheets, it beat Lotus 1-2-3, widely perceived as a high-quality incumbent, by entering early and outspending it. Interestingly, Lotus 1-2-3 itself is another example of a successful later entrant that surpassed the pioneer, Visicalc. Microsoft is pursuing a similar strategy in the web browser market. Typically, the successful later entrant is a multiproduct firm capable of cross-subsidizing some of its business units, using profits generated by a successful product to shore up subsequent new product offerings (e.g. Microsoft's Windows operating system). It is steadily gaining market share for its Internet Explorer product at the expense of the market pioneer, Netscape. While Microsoft mainly outspent its rivals, Sunbeam is an example of a later entrant that overtook the dominant brand by underpricing its brand. In the food processor market, the pioneer Cuisinart is known for its high quality. Sunbeam capitalized on an increasingly price-sensitive market by offering a no-frills compact processor at a low price. In contrast, Cuisinart was stuck selling a high-end processor at a substantially higher price.

When a later entrant is rich in financial resources, is renowned for its technological expertise, and faces a dominant player whose product is perceived to be of high quality, it should innovate and outspend or underprice the incumbents. In the anti-ulcer market, Glaxo's Zantac is a classic example. The pioneer, Smith Kline Beecham's Tagamet, was a highly rated product that took the market by storm. Glaxo, however, made Zantac superior in dosage and side effects, two important attributes in the pharmaceutical industry. Further, it teamed up with Roche's sales force and outspent Tagamet in marketing. As a result, Zantac became not only the highest-selling anti-ulcer drug, but also the best-selling ethical drug in the world by 1991.

UNDEREXPLORED ISSUES, FUTURE RESEARCH AND CONCLUSION

Although we know a great deal about first-mover advantages and disadvantages, late-mover advantages and disadvantages, and late-mover strategies, there are several underexplored issues.

Multibrand Strategies

A firm could pioneer a market with one brand to exploit the sources of pioneering advantage, but, to leverage the sources of late-mover advantage, launch late-mover brands. For example, in the market for anti-cholesterol drugs, Merck first introduced Mevacor, but followed up with an innovative brand, Zocor. This multibrand strategy requires strong financial resources and a high appetite for risk. Not much is known about such strategies. When should firms follow a multibrand strategy? What are the benefits and potential risks of such a strategy?

Phased Obsolescence Strategies

In many markets, the pioneer updates its offering through product improvements or even radically new products. For example, Apple introduces updates of iPhone, iPod and iPad. Its competitors also introduce their newer versions. How should late movers make decisions on when to render their products obsolete by introducing newer versions? Looking for answers to these questions produces fruitful avenues for future research.

Phased Acquisition Strategies

Pioneers and late movers can also compete by looking to acquire successful brands, regardless of whether they are pioneering or late-mover brands. Firms could acquire different brands at different phases in the product life cycle or market, depending on whether they have the resources and whether the brands considered for acquisition are successful or would add value to the firms' portfolio. Not much research has been done on these issues, but they are worthy of further exploration.

Conclusion

Although a number of compelling conceptual arguments have been advanced in support of pioneering advantage, empirical findings are equivocal. Moreover, there are advantages as well for the majority of firms that are later entrants. By adopting the right strategies, later entrants can successfully turn the conventional wisdom of pioneering advantage on its head.

REFERENCES

Bayus, Barry L., Sanjay Jain and Ambar Rao (1997), "Too little and too early: a competitive analysis of the personal digital assistant industry," *Journal of Marketing Research*, **34** (February), 50–63.

Boulding, William and Markus Christen (2003), "Sustainable pioneering advantage? Profit implications of market entry order," *Marketing Science*, **22** (3), 371–92.

Boulding, William and Markus Christen (2008), "Disentangling pioneering cost advantages and disadvantages," *Marketing Science*, **27** (4), 699–716.

Boulding, William and Markus Christen (2009), "Pioneering plus a broad product line strategy: higher profits or deeper losses," *Management Science*, **55** (6), 958–67.

Carpenter, Gregory S. and Kent Nakamoto (1989), "Consumer preference formation and pioneering advantage," *Journal of Marketing Research*, **26** (August), 285–98.

Carpenter, Gregory S. and Kent Nakamoto (1990), "Competitive strategies for late entry into a market with a dominant brand," *Management Science*, **36** (October), 1268–78.

Fischer, Marc, Venkatesh Shankar and Michel Clement (2005), "Can late mover brands use international market entry strategy to challenge the pioneer?" MSI Report, 05-004, 25–48.

Golder, Peter and Gerard Tellis (1993), "Pioneering advantage: marketing logic or marketing legend," *Journal of Marketing Research*, **30** (May), 158–70.

Kardes, F.R., G. Kalyanaram, M. Chandrashekaran and R.J. Dornoff (1993), "Brand retrieval, consideration set composition, consumer choice, and the pioneering advantage," *Journal of Consumer Research*, **20** (1), 62–75.

Kerin, Roger, Rajan Varadarajan and Robert Peterson (1992), "First mover advantage: a synthesis and critique," *Journal of Marketing*, **56** (l), 33–52.

Krishnamurthi, Lakshman and Venkatesh Shankar (1998), "What are the options for later entrants?" in *Mastering Marketing*, London: Financial Times Prentice Hall, pp. 172–8.

Lieberman, Marvin B. and David B. Montgomery (1988), "First-mover advantages," *Strategic Management Journal*, **9**, 41–58.

Lilien, Gary L. and Eunsang Yoon (1990), "The timing of competitive market entry: an exploratory study of new industrial products," *Management Science*, **36** (5), 568–85.

Schmalensee, Richard (1982), "Product differentiation advantages of pioneering brands," *American Economic Review*, **72**, 349–65.

Shankar, Venkatesh (1997), "Pioneers' marketing mix reaction to entry in different competitive game structures: theoretical analysis and empirical illustration," *Marketing Science*, **16** (3), 271–93.

Shankar, Venkatesh (1999), "New product introduction and incumbent response strategies: their interrelationship and the role of multimarket contact," *Journal of Marketing Research*, **36** (3), 327–44.

Shankar, Venkatesh (2006), "Proactive and reactive product line strategies: asymmetries between market leaders and followers," *Management Science*, **52** (2), 276–92.

Shankar, Venkatesh and Barry L. Bayus (2003), "Network effects and competition: an empirical analysis of the videogame industry," *Strategic Management Journal*, **24** (4), 375–94.

Shankar, Venkatesh, Gregory S. Carpenter and Lakshman Krishnamurthi (1998), "Late mover advantage: how innovative late entrants outsell pioneers," *Journal of Marketing Research*, **35** (1), 54–70.

Shankar, Venkatesh, Gregory S. Carpenter and Lakshman Krishnamurthi (1999), "The advantages of entering in the growth stage of the product life cycle: an empirical analysis," *Journal of Marketing Research*, **36** (2), 269–76.

Srinivasan, Raji, Gary L. Lilien and Arvind Rangaswamy (2004), "First in, first out? The effects of network externalities on pioneer survival," *Journal of Marketing*, **68** (1), 41–58.

Vadakkepatt, Gautham Gopal, Venkatesh Shankar and Rajan Varadarajan (2010), "Survival of manufacturing firms in *Fortune* 500: the roles of marketing capital and R&D capital," MSI Working Paper, 10–119.

Varadarajan, Rajan, Manjit Yadav and Venkatesh Shankar (2008), "First-mover advantage in the Internet-enabled environment: a conceptual framework and propositions," *Journal of Academy of Marketing Science*, **36** (3), 293–308.

22 Diffusion and its implications for marketing strategy

Gerard Tellis and Deepa Chandrasekaran

INTRODUCTION

New products, services and innovations are the lifeblood of businesses. There is hence a vast interest in understanding exactly how and how quickly products and services diffuse across a population of adopters, be it within a specific market, country or across countries. A vast literature in marketing has examined the diffusion of new products and innovations in response to this need. The term diffusion has been defined as a special type of communication where the message refers to an innovation (Rogers 1995; Mahajan et al. 2000). In this sense, diffusion refers to the process by which an innovation is communicated through certain channels over time among members of a social system (Chandrasekaran and Tellis 2007). A second use of the term refers to the spread of the innovation across social groups or markets over time, focusing on the phenomenon itself, rather than on its drivers (Chandrasekaran and Tellis 2007; Peres et al. 2010).

This chapter will summarize key research and findings relating to the diffusion of innovations in the marketing literature with implications for new product management. The topics covered include a discussion of the Bass model, estimations and extensions of the Bass model, turning points of the product life cycle (takeoff and saddle), understanding the diffusion patterns across countries, suggestions for future research and conclusions.

THE BASS MODEL

The best-known diffusion model in the marketing literature is the Bass diffusion model. Bass (1969) developed a model for the timing of initial purchase of new products and tested it empirically against data for 11 consumer durables. The model was based on the basic assumption that the timing of a consumer's initial purchase of a new product was related to the number of prior adopters. The model discriminated between the innovators, or those who decided to adopt an innovation independent of others, and imitators, who were susceptible to the influence of prior adopters. We present a brief derivation of the model here (see also Chandrasekaran and Tellis 2007).

The probability that an initial purchase is made at time T, given no purchase was made before, is

$$P(t) = f(t) / (1 - F(t)) = p + q / m \ Y(t) \qquad (22.1)$$

where $P(t)$ is a hazard rate, which depicts the conditional probability of a purchase in a (very small) time interval $(t, t + \Delta)$ if the purchase has not occurred before t. $Y(t)$ refers to the number of prior buyers; m is the total number of initial purchases for the time interval. $F(t)$ denotes the cumulative fraction of adopters at time t and $f(t)$ is the likelihood of purchase at time t. This leads to

$$f(t) = (p + qF(t))[1 - F(t)] \tag{22.2}$$

Where p is the coefficient of innovation and q is the coefficient of imitation. The product $q/mY(t)$ reflects the pressure of prior adopters on imitators. The number of adoptions at time t, $S(t)$, is hence obtained from:

$$S(t) = mf(t) = pm + (q - p) \, Y(t) - q/m \, Y^2(t) \tag{22.3}$$

In order to estimate the model using discrete time series data, equation (22.3) is rewritten as below

$$S_t = a + bY_{t-1} + cY^2_{t-1}, \, t = 2, 3 \ldots \tag{22.4}$$

where S_t refers to sales at time t, Y_{t-1} refers to cumulative sales through period $t-1$ and the three parameters can be identified as

$$p = a/m \tag{22.5}$$

$$q = -mc \tag{22.6}$$

$$m = \frac{-b \pm \sqrt{b^2 - 4ac}}{2c} \tag{22.7}$$

The model enables the researcher to determine the time to, and magnitude of, peak sales (t^*) and $S(t)^*$, respectively. Bass shows that the time to peak sales and the magnitude are, respectively:

$$t^* = (1/(p + q))^* \ln (q/p) \tag{22.8}$$

$$S(t)^* = (m^*(p + q)^2)/4q \tag{22.9}$$

ESTIMATION OF THE BASS MODEL

The original Bass model (Bass 1969) was estimated by ordinary least squares (OLS). This is the simplest and most intuitive method, still used for teaching purposes in marketing academia. However, this method suffers from the following issues: (1) There is likely to be collinearity between the variables, Y_{t-1} and Y^2_{t-1}, making the parameter estimates unstable. (2) The procedure does not provide standard errors for the estimated parameters p, q and m, and hence it is not possible to assess the statistical significance of these estimates. (3) There is a time interval bias because the model uses discrete time series data to estimate a continuous model (Chandrasekaran and Tellis 2007; Mahajan et al. 1990). Maximum likelihood estimation was proposed to eliminate the time-interval bias

Table 22.1   Reported average values of diffusion parameters

	All countries	Developed countries	Developing countries
Coefficient of innovation (p)	0.0007–0.03	0.001	0.0003
Coefficient of imitation (q)	0.38–0.53	0.51	0.56
Market penetration potential (m)	0.39	0.52	0.17

Source: Chandrasekaran and Tellis (2009), based on a meta-analysis of 22 studies of estimates of the Bass diffusion model (reviews, meta-analyses, individual papers) with samples of over ten countries or ten categories.

(Schmittlein and Mahajan 1982). However, this method may underestimate the standard errors of the parameter estimates (Srinivasan and Mason 1986). Srinivasan and Mason (1986) proposed the non-linear least squares (NLLS) estimation, which can be easily estimated using standard software packages and the model is not constrained to be linear in the parameters. Further the model overcomes the time-interval bias of the OLS estimation and provides valid estimated standard errors and T-ratios. However, the estimates can be poor and noisy when obtained from data sets with too few observations (Van den Bulte and Lilien 1997), and the technique does not allow for parameter updating as new data come in. Some researchers propose hierarchical Bayesian techniques, which help to produce more stable forecasts (Lenk and Rao 1990; Neelamegham and Chintagunta 1999; Talukdar et al. 2002), and allow updating of forecasts with new sales data. Kalman filter techniques can estimate the parameters directly, avoid time-interval bias, forecast more accurately than other techniques such as the NLLS and the OLS, and can estimate time-varying parameters (Xie et al. 1997). Venkatesan et al. (2004) propose the use of genetic algorithms to estimate the Bass model. They find in simulations that this technique does not suffer from bias and systematic change in parameter values as more observations are added. As the methods get more sophisticated, we see a trade-off between simplicity and accuracy of estimation. So managers can choose the estimation technique most appropriate to their needs.

Key Findings and Implications

1. *Estimates of* p, q *and* m   Several studies report estimates of p, q and m of various innovations based on the Bass diffusion model. These estimates provide managers with analogy data to develop forecasts for their particular products. One of the most commonly cited references (Sultan et al. 1990) reports average values $p = 0.03$ and $q = 0.38$ for durable goods. Other studies find these values to be typically lower (or much lower) or higher (or much higher) depending on the context. Table 22.1 summarizes the range of average values reported in various studies.
2. *Adopter segments*   The diffusion literature has practical implications beyond forecasting the sales curve. Mahajan et al. (1990) demonstrate how adopter categories can be derived based on the Bass diffusion model. According to their study, innovators comprise 0.2 to 2.8 percent, early adopters 12–20 percent, early majority comprise 29–32 percent, late majority of 29–32 percent and laggards 21–24 percent of the population of adopters. This categorization provides a useful extension to Rogers'

(1995) framework of adopter categories, which, while simple, assumes that all products will see a normal distribution of the adopter segments. Extensions to this research enable marketers to identify optimal targeting strategy, for instance when it is optimal to target the majority rather than innovators (Mahajan and Muller 1998), or identify the role of cross-market communication in influencing diffusion processes (e.g. Goldenberg et al. 2002).

3. *Forecasting* As shown previously, the Bass model enables the researcher to predict two parameters of crucial interest to managers: the magnitude (m) and timing of peak sales. Researchers suggest supplementing some of the estimates with managerial intuition. Particularly, the parameter m may be reasonably estimated by intuition as 100 percent or using analogous data. Heeler and Hustad (1980) demonstrate that such a substitution of m leads to a dramatic improvement in the quality of the estimates. Further, the estimates of the Bass model parameters, as well as software to help estimate these models, are provided for several product categories in relevant review papers and books (e.g. Lilien et al. 2000). These can help managers make predictions for similar product categories, or in other countries.

EXTENSIONS BASED ON THE BASS MODEL

The basic Bass model has been extended in several ways. We note below the key extensions. Interested readers can refer to the original papers or in-depth reviews on the diffusion literature (e.g. Chandrasekaran and Tellis 2007; Mahajan et al. 1990, 1995; Muller et al. 2009; Parker 1994; Shankar 2008).

Bass et al. (1994) include both price and advertising to develop the generalized Bass model:

$$f(t) / [1 - F(t)] = [p + qF(t)]x(t) \tag{22.10}$$

where $x(t)$ is the current marketing effort such that

$$x(t) = 1 + \beta_1 \Delta Pr(t) / Pr(t-1) + \beta_2 \Delta A(t) / A(t-1) \tag{22.11}$$

Here $\Delta Pr(t)$ and $\Delta A(t)$ refer to the rates of changes in prices and advertising. When the coefficients for the decision variables are statistically significant, the Generalized Bass model provides a better fit than the Bass model.

Other models incorporate the effects on diffusion of marketing mix variables such as advertising (Horsky and Simon 1983; Simon and Sebastian 1987), supply restrictions (Jain et al. 1991), competitive effects (e.g. Gatignon and Robertson 1989; Parker and Gatignon 1994; Shankar et al. 1998), as well as try to understand multinational diffusion patterns (e.g. Gatignon et al. 1989; Talukdar et al. 2002). Generalizations based on the Bass model have also been used to understand brand-level diffusion processes (Shankar et al. 1998).

For managers interested in forecasting the diffusion pattern of future technology generations, researchers have developed empirical models that use the information on diffusion model parameters of past technology generations in the same market (Danaher et al. 2001; Kim et al. 2000; Mahajan and Muller 1996; Norton and Bass 1987, 1992). These models help capture the extent of substitution, complementary and competitive effects between generations and across product categories. They also help determine the optimal timing of the introduction of the later generation, whether there has been acceleration in the diffusion of successive generations of technological innovations and for determining the impact of marketing mix variables on the diffusion of technological generations.

Subsequent research has extended and reinterpreted the meaning of the original diffusion parameters. p has been interpreted in subsequent research to reflect the external influence referring to the influence of mass-media communications and q as internal influence referring to the influence of interpersonal communication from prior adopters (Mahajan et al. 1990). Recently, q has been interpreted as the parameter that represents consumer interdependencies, including signals, externalities and interpersonal communications (Peres et al. 2010). Peres et al. (2010) also extend the Bass framework by proposing elements to the imitation coefficient q, beyond word-of-mouth communication. They propose the inclusion of network externalities that exist when the utility of a product to a consumer increases as more consumers adopt the new product. Such externalities are direct if utility is directly affected by the number of other users of the same product, for example e-mail. Network externalities are indirect if the utility increases with the number of users of another, complementary product, for instance DVD players and DVD titles. They also propose the inclusion of social signals that relate to the social information that individuals infer from adoption of an innovation by others. These signals are observed by potential adopters who infer from them the social consequences of adoption.

The mathematical form of the Bass model requires the assumption that the potential adopter population is homogeneous (Chatterjee and Eliashberg 1990). Researchers have developed "disaggregate-level" diffusion models that do not assume an aggregate homogeneous population. Such micro-modeling approaches posit individual adoption time as a function of characteristics of adopters and the resulting aggregate diffusion model thus has a behavioral basis at an individual level.

TURNING POINTS IN THE PRODUCT LIFE CYCLE

We review below some of the key propositions, generalizations and findings from the recent research on diffusion examining product takeoff and growth slowdown.

New Product Takeoff

The Bass model assumes the presence of a certain number of consumers ($p * m$) before "takeoff" (Chandrasekaran and Tellis 2007; Golder and Tellis, 1997; Mahajan et al. 1990). Indeed the depiction of the sales curve in diffusion models and textbooks is smooth (Golder and Tellis 1997). However, most new household durables experience a certain period when sales are low, and witness a dramatic increase in the sales of the new products. Golder and Tellis (1997) define this point of transition as "takeoff," and define it as the transition between the introduction and growth stage of the product life cycle. Figure 22.1 shows the takeoff of microwave ovens in Germany, for instance.

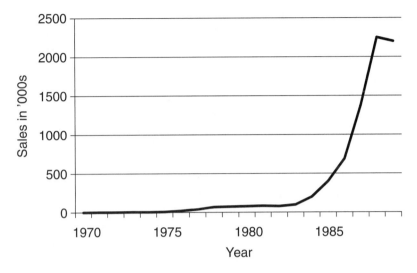

Figure 22.1 New product takeoff

The study of takeoff becomes crucial to managers interested in modeling or predicting the diffusion of new products for the following reasons. First, a sudden and sharp increase in sales requires enormous resources in terms of manufacturing, inventory, distribution and support. Hence knowing when it occurs and what causes it is critical for managers in handling the sales and success of a new product (Peres et al. 2010; Chandrasekaran and Tellis 2007, 2008). Second, takeoff provides an early signal to managers that the product has become desirable to the mass market, while the absence of takeoff may be the sign to cut further support for the new product (Golder and Tellis 1997; Chandrasekaran and Tellis 2007).

How to measure takeoff? Golder and Tellis (1997) provide the first formal measure of takeoff. They develop a threshold of takeoff, which is a plot of percentage sales growth relative to a base level of sales, common across all categories. Takeoff is the first year in which an individual category's growth rate relative to the base sales crosses this threshold. This measure of takeoff successfully fits a visual inspection for 90 percent of the 31 product categories in their sample.

Stremersch and Tellis (2004) and Tellis et al. (2003) use a modification of this measure of takeoff to suit an international sample of countries. The authors define the threshold as a standard plot of growth in sales for various levels of market penetration to provide a more standard comparison across several countries. Takeoff is the first year in which an individual category's growth rate relative to the base sales crosses this threshold.

Key Findings and Implications

1. *Time to takeoff* The reported average time to takeoff of new products in developed countries is six years. Golder and Tellis (1997) report an average time to takeoff for new products in the USA to be six years. Tellis et al. (2003) also report that, on average, new products in Europe take six years to take off. They find that products

take off fastest in Europe in Scandinavian countries. The average time to takeoff of new products in Scandinavian countries is four years, in mid-European countries, the average is six years, and in Mediterranean countries, it is eight years (Tellis et al. 2003). The mean time to takeoff varies considerably between developing countries (11 years) and developed countries (seven years). Chandrasekaran and Tellis (2008) report that products take off fastest in Japan and Norway, followed by other Nordic countries, the USA and some countries of Midwestern Europe. Newly developed countries of Asia (e.g. South Korea) see faster times to takeoff of products than some established, major European countries. These findings can be used to ascertain innovative behavior of countries and to plan launch strategies for durable goods.

2. *Differences across products*   Entertainment and information products take off faster than kitchen and laundry appliances. Tellis et al. (2003) report an average of two years for the former and an average of eight years for the latter. Chandrasekaran and Tellis (2008) find that time to takeoff varies considerably between fun products (seven years) and work products (12 years). Further, they find that time to takeoff of fun products shows smaller differences across cultural clusters than work products.

3. The research also reports diminishing differences in time to takeoff, at least across developed countries (Chandrasekaran and Tellis 2008). This indicates that for new consumer electronics categories, marketers may well use similar marketing strategies.

4. *Penetration at takeoff*   Golder and Tellis (1997) report that an average penetration at takeoff is 1.7 percent of market potential. This level has been found to be consistent in other studies (Tellis et al. 2003; Chandrasekaran and Tellis 2008).

5. *Drivers of takeoff*   The growing literature on takeoff has predominantly used hazard models to determine the drivers of takeoff and to predict takeoff. Golder and Tellis (1997) find that price and market penetration are strongly associated with takeoff. The average penetration at takeoff is 1.7 percent (Golder and Tellis 1997). For post-WWII categories, price at takeoff is 63 percent of original price in an examination of 31 product categories in the USA. Further, they report that every 1 percent decrease in price leads to a 4.2 percent increase in the probability of takeoff (Golder and Tellis 1997). Agarwal and Bayus (2002) find that firm entry dominates price declines in explaining takeoff times. Takeoff in the number of firms in the market precedes product takeoff by at least three years (Agarwal and Bayus 2002). Tellis et al. (2003) examine the diffusion of ten categories across 16 European countries. They find that while culture partially explains inter-country differences in time to takeoff, economic factors are neither strong nor robust explanatory factors. However, Chandrasekaran and Tellis (2008) examine the takeoff of 16 new products across 31 countries and find that, when both developing and developed countries are considered, both culture and wealth drive takeoff. Goldenberg et al. (2010) investigated the effect of network externalities on takeoff and speed of diffusion of innovative products. Using agent-based cellular automata for individual-level analysis, and a Bass model with changing market potential that depends on the threshold level of the adopting population, they find that the higher the network effect, the more pronounced the hockey stick pattern of growth (Peres et al. 2010).

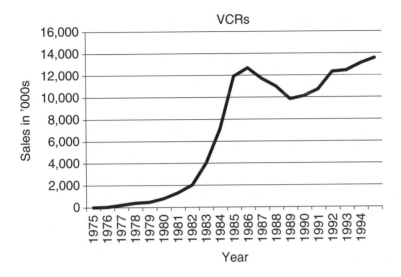

Figure 22.2   Saddle in VCR Sales

The Saddle in New Product Sales

Recent empirical papers have reported a pattern of a sudden trough in sales following takeoff (see Figure 22.2). Goldenberg et al. (2002) define the saddle as a pattern in which an initial peak predates a trough of sufficient depth and duration, followed by sales that eventually exceed the initial peak. They measure the saddle as a trough following an initial peak in sales, reaching a depth of at least 20 percent of the peak, lasting at least two years, followed by sales that ultimately exceed the initial peak. Golder and Tellis (2004) and Stremersch and Tellis (2004) operationalize slowdown, as the first year, of two consecutive years after takeoff, in which sales are lower than the highest previous sales. According to Golder and Tellis (2004), slowdown divides the maturity period of the product life cycle into early maturity and late maturity. Early maturity begins with the year sales slowdown and continues until sales grow to the previous local peak (Golder and Tellis 2004). Late maturity begins with the first year sales being higher than the local peak and continues until a product's sales begin to fall steadily during the decline stage (Golder and Tellis 2004).

The budding research on the saddle offers some explanations as to what may drive this phenomenon. Some researchers posit a segmentation argument (Goldenberg et al. 2002; Muller and Yogev 2006; Van den Bulte and Joshi 2007). This builds on the work by Moore (1991), who argued that a communication gap or a chasm existed between early adopters and early majority, due to the differing nature and characteristics of these adopter segments. Hence the former do not prove to be a good reference point for the latter. Goldenberg et al. (2002) suggest that the chasm leads the early market and the late market to adopt in different ways, and the social contagion process is broken at the point of transition from the early market to the late market. Both Muller and Yogev (2006) and Van den Bulte and Joshi (2007) demonstrate the occurrence of a saddle when there is a division of the market into those who innovate and those who imitate, and if the cross-market communication is low.

Golder and Tellis (2004) posit an alternative explanation based on the theory of informational cascades, building on the work by Bikchandani et al. (1992). Cascades occur when many consumers base their choice on the behavior of a few other consumers rather than on their own private assessments of the utility of alternatives (Chandrasekaran and Tellis 2007). So a positive cascade may cause sales to increase far more than they would have done in the early growth stage. But any small turbulence in the market can reverse this flow and cause a negative cascade, leading to a steep drop in sales of a new product that was previously experiencing growth.

Chandrasekaran and Tellis (2011) examine the specific impact of business cycles, technological cycles and chasms in adopter segments in leading to the saddle in sales, using historical sales data from ten products across 19 countries. They find support for the explanations of chasms and technological cycles for information/entertainment products and business cycles and technological cycles for kitchen/laundry products.

Key Findings and Implications

The saddle is a fairly common phenomenon in the sales history of consumer durables. A sales drop or a slowdown has been seen in 50–96 percent of categories (Goldenberg et al. 2002; Golder and Tellis 2004). Chandrasekaran and Tellis (2011) report that, on average, the saddle occurs nine years post-takeoff, at a mean penetration of 30 percent, lasting for eight years. The sales decline during the saddle is pretty steep. Sales decline by an average 15–32 percent during these drops after slowdown (Chandrasekaran and Tellis 2011; Goldenberg et al. 2002; Golder and Tellis 2004). Managers who find a sharp drop in sales in their product category, following a period of rapid growth, may be encouraged by the findings of a recovery to the prior peak in sales. However, they may need to plan for reduced inventory during the time. The extant research has not yet focused on the best strategies to recover from the saddle– that is, should there be an increase in marketing and R&D expenditure during this time, or a reduction.

DIFFUSION PATTERNS ACROSS COUNTRIES

Several papers on diffusion have focused on the variation in diffusion patterns across countries. These focus mainly on the lead–lag effect, on the heterogeneity issues that lead to an examination of drivers of cross-country diffusion. We briefly review this literature and elaborate on key findings.

Lead–Lag Patterns in Adoption

One of the major findings of the studies on cross-country influences is that countries that introduce a given innovation later show a faster diffusion process (Chandrasekaran and Tellis 2008; Dekimpe et al. 2000a, 2000b; Fischer et al. 2005; Ganesh et al. 1997; Peres et al. 2010; Takada and Jain 1991; Tellis et al. 2003). This impact has been variously termed the lead–lag effect or the cross-country learning effect. The idea is that consumers learn from the previous adoption experiences of countries where the products were commercialized earlier, or took off earlier.

Drivers of Diffusion Processes across Countries

The research also indicates key drivers of cross-country variations in diffusion patterns. These are country characteristics such as the wealth of the country, income inequality, country culture (typically based on the Hofstede 2001 framework as well as cross-country learning effects (Dekimpe et al. 1998, 2000a; Ganesh et al. 1997; Mahajan et al. 2000; Putsis et al. 1997; Stremersch and Tellis 2004; Talukdar et al. 2002; Van den Bulte and Stremersch 2004)). For instance, a 1 percent change in purchasing power parity adjusted per capita income is likely to change the market penetration potential by about 0.3 percent (Talukdar et al. 2002). A 1 percent change in international trade or urbanization is likely to change the market penetration potential by about 0.5 percent and 0.2 percent respectively (Talukdar et al. 2002). Cultural differences matter for cross-country differences in takeoff when developed countries are considered (Tellis et al. 2003), while the role of wealth becomes important when developing countries are considered (Chandrasekaran and Tellis 2008).

Findings and Implications

The cross-country diffusion research also has some implications for entry strategy for the launch of new products. Managers can choose between a waterfall strategy (staggering the commercialization of new products across countries) and a sprinkler strategy (simultaneously introducing the new products across countries). While a simultaneous launch minimizes the risks due to delayed rollouts and competitive environments, conditions such as long product life cycles, small size or slow growth of a foreign market make a waterfall strategy preferable (Chandrasekaran and Tellis 2008). Tellis et al. (2003) argue that a waterfall strategy greatly reduces the scale of operation and exposure to risk of product failure, and increases senior management support when takeoff occurs quickly in the most innovative countries. For instance, Stremersch and Tellis (2004) identify two different types of waterfall strategies in Europe: the first is what companies currently do—introducing in the large countries first; and the second (the North-to-South waterfall)—introducing first in the Nordic countries, then in the Mid-European countries and finally in the Mediterranean countries (see Tellis et al. 2003). Chandrasekaran and Tellis (2008) point out that the market strategy should depend considerably on the type of products. Because times to takeoff of fun products are more similar across countries and takeoff of information/entertainment products is converging faster over time than that for work products, they probably have a universal appeal across cultures. Hence a sprinkler strategy might be feasible for such products. For products that are culturally bound and adopted in some cultures more readily than in others, such as kitchen/laundry appliances, a waterfall strategy may be more appropriate.

FUTURE RESEARCH

We offer the following areas as having the potential for future research. First, the process of diffusion of technology across firms is examined in only a few papers in the marketing literature (Sinha and Chandrasekaran 1992; Gatignon and Robertson 1989), as compared to the vast literature on the diffusion of consumer durables and other household products. Clearly, in the digital age, understanding the diffusion of technologies *per se*, whether across firms or consumers, becomes important. Further, there is a need to better understand diffusion processes at the firm level. Second, new models of diffusion incorporate fine-grained differences in internal influences, pointing to a pressing need to better understand processes of diffusion across social networks (Peres et al. 2010). Third, much progress has been made in developing better estimation techniques based on the Bass model, and for predicting the turning points in the product life cycle. However, there is a need to develop an integrated model to predict the turning points in the S-shaped curve (Hauser et al. 2006). Fourth, much of the diffusion research has focused on either developed markets or on products and innovations originating from developed markets. As interest in emerging markets grows, there is a need to understand the propensity of consumers in emerging markets to adopt innovations that are more specific to their particular needs (Peres et al. 2010).

CONCLUSIONS

Millions of dollars are spent annually in developing new innovations. The success of such innovations depends on how well they are accepted by consumers, how fast they diffuse across a population of adopters and how large a market they create (Shankar 2008). The Bass model has become a simple yet powerful and unifying framework for a great deal of research on the diffusion of innovations across the discipline. This chapter has highlighted the key features of the model, its major findings, and the major extensions of research around the model. The model helps provide strategic directions by explaining some of the key drivers of diffusion, by delineating the differences between external and internal influences, and key parameters of interest, such as the peak sales, time to peak, as well as providing insights on adopter segment classifications. The literature on takeoff and slowdown helps understand the drivers and dimensions of the turning points in the product life cycle, while helping managers plan accordingly in terms of manufacturing, inventory, distribution and support. Diffusion research focusing on cross-country patterns helps managers plan new product entry and understand the impact of lead–lag effects as well as country (economic and cultural) effects on diffusion. We summarize the key findings from the research in Table 22.2. While a great deal of research has been completed, much remains to be done, as the limitations of the above research indicate. Specifically, there is a need to better understand the diffusion of new and emerging technologies, and help understand diffusion processes in different contexts, such as between firms, and across social networks of consumers and in emerging markets.

Table 22.2   Summary of key findings from diffusion research and strategic implications

Paradigm	Key results	Strategic implications	Selected sources
The Bass model	Average values of p and q reported in studies based on the Bass model	These estimates provide managers with analogy data to develop forecasts for their particular products; help determine magnitude and timing of peak sales	Table 22.1 above, Bass (1969); Lilien et al. (2000)
Adopter classifications	Innovators comprise 0.2 to 2.8%, early adopters from 12 to 20%, early majority 29–32%, late majority 29–32% and laggards 21–24% of the population of adopters	Help marketers to identify optimal targeting strategy, and identify the role of cross-market communication in influencing diffusion processes	Mahajan et al. (1990)
Takeoff	The average penetration at takeoff is 1.7% of the market potential; average reported values of time to takeoff is 6 years; mean time to takeoff varies considerably between developing countries (11 years) and developed countries (7 years). Products take off fastest in Japan and Norway, followed by other Nordic countries, the USA, and some countries of Midwestern Europe; time to takeoff varies considerably between fun products (7 years) and work products (12 years). There are diminishing differences in time to takeoff, at least across developed countries	Help managers ascertain innovative behavior of countries and can be used to plan new product launch strategies	Golder and Tellis (1997); Tellis et al. (2003); Chandrasekaran and Tellis (2008)
Saddle	On average, the saddle occurs 9 years post-takeoff, at a mean penetration of 30%, lasting for 8 years. Sales decline by an average 15–32% during these drops after slowdown; there are diminishing differences in time to saddle and year of saddle across countries	The saddle is a fairly pervasive phenomenon that affects most new products. Thus growth is not perennial. At the same time, recovery is also very likely. Helps plan production, inventory and labor to account for a potential slowdown in sales, and recovery from the slowdown	Goldenberg et al. (2002); Golder and Tellis (2004); Chandrasekaran and Tellis (2011)

Table 22.2   (continued)

Paradigm	Key results	Strategic implications	Selected sources
Cross-country diffusion	Countries that introduce a given innovation later show a faster diffusion process. Key drivers or country differences in diffusion include wealth of the country, income inequality, country culture and cross-country learning effects	Managers can choose between a waterfall strategy (staggering the commercialization of new products across countries) and a sprinkler strategy (simultaneously introducing the new products across countries)	Chandrasekaran and Tellis (2008); Dekimpe et al. (1998, 2000a); Ganesh et al. (1997); Mahajan et al. (2000); Putsis et al. (1997); Stremersch and Tellis (2004); Talukdar et al. (2002); Van den Bulte and Stremersch (2004)

REFERENCES

Agarwal, Rajshree and Barry L. Bayus (2002), "Market evolution and sales takeoff of product innovations," *Management Science*, **48** (8), 1024–41.

Bass, Frank M. (1969), "A new product growth model for consumer durables," *Management Science*, **15** (5), 215–27.

Bass, Frank M., Trichy V. Krishnan and Dipak C. Jain (1994), "Why the Bass model fits without decision variables," *Marketing Science*, **13** (3), 203–23.

Bikchandani, Sushil, David Hirshleifer and Ivo Welch (1992), "A theory of fads, fashion, custom and cultural change as information cascades," *Journal of Political Economy*, **100** (5), 992–1026.

Chandrasekaran, Deepa and Gerard J. Tellis (2007), "A critical review of marketing research on diffusion of new products," in N.K. Malhorta (ed.), *Review of Marketing Research*, Armonk, NY: M.E. Sharpe, pp. 39–80.

Chandrasekaran, Deepa and Gerard J. Tellis (2008), "Global takeoff of new products: culture, wealth or vanishing differences?" *Marketing Science*, **27** (5). Available at SSRN: http://ssrn.com/abstract=1017072.

Chandrasekaran, Deepa and Gerard J. Tellis (2011), "Getting a grip on the saddle: chasms or cycles," *Journal of Marketing*, **75** (4), 21–34.

Chatterjee, Rabikar and Jehoshua Eliashberg (1990), "Innovation diffusion process in a heterogeneous population: a micromodeling approach," *Management Science*, **36** (September), 1057–79.

Danaher, Peter J., Bruce G.S. Hardie and William P. Putsis Jr (2001), "Marketing-mix variables and the diffusion of successive generations of a technological innovation," *Journal of Marketing Research*, **38** (November), 501–14.

Dekimpe, Marnik, Philip Parker and Miklos Sarvary (1998), "Staged estimation of international diffusion models: an application to global cellular telephone adoption," *Technological Forecasting and Social Change*, **57**, 105–32.

Dekimpe, Marnik, Philip Parker and Miklos Sarvary (2000a), "Global diffusion of technological innovations: a coupled-hazard approach," *Journal of Marketing Research*, **37** (1), 47–59.

Dekimpe, Marnik, Philip Parker and Miklos Sarvary (2000b), "Multimarket and global diffusion," in Vijay Mahajan, Eitan Muller and Yoram Wind (eds), *New Product Diffusion Models*, Boston MA: Kluwer Academic, pp. 49–73.

Fischer, Marc, Venkatesh Shankar and Michel Clement (2005), "Can late mover brands use international market entry strategy to challenge the pioneer?," MSI Report, 05-004, 25–48.

Ganesh, Jaishankar, V. Kumar and V. Subramaniam (1997), "Learning effect in multinational diffusion of consumer durables: an exploratory investigation," *Journal of the Academy of Marketing Science*, **25** (3), 214–28.

Gatignon, Hubert and Thomas S. Robertson (1989), "Technology diffusion: an empirical test of competitive effects," *Journal of Marketing*, **53** (1), 35–49.

Gatignon, Hubert, Jehoshua Eliashberg and Thomas S. Robertson (1989), "Modeling multinational diffusion patterns: an efficient methodology," *Marketing Science*, **8** (3), 231–47.

Goldenberg, Jacob, Barak Libai and Eitan Muller (2002), "Riding the saddle: how cross-market communications can create a major slump in sales," *Journal of Marketing*, **66**, 1–16.

Goldenberg, Jacob, Barak Libai and Eitan Muller (2010), "The chilling effects of network externalities: perspectives and conclusions," *International Journal of Research in Marketing*, **27** (1), 22–4.

Golder, Peter N. and Gerard J. Tellis (1997), "Will it ever fly? Modeling the takeoff of really new consumer durables," *Marketing Science*, **16** (3), 256–70.

Golder, Peter N. and Gerard J. Tellis (1998), "Beyond diffusion: an affordability model of the growth of new consumer durables," *Journal of Forecasting*, **17** (3/4), 259–80.

Golder, Peter N. and Gerard J. Tellis (2004), "Going, going, gone: cascades, diffusion, and turning points of the product life cycle," *Marketing Science*, **23** (2), 207–18.

Hauser, John, Gerard J. Tellis and Abbie Griffin (2006), "Research on innovation: a review and agenda for marketing science," *Marketing Science*, **25** (6), 687–717.

Heeler, Roger M. and Thomas P. Hustad (1980), "Problems in predicting new product growth for consumer durables," *Management Science*, **26** (10), 1007–20.

Hofstede, Geert (2001), *Culture's Consequences: Comparing Values, Behaviours, Institutions and Organizations across Nations*, 2nd edn, Thousand Oaks, CA: Sage.

Horsky, Dan and Leonard Simon (1983), "Advertising and the diffusion of new products," *Marketing Science*, **2** (1), 1–17.

Jain, Dipak, Vijay Mahajan and Eitan Muller (1991), "Innovation diffusion in the presence of supply restrictions," *Marketing Science*, **10** (1), 83–90.

Kim, Namwoon, Dae Ryun Chang and Allan D. Shocker (2000), "Modeling intercategory and generational dynamics for a growing information technology industry," *Management Science*, **46** (4), 496–512.

Lenk, Peter J. and Amber G. Rao (1990), "New model from old: forecasting product adoption by hierarchical Bayes procedures," *Marketing Science*, **9** (1), 42–53.

Lilien, Gary L., Arvind Rangaswamy and Christophe Van den Bulte (2000), "Diffusion models: managerial applications and software," in Vijay Mahajan, Eitan Muller and Yoram Wind (eds), *New-Product Diffusion Models*, Boston MA: Kluwer Academic Press, pp. 295–336.

Mahajan, Vijay and Eitan Muller (1996), "Timing, diffusion, and substitution of successive generations of technological innovations: the IBM mainframe case," *Technological Forecasting and Social Change*, **51** (2), 109–32.

Mahajan, Vijay and Eitan Muller (1998), "When is it worthwhile targeting the majority instead of the innovators in a new product launch?," *Journal of Marketing Research*, **35** (4), 488–95.

Mahajan, Vijay, Eitan Muller and Frank M. Bass (1990), "New product diffusion models in marketing: a review and directions for research," *Journal of Marketing*, **54**, 1–26.

Mahajan, Vijay, Eitan Muller and Frank M. Bass (1995), "Diffusion of new products: empirical generalizations and managerial uses," *Marketing Science*, **14** (3), Part 2 of 2, G79–G88.

Mahajan, Vijay, Eitan Muller and Rajendra K. Srivastava (1990), "Determination of adopter categories using innovation diffusion models," *Journal of Marketing Research*, **27** (1), 37–50.

Mahajan, Vijay, Eitan Muller and Yoram Wind (eds) (2000), *New-Product Diffusion Models*, Boston, MA: Kluwer.

Moore, Geoffrey A. (1991), *Crossing the Chasm: Marketing and Selling Technology Products to Mainstream Customers*, New York: HarperCollins.

Muller, Eitan and Guy Yogev (2006), "When does the majority become the majority? Empirical analysis of the time at which main market adopters purchase the bulk of our sales," *Technological Forecasting and Social Change*, **73** (9), 1107–20.

Muller, Eitan, Vijay Mahajan and Renana Peres (2009), *Innovation Diffusion and New Product Growth*, MSI Relevant Knowledge Series Monography, Cambridge MA.

Neelamegham, Ramya and Pradeep Chintagunta (1999), "A Bayesian model to forecast new product performance in domestic and international markets," *Marketing Science*, **18** (2), 115–36.

Norton, John A. and Frank M. Bass (1987), "A diffusion theory model of adoption and substitution for successive generations of high-technology products," *Management Science*, **33** (9), 1069–86.

Norton, John A. and Frank M. Bass (1992), "Evolution of technological generations: the law of capture," *Sloan Management Review*, **33** (2), 66–77.

Parker, Philip M. (1994), "Aggregate diffusion forecasting models in marketing: a critical review," *International Journal of Forecasting*, **10**, 353–80.

Parker, Philip M. and Hubert Gatignon (1994), "Specifying competitive effects in diffusion models: an empirical analysis," *International Journal of Research in Marketing*, **11** (1), 17–39.

Peres, Renana, Eitan Muller and Vijay Mahajan (2010), "Innovation diffusion and new product growth models: a critical review and research directions," *International Journal of Research in Marketing*, **27** (2), 91–106.

Putsis, William P. Jr, Sridhar Balasubramanian, Edward Kaplan and Subrata Sen (1997), "Mixing behavior in cross-country diffusion," *Marketing Science*, **16** (4), 354–69.

Rogers, Everett (1995), *Diffusion of Innovations*, New York: Free Press.

Schmittlein, D. and Vijay Mahajan (1982), "Maximum likelihood estimation for an innovation diffusion model of new product acceptance," *Marketing Science*, **1** (1), 57–78.

Shankar, Venkatesh (2008), "The evolution of markets: innovation adoption, diffusion, market growth, new product entry and competitor responses," in Scott Shane (ed.), *Handbook of Technology and Innovation Management*, Cambridge, MA: Blackwell Publishers, pp. 57–112.

Shankar, Venkatesh, Gregory S. Carpenter and Lakshman Krishnamurthi (1998), "Late mover advantage: how innovative late entrants outsell pioneers," *Journal of Marketing Research*, **35** (1), 54–70.

Simon, Hermann and Karl-Heinz Sebastian (1987), "Diffusion and advertising: the German telephone campaign," *Management Science*, **33** (4), 451–66.

Sinha, Rajiv K. and Murali Chandrashekharan (1992), "A split hazard model for analyzing the diffusion of innovations," *Journal of Marketing Research*, **29** (1), 116–27.

Srinivasan, V. and Charlotte Mason (1986), "Nonlinear least squares estimation of new product diffusion models," *Marketing Science*, **5** (2), 169–78.

Stremersch, Stefan and Gerard J. Tellis (2004), "Understanding and managing international growth of new products," *International Journal of Research in Marketing*, **21** (4), 421–38.

Sultan, Fareena, John U. Farley and Donald R. Lehmann (1990), "A meta-analysis of diffusion models," *Journal of Marketing Research*, **27**, 70–77.

Takada, Hirozu and Dipak Jain (1991), "Cross-national analysis of diffusion of consumer durable goods in Pacific Rim countries," *Journal of Marketing*, **55**, 48–54.

Talukdar, Debabrata, K. Sudhir and Andrew Ainslie (2002), "Investigating new product diffusion across products and countries," *Marketing Science*, **21** (1), 97–114.

Tellis, Gerard J., Stefan Stremersch and Eden Yin (2003), "The international takeoff of new products: the role of economics, culture and country innovativeness," *Marketing Science*, **22** (2), 188–208.

Van Den Bulte, Christophe and Gary Lilien (1997), "Bias and systematic change in the parameter estimates of macro-level diffusion models," *Marketing Science*, **16** (4), 338–53.

Van Den Bulte, Christophe and Yogesh V. Joshi (2007), "New product diffusion with influentials and imitators," *Marketing Science*, **26** (3), 400–421.

Van Den Bulte, Christophe and Stefan Stremersch (2004), "Social contagion and income heterogeneity in new product diffusion: a meta-analytic test," *Marketing Science*, **23** (4), 530–44.

Venkatesan, Rajkumar, Trichy V. Krishnan and V. Kumar (2004), "Evolutionary estimation of macro-level diffusion models using genetic algorithms," *Marketing Science*, **23** (3), 451–64.

Xie, J., M. Song, M. Sirbu and Q. Wang (1997), "Kalman filter estimation of new product diffusion models," *Journal of Marketing Research*, **34** (3), 378–93.

23 International entry strategies

Katrijn Gielens, Kristiaan Helsen and Marnik G. Dekimpe

INTRODUCTION

As companies face maturing markets and stiffening domestic competition, they show a growing interest in cross-border initiatives. Many of today's leading companies are making foreign-market entry decisions on a fairly recurring basis whereas others are taking their first steps in this competitive arena (see also Gielens and Dekimpe 2009). For example, Best Buy, the world's largest electronics specialist, continues to internationalize, with market entries into emerging markets such as Mexico and Turkey, and mature markets such as the UK. The world's largest company, Wal-Mart, also actively pursues new foreign operations. As of March 2011, Wal-Mart operated 4587 units in 14 countries outside the USA (walmartstores.com/pressroom/news). The most recently entered country was India (May 2009), where Wal-Mart runs a wholesale operation under a joint venture with India-based Bharti Enterprises (www.time.com). Not to be undone by their Western rivals, rising companies from emerging markets like Tata Motors and Lenovo are also diligently cultivating a global mindset. India-based Tata Motors, for example, recently acquired Jaguar/Land Rover, China's Geely took over Volvo, and Lenovo bought IBM's personal computer division.

The success of these foreign entries obviously depends on the appropriateness of the firm's post-entry decisions, but may also depend on the strategic choices made at the time of entry, as they shape the platform from which competitive advantages can be gained (Gielens and Dekimpe 2001; Green et al. 1995). In this chapter, we reflect on both the antecedents and performance consequences of some of the most important decisions that have to be taken at the time of entry: (1) country selection; (2) timing; (3) mode; (4) scale of entry; and (5) the level of adaptation and standardization. Finally, we discuss how these decisions may be interrelated, and how their effect may change over time after entry. Figure 23.1 summarizes the various aspects that will be discussed in this chapter.

Market-entry decisions are some of a firm's most risky strategic choices, as international market entry requires a major commitment of financial and managerial resources (Mitra and Golder 2002). To most firms, it remains uncertain as to whether a large-scale presence will ever materialize in the hoped-for economies of scale. Similarly, they wonder when it is best to enter a given market, or how much a firm should adapt its concept (such as brands, products, store format) to local tastes, or even whether similar entry strategies will prove to be optimal in mature and emerging markets. This uncertainty helps explain the variability observed in entry strategies adopted by international players, even within the same industry. Given that entry decisions remain difficult, managers often turn to prevailing practices in the industry to learn which decisions are good, or even best (Gielens and Dekimpe 2007). Competitive entry decisions are monitored closely, providing a significant input in the decision process. However, the wide variation in the year of entry, in the scale and mode of entry and in the extent of standardization

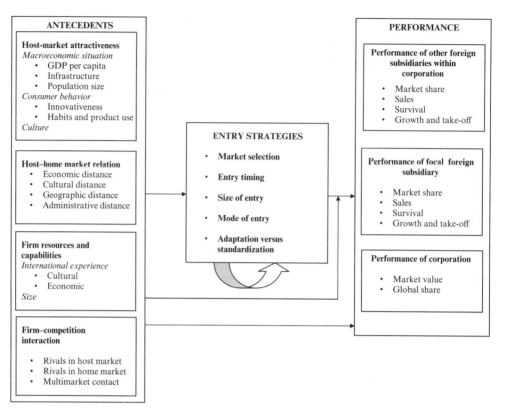

*Figure 23.1   The antecedents and performance consequences of international entry
strategies*

indicates that this does not imply a mere copying of the most popular (modal) pattern;
rather, industry rules suggest different entry decisions contingent on external (e.g. host-
market attractiveness) and internal (e.g. the firm's specific resources) conditions.

Besides looking into the antecedents of these decisions, we provide some insights
into the contribution of different strategic choices at entry on post-entry performance, especially in the longer run. In spite of this growing extent of internationalization, several firms are still struggling to develop the competencies needed to
compete in the global arena (Kumar 1997). Mixed success has been reported when
expanding into foreign markets. Clearly dominating the US retail market, Wal-
Mart's attempts to apply the company's proven US success formula in an unmodified
manner to the German market turned out nothing short of a fiasco. Moreover, many
international companies do not realize comparable margins and/or returns abroad
as in their home market, and few reach break-even volumes in their international
operations. For example, the French retail giant Carrefour loses money in many of
its European and cross-continental markets (bbc.co.uk). In 2010 Carrefour decided
to sell off its 61 supermarkets in Singapore, Malaysia and Thailand,and focus on
markets where it is either the market leader or a strong contender (*Financial Times*
2010a).

Managers expanding abroad are often confronted with trade-offs such as: is it better to quickly enter a market on a more limited scale, or to postpone entry until more resources have accumulated to enable a larger-scale commitment? Are foreign operations more successful when initiated through greenfield expansion, and/or does this depend on how quickly one enters the market? As such, there are clear interdependencies between the various strategic decisions in the middle box of Figure 23.1.

COUNTRY SELECTION

Substantial variation can be observed regarding the countries rivals enter, even within the same industry. In the retailing industry, for example, Germany's Metro Group recently opened a store in the Kazakh capital, Astana. The choice of this country typifies Metro Group's market-entry choices in recent years – frontier markets with growing consumption and very low levels of competition in terms of modern distribution networks. In a similar vein, Metro Group entered Vietnam as far back as 2002, followed by Pakistan in 2007 (www.metrogroup.de). In contrast, its German hard-discount competitor Aldi only enters a foreign market once this market has sufficiently developed. As a testament to this policy, Aldi entered the Polish market in 2008, almost 20 years after that market first opened up to foreign investors, and the first international retail competitors entered (Planet Retail 2010). In this section,we reflect on how country selection decisions are made, and whether this selection impacts the firms' (international) performance.

Several screening methods to evaluate market attractiveness have been suggested in the literature. Kotabe and Helsen (2010) summarize the steps involved as follows. To identify market opportunities for a given product (or service), the international marketer usually starts off with a large pool of candidate countries (say, all Central European countries). To narrow down this pool of countries, the company typically starts with a preliminary screening. The goal of this exercise is twofold: to minimize the mistakes of (1) ignoring countries that offer viable opportunities for your product, and (2) wasting time and/or money on countries that offer no or little potential. Countries that make the grade are scrutinized further to determine the final set of target countries. The second step is to determine the importance weights of each of the different country indicators identified in the previous step. One common method is the "constant-sum" allocation technique. Basically, similar techniques can be used as when weighting criteria in any project-selection process (see, e.g., Urban and Hauser 1993).

Other, far more sophisticated, methods exist to screen target markets. Kumar and colleagues (1994), for example, developed a screening methodology that incorporates multiple objectives a firm could have (instead of just one), resource constraints and its market-expansion strategy (see also Russow and Okoroafo 1996).

Still, relatively little research has explicitly looked into when and why certain selection criteria are more important than others, or whether the emphasis on certain criteria impacts the foreign venture's performance in the long and short term. More research is also needed on the optimal number of countries to select (withhold) at any given time. Is it better to select a single country, or to enter multiple (which raises the question, how many) countries simultaneously? Some general guidelines to prefer either a waterfall (one at a time) or sprinkler (multiple simultaneously) have been provided in Kalish et al. (1995). Still, more research in this domain is needed.

Not surprisingly, many studies suggest that firms should start their international marketing activities by choosing target countries nearest in distance (geographically, culturally, administratively and economically) that offer a large prospective customer base (e.g. Davidson 1980; Johansson and Vahlne 1977) and by tracking rivals' moves.

Overall, firms favor countries with a large prospective customer base as such markets offer better opportunities for good returns (Agarwal and Ramaswami 1992). As for scale, several potential indicators are used to assess and estimate the potential attractiveness of the market. The indicators a company selects are to a large degree driven by the strategic objectives spelt out in the company's global mission. Some indicators are derived from macroeconomic trends, others from consumer behavior and culture. Colgate-Palmolive, for example, views per capita purchasing power as a major driver behind market opportunities. Starbucks looks at economic indicators, the size of the population, and whether the company can locate good joint venture partners (*Asia Inc* 2005). When choosing markets for a particular product, the metrics to consider should depend on the nature of the product and the way local consumers use and perceive this product. Procter & Gamble chose Malaysia and Singapore as the first markets in Asia (ex-Japan) for the rollout of Febreze, a fabric odor remover (*Ad Age Global* 2002). Not only were both markets known for "home-proud" consumers, people there tend to furnish their homes heavily with fabrics. A company might also decide to enter a particular country that is considered as a trendsetter in the industry. Kodak, for example, re-entered the digital camera market in Japan precisely for that reason. As the president of Kodak Japan put it, "what happens in Japan eventually happens in the rest of the world" (*Financial Times* 2004).

As for the relative importance of these indicators, Terpstra and Yu (1988) found that the size of the market in terms of GDP was the most important driver behind US advertising agencies' investment decisions. The critical role of market size in country selection is also supported by several other empirical studies (e.g. Rothaermel et al. 2006; Brewer 2001; Robertson and Wood 2001). Given that there are several measures to proxy market size, the selection of the proper variable is important. A study of small and medium-sized Finnish software enterprises found that the size of the software market in the target country was the most important country selection factor, not GDP or per capita GDP (Ojala and Tyrväinen 2007). Dekimpe et al. (1998) also emphasize the need to adequately match countries on the relevant decision variable, a practice they call sample matching. Apart from the current size, also the future (expected) growth prospects are a key consideration. For example, the growth of the middle class is an important driver for many grocery retailers to enter emerging economies.

Distance is another selection criterion. Like scale, distance is a multi-attribute dimension. It encompasses geographical, cultural, economic and administrative distance (Ghemawat 2001). All of these criteria will determine how similar a prospective host and home market are. In general, the more similar both markets are, the more likely a firm will enter that prospective host market. One way to capture/quantify the firm's knowledge of the economic and cultural environment is through the notion of "near-market" knowledge ("economic" and "cultural") as defined by Mitra and Golder (2002): a firm's understanding of potential new markets based on knowledge generated from operating in similar markets (see also Gielens and Dekimpe 2007).

Several studies have shown a significant impact of geographic distance on target-market selection (Clark and Pugh 2001). However, the evidence is somewhat mixed: one study of the entry decisions of US advertising agencies (Terpstra and Yu 1988) found that firms favor countries with a large market size rather than closer geographic proximity. One might also suspect that the Internet deflates the role of geographic distance in internationalization. The diminishing role of geographic distance on the demand side (i.e. customer preferences and sentiments) was also demonstrated in Lemmens et al. (2007).

Cultural distance is a second component in explaining similarities between a prospect country and the firm's home country. The importance of cultural distance between the home country and the host market is well established. Bell (1995) found that 50–70 percent of the software firms in his cross-country survey chose target countries with a low psychic distance. Likewise, Rothaermel et al. (2006) detected that cultural similarities increase the probability of market entry of US-based Internet firms.

Moreover, economic similarities between home and prospective host markets also play a role. Firms have the greatest ability to leverage their existing knowledge in similar economic markets. Mitra and Golder (2002) demonstrate that when companies have positive experiences in foreign markets, the economic knowledge generated in those markets will lead to earlier entry in similar markets. Especially when firms rely on replicating their existing business model in new markets, this will be easier in countries with similar income distributions, cost structures and quality of resources (Ghemawat 2001).

Finally, administrative distance and hurdles also play a role in a firm's country selection process. Tariffs, trade quota, restrictions on foreign direct investment and preferences to protect domestic competition by prospective host countries' governments will directly impede a firm from selecting a country as potential new market (for an extensive overview of protectionist measures, see Ghemawat 2001). On the other hand, when administrative borders erode, cross-border diffusion will accelerate, as demonstrated by Mahajan and Muller's (1994) study of the impact of the European unification.

The importance of (the various components of) distance tends to evolve as the firm gains more international experience. As the firm gathers more international expertise, it can expand into countries that are geographically or culturally more distant. For instance, Starbucks opened its first store in Canada in 1987, Wal-Mart chose Mexico as its first country for international expansion in 1991, and Microsoft picked Canada as its first market outside the USA for the launch of the Xbox 360 game console (Kotabe and Helsen 2010). When operating in "similar" countries, it is assumed (hoped) that relevant knowledge can be transferred from one country to another. We will further reflect on the dynamic nature of this process later in this chapter.

Tracking competitors' moves also plays an important role in country selection. As firms meet their competitors more and more in several different international markets, the mere presence of those rivals can become an important selection criterion (Gimeno 1999, Kirmani and Wernerfelt 1985). Previous studies showed that such multimarket contact (MMC) often leads to a situation of "mutual forbearance": firms understand that their overlapping rivalries enhance the risk of costly retaliation not only in the challenged market, but also in other markets where they compete with each other (Jayachandran et al. 1999). MMC insights have been applied in marketing by several earlier studies (e.g. Gielens et al. 2008, Shankar 1999, Kang et al. 2010). In the area of country selection, such insights could be relevant in terms of both direct effects (i.e. how MMC affects the internationalizing firm's decision to enter and/or exit target countries) and more indirect strategic effects (i.e. how it affects the firm's reactions to its competitors' decisions).

With respect to the relative importance of these different antecedents in determining country selection, empirical findings are ambiguous: some studies suggest that cultural distance is the most important driver (e.g. Jones and Teegen 2001; Rothaermel et al. 2006); others find that the market size of the target markets is the key driver (e.g. Ojala and Tyrväinen 2007). Clearly, the question what variables should matter most in (first-) country selection will be context-dependent. Several important variables in this area have received scant or no consideration thus far. Potential moderators could include the nature of the industry, the size of the company (large versus SMEs), the internationalizing firm's home country/region (e.g. developed countries versus emerging markets). Also, the strategic aspects of country selection – in particular, the role of competition (global, pan-regional and/or local) – have thus far been largely ignored. Finally, research on country selection has so far been primarily descriptive, without much exploration of the subsequent performance implications.

TIMING OF ENTRY

In April 2010, Best Buy opened its first superstore in the UK. The entry of the world's largest electronics specialist into the highly competitive UK marketplace sent shockwaves among existing players across Europe. However, business analysts believe that Best Buy's influence and ambitions for Europe have been widely overstated. Crucially, the delays in the retailer's opening plans have given established players time to react, which they have exploited with moves to counter the threat. Timing is indeed crucial in international operations. We first reflect on how competitive moves and international experience act as important antecedents in shaping the timing decision before elaborating on the performance consequences of one's international entry timing.

Antecedents

Because of the perceived opportunity costs, or because they do not want to commit themselves (yet) in the midst of high uncertainty, firms may be reluctant to enter a specific market. Indeed, early and extensive commitments tend to reduce flexibility and increase risk exposure. Lack of accurate information on the opportunities in a new market increases uncertainty, and may delay entry. Prior decisions by rivals, however, may provide crucial information on the success potential of a foreign venture (see, e.g. Henisz and Delios 2001). Following what seems like the industry norm reduces uncertainty and enhances legitimacy, as a given practice is seen as appropriate (e.g. Anderson 1988; Geletkanycz and Hambrick 1997). A firm's initial urge to remain cautious is thus expected to decrease when rival players enter the host market. On the other hand, rival players tend to reduce host-market opportunities (Martin et al. 1998). With every rival entering, market competition becomes tougher, raising a barrier to further entry. Combined, these insights suggest that initially the presence of rivals facilitates a process of social recognition or legitimization, and therefore attracts new entrants into the host market (see Hannan and Freeman 1977). Still, as competitive investments in the host country increase, the best geographical locations get preempted and some interesting market opportunities become depleted, creating a deterrence effect that eventually dominates the legitimization effect. Moreover, companies may not see their competitive landscape as homogeneous, and not attach equal weight to all potential competitors (e.g. Debruyne and Reibstein 2005). As such, the relevant consideration set may not consist of all players in the industry, but only those with which they share some key attributes.

Gielens and Dekimpe (2007) find empirical evidence for the existence of such interorganizational learning with respect to entry timing of retailers into Central and Eastern Europe. Faced with the considerable uncertainty surrounding entry decisions in markets that only recently opened their borders, managers looked at prevailing practices in the industry to guide their own decisions. Especially the moves made by their home rivals were carefully followed. Their presence reduced the perceived uncertainty, as firms with similar backgrounds had already made the move. France's Auchan, for example, cites the presence of its French rivals Leclerc and Casino as a key driver to also enter Poland. Foreign rivals were not ignored, however. Interestingly, the deterrence effect of the latter's presence was found to be much more prominent. Anecdotal support for this is found in Carrefour's announcement that it postponed its Hungarian expansion in favor of Romania and China to avoid competition of chains such as the UK's Tesco or Germany's Metro (*Grocer* 2000).

Learning and deterrence are also derived from product- or concept-based reference groups. A player offering a similar value proposition or product clearly sends a positive signal. However, such entries compete directly for the same consumers, and therefore tend to quickly exert a deterrent effect on the timing decision. Rivals with a sufficiently different product or service offer, in contrast, accelerate their own entry decision. While informative about the market potential, they are perceived as less threatening.

Competitive actions are, of course, not the only relevant source of information for the entry-timing decision. Prior internal experience, especially in culturally and economically similar markets, may also be an important source of knowledge (Mitra and Golder 2002). As firms gain experience in assessing prevailing business practices and consumer preferences in a variety of host markets, the perceived risk of further international expansion is reduced. The more similar a potential host market is to other markets the firm already has experience with, the easier the transfer of knowledge will be. Mitra and Golder (2002) consider in this respect the impact of prior experience in both culturally and economically similar markets. The former, referred to as near-market cultural knowledge, reduces potential acculturation problems, while its economic counterpart helps to replicate the firm's business model in countries where customer income, as well as the cost and quality of resources, is similar. Both forms of market knowledge are believed to positively impact the speed of entry.

Performance Consequences

Turning to the performance implications, a substantial body of literature has documented the impact of (early) entry timing on post-entry performance. The advantages and disadvantages of early entry in a domestic (product entry) setting have been discussed at great length in the marketing literature (see e.g. Golder and Tellis 1993; Lieberman and

Montgomery 1998; Shankar et al. 1998), stating resource preemption, consumer preferences, learning curve effects and imitation costs as the main drivers underlying the potential advantages and disadvantges.[1] Although the role of market entry timing is believed to be critical, the direction of the effect is not clear, with some researchers suggesting a non-monotone influence (see, e.g., Geyskens et al. 2002).

Translating these first-mover (dis)advantages from a product entry into an international context, Johnson and Tellis (2008) suggest several reasons why early entry into international markets could favor or hurt success. They outline that early entry can lock up access to distribution channels and suppliers, while also shaping the pattern of consumer preferences. Moreover, early entrants can benefit from being the first to secure governmental concessions and incentives. Early entrants can also observe and learn market attributes for a longer period without the presence of rivals. On the other hand, in an international context, pioneers may fail because of a lack of knowledge as they may not be aware of the pitfalls of the new market, or they may have to deal with an infrastructure which is not yet fully developed.

Using a sample of almost 200 entries in China and over 60 in India, Johnson and Tellis (2008) find that earlier entrants in an important market such as India enjoy greater success than later entrants. For the Chinese market, no significant effect was found. More positive evidence is provided by Mascarenhas (1992, 1997), who demonstrates that new products indeed perform better in an international market if they are introduced early. Likewise, Gielens and Dekimpe (2001) find that in the retailing industry time of entry appears to be a prime source of persistent competitive advantage, particularly when entering through greenfield expansion. Fischer et al. (2005), on the other hand, demonstrate in the context of pharmaceutical brand rollouts in eight European markets that later movers can challenge the market pioneer through an international market entry strategy that involves a sequential entry into many large international markets.

MODE OF ENTRY

In 1996, France's food group Danone signed an agreement with the Wahaha Group, a Chinese beverage company, to set up a series of joint ventures in China in which Danone held a 51 percent stake. The agreement led to 39 joint ventures to produce and market various Wahaha-branded beverages and snacks. *Forbes* magazine hailed the partnership as a "showcase" joint venture. Danone left most of the day-to-day management in the hands of Zong Qinghou, Wahaha's chairman, and one of China's wealthiest businessmen. The joint venture turned into a $2 billion behemoth with Wahaha becoming one of China's leading beverage brands. Despite its phenomenal success, the Sino-French relationship turned sour in 2007 when Danone openly accused its Chinese partner of violating the joint venture agreement by setting up competing joint ventures that sold Wahaha-branded products through distributors outside the ones selected by Danone's joint ventures. Danone filed a lawsuit against companies linked to Mr Zong's. The latter struck back by orchestrating a campaign against Danone with rallies and news conferences, and comparing Danone's tactics to the Western powers that bullied China a century ago (*The New York Times* 2009). The nationalist backlash in the Chinese press crippled Danone's reputation in China. The yearlong dispute was finally resolved at the end of 2009 when the two companies agreed to drop all legal proceedings and Danone agreed to exit the joint venture by selling its entire 51 percent stake in partnership to the Wahaha Group for an estimated $500 million (*Forbes* 2009). The Danone/Wahaha joint venture saga illustrates to some extreme the challenges multinational marketers can face in choosing international entry-mode strategies.

A firm entering a foreign market faces an array of entry-mode choices to penetrate the target market. The alternative entry modes provide a managerial trade-off between risk and control. At one end of the spectrum is the export of goods, which has the lowest degree of control, but also the lowest amount of risk. Licensing, franchising and various forms of joint venture offer a progressively increasing degree of control for the firm coupled with higher levels of risk. At the other end of the spectrum are high-intensity ownership-based entries, such as majority-stake joint ventures, wholly owned subsidiaries and foreign acquisitions that entail the highest control but also the greatest risk. We first reflect on the antecedents of these decisions, before elaborating on their performance outcomes.

Antecedents

Research on the determinants of foreign-entry mode-choice patterns is abundant.[2] The literature identifies several decision criteria that could influence the choice of entry mode. These decision criteria are related to the transaction cost involved when entering a new market, the resources and capabilities the firm possesses, and the institutional environment in which the entry occurs.

Transaction cost economics (TCE) argues that the desirable governance structure (high- versus low-control mode) depends on the comparative transaction costs, that is, the cost of running the operation, which are determined by the degree of specificity of the assets involved in the transaction, the uncertainty surrounding the transaction and the frequency of the transaction. These three factors influence the choice between market and hierarchy (Williamson 1975; see Kim and Hwang 1992 for an excellent review of this literature in the context of international entry decisions). The starting premise is that markets are efficient and competitive. Therefore market pressure minimizes the need for control. Under such circumstances, low-control modes are preferable because market pressures will force the outside partner to comply with his/her contractual duties. When the market mechanism breaks down, however, high-control entry modes become more desirable. This is most likely to happen for transactions that involve highly specific assets in which there is room for potential opportunistic behavior by the foreign partner, as was illustrated in the Danone/Wahaha example discussed earlier. Examples of such assets could include brand equity and proprietary technology or know-how. When these assets are valuable, the firm might be better off adopting a high-control entry mode in order to safeguard these assets against opportunistic behavior (see also Zhao et al. 2004). The TCE paradigm thus tends to focus on the extent of uncertainty in the new environment and the need for control.

The resource-based view (RBV), on the other hand, focuses on the overall strategic posture of the firm. According to this perspective, firms with imperfectly imitable resource-based competitive advantages prefer to expand through wholly owned subsidiaries for two main reasons. First, through such an entry move, the firm is in a better position to protect its resource-based advantages against value erosion. Second, by having a wholly owned subsidiary, the firm can capture and transfer information between the parent and its foreign unit more efficiently (Brouthers et al. 2008).

The institutional theory (IT) paradigm, in turn, centers around the pressures of the host country's institutional environment in which the firm operates. Each country, with its own institutional environment, prescribes the economic "rules of the game," and shapes the nature of competition (Scott 2005). IT scholars view alliances as a response to the pressures stemming from the institutional environment. A firm entering a foreign market in an industry deemed sensitive or strategic by the host government is often forced to enter into an alliance with a local partner. In countries with weak institutions, a firm may enter an alliance with a local partner to reduce the risks of doing business there. Several studies underscore the importance of institutions in determining the success of entry-mode strategies. Makino and Beamish (1998) observe that in some Asian countries that exhibit high institutional uncertainty (e.g. the Philippines), joint ventures had a higher survival rate than wholly owned subsidiaries. Likewise, Delios and Beamish (2004) and Li (1995) find that wholly owned subsidiaries are more likely to survive than joint ventures in countries with a relatively stable institutional environment. A recent empirical study on entry-mode choices in transition economies (Dikova and van Witteloostuijn 2007) shows that greater institutional advancement is positively correlated with the likelihood of acquisition establishments.

Combined, these different paradigms lead, roughly speaking, to two classes of decision criteria: internal (firm-specific) criteria and external (environment-specific) criteria. Key external factors that could influence entry-mode selection include market size and growth, risk, market openness, the nature/extent of competition and the target country's culture. Internal considerations that could be relevant include company goals, international experience, and internal resources and capabilities.

A key external determinant of entry-choice decisions is the market size of the host country. Large markets justify major resource commitments in the form of equity joint ventures or wholly owned subsidiaries. Market size can relate to the current size of the market. However, for rapidly growing markets, the future market potential implied by the growth rate is often more critical, especially when the host country is an emerging market.

Another major concern when choosing one's entry mode is the level of risk the company is willing to accept. Note that a distinction should be made between political/financial and marketing risk (Arnold 2004). The standard concept of risk refers to the instability in the market environment (e.g. uncertainty about market demand) that may impact the company's profitability in the host country. Generally speaking, the greater the market risk, the less eager companies are willing to make substantial resource commitments (note that this will depend on the company's amount of risk tolerance). However, low-intensity modes (e.g. exporting, licensing) in which the local partner takes all the key marketing decisions may limit or cut off the market information that could benefit the firm. The reason is that foreign partners often have a major incentive to jealously guard information about their market (e.g. buying patterns, consumer preferences) out of fear of disintermediation (Arnold 2004). This type of risk is sometimes referred to as marketing risk.

Market openness (institutional barriers) is another important concern. Government regulations and red tape can heavily constrain the set of available entry-mode alternatives. Major acquisitions often need to be cleared by the host government, especially when the planned takeover occurs in a strategic industry. For instance, in 2009 the Chinese government blocked Coca-Cola's attempted takeover of Huiyuan Juice, a leading local juice brand (Bloomberg 2009).

Competitive pressure is another crucial driver that may influence the preferred entry mode. The dominance of Kellogg's as a global player in the breakfast-cereal market was a key motivation behind the creation in the early 1990s of Cereal Partners Worldwide, a joint venture between Nestlé and General Mills (Kotabe and Helsen 2010).

Research suggests that culture also could have a major impact on entry-mode choice decisions. Several researchers have examined the effect of national culture or cultural distance on entry-mode choices (e.g. Kogut and Singh 1988). Tihanyi and colleagues (2005) provide an excellent overview of recent contributions in this area. Opinions about the nature of the relationship differ. Some studies suggest that through higher levels of equity ownership, firms are able to bridge cultural gaps. Others note that by entering through a joint venture instead of a wholly owned subsidiary, firms are able to lower their risk exposure in culturally distant markets. A meta-analysis of a wide range of studies in the literature found no clear-cut evidence in favor of either argument (Tihanyi et al. 2005).

Looking at the internal criteria, company objectives are obviously a key influence in choosing an entry mode. Firms that have limited aspirations typically favor low-intensity modes (e.g. licensing). Companies with more ambitious strategic goals would pick entry modes that provide the flexibility and control needed to achieve their goals. In the fiercely competitive beer industry, InBev[3] made an aggressive offer in 2008 to buy Anheuser-Busch, America's leading beer brewer. In the words of InBev's CEO, Carlos Brito, the merger would lead to a "stronger, more competitive, global company with an unrivaled worldwide brand portfolio and distribution network" (*Forbes* 2008). In the service industry, firms are more likely to use full-control modes when they pursue global strategies and when they are driven by asset exploitation motives. However, service firms prefer shared-control modes when they enter markets in search of complementary assets and new clients (Sanchez-Peinado et al. 2007).

Cumulative international experience is generally recognized as a key factor in entry-mode choice. With rising experience, firms gather knowledge of foreign markets, perceive less uncertainty and, as a result, become more aggressive in committing resources and taking control. Indeed, Gatignon and Anderson (1988) found that a firm's propensity to use wholly owned subsidiaries increased with the amount of international experience (measured as the number of foreign market entries to date). Some studies, however, found no effect of international experience on degree of control (e.g. Kogut and Singh 1988; Sharma and Johanson 1987). Interestingly, Erramilli (1991) found a U-shaped relationship between experience and desire for control in his study of the entry behavior of US service firms: they preferred high-control modes in the early and late stages of their international expansion.

Another important determinant deals with internal resources, assets and capabilities. Companies with tight resources (e.g. human, access to capital) or limited assets (tangible or intangible) are typically constrained to low-intensity entry modes such as exporting and licensing. Internal competencies can also influence the entry-mode choice. When the firm lacks certain skills or assets that are critical for the success of its entry strategy, it can try to bridge the gap by forming a strategic alliance with a local partner.

Performance Consequences

Johnson and Tellis (2008) find that in emerging markets such as India and China entry strategies that involve high levels of control (e.g. wholly owned subsidiaries) are more successful than those that involve low levels of control (e.g. licensing). Likewise Gielens and Dekimpe (2001) observe that greenfield operations perform better than acquisitions and joint ventures. Moreover, the effect of the mode of entry depends on entry timing. On the one hand, being early offers an opportunity to select the best partners available in the target market, thereby mitigating the potential disadvantages of acquisitions and joint ventures. Moreover, greenfield expansion requires a larger and longer-term commitment, which may cause a reduction in flexibility. For example, joint venture contracts can typically be renewed or renegotiated on shorter notice than the time needed to establish new entities in the foreign market. This flexibility is argued to be most critical in the early stages of market development. On the other hand, being early also offers the best opportunities to select the most suitable channels, stores and shelf position, which is a decision critical to the success of greenfield operations. Especially in service-related industries where physical contact with consumers is required, store locations determine both the number and type of consumers a store will attract. Being able to preempt the most attractive store sites may substantially increase the sales potential of *de novo* stores. This issue may be less important when dealing with acquisitions or joint ventures, as one may still acquire or join forces with the earlier entrants that occupy the better locations.

SCALE OF ENTRY

Lack of scale was one of the fundamental problems that Wal-Mart encountered in the countries were it failed, South Korea and Germany. In South Korea, Wal-Mart had only 16 stores – a small presence that contributed to its decision in May 2006 to sell out to a Korean discount chain. Many Koreans had never heard of Wal-Mart. In Seoul, a sprawling area of 10 million, there was only a single store. In Germany, Wal-Mart acquired a relatively small chain (representing less than 1 percent of the market) that did not allow them to replicate their power base in the German market and to deliver their EDLP (everyday low pricing) promise (Lander 2006). In both countries, lack of scale ultimately led to the retailer's inability to compete with established discounters, like the Aldi chain in Germany and E-Mart in Korea. In contrast, Wal-Mart's most successful markets, like Mexico, are those in which it started big. There, the company bought the country's largest and best-run retail chain, Cifra. Also in the UK, Wal-Mart bought one of the leading players, Asda (Gielens et al. 2008).

Antecedents

Entry scale is indeed a fundamental element of strategic diversification. On the one hand, many firms are reluctant to quickly commit substantial resources to a new host market, especially in light of the considerable uncertainty that often accompanies foreign-market entries, and the realization that investments are largely sunk when initial expectations fail to materialize. On the other hand, firms in many industries tend to be confronted with a saturated market demand in their home country, and fear being left out of interesting growth opportunities abroad when investing too little, too late.

Performance Consequences

A variety of reasons may cause a positive relationship between entry scale and post-entry performance. First, large-scale entry may induce volume-driven cost advantages. The greater the scale of the initial set-up, the less growth is needed before the minimum-efficient scale of the industry is obtained (Biggadike 1979). Second, large-scale entry (e.g. with many outlets) may ensure preemption of the more attractive locations in both geographic (location of the outlets) and perceptual (product-characteristics) space (Lieberman and Montgomery 1988). Third, incumbents are less likely to react aggressively when the entrant has made substantial hard-to-reverse investments, and other potential entrants may be less inclined to actually enter the market afterwards. The scale of the entry is therefore used as a signal of managerial commitment. Fourth, entrants holding more positive expectations are likely to make larger initial commitments (Caves 1998). As such, entry scale may reflect the entrant's performance expectations, and may already capture an option for further expansion. Finally, start-up scale can reflect the ability of the entrant to attract financial resources, a proxy for its future growth potential.

Moreover, the scale of entry may not only have direct performance implications, it may also interact with the timing of entry. A substantial entry scale by early firms is thought to be effective in preempting the best locations, to signal commitment for their move, and to create barriers for later entrants. The larger the capacity utilized by early movers, the greater the performance benefits of being early. Late entrants find it harder to digest large initial investments than innovators. Indeed, the former's investments are likely to become less effective given the more competitive environment they encounter.

MARKET ADAPTATION VERSUS STANDARDIZATION

Best Buy has made adaptability the cornerstone of its globalization strategy. For example, Best Buy's growth in China is due to the fact that it designed its local stores to be less transactional (as in the USA) and more experiential, giving Chinese customers plenty of space to browse and try out products before actually buying them. Other quintessential American brands have localized themselves around the world. To develop its business in India, a country where 80 percent of people do not eat beef, McDonald's introduced vegetarian burgers and other Indian dishes whilst meat burgers (the Maharaja Mac with lamb or chicken) for non-beef eaters were introduced in New Delhi. Wal-Mart's failure in Korea was partially attributed to the lack of strategic fit between Wal-Mart's EDLP strategy and the nature of Korean consumers. Korean consumers were unwilling to compromise customer service and quality for a lower price, and expected to see sales people in each aisle of the retail store. As a consequence, Wal-Mart's EDLP was perceived to be of insufficient "value" in the minds of Korean consumers. Still, not all global companies need to adapt to different cultures. Companies such as Apple compete on their pace of innovation rather than localization, and sell the same iPad worldwide. Also Ryanair does not worry about adapting its product to local markets. Its competitiveness lies in price: "Whether you decide to differentiate your market is entirely dependent on your product" (Jacobs 2010).We briefly touch upon the antecedents of the adaptation decision before elaborating on its performance decisions.

Antecedents

One of the most important drivers underlying the adaptation versus standardization debate is the level of market homogenization. In general, it has been argued that markets have become so homogenized that firms can market identical products and services around the globe through standardized marketing programs, and thereby capitalize on the company's existing capabilities and knowledge. Critics, however, argue that because of long-existing cultural, political and/or economic differences among nations, one should adapt marketing programs (e.g. products, advertising campaigns, pricing and store formats) to the local market and environmental conditions (see, e.g. Parker and Tavassoli 2000). At a more meta-level, the question is raised whether relatively homogeneous segments can be found across national borders (Bolton and Myers 2003), and what variables should be used as a basis for international marketing segmentation (Steenkamp and Ter Hofstede 2002; Lemmens et al. 2007).

Irrespective of the level of homogenization of markets, the more remote the foreign operations are from the firm's core product or business, the greater the uncertainty involved. In addition, the previously acquired expertise may then not be directly transferable to the new setting. To reduce the uncertainty involved, and to benefit as much as possible from the parent firm's commercial and logistic experience, the parent firm may want to enter foreign markets with the concept it is most familiar with (Li 1995).

Performance Consequences

Thus far, little agreement exists as to whether and when standardization or adaptation is most appropriate in foreign markets.[4] Szymanski et al. (1993), for example, find that businesses may be better off standardizing their strategic resources to capture the benefits when serving multiple Western markets. Still, one of the main obstacles in researching this question is the lack of adequate samples that allow comparing adaptation and standardization decisions without incurring serious selection biases. Moreover, the positive effects of a related entry are thought to be intertwined with the mode of entry used. The more related the two formats, the more the firm is able to build on existing routines, and the less likely it is that the firm will have to acquire externally the needed capabilities. Entry through acquisitions or joint ventures, while using a familiar business format, in contrast, is likely to result in the purchase of unwanted or duplicate assets, and therefore result in less profitable outcome situations.

In sum, companies often find themselves in a bind on the appropriate format to choose when entering a foreign market. This choice can be dictated by demand (adaptation to host-market conditions) or supply (expertise in the home market) considerations. Gielens and Dekimpe (2001) demonstrate that especially when entering through acquisitions or joint ventures, one should try to fully exploit the expertise of the local partners, and adapt the format to local market conditions, rather than trying to impose one's own preferred format.

DYNAMICS OF ENTRY STRATEGIES

The impact of an entry decision can change over time. Some decisions will have a long-term impact, while in other cases their effect will be relatively short lived. Moreover, the importance of certain factors can change as firms grow more familiar with foreign operations. For example, as the firm builds more international experience, the cultural/economic distance to the home country may become less of an impediment. A study of the international expansion paths of US service firms found that as their international experience increases, these firms indeed seek out markets that are geographically and culturally more distant (Erramilli 1991).

An important factor in this evolution is the firm's ability to transfer knowledge across countries. Conventional wisdom appears to be that firms should gradually enter into more "remote" (culture- and economy-wise) countries, where each time one's knowledge base is updated (upgraded) in a rather incremental fashion (i.e. without major shocks). However, at some point, the firm may adopt an alternative strategy to immediately go to a variety of vastly different target markets, in order to quickly enrich its knowledge base through a wide variety of experiences. The former corresponds to a waterfall strategy, while the latter is associated with a sprinkler strategy of international expansion (Kalish et al. 1995). More research is needed on determining which strategy is more called for at various stages in the internationalization process.

Firms may also adapt their entry mode over time. The drivers that resulted in the initial entry-mode selection tend to evolve over time. As a result, the firm may feel the urge to switch its presence mode. Conventional wisdom suggests that firms progressively move to greater control modes. For instance, Starbucks initially entered China through three joint ventures covering different regions. Over time, the firm raised its control in the three ventures. In 2006, the coffee chain increased its ownership in the North China partnership to 90 percent so that it could achieve greater operational efficiencies and accelerate its market expansion (www.starbucks.com). So far, scant attention has been paid to the dynamics of entry-mode choices. The limited research that does exist has primarily focused on the antecedents of an internationalization mode change, not so much on the performance consequences. Chetty and Agndal (2007) explore how social capital influences a change in internationalization mode using an in-depth qualitative study of a sample of New Zealand and Swedish small and medium-sized enterprises. Social capital refers to the ability of a firm to acquire resources through its business networks. The authors find that the most frequent form of change was toward a higher-control mode, mainly because firms wanted to be closer to their customers. As firms develop their knowledge base and gain a better understanding of their customers, they increase their social capital. High-control entry modes that facilitate further development of social capital then become preferable to the internationalizing firm. Puck et al. (2009) focused on the conversion of joint ventures into wholly owned subsidiaries by foreign firms in China. Their results reveal that the generation of local market knowledge and a reduction of uncertainty have a positive impact on the conversion likelihood, whereas the effect of government regulations and cultural distance was negative.

Finally, while previous research has often focused on the scale of the initial entry, interesting research opportunities are present when studying the subsequent evolution in the investments (e.g. number of stores operated) in different countries, especially for companies with an extended country portfolio. Indeed, trade-offs have to be made then on where to grow first. This may require divestments in other countries, even when the operations in the latter are profitable as well.

CONCLUSION

More and more firms are no longer confined to their local (domestic) market, but extend their operations across multiple countries. This involves considerable risks, as major decisions with long-lasting performance implications need to be made under considerable uncertainty. Indeed, various decisions have to be made when entering foreign markets, including the selection of the target countries, the timing, scale and mode of entry, and the extent of standardization versus local adaptation. In this chapter, we have reviewed relevant literature on each of these decisions. Still, various avenues for future research remain open.

More attention should be given to capture simultaneously the impact of certain variables on both the selection decision and the subsequent post-entry performance of the foreign venture. One challenge in addressing this concern is that researchers usually restrict their samples to countries that the firm decided to enter. Typically, information on the firm's consideration set of countries at the time of the entry decision is ignored, thereby creating potential sample-selection biases. Still, one could envision explicitly modeling the "selection" issue and incorporating it in the performance evaluation. By looking simultaneously at an outcome and selection equation, less biased results may be obtained with respect to the relative importance of various selection criteria.

Even less knowledge is available as to the different impact of selection criteria between emerging (EM) and developed markets. We speculate that near-market knowledge would likely be weighted more by companies from developed countries than by EM firms. The latter will often select target countries that are very dissimilar from their home market, but which are lead markets in the firm's industry. The learning built up in such lead markets is likely to be bigger for such firms than from markets similar to their home market. A case in point is Sany, one of China's flagship machinery companies. Sany recently decided to set up a manufacturing presence in Germany, the world's lead market for engineering. Sany Germany's managing director commented that "Germany has the highest level of regulatory requirements. If you are successful here, you can easily expand into other markets" (*Financial Times* 2010b).

Another lacuna is that most entry decisions have been studied at the company level (i.e. the firm's decision to establish a presence in a target country). Very little research has been done at the brand (launch of a new brand) or product-line level. Companies often use a particular country or group of countries as a test market for a new product or brand introduction. Our understanding of the geographic rollout strategies for global brands, and their performance consequences, is still extremely limited. Townsend and colleagues (2009) tested several hypotheses on global brand expansion in the context of the automotive industry using event history analysis. Their study indicates that brands are less likely to enter countries with population sizes and economic conditions much different from their home market. They also find strong evidence of mimetic behavior: brands tend to mimic the market entries of their competition. In the consumer packaged goods sector, the question becomes even more intricate, as brand managers have to select both the country sequence to launch their products, as well as the retail banners within a given country through which they will try to reach their customers (Gielens and Steenkamp 2007). As retailers themselves become more international (Gielens and Dekimpe 2001, 2007), this raises additional questions as to who is in control as to where the product will be sold when.

Moreover, a wider set of performance criteria could be considered to evaluate entry strategies. So far, the extant literature has concentrated on the performance of the foreign ventures in each new market individually, mostly focusing on sales and market shares. Still, a new venture may well have (performance) implications on other foreign ventures within a firm's portfolio of markets in which it operates. Even though the literature has looked into how international presence in one market can influence the strategic decisions related to venturing into a new host market, the performance consequences and trade-offs have been largely neglected. Moreover, the impact on the firm as corporate entity has been neglected as well. Can a decision that benefits the performance of the firm's branch in a new market negatively impact the performance in other markets, or are there synergy effects? Moreover, no distinction between the short- and long-term sales and market-share implications is typically made, whereas the impact of entry strategies on the growth and take-off in new markets has been neglected. Whereas the large body of literature on international diffusion (see, e.g., Stremersch and Tellis 2004, Takada and Jain 1991; Talukdar et al. 2002; Tellis et al. 2003)[5] has looked into the antecedents of growth and international take-off, it (rarely) has looked into the impact of entry strategies on these performance dimensions.

Finally, while we have concentrated on international entry strategies, exits in global marketing are not uncommon. In 2001, Colgate-Palmolive sold its laundry detergent brands in Mexico to Henkel, its German competitor. In 2006, Wal-Mart retreated twice in a row: the American mega-retailer first sold its stores in South Korea and then, barely two months later, it also sold its German stores to Metro (Lander 2006). Similarly, Nokia, the world's largest mobile phone maker, decided to stop making phones for the Japanese market in 2008. The literature on market exits is much more limited than the one on market entries. Originally, firm exits were mostly described as failures, with a focus on poor market shares, low profitability or lack of financial resources (Kotabe and Ketkar 2009). More recently, more strategic motives have also been identified, such as the need to exit because of a lack of strategic fit, restructuring and/or other proactive moves. Within the more resource-based view of the firm, divestments are then described as a move towards the core business by getting rid of non-core assets (e.g. Waddock 1989), while portfolio theory has focused on how firms may want to realign their country portfolio to optimally exploit market opportunities (see, e.g., Pauwels and Matthyssens 1999). In line with the entry literature, the antecedents and performance consequences for the firms as a whole should be investigated in more detail, so that we can learn when exits may benefit the firm or when they were made in vain. As such, one should consider both the economic costs of exit, including the sunk costs made during entry that will not be recovered, and the more strategic costs coming from the ties between the subsidiary that has to be divested and the rest of the firm's network.

In sum, even though considerable research on the antecedents and consequences of international entry (and exit) decisions already exists, numerous research opportunities remain. We hope the current review will contribute to a renewed and/or intensified interest in this fascinating domain.

NOTES

1. For further details on this subject, see Lieberman and Montgomery, Chapter 20 and Shankar and Carpenter, Chapter 21 in this volume.
2. For recent reviews, see Katsikeas et al. (2009) on exporting, Brouthers and McNicol (2009) on international franchising and licensing, Rivera-Santos and Inkpen (2009) on joint ventures and alliances, and Dikova and Brouthers (2009) on acquisition versus greenfield entry.
3. The company was renamed AB InBev after the successful completion of the merger.
4. For a recent review, see Samiee et al. (2009).
5. For further details on this subject, see Tellis and Chandrasekaran, Chapter 22 in this volume.

REFERENCES

Ad Age Global (2002), "Grey showers Febreze over Southeast Asia," *Ad Age Global*, May, 18.
Agarwal, J. and W.A. Ramaswami (1992), "Choice of foreign market entry mode: impact of ownership, location and internalization factors," *Journal of International Business Studies*, **23**, 1–27.
Anderson, E. (1988), "Strategic implications of Darwinian economics for selling efficiency and choice of integrated or independent sales forces," *Management Science*, **34**, 599–618.
Arnold, D. (2004), *The Mirage of Global Markets*, Upper Saddle River, NJ: Prentice-Hall.
Asia Inc (2005), "Coffee talk," March, 16–17.
Bell, J. (1995), "The internationalization of small computer software firms: a further challenge to 'stage' theories," *European Journal of Marketing*, **29** (8), 60–75.
Biggadike, R. (1979), "The risky business of diversification," *Harvard Business Review*, **57**, 103–11.
Bloomberg (2009), "China blocks Coca-Cola's $2.3 billion Huiyuan bid," http://www.bloomberg.com/apps/news?pid=newsarchive&sid=avk88z.Ww108.
Bolton, R.N. and M.B. Myers (2003), "Price-based global market segmentation for services," *Journal of Marketing*, **67**, 108–28.
Brewer, P. (2001), "International market selection: developing a model from Australian case studies," *International Business Review*, **10** (2), 155–74.
Brouthers, K.D., L.E. Brouthers and W. Steve (2008), "Resource-based advantages in an international context," *Journal of Management*, **34**, 189–217.
Brouthers, L.E. and J.P. McNicol (2009), "International franchising and licensing," in M. Kotabe and K. Helsen (eds), *The Handbook of International Marketing*, Thousand Oaks, CA: Sage Publications, pp. 183–97.
Caves, R.E. (1998), "Industrial organization and new findings on the turnover and mobility of firms," *Journal of Economic Literature*, **36**, 1947–82.
Chetty, S. and H. Agndal (2007), "Social capital and its influence on changes in internationalization mode among small and medium-sized enterprises," *Journal of International Marketing*, **15** (1), 1–29.

Clark, T. and D.S. Pugh (2001), "Foreign country priorities in the internationalization process: a measure and an exploratory test," *International Business Review*, **10**, 285–303.

Davidson, W.H. (1980), "The location of foreign direct investment activity: country characteristics and experience effects," *Journal of International Business Studies*, **11**, 9–22.

Debruyne, M. and D.J. Reibstein (2005), "Competitor see, competitor do: incumbent entry in new market niches," *Marketing Science*, **24**, 55–66.

Dekimpe, M.G., P.M. Parker and M. Sarvary (1998), "Staged estimation of international diffusion models: an application to global cellular telephone adoption," *Technological Forecasting and Social Change*, **57**, 105–32.

Delios, A. and P.W. Beamish (2004), "Geographic scope, product diversification and the corporate performance of Japanese firms," *Strategic Management Journal*, **20**, 711–27.

Dikova, D. and K.D. Brouthers (2009), "Establishment mode choice: acquisition versus greenfield entry," in M. Kotabe and K. Helsen (eds), *The Handbook of International Marketing*, Thousand Oaks, CA: Sage Publications, pp. 218–44.

Dikova, D. and A. van Witteloostuijn (2007), "Foreign direct investment mode choice: entry and establishment modes in transition economies," *Journal of International Business Studies*, **38**, 1013–33.

Erramilli, M.K. (1991), "The experience factor in foreign market entry behavior of service firms," *Journal of International Business Studies*, **22**, 479–501.

Financial Times (2004), "Kodak sets for gamble on re-entry to Japan," December 15, p. 21.

Financial Times (2010a), "Carrefour's supermarket selloff defies growth potential," http://www.ft.com/cms/s/0/fb4cdbe8-baa2-11df-b73d-00144feab49a.htmlwww.ft.com.

Financial Times (2010b), "Chinese push into Germany's heart and soul," http://www.ft.com/cms/s/0/98828a00-a4d4-11df-8d8c-00144feabdc0.html.

Fischer, M., V. Shankar and M. Clement (2005),"Can late movers challenge the pioneer through international market entry strategy?" MSI report 05-004.

Forbes (2008), "InBev bags Anheuser-Busch," http://www.forbes.com/2008/07/14/inbev-anheuser-busch-markets-equity-cx_jb_0714markets1.html.

Forbes (2009), "Danone gives up China fight," http://www.forbes.com/2009/09/30/danone-wahaha-dispute-markets-business-trademark.html.

Gatignon, H. and E. Anderson (1988), "The multinational corporation's degree of control over foreign subsidiaries: an empirical test of a transaction cost explanation," *Journal of Law, Economics and Organization*, **4**, 89–120.

Geletkanycz, M.A. and D.C. Hambrick (1997), "The external ties of top executives: implications for strategic choice and performance," *Administrative Science Quarterly*, **42**, 654–81.

Geyskens, I., K. Gielens and M.G. Dekimpe (2002), "The market valuation of Internet channel additions," *Journal of Marketing*, **66** (2), 102–19.

Ghemawat, P. (2001), "Distance still matters," *Harvard Business Review*, September, 27–35.

Gielens, K. and M.G. Dekimpe (2001), "Do international entry decisions of retail chains matter in the long run?," *International Journal of Research in Marketing*, **18**, 235–59.

Gielens, K. and M.G. Dekimpe (2007), "The entry strategy of retail firms into transition economies," *Journal of Marketing*, **71**, 196–212.

Gielens, K. and M.G. Dekimpe (2009), "Global trends in grocery retailing," in M. Kotabe and K. Helsen (eds), *The Handbook of International Marketing*, Thousand Oaks, CA: Sage Publications, pp. 413–28.

Gielens, K. and J.-B.E.M. Steenkamp (2007), "Drivers of consumer acceptance of new packaged goods: an investigation across products and countries," *International Journal of Research in Marketing*, **24** (2), 97–111.

Gielens, K., L.M. Van de Gucht, J-B.E.M. Steenkamp and M.G. Dekimpe (2008), "Dancing with a giant: the effect of Wal-mart's entry into the U.K. on the performance of European retailers," *Journal of Marketing Research*, **45**, 519–34.

Gimeno, J. (1999), "Reciprocal threats in multimarket rivalry staking out spheres of influence in the US airline industry," *Strategic Management Journal*, **20**, 101–28.

Golder, P. and G. Tellis (1993), "Pioneering advantage: marketing fact or marketing legend?," *Journal of Marketing Research*, **30** (May), 158–70.

Green, D.H., D.W. Barclay and A.B. Ryans (1995), "Entry strategy and long-term performance: conceptualization and empirical examination," *Journal of Marketing*, **59**, 1–16.

Grocer (2000), "Hungary: Carrefour pulls out but Tesco digs in," **223** (7479), 16–17.

Hannan, M.T. and J.H. Freeman (1977), "The population ecology of organizations," *American Journal of Sociology*, **82**, 929–64.

Henisz, W. and A.D. Delios (2001), "Uncertainty, imitation and plant location: Japanese multinational corporations," *Administrative Science Quarterly*, **46**, 443–77.

Jacobs, E. (2010), "Navigating cultural differences," *Financial Times*, July 19.

Jayachandran, S., J. Gimeno and P.R. Varadarajan (1999), "The theory of multimarket competition: a synthesis and implications for marketing strategy," *Journal of Marketing*, **63**, 49–66.

Johansson, J. and J.-E. Vahlne (1977), "The internationalization process of the firm: a model of knowledge development and increasing foreign market commitments," *Journal of International Business Studies*, **8**, 23–32.

Johnson, J. and G.J. Tellis (2008), "Drivers of success for market entry into China and India," *Journal of Marketing*, **72**, 1–13.

Jones, G.K. and H.J. Teegen (2001), "Global R&D activity of U.S. MNCS: does national culture affect investment decisions?" *Multinational Business Review*, **9**, 1–7.

Kalish, S., V. Mahajan and E. Muller (1995), "Waterfall and sprinkler new-product strategies in competitive global markets," *International Journal of Research in Marketing*, **12**, 105–19.

Kang, W., B. Bayus and S. Balasubramanian (2010), "The strategic effects of multimarket contact: mutual forbearance and competitive response in the computer industry," *Journal of Marketing Research*, **47**, 564–76.

Katsikeas, C.S., L.C. Leonidou and S. Samiee (2009), "Research into exporting: theoretical, methodological, and empirical insights," in M. Kotabe and K. Helsen (eds), *The Handbook of International Marketing*, Thousand Oaks, CA: Sage Publications, pp. 165–82.

Kim, W.C. and P. Hwang (1992), "Global strategy in multinationals' entry mode choice," *Journal of International Business Studies*, **22**, 29–53.

Kirmani, A. and B. Wernerfelt (1985), "Multiple point competition," *Strategic Management Journal*, **6**, 87–96.

Kogut, B. and H. Singh (1988), "The effect of national culture on the choice of entry mode," *Journal of International Business Studies*, **19**, 411–32.

Kotabe, M. and K. Helsen (2010), *Global Marketing Management*, 5th edn, New York: John Wiley & Sons.

Kotabe, M. and S. Ketkar (2009), "Exit strategies," in M. Kotabe and K. Helsen (eds), *The Handbook of International Marketing*, Thousand Oaks, CA: Sage Publications, pp. 238–60.

Kumar, N. (1997), "The revolution in retailing: from market driven to market driving," *Long Range Planning*, **30**, 830–35.

Kumar, V., A. Stam and E.A. Joachimsthaler (1994), "An interactive multicriteria approach to identifying potential foreign markets," *Journal of International Marketing*, **2**, 9–52.

Lander, M. (2006), "Wal-Mart gives up Germany," *International Herald Tribune*, July 28.

Lemmens, A., C. Croux and M.G. Dekimpe (2007), "Consumer confidence in Europe: united in diversity," *International Journal of Research in Marketing*, **24**, 113–27.

Li, J. (1995), "Foreign entry and survival: effects of strategic choices on performance in international markets," *Strategic Management Journal*, **16**, 333–51.

Lieberman, M.B. and D.B. Montgomery (1988), "First-mover advantages," *Strategic Management Journal*, **19**, 1111–25.

Mahajan, V. and E. Muller (1994), "Innovation diffusion in a borderless global market: will the 1992 unification of the European Community accelerate diffusion of new ideas, products and technologies?," *Technological Forecasting and Social Change*, **45**, 221–35.

Makino, S. and P.W. Beamish (1998), "Performance and survival of joint ventures with non-conventional ownership structures," *Journal of International Business Studies*, **29**, 797–818.

Martin, X., A. Swaminathan and W. Mitchell (1998), "Organizational evolution in the interorganizational environment: incentives and constraints on international expansion strategy," *Administrative Science Quarterly*, **43**, 566–601.

Mascarenhas, B. (1992), "First-mover effects in multiple dynamic markets," *Strategic Management Journal*, **13**, 237–43.

Mascarenhas, B. (1997), "The order and size of entry into international markets," *Journal of Business Venturing*, **12**, 287–99.

Mitra, D. and P.N. Golder (2002), "Whose culture matters? Near-market knowledge and its impact on foreign market entry timing," *Journal of Marketing Research*, **39**, 350–65.

The New York Times (2009), "Danone exits Chinese venture with Wahaha," http://www.nytimes.com/2009/10/01/business/global/01danone.html.

Ojala, A. and P. Tyrväinen (2007), "Market entry and priority of small and mediumsized enterprises in the software industry: an empirical analysis of cultural distance, geographical distance, and market size," *Journal of International Marketing*, **15**, 123–49.

Parker, P.M. and N.T. Tavassoli (2000), "Homeostasis and consumer behavior across cultures," *International Journal of Research in Marketing*, **17**, 33–53.

Pauwels, P. and P. Matthyssens (1999), "A strategy process perspective on export withdrawal," *Journal of International Marketing*, **7**, 10–37.

Planet Retail (2010), www.planetretail.net.

Puck, J.F., D. Holtbrügge and A.T. Mohr (2009), "Beyond entry mode choice: explaining the conversion of joint ventures into wholly owned subsidiaries in the People's Republic of China," *Journal of International Business Studies*, **40**, 388–404.

Rivera-Santos, M. and A.C. Inkpen (2009), "Joint ventures and alliances," in M. Kotabe and K. Helsen (eds), *The Handbook of International Marketing*, Thousand Oaks, CA: Sage Publications, pp. 198–217.

Robertson, K.R. and V.R. Wood (2001), "The relative importance of type of information in the foreign market selection process," *International Business Review*, **10** (3), 363–79.

Rothaermel, F., S. Kotha and H.K. Steensma (2006), "Technological sophistication versus cultural similarity: an empirical analysis of country factors influencing location decision in the internationalization of Internet firms," *Journal of Management*, **32**, 56–82.

Russow, L.C. and S.C. Okoroafo (1996), "On the way towards developing a global screening model," *International Marketing Review*, **13**, 46–64.

Samiee, S., C.S. Katsikeas and M. Theodosiou (2009), "Uniformity versus conformity: the standardization issue in international marketing strategy," in M. Kotabe and K. Helsen (eds), *The Handbook of International Marketing*, Thousand Oaks, CA: Sage Publications, pp. 303–22.

Sanchez-Peinado, E., J. Pla-Barber and L. Hérbert (2007), "Strategic entry variables that influence entry mode choices in service firms," *Journal of International Marketing*, **15**, 67–91.

Scott, W.R. (2005), *Institutions and Organizations*, Thousand Oaks, CA: Sage.

Shankar, V. (1999), "New product introduction strategies: their interrelationship and the role of multimarket contact," *Journal of Marketing Research*, **36**, 327–44.

Shankar, Venkatesh, Gregory Carpenter and Lakshman Krishnamurthi (1998),"Late mover advantage: how innovative late entrants outsell pioneers,"*Journal of Marketing Research*, **35** (1), 54–70.

Sharma, D.D. and J. Johanson (1987), "Technical consultancy in internationalisation," *International Marketing Review*, **4** (Winter), 20–29.

Steenkamp, J-B.M. and F. ter Hofstede (2002), "International market segmentation: issues and perspectives," *International Journal of Research in Marketing*, **19**, 185–213.

Stremersch, S.B. and G.J. Tellis (2004), "Understanding and managing international growth of new products," *International Journal of Research in Marketing*, **21** (4), 421–38.

Szymanski, D.M., S.G. Bharadwaj and P.R. Varadarajan (1993), "Standardization verus adaptation of international marketing strategy: an empirical investigation," *Journal of Marketing*, **57** (4), 1–17.

Takada, H. and D. Jain (1991), "Cross-national analysis of diffusion of consumer durable goods in Pacific Rim countries," *Journal of Marketing*, **55** (2), 48–54.

Talukdar, D., K. Sudhir and A. Ainslie (2002), "Investigating new product diffusion across products and countries,"*Marketing Science*, **21** (1), 97–114.

Tellis, G.J., S. Stremersch and E. Yin (2003), "The international takeoff of new products: the role of economics, culture, and country innovativeness," *Marketing Science*, **22**, 188–208.

Terpstra, V. and C. Yu (1988), "Determinants of foreign investment of US advertising agencies", *Journal of International Business Studies*, **19**, 33–46.

Tihanyi, L., D.A. Griffith and C.J. Russell (2005), "The effect of cultural distance on entry mode choice, international diversification, and MNE performance: a meta-analysis," *Journal of International Business Studies*, **36**, 270–83.

Time (2009), "Why Wal-Mart's First India Store Isn't a Wal-Mart," http://www.time.com/time/world/article/0,8599,1898823,00.html.

Townsend, J.D., S. Yeniyurt and M.B. Talay (2009), "Getting to global: an evolutionary perspective of brand expansion in international markets," *Journal of International Business Studies*, **40**, 539–58.

Urban, G.L. and J.R. Hauser (1993), *Design and Marketing of New Products*, 2nd edn, Eaglewood Cliffs, NJ: Prentice-Hall.

Waddock, S. (1989), "Core strategy: end result of restructuring?" *Business Horizons*, May–June, 49–55.

Wal-Mart China (2010), http://www.wal-martchina.com/english/walmart/fastfact.htm.

Williamson, O.E. (1975), *Markets and Hierarchies*, New York: The Free Press.

Zhao, H., Y. Luo and T. Suh (2004), "Transaction cost determinants and ownership-based entry mode choice: a meta-analytical review," *Journal of International Business Studies*, **35**, 524–44.

PART VII

IMPACT OF MARKETING STRATEGY

24 Marketing strategy and firm value
Venkatesh Shankar

INTRODUCTION

Marketing executives are under increasing pressure to justify marketing spending and the marketing strategy underlying that spending. The value of marketing expenditures is constantly called into question in many organizations. Marketing models that estimate the effects of marketing spending on metrics such as sales, market share and even profits exist (Shankar 2011). Furthermore, we know much about the short- and the long-term effects of marketing strategy on sales and market share (Hanssens and Dekimpe, Chapter 26 in this volume). However, there is a growing desire from both managers and academics to understand the effects of marketing strategy on a metric that is critical to investors, namely, firm value or shareholder value (Srinivasan and Hanssens 2009).

To better understand the value investors derive from a firm's marketing strategy, we need to examine what we know and what we do not know about how marketing strategy is related to firm value. Decisions relating to marketing strategy and changes in marketing strategy affect sales, profits and cash flow. In particular, they influence both the magnitude and variability or volatility of cash flows (Srivastava et al. 1998). The magnitude of cash flows affects shareholder value and the variability of cash flows determines shareholder risk (Srivastava et al. 1999).

Prior research examines the link between the elements of marketing strategy and firm value. These elements include branding strategy, product strategy, new product or innovation strategy, pricing strategy, advertising strategy, distribution channel strategy and customer satisfaction management. Prior research focuses on the relationship between any one of these elements and firm value. Previous studies typically examine how changes to a firm's marketing strategy elements or announcements impact firm value and risk.

Results from previous research offer interesting findings regarding the effects of marketing strategy on shareholder value. Some are consistent. Others are contradictory. In this chapter, we review prior research and highlight its key results. We also discuss the measures of shareholder value, point out the key unresolved issues, and offer suggestions for future research.

The rest of this chapter is organized as follows. In the next section, we summarize the major metrics and methods used in this research stream. Next, we present a conceptual model of the effect of marketing strategy on firm value. We review research linking the different elements of marketing strategy and firm value. We highlight the key findings and point out important caveats about the conclusions. We conclude by outlining underexplored issues and suggestions for future research.

MEASURES OF FIRM VALUE

Measures of firm value are based on stock market responses. Firm value is the present value of its future cash flows, discounted at the risk-adjusted cost of equity (Fama and Miller 1972). The announcement of a change in marketing strategy causes investors to change their expectations about the firm's future cash flows, which, in turn, results in a change in stock prices.

The economic rents associated with changes in cash flows are passed on to the firms' shareholders as compensation for the risk involved in owning the firm's stocks. These excess returns, or abnormal returns, can be measured by pricing models, such as the Capital Asset Pricing Model (CAPM) or the Fama French model. Abnormal returns can manifest in the short term (a few days or weeks) or over the long term (several months or years) based on the speed of changes in the investors' value perceptions.

Tobin's Q

Tobin's Q is defined as the ratio of the market value of the firm's assets to the replacement value of the assets (Tobin 1969). Because Tobin's Q is a stock variable, it is particularly useful in cross-sectional or panel-data studies where the stock of shareholder wealth is compared to the stock of a variable related to the firm's marketing strategy. Several studies in marketing use this metric to capture firm value (e.g. Grewal et al. 2010; Sorescu and Spanjol 2008).

However, Tobin's Q has some limitations. Results from studies using this measure are difficult to interpret because cross-sectional differences in Q values do not necessarily reflect differences in economic rents. Due to differing accounting choices in reporting total assets, Q values can differ across firms. Moreover, Q values vary significantly across industries due to differences in growth rates and discount rates, making it a weak metric for cross-industry studies. Q values are also not directly comparable for the same firm over time periods because they can change significantly due to depreciation, mergers, acquisitions or changes in accounting practices. Furthermore, Tobin's Q assumes that the stock market is perfectly efficient; that is, stock prices reflect all future effects.

Abnormal Returns

Abnormal returns overcome many of the limitations associated with Tobin's Q. Unlike Tobin's Q, abnormal returns are dynamic and measure firm-specific changes in shareholder value due to economic rents. Abnormal returns can be measured in the short term (typically, during the few days surrounding an event or announcement) or over the long term (typically, between one and three years). Measuring abnormal returns involves the comparison of realized stock return with investors' risk-adjusted rate of return. Choosing an appropriate benchmark for this comparison is critical for long-term abnormal returns because an incorrect benchmark could lead to wrong conclusions about the long-term effect of marketing strategy on firm value. Abnormal returns differ from Tobin's Q in one important aspect. Unlike Tobin's Q, abnormal returns are a flow variable because they capture the present value of economic rents earned during a specific time period.

Short-term cumulative abnormal returns (CARs)

The standard measure of abnormal returns is the short-term cumulative abnormal returns (CARs) (Brown and Warner 1985). CARs have been used extensively in the firm value literature (e.g. Chaney et al. 1991; Sorescu et al. 2007). CARs are computed as follows. First, firm-specific stock returns are added over a three- to seven-day window surrounding a change in marketing strategy. Second, the cumulative rate of return for a benchmark capturing investors' expected rate of return during that same period is subtracted from the cumulative stock returns. A commonly used benchmark model is the "market-adjusted" model in which the benchmark is the stock market's average return. An alternative benchmark is the "market model," which adjusts for systematic risk. The results from these benchmarks are unlikely to be different (Brown and Warner 1985), so the benchmark typically does not matter much. Some studies use an NPV measure, which is equal to CARs multiplied by the market value of equity (e.g. Sorescu et al. 2003; Kalaignanam et al. 2007).

A major advantage of the CARs metric is that it is forward looking. It measures the change in marketing strategy's economic rents earned not only during the time period when the CARs are measured, but also in the future. However, CARs assume that stock markets are efficient and that investors can accurately estimate the firm's future cash flows associated with a change in marketing strategy. Research in behavioral finance has reexamined these assumptions and developed alternative measures based on long-term event windows.

Long-term abnormal returns

Long-term abnormal return measures capture the discounted value of all future cash flows (including the cash flows during the measurement period) resulting from a change in marketing strategy. Unlike CARs, long-term abnormal return measures do not assume that all information is instantly incorporated into stock prices. Rather, they allow for the information to be included over a longer period of time. Two common methods of measuring long-term abnormal returns are buy-and-hold abnormal returns (BHARs) and calendar time portfolio abnormal returns (CTARs).

Buy-and-hold abnormal returns (BHARs)

The BHARs capture the returns for a hypothetical investor who buys and holds the stock for a predetermined period. They are computed by taking the cumulative returns of a firm's stock over one year or longer, and subtracting the cumulative performance of a benchmark comprising stocks whose risk profile closely matches that of the firm over the same period. A commonly used benchmark is a portfolio of stocks with similar size, book-to-market and momentum (Daniel et al. 1997).

BHARs are most useful in cross-sectional analysis of long-term returns because they preserve rank ordering. Several studies in marketing have used BHARs as the dependent variable in cross-sectional and panel models (e.g. Sorescu, Chandy, and Prabhu 2007). However, due to high cross-sectional correlation, the BHARs tend to have inflated t statistics.

Calendar time abnormal returns (CTARs)

The calendar time measure overcomes BHARs' main limitation. CTARs are computed for a portfolio of firms that have a common characteristic, such as a change in marketing strategy. For example, all firms changing their marketing strategy in the focal year constitute a portfolio. First, a portfolio that invests in the stocks of firms experiencing a marketing strategy change for exactly one year is created. Second, the monthly returns of the portfolio are regressed on factors that affect stock returns, such as size, book-to-market and momentum. The intercept (alpha) from this regression provides an estimate of the portfolio's abnormal return during the year. This measure has been used to assess stock market returns to R&D expenditures (Chan et al. 2001) and new product pre-announcements (Sorescu, Shankar and Kushwaha 2007).

However, CTARs also have their own limitations. First, they can only be computed at a portfolio level and not at an individual firm level, making them not ideal for cross-sectional analysis. To extend CTARs for studying cross-sectional differences among firms with different strategies, we need to group the firms into several portfolios according to the values of the independent variable of interest and determine separate "alphas" for the portfolios. By comparing the "alphas" across the portfolios, we can draw conclusions on cross-sectional effects of the independent variable. Second, the power of CTARs is low (Loughran and Ritter 2000), suggesting caution in interpreting tests with insignificant *t*-statistics as zero abnormal returns. Given their low power, CTARs should be predominantly used for rejecting the null hypothesis. The test result should be typically treated as inconclusive, except when the estimate of alpha is very small or if its sign is not in the expected direction.

ELEMENTS OF MARKETING STRATEGY AND THEIR EFFECTS ON FIRM VALUE

Decisions regarding the different elements of marketing strategy influence firm value as outlined in Figure 24.1. A change in each element of marketing strategy influences the

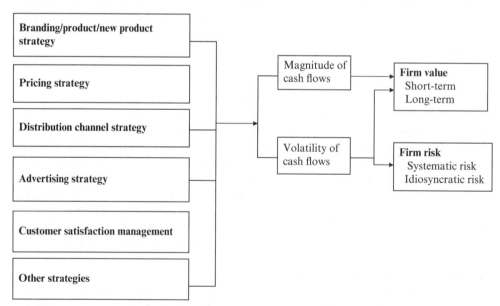

Figure 24.1   Conceptual model of marketing strategy, firm value and firm risk

magnitude and the variability of cash flow. Changes in cash flow are associated with changes in shareholder value, while variability in cash flow is related to firm risk.

A summary of selected research papers examining the effect of changes in marketing strategy on shareholder value appears in the Appendix. The articles in the table are organized by different elements of marketing strategy. The table highlights the key findings and limitations of each relevant paper. It also outlines the metrics used to assess shareholder value, and includes the data source(s) used in the empirical analysis.

Branding Strategy

Brands are strategic assets (Keller, Chapter 17 in this volume). Branding strategy includes decisions that influence the customer's perceptions of the brand, its value and the composition of the brand portfolio. Morgan and Rego (2009) examine the value of brand portfolio. They find that market share is a useful metric for assessing marketing effectiveness and that high customer loyalty is significantly related to a low level of intra-portfolio competition and strong quality perceptions. Rego et al. (2009) analyze customer-based equity and firm value. They conclude that consumer-based brand equity predicts unsystematic risk and protects the firm from downside systematic risk, highlighting the importance of brand management during economic uncertainty.

Mizik and Jacobson (2009) find that changes in brand assets are associated with changes in financial value. Mizik and Jacobson (2009) further conclude that a firm's valuation accuracy can be improved upon by incorporating brand asset information, while brand metrics can explain shareholder value more fully than just accounting variables used in isolation. Shankar et al. (2008) show that brand equity is negatively associated with volatility in shareholder value, and that brand equity mediates the effect of advertising on firm value. Their result on brand equity–shareholder value relationship is consistent with Rego et al. (2009). Bharadwaj et al. (2011) also find that brand quality enhances shareholder wealth and that unanticipated changes in brand quality can erode shareholder wealth.

Thus there is evidence to support a positive relationship between brand equity and shareholder value and a negative relationship between brand equity and firm risk. An improvement in brand equity not only enhances shareholder value but also reduces firm risk.

Product Strategy

A firm's product mix refers to the make-up of different products or product categories in its portfolio. A product mix can be made of goods and services. A firm may be selling several types of goods and services in different product markets. In each product market, a firm may have multiple products targeted at different segments. A firm could change its product mix by changing the products it offers at one or more of these levels. The firm expects investors to understand and view these changes positively (e.g. Chaney et al. 1991; Pauwels et al. 2004).

A change in the product mix may also affect a firm's systematic and idiosyncratic risks. A reduction in systematic risk could occur if the changes to the firm's product mix are consistent with the overall trends in the industry (Chaney et al. 1991). Furthermore, if such changes lead to an improvement in the firm's overall product quality or performance, then systematic risk could decline (Kroll et al. 1999). A change in the product mix may affect idiosyncratic risk by reducing volatility in customer demand and by improving the odds of firm survival. In a study of the wine industry, Delacroix and Swaminathan (1991) find that additions to a firm's product mix reduce its mortality rate, implicitly reducing its idiosyncratic risk.

New Product/Innovation Strategy

A disproportionately large number of studies focus on the effects of new product introductions on firm value. Successful new products can increase shareholder value directly through firm revenues and indirectly through brand equity. Prior research explores if this relationship is positive by examining if new products are associated with an increase in shareholder value under different conditions and with different types of innovation.

The new product development (NPD) process comprises different stages, from idea generation to commercialization (Shankar 2008). Different studies operationalize firm-level innovation in different ways, ranging from innovation in its earliest stages, such as R&D expenditures and patents, to the launch of new products. Returns to innovation vary significantly depending on the innovation stage. A study of stock market returns across the stages of an innovation project shows that returns in the launch stage are the lowest among all the stages (Sood and Tellis 2009). Further, the study shows that the total stock market returns to innovation, or the sum of returns across the stages of NPD are 13 times higher than the returns at any stage in the NPD.

Research focusing on the early stages of innovation examines the effect of R&D expenditures, patent output and product preannouncements on firm value. In general, R&D expenditures positively influence market value (Chauvin and Hirschey 1993; Greenhalgh and Rogers 2006), Tobin's Q (Ceccagnoli 2009; Hall and Oriani 2006), and stock returns (Lev and Sougiannis 1996; Pakes 1985).

The results on the effect of patents on firm value are mixed. Some studies question their economic value. Pakes (1985, p. 407) states: "Most of the variance in the stock market rate of return has little to do with the firm's inventive endeavors, at least as measured by its R&D input and its patent output." Similarly, Greenhalgh and Rogers (2006) find that firms that receive only UK patents have no significant market premium. Other studies show that patents are a significant determinant of Tobin's Q, only for the firms in the top Tobin's Q quintiles (Coad and Rao 2006). Rather than the absolute number of patents, the number of patents relative to R&D expenditures and patent citations relative to patent counts actually determine stock market value (Hall et al. 2005).

Some firms may preannounce their new products. Preannouncements of new products may be associated with positive stock market returns (Mishra and Bhabra 2002; Sood and Tellis 2009; Sorescu, Shankar and Kushwaha 2007). This finding suggests that firms have the option of incorporating the expected cash flows from a new product into its market value prior to the product's market introduction. However, there are caveats. Delaying a previously preannounced product decreases the market value of the firm by 5.25 percent (Hendricks and Singhal 1997), while not keeping promises also tarnishes firm value (Sorescu, Shankar and Kushwaha 2007).

There is generally a positive relationship between new product launch and a firm's market value (e.g. Blundell et al. 1999), Tobin's Q (e.g. Sorescu and Spanjol 2008) and long-term abnormal returns (e.g. Sorescu and Spanjol 2008). There is also a positive link between announcements of new product introductions and short-term cumulative abnormal returns (e.g. Chaney et al. 1991) and long-term abnormal returns (e.g. Pauwels et al. 2004). Breakthrough or radical new products are associated with greater shareholder returns than are incremental products. Srinivasan et al. (2009) show that new-to-the-market innovations are associated with the highest stock returns. Sorescu and Spanjol (2008) find that breakthrough consumer packaged goods innovations have positive abnormal returns both in the short and the long run.

Many innovations are developed through alliances. Das et al. (1998) find that stock market responses to announcements of technological alliances are more favorable than responses to marketing alliances. Kalaignanam et al. (2007) find that abnormal stock returns to NPD alliance announcements are asymmetric across large and small alliance partners.

Pricing Strategy

Different firms use different pricing strategies. For example, some firms adopt a variable pricing strategy, while others follow a fixed fee pricing model. Similarly, some companies practice a uniform or linear pricing model, while others adopt a tiered pricing approach.

A firm typically undertakes a change in the pricing strategy when it believes that it may soon be out of line with market demand. When its products are not differentiable from its competitors', a firm can increase the complexity of its pricing strategy to gain economic rents by charging a premium price (Carlin 2009).

To the extent that a firm changes its pricing strategy to be more flexible, that is, increases the likelihood that it will extract maximum rents from each customer segment, the new pricing strategy can yield greater cash flows. Such a pricing strategy can also smooth cash flows and lead to a decrease in idiosyncratic risk. However, the consequences of changes in pricing strategy may also be difficult to grasp for many investors. For instance, changing to a complex, customized pricing strategy may lead to negative net cash flows in the short run due to high customer acquisition costs. However, in the long run, through upselling and cross-selling of high-margin items, the net cash flows and the net present value of the change in the pricing strategy may become positive. If investors need some time to assess the true impact of a change in pricing strategy, the market reaction to such a change will only be apparent in the long term.

Furthermore, a change in pricing strategy may affect firm risk. For example, if a firm changes its pricing strategy from an upfront fee-based pricing model to a subscription model, then its revenue stream becomes more stable. Consequently, its stock returns will likely be less volatile. Indeed, changes in pricing strategy are associated with lower idiosyncratic risk (Shankar and Sorescu 2011).

Distribution Channel Strategy

Organizations distribute their products through one or more channels. A distribution channel strategy encompasses various approaches, such as direct versus indirect methods of delivery and the choice of single or multiple channels.

A change in distribution channel strategy could involve any of the following: (1) a significant change in the proportion of products distributed through the direct channel, (2) a move from delivering products through a single channel to multiple channels, (3) a streamline of the existing channel, or (4) the addition of a new channel (Geyskens et al. 2002). Investors may treat a change in the channel strategy as an indicator of profit expansion through a new channel, or a more efficient method of distribution through existing channels. Consistent with this argument, Geyskens et al. (2002) find that the addition of the Internet channel is associated with an increase in shareholder value. However, similar to changes in pricing strategy, changes to channel strategy may not always have an immediate and clear impact on cash flows. Investors may need to go through a learning process over a longer period to fully evaluate the consequences of such actions.

When a firm announces a change in its channel strategy, it aims to assure investors that it is moving toward a more stable and/or a more profitable distribution strategy. Because the firm derives its revenues directly from channel members, the stability of the firm's distribution will directly impact the stability of its cash flows, influencing firm risk. If the firm's change in the channel strategy follows its competitors', then the firm should experience a reduction in its systematic risk. However, if the firm's channel strategy change is unique to the firm, then it is likely to be associated with changes in its idiosyncratic risk. There is scant research on changes in distribution channel strategies, so the effects on firm risk are open research questions.

Advertising Strategy

In general, studies support a positive relationship between advertising strategy and firm value. Joshi and Hanssens (2010) show that, in general, advertising spending has a positive, long-term impact on market capitalization and a negative impact on the market values of competitor firms.

However, some studies do not find a positive link between advertising and firm value in certain product category or industry contexts. For example, in the entertainment context, Joshi and Hanssens (2009) find that movies with above average pre-launch advertising have lower post-launch stock returns than films with below average advertising; this suggests a dissipating effect of advertising spending for products with a short life cycle. Furthermore, Joshi and Hanssens reveal that hit movies may experience low stock prices if given high media support. In the pharmaceutical context, Osinga et al. (2011) reveal that direct-to-consumer advertising leads to higher stock returns and lower systematic risk, while direct-to-physician marketing only has a modest, positive effect on stock returns.

There are differences across B2C and B2B firms as well with regard to advertising impact on firm value. By analyzing the effects of advertising on shareholder value, Srinivasan et al. (2011) reveal that a majority of B2C firms overspend on advertising and realize diminishing stock returns, while a majority of B2B firms are spending the right amount on advertising.

Among the components of advertising, some influence firm value more than others. Karniouchina et al. (2009) show that traditional advertising variables, such as the length of the ad, the recency and primacy of the ad, the information clutter and the source credibility for the advertising message, all influence market value.

Managing Customer Satisfaction

Like brands, customers are important assets. Therefore, managing customer satisfaction is an important task for the firm (Mittal and Frennea, Chapter 16 in this volume). The relationship between customer satisfaction and shareholder value has been well researched. There are two broad countervailing conclusions. One conclusion is that customer satisfaction is significant and positively related to shareholder value and negatively associated with firm risk. Ittner and Larcker (1998) show that a five-point increase on a 0–100 scale of customer satisfaction is positively related to a 1 percent increase in cumulative abnormal stock returns. Furthermore, Anderson et al. (2004) show that a 1 percent change in the American customer satisfaction index (ACSI) is positively associated with a 1.016 percent change in Tobin's Q. Gruca and Rego (2005) reveal that improvements in customer satisfaction scores are positively related to increases in cash flow and decreases in cash flow variability. Fornell et al. (2006) and Mittal et al. (2005) discover strong links among customer satisfaction, firm profitability and market value. Luo et al. (2010) find that positive changes in customer satisfaction improve analyst recommendations, which mediates the effect of satisfaction changes on firm metrics. In fact, Tuli and Bharadwaj (2009) state that customer satisfaction provides valuable information to financial markets, so firms should disclose their customer satisfaction scores. Grewal et al. (2010) offer a nuanced result – shareholder value is influenced by the interplay of satisfaction levels and customer satisfaction heterogeneity, thus suggesting that both the mean level and the variability in customer satisfaction scores influence firm value.

The other conclusion is that customer satisfaction scores are not value relevant (Jacobson and Mizik 2009). Ittner et al. (2009) also find no evidence for ACSI as a driver of long-run returns. While Ittner et al. show that customer satisfaction information is value relevant in the short term, their long-run results are consistent with those of Jacobson and Mizik (2009).

However, Fornell et al. (2009) maintain that above-market returns to customer satisfaction persist and are both economically and statistically significant. They attribute the failure to reject the null hypotheses of no effects by Jacobson and Mizik (2009) to a lack of statistical power.

Other Elements Related to Marketing Strategy

Change in business model is another element of marketing strategy that is gaining some momentum in academic research (Shankar and Sorescu 2011). A business model can be viewed as a mechanism that outlines how a firm creates and appropriates value (Zott and Amit 2008). Stock prices react to changes that improve the effectiveness or efficiency of a firm's business model. A 2010 Boston Consulting Group study reports that firms pursuing business model innovations earned, on average, 2.7 percent in excess stock returns over a ten-year period, compared to 1.7 percent in excess stock returns for firms pursuing only product and process innovations (Lindgardt et al. 2009).

Shankar and Sorescu (2011) find that changes in business model are positively associated with changes in firm value and that changes in the marketing mix components of the business model are related to positive short-term abnormal returns. However, they show that changes to multiple components of the business model are associated with negative short-term returns and higher idiosyncratic risk. These results suggest that the effects of changes to business models on firm value are complex and nuanced.

Another element of a firm's marketing strategy is an adverse or negative marketing event, such as a product recall. Wiles et al. (2010) find that firms have an average abnormal return of −0.91 percent for such events and that investors penalize commission violations more than omission violations. Furthermore, Tipton et al. (2009) show that adverse marketing events are associated with significant abnormal returns of 1 percent and that event characteristics are more significant than are firm and brand characteristics.

An important element related to marketing strategy is marketing alliances. Among the components of marketing alliances, network efficiency, network density and alliance capability have a positive effect, while network reputation and network centrality have no impact on firm value (Swaminathan and Moorman 2009).

Other elements of marketing strategy that have been shown to have effects on firm value include customer equity and corporate social responsibility (CSR). Kumar and Shah (2011) show that strategies focused on customer equity increase the stock price and beat investor expectations. Luo and Bhattacharya (2009) find that greater CSR activities lower idiosyncratic risk but a simultaneous pursuit of CSR, advertising and R&D activities may not have an overall positive effect on firm value.

FUTURE RESEARCH

Although much is known about the effects of marketing strategy on firm value, a number of underexplored issues exist. Hanssens et al. (2009) call for research efforts to address the following areas: (1) main drivers of market value; (2) understanding brand valuation; (3) challenging the efficient market hypothesis; (4) the investor community as a customer (investor relations); and (5) analyzing the analysts. In addition, we outline several areas for future research.

A growingly popular new product strategy involves the development of innovations through outsiders such as customers, suppliers and channel partners. This process, known as "open innovation" (Chesbrough 2010) or "customer co-creation" (Hoyer et al. 2010), offers a large pool of ideas for commercialization. Future research could examine the link between open innovation strategy and shareholder value. Future research could also address questions relating to changes in marketing strategy and firm value at a macro level.

At a country level, what is the relationship between aggregate changes to marketing strategy of all firms and the returns to the stock market index? How do these returns differ across countries?

While there is an inordinate amount of research on the relationship between new product strategy and firm value, more research is needed to better understand the linkages between pricing strategy and firm value, and between channel strategy and shareholder value. Moreover, while we know much about first-mover and late-mover advantages with regard to market share (Shankar and Carpenter, Chapter 21 in this volume), we do not have a good grasp of the relationship between entry strategy and shareholder value. These are useful avenues for future research.

Advertising is a significant moderator of the relationship between new product strategy and market value. However, we do not know how different elements of marketing strategy interact with one another to affect shareholder value. For example, what is the combined effect of changes in pricing and distribution strategies on shareholder value? More studies on the interactive effects of changes in different elements of marketing strategy are required to better understand the overall effects on firm value.

The literature on marketing strategy and shareholder value suffers from a selection or publication bias. Studies showing null effects are unlikely to be published (for an exception see Eddy and Saunders 1980). Therefore it is possible that a change in marketing strategy may not be valuable under certain conditions. Managers need a critical understanding of the factors that negatively impact the rents from a change in marketing strategy.

Finally, as firms are increasingly investing in social and mobile media (Hoffman and Novak, Chapter 12; Shankar, Chapter 13 in this volume), managers need a clear understanding of how changes in digital or mobile marketing strategy affect firm value. Future research should examine this issue in depth.

ACKNOWLEDGMENT

I thank Nicole Hanson for research assistance.

REFERENCES

Anderson, Eugene W., Claes Fornell and Sanal K. Mazvancheryl (2004), "Customer satisfaction and shareholder value," *Journal of Marketing*, **68**, 172–85.

Austin, D.H. (1993), "An event-study approach to measuring innovative output: the case of biotechnology," *American Economic Review*, **83** (2), 253–8.

Bharadwaj, Sundar, Kapil Tuli and Andre Bonfrer (2011), "The impact of brand quality on shareholder wealth," *Journal of Marketing*, forthcoming.

Blundell, R., G. Rachel and J. Van Reenen (1999), "Market share, market value and innovation in a panel of British manufacturing firms," *Review of Economic Studies*, **66** (3), 529–54.

Brown, S.J. and J.B. Warner (1985), "Using daily stock returns: the case of event studies," *Journal of Financial Economics*, **14** (1), 3–31.

Carlin, Bruce I. (2009), "Strategic price complexity in retail financial markets," *Journal of Financial Economics*, **91**, 278–87.

Ceccagnoli, Marco (2009), "Appropriability, preemption, and firm performance," *Strategic Management Journal*, **30** (1), 81–98.

Chakravarty, Anindita and Rajdeep Grewal (2011), "The stock market in the driver's seat! Implications for R&D and marketing," *Management Science*, **57** (9), 1–16.

Chan, L.K., J. Lakonishok and T. Sougiannis (2001), "The stock market valuation of research and development expenditures," *Journal of Finance*, **56** (6), 2431–56.

Chaney, P.K., T.M. Devinney and R.S. Winer (1991), "The impact of new product introductions on the market value of firms," *Journal of Business*, **64** (4), 573–610.

Chauvin, K.W. and M. Hirschey (1993), "Advertising, R&D expenditures and the market value of the firm," *Financial Management*, **22** (4), 128–40.

Chen, Yubo, Shankar Ganesan and Yong Liu (2009), "Does a firm's product-recall strategy affect its financial value? An examination of strategic alternatives during product-harm crises," *Journal of Marketing*, **73** (6), 214–26.

Chesbrough, H. (2010), "Business model innovation: opportunities and barriers," *Long Range Planning*, **43** (2/3), 354–63.

Coad, A. and R. Rao (2006), "Innovation and market value: a quantile regression analysis," *Economics Bulletin*, **15** (13), 1–10.

Cockburn, I. and Z. Griliches (1988), "Industry effects and appropriability measures in the stock market's valuation of R&D and patents," *American Economic Review*, **78** (2), 419–23.

Connolly, Robert A. and Mark Hirschey (1988), "Market value and patents: a Bayesian approach," *Economics Letters*, **27** (1), 83–7.

Daniel, Kent, Mark Grinblatt, Sheridan Titman and Russell Wermers (1997), "Measuring mutual fund performance with characteristic-based benchmarks," *Journal of Finance*, **52**, 1035–58.

Das, S., P. Sen and S. Sengupta (1998), "Impact of strategic alliances on firm valuation," *Academy of Management Journal*, **41** (1), 27–41.

Delacroix, Jacques and Anand Swaminathan (1991), "Cosmetic, speculative, and adaptive organizational change in the wine industry: a longitudinal study," *Administrative Science Quarterly*, **36** (4), 631–61.

Dotson, Jeffrey and Greg Allenby (2010), "Investigating the strategic influence of customer and employee satisfaction on firm financial performance," *Marketing Science*, **29** (5), 895–908.

Eddy, A.R. and G. Saunders (1980), "New product announcements and stock prices," *Decision Sciences*, **11** (1), 90–97.

Fama, Eugene F. and Merton H. Miller (1972), *The Theory of Finance*, Hinsdale, IL: Dryden Press.

Fang, Eric (Er), Robert Palmatier and Rajdeep Grewal (2011), "Effects of customer and innovation asset configuration strategies on firm performance," *Journal of Marketing Research*, **48** (3), 587–602.

Fornell, Claes, Sunil Mithas and Forrest Morgeson III (2009), "The economic and statistical significance of stock returns on customer satisfaction," *Marketing Science*, **28** (5), 820–25.

Fornell, Claes, Sunil Mithas, Forrest V. Morgeson III and M.S. Krishnan (2006), "Customer satisfaction and stock prices: high returns, low risk," *Journal of Marketing*, **70** (January), 3–14.

Geyskens, Inge, Katrijn Gielens and Marnik G. Dekimpe (2002), "The market valuation of internet channel additions," *Journal of Marketing*, **66** (April), 102–19.

Greenhalgh, Christine and Mark Rogers (2006), "The value of innovation: the interaction of competition, R&D and IP," *Research Policy*, **35** (4), 562–80.

Grewal, Rajdeep, Murali Chandrashekaran and Alka Citrin (2010), "Customer satisfaction heterogeneity and shareholder value," *Journal of Marketing Research*, **47** (4), 612–26.

Gruca, Thomas S. and Lopo L. Rego (2005), "Customer satisfaction, cash flow, and shareholder value," *Journal of Marketing*, **69** (3), 115–30.

Hall, B.H. and R. Oriani (2006), "Does the market value R&D investment by European firms? Evidence from a panel of manufacturing firms in France, Germany, and Italy," *International Journal of Industrial Organization*, **24** (5), 971–93.

Hall, B.H., A. Jaffe and M. Trajtenberg (2005), "Market value and patent citations," *RAND Journal of Economics*, **36** (1), 16–38.

Hanssens, Dominique, Roland Rust and Rajendra Srivastava (2009), "Marketing strategy and Wall Street: nailing down marketing's impact," *Journal of Marketing*, **73** (6), 115–18.

Heeley, Michael B. and R. Jacobson (2008), "The recency of technological inputs and financial performance," *Strategic Management Journal*, **29** (7), 723–44.

Hendricks, K.B. and V.R. Singhal (1997), "Delays in new product introductions and the market value of the firm: the consequences of being late to the market," *Management Science*, **43** (4), 422–36.

Henock, Louis and Amy Sun (2010), "Investor inattention and the market reaction to merger announcements," *Management Science*, **56** (10), 1781–93.

Hoyer, Wayne D., Rajesh Chandy, Matilda Dorotic, Manfred Krafft and Siddharth S. Singh (2010), "Consumer cocreation in new product development," *Journal of Service Research*, **13** (3), 283–96.

Ittner, C.D. and D.F. Larcker (1998), "Are non-financial measures leading indicators of financial performance? An analysis of customer satisfaction," *Journal of Accounting Research*, **36** (supplement), 1–46.

Ittner, Christopher, David Larcker and Daniel Taylor (2009), "The stock market's pricing of customer satisfaction," *Marketing Science*, **28** (5), 826–35.

Jacobson, Robert and Natalie Mizik (2009), "The financial markets and customer satisfaction: reexamining possible financial market mispricing of customer satisfaction," *Marketing Science*, **28** (5), 809–18

Jaffe, A.B. (1986), "Technological opportunity and spillovers of R&D: evidence from firms' patents, profits, and market value," *American Economic Review*, **76** (Dec.), 984–1001.

Joshi, Amit and Dominique Hanssens (2009), "Movie advertising and the stock market valuation of studios: a case of "great expectations?," *Marketing Science*, **28** (2), 239–50.

Joshi, Amit and Dominique Hanssens (2010), "The direct and indirect effects of advertising spending on firm value," *Journal of Marketing*, **74** (1), 20–33.

Kalaignanam, K., V. Shankar and R. Varadarajan (2007), "Asymmetric new product development alliances: win–win or win–lose partnerships?," *Management Science*, **53**(3), 357–74.

Karniouchina, Ekaterina, William Moore and Kevin Cooney (2009), "Impact of mad money stock recommendations: merging financial and marketing perspectives," *Journal of Marketing*, **73** (6), 244–66.

Kelm, K.M., V.K. Narayanan and G.E. Pinches (1995), "Shareholder value creation during R&D innovation and commercialization stages," *The Academy of Management Journal*, **38** (3), 770–86.

Krasnikov, Alexander, Saurabh Mishra and David Orozco (2009), "Evaluating the financial impact of branding using trademarks: a framework and empirical evidence," *Journal of Marketing*, **73** (6), 154–66.

Kroll, Mark, Peter Wright and Richard A. Heiens (1999), "The contribution of product quality to competitive advantage: impacts on systematic variance and unexplained variance in returns," *Strategic Management Journal*, **20** (4), 375–84.

Kumar, V. and Denish Shah (2009), "Expanding the role of marketing: from customer equity to market capitalization," *Journal of Marketing*, **73** (6), 119–36.

Kumar, V. and Denish Shah (2011), "Marketing's profit impact: quantifying online and off-line funnel progression," *Marketing Science*, **30** (4), 595–603.

Laursen, Keld and Ammon Salter (2006), "Open for innovation: the role of openness in explaining innovation performance among U.K. manufacturing firms," *Strategic Management Journal*, **27** (2), 131–50.

Lee, R.P. and Q. Chen (2009), "The immediate impact of new product introductions on stock price: the role of firm resources and size," *Journal of Product Innovation Management*, **26** (1), 97–107.

Lev, Baruch and Theodore Sougiannis (1996), "The capitalization, amortization, and value-relevance of R&D," *Journal of Accounting and Economics*, **21** (1), 107–38.

Lindgardt, Zhenya, Martin Reeves, George Stack and Michael Deimler (2009), "Business model innovation. When the game gets tough, change the game." Available from http://www.bcg.com/documents/file36456. pdf, accessed 17 September.

Loughran, Tim and Jay R. Ritter (2000), "Uniformly least powerful tests of market efficiency," *Journal of Financial Economics*, **55** (3), 361–89.

Luo, Xueming (2009), "Quantifying the long-term impact of negative word of mouth on cash flows and stock prices," *Marketing Science*, **28** (1), 148–65.

Luo, Xueming and C.B. Bhattacharya (2009), "The debate over doing good: corporate social performance, strategic marketing levers, and firm-idiosyncratic risk," *Journal of Marketing*, **73** (6), 198–213.

Luo, Xueming, Christian Homburg and Jan Wieseke (2010), "Customer satisfaction, analyst stock recommendations, and firm value," *Journal of Marketing Research*, **47** (6), 1041–58.

Mehra, Rajnish and Edward C. Prescott (2003), "The equity premium in retrospect," in G.M. Constantinides, M. Harris and R. Stulz (eds), *Handbook of the Economics of Finance*, Amsterdam: North-Holland.

Mishra, D.P. and H.S. Bhabra (2002), "Assessing the economic worth of new product pre-announcement signals: theory and empirical evidence," *Journal of Product and Brand Management*, **10** (2), 75–93.

Mittal, Vikas, Engene W. Anderson, Akin Sayrak and Pandu Tadikamalla (2005), "Dual emphasis and the long-term financial impact of customer satisfaction," *Marketing Science*, **24** (4), 544–55.

Mizik, Natalie and Robert Jacobson (2009), "Valuing Branded Businesses," *Journal of Marketing*, **73** (6), 137–53.

Morgan, Neil and Lopo Rego (2009), "Brand portfolio strategy and firm performance," *Journal of Marketing*, **73** (1), 59–74.

Osinga, Ernst, Peter Leeflang, Shuba Srinivasan and Jaap Wieringa (2011), "Why do firms invest in consumer advertising with limited sales response? a shareholder perspective," *Journal of Marketing*, **75** (1), 109–24.

Oxley, Joanne, Rachelle Sampson and Brian Silverman (2009), "Arms race or détente? How interfirm alliance announcements change the stock market valuation of rivals," *Management Science*, **55** (8), 1321–37.

Pakes, A. (1985), "On patents, R&D, and the stock market rate of return," *Journal of Political Economy*, **93** (2), 390–409.

Pauwels, K., J. Silva-Risso, S. Srinivasan and D.M. Hanssens (2004), "New products, sales promotion, and firm value: the case of automobile industry," *Journal of Marketing*, **68** (4), 142–56.

Rao, Ramesh K.S. and Neeraj Bharadwaj (2008), "Marketing initiatives, expected cash flows, and shareholders' wealth," *Journal of Marketing*, **72** (1), 16–20.

Rego, Lopo, Matthew Billett and Neil Morgan (2009), "Consumer-based brand equity and firm risk," *Journal of Marketing*, **73** (6), 47–60.

Shankar, Venkatesh (2008), "The evolution of markets: innovative adoption, diffusion, market growth, new product entry and competitor responses," in Scott Shane (ed.), *Handbook of Technology and Innovation Management*, Cambridge, MA: Blackwell Publishers, pp. 57–112.

Shankar, Venkatesh (2011), "Marketing strategy models," *Wiley Encyclopedia in Marketing*, Wiley.

Shankar, Venkatesh and Alina B. Sorescu (2011), "The impact of business model changes on shareholder value," Working Paper, Texas A&M University, College Station, TX.

Shankar, Venkatesh, Pablo Azar and Matthew Fuller (2008), "BRAN*EQT: a model for estimating, tracking, and managing brand equity for multicategory brands," *Marketing Science*, **27** (4), 545–66.

Sharma, A. and Nelson Lacey (2004), "Linking product development outcomes to market valuation of the firm: the case of the U.S. pharmaceutical industry," *Journal of Product Innovation Management*, **21** (5), 297–308.

Sood, A. and G.J. Tellis (2009), "Do innovations really pay off? Total stock market returns to innovation," *Marketing Science*, **28** (3), 442–56.

Sorescu, A. and J. Spanjol (2008), "Innovation's effect on firm value and risk: insights from consumer packaged goods," *Journal of Marketing*, **72** (2), 114–32.

Sorescu, A., R. Chandy and J.C. Prabhu (2003), "Sources and financial consequences of radical innovation: insights from pharmaceuticals," *Journal of Marketing*, **67** (4), 82–101.

Sorescu, A., R. Chandy and J.C. Prabhu (2007), "Why some acquisitions do better than others: product capital as a driver of long-term stock returns," *Journal of Marketing Research*, **44** (1), 57–72.

Sorescu, A., V. Shankar and T. Kushwaha (2007), "New product preannouncements and shareholder value: don't make promises you can't keep," *Journal of Marketing Research*, **44** (2), 468–89.

Srinivasan, Raji, Gary Lilien and Shrihari Sridhar (2011), "Should firms spend more on research and development and advertising during recessions?" *Journal of Marketing*, **75** (3), 49–65.

Srinivasan, Shuba and Dominique M. Hanssens (2009), "Marketing and firm value: metrics, methods, findings, and future directions," *Journal of Marketing Research*, **46** (3), 293–312.

Srinivasan, Shuba, Koen Pauwels, Jorge Silva-Risso and Dominique M. Hanssens (2009), "Product innovations, advertising, and stock returns," *Journal of Marketing*, **73**, 24–43.

Srivastava, Rajendra K., Tasadduq A. Shervani and Liam Fahey (1998), "Market-based assets and shareholder value: a framework for analysis," *Journal of Marketing*, **62** (January), 2–18.

Srivastava, Rajendra K., Tasadduq A. Shervani and Liam Fahey (1999), "Marketing, business processes, and shareholder value: an organizationally embedded view of marketing activities and the discipline of marketing," *Journal of Marketing*, **63** (October), 168–79.

Stam, Erik and Karl Wennberg (2009), "The roles of R&D in new firm growth," *Small Business Economics*, **33** (1), 77–89.

Swaminathan, Vanitha and Christine Moorman (2009), "Marketing alliances, firm networks, and firm value creation," *Journal of Marketing*, **73** (5), 52–69.

Tellis, Gerard J., Jaideep C. Prabhu and Rajesh K. Chandy (2009), "Radical innovation across nations: the preeminence of corporate culture," *Journal of Marketing*, **73** (1), 3–23.

Thirumalai, Sriram and Kingshuk Sinha (2011), "Product recalls in the medical device industry: an empirical exploration of the sources and financial consequences," *Management Science*, **57** (2), 376–92.

Tipton, Martha Myslinski, Sundar Bharadwaj and Diana Robertson (2009), "Regulatory exposure of deceptive marketing and its impact on firm value," *Journal of Marketing*, **73** (6), 227–43.

Tobin, James (1969), "A general equilibrium approach to monetary theory," *Journal of Money, Credit and Banking*, **1** (1), 15–29.

Tuli, Kapil and Sundar Bharadwaj (2009), "Customer satisfaction and stock returns risk," *Journal of Marketing*, **73** (6), 184–97.

Wiles, Michael, Shailendra Jain, Saurabh Mishra and Charles Lindsey (2010), "Stock market response to regulatory reports of deceptive advertising: the moderating effect of omission bias and firm reputation," *Marketing Science*, **29** (5), 828–45.

Yang, C.H. and J.R. Chen (2003), "Patent and productivity: evidence from the Taiwan manufacturing firm," *Taiwan Economic Review*, **30** (4), 28–48.

Zott, Christophe and Raphael Amit (2008), "The fit between product market strategy and business model: implications for firm performance," *Strategic Management Journal*, **29**, 1–16.

Paper	Focus	Firm value metric	Data	Key findings	Key limitations
Branding strategy					
Morgan and Rego (2009)	Brand portfolio strategy	Tobin's Q; cash flow	American Customer Satisfaction Index; 72 large publicly traded firms	(1) Market share is a useful metric for assessing marketing effectiveness (2) Customer loyalty linked to low level of intraportfolio competition and strong quality perceptions	(1) Data contains only large, publicly traded companies; (2) Lack of control for industry differences
Rego et al. (2009)	Consumer-based brand equity	Credit ratings; total equity risk	252 firms from EquiTrend, COMPUSTAT	(1) Consumer-based brand equity (CBBE) associated with firm risk; (2) CBBE predicts unsystematic risk and protects from downside systematic risk; (3) make brand management part of a firm's mgmt. strategy during economic uncertainty	(1) None given
Mizik and Jacobson (2009)	Valuing branded businesses	Market capitalization; enterprise value; operating income; sales	Y&R BAV database, COMPUSTAT	(1) Valuation accuracy can be improved by incorporating brand asset information; (2) brand metrics are significant and improve model fit more than just accounting variables	(1) Could add other brand metrics to the model; (2) look at other intangible assets such as mgmt. quality, satisfaction, innovation strategy, product pipeline

Paper	Focus	Firm value metric	Data	Key findings	Key limitations
Branding strategy					
Bharadwaj et al. (2011)	Brand quality and shareholder wealth	Stock returns, systematic risk and idiosyncratic risk	132 firms from multiple industries over 2000–2005; used "mono-branded" firms	(1) Brand quality enhances shareholder wealth; (2) unanticipated changes in brand quality can also erode shareholder wealth	(1) Does not control for other brand-related metrics such as brand esteem and brand equity; (2) short time frame
Shankar et al. (2008)	Relationship among advertising, brand equity and shareholder value	Abnormal returns	Insurance industry	Brand equity is negatively related to volatility in shareholder value. Brand equity mediates the effect of advertising on shareholder value	Single firm and industry
Product/new product/innovation strategy					
Chakravarty and Grewal (2011)	R&D and marketing – stock market reaction	Bayesian VAR model – DVs are unanticipated R&D and marketing budgets	141 high-tech firms over 1995–2009	(1) Firms display moderate myopic reactions, in the form of unanticipated decreases in R&D budgets but increased budgets for marketing functions; (2) as firm size or industry concentration decreases, there is a tendency to manage myopically in response to past stock returns and volatility increases	(1) Need to account for long-term effects on firm value; (2) limited industry analysis
Chan et al. (2001)	The stock market valuation of R&D expenditures	CTAR	COMPUSTAT	(1) Companies with high R&D to equity market value earn large excess returns; (2) R&D intensity is positively associated with return volatility	None given

Study	Focus	Measure	Data	Findings	Limitations/future research
Chaney et al. (1991)	The impact of new product introductions on the market value of firms	ST CARs	WSJ announcements	(1) The aggregate impact of a new product introduction on the market value was 0.75% over a 3-day period	(1) Did not incorporate unanticipated trading volume around the event date; (2) results would be strengthened by using time series data
Cockburn and Griliches (1988)	Industry effects and appropriability measures in the stock market's valuation of R&D and patents	Market value	NBER patent database	(1) Find evidence for an interaction between industry level measures of the effectiveness of patents and the market's valuation of a firm's past R&D, patenting performance and current R&D	(1) High within industry variance leading to unstable estimates; (2) need to incorporate if different appropriability environments imply different depreciation rates for R&D investment
Fang et al. (2011)	Customer and asset innovation configuration strategies on firm performance	Stock prices and idiosyncratic risk	Firms in high-tech industries; survey of senior managers; COMPUSTAT	(1) Performance is highest when firms employ configurations using deep customer and broad innovation assets or deep innovation and broad customer assets; (2) performance decreases in deep–deep and broad–broad asset configurations	(1) Managers reports may include bias; (2) used patent data to calculate measures of innovation asset depth and breadth
Heeley and Jacobson (2008)	Recency of technological inputs and financial performance	Stock returns	USPTO data	(1) Higher recency leads to higher stock returns; (2) firms operating at the technological input frontier have market returns significantly below the mean	(1) Future research questions include: what factors allow a firm to leverage inventions at the right time? Does the decision to use knowledge inputs of different recency depend on firm characteristics?

Paper	Focus	Firm value metric	Data	Key findings	Key limitations
Product/new product/innovation strategy					
Hendricks and Singhal (1997)	Delays in new product introductions and the market value of firms	ST CARs	Archival searches in news databases	(1) Delay announcements decrease the market value of the firm by 5.25%; (2) significant penalties for not introducing new products on time	(1) Would be beneficial to also look at the impact on market share, sales growth and profitability; (2) useful to consider the impact on competitors
Krasnikov et al. (2009)	The financial impact of trademarks	Cash flow, Tobin's Q, ROA, stock returns	108 firms – a mixture of manufacturing and service firms	(1) The total number of trademarks available to a firm increases their cash firm value metrics	(1) Restricted to larger firms; (2) need to complement trademark information with consumer attitudes
Lee and Chen (2009)	The immediate impact of new product introductions on stock price: the role of firm resources and size	ST CARs	WSJ announcements	(1) Firm resources with emphases on R&D are imperative to materialize new product concepts	None given
Pakes (1985)	Patents, R&D and the stock market rate of return	Annual stock returns	USPTO data	(1) Interfirm differences in patent applications seem to follow interfirm differences in the market value of a firm's research output quite closely; (2) intertemporal differences in a firm's patent applications are largely a result of its propensity to patent	None given

432

Author (Year)	Topic / Variables	Measures	Data source	Findings	Limitations
Rao and Bharadwaj (2008)	Innovation and firm value	ST CARs	FDA	(1) New ventures with external legitimacy through alliances with established firms gain more from their new products	(1) Four types of internal legitimizing actions may not be exhaustive; (2) assume that all alliances provide external legitimacy; (3) do not study returns from established firms
Sood and Tellis (2009)	Total stock market returns to innovation	ST CARs	Archival searches in news databases	(1) Total market returns to an innovation project are more than 13 times returns from an average innovation event	(1) Limited set of industries; (2) potential selection bias
Sorescu and Spanjol (2008)	Innovation's effect on firm value and risk	BHARs, Tobin's Q	Product scan	(1) Breakthrough innovation is associated with increases in both normal profits and economic rents; (2) breakthrough innovation is associated with increases in the risk of the innovating firm, and is offset by above-normal stock returns	(1) Further research can incorporate the link between the propensity to innovate and various governance variables
Srinivasan et. al. (2009)	Product innovations, advertising, and stock returns	Weekly stock returns	J.D. Power and Associates	(1) Adding these marketing actions to the established finance benchmark model greatly improves the explained variance in stock returns	(1) Industry specific; (2) did not consider specific launch strategies or innovation process measures; (3) censored out data that did not make it to the market
Tellis et al. (2009)	Radical innovation across nations, corporate culture, firm value	Market-to-book ratio	Archival searches	(1) Corporate culture is the strongest drive of radical innovation across nations; (2) the commercialization of radical innovations translates into a firm's financial performance	(1) Do not explore whether radical innovation leads to national wealth in addition to firm value; (2) need to join consumer innovativeness and firm innovation; (3) do not study subsidiaries of multinational firms

Paper	Focus	Firm value metric	Data	Key findings	Key limitations
Advertising strategy					
Karniouchina et al. (2009)	Television advertising, persuasive communications and market reaction	Event study	Stock recommendations from TV show	(1) Traditional advertising variables (length, recency–primacy effects, information clutter and source credibility) influence the market	(1) Only evaluates one show; (2) beneficial to examine a continuum of financial programming
Joshi and Hanssens (2009)	Movie advertising and stock market valuation	Event study–stock price	300 movies released by large studios between 1995 and 1998	(1) Movies with above average pre-launch advertising have lower post-launch stock returns than films with below-average advertising; (2) movies that are hits may result in a lowering of stock price if they had high media support	(1) Opportunity to analyze the effect of other variables such as limited release, movie piracy and lead actor endorsement; (2) look at the impact of sequels, DVDs and video games sales
Joshi and Hanssens (2010)	Advertising spending and firm value	VAR model with advertising, sales revenue, profit, R&D, stock return	15 years of monthly data for PC industry and sporting goods industry	(1) Advertising spending has a positive, long-term impact on own firms' market capitalization and may have a negative impact on the valuation of a competitor	(1) Two industries used; (2) need to look at the differential impact of advertising media on market valuation; (3) advertising data did not breakout spending on product advertising vs brand image advertising
Osinga et al. (2011)	Advertising with limited sales response	Stock returns, systematic risk and idiosyncratic risk	Eight of the largest US drug manufacturers; monthly data for 1993–2000	(1) Direct to consumer advertising lead to higher stock returns and lower systematic risk; (2) direct to physician marketing has modest positive effects on stock returns	(1) Used aggregate data; (2) need to see how investors form expectations; (3) did not take into account the rise of web trading

Srinivasan et al. (2011)	Advertising and R&D spending during recessions	Profits; stock market returns	10000 firms from 1969 to 2008	(1) The majority of B2C firms are underspending on R&D while overspending on advertising; (2) the majority of B2B firms are spending the right amount on advertising	(1) Did not distinguish between service firms with contractual relationships; (2) do not consider the role of firms' global economic activity; (3) could include firm survival metric
Customer satisfaction management					
Dotson and Allenby (2010)	Customer and employee satisfaction on firm financial performance	Hierarchical Bayesian model of simultaneous supply and demand	Retail banking; 13 months of data for 898 retail locations; customer survey for satisfaction	Significant relationship between customer and employee satisfaction and firm technology	(1) Did not account for the existence of competitive effects; (2) assumed strict normality in the model; (3) modeled on optimal behavior, not necessarily actual behavior
Fornell et al. (2009)	Customer satisfaction and stock returns	All	Rejoinder	(1) The failure to reject the null hypotheses by Jacobson and Mizik (2009) is probably due to a lack of statistical power; (2) above-market returns persist and are both economically and statistically significant	NA
Grewal et al. (2010)	Customer satisfaction heterogeneity and shareholder value	Shareholder value	US airlines industry (1997–2005)	(1) Service quality and advertising affect the heterogeneity in customer satisfaction; (2) shareholder value is shaped by the interplay of satisfaction level and heterogeneity	(1) Single industry; (2) missing data on the actual service experience

Paper	Focus	Firm value metric	Data	Key findings	Key limitations
Customer satisfaction management					
Ittner et al. (2009)	Customer satisfaction and stock market returns	Event study for both short-term and long-term results	ACSI scores; 1450 firm-year observations (substantially larger than other samples)	(1) Find no evidence that ACSI predicts long-run returns; (2) customer satisfaction information is value relevant, but they are also consistent with Jacobson and Mizik's conclusion	(1) None given but suggests that researchers provide long-term market returns for stock market returns rather than just short-term returns
Luo et al. (2010)	Customer satisfaction, analyst recommendations and firm value	Abnormal return, systematic risk and idiosyncratic risk	Large-scale longitudinal data set; ACSI, COMPUSTAT	(1) Positive changes in customer satisfaction improve analyst recommendations; (2) they mediate satisfaction changes on firm metrics	(1) Further examine marketing's direct impact on firm value and its indirect impact through financial analysts and their recommendations
Tuli and Bharadwaj (2009)	Customer satisfaction and risk of stock returns	Systematic and idiosyncratic risk	Panel data sample of publicly traded US firms and American Satisfaction Index	(1) Satisfaction provides valuable information to financial markets (2) Firms should disclose their customer satisfaction scores	(1) SIC codes may not include firms that are direct competitors
Negative marketing					
Chen et al. (2009)	Product-recall strategy and financial value	Event study	Consumer Product Safety Commission recalls; 12-year time period 1996–2007	(1) Proactive strategies have a more negative effect on firm value than passive strategies	(1) Beneficial to have a more comprehensive study of recall strategies; (2) useful to look at long-term effects;(3) did not include the role of news media

Author (Year)	Topic	Method	Data/Context	Findings	Limitations/Future research
Luo (2009)	Negative word of mouth on cash flows and stock prices	Use a VAR model – negative word of mouth, cash flow, stock return, and stock volatility	NWOM data from airline industry (USDT); covers 84 months from nine airlines	(1) Takes a number of months before the stock price impact of NWOM reaches the peak point; (2) takes several months after the peak before the stock price impact of NWOM dies out completely	(1) None explicitly given – future areas of research include: look at NWOM's asymmetric effects in line with prospect theory
Thirumalai and Sinha (2011)	Product recalls and financial consequences	Event study	Medical device industry over a four year period (2002–2005); FDA recalls	(1) At an aggregate level, the market penalties for medical device recalls are not significant – the costs of poor service quality are not severe; (2) firms with an R&D focus have a higher likelihood of device recalls; (3) learning effects exist	(1) Need to look at the long-term impact of recalls; (2) did not study the mechanisms by which firms learn; (3) understanding the role of spillover effects would be beneficial
Tipton et al. (2009)	Regulatory exposure of deceptive marketing and firm value	Event study	In-depth interviews with practitioners; FDA warning letters	(1) Incidents are associated with significant abnormal returns of 1%; (2) event characteristics are more significant than firm and brand characteristics	(1) Beneficial to include competitor effects; (2) did not account for the effect on each stakeholders; (3) did not use alternative risk metrics
Wiles et al. (2010)	Omission bias and firm reputation as moderating factors for stock market response to deceptive advertising	Event study for both short-term and long-term results	Pharmaceutical industry; DDMAC warning letters of FDA ad violations	(1) Find an average abnormal return of −0.91%; (2) related to an omission bias – investors penalize commission violations more than omission violations	(1) One industry limitation; (2) need to examine potential welfare implications; (3) MBA students were used instead of actual investors

Paper	Focus	Firm value metric	Data	Key findings	Key limitations
Mergers and alliances					
Henock and Sun (2010)	Investor inattention and merger announcements – market reaction	Event study	Stock swaps between 1994 and 1996 using EDGAR; sample comes from SDC database	(1) Inattention affects information processing even with merger announcements; (2) find evidence that investors are less attentive to Friday announcements	(1) None given
Oxley et al. (2009)	Interfirm alliances and the stock market valuation of rivals	Event study	Alliance announcements in the telecommunications and electronic industries during 1996–2004	(1) Find evidence consistent with competition attenuation in some alliances	(1) Narrow set of industries used; (2) gap exists to look at rivals impact form alliances and mergers
Swaminathan and Moorman (2009)	Alliances and firm networks	Event study – abnormal stock returns	230 alliance announcements in the software industry	(1) Marketing alliances create value; (2) network efficiency, network density and alliance capability have a positive effect; (3) network reputation and network centrality have no effect	(1) Did not examine all the structural, relational and legal factors that might influence how alliances operate; (2) did not look at marketing alliance type

Other topics				
Kumar and Shah (2009)	Linking customer equity (CE) to market capitalization (MC)	CLV, contribution margin	Two field experiments with two firms	(1) CE framework can predict the MC of a firm; (2) CE focused strategies increase the stock price and beat expectations	(1) Need to see if stock price gains are sustained when factoring in competitive actions and reactions; (2) results may not hold for long time horizons and for all industries
Luo and Bhattacharya (2009)	CSR and firm-idiosyncratic risk	Idiosyncratic risk	COMPUSTAT, Fortune's Mac – 541 large companies	(1) Higher CSP lowers firm-idiosyncratic risk; (2) simultaneously pursuing CSP, advertising and R&D is harmful	(1) Need to model the heterogeneous, differential effects of CSP and the trade-offs among various strategic assets

25 Productivity of marketing strategy
Brian T. Ratchford

PRODUCTIVITY OF MARKETING STRATEGY

I shall begin by defining the domain of this review. In general, productivity is a ratio of inputs to outputs, and marketing strategy refers to basic decisions about segmentation, targeting, positioning, marketing mix and expenditures on these variables.[1] Thus the domain of this review is research related to the ability of resources expended on implementing marketing strategies to affect some measure of output. The focal organization might be engaged in manufacturing, retailing, services or any other line of endeavor.

The topic of marketing productivity was prominent in the 1950s and 1960s, when a literature centered on minimizing distribution costs developed (Sheth and Sisodia 2002). While research on retail productivity and sales force productivity continued after 1970, little attention was paid to the productivity of the overall marketing function between 1970 and the 1990s, when the need to pay more attention to the financial payoffs of marketing activities became apparent (Sheth and Sisodia 2002). Since that time an extensive literature on marketing productivity has emerged. This literature can be divided into three general topics: (1) conceptual approaches to productivity measurement, that is, what should be measured; (2) techniques for measuring productivity, that is, how to measure it; and (3) applications of the conceptual approaches to productivity and the resulting findings. This review will cover these literatures in turn.

CONCEPTUAL APPROACHES

A considerable literature postulates that marketing influences financial returns through a sequence of steps similar to that outlined in Figure 25.1. Resource inputs form the denominator of a productivity measure. These might be expenditures on advertising and other marketing efforts, number of salespeople, investments in product development and so on, depending on the particular problem being studied. The ratio of financial performance to resource inputs would be a measure of return on marketing investments. However, while productivity might be measured as financial returns relative to marketing inputs, this is not very diagnostic. Thus, again depending on the situation, productivity might be measured at each stage of the process, for example customer impact/resource inputs, customer equity/customer impact, market outcomes/customer equity, financial return/market outcomes. Customer impact in the value chain would be measured by variables such as awareness, attitudes, purchasing and satisfaction. Customer equity is the total of discounted lifetime values summed over all of the firm's current and potential customers (Rust et al. 2004a). Market outcomes would be measured by variables such as market share, share of wallet and so on.

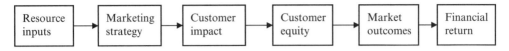

Figure 25.1   Value chain

Conceptual versions of the framework in Figure 25.1 are presented in Morgan et al. (2002), Rust et al. (2004), and Heskett et al. (1994).[2] Many empirical studies attempt to capture the financial return on marketing by employing some or all of the above links (see Srinivasan and Hanssens 2009 for a review).[3] Some of the studies of financial returns that also incorporate productivity measures for one or more of the above links are Kamakura et al. (2002); Mittal et al. (2005); Narasimhan et al. (2006); Luo and Donthu (2006); Keh et al. (2006).

Rust et al. (2004) expand the chain in Figure 25.1 into two rows, one for marketing actions, the other for their impact on the firm, and emphasize feedback from financial impact to strategy and actions (deployment of resources). The authors go on to discuss measures that could be used to evaluate productivity at each stage in the chain, and review existing research on the various stages. Their paper contains a detailed list of topics for further research.

Heskett et al. (1994) construct a chain linking strategy to profitability for services. They emphasize employee satisfaction, productivity and retention in addition to customer satisfaction. Customer satisfaction leads to loyalty and profits. They develop an extensive list of questions that should be asked in constructing an audit of the service–profit chain.

Based on the resource-based view of the firm, Morgan et al. (2002) present a conceptual framework that expands on the input box in Figure 25.1 to include a flow from resources to capabilities to positional advantages that lead to consumer perceptions and the remaining boxes in Figure 25.1. Consistent with this, Narasimhan et al. (2006) and Dutta et al. (2005) argue that the capabilities are the source of productivity differences between firms. These are not measured directly but inferred from relating outputs to the resources used as inputs.

Morgan et al. (2002) outline the factors that would be involved in developing a system for marketing performance assessment, which the authors envision as an integrated version of traditional productivity measurement and the traditional marketing audit. The authors also make a distinction between efficiency and effectiveness. They define the role of traditional productivity measurement as measuring efficiency – the ratio of inputs to outputs. Conversely they define effectiveness as measuring factors associated with the broad selection and performance of marketing strategy, such as assessing the consistency of marketing strategy with environmental opportunities and threats, assessing the interactions between marketing and the rest of the organization, and evaluating procedures used to obtain marketing information. The authors present a detailed list of the factors that should be considered in a marketing performance assessment, but not much in the way of concrete guidance about actual measures of efficiency and effectiveness. In particular, exactly how they define effectiveness is unclear.

Although it is not clear that their definitions are consistent with Morgan et al. (2002), definitions of efficiency and effectiveness are also provided by Sheth and Sisodia (2002).

They define effectiveness as the right allocation of resources, while efficiency is producing this allocation with the minimum feasible amount of resources. For example, spending too much on advertising, and not enough on call center staffing, would be ineffective. Producing advertisements that fall short of having maximum sales impact would be inefficient. Sheth and Sisodia (2002) argue that these two dimensions of productivity are multiplicative. They also define the productivity of marketing as the quantifiable value added by the marketing function relative to its costs. The authors contend that marketing efficiency might be improved by adopting successful practices from manufacturing and accounting, such as cycle time reduction, adopting a process orientation of developing ways to successfully deal with customers, improving the accounting for marketing costs, and developing better standards for measuring marketing performance. On the other hand, effectiveness might be improved by leveraging database technology to deliver better value, making information systems available to front-line personnel, and focusing on hiring and retaining the right employees.

Sheth and Sisodia (2002) may have had the economics literature in mind when they defined effectiveness and efficiency as multiplicative dimensions of productivity. Related concepts in the economics literature are allocative and technical efficiency (e.g. Fare et al. 1994). Allocative efficiency refers to choosing the optimal combination of inputs, for example choosing the combination that equates marginal returns per dollar spent across inputs. This appears to be similar to Sheth and Sisodia's concept of effectiveness. Technical efficiency refers to maximizing the quantity produced with the chosen quantities of inputs, and therefore seems similar to Sheth and Sisodia's concept of efficiency. Because a technical efficiency measure eliminates the confounding effect of differences in input and output prices, it is generally superior to return on investment for making efficiency comparisons between firms or other units (bank branches, stores, sales territories). Possibly because data on input prices are hard to obtain, studies of productivity in marketing generally concentrate on technical efficiency, and do not measure allocative efficiency.

Although different studies offer differing views of the concepts relating to productivity, we can summarize the concepts as follows. Productivity refers to the extent of output for a given level of input. To maximize productivity means to maximize the output for a given input. Efficiency is a measure of the extent of input for a given level of output. A firm is most efficient in obtaining a desired outcome (e.g. sales level, market share) if it expends the minimal level of inputs. While efficiency is doing things right, effectiveness is doing the right things. In the context of marketing strategy, efficiency is achieving the marketing goals with the least use of resources, whereas effectiveness is pursuing and realizing the most appropriate goals. Marketing return on investment (MROI) is a financial measure of net profits achieved as a ratio of marketing expenditures. The key concepts and differences among these terms are summarized in Table 25.1.

In order to be informative about performance, productivity must be measured relative to something. While it might be useful to study changes in productivity over time, relative productivity is usually measured through comparisons with other firms in the same industry, other units such as retail outlets of the same firm, or other sales territories. Again, the choice of a benchmark against which to measure productivity depends on the problem at hand. In the next section I outline two commonly used approaches to measuring productivity, and discuss their strengths and limitations.

Table 25.1   Summary of concepts related to productivity

Concept	Definition	Examples	References
Productivity	Output/input	Ratio of communication outputs to inputs	Luo and Donthu (2006)
Efficiency/ technical efficiency	Input/output	Comparing efficiency of branch banks in using marketing resources	Kamakura et al. (1996), Kamakura et al. (2002)
Maximum productivity	Maximum (output/input)	Identifying most productive branch banks	Kamakura et al. (1996), Kamakura et al. (2002)
Maximum efficiency	Minimum (input/output)	Identifying most efficient retail outlets in a chain	Grewal et al. (1999)
Effectiveness	Choosing the best combination of outputs and/or inputs	Allocating funds between advertising and call centers so output is maximized	Sheth and Sisodia (2002)
Allocative efficiency	Optimal combination of inputs given their prices	Investing in technology as labor costs rise	Fare et al. (1994)
ROI	Profit/assets	Comparisons of profitability of branch banks	Kamakura et al. (2002)
Marketing ROI	Profit/marketing expenditure	Comparison of marketing performance of different subsidiaries	Grewal et al. (2009)

MEASURING PRODUCTIVITY

Two commonly used approaches to measuring the relative productivity of a decision-making unit (DMU) are data envelopment analysis (DEA) and stochastic frontier analysis (SFA). DEA is a linear programming procedure for evaluating the ratio of outputs to inputs of a DMU (firm, outlet, sales territory) relative to other units, while SFA is a regression procedure for evaluating the output of a DMU relative to a frontier describing the maximum attainable output for a given set of inputs. I will present a description of the two approaches, and discuss their strengths and limitations (a similar discussion is presented in Dutta et al. 2004). The key features and differences between the two approaches are highlighted in Table 25.2.

DEA

DEA was originally proposed by Charnes et al. (1978), and has been extended in many different directions since then (see, e.g., Coelli 2008). In this model, the frontier describing maximum output for a given set of inputs is assumed to be piecewise linear. The objective is to determine how close a given DMU's ratio of outputs to inputs is to the frontier. Let y_{jk} be output j of DMU k, and x_{ik} be input i of DMU k. Then the objective is to choose a set of weights w_j and v_i that maximize the weighted sum of outputs relative to inputs subject to the constraint that the maximum ratio of outputs to inputs across all k DMU = 1.

Table 25.2   Summary comparison of DEA and SFA techniques

Attribute	DEA	SFA
Analytical approach	Linear programming	Regression analysis
Productivity measure	Outputs/inputs relative to maximum outputs/inputs	Distance of inefficiency error from efficiency frontier
Functional form	Piecewise linear	Must be specified – often double log or translog
Error structure	None (except for recent extensions)	Random error and one-sided inefficiency error
Flexibility	Non-parametric	Requires specification of functional relation between outputs and inputs and shape of error term
Outputs	Handles multiple outputs	One output (except for recent extensions)
Major drawbacks	Sensitivity to outliers	Need to specify functional forms

$$\max \frac{\sum_j w_j y_{j0}}{\sum_i v_i x_{i0}} \tag{25.1}$$

$$\text{subject to } \frac{\sum_j w_j y_{jk}}{\sum_i v_i x_{ik}} \leq 1 \text{ for all DMU } k$$

$$w_j, v_i \geq 0$$

In effect, the weights are chosen to make the focal DMU the as productive as possible subject to a normalization constraint that makes the maximum productivity = 1. In this formulation the weights are identified only up to multiplication by a constant. This problem can be alleviated by imposing the constraint $\sum_i v_i x_{i0} = 1$, and converting the problem in Equation (25.1) into a linear programming problem:

$$\max \sum_j w_j y_{j0} - \varnothing_0$$

subject to the constraints:

$$\sum_i v_i x_{i0} = 1$$

$$\sum_j w_j y_{j0} - \varnothing_0 \leq \sum_i v_i x_{ik} \text{ for all DMU } k$$

$$w_j, v_i \geq 0$$

In practice the dual to this program is usually solved:

$$\min T_0$$

Table 25.3   Hypothetical DEA example

Hotel	1	2	3	4	5	6
Outputs						
Room	80	85	90	50	70	60
Food	20	20	22	8	23	39
Inputs						
Capital	20	15	25	12	20	18
Labor	30	35	30	18	25	18
Efficiency	0.959	1.000	1.000	1.000	0.933	1.000
L1	0.000	0.000	0.000	0.000	0.000	0.000
L2	0.395	1.000	0.000	0.000	0.189	0.000
L3	0.337	0.000	1.000	0.000	0.176	0.000
L4	0.000	0.000	0.000	1.000	0.000	1.000
L5	0.000	0.000	0.000	0.000	0.000	0.000
L6	0.267	0.000	0.000	0.000	0.635	0.000
Surplus cap.	0.000	0.000	0.000	0.000	0.000	0.000
Surplus lab.	0.000	0.000	0.000	0.000	0.000	0.000
Surplus room	0.000	0.000	0.000	0.000	0.000	0.000
Surplus food	5.757	0.000	0.000	0.000	9.418	0.000

subject to the constraints:

$$y_{j0} \leq \sum_{k} \lambda_{k} y_{jk} \text{ for all outputs } j$$

$$T_{0} x_{i0} \geq \sum_{k} \lambda_{k} x_{ik} \text{ for all inputs } i$$

$$\lambda_{k} \geq 0 \text{ for all } k$$

$$\sum_{k} \lambda_{k} = 1$$

where T_0 is the measure of the DMU's technical efficiency relative to the frontier. If the focal DMU is efficient, it occupies an extreme point on the frontier, and $T_0 = 1$. Otherwise the frontier is defined by a linear combination of the best DMU given the weights assigned to the focal DMU and T_0 is measured relative to this linear combination. In this case T_0 will vary between 0 and 1, depending on how efficient it is. The model described here is a basic DEA model. If there are inputs that are fixed or uncontrollable by the DMU, additional constraints for each of these inputs are introduced (Dutta et al. 2004, p. 53).

An example of DEA calculations is presented in Table 25.3. The objective is to compare the efficiency of six hotels in converting two inputs, capital and labor, into two outputs, room revenue per room and food revenue per room. The dual linear program listed above is solved six times, once for each hotel. The results in Table 25.3 indicate that four of the six hotels are efficient: no other combination of hotels can produce more of the two outputs with the same amount of inputs. Hotel 1 has an efficiency ratio of 0.959: it produces only 0.959 of what a combination of Hotels 2, 3 and 6 could produce with the same inputs. Similarly Hotel 5 is inefficient relative to a combination of Hotels 2, 3 and 6. Since the combination of L2, L3 and L6 would produce 25.757 units of food output, this combination would still produce 5.757 units of food more than Hotel 1 would even if Hotel 1's inputs were reduced enough to make it efficient. This produces the value of the surplus variable for food for Hotel 1. If these extra 5.757 units were worth something, it would be hard to say that Hotel 1 is efficient even if its inputs were reduced enough to put it on the frontier. Thus values of surplus variables (or slack variables if constraints are less than or equal) provide important diagnostic information in DEA.

The DEA model described above measures technical efficiency, and does not consider allocative efficiency – whether the cost-minimizing mix of inputs was chosen given their prices. To calculate allocative efficiency, start with the following cost minimizing DEA (e.g. Coelli 2008):

$$\min \sum_i c_i x_i^*$$

subject to the constraints:

$$y_{j0} \leq \sum \lambda_k y_{jk} \text{ for all outputs } j$$

$$x_i^* \leq \sum \lambda_k x_{ik} \text{ for all inputs } i$$

$$\lambda_k \geq 0 \text{ for all } k$$

$$\sum_k \lambda_k = 1$$

where c_i is the price of input i, and x_i^* is the cost minimizing quantity of input i, which is calculated by the linear program. Then cost efficiency (CE) is the ratio of minimum cost to observed cost: $CE = \sum_i c_i x_i^* / \sum_i c_i x_i$. Allocative efficiency is then the ratio of cost efficiency to technical efficiency: $AE = CE/TE$.

A key advantage of the DEA model is that it is non-parametric, and allows for a flexible frontier. A disadvantage of the basic DEA model described above is that it does not allow for measurement errors or the effects of unobservable variables. However, there has been work to develop a statistical foundation for DEA, for example Banker (1993), Gstach (1998). Recently Banker and Natarajan (2008) developed a model in which a regression of the log of the DEA technical efficiency estimate on contextual variables yields a consistent estimate of the impact of the contextual variables on productivity. Banker et al. (2010) develop statistical tests for determining whether DEA estimates of efficiency differ between two groups of decision-making units.

SFA

While DEA does not impose parametric restrictions on the relation between inputs and outputs, SFA assumes a parametric relationship between inputs and outputs that is similar to a standard regression, such as:

$$\text{In } y_k = f(x_k) + e_k$$

where y_k is output of DMU k, x_k is a vector of inputs of DMU k, and e_k is a random error term. The two common forms of the function f are the Cobb–Douglas form, which is log-linear, or the translog form, which adds squares and cross products of the log x terms to the Cobb–Douglas function.

The point of departure of SFA from the standard regression is that the error term e_k includes two components, random error ε_k, and an inefficiency error that has its minimum value at zero, η_k.

$$e_k = \varepsilon_k - \eta_k$$

where $\varepsilon_k \sim N(0, \sigma_\varepsilon^2)$ and $\eta_k \geq 0$. The inefficiency error, η_k, is often assumed to have a truncated normal distribution (the half of the distribution ranging from 0 to ∞), or an exponential distribution. The model parameters, including the two error components, can be estimated by maximum likelihood, and η_k can be estimated for each DMU from knowledge of the error term for k and the size of the two error components (see, e.g., Greene 2008, pp. 538–42). While a drawback of the model described above is that it can accommodate only one output, an extension of the frontier regression model to estimating a distance function with multiple outputs has recently been developed (Atkinson et al. 2003). An excellent summary of procedures for SFA is provided by Cornwell and Schmidt (2008). As discussed in Cornwell and Schmidt (2008), the restrictive functional form of the inefficiency error, η_k, can be relaxed if panel data are available.

Comparison of DEA and SFA

The DEA model has been very widely applied, and admits of extensions to fixed and qualitative inputs. Its major advantage is its flexible piecewise linear structure, and its major disadvantage is a corresponding sensitivity to outliers. While extensions of DEA that allow for stochastic errors might remedy this problem, these have not been widely used in the marketing literature. While the SFA approach requires assumptions about the shape of the efficiency frontier, flexible functional forms such as translog mitigate this drawback. Moreover, recently developed procedures (Atkinson et al. 2003) allow the use of SFA in estimating frontiers with multiple outputs. Perhaps the most restrictive part of the SFA model is a need to make assumptions about the shape of the inefficiency error; however, attempts to add a stochastic structure to DEA also require similar restrictions. As noted above, applications of SFA to panel data can limit the restrictiveness of assumptions about the shape of the inefficiency error (Cornwell and Schmidt 2008). In general, DEA has the advantage of flexibility at the expense of sensitivity to the effects of unobserved variables, while SFA has the advantage of addressing the possible impact of unobservable variables at the expense of a need to impose a parametric structure on the error terms in the SFA model. Recent extensions of both models attempt to address their limitations. Both models are easy to implement with standard software, and there is no clear advantage of one approach over the other.

MEASURING INPUTS AND OUTPUTS

Starting with the Resource input box in Figure 25.1, I shall discuss potential measures of the boxes in the figure that capture inputs and outputs (since marketing strategy provides the mechanism for transforming the inputs to outputs, it is not relevant to this discussion). In addition to outlining measurement methods and sources, I shall discuss measurement problems that may arise at each stage.

Resource Inputs

The exact measures of marketing resource inputs depend on the nature and scope of the problem being studied. Physical measures such as employees, selling space and inventories are sometimes employed, and in other cases expenditures on various marketing activities are used. An example would be expenditures on different types of advertising. When expenditures are used, care must be taken to assure that prices are comparable across data points. Otherwise estimated productivity changes will be confounded by price differences.

While measuring marketing inputs may seem straightforward, consumers also participate in the production process, and are rightly regarded as supplying an input to the process. As an extreme example, there are no sales unless some consumer buys the item. More common examples are in services, such as banks, where some consumers may be harder to serve because they lack skill; in retail businesses where some consumers may require more attention, or where some consumers may free-ride on the salesperson's time and buy elsewhere; and in many retail and service settings where waiting lines form and consumers may impose costs on others (see, e.g. Oi 1992). Differences in the mix of consumers across firms, retail outlets or sales territories can affect marketing productivity measures unless some correction is made. Approaches to this problem are provided in Kamakura et al. (1996), Xue and Harker (2002) and Xue et al. (2007). The latter two studies provide approaches to measuring customer efficiency empirically.

Customer Impact

According to Rust et al. (2004b), customer impact can be measured by awareness, associations, attitudes, attachment and experience, all of which are measured in standard tracking studies. Customer satisfaction has been linked to profits in a number of studies (e.g. Gruca and Rego 2005; Mittal et al. 2005; Gupta and Zeithaml 2006), and has been used as an output measure in studies of productivity (Kamakura et al. 2002; Mittal et al. 2005).

Customer Equity

Drèze and Bonfrer (2009) clarify the distinction between customer equity, which is the sum of lifetime values of current and future customers, and customer lifetime value (CLV), which is the discounted present value of profits from current customers. They show that maximizing customer equity is a more profitable objective because it implies decisions that give more weight to customer retention and less to customer acquisition than CLV. There are several different approaches to measuring customer equity, and Kumar and George (2007) present a detailed comparison of several different methods for determining customer equity, including Berger and Nasr (1998), Blattberg et al. (2001), Gupta and Lehmann (2003), Rust et al. (2004a), Venkatesan and Kumar (2004). An approach to measuring customer equity is also provided by Gupta et al. (2004). See also the review by Blattberg et al. (2009).[4]

Market Outcomes

Market outcomes refer to the marketplace aggregation of the individual customer impacts. Some commonly used measures of market outcomes are sales, market shares and sales growth. Rust et al. (2004b) stress the importance of measuring brand equity, the value of the brand defined as the incremental discounted cash flow resulting from brand associations.

Financial Performance

Srinivasan and Hanssens (2009) present a detailed discussion of the strengths and limitations of measures of financial performance that might be used in measuring the final box in Figure 25.1. These include both measures of returns and measures of risk. Alternative measures of returns are profits, firm valuation (stock price × number of shares), Tobin's Q (ratio of market value to replacement cost of assets) and stock returns. Measures of risk are cash flow volatility, systematic market volatility and idiosyncratic volatility (variability of returns that is not explained by changes in the average market portfolio). Although they do not focus on productivity, Srinivasan and Hanssens (2009) present an extensive review of the literature relating different marketing metrics to financial performance.

SUMMARY OF RESULTS OF STUDIES OF MARKETING PRODUCTIVITY

While many empirical studies have established links between the boxes in Figure 25.1, I shall focus on the subset that have studied the relative productivity of firms, or units within a firm such as stores, restaurant locations, sales territories and branch banks. The existing marketing literature on productivity, which is sparse compared to literatures in economics and operations, can be usefully divided between firm comparisons and comparisons of units within firms.

Studies of Relative Productivity of Firms

Using data from the American Customer Satisfaction Index (ACSI) over a six-year period, Mittal et al. (2005) studied the impact of satisfaction and efficiency on the Tobin's Q measure of financial performance. Efficiency is determined by a firm-level DEA with satisfaction as the output, and employees, advertising and cost of goods sold as inputs (the input measures were per dollar sold). Both revenue enhancement and efficiency were found to affect Tobin's Q.

Luo and Donthu (2006) studied the relative efficiency of a sample of firms in converting expenditures on four communication inputs (broadcast, print, outdoor and sales promotion) into three outputs (sales level, sales growth and corporate reputation). The authors compared 712 *Fortune 1000* firms over an eight-year period. To achieve their objective of measuring changes in the productivity of communication over time, the authors compute Malmquist indexes for each firm for each pair of time periods. Malmquist indexes are the geometric mean of two indexes of efficiency change from t to $t + 1$, and require solutions to four DEA analyses for each firm and pair of time periods. Using this methodology, the authors find evidence of increasing productivity of marketing communications over time. Regression relationships between the firm-level productivity changes and Tobin's Q indicated that there is an inverted-U relation between Tobin's Q and communication productivity. The year-to-year productivity changes reported in the paper tend to be on the order of 20 percent, which seems implausibly large.

Murthi et al. (1996) present an early marketing application of DEA, which employed the PIMS (Profit Impact of Market Strategy) data to measure the impact of efficiency on the relationship between market share and pioneering (pioneering advantage). The authors use ten input variables that measure marketing and other inputs, and two output variables, ROI (return on investment) and market share. They interpret the resulting efficiency indexes as managerial skill. Although the pioneers were found to be more efficient than early followers and late entrants, the authors did not find that efficiency moderated the effect of pioneering on market share.

Dutta et al. (2005) used stochastic frontier analysis to study the relative R&D capability of 64 firms. The authors define capabilities as the efficiency with which a firm converts inputs to outputs, which is inferred from the stochastic frontier analysis, and the authors explain how their model follows from the resource-based theory of the firm.

Also employing stochastic frontier analysis, Narasimhan et al. (2006) studied the relative efficiency of the 64 firms in absorbing know-how from outside. The authors define absorptive capacity as the efficiency with which a firm absorbs know-how from outside relative to what it could have absorbed with the same resources. The inputs in this study are R&D expenditure, marketing expenditure and innovation stock, and the dependent measure is technical know-how absorbed from outside, which is estimated from patent data. The authors find that absorptive capacity (efficiency at converting the inputs to know-how) is related to profitability.

In another application of stochastic frontier analysis, Sellers-Rubio and Mas-Ruiz (2009) compared the relative efficiency of 42 Spanish supermarket chains. Instead of allowing the inefficiency error to be purely random, the authors model the expected value of this error term as a function of inventory investment, wage per employee, age of the firm and a time trend. They find that all of these factors are associated with increased efficiency.

Studies of the Relative Productivity of Units within Firms

The literature on comparisons of marketing productivity might be divided into distinct application areas: comparisons of the marketing performance of multinational subsidiaries; comparisons of branch banks, and restaurants, which might apply more generally to providers of services; comparisons of retail outlets providing tangibles, including supermarkets; and comparisons of sales territories. I shall discuss research in each of these areas.

Multinational subsidiaries

Grewal et al. (2009) evaluate the relative marketing performance of 18 subsidiaries of a *Fortune 50* corporation that operate in different countries. They employ a two-stage version of the model portrayed in Figure 25.1, where the first stage evaluates the link between marketing inputs and marketing assets, and the second stage evaluates the link between marketing assets and overall subsidiary performance. At the first stage, inputs are marketing expenses and personnel deployed, and outputs are number of brand aware customers, number of retail outlets and number of industrial customers. These outputs are, in turn, used as inputs at the second stage, in which the outputs are sales, market share and profits. Controls for market competitiveness and regulation were employed at each stage. The authors ran DEA models at both stages and classified the 18 firms as efficient or inefficient at each stage based on the DEA results. The results indicated that nine of the 18 subsidiaries were efficient at both stages, and an evaluation of the DEA results for the subsidiaries that were inefficient at one or both stages led to insights into how to improve the inefficient subsidiaries.

Services

In one of the more complete attempts to model the stages between marketing inputs and marketing performance, Kamakura et al. (2002) implement a modified version of the service–profit chain (Heskett et al. 1994) discussed earlier. Kamakura et al. estimate two models, a strategic model aimed at capturing the most important drivers of profitability, and an operational model aimed at benchmarking the performance of individual units (branch banks in this case) to determine operational improvements that will help in attaining the strategic objectives. The strategic model has the following recursive structure:

Customer attribute perceptions = *f*(investments in inputs);
Behavioral intentions = *f*(attribute perceptions);
Customer retention = *f*(behavioral intentions, competition);
Profit = *g*(*f*(customer retention), *f*(resource investments)).

Estimates of the strategic model on consumer survey data indicated that the model outlined above is supported.

The operational model comprises two DEA models estimated across branches of a bank. The first model is an operational efficiency model comparing the relative ability of the branches to convert operational inputs (tellers, managers, employees, ATMs) into outputs (customers, transactions, proportion who would highly recommend the branch). The second model links the proportion of a branch's customers who would highly recommend the branch to share, retention and bank balances. A key finding is that branches that were efficient in both DEA models were also more profitable than those that were efficient at only one stage, or those that were not efficient at either stage. This paper provides an excellent case example of how an audit of the service performance of individual units might be implemented in practice.

Keh et al. (2006) also employed a two-stage DEA model to assess the relative efficiency of hotels in a chain. Stage 1 determined the allocative efficiency of each hotel's budget allocation to marketing, using ADEA, allocative DEA. Stage 2 determined the relative productivity of each hotel in producing output for a given marketing budget. One finding was that hotels that overspent on marketing relative to other inputs tended to have a more efficient output.

Donthu and Yoo (1998) compared the efficiency of 24 fast-food outlets using DEA. Inputs are store size, store manager experience, whether outlet is in a mall or not, and promotional expenditures. Outputs were sales and customer satisfaction. The authors showed that the DEA results were superior to those obtained from regressions, and that they were quite stable over a three-year period. Donthu et al. (2005) contains a similar study, and provides an extensive discussion of how DEA might be used in benchmarking. In both studies the authors stressed the sensitivity of the DEA results to outliers.

Kamakura et al. (1996) focused on the potential impact of unobservable factors on measured productivity; one of these unobservable factors is likely to be differences in the difficulty of serving customers of different units. Their approach to the problem was to extend the stochastic frontier model to accommodate multiple frontiers, which are modeled as latent classes. They apply this multiple frontier approach to longitudinal data on the performance of 188 branch banks, and identify five groups of banks with distinctive production functions. The authors contend that productivity comparisons within groups are more meaningful than employing one frontier in which all units are assumed to have the same production function.

Retailing

While there is a large literature on retail productivity, most of it is concerned with more macro issues such as productivity changes in the sector, comparing ownership types (company owned versus franchised), and isolating variables that affect productivity. Relatively few studies have been aimed at comparing the productivity of individual stores as a means of benchmarking performance and developing marketing strategies.

One of the studies that does focus on benchmarking is Grewal et al. (1999). This study presents an evaluation of the relative performance of 59 outlets of a retail chain. The authors employ three inputs, store operating expenses, square footage and inventory, and run one DEA model with aggregate sales as the output, and a second model with output for two categories separated. The authors also considered a model limited to specific geographic regions. The paper contains an extensive discussion of how the study results might be used in identifying best practices that can be emulated by inefficient units, and in establishing performance goals.

While the studies reviewed above tend to focus internally and to take output as a given, the study by Gauri et al. (2009) takes a more output-oriented approach. Using frequent shopper data from all stores in a chain, the authors perform a detailed analysis of factors affecting demand at the block group level to develop benchmark measures of expected demand at each store. Comparisons between the actual and expected output then become a measure of how well each store performs in its trade area. The authors discuss how their benchmarking approach can be used in a diagnostic manner to provide insights into evaluating the performance of a given store.

Vaz et al. (2010) present an analysis of the relative efficiency of 78 stores in a chain of hypermarkets and supermarkets. Inputs are selling area, number of items, inventories and losses due to spoilage (the authors explain why this is used as an input). The output is sales. The first stage of the analysis uses a conventional DEA to compare the efficiency of five individual departments across stores. A second-stage analysis applying a technique called Network DEA then considers the reallocation of the existing set of resources employed by a given department to other departments so that sales are maximized.

Sales territories
Horsky and Nelson (1996) used a procedure that is equivalent to DEA in relating a number of input variables that relate sales potential to sales, the output variable. The procedure was used to compare the efficiency of sales territories, and to determine how the current sales force could be redeployed and sized to improve profitability. Mahajan (1991) presented an application of DEA to assessing the relative efficiency of the sales function of multiple insurance agencies.

CONCLUSIONS AND SUGGESTIONS FOR FURTHER RESEARCH

As shown in Figure 25.1, there is a chain of inputs and outputs that link the input of marketing resources to the ultimate long-run return on the marketing function. The need to account for the productivity of the marketing function has become critical, and an assessment of each link in the chain can yield the information required to provide this accounting. The studies reviewed in this chapter demonstrate that differences in productivity across firms or units within firms at various points in the chain can be substantial, and that there are potentially large gains to benchmarking marketing efforts of a firm or unit against best practices.

This study has provided a review of the DEA and SFA techniques, two approaches to productivity assessment that have been widely applied in practice, and are relatively easy to implement. It has also summarized a number of examples of marketing productivity analyses that use different approaches and focus on different links in the chain. These provide a number of examples that can guide actual productivity assessments. One key conclusion from the review is that many studies incorporate intermediate links in the chain outlined in Figure 25.1, and that it is feasible to do so with readily available data.

The studies reviewed in this chapter also suffer from some common weaknesses. One is that they differ greatly in the amount of care used in defining relevant inputs and outputs, which is a critical first step in obtaining useful results. In particular there is a tendency to use expenditures on marketing activities as inputs, and sales as outputs, without taking care to assure that the influence of different prices is eliminated from the analysis. If all units face the same prices, this is not an issue. But if they do not, the efficiency assessments will be biased. Another common weakness is that studies commonly ignore the role of the consumer in the production process, which is particularly important for retailers and providers of services. However, it is important for manufacturers and others as well. For example, customers in an area or country that are avid users of the Internet may be cheaper to reach than others for manufacturers of such items as automobiles or electronics.

Over the past 20–25 years the productivity measurement techniques reviewed in this study have developed to a high degree of sophistication and have been incorporated into standard software. Similarly, theories of production and cost functions and types of efficiency have been developed to a high degree of sophistication, especially in the economics literature. However, less is known about how to translate these measures into practice in order to get valid comparisons of productivity. For example, little is known about how to measure the customer input to the production process, and this is one important area for further research. Moreover, observed productivity differences between firms or units raises the question of why these differences exist. This is another area for further research.

NOTES

1. The American Marketing Association defines marketing strategy as a "statement (implicit or explicit) of how a brand or product line will achieve its objectives. The strategy provides decisions and direction regarding variables such as the segmentation of the market, identification of the target market, positioning, marketing mix elements, and expenditures. A marketing strategy is usually an integral part of a business strategy that provides broad direction to all functions" (http://www.marketingpower.com/_layouts/Dictionary.aspx).
2. See also Shankar, Chapter 13 in this volume.
3. See also Hanssens and Dekimpe, Chapter 26 in this volume.
4. Also see the discussion of lifetime value measurement in Kumar and Rajan, Chapter 7 in this volume.

REFERENCES

Atkinson, S.E., C. Cornwell and O. Honerkamp (2003), "Measuring productivity change using a Malmquist index: stochastic distance function estimation vs. DEA," *Journal of Business and Economic Statistics*, **21**, 284–5.
Banker, R. (1993), "Maximum likelihood consistency and data envelopment analysis: a statistical foundation," *Management Science*, **39** (10), 1265–73.
Banker, R.D. and R. Natarajan (2008), "Evaluating contextual variables affecting productivity using data envelopment analysis," *Operations Research*, **56** (1), 48–58.
Banker, R.D., Z.Q. Zheng and R. Natarajan (2010), "DEA-based hypothesis tests for comparing two groups of decision making units," *European Journal of Operational Research*, **206** (1), 231–8.
Berger, P. D. and N. Nasr (1998), "Customer lifetime value: marketing models and applications," *Journal of Interactive Marketing*, **12** (1), 17–30.
Blattberg, R., G. Getz and J. Thomas (2001), *Customer Equity: Building and Managing Relationships as Valuable Assets*, Boston, MA: Harvard Business School Press.
Blattberg, R., E. Malthouse and S. Neslin (2009), "Customer lifetime value: empirical generalizations and some conceptual questions," *Journal of Interactive Marketing*, **23** (2), 157–68.
Charnes A., W. Cooper and E. Rhodes (1978), "Measuring the efficiency of decision making units," *European Journal of Operational Research*, **3** (4), 429–44.
Coelli, T. (2008), "A guide to DEAP Version 2.1: a data envelopment analysis (computer) program," CEPA Working Paper 96/08, Center for Efficiency and Productivity Analyis, Univsity of New England, Armidale, NSW, 2351, Australia.
Cornwell, C. and P. Schmidt (2008), "Stochastic frontier analysis and efficiency estimation," in L. Matyas and P. Sevestre (eds), *The Econometrics of Panel Data*, Berlin: Springer-Verlag, pp. 697–726.
Donthu, N. and B. Yoo (1998), "Retail productivity assessment using data envelopment analysis," *Journal of Retailing*, **74** (1), 89–105.
Donthu, N., E. Hershberger and T. Osmonbekov (2005), "Benchmarking marketing productivity using data envelopment analysis," *Journal of Business Research*, **58** (11), 1474–82.
Drèze, X. and A. Bonfrer (2009), "Moving from customer lifetime value to customer equity," *Quantitative Marketing and Economics*, **7** (3), 289–320.

Dutta S., W. Kamakura and B. Ratchford (2004), "Deterministic and stochastic approaches to measuring marketing productivity," in C. Moorman and D. Lehmann (eds), *Assessing Marketing Strategy Performance*, Cambridge, MA: Marketing Science Institute, pp. 47–68.

Dutta, S., O. Narasimhan and S. Rajiv (2005), "Conceptualizing and measuring capabilities: methodology and empirical application," *Strategic Management Journal*, **26** (3), 277–85.

Fare, R., S. Grosskopf and C. Lovell (1994), *The Measurement of Efficiency of Production*, Cambridge: Cambridge University Press.

Gauri, D., J. Pauler and M. Trivedi (2009), "Benchmarking performance in retail chains: an integrated approach," *Marketing Science*, **28** (3), 502–15.

Greene, W. (2008), *Econometric Analysis*, 6th edn, Upper Saddle River, NJ: Pearson Prentice-Hall.

Grewal, D., M. Levy, A. Mehrotra and A. Sharma (1999), "Planning merchandising decisions to account for regional and product assortment differences," *Journal of Retailing*, **75** (3), 405–24.

Grewal, D., G. Iyer, W. Kamakura, A. Mehrotra and A. Sharma (2009), "Evaluation of subsidiary marketing performance: combining process and outcome performance metrics," *Journal of the Academy of Marketing Science*, **37**, 117–29.

Gruca, T. and L. Rego (2005), "Customer satisfaction, cash flow, and shareholder value," *Journal of Marketing*, **69** (3), 115–30.

Gstach, D. (1998), "Another approach to data envelopment analysis in noisy environments: DEA+," *Journal of Productivity Analysis*, **9**, 161–76.

Gupta, S. and D. Lehmann (2003), "Customers as assets," *Journal of Interactive Marketing*, **17** (1), 9–24.

Gupta, S. and V. Zeithaml (2006), "Customer metrics and their impact on financial performance," *Marketing Science*, **25** (6), 687–717.

Gupta, S., D. Lehmann and J. Stuart (2004), "Valuing customers," *Journal of Marketing Research*, **41** (1), 7–18.

Heskett, J., T. Jones, G. Loveman, W. Sasser and L. Schlesinger (1994), "Putting the service–profit chain to work," *Harvard Business Review*, **72** (2), 164–74.

Horsky, D. and P. Nelson (1996), "Efficient frontier benchmarking," *Marketing Science*, **15** (4), 301–20.

Kamakura, W.A., Thomasz Lenartowicz and Brian T. Ratchford (1996), "Productivity assessment of multiple retail outlets," *Journal of Retailing*, **72** (4), 333–56.

Kamakura, W., V. Mittal, F. de Rosa and J. Mazzon (2002), "Assessing the service–profit chain," *Marketing Science*, **21** (3), 294–317.

Keh, H., S. Chu and J. Xu (2006), "Efficiency, effectiveness and productivity of marketing in services," *European Journal of Operational Research*, **170** (1), 265–76.

Kumar, V. and M. George (2007), "Measuring and maximizing customer equity: a critical analysis," *Journal of the Academy of Marketing Science*, **35** (2), 157–71.

Luo, X. and N. Donthu (2006), "Marketing's credibility: a longitudinal investigation of marketing communication productivity and shareholder value," *Journal of Marketing*, **70** (4), 70–91.

Mahajan, J. (1991), "A data envelopment analytic model for assessing the relative efficiency of the selling function," *European Journal of Operational Research*, **53** (2), 189–205.

Mittal, V., E. Anderson, A. Sayrak and P. Tadikamalla (2005), "Dual emphasis and the long-term financial impact of customer satisfaction," *Marketing Science*, **24** (4), 544–55.

Morgan, N., B. Clark and R. Gooner (2002), "Marketing productivity, marketing audits, and systems for marketing performance assessment – integrating multiple perspectives," *Journal of Business Research*, **55** (5), 363–75.

Murthi, B.P.S., Kannan Srinivasan and Gurumurthy Kalyanaram (1996), "Controlling for observed and unobserved managerial skills in determining order-of-entry effects on market share," *Journal of Marketing Research*, **33**, 329–36.

Narasimhan, O., S. Rajiv and S. Dutta (2006), "Absorptive capacity in high-technology markets: the competitive advantage of the haves," *Marketing Science*, **25** (5), 510–24.

Oi, W. (1992), "Productivity in the distributive trades: the shopper and the economics of massed reserves," in Zvi Griliches (ed.), *Output Measurement in the Service Sectors*, Chicago, IL: University of Chicago Press.

Rust, R., K. Lemon and V. Zeithaml (2004a), "Return on marketing: using customer equity to focus marketing strategy," *Journal of Marketing*, **68** (1), 109–27.

Rust, R., T. Ambler, G. Carpenter, V. Kumar and R. Srivastava (2004b), "Measuring marketing productivity: current knowledge and future directions," *Journal of Marketing*, **68** (4), 76–89.

Sellers-Rubio, R. and F. Mas-Ruiz (2009), "Technical efficiency in the retail food industry: the influence of inventory investment, wage levels, and age of the firm," *European Journal of Marketing*, **43** (5–6), 652–69.

Sheth, J. and R. Sisodia (2002), "Marketing productivity – issues and analysis," *Journal of Business Research*, **55** (5), 349–62.

Srinivasan, S. and D.M. Hanssens (2009), "Marketing and firm value: metrics, methods, findings, and future directions," *Journal of Marketing Research*, **46** (3), 293–312.

Vaz, C., A. Camanho and R. Guimaraes (2010), "The assessment of retailing efficiency using network data envelopment analysis," *Annals of Operations Research*, **173** (1), 5–24.

Venkatesan, R. and V. Kumar (2004), "A customer lifetime value framework for customer selection and optimal resource allocations," *Journal of Marketing*, **68** (4), 106–25.

Xue, M. and P. Harker (2002), "Customer efficiency: concept and its impact on e-business management," *Journal of Service Research*, **4** (4), 253–67.

Xue, M., L. Hitt and P. Harker (2007), "Customer efficiency, channel usage, and firm performance in retail banking," *M&SOM-Manufacturing & Service Operations Management*, **9** (4), 535–58.

26 Short-term and long-term effects of marketing strategy
Dominique M. Hanssens and Marnik G. Dekimpe

INTRODUCTION

There is general agreement on the premise that the firm's scarce marketing resources should be managed for the purpose of long-term and profitable growth. Putting that premise into practice is difficult, in part because there is little agreement on what exactly constitutes the long term, and how it is different from the short term. Even with common definitions of short term and long term, there is further ambiguity on how to quantify (measure) the impact of marketing tactics and strategies across both time horizons.

The important questions for marketing strategists are twofold: first, is my marketing strategy producing the necessary short-term returns without jeopardizing future returns? Indeed, without short-term results, long-term impact is an idle construct. Conversely, if short-term performance undercuts future performance, then marketing is bound to become more challenging over time, with profit erosion, brand-value dilution and sometimes bankruptcy as possible consequences. Second, if the answer to the first question is negative, how do I diagnose the problem and make the necessary adjustments?

The purpose of this chapter is to bring clarity to these important issues. First, we will propose workable definitions of the key terms in the title, and we point out how various data analyses can be used to operationalize these definitions. Next, we will summarize what has been learned about marketing's impact on both short-term and long-term business performance. In the process we will also discuss the relationship between these learnings and the use of commonly used "long-term" constructs such as brand equity and customer equity. Finally, we will review some generalizations around the long-term effects of the major elements of marketing strategy.

RESOLVING THE AMBIGUITY AROUND THE "LONG TERM"

The difficulty around the distinction between short term and long term arises primarily because of ambiguity around the time dimension, and because of a predisposition that short term is viewed as observable and therefore practical, but possibly unhealthy. As such, there is general agreement that short-term profit maximization may not be the best paradigm for allocating resources (Dekimpe and Hanssens 1999). By contrast, the long term is unobservable and therefore impractical (some call it theoretical), but healthy. For example, daily sales are short term, as are quarterly earnings reported by public companies. By contrast, a five-year market penetration plan for a new product would typically be construed as long term.

However practical, these definitions are not that useful because the time windows are arbitrary, and do not necessarily relate to marketing strategy. For example, discounting your products or services often produces immediate lifts in demand (practical and healthy), but may erode brand equity in the long run (but when is the long run?). Investing in R&D for product innovation is viewed as good long-run strategy, but the resulting short-run cash drain on the company may prevent the realization of this beneficial long-run outcome.

What short-term and long-term considerations have in common is that they are both concerned with change, either in marketing strategy, business outcomes or environmental conditions. Consequently, the arbitrary time-based distinction between short run and long run can be replaced by a distinction in the nature of that change, that is, a temporary change or a permanent (persistent) change. We will see that this distinction provides a useful and readily implementable framework for evaluating the impact of marketing actions on business performance. In addition, the resulting metrics will be time-subscript independent, that is, separating the definition of long-term from a specific calendar time or time window.

Proposed Definitions

Short-term effects are temporary in nature. After the effects are dissipated, sales performance returns to the level it enjoyed before the marketing action took place. In most cases that will be a "return to the mean," but sometimes it can be a "return to the trend" (Dekimpe and Hanssens 2004). If desired, we can further break down "short term" in immediate and dust-settling effects (Pauwels et al. 2002). By contrast, long-term effects are permanent or persistent in nature. That means that, after the marketing action is completed, business performance reaches a different (higher or lower) level and stays at that new level. Thus, in that case, the marketing action would have both a short-term and a long-term effect.

Note that, in empirical work, these definitions will be supplemented with an additional metric, time to mean reversion, sometimes called decay, carryover, inertia or stickiness. For example, brand awareness may exhibit only temporary shifts as a result of brand advertising, however, its inertia may be high; that is, it takes a long time for the mean reversion to be completed. See, for example, Hanssens et al. (2011) for an elaboration on measuring inertia.

Illustration

To illustrate, imagine that, in reviewing the past marketing actions and business performance of a brand, a certain marketing campaign initiated, say, 24 months ago, had never taken place. In that case, would the company's current business performance, for example sales level, be any different from what it actually is? If no, then that past marketing campaign could have had, at best, only a temporary impact on performance. If yes, then the campaign effect would have been permanent; that is, the brand's current performance level can be traced back – in full or in part – to the marketing campaign initiated two years ago. Statistical techniques using high-quality time-series data exist to diagnose which of the two scenarios above applies (see, e.g., Dekimpe and Hanssens 1995a, 2004).

Implications

By defining short term and long term in terms of the dynamics of change, we do away with arbitrary calendar-based time horizons such as weeks, quarters or years. We also set up a framework for understanding the need to spend marketing money continuously versus only sporadically. Indeed, suppose that in a certain category, consumer brand choice is predominantly zero-order, that is, responsive only to the conditions that are present at the time of purchase. In such an environment, each purchase needs to be supported by current marketing, as there are no memory effects. Consequently, long-term marketing impact would require repetitive spending; that is, the long-term effect is simply the sum of the short-term impacts of these actions. The opposite would hold for a scenario with very high consumer-memory effects that convert into purchase behavior, for example habitual buying. A long-term impact could then be obtained by perhaps a single marketing action that generated a long customer revenue stream for the brand, without the need for marketing reinforcement. Needless to say, the financial ramifications of such scenarios are major. In what follows, we will investigate in more detail the driving forces that generate such long-term marketing impact.

Measurement Approaches

There are two fundamentally different approaches to assessing long-term impact. The first is a "flow projection" approach, whereby the movements in business performance and marketing activity are used to project the long-term outlook for a brand. For example, the demand- or revenue-generating process of a brand is typically described by flow metrics. The second is a "stock metric" approach, in which a new and additional metric is created that supposedly discounts the brand's future outlook into a current position. Examples of such stock metrics include brand equity (see Keller, Chapter 17 in this volume), customer satisfaction (see Mittal and Frennea, Chapter 16 in this volume) and customer lifetime value (see Kumar and Rajan, Chapter 7 in this volume). Likewise, the cumulative sales of a new durable, or its installed base, is a stock variable, which can be instrumental in convincing other users to adopt the product as well (i.e. a diffusion effect; see Tellis and Chandrasekaran, Chapter 22 in this volume). A more extensive discussion of flow and stock metrics in marketing is provided in Hanssens and Dekimpe (2008) and Leeflang et al. (2009).

THE COMPONENTS OF LONG-TERM MARKETING IMPACT

Suppose you are a marketing executive contemplating the launch of a costly marketing campaign whose objective is to lift the sagging sales performance of a brand. Naturally, the degree of sales increase anticipated as a result of the campaign should be a deciding factor in whether or not to initiate the campaign. Indeed, the campaign should be viewed as an investment of the company's time, money and reputation. This investment is expected (hoped) to yield a net positive return that is higher than that of alternative uses of the company's scarce resources.

However, the potential impact of marketing campaigns on sales and, ultimately, profits extends well beyond the spending period. Both the marketing literature and managerial experience teach us, for example, that advertising effects are subject to a wear-in or build-up phase, followed by a wear-out phase (Hanssens et al. 2001). These and other over-time effects of marketing are not limited to consumer response. Indeed, a successful campaign may result in feedback effects on internal decision making, for example when the observed sales lift attributed to advertising results in subsequent increases in advertising budget allocations. Similarly, competitors may imitate or retaliate against a campaign that they perceive as a threat to their business performance.

Whether or not our hypothetical marketing campaign is ultimately successful will depend on the combined forces of consumer response, performance feedback and competitive reactions, and how these forces shape the financial return of the initial campaign. Therefore an accurate assessment of marketing effectiveness should pay particular attention to so-called long-run sales response, that is, to movements in business performance that continue in the future but that can be attributed to a particular short-term marketing activity. In addition, there may be subsequent marketing-mix adjustments that persist over time as well.

Marketing impact is usually interpreted in the context of consumer response. For example, a persuasive advertising for an appealing product generates consumer interest and lifts demand for the product. There is, however, very little evidence that such demand shift can be sustained without further inducement. Following Dekimpe and Hanssens (1995a), six components have been identified that make up the "chain reaction" from initial marketing campaign to persistent demand impact: (1) contemporaneous; (2) carryover; (3) purchase reinforcement; (4) feedback effects; (5) firm-specific decision rules; and (6) competitive reactions. In quantifying the total long-run impact of a marketing action, all channels of influence should be accounted for. A similar logic can be found in Bass and Clarke (1972, p. 300), who state that "credit for the second purchase should be assigned to the expenditure which induced trial" and Leeflang and Wittink (1992, 1996), who make a case for incorporating competitive reaction patterns in assessing the total effect of marketing activities. In what follows, we present a brief motivation for considering each of these effects. For expository purposes, we focus on the advertising–sales relationship.

Contemporaneous Effects

Consensus exists in the marketing field that advertising often has a considerable immediate impact. For example, Leone and Schultz (1980) call the positive elasticity of selective advertising one of marketing's first empirical generalizations.

Carryover Effects

Numerous studies have argued that the effect of advertising in one period may be carried over, at least partially, into future periods (see, e.g., Givon and Horsky 1990). Consumers are supposed to remember past advertising messages and create "goodwill" towards the brand. However, because of a gradual forgetting, only part of an initial effect may remain effective in subsequent periods. This phenomenon has often been captured by imposing a geometric decay on the response coefficients.

Purchase Reinforcement

Givon and Horsky (1990) argue that the dynamic impact of advertising on sales can also work indirectly through purchase reinforcements: a given outlay may create a new customer who will not only make an initial purchase, but also repurchase in future periods. Using a similar logic, Horsky and Simon (1983) argue that advertising gives innovators an incentive to try the product, after which an imitation effect takes over, creating a larger customer base and higher future sales. According to Bass and Clarke (1972) and Hanssens et al. (2001, p. 141), current advertising outlays should receive credit for these subsequent sales, since, without the effort, no incremental sales would have occurred.

Feedback Effects

Bass (1969) warned that advertising spending may be influenced by current and past sales, and should not be treated as exogenous. This is certainly the case when percentage-of-sales budgeting rules are applied. To illustrate the importance of feedback effects in the derivation of an expenditure's total impact, consider the following chain reaction initiated by a one-period advertising increase: increased advertising in period $t \rightarrow$ increased sales in $t \rightarrow$ increased advertising in $t + 1 \rightarrow$ increased sales in $t + 1 \rightarrow \ldots$ Credit should be given to the initial advertising increase for the subsequent sales increases since without it, none of these effects would have occurred.

Firm-specific Decision Rules

Traditional single-equation models treat advertising as exogenous, and do not model the dependence of current spending on previous expenditure levels. Empirical evidence contradicts this "independence" assumption: published time-series models often find significant autoregressive components in a firm's spending pattern (see, e.g., Hanssens 1980). In other words, spending this January tends to be related to last December's and/or last January's advertising. Here again, a chain reaction may occur that affects the total long-run impact. Similarly, one should allow for coordinated marketing decisions, where one marketing instrument affects the level of another instrument in the same firm, either positively or negatively.

Competitive Reactions

Competitive activities may change advertising's effectiveness drastically. For example, even though the instantaneous sales response may be positive, its long-run effect could be zero because of competitive reactions. We refer to Leeflang and Wittink (1992, 1996) and Metwally (1978) for a detailed discussion on such self-canceling effects.

Summary

While there is a consensus that each of these effects should be allowed for, most studies have only considered a subset of them. Moreover, previous work has focused on the measurement of short-term effects, rather than on the derivation of the total long-run

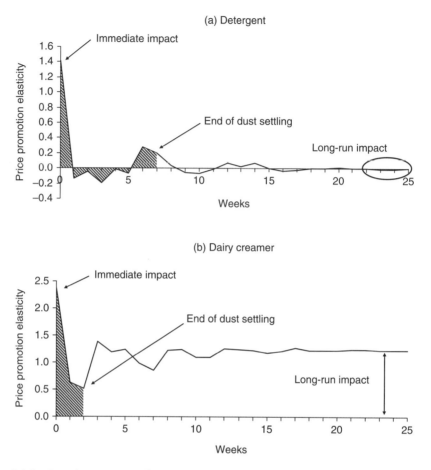

Figure 26.1   Impulse–response functions derived in a persistence analysis

impact. Persistence calculations try to incorporate all channels of influence, enabling one to draw managerially relevant long-run inferences. Persistence calculations typically start with the estimation of a vector-autoregressive (VAR) model. The model is specified in the levels of the variables, in the first difference, or in error-correction format, depending on the outcome of preliminary unit-root and cointegration tests; see for example Dekimpe and Hanssens 2004 or Enders 1995 for a technical discussion. These VAR models allow for the complex feedback loops needed to incorporate the aforementioned effects. From the VAR parameters, impulse–response functions can be derived. Technically speaking, an impulse–response function traces the incremental effect of a one-unit (or one-standard-deviation) shock in one of the variables on the future values of the other endogenous variables in the VAR system, taking into account each of the factors. Impulse–response functions are typically depicted in a graphical way, as illustrated in Figure 26.1.

A comprehensive study by Pauwels (2004) shed important light on the relative contributions of these six factors in generating long-term impact. A key finding is that feedback and firm decision rules can amplify the observed consumer response effects by a factor of five. Similarly, Nijs et al. (2007) and Srinivasan et al. (2008) quantified the relative contribution of the various factors in the price-setting process of grocery products. A key result of their research is that inertia in pricing is costly to retailers; that is, it results in suboptimal profitability.

ADDING THE COST DIMENSION: FOUR STRATEGIC SCENARIOS

Discussions about marketing effectiveness cannot be complete without considering the cost side. Much as response can be temporary or permanent, so can marketing spending. For example, if a brand engages in a sports-event sponsorship that turns out to be successful, it may well include such sponsorships in the future; that is, the expenditure becomes recurring. In that case, the firm commits itself to spending in the future, so the current expenditures have a permanent character.

Following Dekimpe and Hanssens (1999), the combinations of temporary and permanent response and spending produce the following four strategic scenarios: business as usual; escalation; hysteresis; and co-evolution. Most of the marketing-impact literature applies to the "business-as-usual" case, even though that may not be explicitly acknowledged. For example, the brand sets a "promotion schedule" for the coming year, which looks similar to last year's schedule. So long as individual marketing actions are profitable (i.e. the net revenues they generate exceed their costs), business-as-usual scenarios are sustainable; that is, they can be repeated year after year. The "co-evolution" scenario is similar to "business as usual", except that it takes place in an evolving environment.

There are many real-world illustrations of and explanations for the four scenarios described in Figure 26.2.[1] They are as follows.

Empirical evidence from scanner-panel data suggests that the performance and spending behavior of several frequently purchased consumer brands and categories is predominantly stationary (e.g. Dekimpe et al. 1998; Lal and Padmanabhan 1995). Yet companies resort repeatedly to promotional tactics in order to create temporary sales gains. This case can be classified as temporary marketing activity creating temporary incremental results, a scenario referred to above as "business as usual." Such scenarios often exist in market shares, which have been shown to predominantly fluctuate around fixed means over time (Dekimpe and Hanssens 1995b, p. G114). Ehrenberg (1988) argues that consumers' habitual buying propensities explain such stationary behavior, both in repeat buying and in brand switching. Companies that can profitably play the repeated "business-as-usual" game can sustain their positions for a long time; for example, the alternating price promotions by leading national brands such as Pepsi and Coke can be seen as a long-run strategy to defend their stable market shares from possible encroachment by a third firm (Lal 1990).

Other markets are characterized by escalating marketing expenditures or prices without long-run sales movements. Metwally (1978) examined six Australian markets (instant coffee, bottled beer, cigarettes, toothpaste, toilet soap and washing powder). In all instances, industry advertising outlays had increased by more than 300 percent over a 16-year period, while total sales increased by less than 70 percent and market

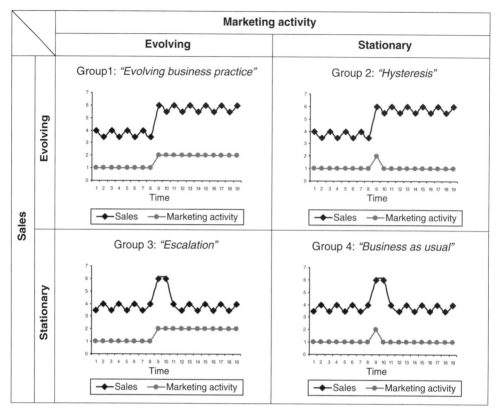

Figure 26.2   The four basic business scenarios

shares remained largely the same. A detailed analysis of the relevant response and reaction elasticities confirmed the notion that advertising expenditures in all industries were self-canceling and escalating. Marketing escalation suggests that competitive action and reaction create sustained marketing engagements without persistent sales or market share gains for any of the players. Price wars are another example of such escalating behavior (see, e.g., Van Heerde et al. 2008). While they may be profitable at the onset, spending escalation scenarios are typically not sustainable to the players.

"Hysteresis" is a phenomenon of temporary marketing action causing sustained sales change. Little (1979) first used the term in marketing, and Simon (1997) presents conceptual evidence (e.g. loyalty after brand switching, organizational inertia etc.) in support of its existence. Marketing actions that exhibit hysteresis are particularly attractive to companies, because temporary investments generate permanent benefits. For example, Simon (1997) illustrates that the Gorbachev era in the former Soviet Union provided a fortuitous boost to brand equity and sales of the Gorbachev vodka label in Germany. During that political era, its sales rose by 500 percent and remained at that high level long after the resignation of the political leader in 1990. Similarly, in a scanner market environment, Dekimpe et al. (1998) found that temporary price reductions by a private-label soup brand could create hysteretical primary-demand effects.

The 1970s and 1980s have witnessed a gradual increase in the market performance of Japanese automobile makers worldwide (e.g. Hanssens and Johansson 1991). At the same time, Japanese firms invested sustained efforts in quality improvement, image building, distribution channels and aggressive pricing. This is an example of sustained marketing effort leading to persistent results, which we call the "evolving-business practice" scenario. This scenario has been empirically verified by Baghestani (1991) in the context of advertising spending and sales performance for a consumer product. Similarly, Bronnenberg et al. (2000) showed how consumer acceptance (market share) and retailer distribution codetermine each other in emerging product categories. Hanssens (1998), in turn, showed that factory orders and retail sales are in a long-run equilibrium, even though shocks to either have different long-run consequences. At the strategic level, Johnson and Russo (1997) argue that competitors co-evolve, or adapt interdependently, to ever-changing market conditions. In their view, principles of co-evolution augment those of game theory and behavioral theory in our understanding of the dynamics of competitive strategy. The joint condition of evolving market performance and evolving marketing spending among competitors is a logical empirical test for the presence of co-evolution.

MARKETING INSIGHTS OBTAINED THROUGH THE PERSISTENCE LENS

Over the years, persistence modeling has seen numerous applications in the marketing literature. Recent reviews include Dekimpe et al. (2008) and Dekimpe and Hanssens (2010). These applications reflect an evolution through three stages.

In a first stage, the various concepts were introduced (both conceptually and technically), and illustrated for a variety of marketing instruments, such as advertising (Dekimpe and Hanssens 1995a), price promotions (Dekimpe et al. 1999), and for a variety of conventional performance metrics, such as brand sales, market share, primary demand and profitability. These studies typically establish that long-term marketing effects (i) exist, and (ii) can be quantified. In Figure 26.1a, for example, the impulse–response function showing the over-time effect of a promotion in the detergent market converges to zero, illustrating the absence of a long-run impact, even though the short-term effect could be obtained by summing the areas under the curve. In Figure 26.1b, by contrast, the impulse–response function converges to a positive level, which quantifies the long-run impact of a promotion in the dairy-cream market.

Following these initial illustrations, and spurred by the growing availability of large data sets in the consumer packaged goods (CPG) sector, several studies have developed empirical generalizations.[2] Illustrative of this stage are the studies by Nijs et al. (2001), Steenkamp et al. (2005), Pauwels and Srinivasan (2004), and Srinivasan et al. (2004), among others. They typically report average values for the short- and long-run elasticities, frequency distributions on the number of significant effects, while testing in a second stage both brand- and category-related drivers for the magnitude of these elasticities. Nijs et al. (2001), for example, studied the primary-demand effects of price promotions in 560 different frequently purchased consumer-good (FPCG) categories, and found an average short-run elasticity of 2.21 and an average long-run elasticity of 0.02. Significant positive effects were found in 58 percent of the categories in the short run, but only in 2 percent for the long-run effects. Moreover, the size of the elasticity was linked to covariates such as the advertising intensity in the category, the promotional frequency in the category, and the perishable nature of the product. Given the nature of the variables considered (e.g. price promotions, competitive reactions etc.), the focus of these applications was more on the tactical interactions that could, in some instances, result in long-run (persistent) performance (sales, market share etc.) gains.

More recent applications have started to tackle more strategic questions. Villanueva et al. (2008) used persistence modeling to compare the impact of marketing-induced versus word-of-mouth customer acquisition on customer-equity growth. Customers are valuable assets to a firm, but they can be costly to acquire and retain. Using data from a Web-hosting company, they found that marketing-induced customers add more short-term value, while customers acquired through slower but cheaper word-of-mouth processes add nearly twice as much long-term value to the firm. Trusov et al. (2009), in turn, studied the effect of word-of-mouth marketing on member growth at an Internet social network, and compared it with more traditional marketing vehicles. Word-of-mouth referrals were found to have a substantially longer carryover effect than more traditional marketing actions, and to have higher elasticities. Similarly, Gupta and Lehmann (2008) reviewed how persistence models can be used to evaluate the lifetime value of a firm's or brand's customer base, which is one of the aforementioned stock metrics.

As a second illustration, persistence models have also been used to establish the relevance of marketing activities to the financial value of the firm (see Shankar, Chapter 24 in this volume). Pauwels et al. (2004), using data from the automobile industry, showed that new-product introductions increase long-term financial performance and firm value, while promotions do not. Here the performance metric went beyond the more conventional sales/market-share metrics to include stock-price information. Similarly, Joshi and Hanssens (2010) showed how advertising has a positive effect on firm valuation in both the computer and sportswear industries. Contributions of long-run persistence modeling to the marketing–finance interface have recently been reviewed in Srinivasan and Hanssens (2009).

Aside from examining more strategic metrics, such as customer equity and stock prices, recent applications have also taken a more refined look at certain marketing problems. Earlier (i.e. stage 1 and 2) applications typically examined time series at a fairly aggregate level. As a first departure, Pauwels and Hanssens (2007) used persistence modeling in a moving-window setting to diagnose strategic marketing turnarounds. Indeed, early work in persistence modeling revealed that many performance measures are stationary over time, especially measures of market share (Dekimpe and Hanssens 1995b), but also measures of primary demand (Nijs et al. 2001). However, this is not necessarily compatible with the firm's objectives for sustainable profitable growth. Pauwels and Hanssens demonstrated that brands tend to systematically improve or deteriorate their performance outlook in clearly identifiable time windows, which typically are shorter than the intermediate periods of stability. Moreover, shifts in performance regime were found to be associated with the brand's marketing actions and policy shifts, and therefore (to some extent) under managerial control.

Second, rather than studying aggregate and/or "final" performance metrics, recent studies have looked at either more disaggregate (e.g. Sismeiro et al. 2008) or more intermediate (e.g. Srinivasan et al. 2010) metrics. Sismeiro et al. (2008) no longer analyzed a single, aggregate performance series in their study on the impact of detailing in the pharmaceutical sector, but segmented[3] physicians according to the classification shown in Figure 26.2, while Srinivasan et al. (2010) included intermediate customer-mindset metrics (such as advertising awareness, brand consideration and brand liking) in a sales–response model that already accounted for the short- and long-run effects of advertising, price, distribution and promotion. It was shown how variations in these metrics can be used as early warning signals that provide sufficient time for corrective managerial actions before brand performance itself is affected.

CONCLUSION

Marketing managers have an intrinsic interest in knowing (and quantifying) whether their actions, tactical as well as strategic, have a long-run impact on certain performance metrics. Persistence thinking offers a useful and flexible lens to do so, since it

- can be applied to both conventional performance metrics (such as sales, market shares) and more strategic metrics such as customer lifetime value and stock prices;
- allows us to simultaneously consider the revenue and the cost side;
- resolves the ambiguity about the length of the time horizon;
- can be applied at different levels of aggregation, with both "final" and "intermediate"metrics; and
- can be used to identify strategic turning points, which can be linked to managerial actions.

Given these properties, it should come as no surprise that persistence modeling is used increasingly to not only quantify the long-run implications of tactical marketing decisions, but also to study a wide variety of strategic marketing problems. The settings for these studies have evolved from traditional bricks-and-mortar markets to Internet environments[4] (e.g. Wiesel et al. 2009; Joshi and Trusov 2009; or Shin et al. 2011). They have also opened up the debate on the value relevance of marketing activities to the financial community (e.g. Pauwels et al. 2004), and on the optimal use of marketing during economic crises (e.g. Gijsenberg et al. 2009). We are confident that the advent of high-quality marketing databases over prolonged time periods, combined with an increasing need for marketing accountability in corporate and government circles, will contribute further to this evolution of quantifying the short- and long-run implications of marketing strategies.

NOTES

1. In Figure 26.2, we depict the over-time impact (impulse–response function) of a shock to the marketing support variable on both the associated performance metric and the shocked series itself.
2. Many of these generalizations are summarized in Hanssens (2009).
3. Lim et al. (2005) contribute another example of combining segmentation with persistence modeling.
4. As such, Pauwels and Weiss (2008) studied the strategic problem faced by many online content providers, that is, how to go from a free Internet business model to a fee-based model, and derived actionable recommendations on how to use different marketing-mix instruments (e.g. search-engine referrals, targeted e-mail offerings etc.) during this transition.

REFERENCES

Baghestani, H. (1991), "Cointegration analysis of the advertising–sales relationship," *Journal of Industrial Economics*, **39** (December), 671–81.

Bass, F.M. (1969), "A simultaneous equation regression study of advertising and sales of cigarettes," *Journal of Marketing Research*, **6** (August), 291–300.

Bass, F.M. and D.G. Clarke (1972), "Testing distributed lag models of advertising effect," *Journal of Marketing Research*, **9** (August), 298–308.

Bronnenberg, B.J., V. Mahajan and W.R. Vanhonacker (2000), "The emergence of market structure in new repeat-purchase categories: the interplay of market share and retailer distribution," *Journal of Marketing Research*, **37** (February), 16–31.

Dekimpe, M.G. and D.H. Hanssens (1995a), "The persistence of marketing effects on sales," *Marketing Science*, **14** (1), 1–21.

Dekimpe, M.G and D.H. Hanssens (1995b), "Empirical generalizations about market evolution and stationarity," *Marketing Science*, **14** (summer, part 2), G109–G121.

Dekimpe, M.G. and D.H. Hanssens (1999), "Sustained spending and persistent response: a new look at long-term marketing profitability," *Journal of Marketing Research*, **36** (November), 397–412.

Dekimpe, M.G. and D.H. Hanssens (2004), "Persistence modeling for assessing marketing strategy performance," in Christine Moorman and Donald R. Lehmann (eds), *Assessing Marketing Strategy Performance*, Cambridge, MA: Marketing Science Institute, pp. 69–93.

Dekimpe, M.G. and D.H. Hanssens (2010), "Time series models in marketing: some recent developments," *Marketing Journal of Research and Management*, **1**, 93–8.

Dekimpe, M.G., D.H. Hanssens and J.M. Silva-Risso (1998), "Long-run effects of price promotions in scanner markets," *Journal of Econometrics*, **89**, 269–91.

Dekimpe, M.G., P.H. Franses, D.M. Hanssens and P.A. Naik (2008), "Time-series models in marketing," in B. Wierenga (ed.), *Handbook of Marketing Decision Models*, New York: Springer, pp. 373–98.

Ehrenberg, A.S.C. (1988), *Repeat Buying: Facts, Theory, and Data*, 2nd edn, New York: Oxford University Press.

Enders, W. (1995), *Applied Econometric Time Series*, New York: John Wiley.

Gijsenberg, M., H.J. van Heerde, J-B.E.M. Steenkamp and M.G. Dekimpe (2009), "Price and advertising effectiveness over the business cycle," paper presented at the 2009 ANZMAC Conference.

Givon, M. and D. Horsky (1990), "Untangling the effects of purchase reinforcement and advertising carry-over," *Marketing Science*, **9** (Spring), 171–87.

Gupta, S. and D.R. Lehmann (2008), "Models of customer value," in B. Wierenga (ed.), *Handbook of Marketing Decision Models*, New York: Springer, pp. 255–90.

Hanssens, D.M. (1980), "Market response, competitive behavior, and time series analysis," *Journal of Marketing Research*, **17**, 470–85.

Hanssens, D.M. (1998), "Order forecasts, retail sales, and the marketing mix for consumer durables," *Journal of Forecasting*, **17** (3), 327–46.

Hanssens, D.M. (ed.) (2009), *Empirical Generalizations about Marketing Impact*, Cambridge, MA: Marketing Science Institute, Relevant Knowledge Series.

Hanssens, D.M. and M.G. Dekimpe (2008), "Models for the financial-performance effects of marketing," in B. Wierenga (ed.), *Handbook of Marketing Decision Models*, New York: Springer, pp. 501–23.

Hanssens, D.M. and J.K. Johansson (1991), "Rivalry as synergy? The Japanese automobile companies' export expansion," *Journal of International Business Studies*, **22** (3), 503–26.

Hanssens, D.M., L.J. Parsons and R.L. Schultz (2001), *Market Response Models: Econometric and Time-Series Research*, 2nd edn, Boston, MA: Kluwer Academic Publishers.

Hanssens, D.M., K. Pauwels, S. Srinivasan and M. Vanhuele (2011), "Consumer attitude dynamics and effective marketing spending," UCLA Working Paper, July.

Horsky, D. and L.S. Simon (1983), "Advertising and the diffusion of new products," *Marketing Science*, **7** (Fall), 356–67.

Johnson, E.J. and J.E. Russo (1997), "Coevolution: toward a third frame for analyzing competitive decision making," in G.S. Day and D.J. Reibstein (eds), *Dynamic Competitive Strategy*, New York: John Wiley & Sons, pp. 177–97.

Joshi, A.M. and D.M. Hanssens (2010), "Direct and indirect effects of advertising spending on firm value," *Journal of Marketing*, **74** (1), 20–33.

Joshi, A.M. and M. Trusov (2009), "Double jeopardy! Modeling the dual role of online search when marketing through social and commercial media," Working Paper, University of Central Florida.

Lal, R. (1990), "Price promotions: limiting competitive encroachment," *Marketing Science*, **9** (3), 247–62.

Lal, R. and V. Padmanabhan (1995), "Competitive response and equilibria," *Marketing Science*, **14** (3), 247–62.

Leeflang, P.S.H. and D.R. Wittink (1992), "Diagnosing competitive reaction using (aggregated) scanner data," *International Journal of Research in Marketing*, **9** (1), 39–57.

Leeflang, P.S.H. and D.R. Wittink (1996), "Competitive reaction versus consumer response: do managers overreact?," *International Journal of Research in Marketing*, **13** (2), 103–19.

Leeflang, P.S.H., T.H.A. Bijmolt, J. Van Doorn, D.M. Hanssens, H.J. van Heerde, P.C. Verhoef and J.E. Wierenga (2009), "Creating lift versus building the base: current trends in marketing dynamics," *International Journal of Research in Marketing*, **26** (1), 13–20.

Leone, R.P. and R.L. Schultz (1980), "A study of marketing generalizations," *Journal of Marketing*, **44** (Winter), 101–18.

Lim, J., I.S. Currim and R.L. Andrews (2005), "Consumer heterogeneity in the longer-term effects of price promotions," *International Journal of Research in Marketing*, **22** (December), 441–57.

Little, J.D.C. (1979), "Aggregate advertising models: the state of the art," *Operations Research*, **27** (July–August), 629–67.

Metwally, M.M. (1978), "Escalation tendencies of advertising," *Oxford Bulletin of Economics and Statistics*, **40** (2), 153–63.

Nijs, V.R., Marnik G. Dekimpe, Jan-Benedict E.M. Steenkamp and D.M. Hanssens (2001), "The category-demand effects of price promotions," *Marketing Science*, **20** (1), 1–22.

Nijs, V.R., S. Srinivasan and K. Pauwels (2007), "Retail-price drivers and retailer profits," *Marketing Science*, **26** (July–August), 473–87.

Pauwels, K. (2004), "How dynamic consumer response, competitor response, company support, and company inertia shape long-term marketing effectiveness," *Marketing Science*, **23** (Fall), 596–610.

Pauwels, K. and D.M. Hanssens (2007), "Performance regimes and marketing policy shifts," *Marketing Science*, **26** (May–June), 293–311.

Pauwels, K. and S. Srinivasan (2004), "Who benefits from store brand entry?," *Marketing Science*, **23** (Summer), 364–90.

Pauwels, K. and A. Weiss (2008), "Moving from free to fee: how online firms market to change their business model succesfully," *Journal of Marketing*, **72** (3), 14–31.

Pauwels, K., D.M. Hanssens and S. Siddarth (2002), "The long-term effects of price promotions on category incidence, brand choice and purchase quantity," *Journal of Marketing Research*, **39** (November), 421–39.

Pauwels, K., J. Silva-Risso, S. Srinivasan and D.M. Hanssens (2004), "The long-term lmpact of new-product introductions and promotions on financial performance and firm value," *Journal of Marketing*, **68** (4), 142–56.

Shin, H.S., D.M. Hanssens and B. Gajula (2011), "The impact of positive vs. negative online buzz on retail prices," UCLA Working Paper.

Simon, H. (1997), "Hysteresis in marketing – a new phenomenon?," *Sloan Management Review*, **38** (Spring), 39–49.

Sismeiro, C., N. Mizik and R. Bucklin (2008), "Modeling co-existing business sceneries with time series panel data: a new dynamics-based segmentation approach," MSI Reports, 2008-02.

Srinivasan, S. and D.M. Hanssens (2009), "Marketing and firm value: metrics, methods, findings, and future directions," *Journal of Marketing Research*, **46** (3), 293–312.

Srinivasan, S., K. Pauwels and V. Nijs (2008), "Demand-based pricing versus past-price dependence: a cost-benefit analysis," *Journal of Marketing*, **72** (1), 15–27.

Srinivasan, S., M. Vanhuele and K. Pauwels (2010), "Mind-set metrics in market response models: an integrative approach," *Journal of Marketing Research*, **47** (4), 672–84.

Srinivasan, S., K. Pauwels, D.M. Hanssens and M.G. Dekimpe (2004), "Do promotions benefit manufacturers, retailers, or both?," *Management Science*, **50** (5), 617–29.

Steenkamp, J.B.E.M., V.R. Nijs, D.M. Hanssens and Marnik G. Dekimpe (2005), "Competitive reactions to advertising and promotion attacks," *Marketing Science*, **24** (1), 35–54.

Trusov, M., R.E. Bucklin and K. Pauwels (2009), "Effects of word-of-mouth versus traditional marketing: findings from an Internet social networking site," *Journal of Marketing*, **73** (5), 90–102.

Van Heerde, H.J., E. Gijsbrechts and K. Pauwels (2008), "Winners and losers in a major price war," *Journal of Marketing Research*, **45** (October), 499–518.

Villanueva, J., S. Yoo and D.M. Hanssens (2008), "The impact of marketing-induced versus word-of-mouth customer acquisition on customer equity growth," *Journal of Marketing Research*, **45** (February), 48–59.

Wiesel, T., K. Pauwels and J. Arts (2009), "Marketing's profit impact: quantifying online and offline funnel progression," Working Paper, Dartmouth College.

27 Marketing and democracy
John A. Quelch and Katherine E. Jocz

OVERVIEW

Marketing at its best shares fundamental characteristics with democracy. Both seek to include as many people as possible, consumers and citizens are actively engaged, information flows freely, decisions involve free choice, exchange is fair and equitable, and a desired outcome is improved well-being for individuals and for society. A focus on these core benefits enables companies to tune marketing strategies to deliver greater value to their shareholders, to customers and to society.

MARKETING IS IMPORTANT TO SOCIETY

Marketing is both an economic and social accelerant. The economic function is widely recognized: for instance, if a business is introducing a new product, it needs marketing to inform consumers about product features and availability. Overall, marketing performs a highly significant function in the economy in terms of accelerating the pace of adoption of new products and services in the marketplace, the creation of business opportunities and national economic development.

The social function that marketing performs is often overlooked. Marketing-based exchanges are a vital means for bringing societies and communities closer together. Consider that every day there are billions of transactions where a buyer buys something from a seller. For the most part, with very few exceptions, those billions of transactions occur satisfactorily with no problem of bad or untrustworthy behavior on either party's side. This provides a very important social glue to bond people into a collaborative effort of mutual trust, or social capital. As depicted in Figure 27.1, social capital, along with economic capital and specific historical and cultural factors, is correlated with democratization (Halpern 2005; Norris 2001; Przeworski et al. 1996).

DEMOCRACY IS IMPORTANT TO MARKETING

Equally important, marketing flourishes best in healthy democracies. Modern representative democracies are rooted in the idea of a social contract, by which people create, or consent to governments to achieve, common ends and to provide for collective needs (e.g. see Locke 1689). In modern democracies, representatives are empowered to coordinate and resolve conflicts among individuals and groups, including, according to a number of theorists, balancing production and consumption activities (Dahl 1998). Majority rule is tempered by minority rights. In addition to political

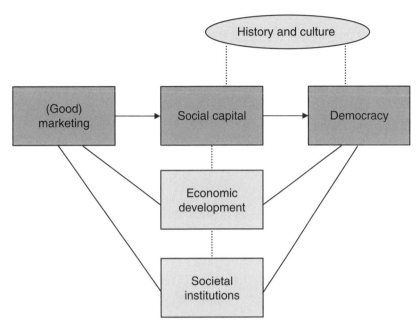

Figure 27.1 Marketing and society

rights, modern democratic states guarantee citizens basic human rights, civil liberties, and equal rights and due process before the law (Pennock 1979). Democracy in one respect is "a meta-institution for building good institutions" (Rodrik 2000). In seeking to ensure sufficient levels of economic and social well-being for all their citizens, modern democracies, to varying degrees, have created conditions conducive to healthy, competitive marketplaces, including effective legal and regulatory frameworks.

WHAT MARKETING AND DEMOCRACY HAVE IN COMMON

In the 1950s, management expert Peter Drucker formulated the "marketing concept," which asserted that, above all, firms must create value for customers and see the business from the customer's point of view (Drucker 1954, p. 39). Ever since, the idea that the purpose of a company is to create satisfied customers has been widely accepted as a guiding principle of marketing. This principle closely parallels the guiding philosophy of democracy, that the purpose of government is to serve its citizens. Individual sovereignty is central to both. In the marketplace, "consumers, by registering their dollar votes, determine which goods and services shall be provided and in what quantities" (Baumol and Blinder 1982, p. 786). However, companies do not serve consumers out of altruism; rather, the rationale is that by producing what consumers want and are willing to pay for, companies simultaneously maximize consumer welfare and their long-run profits.

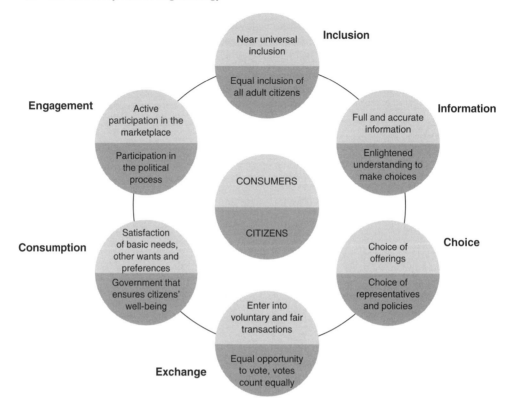

Figure 27.2   Marketing and democracy

Six Shared Characteristics

According to political theorist Robert Dahl, an ideal representative democracy must meet the following conditions: equal opportunity to vote and votes that count equally, the opportunity for citizens to control and choose items placed on the agenda, enlightened understanding on the part of citizens, effective participation by citizens and, finally, inclusion of all adults (Dahl 1998, ch. 4).

Grounded in consumer sovereignty, modern marketing shares equivalent characteristics. At its best, it offers consumers the core benefits of voluntary and fair transactions (exchange), control and choice over offerings (choice), informed understanding (information), active participation in shaping the marketplace (engagement), and near universal inclusion (inclusion) (Quelch and Jocz 2008). These benefits correspond to the five ideal conditions for democracy identified by Dahl. In addition, satisfaction of basic needs and other wants and preferences (consumption) is consistent with the obligation of governments to ensure citizens' well-being (see Figure 27.2).

Note, however, that the rationale for putting customers first hinges on the assumption of consumer sovereignty, yet the degree of consumer sovereignty depends on market conditions. It is no accident that the marketing concept was formulated during the post-World War II period of huge market expansion. Vigorous competition in a mixed, if not free-market, economy, an excess of supply over demand, and rising disposable incomes generally tip the balance of power to consumers versus producers. Consumer sovereignty may be lower in other conditions, such as in less developed countries, where purchasing power is low, where demand exceeds supply, where information is scarce, or where governments attempt to control the marketplace. Keeping this caveat in mind, the core benefits of marketing are discussed in more detail below.

Marketing's Benefits: Key Features and Issues

We have argued that good marketing provides six democratic benefits: marketers offer consumers choice. They give information. They want to engage consumers, to earn their interest and loyalty. Most marketers seek to be inclusive, to bring quality and innovation to the masses. A marketer's success depends on a fair exchange of value with a customer and subsequent consumption of goods and services that satisfy needs and improve quality of life. Table 27.1 summarizes key features of these benefits as well as issues raised when marketing fails to provide them.

Exchange

In the USA, Europe and other industrialized countries, consumers obtain virtually all their goods and most services through voluntary transactions. A buyer and a seller enter into an exchange because it creates value for both. A key feature of marketing exchanges is that what consumers give up and what they acquire extend beyond narrow economic considerations. That is, consumers obtain functional and emotional benefits, as well as products and services, in return for both monetary and nonmonetary compensation. For instance, consumers spend time viewing ads (which may be enjoyable) in return for free or subsidized entertainment. They acquire goods to gain the symbolic value of the brand as well as the functional benefits delivered by the product.

Consumers expect to find good-quality, well-priced products at convenient times and locations. They expect marketers to help them solve problems, and to treat them with respect. Marketing "makes goods and services more valuable by getting them where they are wanted, when they are wanted, and transferred to the people who want them" (Converse and Huegy 1952, p. 1). Helping to strengthen the social fabric, the billions of daily marketplace transactions are based on mutual trust. These marketing exchanges depend largely on voluntary good behavior by marketers and consumers.

On the other hand, there obviously are unscrupulous marketers who try to take advantage. Like democracy, marketing depends on checks and balances to protect consumers against abusive marketers and marketing practices that cause consumers harm. These checks and balances include competitors, consumers, the media, and ultimately the power of government. It is also up to good marketers to protect consumers' interests. Marketing is not a licensed profession with specified codes of conduct, but marketers can form strong trade associations to develop codes of conduct and police those who step out of line and treat consumers poorly.

Table 27.1   What marketing does well and where it can go wrong

Core benefit	Marketing at its best	Issues and problems
Exchange	• Win–win based on mutual trust and satisfaction • Fair prices and good deals • Value is more than just functional performance • From Main Street to buy anytime, anywhere	• Unscrupulous marketers and bad behaviors • Excessive market power • Consumers locked in or penalized
Consumption	• Access to a wide range of goods and services • Contributes to economic growth and national well-being	• Too much consumption • Too little consumption • Imprudent consumption
Choice	• Addresses individual needs, desires, preferences, goals • Allows expression of singular identity and social belonging • Expert agents for difficult decisions	• Creation of false needs • Too little real choice • Too much choice
Information	• Informed consumers make better choices • Brands and advertising inform and assure • Product/service benefits in exchange for personal information • Ad-supported media provides media diversity for diverse consumers	• Information asymmetries between marketers and consumers • Persuasion rather than facts • Untruthfulness, deception, partial disclosure • Privacy • Unequal access to information among consumers
Engagement	• Consumers co-create brand meaning • Consumers co-produce the product/service experience • Products and brands as focus of consumer communities and exchanges	• New norms (everything for free) around digital and online • Shifting costs to consumers • Civic engagement displaced by marketplace engagement
Inclusion	• Equality of opportunity to buy • Expanding marketplace • Cultural exchange and cosmopolitanism	• Profits and the poor • Market failures • Cultural imperialism

Consumption

An essential benefit of marketing is individuals' ability to consume goods and services necessary for health and well-being. Marketers have helped to democratize consumption. They compete vigorously to sell more things to more people. They have incentives to introduce new products and to make available to a broader segment of the population products initially affordable only to the elite. Although consumption is tied to social and economic status, mass marketers have enabled even low-income consumers to raise living standards far beyond those of a century or even 50 years ago.

Consumption has been a strong driver of economic growth as well as a contributor to individual well-being. However, individual consumption above a modest level is not necessarily correlated with happiness. A looming social question is whether individuals and societies are consuming too much or consuming unwisely, not saving for the future, or damaging environmental resources or the social fabric. Increasingly, the public expects marketers to address the social impacts of consumption, for example, designing products to minimize post-consumer waste or cutting back on advertising high-sugar foods to children. At the same time, underconsumption of necessary goods and services continues to be a problem in many developing nations and in impoverished segments of developed societies.

Choice
The proliferation of products, retail channels and media adds up to a vast number of consumption alternatives. The range of marketplace choice is democratic in that, increasingly, marketers have tailored their offerings to satisfy differing needs among different segments within a diverse consumer population. Choice respects individuality and allows consumers to achieve their own goals. In addition to allowing people degrees of freedom to buy and consume in accord with their individual needs and preferences, marketplace choice is also a means for members of social groups to construct shared identity and social belonging.

At the same time, choice brings complexity. So far, consumers have coped by using a variety of rules-of-thumb and shortcuts, including relying on brand name or trusted retailers, or using experts to simplify decisions. Yet marketplaces may be approaching a limit where too many choices can burden and confuse consumers, or where they may grow more dependent on expert agents to help make decisions.

A recurrent critique of marketing, especially in regard to global markets, is the idea that marketers teach consumers to make choices based on inauthentic or false desires. In other words, marketers are accused of creating false needs for their brands that replace "genuine" needs. Defenders of marketing say that this critique underestimates consumers and their real desires for new experiences or their capacity to mix and match the traditional and the new.

Information
Like democracies, the consumer marketplace depends on free flows of information in order to function well. Consumers need accessible, complete, accurate and timely information from marketers in order to make intelligent choices. Brand names serve as shorthand for more detailed information and offer quality assurances. Information about consumers enables marketers to target consumers with appropriate communications and to offer the right product at the right place, the right time and the right price. With customer information systems, marketers can more easily balance supply and demand and meet consumers' ever-changing needs in cost-effective ways.

Because marketers need to reach diverse groups of consumers, they provide the financial foundation for a wide array of media, including early support for new media. However, from the advent of mass advertising, a long-standing debate has posed the question of whether consumers can hold their own against advertising or whether marketers succeed in manipulating consumers against their will. Most industrialized nations have advertising regulations aimed at protecting consumers from false, misleading or deceptive information practices. There is also evidence that consumer word of mouth and expert opinion perceived as objective trump corporate advertising in terms of consumers viewing information as trustworthy and credible (Nielsen Company 2007).

Issues concerning proper use of information are increasingly salient. Evolving technology allows marketers access to huge amounts of sensitive personal information, so privacy is a growing concern. Marketers, consumers and government regulators are still grappling with negotiating evolving standards of privacy and means of enforcement. Public policy is also concerned with mitigating potential information asymmetries favoring businesses over individuals through such means as ensuring public access to airwaves.

Engagement

Marketing engages consumers, in part because consumers have to engage with the marketplace if they want access to goods and services. But many consumers engage with marketing because it offers additional emotional and psychic benefits (Bagozzi 1975). They relish expressing their identity, being part of a community, and exercising their creativity – not through every purchase decision they make but through those in which they have chosen to be more involved. Quite a few become experts on particular brands or product categories.

Enabled by interactive communication technologies, consumers are engaging with marketers in customizing products or adopting self-service options. In the digital world, consumers are contributing content and forming communities around consumption. Some are even creating advertising, for example the popular Doritos commercials aired during the 2009 Super Bowl and subsequently online. Others, either alone or as part of a network, are helping to design new products.

Against a natural reluctance to cede control to consumers, marketers increasingly take the view that consumer engagement will bolster, and not weaken, marketing, in the same way that political democracies grow more robust and more representative of the public when more citizens engage in public affairs. They see that letting consumers participate better reveals their wishes; that some consumers want deeper relationships with marketers and brands and are willing to pay for customized service; and that turning over marketing tasks and functions to consumers can simultaneously reduce costs and increase consumers' sense of empowerment.

Among possibly deleterious effects, an issue for society is whether such engagement with brands may be displacing other social ties and civic values. An issue for marketers is that consumers engaged with creating and sharing content in the digital world are developing new norms about paying for content and services, namely, that most things should be free. An issue for consumers is that even though self-service participation may reward them with lower prices, greater control and liberation from long lines, it may also burden them with more of the work and time costs.

Inclusion

Consumer marketplaces are naturally inclusive, because marketers benefit from expanding the number of customers. On the whole they are not elitist; they serve the vast majority of the population, and the rich pay a price premium if they want unique, specialized or luxury items. Starbucks is not atypical in starting out as a specialty up-market brand that over time expanded into being more of a mass-market brand competing with Dunkin Donuts and McDonald's. In some situations, more affluent consumers subsidize others; for example, higher airfares paid by business travelers subsidize low fares paid by tourist passengers on the same flight; early adopters of technology pay more than later adopters.

That is not to say that all consumers have equal access to goods or that retailers and other marketers do not discriminate against various ethnic, religious or racial groups. There remain populations who have little, if any, access to marketing systems that could raise living standards by linking consumers with multiple producers and by consistently delivering good-quality products and services. However, seeing attractive opportunities at the bottom of the pyramid, global marketers have displayed growing interest in participating in underserved markets and emerging economies, sometimes in partnership with local or global not-for-profit organizations (Prahalad 2005).

Marketing to the bottom of the pyramid should provide poorer consumers with better access to goods and services. But it also raises the social issue of whether marketing ultimately serves the interests of poor consumers. Marketers selling to these populations walk a tightrope between exploiting consumers and liberating them. Alternative approaches such as corporate philanthropy programs don't seek to profit from the poor, but they may be short-lived. On the other hand, profitable marketing programs may allow companies to stay in for the long haul and therefore have a greater long-term positive impact.

Inclusion also rubs up against heterogeneity. Global marketing and branding, and the shared consumer experience they have created, have in some ways brought the world closer together. But local populations do not want Western-style marketing practices imposed upon them with no respect for their particular social and cultural contexts.

SOME MANAGERIAL IMPLICATIONS

Marketing strategies aim to create value through a strategic process of identifying and selecting segments to serve, defining the value proposition, and designing the systems and networks for delivering the value proposition. Approaching the strategic process from the perspective of democratization underlines the importance of creating value for both the business and the customer through providing the six core benefits described above. For example, efficient distribution and logistics systems enable exchange with broad segments of customers quickly and cheaply. Wal-Mart may be disparaged, but its mission of bringing low prices to everyone is democratic and inclusive. Marketing communications that inform consumers of the choices that suit their needs stimulate consumption. Creative marketing communications, good product design, and enjoyable retail experiences engage consumers and accelerate information sharing and new-product adoption.

Approaching strategy through this framework is particularly relevant in light of three major trends affecting marketing: empowered consumers, opportunities opening up in emerging markets, and scrutiny of the social impact of business practices.

Empowered Consumers

Beginning in the late nineteenth century and continuing through the first half of the twentieth century, corporations courted a mass market of consumers with low prices and consistent products achieved through economies of scale in supply, production and distribution, and from national selling, advertising and branding. A shift toward market fragmentation occurred in the last half of the twentieth century, when marketers sought to optimize profits by serving different niches of consumers with different value propositions, thus splintering the mass market into segmented markets. Intense market competition, increasing incomes and expanding consumption meant that consumers played an ever more powerful role in the marketplace. If customers weren't satisfied with the value they received from products or services, marketers knew they would switch their business elsewhere as soon as they could. More than that, consumers expected marketers to supply relevant information, an abundance of choices and satisfying, convenient transactions.

Increasingly, consumer power is founded on information and communication technologies that allow consumers to access extensive repositories of data about brands and products, to contribute their own opinions, and to share information with friends and strangers. Twenty-first-century consumers want marketers to respect them, to engage them, and to earn their interest and loyalty. With the first generation of the Web, marketers could offer better information, interactive engagement between consumer and marketer, a wide range of product choices with more customization, and around-the-clock availability. Online marketers like eBay, Amazon and IngDirect capitalized on these possibilities for delivering value, while consumers gained from reduced search and transaction costs, including easier ability to make product feature and price comparisons. The second generation of the Web is dominated by consumer-created content and social networks: from blogs, Twitter, Facebook, YouTube and MySpace to the Huffington Post. The explosion of smart mobile phones means that consumers can participate in this digital world virtually anywhere, anytime.

This new media environment promises new possibilities for marketers to create and deliver value to consumers around the world. In 2008, the mobile content market in Japan was already worth over $6 billion; the mobile value-added service market exceeded $1 billion in India and $18 billion in China. In the past couple of years, Adidas found that placing messages in social media delivered a five times higher return than television and has attracted over 2 million fans to a Facebook page. Dell uses Twitter to alert consumers about promotions and to generate sales. On the other hand, marketers face twin challenges: they have less control over social media than traditional media and the reach and frequency of consumer word of mouth is greatly amplified – a particular concern given that consumers trust their peers more than marketers.

In this increasingly democratized marketplace, the starting point is not the "customer is king," but the "customer and the company are in it together." The best marketers have always entered into a conversation with consumers. But increasingly, thanks to mobile and social media, that dialog will take place in real time. In response to marketing strategies that engage customers, consumers will lend their creativity to marketers by creating ads, participating in market research, suggesting product improvements and joining in viral marketing campaigns. For instance, Mountain Dew, whose soft drinks are aimed at the younger demographics, spent almost the entire 2009 budget for its yearlong "DEWmocracy 2" campaign online. Using Facebook, Twitter, YouTube and other social media networks and tools, 4000 of the brand's most loyal consumers helped to co-create three new beverages. In addition to selecting flavors, colors, names and package design, the fans also collaborated in creating television ads, online media planning and buying, and leading grassroots campaigns in a nationwide contest to select the final winning addition to the product line. More than a gimmick, the point of DEWmocracy was to introduce a successful mass-market product based on superior market research, targeting, positioning and buzz.

Not every consumer will want close relationships with marketers and their brands, and those who do will be selective. All, however, appreciate good quality at an equitable price, more convenient ways to obtain products and services, and lower purchase risk. Consider consumers battered by the recession who could consume less. Marketing strategies needed to be inclusive, offering new choices to suit new circumstances, and focused on alternative forms of exchange value. Consumers who turned to do-it-yourself, for instance, traded status value for functional value, self-service for price, and derived satisfaction from engagement and control. The recession further elevated the power of information: more consumers stayed at home, additional time on the Internet was free, there was an increased need for the comfort of social networks, and trust deficits favored word of mouth. As a result, consumers increased their information search, including consulting social networks and online recommendations and reviews, in order to obtain better deals from marketers. The democratic framework is a useful reminder that, at a minimum, marketing depends on mutually satisfying exchanges between consumers and marketers. Or, as Leonard Marsh, one of the three original founders of the Snapple Beverage Company, explained the brand's success: "We never thought of ourselves as being any better than our customers."

Emerging Markets

Poor consumers in developing countries have limited access to goods and services, and may have little (if any) choice over the purchases they make. Typically, they start off with little marketplace clout. But global marketing is expanding, in large part because population growth is slow or stagnant in developed markets. As it does, marketers should treat all individuals as potential customers who all want the same core benefits. They should also recognize that consumer power is growing, thanks in large part to the explosive growth in mobile communications and the Internet that is enabling unprecedented access to product information. Six out of ten people in the world now use cellphones; more than 60 percent of them live in developing countries. A quarter of the world's population has Internet access; 40 percent of them live outside Europe or North America.

Consumption aspirations are much the same worldwide. More than 25 years ago, Theodore Levitt (1983) observed that "Almost everyone everywhere wants all the things they have heard about, seen, or experienced via the new technologies." Adoption cycles of many items track very clearly per capita income growth from country to country. People want a cellphone at $1500 per capita annual income, a TV at $2500, and a car at $5000. Consumers want functional benefits and value, but brands also play an aspirational and status role, as witness the success of brands like Shisheido in China. Online social networking and digital buzz promise to accelerate new product adoption.

Perhaps the key deficit for consumers in emerging markets is in the area of exchange. Vital marketing infrastructure is lacking in much of the developing world. This includes physical infrastructure necessary for distribution, such as roads and warehouses, and financial infrastructure necessary for payments, such as banks and credit. According to the United Nations Food and Agriculture Organization, the number of hungry people rose to over a billion, or nearly one in seven people, not just because of deficiencies in growing sufficient supplies of food, but also because the necessary distribution systems are lacking. Retailing and distribution remain largely local activities – presenting significant opportunities for global marketers to contribute to improved systems of exchange. In a number of instances, corporations have partnered with local suppliers, distributors, governments or non-governmental organizations to build infrastructure. Ericsson, for example, set up local franchises to own and operate telecommunications centers serving poor communities. ABB and the Worldwide Fund for Nature collaborated on a pilot project to bring commercially viable delivery of electricity to rural Tanzanian villages. Hindustan Lever's large distribution network reaches rural areas through mom-and-pop stores, door-to-door salesforces employing local women, and bicycle deliveries to more remote villages. In Vietnam, German retailer and wholesaler Metro Group offered expertise and a financial grant to the Ministry of Transportation to modernize the country's product distribution network, including upgrading hygiene, health and packaging standards; the firm also invested in refrigerated transportation and warehouses to enable fish and meats from rural areas to be sold in urban areas.

Providing the benefits of inclusion means adapting to heterogeneity within emerging nations. Typically there are significant urban versus rural differences, ethnic and language diversity, and perhaps differences in physical geography. Like consumers everywhere, those in emerging markets want a choice of quality, affordable products that suit their needs and solve their particular problems. In many cases, products and services must be modified or redesigned based on indispensable local knowledge, while simultaneously retaining as many standardized components as possible to keep costs down. Both the delivery and content of marketing communications must demonstrate respect for consumers of very different cultural and linguistic backgrounds. Advertising is an obvious area where adaptation is essential. A model in a Saudi Arabian cosmetic advertisement cannot be shown in the same way as in the West. In many cases, creative approaches to addressing these challenges will be invented by local marketers, who may then – like Tata in India, for example – become potent competitors to multinational corporations.

What Does Social Responsibility Entail?

There is an expectation that democratic government benefits society. The same criterion holds true of marketing. Part of good marketing is ensuring that individual consumers receive value in marketing exchanges, that brand names signify assurance and trust, and that customers do not hesitate to enter into long-term relationships or contracts. If problems arise, the company takes immediate steps to redress the situation. When 20 million toys manufactured in China for Mattel were found to have lead paint, the CEO apologized publicly, took full responsibility, quickly reached out to consumers using, among other media, attention-getting ads on high-traffic Internet sites such as Yahoo that linked to the infomative Mattel website, and empowered consumers to return the affected products directly to Mattel with minimal hassle.

Beyond treating individual consumers well, socially valuable marketing solves important problems and makes the world a better place. It is not just a matter of diverting time and money into a veneer of charitable activities or social-responsibility campaigns; it is a matter of ensuring that all marketing is socially valuable.

Of course, this is easier said than done. For example, sales of bottled water soared in the 1990s, related to health consciousness; lately, a backlash from environmental groups opposed to the production of billions of plastic water bottles, as well as from critics of water privatization and watchdogs worried about chemical pollutants in the packaging and contents, have altered public perceptions of the benefits of bottled-water consumption.

There is an inevitable tension – for both consumers and marketers – when what pleases consumers in the short run may not be good for them individually or for society as a whole in the long run. Myopic marketers concerned only with their firm's short-term interests shy away from such problems. More far-sighted marketers care about the kinds of consumption they promote. In response to increasing concerns about childhood obesity, for example, Kraft Foods Inc. shifted advertising of sugar-laden Oreos and Kool-Aid away from children between the ages of six and eleven. Knowing there is no easy solution, marketers truly conscious of social value work to contribute to solving such dilemmas. Measuring marketing activities against the six democratic benefits provides a framework for approaching such problems.

Unilever's internationally lauded Real Beauty campaign for Dove soap, for example, focused on inclusiveness. The global beauty industry had long relied on women's desires for self-expression and self-improvement. But increasingly, rather than consider the physical ideals promulgated by beauty-industry advertising to be aspirational, many women and girls perceived them as unattainable and ended up feeling worse about themselves. Although the industry was nominally inclusive, a large segment of consumers felt excluded from a value-creating exchange. Dove broke ground by deploying typical girls and young women as models in ads that celebrated the diversity of beauty. The low-budget "Evolution" spot, which aired on YouTube, tackled distorted beauty stereotypes head on by charting the transformation of a typical young woman into a billboard model through the artifices of make-up and Photoshop. It inspired dozens of parodies and stimulated volumes of discussion on the Internet (as well as in commercial broadcast and print media) on the themes of self-esteem, beauty-industry stereotypes, the desirability or undesirability of picturing ordinary "unbeautiful" women in ads and the sincerity and motives of the marketers. Particularly in Europe and North America, sales of the brand rose – indicating that consumer trust exceeded misgivings and suggesting that the campaign both resonated with consumers and engaged them in choosing a new path to express their individuality.

Socially responsible marketing also tries to protect consumers against the worst excesses of bad marketers. Responsible marketers can influence the behaviors of other corporations and leaders through structures such as trade associations and through supporting an appropriate regulatory environment. In particular, it's important to watch out for early warning signals that industry practices are eroding the trust and respect that hold marketplaces together. For example, the profitability of the credit-card industry long relied heavily on charges and fees that punished consumers for not obeying often opaque rules. If there are warning signs, the best course of action is to adopt a leadership position beyond what the law may currently demand – to set the bar higher for expected good practice, or to steer the industry toward self-regulation that will underpin its long-term reputation with customers. That does not mean, however, that consumers should not be expected to look out for themselves and prudently seek the best deal and check with friends and online as to whether or not they are dealing with legitimate marketers who are going to live up to their word.

ADDITIONAL QUESTIONS CONCERNING MARKETING AND DEMOCRACY

We have highlighted a number of the rich implications for marketers that arise from comparing democracy and marketing. The comparison also raises at least three important political, economic and social issues concerning the interface of marketing and democracy.

Balancing Marketing and Democracy

The marketing profession's assumption is that what's good for the customer is good for the firm and, by extension, for society. An alternative perspective is that marketing is "sucking up the air from every other domain to sustain the sector devoted to consumption" (Barber 2007, p. 12). If Starbucks achieves its goal of becoming the "third place in your life," does that undermine civic engagement or are engaged consumers just as likely as anyone else to be engaged citizens?

Does greater use of political marketing lead to a better field of candidates ("products") or better understanding of and responsiveness to what issues matter to voters? Does it help people to make better choices or the reverse?

Marketing in Non Democracies

Can marketing create institutions and values conducive to emerging democracies, for example through building marketing distribution systems that satisfy consumption needs or through fair, transparent, trustworthy marketing exchanges that contribute to social capital?

What are the ethical implications of marketing in undemocratic nations? Google gained entry into China by agreeing to ban search results on topics deemed sensitive by the Chinese government. Arguments in favor were that Google could do more good for Internet freedom and human rights by working inside the country to create value for its Chinese users, employees and business partners. Arguments against were that Google, the "don't be evil" company, was selling out its core principles to play in the world's second-largest economy. A decade later, the latter argument prevailed when Google announced it would pull up stakes unless China agreed to stop censoring search.

Promoting "Best Practices" to Benefit Consumers and Citizens

Public policy to provide public goods or to balance societal costs and benefits of consumption may require shifts in consumer demand and preferences, for example as related to global climate change or provision of healthcare or education. How should marketing strategies adapt to needs to decrease consumption? What are the most efficient and effective roles for marketing *vis-à-vis* the public and non-profit sectors?

Within corporations, how can marketers effectively advocate for treating consumers democratically and putting social value first, for example embedding environmental, social and ethical considerations into the DNA of the organization rather than taking on these causes merely for public relations purposes or to satisfy legal requirements?

REFERENCES

Bagozzi, Richard P. (1975), "Marketing as exchange," *Journal of Marketing*, **39** (4), 32–9.

Barber, Benjamin R. (2007), *Consumed: How Markets Corrupt Children, Infantilize Adults, and Swallow Citizens Whole*, New York: W.W. Norton.

Baumol, William J. and Blinder, Alan S. (1982), *Economics; Principles and Policy*, 2nd edn, New York: Harcourt Brace Jovanovich.

Converse, Paul D. and Huegy, Harvey W. (1952), *The Elements of Marketing*, 5th edn, Englewood Cliffs, NJ: Prentice-Hall.

Dahl, Robert A. (1998), *On Democracy*, New Haven, CT: Yale University Press.

Drucker, Peter F. (1954), *The Practice of Management*, New York: Harper & Row.

Halpern, David (2005), *Social Capital*, Cambridge, UK: Polity Press.

Levitt, Theodore (1983), "The globalization of markets," *Harvard Business Review*, **61** (4), 92–102.

Locke, John (1689), *Second Treatise on Government*, Project Gutenberg, available at www.gutenberg.org.

Nielsen Company (2007), "'Word-of-mouth' the most powerful selling tool: Nielsen global survey," Global Online Consumer Survey, New York (April).

Norris, Pippa (2001), "Making democracies work: social capital and civic engagement in 47 societies," Faculty Research Working Papers, RWP01-036, John F. Kennedy School of Government, Harvard University, Cambridge, MA, October.

Pennock, J. Roland (1979), *Democratic Political Theory*, Princeton, NJ: Princeton University Press.

Prahalad, C.K. (2005), *The Fortune at the Bottom of the Pyramid*, Upper Saddle River, NJ: Wharton School Publishing.

Przeworski, Adam et al. (1996), "What makes democracies endure?," *Journal of Democracy*, **7** (1), 39–55.

Quelch, John A. and Jocz, Katherine E. (2008), *Greater Good: How Good Marketing Makes for Better Democracy*, Boston, MA: Harvard Business Press.

Rodrik, Dani (2000), "Institutions for high-quality growth: what they are and how to acquire them," Working Paper, No. 7540, National Bureau of Economic Research, Cambridge, MA, February, 48.

Index